THE POLITICS OF TOTALITARIANISM

The Communist Party of the Soviet Union from 1934 to the present

THE POLITICS OF TOTALITARIANISM

THE COMMUNIST PARTY OF THE SOVIET UNION FROM 1934 TO THE PRESENT

BY

JOHN A. ARMSTRONG

RANDOM HOUSE · NEW YORK

First Printing

© Copyright, 1961, by John A. Armstrong

Library of Congress Catalog Card Number: 61-6242

The author gratefully acknowledges permission to use passages from the following:

E. D. Simon *et al.*, *Moscow in the Making.* Longmans, Green & Co. Limited. Article by Jozsef Revai in *Foreign Affairs*, October 1949.
Joseph S. Berliner, *Factory and Manager in the USSR.* Harvard University Press.
Gustav Hilger and Alfred E. Meyer, *The Incompatible Allies: A Memoir-History of German-Soviet Relations, 1918-1941.* The Macmillan Company
Selections from *The Current Digest of the Soviet Press,* Leo Gruliow, editor. Published by The Joint Committee on Slavic Studies.
Selections from *Current Soviet Policies* and *Current Soviet Policies* II, Leo Gruliow, editor. Frederick A. Praeger, Inc.

Manufactured in the United States of America

This is Part III of a study
of the Communist Party of the
Soviet Union prepared under
the general sponsorship of the
Research Program on the History
of the Communist Party of the
Soviet Union.

TABLE OF CONTENTS

PREFACE

Anyone who studies the recent development of Soviet Communism will
certainly not have a dull time, but he is most likely to have some exceedingly frustrating moments. When I set out to write a chronological account
of the last quarter-century of the Communist Party of the Soviet Union,
I was quite aware, from my earlier investigations, of the limits of possible
accomplishment. My previous studies had analyzed particular aspects of
Soviet politics; though speculative in some measure, these monographs were
largely limited to topics for which reasonably complete evidence was available. While the gaps and uncertainties in a chronological treatment are
necessarily more extensive, such a treatment has long been urgently needed.
Many—I believe the most fundamental—aspects of the Communist Party
have remained unaltered in their essentials during the last twenty-five years,
if not since the Bolshevik Revolution of 1917. But the considerable changes
can be understood only by examination in temporal sequence of the overall
development of the Party. In view of its lack of definitiveness one hesitates
to label such a narrative "history." It may provide, however, the framework
in which the fragmentary information now available can be interpreted and
serve as a scaffolding for the erection of a future history. If the framework
I have offered serves even as a temporary support for new items of evidence
as they become available, it will have fully served its purpose.

The choice of December 1934 as the starting point for my narrative was
determined in considerable measure by convenience of division of labor
with my colleagues in the Research Program on the History of the Communist Party of the Soviet Union. Certainly one can present persuasive
arguments for beginning a treatment of the third phase of CPSU history
in 1929 or in 1939. But I feel that the end of 1934 presents great advantages
for starting the examination of what I consider the key element of my

work—the politics of totalitarianism. Russian Communism has always had a strong bent toward totalitarianism, but before the mid-thirties circumstances were not ripe for the institution of a full-blown totalitarian regime. Until 1933, when the first Five Year Plan for industrialization had been fulfilled and collectivization of agriculture carried out, it was uncertain that the indispensable economic basis would exist for a regime penetrating all aspects of life. Consequently, the "Congress of Victors" (January-February 1934) which celebrated these accomplishments precedes my study, as its immediate background. Equally important is the fact that in 1934 Joseph Stalin was in the final phase of establishing his absolute control over the Party, a process which was drastically speeded up after the assassination of Sergei M. Kirov at the end of that year. Finally, from 1934 on, the imposition of complete political control upon cultural and social life proceeded at a quickening pace.

This study allots approximately equal coverage to the major periods of CPSU history after 1934. To some extent the materials for the first period (1934-38) are more extensive and reliable, but so much has been written on this portion of Soviet history (especially the purge trials) that I have felt a somewhat summary treatment would be adequate. Though the period since Stalin's death (1953-60) is so recent that it can hardly be seen in perspective, material concerning it is also relatively abundant, and at least as reliable as the evidence for any other period since 1938. Consequently, I have devoted nearly one-third of my treatment to these years.

It is the intervening period (1939-52) which is most difficult to treat, for materials concerning it are scarce and heavily distorted. As a result, many treatments of Soviet affairs tend to neglect these years. In my view, however, they are crucially important to an understanding of the evolution of Soviet Communism, for they include the traumatic experience of World War II, the preceding expansion of Soviet territory, and the subsequent consolidation of Soviet power. Therefore, I have devoted some two-fifths of my treatment to this period.

Occasionally the reader may feel that I devote more space to certain events or personages than their importance in the overall account warrants. Given, however, the difficulty of establishing the validity of so many details of CPSU history, I have thought it desirable from time to time to present little-known but well-established incidents which, though perhaps relatively unimportant in themselves, throw a vivid light upon significant aspects of this history. For example, the "Münzenberg affair" described in Chapter II is not very important in itself; but it harshly illuminates the connection between the Soviet Communist Party and the Comintern forces.

I have noted that this volume cannot be considered a definitive history, for the available information is too scanty. This being the case, it has seemed to me that the only proper procedure is to present not only the fragmentary record of unassailable fact but, where gaps of crucial importance exist, to indicate the rumors and unverifiable data which might fill them. Moreover, in the most important cases where coherent but unproven explanations of the data by outside observers exist, I have noted and criticized them. Finally, I have presented my own speculative explanations. Not to set forth my personal interpretations explicitly would be misleading, for the author of a work of this kind must inevitably form assumptions in order to select and organize his material. At every point I have endeavored to make clear the lines between what I consider established fact, unsubstantiated allegation, and hypothesis. Scrupulous attention to these distinctions, rather than mere refusal to consider the speculative, marks, it seems to me, the boundary between scholarship and sensationalism in the field of contemporary political affairs.

This is not the place to present a detailed comment on the sources which I have used.* I have relied mainly on Soviet publications, particularly newspapers and periodicals. But I have not hesitated to employ memoir material, including works of émigrés; I see no fundamental distinction between the reliability of these two classes of materials. Though I cannot claim that unpublished sources constitute a major portion of my evidence, I have occasionally drawn upon the oral or manuscript testimony of observers of the events described, and I was able to examine a considerable number of unpublished dissertations by Soviet students. Finally, secondary treatments, published or in thesis form, have been indispensable, both as guides to my research and as sources of information on innumerable peripheral aspects of my subject.

My theme is the Communist Party of the Soviet Union, not Soviet society as a whole. In my opinion, the history of the Party comprises (though it is not confined to) all the topics, aside from the purely legal, which we customarily treat under the rubric of political history. But because the Soviet system is totalitarian the examination of the ruling Party tends to embrace the entire history of the USSR. The problem in treating the CPSU

---

* "An Essay on Sources for the Study of the Communist Party of the Soviet Union, 1934-1960," issued by the External Research Division, U.S. Department of State, Washington, D.C., 1961, contains my detailed comment on materials used in preparing this volume.

is, then, primarily one of focus and emphasis. Like Alan Bullock, I believe that the essence of totalitarianism, Nazi or Soviet, is political power. Consequently, I have dealt in detail with other Soviet institutions—particularly the army and the police—insofar as they have constituted power factors.

A key aspect of CPSU history—though certainly not always the most important aspect—has been the struggle for power among Party leaders. That such struggles play an important role in totalitarian dictatorship is demonstrated not only by many earlier studies of the USSR, but by more definitive investigations of Nazi totalitarianism. Consequently, I have devoted much attention to personalities and personal relationships in the Party command and in the other Soviet bureaucratic apparatuses. No doubt this approach will appear superficial to those analysts who view developments in the USSR almost exclusively from the standpoint of "broad social forces," but I remain unconvinced that one's view can encompass the Soviet forest before one has scrutinized the trees.

Setting the proper limits for the treatment of Party policy is difficult. In its formation, policy is inextricably related to power considerations. Public manifestations of Party policy, however, usually relate to economic or ideological matters. I have not tried to present in detail the ephemeral shifts of emphasis in Party propaganda, but I have endeavored to describe and analyze the more basic shifts in Party doctrine. Since fundamental Communist doctrine is inseparable from Marxist-Leninist philosophy, discussion of ideological matters has tended to verge on the sphere of philosophy, though I do not pretend to treat the latter topic as such. It has been very difficult to decide how much attention to devote to cultural controls. A major aspect of totalitarianism is a pervasive domination of cultural affairs, but it is obviously infeasible to discuss all aspects of literature and the arts. Consequently, I have concentrated my attention on the aspects most closely related to changes in the Party line and Party alignments.

The problem of presentation of Party policy in economic affairs has been even thornier. Much the larger portion of Party pronouncements deals with economic matters. To discuss these pronouncements in detail, analyzing their relation to the real economic situation of the USSR, would greatly exceed the scope of this work, even if my own competence permitted such an extended excursion into the field of the economist. In most instances, therefore, I have only summarized the nature of economic policies pursued during the principal periods of Party history. However, those economic matters which have been most closely related to the exercise of Party control of Soviet society, and especially those which have been directly related to the power struggle within the Party, have received more detailed treatment.

Obviously, a discussion of the CPSU must stress developments within the Soviet Union. But to treat the Soviet Communist Party in isolation from world Communism would obscure the true significance of the Party. Consequently, I have felt obliged to devote some attention to developments outside the USSR. The problem is a complex one, for, in addition to major chronological shifts in the Communist "line," Communist tactics and activities have differed so much from country to country that no simple formula can summarize them even year by year. Obviously, a detailed treatment of all major Communist parties is impossible in this volume. I have felt it best, therefore, to describe briefly the major temporal and regional changes in world Communist policies, while focusing my attention upon those developments outside the USSR which were most intimately related to developments in the CPSU itself. For example, I summarize briefly the shift toward hostility toward the Western allies following World War II, while treating in detail aspects of the East European satellite purges which seem to be related to power alignments in Moscow, although from the standpoint of contemporary history in general, the former development was doubtless more important.

I have already mentioned that this study is one of a series sponsored by the Research Program on the History of the Communist Party of the Soviet Union. The generous financial assistance provided by the Program under a grant from the Ford Foundation made it possible for me to travel, collect materials, and above all to devote some eighteen undisturbed months to the completion of this volume. Beyond this material assistance, the advice and encouragement of the members of the Committee in charge of the Program—Geroid T. Robinson, Harold H. Fisher, Merle Fainsod, and its Chairman, Philip E. Mosely—have been invaluable. Drawing on his wealth of experience with Soviet sources as editor of the *Current Digest of the Soviet Press,* Leo Gruliow gave me numerous very useful suggestions. Aside from this personal assistance, I must acknowledge that without the comprehensive coverage of the Soviet press contained in the files of the *Current Digest* for the past twelve years I would have found it impossible to examine this recent period in the time available to me. To Alfred G. Meyer, former Director of the Program, I am most grateful both for his gathering of important manuscript materials and for his advice. To my co-author in the series, Leonard Schapiro, I am indebted both for personal advice and for the guidance provided by his pioneering volume, *The Communist Party of the Soviet Union.* Leo Gruliow, Alfred G. Meyer, Leonard Shapiro, Merle Fainsod, and Boris I. Nicolaevsky read the first draft of this study and made very valuable suggestions. To all of these, and to many others, I am indebted for advice, but I alone bear the responsibility for both the factual material and the interpretations presented in this book.

Josephine B. Bruno, Executive Director of the Program, has smoothed my path in innumerable ways. My research assistant, George J. Svejda, has contributed very substantially to this work by his analysis of the Union Republic Party plenums and of Czechoslovak Communist sources. I am grateful to Norma M. Smith, Mary Holbrow, Stephanie Posner, and Norma Lynch for typing the complex manuscript.

Aside from those most intimately involved in the work of the Research Program on the CPSU, persons who have assisted me in the course of preparing this volume are too numerous to cite by name—and for understandable reasons some prefer to retain their anonymity. I cannot fail, however, to mention the staffs of the libraries and institutes where I carried out my basic research. In Europe the Lenin State Library (Moscow), the Bibliothèque de Documentation Internationale Contemporaine (Paris), and the Institute for the Study of the USSR (Munich) were very helpful. In this country the libraries of the University of Wisconsin and Columbia University, the New York Public Library, and the Library of Congress provided my principal research bases. I am especially grateful to the staff of the Library of Congress, which received me most hospitably for more than a year. I owe a very heavy debt of gratitude in particular to Sergei Yakobson, Fritz T. Epstein, and Paul Horecky of the Slavic and Central European Division, and to Leon Herman of the Legislative Reference Service.

To my colleagues at the University of Wisconsin I am indebted for less specialized, but equally stimulating advice and criticism. The able and helpful staff at Random House—in particular, Jason Epstein, Nathan Glazer, and Berenice Hoffman—has provided most welcome editorial advice. Finally, I must mention in this connection that my wife, Annette Taylor Armstrong, in addition to her unflagging encouragement in this lengthy project, meticulously edited the entire first draft.

JOHN A. ARMSTRONG

Madison, Wisconsin
September 1960

GLOSSARY*

Aesopian language—esoteric communication by hints or allusions

Agitprop—propaganda and agitation organization

ASSR—Autonomous Soviet Socialist Republic

Brigade—large collective farm work unit

Cadres—personnel

Candidate—probationary member of Party

Chekist—police agent (archaic or honorific at present)

Cominform—Communist Information Bureau

Comintern—Communist International

Commissar—Communist official: (1) head of major government department prior to 1946; (2) political officer in military forces prior to 1942

Commissariat—ministry

CPSU—Communist Party of the Soviet Union

Fascist—when related to Soviet ideas or allegations, refers to any regime accused by Communists of resembling Italian Fascism, Nazism, or representing particularly "reactionary" capitalists

Five year plan—period of economic development

Fraction—intra-Party faction

Glavk—Chief Administration, major subdivision of a department or ministry

GOKO—State Defense Committee— also GKO

GorKO—City Defense Committee

Gorkom—city Party committee

Gosplan—State Planning Commission

Instructor—Party official for supervision and inspection

KGB—Committee of State Security

Kolkhoz—collective farm

Kolkhoznik—collective farm member (peasant)

Krai—territory

Kulak—"richer" peasant using hired labor—term of opprobrium

Link—small collective farm work unit

MGB—Ministry of State Security

MTS—Machine Tractor Station

MVD—Ministry of Internal Affairs

* This brief list includes only the Soviet and Communist terms which are used most frequently in this book and which are most apt to be confusing to the reader. For additional clarification of these and other terms the reader is referred to the appropriate index entries.

NKGB—Commissariat of State Security

NKVD—Commissariat of Internal Affairs

Nomenklatura—sphere of personnel assignment

Norm—labor output quota

Obkom—oblast (province) Party committee

Oblast—province or region

OGPU—General State Political Administration (political police)

Orgburo—Organizational Bureau of Party

Politburo—Political Bureau of Party

Presidium—unless otherwise noted, refers to Presidium of CPSU; when uncapitalized and so indicated, refers to presidium of Ukrainian Party; otherwise is used (with special indication) to refer to higher bodies of various state organizations

Rabfak—special school for workers (in twenties)

Raikom—district Party committee

Raion—district

RAPP—Russian Association of Proletarian Writers

RSFSR—Russian Soviet Federated Socialist Republic

Sector—subdivision of sections (as of Secretariat of Party)

SED—Socialist Unity Party (Communist), East Germany

Socialist—when uncapitalized (unless otherwise indicated by context) refers to Soviet term for stage of development toward Communism; when capitalized, or in form "social democratic" or "democratic socialist," refers to groups or persons adhering to Western democratic principles

Soviet—adjective referring to USSR and its regime

Soviets—state legislative bodies

Sovnarkhoz—council of national economy

Union Republic—constituent member of USSR

USSR—Union of Soviet Socialist Republics

VKP(b)—All-Union Communist Party (Bolshevik)

WFDY—World Federation of Democratic Youth

WFTU—World Federation of Trade Unions

THE POLITICS OF TOTALITARIANISM

The Communist Party of the Soviet Union Since 1934

CHAPTER

I

TO THE VICTORS...

As the Russian winter of 1934 approached, the leaders of the Soviet Communist Party regarded their position with measured satisfaction. Their regime was entering upon its eighteenth year. This in itself was no small sign of success for a system which had made as sharp a break with the political traditions of its country as had Soviet Communism. To draw the Communists' own favorite parallel, the period of their rule was not much shorter than the entire period between Revolution and Bourbon Restoration in France; to anticipate history, the Communists as a ruling power far surpassed the record of the Nazis.

But this was not all. Unlike the French Revolution, the reign of Communism had not been marked by a series of physically violent clashes among its adherents or by forceful overthrows of ruling groups. When Lenin, the recognized leader of the Revolution, died, the battles for succession were carried on by oratory and intrigue rather than arms. To the outside observer this was a distinction of dubious merit, for the arms which the Communists had so sparingly used against one another were mercilessly applied to their "non-Party" countrymen. To the defeated contenders for the succession—and particularly to that giant among them, Leon Trotsky—the triumph of the General Secretary, Joseph V. Stalin, had meant the perversion of the Communist aims. Even Trotsky, however, contended that the Soviet system, because founded on a transfer of the ownership of the means of production, was an essentially higher form of social organization which would eventually overcome the errors and corruption of the present.

Even in this considerable reservation Trotsky was, on the surface, almost alone. Every Communist opposition leader of stature still residing in the USSR had formally made his peace with Stalin. The "capitulation" in the closing months of 1934 of Khristian Rakovskii, Trotsky's last major open supporter in the Soviet Union, was a heavy blow to him.[1] Opposition leaders like Grigorii Zinoviev, Lev Kamenev, and Nikolai Bukharin, once far more powerful than Rakovskii, repeated their confessions of error at the Seventeenth Party Congress held at the beginning of the year.

No doubt the principal motivations of the "capitulators" were personal —the desire to return from exile and to obtain a minimum of security and comfort for themselves and for their families—and tactical—the hope of maintaining a foothold in political life, i.e., the Communist Party. Stalin and his followers, however, supported by the text of the confessions, could claim that the material successes achieved by the Soviet regime under their direction had proved the opposition to be wrong. The *Pravda* editorial celebrating the opening of the Congress called it the "Congress of Victors." [2] Stalin himself pointed out the significance of the "victory":

Victorious is the policy of industrialization of the country. Its results are now apparent to everyone. What can be argued against this fact?

Victorious is the policy of liquidation of the kulaks and complete collectivization. Its results, too, are now apparent to everyone. What can be argued against this fact?

The experience of our country demonstrates that the victory of socialism in one, separate country is fully possible. What can be argued against this fact? [3]

Stalin's claim to victory rested on the assertion of economic progress. In the industrial field, there is much to substantiate Stalin's contention. He said that value of large-scale manufacturing in 1933 (the opening year of the second Five Year Plan for industrial development) had been almost twice that of 1929 at the beginning of the industrialization process.[4] Very likely this claim was inflated. Aside from the usual difficulties in estimating the real value of the heterogeneous output of a huge industrial system, the changes in Soviet industry, particularly the production of many machinery products which had no value-prototypes in the earlier period, make the most objective appraisals uncertain. We may assume that Stalin's statisticians resolved the doubt in favor of the Soviet system. Nevertheless, a painstaking critical analysis indicates that the overall increase in Soviet industry was approximately 50 per cent during that period, certainly a sizable figure.[5]

More significant than the overall figure, however, was the rate of development in specific industrial branches. Consumer goods, according to Stalin's figures, had increased about two-thirds in value. Estimates by the economist cited above suggest the true increase was nearer one-fourth.[6] On the other hand, armaments and means of production had increased, according to Stalin, by 140 per cent; estimates by several non-Soviet analysts indicate that his figure is not incredible.[7]

Two features of heavy industrial development demand special attention. One was the extraordinary emphasis on producing tools and machinery which would make the USSR economically independent. During the first Five Year Plan (1928-32) foreign machinery and technical assistance had been imported lavishly, but they were used to construct facilities which would eliminate the need for foreign help. By 1933 Soviet imports showed a very sharp decline as compared with the years of the first Five Year Plan; they were not to recover before World War II.[8] A second feature of crucial importance was the shift of emphasis in industrial development to the strategically secure Urals and West Siberian regions. While—as we shall see later—the share of these areas in the USSR's total industrial production remained relatively small up to the war, the basis was laid for rapid development.

Indeed, laying the basis for development was the most significant aspect of Soviet industrial progress down to 1934, although Stalin and other Soviet speakers preferred to describe it in terms of material accomplishments. We have seen what a relatively small place consumer goods occupied; even if one accepts the official figures as accurately reflecting material output, they have little relevance to the essential welfare of the population. The vast population transfers incident to industrialization, even when they involved no overt compulsion, worked extreme hardships on those involved. The acute shortage of housing in the older urban areas was far outmatched by the crowded, primitive conditions in the new industrial centers, though the barracks built there figured in the overall increase in consumers goods. The excessive strains and physical dangers arising from construction and operation of industrial facilities by half-trained personnel working at fever tempo involved considerable human loss. On the whole it is still an open question whether the industrial working force, the technicians and the managers, regarded the industrialization process of 1928-34 as a triumph or a trial.[9]

From this point of view, the agricultural picture is less ambiguous. The regime indeed insisted that here, too, a great victory had been won. Anastas I. Mikoian, rapidly rising in the ranks of Stalin's followers, declared, ". . . Comrade Stalin, with steel tenacity and the sagacity of genius, roused the spirit and will of our Party and all toilers for the struggle, and after a few months secured for our Party the greatest victory in the collective and state farm fields." [10] Even the official record suggests, however, that the campaign organizing agriculture around the kolkhoz (collective farm), though begun in 1928, was still a sore point. Stalin did not claim here, as he had for industry, that an actual material increase of large dimensions had been accomplished, but that conditions had been created "for such a rise and such a leap in the near future." [11] At the same time, the defeated opposition leaders, especially Bukharin, were forced to testify that the "extraordinary and acute struggle with the kulaks, a struggle which then turned into the slogan of the liquidation of the kulaks as a class" was thoroughly justified.[12]

It was indeed essential to Stalin's regime to have justified the struggle against the kulaks (officially defined as the "richer"—purely a relative term—peasants who from time to time used hired labor, but extended to any peasant groups which opposed the regime). In terms of social upheaval and human suffering this was the most catastrophic episode of Soviet rule between the Civil War and World War II. By passive resistance, especially the slaughtering of their livestock just before it was to be taken for the collectives, and sometimes by violence, the kulaks opposed the absorption of their farms into the kolkhozes. In many instances a large proportion of the other peasants made common cause with the kulaks, and in some areas—especially the more prosperous black-earth regions of the Ukraine, the North Caucasus, and south-central Russia—almost the entire village was united in opposition to collectivization. Under these circumstances, even Stalin's private admission that the "great bulk" of ten million opponents of collectivization had been "wiped out by their labourers" was short of the truth.[13] As the struggle in the countryside went on, the term "kulak" came to be applied not only to any opponent of collectivization, but to their families as well: "Don't think of the kulak's hungry children; in the class struggle philanthropy is evil," wrote a minor Communist official.[14] Grain quotas were ruthlessly collected, regardless of the amount left for the peasants; whole villages were deported to Siberia in wintertime. The effects, as far as children were concerned, can be roughly estimated from the number expected in the elementary-school grades eight years after the worst of the collectivization period. For the USSR as a whole, over one million fewer seven-year-old children were to enter the first grade in 1941 than were to leave the fourth grade (at the age of eleven) in the same year. Consequently, infant mortality and the deficit of births in 1933-34 must have much exceeded one million, since the children born in 1929-30 were, of course, also affected by famine resulting from the beginning of collectivization. In Kazakhstan, where the famine was worst, the 1933-34 group was *less* than three-fifths the size of the 1929-30 group, while in Moldavia (which, almost entirely outside the USSR in 1933, had not been affected by collectivization) the 1933-34 group was two-thirds *larger* than the 1929-30 group.[15]

The most extreme period of hardship for the rural population ended in late 1933, when the harvest was unusually good, though of course the 1934 birth rate was heavily depressed. Having liquidated its most determined opponents and secured collectivization of 69 per cent of the peasant households, the Party relaxed its repressive measures. Local Party organizations ordered an end to "mass violations of revolutionary legality, administrative excesses in regard to individual farmers and kolkhozniks." [16] *Only* 12,000 *more* families, whose heads were "actively struggling against the kolkhozes, sowing and procurement," instead of the 100,000 requested by local authorities, were to be deported. Women with small children, the aged, and the infirm could be assigned to forced labor in their villages instead of being deported. The 800,000 actually under arrest were to be reduced to 400,000, according to Stalin's secret instructions of the same period.[17] This did not affect the much larger number confined to concentration camps or deported in groups to distant parts of Siberia.

These ameliorations could not, however, overcome the traumatic effects of collectivization. While Soviet figures claimed the unusually good harvest of 1933 provided an increase of grain and other field crops over 1929, even this is doubtful. Stalin admitted that the number of farm animals had been halved.[18] It was obvious that it would be a long time before much more food was available to the people.

Not as obvious as the effects upon agricultural output, nor as horrifying as the human suffering, but in some respects even more debilitating in the long run was the moral impact of collectivization. A surface manifestation, of relatively minor significance in itself, was the prevalence of bandits where impenetrable terrain enabled them to survive police measures. Nine new bandit groups, with thirty-three members, appeared in the Western Oblast (region) in August 1934 alone, according to the official police report.[19] Much more important was the calloused attitude toward human suffering induced among many of the "victors" themselves—but that can be considered later.

If the social and economic aspects of the Communist "victory" were ambiguous, attainments in the international field were still more doubtful. The thesis of "socialism in one country," adumbrated by Lenin, explicitly formulated and constantly more strongly emphasized by Stalin, made the strengthening of the Soviet state the principal immediate aim. But this goal, as well as the more distant one of world revolution, had been seriously threatened by the rise of the Nazis in 1933.

Before the Nazis attained power the German Communist Party, in accordance with the "general line" of the Comintern (Communist International), had believed that a period of Nazi rule would be merely a transition to Communism. Consequently, the German Communists refused to ally with other anti-Nazi parties, particularly the largest, the Social Democrats. When the Nazis actually achieved power, they quickly and ruthlessly suppressed the Communist Party. Nevertheless, the Comintern— perhaps encouraged by such Nazi blunders as the Reichstag fire trial which enabled the Comintern leader Georgi Dimitrov to attain world fame by his defense speeches—maintained the old line. The Nazi regime and other "Fascist" systems were regarded as just another, and weaker, form of bourgeois rule, which was compelled by the "general crisis of capitalism" to abandon its parliamentary screen for overt terrorism.

Such theorizing did not, of course, obviate the threat which a Nazi-ruled Germany, perhaps as "the gendarme of capitalism," might pose to the Soviet Union itself. At first the Soviet leaders tried to counter the danger by diplomatic means.

Early Soviet suggestions that the Nazi ideological opposition to Communism need not stand in the way of good relations between the USSR and Germany were repeated by Stalin at the Seventeenth Congress. As the year wore on, however, the Soviet leaders appeared to recognize the futility of efforts to come to terms with the Nazi regime.[20] By June 1934, the durability of that regime appeared demonstrated by Hitler's drastic suppression of the Röhm faction in his party; consequently the Soviet leadership was faced with the necessity of considering it as a factor in long-range policy calculations.

Discussions for a Franco-Soviet mutual security pact began in the spring of 1934. In September, fulfilling a French condition for making the alliance, the USSR joined the League of Nations. Although the assassination a few weeks later of the French architect of the alliance, Louis Barthou, was recognized as a serious setback, the new policy of "collective security" seemed at the end of 1934 to offer the USSR a certain compensation for the rise of Nazism.

International Communism, on the other hand, did not gain even this compensation. By the end of 1934 the German Communist Party, its strongest member (outside the Soviet Union), was smashed. Before long the French Communist Party was to grow into a replacement for the Germans, but in the autumn of 1934 this was far from apparent to the Comintern leaders. As late as December, the Comintern magazine, *Kommunisticheskii Internatsional,* stressed the Spanish and the Chinese parties, which were, it said, confronted by a revolutionary crisis, as the vanguard of the international movement.[21]

If such was the nature of the "victory" proclaimed in 1934, what of the victorious Party itself? It had, to use Stalin's phrase, "no more enemies to fight"; the superficial observer, taking this remark at its face value, might have anticipated a long period of tranquillity. In fact, even as Stalin spoke, the Party ranks were being subjected to a far-reaching purge. Although at the Seventeeth Congress Nikolai Ezhov reported 2,807,786 members and candidates (probational members) as compared to 1,972,483 at the Sixteenth Congress (mid-1930), his figures conceal the violent fluctuations in membership during the intervening period.[22] In the two years preceding the opening of the purge in mid-1933, the Party had grown by 69 per cent.[23] By the end of 1933, however, the purge had led to the expulsion of 17 per cent of more than a million Communists checked, while 6.3 per cent more were placed in the "preprobation" sympathizer groups.[24]

While the purge of 1933-34 indicated considerable instability in the mass membership of the Party, it did not, apparently, reflect factional struggles for power. The purge, as the decree initiating it indicated, was aimed primarily at two elements. First were those who, though sincere members, were too weak-willed or ignorant to carry out the Party's demands. This element was viewed relatively leniently, and most persons in it were transferred to the sympathizer groups for further preparation for Party status. The second element, consisting of persons who had joined the Party for reasons of expediency, was regarded as a real threat. In it were "class alien" persons such as kulaks who had joined the Party to escape the rigors of collectivization, and perhaps to try to modify the agricultural policies; "careerists" who took advantage of the upheaval in the rural areas for personal advancement and frequently for downright robbery or blackmail; and "degenerates" who, while perhaps carrying out their Party assignments, presented bad examples in their personal conduct.[25]

That the purge was primarily directed at the group which had entered the Party during the collectivization period is indicated by the statistics concerning Party members examined in 1933. While 16.5 per cent of the examinees admitted to Party membership in 1932 and 1933 were ousted, only 10.3 per cent of the "Civil War" members (1918-20) were dismissed, as was a bare 2.7 per cent of the "Old Bolsheviks" admitted before 1918.[26] Since "the directing role fell to this basic, tested level of Party members, who have gone through the school of Civil War and underground," the 1933 purge had little effect on the real governing force in the apparatus.[27]

It would be hard to exaggerate the importance of the place in the Soviet system which the apparatus had attained by 1934. By that time the real strength of the Party lay not in the general membership, but in the minority of members who were full-time members of the Party bureaucracy itself, or who were assigned to equally important posts in the bureaucracies of the state. Among these bureaucracies the superior position of the Party apparatus was well established. After becoming General Secretary in 1922, Stalin had skillfully developed the Party apparatus as a mechanism first to oust his rivals, and then to establish undisputed control of the Soviet Union. From the mid-twenties on, the Party apparatus remained the fulcrum of political rivalries in the USSR; any alteration in its organization might well constitute a significant step in the development of Party history.[28]

Throughout the history of the CPSU "democratic centralism," established by Lenin as the guiding principle of Party organization, has nominally prevailed.[29] According to this principle, all higher officers are elected by the representatives of lower Party organizations; but once elected the officers are entitled to complete obedience during their term of office. Long before 1934, however, the election of Party officers had become a formality, for the central Party authorities dictated the nominations at all levels. The upper level of the apparatus was in fact self-selecting and self-perpetuating.

The basic unit of the Party remained the primary Party organization in the members' place of work, though in rural districts (as discussed in Chapter VII) the primary organization was often formed on a territorial basis. At higher levels the general system of Party organization was territorial. In the countryside the principal unit was the raikom, or raion (district) committee, dominated by its first secretary. In the city the gorkom (city committee) and its first secretary occupied parallel positions. The next higher level (aside from special variations in nationality areas) was the obkom, or oblast committee. The obkom first secretary, who supervised a territory with a million or more inhabitants, was an official of proconsular powers. Nevertheless, he, like all territorial levels of apparatus officials, was completely subordinate to the great central Party apparatus which was the bulwark of Stalin's rule.

Nominally the supreme central authority was the Party Congress. The convocation of a Congress, like the Seventeenth Congress of 1934, was still a very important matter, often a turning point in Party history. The infrequency of these meetings—the Sixteenth Congress had been held in 1930, and even nominally the Party Conference of 1932 had less extensive authority—was one reason for their inability to supervise the dynamic flow of Party affairs. More important was the fact that the apparatus and the Congress were in practice almost identical. High- or middle-level position in the apparatus almost automatically led to unopposed nomination as a Congress delegate from one or more lower Party organizations. While the Congress delegations contained some persons who were not apparatus officials, the Central Committee, elected as the "permanent" organ of the Congress (though it convened for only a few days each year), was almost entirely composed of higher Party officials.

In practice, the truly permanent central bodies of the apparatus were more powerful than either Congress or Central Committee. In 1934 the Politburo (Political Bureau) and the Orgburo (Organization Bureau) were still key positions, though Stalin had relied more and more on the Secretariat, which exercised day-to-day control over the Party apparatus. Consequently, it is most often changes in the organization of the Secretariat which provide clues to major Party developments. Very frequently these changes simply reflect the exigencies of political and economic control. Often, however, alterations in Secretarial organization reflect efforts of rival Party leaders—in Stalin's day, his lieutenants—to enhance their positions. All such changes, therefore, deserve close attention.

Of the major subdivisions of the apparatus, that dealing with indoctrination was least subject to change. Even here, however, a certain measure of reorganization was undertaken at the Seventeenth Congress, where two sections dealing with indoctrination were combined into the Section for Culture and Propaganda of Leninism. More fundamental was the change in the organizations supervising Party operations, personnel, and economic development. Assignment of personnel ("cadres") was probably the most crucial element of Party activity, for it not only affected the efficiency of the entire Soviet system, but provided an arena for political rivalry. Stalin had used his control of the Secretariat to place his adherents in key positions throughout the apparatus, and to render his antagonists impotent by assigning their supporters to distant or insignificant posts. The lesson was not lost on the dictator's own lieutenants; control of cadres sections was, therefore, a major prize in internecine power rivalry. The implications of the major change in Party structure affecting personnel made at the Seventeenth Congress can be best treated in detail in Chapter II, for they are intimately connected to economic and political changes of a longer-range nature; but the most essential aspects can be summarized here. Up to 1934 the basic organization of the Secretariat had been by "functional" sections. An organization-instruction section supervised the work of various levels of the Party apparatus and assigned Party apparatus personnel. A secret section maintained liaison with the police, while an administration of affairs directed routine Party activities. Finally, an assignments section, with numerous subdivisions, supervised the apportionment of personnel to all aspects of Soviet activity outside the Party apparatus itself. Obviously, this organization provided a powerful instrument for centralized control of personnel assignment.

The great defect of this scheme, according to Lazar M. Kaganovich, was its failure to grapple with "basic questions of life," i.e., primarily with economic matters.[30] To remedy this situation, the Seventeenth Congress created "integral production-branch" sections, designed to supervise entire branches of economic and administrative activity. In this way the assignment of personnel, while still directed from Moscow, was subdivided in accordance with economic branch requirements. In principle the decision seemed a complete triumph for Kaganovich's ideas. In practice, as will appear later, the new system was soon watered down.

Kaganovich was also closely connected with another significant change in Party organization carried out at the Seventeenth Congress. In January 1933 political sections had been established in the MTS (machine tractor stations), which constituted the framework for mechanization of agriculture. The political sections were designed to see that the kolkhozes supplied the products demanded by the government, to root out unreliable and opposition elements in the village, and to lay the groundwork for Party and

Komsomol (Communist Youth) organizations there. In the first task the political sections worked with the general director of the MTS, in the second with the MTS police deputy, and in the third with the raion, or district, Party organization.[31] The importance of the political sections is suggested by the fact that in 1933-34 eighteen thousand "tried" Party members were sent to staff them, and the similar political sections of the state farms. The 3,368 political sections practically ran Party propaganda activities in rural areas. According to a recent Soviet account they issued over two thousand newspapers (albeit mostly single-sheet, weekly publications), and operated almost as many small local radio stations.[32]

Since the basic principle of Party structure was territorial, the formation of the MTS political sections, each supervising Party activities in a group of kolkhozes, was an expedient explicitly designated as temporary; it was nonetheless resented by the regular raion Party committee or raikom. The resentment was repaid by the MTS political directors, who pointed out that they had been given their assignments because the raikoms were weak, yet the latter deliberately hampered the directors' activities.[33]

Discussion at the Seventeenth Congress suggests that this friction was reflected at higher Party levels. Lazar M. Kaganovich vigorously defended the political sections, noting sarcastically that

> Many are interested in the question just what will become of the political sections and the raikoms, and point to a certain contradiction. Of course from the point of view of formal logic there is a contradiction here. . . . I think that one should not conjecture, and one should not give schematic recipes in an organizational question.[34]

Subsequently the Congress adopted Kaganovich's suggestion that the MTS-raikom friction be solved *either* by transforming the political section into the raikom of a new raion, formed by subdividing the old, *or* by subordinating the political section to the existing raikom, as the Central Committee should decide in specific circumstances.[35]

At its plenum (plenary session) late in November 1934, the Central Committee ordered the political sections dissolved. Only the largest raions were divided; eventually nine hundred new ones were formed. This permitted over one-fourth of the political sections to become independent raikoms. Traces of the old friction remained even in these cases, for the old raikoms were reluctant to assist the new with equipment and personnel.[36] In most cases the political sections were changed into ordinary primary party organizations. The post of MTS deputy director for political affairs replaced that of political section director. The new post carried much less authority, for kolkhoz and MTS Party activities were subordinate to the raikoms. In a number of raikoms the post of second secretary was created, and often filled by former political section directors. Although Kaganovich had delivered the speech proposing the Central Committee decision, the position of the territorial apparatus appears to have triumphed.

The various policy divergences in organizational matters may have had little bearing on the power balance within the Communist ruling group. Clearly Joseph Stalin was the dominant figure. Next to him in prominence was Kaganovich, who was first secretary of the Moscow Party organization, Chairman of the Party Control Commission, and who exercised, as indicated above, a general supervision over the economy. V. M. Molotov, Chairman of the Council of People's Commissars, though rarely taking the initiative, had a powerful position. V. V. Kuibyshev, Chairman of the Commission of Soviet Control; M. I. Kalinin, formal chief of state; and K. E. Voroshilov, Commissar of Defense, were no longer at the peak of power, though very important. A. A. Andreev, Commissar of Transportation, and S. V. Kosior, first secretary of the Ukrainian Party, were never top figures. "Sergo" Ordzhonikidze, Commissar of Heavy Industry, and S. M. Kirov, first secretary of the Leningrad Party organization, were clearly dynamic leaders.

These ten comprised the membership of the Politburo, or policy committee of the Party. The five candidate (non-voting) members of the Politburo—Mikoian, V. Ia. Chubar', G. I. Petrovskii, P. P. Postyshev, and Ia. E. Rudzutak—held nominally less important posts in the territorial apparatus or in economic supervision. Several, however, like Postyshev, were actually more influential than many full members of the Politburo.

Was the 1934 Politburo fully subordinate to Stalin, or did its members show some signs of independence? A. S. Enukidze assured the Seventeenth Congress that complete harmony prevailed.

> Comrade Stalin knew how to surround himself with the best people in our country. . . . I don't refer to this to acquaint you with these comrades, whom you know as well as I, but just let those beyond the frontier of our country, who often babble about all kinds of controversies in the directing head of our Party, remember this and never get it out of their heads.[97]

Perhaps Enukidze was being completely frank. To all appearances he was then one of Stalin's closest friends. But Enukidze was also, according to all accounts, a man of extraordinary good will; it would not be surprising if he had tried to smooth over incipient friction among his associates, though there is no direct evidence that he sought to do so in 1934. Within a year and a half from the time Enukidze made this statement he was in disgrace, and within three years he was shot. In the meantime, one of his listeners at the Congress had taken advantage of a trip abroad to give the world materials which Boris Nicolaevsky used to write the remarkable *Letter of an Old Bolshevik*.[38]

According to this document, Kirov had advocated a "policy of reconciliation": lenient treatment for opposition elements, and an effort to draw them back into the Party; relaxation of pressures on the peasantry; and firm alignment with the West against the Nazi danger. Stalin demanded stern measures, including execution of Party opponents, particularly M. N. Riutin in 1932, to enforce his will. Nevertheless, Kirov triumphed, especially at the November Central Committee plenum, which is supposed to have contained a strong majority favoring "liberalization." According to the *Letter* the plenum decided to relieve Kirov of his Leningrad duties to permit him to devote himself to work in the central Secretariat. There, in Moscow, Kirov would have been in a position to implement the "reconciliation" or at least to impose a constant check on Stalin.

Such, in bare outline, is the story of the *Letter*. Boris Nicolaevsky, the veteran émigré analyst who first published it, maintains that Ordzhonikidze and Kuibyshev were aligned with Kirov.[39] Most émigré accounts agree that Kaganovich was Stalin's firmest adherent at that time, and point to Kirov's great personal popularity to explain his success.[40] But an early (April 1934) letter from Moscow in *Sotsialisticheskii Vestnik* (the journal which originally published the *Letter*), alleged that Kirov and Kaganovich, in contrast to Stalin, Voroshilov, Molotov, and Kalinin, were *against* privileges for the peasants.[41] To mention just one more divergence in accounts, Grigorii Tokaev, a secret oppositionist in the Leningrad Party in 1934, says that Kirov was, next to Stalin, the most hated leader.[42]

As will unfortunately appear again and again in the course of this treatment, mere evaluation of the qualifications of conflicting witnesses does not help much in resolving disputes about the nature of high politics in the USSR. According to Nicolaevsky (in 1959), the disaffected Communist officials who provided background material for the *Letter* had direct access to the circle in which the controversy was taking place. The *Letter* itself does not claim such access, however, and it seems doubtful that Bukharin, the only official named, was by 1934 in a position to know just what the top Soviet leaders planned. Reports other than Nicolaevsky's are obviously based on second- or third-hand information.

The alternative approach is to examine the known course of events to see if it conforms to the "inside" explanations. Here two questions may be asked: Is it probable that Kirov was in a position to defeat Stalin, assuming he wished to do so? Was a policy of "reconciliation" actually apparent in 1934?

The accounts sketched above emphasize a struggle in the Politburo. According to the Party statute, the Politburo was the highest body functioning between Central Committee plenums, but in fact the Secretariat had usurped much of its power. Stalin, as General Secretary, had used the Secretariat, the continually operating staff agency, as the principal lever in overturning the opposition groups.[43] As most of the 1934 Politburo members (and indeed Central Committee members) indirectly owed their positions to the efficacy of the Secretariat as a political weapon, they might well have hesitated to challenge its power. Kirov was, to be sure, a member of the Secretariat; but so, of course, was Stalin. Kaganovich, who, most accounts agree, opposed Kirov's "reconciliation," and who in any case was probably at odds with him on the question of MTS political sections, was also a Secretary. The fourth member, Andrei Zhdanov, though still in a junior position, was an intransigent supporter of extreme measures in many fields. While these considerations do not rule out Stalin's temporary defeat —or retreat—in 1934, they do cast some doubt on its likelihood.

Many developments, on the other hand, do suggest a "policy of reconciliation." The curb on the harshest measures directed at the peasantry has already been described. Proponents of the "reconciliation" interpretation have stressed this change, though pointing out that Kirov was never willing to "retreat" from collectivization of agriculture.[44] The July 1934 transformation of the dread OGPU (General State Political Administration—a euphemistic title for the political police) into a branch of the Commissariat of Internal Affairs (NKVD) also appeared to many as a step to replace arbitrary measures by legal action. The *Pravda* editorial announcing the change stressed the importance of the establishment (through the dissolution of the special tribunal of the OGPU) of the single court system.[45] Andrei Vyshinskii, as Procurator of the USSR, an office formed just a year earlier to supervise the legality of OGPU activities, also stressed dependence on the courts.[46] In view of Vyshinskii's earlier association with police activity, neither his remarks nor his position was very reassuring. Genrikh Iagoda's appointment to head the NKVD, however, did appear to mean a certain curb on Stalin, for there was a long history of friction between them.[47]

Offsetting the restrictions on the police was a series of measures which potentially increased its arbitrary power. A decree of June 8, 1934, provided for punishment of relatives of Soviet officials who fled abroad. The decree founding the NKVD set up a special board empowered to impose five years' exile; thus the nominal transfer of jurisdiction to the courts was undone.[48] A further decree of November 5, 1934, gave the special board power to impose exile or imprisonment on all considered "socially dangerous." [49] Finally, as the Communist press boasted, the internal passport system, established in 1932, established a net of control which no "enemy" in the USSR could escape.[50]

In many respects, 1934 developments in cultural and ideological aspects of Soviet life seemed to parallel those in the fields of police control. With the complete victory of the program of socialism in one country, the era of radical "proletarian experimentalism" was ended. In the economic and social field this meant that equality of reward was bitterly attacked as "petit bourgeois" and utopian, wholly incompatible with socialism.[51] In philosophy, the Central Committee, obviously following up Stalin's speech to the Institute of the Red Professors a month earlier, condemned both major schools of thought. The "mechanists," including Bukharin, were denounced for presenting a "vulgarized" concept of Marxism devoid of the dialectic element. The principal proponent of the dialectic, on the other hand, A. M. Deborin, was attacked as a "Menshevizing idealist" who divorced theory and practice.[52]

In the short run, by reducing the power of dominant philosophers, especially Deborin, the Party intervention appeared to provide a little more scope for independent thought. In the long run, Stalin's intervention set a precedent which eventually turned Soviet philosophy into a servile exposition of his dicta. The same tendency was visible in artistic expression. In 1934 the fine arts were still relatively free, but the RAPP (Russian Association of Proletarian Writers) controversy had made deep inroads upon literary independence. The downfall of RAPP, which had insisted on a radical interpretation of Marxist requirements in literature, meant a certain toleration for non-Party writers, the so-called "fellow travelers." In 1931 Stalin had hinted that the co-operation of non-Party intellectuals was needed —especially in glorifying the Five Year Plan—and, as in the philosophy dispute, the Central Committee complied the next year by dissolving RAPP. But the major reason for the dissolution of RAPP was the unwillingness of its leaders to recognize that literature, whether "Marxist or not," must refrain from criticizing the Soviet system. The new dispensation in Party control of literature soon proved to be more debilitating in its regimentation of literature, though less doctrinaire, than RAPP.[53]

The opening act of the new phase of Party control was the Soviet Writers' Congress of August 1934. Nominally the dominant figure was Maxim Gor'kii, most famous of Soviet Marxist writers. There was a considerable range of expression at the Congress. Not too obtrusively, but firmly, however, the real meaning of the Congress was set forth by the Party spokesmen. Chief among the latter was Andrei Zhdanov, the Central Committee Secretary, who sharply attacked Western literature, and praised the "tendentiousness" of Communist writing. Soviet writers, he said, must be "engineers of human souls," presenting under the rubric "social realism," not "objective reality" but "reality in its revolutionary development."[54] To ensure constant guidance of literature, a Union of Soviet Writers, dominated by the Presidium of its Executive Board, was established by the Congress.[55]

The victory celebrated by the Party in 1934 boded no good for articulate non-Russians in the USSR. Indeed, the "victory" itself, as several speakers implied, was won on the corpses of several of the most zealous "national Marxists." Foremost among them was the Old Bolshevik Mykola Skrypnyk, minister of education in the Ukraine, who had committed suicide in May 1933. Skrypnyk's death was the culmination of a long struggle to create a thoroughly Marxist Ukrainian culture independent of the Russian. Stalin, though a non-Russian by origin himself, evidently recognized at an early date the importance of Russian national feeling in strengthening the Soviet state, and thereby his own dictatorship. The Ukrainian Communists' struggle for cultural independence from "Moscow" could all too easily turn into a political rejection of Stalin's dominance.[56] Consequently, from 1926 on he gradually narrowed the limits of national expression in the Ukraine. At the Seventeenth Congress he explained this tactic as follows:

> Even until very recently the deviation toward Ukrainian nationalism did not constitute the principal danger in the Ukraine, but when they stopped fighting it and let it grow until it merged with interventionism, this deviation became the main danger.[57]

We have seen that the "victory" achieved in 1934 was a rather dubious amalgam of many elements: some, like the industrial advance, spectacularly favorable from the Soviet standpoint, some fraught with suffering in the past and danger for the future. Similarly, the surface relaxation, whether or not it concealed conflict at the highest Party levels, undoubtedly covered a multitude of conflicting tendencies in the Soviet body politic. The shot fired on December 1 was the catalyst of a far greater explosion.

CHAPTER

▌▌

KIROV'S ASSASSINS

Kirov was shot to death in his Smolny Institute office on the afternoon of December 1, 1934, a few days after his return to Leningrad from the Central Committee plenum. The assassin was Leonid V. Nikolaev, a Party member and former government worker in Leningrad. The deputy director of the Leningrad NKVD, Ivan Zaporozhets, had stimulated and assisted Nikolaev in preparing for the killing.

These are facts—if anything can be called fact in the obscurity surrounding this strange affair. The strangest aspect, the role of Zaporozhets, and almost certainly of higher figures in the police, is demonstrated not only by the testimony of numerous witnesses, but by the undisputed circumstances of the case. Some time before the killing, Nikolaev had been detained by guards in the Leningrad Party headquarters in the Smolny. In his briefcase they found a revolver and a diary, which apparently contained allusions to his intention of assassinating Kirov. Later evidence indicated that Nikolaev had indeed intended to make an attempt on Kirov's life at this time. Nevertheless, Nikolaev was freed, and even given back his revolver. When he returned on December 1, the guards were curiously absent, with the exception of Kirov's aide Borisov, nominally an NKVD employee, who was mysteriously killed in an automobile accident the following day.

Why did Nikolaev undertake this desperate assault upon a top Party leader? It is quite improbable that Nikolaev was a knowing tool of the secret police. It is, of course, possible that he was, as the series of Soviet official versions cited below maintain, a member of some opposition group, or at least in sympathy with some opposition tendency. If this is the case, Zaporozhets evidently knew of Nikolaev's political views, and took advan-

20

tage of them. A second possibility is that Nikolaev bore a grudge against Kirov as head of the Leningrad Party. Nikolaev had lost his job in the Leningrad apparatus, or had been assigned to less desirable duties outside the city, and had also been expelled for a time from the Party itself. Then there is the banal possibility that Nikolaev acted because his attractive wife had been seduced by Kirov. This explanation was rumored in Moscow very soon after the assassination.[1] Trotsky, not much inclined to accept the trivial or accidental explanation when a more impressive one was available, apparently found this theory thoroughly credible.[2] Elizabeth Lermolo, who claims to have met Nikolaev's wife, dismisses the explanation on the ground that she was too ugly to have attracted the rather handsome Kirov.[3] Alas, we have no picture of this Helen (or Milda, to give her real name) whose face *may* have launched ten thousand executions.

A more serious, but related, question is why Zaporozhets and his accomplices undertook to prod and help Nikolaev. As will be shown, the official Soviet versions are so contradictory and implausible as to deserve little credence, except insofar as they admit the fact—apparent to outside observers as soon as the first descriptions of the assassination were released —of police involvement. The natural supposition, then, has been that these versions were covers for the real instigators, in the highest levels of the Communist regime. The final version during Stalin's lifetime made Iagoda, the Commissar of the NKVD, the author of the plot.[4] Highly placed defectors from the NKVD, however, found this explanation ridiculous.[5] Zaporozhets would not have dared act on Iagoda's order alone, even had Iagoda himself had the courage—and the motive—to kill Kirov.[6]

Since the only person possessing the power to compel Iagoda to undertake such an assignment was Stalin, the suspicion of his opponents outside the USSR (and, if their reports are correct, the suspicion of many Soviet citizens) immediately focused on him. Moreover, those who have believed that Kirov and Stalin advocated sharply opposed policies during 1934 have a plausible motive for Stalin's instigation of the assassination. However, part of this explanation is that Stalin wished to have Kirov done away with before Kirov could appear at the November 25-28 plenum in which his "reconciliation" policy is supposed to have triumphed, and his personal power advanced.[7] This would be more plausible, evidently, had the abortive attempt occurred shortly before the plenum. Alexander Orlov, one of the NKVD defectors, does in fact maintain that it took place about ten days before the assassination, i.e., during the week preceding the plenum.[8] Another defector, Walter Krivitsky, on the other hand, placed the failure

two months earlier than the success, and this approximate date is corroborated by both the first official Soviet announcement and by Nikita Khrushchev's secret speech to the Twentieth Party Congress.[9]

Several observers have felt that the case against Stalin was practically
proven by Khrushchev's revelation that the "top functionaries of the Leningrad NKVD" were shot in 1937 "in order to cover the traces of the organizers
of Kirov's killing."[10] While these remarks make it extremely probable that
Stalin had foreknowledge of the plot, they do not rule out an explanation
which accepts Stalin's involvement without admitting enmity between
him and Kirov. This explanation maintains that Stalin valued Kirov as a
lieutenant. But in order to justify extreme measures against all forms of
opposition Stalin needed a striking demonstration of his theory that

> the growth of the power of the Soviet state will intensify the resistance of the
> last remnants of the dying classes. It is precisely because they are dying and
> their days are numbered that they will go on from one form of attack to other,
> sharper forms of attack. . . .[11]

Consequently, he arranged that Nikolaev—a real malcontent, for whatever
reason—be helped to attempt the assassination, which was to be "narrowly"
averted at the last moment. To Stalin's dismay, Nikolaev's attempt succeeded. While the most circumstantial version of this explanation has been
advanced recently by a former NKVD official,[12] Trotsky suggested it not
long after the assassination.[13]

It is worth devoting some consideration to the circumstances (unsatis-
factorily explained as they are) of Kirov's death because of the tremendous
repercussions of the assassination. Within hours after the shooting, Stalin,
Iagoda, his deputy, Ia. S. Agranov, and probably Zhdanov and other high
officials, arrived in Leningrad. That same night, Stalin secured two special
decrees by the presidium of the Soviet legislature, the Central Executive
Committee, authorizing the death penalty without right of appeal for
"terrorists."[14] On December 2 the Soviet press announced the assassination
without details, though a *Pravda* editorial said it showed the "enemies are
still creeping into the camp of the revolution." The following day the NKVD
announced the assassin's name. On December 4 the bare physical details
of the slaying were given. The head of the Leningrad NKVD, F. D. Medved
(who two days earlier had signed an obituary statement), and several of
his subordinates (not, however, Zaporozhets) were accused of negligence.
On the same page of *Pravda* were printed lengthy lists of "White Guards"

recently arrested in Leningrad and Moscow for "preparation of terrorist acts." The "White Guards" (anti-Communists) were not explicitly linked to Nikolaev at this time; but the publication of these lists and long stories on subsequent days concerning the infiltration of numbers of such "terrorists" into the USSR gave the impression that Kirov's assassination was part of a vast anti-Soviet plot. As late as the end of December and the first week of January *Pravda* continued to charge that anti-Soviet émigré newspapers in the United States, Germany, and Yugoslavia had covertly advocated Kirov's murder beforehand and afterward condoned it.[15]

Two weeks before these last articles appeared, the Soviet press began to advance quite a different version. To the careful outside observer this shift suggests that Stalin was either confused because the "staged" assassination had accidentally succeeded, or because he failed to extract a confession from Nikolaev. The Soviet press, however, pictured the new version as entirely compatible with the first, emphasizing the diabolical interrelations among opponents of socialism. This new version was circulated in a secret Central Committee letter in mid-December, and publicly adumbrated at a meeting of the Moscow Party organization, reported in *Pravda* on December 17, where "agents of the class enemy, foul dregs of the former Zinoviev anti-Party group" were accused.[16] This accusation increased in intensity and broadened in scope until the December 30 announcement of the trial *in camera* of Nikolaev and seven "accomplices" by a special Leningrad session of the Military Collegium of the Supreme Court. According to the prosecution, Nikolaev was a member of the "Leningrad center" of Zinoviev's followers, who "after losing hope of mass support" turned to terrorism in order to put through Trotsky's and Zinoviev's program. Trotsky was directly linked to the assassination by the allegation that he was in touch with a foreign consul (it is said that the Latvian Bissinieks was meant) who subsidized Nikolaev.[17]

A week before Nikolaev's death sentence was announced, *Pravda* (December 23) reported the arrest in Moscow on December 16 of Zinoviev, Kamenev, and thirteen other "members of the former Zinoviev group." As evidence was insufficient to try several, including Zinoviev and Kamenev, in court, they had been transferred to the NKVD special board.[18] On January 16, however, the Procurator's accusation against these erstwhile opposition leaders contended that they, as "the Moscow center," had known of the terrorist tendencies of the Nikolaev group and indeed had inflamed them. Zinoviev admitted the "political responsibility" of the "former anti-Party 'Zinoviev' group for the murder committed."[19] On this basis Zinoviev and several other defendants were sentenced by the Military Collegium of the Supreme Court to ten years imprisonment; Kamenev and others to five.[20]

During the months immediately following these trials, the Soviet press did not often mention further arrests. Numerous reports indicate, however, that thousands of Leningrad citizens had been arrested and sent to "isolator" camps in the weeks following Kirov's death.[21] Meanwhile, the Communist propaganda machinery was conducting an intense campaign on the significance of the assassination as exemplifying Stalin's theory of the heightened intensity and unscrupulousness of opposition as socialism advanced. The Central Committee secret letter cited above ordered the cultural and propaganda sections of the territorial apparatus to form groups for the study of Party history emphasizing the pernicious role of anti-Party elements.[22] A second secret letter of January 29, 1935, reiterated this instruction.[23] Innumerable articles in the Soviet daily and periodical press reviewed the charges made at the trials described above. They stressed the need for heightened vigilance to combat the growing violence and duplicity of the opposition, and the danger of *any* deviation as eventually leading to criminal activity in collaboration with foreign and domestic reactionaries.

Either because action of the Party organization at the scene of the assassination was thought to provide a better object lesson, or because Andrei Zhdanov, who had replaced Kirov in Leningrad, was an especially vigorous and implacable foe of all deviations, the Party organization there took the public lead in the new line of indoctrination. The gorkom (city Party committee) passed a resolution on March 29 which reiterated the points made in the secret letters; it emphasized study of Party history, especially for the post-Revolutionary period, as the key to the understanding of the theory of Marx-Engels-Lenin-Stalin.[24]

With the justification that Communist theory is intimately related to practice, Stalin's version of his triumph over his rivals was thenceforth to be the main subject of indoctrination. This tendency, which was foreshadowed by the creation of a Party committee on history—including Zhdanov in its membership—will be treated in detail later. Here it is important to note the enormous stimulus which this tendency received from the Kirov affair.

The Leningrad resolution ascribed primary importance to forming a net of study circles, though it also made provisions for consultations with individuals studying Party history alone. Later in the spring the whole indoctrination apparatus of the Central Committee was reorganized. The Culture and

Propaganda Section was dissolved. First place in the new organization was given to a Section of Propaganda and Agitation in charge of indoctrination within the Party. Its supervision extended to the study circles and Party schools; it also directed mass agitation campaigns. The other sections were: Schools; Press and Publications; Science, Scientific-Technical Inventions and Discoveries; and Cultural-Enlightenment Work. The mere list of these sections suggests the increasing totalitarian control by the Party machine. The Cultural-Enlightenment Work Section, under the direction of Zhdanov's close associate, Aleksandr Shcherbakov, was especially significant in this regard, for its duties were to include supervision of motion pictures, radio, theaters, writers' organizations, artists, and architects.[25]

The reorganization of propaganda activities was one of a series of highly important organizational measures introduced in the winter and spring of 1935. Two plenums of the Central Committee were held in February, on the first and the twenty-eighth.[26] On January 25 Kuibyshev had died, ostensibly from heart failure. His relative youth, rumored opposition to Stalin, and the coincidence with Kirov's death have led many to suspect foul play. There were then two vacancies in the Politburo, which were filled by promoting Mikoian and Chubar'. Zhdanov and R. I. Eikhe replaced them as candidates. Ostensibly all were Stalin's followers; but Eikhe and Chubar' were later purged, while Zhdanov and Mikoian remained in favor. Consequently, it is hard to see any special political significance in these appointments.

The appointment of N. I. Ezhov to the Secretariat and to the chairmanship of the Commission of Party Control (replacing Kaganovich, who became Minister of Rail Transport) was crucially significant. This signaled the appearance of members of Stalin's personal staff as overt wielders of power. A. N. Poskrebyshev, perhaps Stalin's most trusted aide, received little public attention until 1937.[27] Another aide, M. F. Shkiriatov, became Ezhov's deputy in the Commission of Party Control, and G. M. Malenkov his second-in-command in the Section of Directing Party Organs of the Party Secretariat.[28]

The Commission of Party Control was created by the Seventeenth Congress, replacing the Central Control Commission. Its principal tasks were to increase control over fulfillment of Party decisions and to heighten Party discipline. In carrying out the latter task, the Commission issued directives on such matters as expulsion of Party members for economic mismanagement or for having recommended Party membership for persons who turned

out to be Zinoviev supporters.[29] "Groups" of the Commission were established to watch over every major aspect of the Soviet economy and administration.[30] Especially important instruments for centralized Party control
were the plenipotentiaries of the Commission, who were sent to territorial
secretaries. Ezhov's speech to the third plenum of the Commission in the
spring of 1936 cautioning the plenipotentiaries to inform the territorial
Party officials of the plan of inspection which the plenipotentiaries wished
to follow, and the central directives which they were charged to enforce
suggest that their high-handed behavior may have made matters worse.[31]

Much more prominence was accorded the Commission of Party Control
than was given the Section of Directing Party Organs of the Secretariat.
Nevertheless, it seems probable that the latter was really more important
in Ezhov's process of reducing the Party organization to complete submission to Stalin. The "production-branch" reorganization of the Secretariat
at the Seventeenth Congress had left this section in complete charge of
internal Party activities other than indoctrination. Nominally Party members
employed outside the apparatus in economic activities were supervised by
the industrial sections of the Secretariat. Gradually, however, the Directing
Party Organs Section seems to have gathered into its hands more and more
of the real control over all personnel.

The first steps toward establishing personnel, or cadre, sections were
taken at the local level. Some time in February 1935, probably at one of
its plenums, the Central Committee "on the initiative of Stalin" decided to
form cadres sections in a large number of gorkoms.[32] The first public notice
was issued on March 27; it ordered the formation, with the assistance of
the Directing Party Organs Section, of cadres sections in fifty gorkoms.
This directive was followed in two days by the resolution of the Leningrad
Party organization which set the pattern in personnel, as in propaganda,
reorganization. The Leningrad resolution stated that lack of cadres sections
had hampered the work of training, choosing, and distributing Party
personnel, and diminished day-to-day contacts between the gorkom and
the primary Party organizations. The size of the Leningrad cadres section
—which included the director, his deputy, ten assistants, sixteen instructors,
and five technical workers—increases the impression that it was designed
to play a key role in all phases of Soviet activity in the city.[33] Officially,
however, the duties of the cadres section were: to form a reserve for the
apparatus from suitable Communists not then employed in it, to assist in
verification of Party documents, and to strengthen the flow of information
within the Party.[34] At this stage, then, the cadres section was nominally

confined to supervision of personnel related to the Party apparatus itself.

On September 26, 1935, a significant reorganization of the Directing Party Organs Section began. A "sector" (subsection) for accounting for directing cadres was established. Under this sector were placed two "groups" —one for accounting for Party apparatus cadres, a second for maintaining records on their assignments. In addition, three "groups" were designed to account for directing personnel in all phases of Soviet activity: industry and transport; agriculture, trade, finance, and planning; and administrative, cultural, and scientific organizations. Just as significant were the eleven territorial "groups." Each was headed by an instructor who had to know the area "not worse than the area secretary." His staff included an instructor for cadres. Each "group" supervised a large area of the USSR overlapping the established administrative divisions. The wording of the decree and Ezhov's explanation of it imply that the Section of Directing Party Organs did not as yet assign personnel outside the apparatus.[35] All the same, the complete centralization of personnel information and the dispatch of cadres instructors to the territorial apparatus were powerful instruments for over-all control.

The organizational measures adopted in 1935 were closely related to the progress of the Party purge. An enormous number of Communists—about seven hundred thousand—were expelled in mid-1933. The pace slowed down during the remainder of 1933 and 1934. Anyone who closely analyzes published Party statistics for this period soon becomes aware of their frequent inaccuracy and even contradiction—a state of affairs often enough criticized by the Party itself. Consequently, it does not seem worth while, unless a Communist speaker is directly cited, to burden the reader and the printer with precise numbers, which merely give a spurious appearance of exactitude. In round numbers, then, the Party comprised 2,700,000 in late 1933, and 2,350,000 a year later, a decline of about 350,000 in more than a year of purging. Despite the Kirov assassination, the rate of purge continued to diminish in the first months of 1935; only about 100,000 were expelled before May.[36] The bulk of the expellees appears still to have been recent Party entrants, predominantly rural; by 1935, however, the purge was beginning to strike down a considerable number of the Party apparatus workers in the countryside.[37]

Although many Party organizations had not even after two years completed the purge, the Central Committee decided on May 13, 1935, to start a new process, the "verification" of Party documents. It charged (with some reason) that there had been "chaos" in issuance and safeguarding of documents, but related this to the political situation of the spring of 1935 by alleging that this confusion had permitted the infiltration of "enemies."[38] In effect verification was the occasion for a second screening, much more closely related than the first purge to Stalin's political objectives.

Highly important among these was the elimination of the influence of the Old Bolsheviks—the "founding fathers" of the Revolution. Unfortunately, Soviet sources do not provide statistics on the length of Party membership of those expelled during verification. In view of the Soviet stress on expulsion of recent entrants during the earlier purge, this omission is probably significant in itself. At any rate, anti-Stalinist accounts, especially the *Letter of an Old Bolshevik*,[39] and an examination of official reports on other Soviet moves during mid-1935, demonstrate the existence of a campaign against the Old Bolsheviks. Most obvious was the formal dissolution by a Central Committee decree of May 25 of the Society of Old Bolsheviks.[40] Then there was the increasing tendency to place "non-Party Bolsheviks" on a par with Party members. For example, a *Pravda* editorial of May 30 declared that

> Bolshevik is he who is dedicated finally to the cause of the proletarian revolution. Such are many non-Party persons. Either they have not succeeded in entering the ranks of the Party, or they so highly esteem it, regard it as so sacred that they want to prepare for entrance into the Party ranks.

Stalin's anger against the Old Bolsheviks seems to have arisen because of certain mysterious events in the spring of 1935. It is said that a group of Komsomols was discovered plotting the assassination of Stalin himself, and that officers of the Kremlin guard were involved. The young terrorists were supposed to have been stimulated by speeches or writings of members of the Society of Former Political Exiles which, like the Old Bolsheviks, consisted of revolutionaries from Tsarist times.[41] At any rate, this society was also dissolved, and propaganda directives emphatically denounced the "*narodnichestvo*," or terroristic tactics once advocated by Social Revolutionaries.[42]

Almost certainly these obscure events are related in some manner to the action of the June 5-7 plenum of the Central Committee in expelling A. S. Enukidze from his post as secretary of the Central Executive Committee and from the Party itself, but it is not clear whether the real ground for the dismissal was Enukidze's protection of suspect elements or his affront to Stalin's vanity. Officially, Enukidze was charged at this point with filling the apparatus of the Central Executive Committee secretariat with "alien and immoral" elements—elsewhere a "Tsarist princess" was mentioned —and through his "liberal" attitude letting himself be used by them.[43]

Since Enukidze, a Georgian, was thought to be one of Stalin's few intimate friends, his sudden disgrace was startling. Speculation about Stalin's psychological development is not very fruitful. Still, it does seem clear that his morbid suspicion, complete intolerance of contrary views, and insatiable craving for adulation developed at a rapid rate in the early thirties. The death in 1932 of his second wife, rumored a suicide caused by his brutal behavior, seems to have been a major turning point. It is said also that Gor'kii, whom Stalin had known well and perhaps to some degree respected, broke with Stalin in 1935 over his treatment of the opposition.[44]

Bitter assaults on Enukidze as a "degenerate" and "Philistine" by Stalin's favorites of the time, such as Nikita S. Khrushchev, then Moscow obkom secretary, suggest that Stalin's friendship had turned to hatred.[45] Other attacks imply that Enukidze was punished not for what he did but for what he failed to do for Stalin:

> He is a typical representative of just that category of people the philosophical thought of whose life is contained in the following "We have already done our business, and now we may live quietly, not disturbing ourselves and not disturbing others."[46]

This may refer to Enukidze's rumored pleas for mercy for his Old Bolshevik associates allegedly implicated in Kirov's assassination, for Enukidze's "lack of vigilance" was explicitly related to the assassination.[47] In any case, it is fairly certain that Stalin felt Enukidze was not a sufficiently pliable tool to be trusted to direct the Secretariat of the Central Executive Committee during the approaching purge. It is significant that in mid-1935 a second trial—kept quiet at the time—doubled Kamenev's term of imprisonment,[48] and that closed Party meetings were by autumn denouncing "Right opportunists" as well as the followers of Zinoviev and Trotsky.[49] The accusation of Enukidze may, on the other hand, relate to his rumored refusal to rewrite Transcaucasian Bolshevik history to glorify Stalin's role.[50]

Dark a prospect as the events just described implied, it would be wrong to give the impression that the general public in the USSR was absorbed by the intra-Party strife. Foreign affairs, especially the continued advance of the Nazis, and the countermovement toward the Popular Front, occupied a prominent, though secondary, place in the Soviet press. Greatest emphasis was devoted to the project for a new Soviet Constitution, fulsomely praised

as the "most democratic in the world." Even the plenums which, as we
have seen, dealt with key Party matters, also were described as devoting
much of their attention to the Constitution. Economic affairs, as always,
occupied the major place in the Soviet newspapers. Especially stressed
was the Stakhanovite movement for above-norm production in industry,
described in Chapter VII.

Numerous reports from defectors, and the abundant documentation contained in the Smolensk Party archives captured by the Germans, indicate,
however, that the more articulate classes—intellectuals, managers, and
officials—were swept by a feeling of uneasiness. Meetings became almost
hysterical in tone.[51] Libraries, always censored, were torn by indiscriminate
purges of books by oppositionist authors.[52] For Party members, the verification process was a frightening experience. Zhdanov explicitly called it
"repression" though he explained that this meant extensive purge and
investigation with an "educative significance."[53] To be sure, the expulsions
were not as numerous as in the Party purge proper. Ezhov reported to the
December 21-25, 1935, Central Committee plenum that 81.1 per cent of
the members and candidates had been verified by December 1; of these,
9.1 per cent, or about 190,000 had been dropped.[54] But the purge had for
the most part excluded recent entrants, while those dropped at verification
were frequently old members whose whole lives had been bound up with
their Party status. Moreover, the charges of association with terrorism or
lack of vigilance in dealing with it were far more dangerous than the earlier
accusations of passivity, careerism, or even corruption. To make matters
worse, a third process of investigation was ordered even before verification
was finished. The December plenum at which Ezhov reported ordered that
all Communists exchange their cards. A supplementary instruction of
January 14, 1936, required that this exchange, which was utilized to inquire
once more into the social backgrounds and deviations from the Party line
of the members, take place from February through May, 1936.[55]

The end of the first phase of tension and the beginning of the second
was marked by the public trial, held in Moscow, August 19-24, 1936, of
Zinoviev, Kamenev, and fourteen others.[56] The trial was preceded by the
circulation of another Central Committee secret letter setting forth the
prosecutor's accusations as established facts.[57] In this way, the Party propaganda machine at all levels was prepared in advance to utilize the trial as a
demonstration of the evil of opposition.

The trial of the "sixteen," has been subjected to well-nigh endless discussion outside the USSR.[58] Since the accusations relate to events and cir-

cumstances already analyzed above, we need treat only a few of the outstanding features here. All of the defendants confessed (though I. N.
Smirnov made some reservations), a fact which has given rise to much
speculation and many "inside" explanations. Most likely a combination of
physical pressure, promises to spare the defendants or their families, and
appeals to a peculiar Communist concept of service to the "revolution" even
at the cost of one's own reputation was used. Which elements predominated
in individual cases is a fascinating but insoluble riddle. The simplest explanation for the unanimity of the confessions is that recalcitrant defendants
were just not brought to public trial. Only four of the nineteen tried in
January 1935 appeared in the 1936 court, although nine of the earlier group
had been explicitly charged as members of the "Moscow center." Moreover,
the secret letter refers to interrogations of more than a score of implicated
persons who were not publicly tried then or later.[59]

The official reason for retrying Zinoviev and Kamenev was that new
evidence revealed not only that they were directly implicated in Kirov's
assassination, but that they had plotted the murder of the entire Soviet
leadership except Molotov. This strange omission gave rise to the rumor
that Molotov was himself scheduled for trial. If there had been any coolness
between Molotov and Stalin it soon vanished, however.[60]

Eleven of the defendants were Jews.[61] In view of the considerable proportion of Jews among the Communist leaders, this circumstance could not at
the time be taken as a clear indication of anti-Semitism, but later developments seem to indicate that Stalin began then to identify his enemies with
Jews in general. All the more grotesque was the charge that these Jews were
linked to the Nazi police, and planned to betray the Soviet Union by
adopting a defeatist attitude in case it became involved in war with Germany
and other Fascist powers.[62] The true aim of these charges, which were
based primarily on the testimony of hitherto obscure German-Jewish Communists living in the USSR, was to destroy Trotsky's reputation. He was,
as has often been said, the real defendant at the Moscow bar. Ironically, it
was precisely in his effort to provide evidence of Trotsky's link to the
defendants that Andrei Vyshinskii, the prosecutor, made the most ludicrous
blunders. For example, he described a long-demolished Copenhagen hotel
as the place where Trotsky and his coconspirators met.[63]

For the higher echelons of the Party the most ominous aspect of the
trial was its obvious promise of more trials to come, for the police and the
Right opposition were clearly implicated. Again, however, it should be
clearly understood that the trial, heavily stressed as it was in the Soviet

press, was not the only, or probably even the principal, preoccupation of the average Soviet citizen. Though material conditions had improved somewhat, the business of living was sufficient to occupy the attention of most. The discussion of the Constitution was approaching its final stage. Chkalov's spectacular flight across the North Pole occupied much of the newspaper space at the end of July and the first part of August. Finally—most important to many articulate Soviet citizens and certainly to pro-Soviet foreign observers—the Popular Front policy seemed in Spain to have finally checked the advance of Fascism.

CHAPTER

COMINTERN AND POPULAR FRONT

Superficially the contrast between Soviet domestic politics and international Communist policies during the middle thirties is enormous. While all independence was being suppressed within the Soviet Party and totalitarian control extended over every nonpolitical aspect of Soviet life, foreign Communist parties were proclaiming the defense of democracy and individual liberty. Ostensibly Soviet foreign policy firmly opposed the Nazi and Fascist governments, but internally the Soviet regime more and more resembled a Fascist police state.

In trying to explain this paradox, Boris Nicolaevsky and, with some reservations, Franz Borkenau, have contended that Stalin was always intent on making an alliance with Hitler.[1] This theory is linked to Kirov's supposed policy of reconciliation. Kirov and his associates, so the argument runs, were consistent in pursuing a policy of relative relaxation of oppression at home and alignment with liberal democratic forces abroad. To be sure, the advocates of this explanation admit, such a policy could not be derived from Leninist theory, but the concern for welfare and freedom at home was logically related to emotional revulsion against Fascism abroad. Stalin, on the other hand, secretly admired Hitler, especially for his 1934 "blood purge" of opponents in the Nazi Party. This explanation points out that the earliest, yet in many respects the most crucial, steps of the anti-Nazi orientation—the Franco-Soviet alliance and the French Popular Front —were taken before Kirov's assassination. After that, the argument continues, Stalin felt bound to continue the orientation until he could demonstrate to Hitler that it was worth while cultivating Soviet friendship.

Though policy of obtaining an ally by blackmail is not unprecedented—

Hitler evidently had somewhat the same idea regarding Great Britain —the explanation is devious. If it were merely an ex post facto deduction based on the fact that a Nazi-Soviet alliance was eventually made, it would carry little weight. It is strongly supported, however, by the testimony of two extraordinarily well-informed defectors, Walter Krivitsky and Erich Wollenberg. Both contended that Stalin wished an alliance with Hitler, though Krivitsky's account makes much more of Stalin's crafty persistence in this course.[2]

Neither Krivitsky nor Wollenberg was, or claimed to be, Stalin's confidant. They, like non-Soviet observers, based their analysis on deduction, strengthened by second-hand accounts of Stalin's remarks. Insofar as the literal force of these remarks can be deduced, nearly all could just as easily mean that Stalin was pursuing a course of cold-blooded opportunism, as that he was devoted to a pact with Hitler. The principal overt move adduced by Krivitsky, as contrasted to these oral indications of Stalin's intentions, is the Berlin mission of David Kandelaki in 1936-37. Kandelaki, of a Georgian family apparently very close to Stalin, and possibly to Mikoian, was ostensibly engaged in a trade mission.[3] Actually, according to Krivitsky, he put out feelers for a political *détente* between Germany and the USSR. Moreover, German foreign office files reveal that Kandelaki did suggest an improvement of German-Soviet political relations,[4] but, as one competent observer has pointed out,

> it would be rash indeed to imagine that the repeated advances made by men outside diplomatic channels, like Tukhachevskii or Kandelaki, represented views opposing the official foreign policy. It can well be imagined that Litvinov himself believed it necessary to extend such feelers again and again, if only to sound out Hitler's intentions and moods.[5]

Additional evidence against the concept of Stalin's inflexible preference for a Nazi pact is the fact that even after the alliance was actually formed a secret high-level propaganda directive denounced the Germans and set world revolution as the goal.[6]

In view of the contradictory nature of the evidence just described, it is safest to assume, except in cases where specific information is available, that Stalin pursued a *Realpolitik* aimed at maximizing Soviet and world Communist strength. This does not imply, however, that the unfolding of the policy was itself devoid of contradiction. Such complications were especially evident in the emergence of the Popular Front in France. The reversal of Franco-Soviet relations in 1934 was undoubtedly the most important event in Soviet foreign relations between 1933 and 1936. It is true that recognition by the United States (1933) brought increased prestige to the USSR, and made it easier to secure a certain amount of American public sympathy for some Soviet objectives. The American Communist Party was in no position to become a major political factor, however, and the United States was not involved in political relations directly affecting the USSR. France, on the other hand, was a key to collective security—as long as she herself did not adopt a Fascist-like regime.

On February 6, 1934, taking advantage of the financial scandal known as the *affaire Stavisky,* various quasi-Fascist groups rioted against the French parliament and Edouard Daladier's government. As in the last days of Weimar, the Communists also joined in the demonstrations aimed at the Republican government. Ossip Piatnitskii, a major Soviet Comintern leader, implied as much shortly afterward:

> In answer to this [Fascist] demonstration the workers spontaneously went into the street. One part of the workers openly demonstrated against the Fascists, the other part of the workers also went toward parliament with their own demands, but not separating their demonstration sufficiently clearly from the Fascist. Direction by the Communist Party of the spontaneously arising worker demonstrations was not visible that day.[7]

Communist leadership was in fact "not visible" it seems because the Comintern representative in Paris, who had himself given the instructions for the demonstration, kept carefully out of sight.[8]

Apparently the Communist leaders—French or Comintern—quickly felt some misgivings concerning the effects of their actions, for as Piatnitskii puts it, "as early as February 7 the Communist Party not only advanced the correct slogans, but developed an energetic campaign against the Fascists."[9] During the following week the Communists co-operated with Socialist and CGT (the largest labor union confederation, then non-Communist) demonstrations, though in a manner designed to put the non-Communist leadership in a bad light.

At this point, international Communism was by no means decided on real collaboration with the *leadership* of other left-wing organizations, the so-called "united front from above." In April the Comintern journal, *Kommunisticheskii Internatsional,* denounced a Czechoslovak Communist senator for failing to take a revolutionary line and for implying that the Party would support military defense against Fascism.[10] Probably there was some controversy in the Comintern leadership—Borkenau cites an anonymous French ex-Communist as saying that the Ukrainian Comintern leader, Dmitrii Manuil'skii, favored co-operation, as opposed to Piatnitskii and the Hungarian Béla Kún. There seems also to have been some opposition to the general policy of rapprochement with France favored by Maxim Litvinov.[11] Apparently these divergences were complicated by a leadership struggle in the French party. In any case, as late as mid-April the French leader, Maurice Thorez, denounced the idea of a Communist-Socialist bloc.[12]

By June the French Communists entered into negotiation for an alliance with the national board of the Socialist party.[13] The agreement concluded the following month provided for joint manifestations against German and Austrian Fascism, against preparation for war, and for democracy.[14] The really big change in Communist tactics was the willingness to enter into an agreement with the "top," including a Communist pledge to cease polemics against the Socialists. The Communists reserved, however, the right to attack those who "departed" from the principles of the united front—and indeed the Socialist leaders were attacked, soon and often.[15]

During the following two years the French Communist Party increased both its own strength and the scope of its political alliances. Two key events occurred in May 1935. Pierre Laval, then French Foreign Minister, journeyed to Moscow in connection with the formal signing of the alliance which had been arranged the previous year. In marked contrast to the earlier intransigent opposition of all Communist parties toward defense measures in capitalist states, Stalin publicly told Laval that he unreservedly supported French national defense. Comintern and French Communist leaders hedged on this point by warning that they would only support an army which was "democratic," and consequently not available for use against the workers or colonial peoples.[16] Essentially, however, Communists were obliged at least to refrain from undermining the armed forces in countries allied to the USSR.[17]

In the May 1935 municipal elections in France, the Communist Party co-operated informally and successfully with the Radical Socialists (left-wing republicans) as well as with the Socialists. This "Popular Front" (i.e., extension of the "united front" to include "bourgeois" parties) was formalized for the legislative elections in the spring of 1936; it resulted in a sweeping victory for the left wing, and especially for the Communists. The latter refused to join the Socialist Léon Blum's government, however, and embarrassed it considerably by supporting a wave of sit-down strikes which impeded defense production.[18]

In the meantime the Seventh (and last) Congress of the Comintern had taken place in Moscow in August 1935. Essentially it was an endorsement of the Popular Front tactic, though the "united front" with working-class parties was mentioned most frequently. Georgi Dimitrov, the Bulgarian hero of the Reichstag fire trial, was the most prominent figure and was elected General Secretary. Though less prominent, Manuil'skii took the lead in defending the Soviet position on collective security, including League of Nations membership, for, he said, the proletariat had an interest in defending the USSR against German, Japanese, and Italian aggression. He also said that small countries might properly be defended by Communists against foreign aggression since the struggle of the bourgeois of the former might lead to a "national liberation" struggle; but he denied such support to the "great imperialist" powers.[19] The Italian Palmiro Togliatti ("Ercoli") pointed out also that bourgeois democratic freedoms, unsatisfactory as they were to the proletariat, were much preferable to Fascism.[20] While the emphasis throughout was on the "united front," the resolutions of the Congress carefully pointed out the essentially transitory nature of this tactic. They denounced the "right opportunistic" illusions that socialism could be achieved by a legal, peaceful road, and that reliance in the fight against Fascism could be placed on "automatism" or "spontaneity" of the masses, which might lead to a reduction of the role of the Party "at the moment of decisive action."[21]

While the French Popular Front was praised, the Congress was much less enthusiastic over relations with Social Democrats in other countries. As Piatnitskii pointed out, Social Democrats which were represented in the governments of their countries (as in Scandinavia), or which had a good prospect of becoming the governing party (Great Britain), had rejected the united front with the Communists.[22] Piatnitskii explained this lack of co-operation on the ground that those Socialists really defended the interests of their bourgeoisie. The relations with British Labour particularly reflected the continued Communist distrust of Great Britain as the bulwark of imperialism, inclined to sympathize with Fascism.

This attitude did not mean that the Communist parties were unwilling to extend their alliances even to conservative groups, if such alignments appeared to enhance the growth of Communist influence and to strengthen the anti-German front. In early 1936 the exiled German Communist Party proposed a league with German Catholic groups against Nazi persecution.[23] André Marty in France noted the increase of the Christian Popular Democrats as a result of sympathy for the Popular Front; evidently considerable efforts were made to secure the support of French Catholic leaders.[24] Early in 1938 Thorez denounced those who ridiculed Catholic or Masonic vestments and ceremonies.[25] According to one report, Moscow even directed the Italian Communist Party to offer to cease its opposition to Mussolini, in order to facilitate Soviet-French-Italian co-operation for mutual security against Germany.[26]

The Communist effort to extend its contacts to the right was logical because a viable anti-Nazi front in many countries required co-operation with groups which had no sympathy for Marxism or radically leftist labor movements. This was true in France as far as the pursuit of a strong anti-Nazi foreign policy and the preparation of adequate defense forces were concerned. In Spain it was necessary to avert a domestic right-wing dictatorship aided by the Nazis.

The Communists long-standing interest in Spain became intense in 1934 when a violent insurrection of Asturian workers appeared to open the prospect of a "dictatorship of the proletariat." In September 1934 the weak Spanish Communist Party joined in a united front with the Socialists and other "workers" parties. In early 1936 the adherence of the left-wing Republicans transformed this alignment into a "Popular Front" which won a decisive, though narrow, victory in the general elections. A few months later civil war broke out when a right-wing army junta, soon to be led by General Francisco Franco, endeavored to seize power. In September 1936, after hostilities had begun, the Spanish party entered the government; by this time, however, it categorically rejected dictatorship of the proletariat as an immediate aim.[27]

The change in program of the Spanish Communist Party was based on the realization that only the support of a part of the middle class and the peasantry would enable the Republican regime to survive. Moreover, any attempt to establish an extreme revolutionary regime would alienate moderate opinion in the Western countries. The stakes were much larger than Spain alone, for Germany and Italy were openly aiding the rebel, or Nationalist, forces. If, then, moderate opinion identified the Communists with revolution in Spain, moderates would feel that the choice was not between Fascism and anti-Fascism of the Popular Front, but between Fascism and violent social upheaval.

In these circumstances, Soviet policy was faced with a dilemma. If it failed to support the Spanish Popular Front, the powerful French Popular Front would collapse, and with it, perhaps, the lagging Franco-Soviet alliance and the whole policy of collective security. Maxim Litvinov apparently told the French ambassador, Robert Coulondre, that Stalin, feeling no vital Soviet interests were at stake in Spain, wished to keep aloof at first, but feared defection of the French Communist Party if he did so.[28] On the other hand, if the USSR intervened openly, conservative elements in France and Great Britain would denounce it as a revolutionary aggressor, with equally fatal results to the policy of collective security.

The solution—an unsatisfactory one, which we may guess caused Stalin to regard the whole Spanish affair with distaste—was to have the Spanish Communist Party induce the Republican elements to pursue ostensibly moderate policies. In similar vein, Soviet nonmilitary aid to Spain was widely publicized, while the Soviet Union worked diplomatically for nonintervention by all powers. Behind the scenes, on the other hand, the USSR provided enough military support to enable the Republican government to maintain itself for more than two years.

By far the larger part of the manpower support given the Republican government, and a considerable portion of the military supplies, were not sent from the Soviet Union itself but were obtained in other countries by the Comintern. The key elements were non-Spanish volunteers for the International Brigades. Though many non-Communists sympathetic to the Republican cause were recruited, the recruiting mechanism was the Comintern; the hard core of personnel consisted of Communists; and the Soviet Communist Party, through its agents in Spain, completely controlled the Brigades throughout the war. A careful impartial analysis of the strength of the Brigades puts them at about 60,000 over the entire period of the war, and 30,000 as the maximum at any one time.[29] A recent Soviet source, which fully recognizes the Communist inspiration and control of the Brigades, cites various non-Soviet Communist estimates of 20,000-50,000.[30] The same source indicates losses in killed or missing as 3,000 French, 600 Italians, 1,800 Americans, and 500 British.[31] These figures demonstrate the deep interest of French Communism in the Spanish war, a factor which Manuil'skii later recognized explicitly.[32] International Brigade contingents from East and Central Europe, however, though not as large as those from West Europe, were first on the scene.[33] More important, they were composed to a greater extent of Communist cadres, some of whom, like the Bulgar Stepanov and the Hungarian Ernö Gerö, played very significant

roles in maintaining Communist power in Spain. Still more important, as
we shall see, has been the role of the "Spanish veterans" in Communist
politics in East Europe since World War II.

More pertinent to our immediate subject is the role of Soviet personnel.
While the numbers involved probably did not exceed five thousand, the
importance of Soviet soldiers was considerable, for most were skilled military experts or technicians. In the latter category, tank operators (at first
nearly all of the Republican tanks were Soviet in origin) and aviators
predominated. The chief aviation advisor was the Soviet general Ia. V.
Smushkevich ("Douglas"), and as Soviet sources now indicate, such
famous Soviet figures as the pilot A. K. Serov participated in the air operations. The tank commander during the early part of the war was Gorev.[34]
Among the major military figures involved were Ian Berzin, former director
of Soviet military intelligence, who as "Grishin" served as chief of staff of
the Republican forces for a time in 1937; Shtern ("Kleber"), who exercised
a decisive command in the early defense of Madrid; and future marshals
Aleksander I. Rodimtsev and Kirill A. Meretskov. In addition, Rodion Ia.
Malinovskii and the future admiral Nikolai G. Kuznetsov were apparently
advisors, while it is rumored that future marshals G. I. Kulik and Georgii K.
Zhukov were at one time in Spain.

A more sinister role was played by the civilian and NKVD advisors in
Spain. Through the Spanish Communist Party, they actively intervened in
Spanish politics, and at certain periods of the war they exercised a considerable measure of control over Republican policies. Aside from the
efficiency of the Soviet political experts at devious political maneuvering,
they possessed a number of crucial advantages in dealing with Spanish
politicians. The importance of Soviet military aid—including the International Brigades—in the early stages of the war made it very difficult to
reject Soviet "advice." The fact that a large portion of the Spanish gold
reserve was secretly deposited in the USSR increased the Soviet advisors'
leverage.[35] Through the institution of military commissars controlled by
pro-Soviet elements, Soviet influence in the army extended far beyond the
International Brigades and the Soviet soldiers themselves.

One instance of Soviet intervention in Spanish affairs stands out because
of its importance for the general development of Soviet and Comintern
policies during this period. The new Comintern line of co-operation with
left-wing parties did not mean the slightest concession to dissident Communist elements abroad, or to anyone who questioned Soviet policy. Socialist leaders like Blum who questioned the justice of the arrests following

Kirov's assassination were bitterly attacked.[36] Denunciation of foreign left-wing critics of Stalin's policy, including former Communist groups not directly associated with Trotsky, was violent even before Kirov's assassination, however. The principal attack, though, was reserved for Trotsky and his adherents; as early as 1935 French Communists were accusing the Trotskyites of assassinating a member of the French party.[37] But the campaign mounted feverishly as the public trials in Moscow progressed.

The Spanish situation was especially delicate because of the membership of the POUM (Workers' United Marxist Party) in the Popular Front. This group, centered in Barcelona, disclaimed connection with Trotsky, and he heartily reciprocated the disclaimer. Nevertheless, it shared many ideas with him, and foreign Trotskyites appearing in Spain seem to have found Barcelona especially congenial. Most important, perhaps, the POUM leader, Andrés Nin, while in the Soviet Union had been an oppositionist associated with Trotsky. These reasons were sufficient to make the POUM the prime target for the NKVD advisors operating with the Republican political police. In addition, the POUM, allied to the much more powerful Anarchist party in Catalonia, was a serious hindrance to the policies which the Communists wished to carry out in Spain. Both the POUM and the Anarchists advocated extremely radical social measures, and physically attacked conservative elements. Their separatist tendencies and lack of military discipline hindered effective prosecution of the war. Consequently, the Communists were by no means the only Republican group which desired to curb the POUM.

At the end of 1936 the POUM was ousted from the Catalonian government; in the following spring the political police began a terroristic suppression of the party. On May 3 the POUM and some Anarchist groups, in physical danger and feeling their political power undermined, rebelled against the central government, but were soon suppressed. On June 16 the Communists succeeded in having the leadership and more than a thousand members of the POUM arrested.[38]

Having destroyed the POUM as a political force, the Communists might easily have secured the quick conviction for rebellion of many of the leaders. The principal purpose of the Soviet advisors, however, was to stage a show trial in Spain which would demonstrate that "Trotskyites" there, as in the USSR, were part of a vast international network of Fascist agents. Immediately after the rebellion, *Kommunisticheskii Internatsional* related the event to the Moscow trials.[39] In the meantime, the key link to Trotsky, Nin, was tortured to death—it is said by the chief NKVD agent

Alexander Orlov—in a vain attempt to secure his confession.[40] The Comintern press covered up this dark fiasco by asserting Nin had escaped from Catalonia.[41] The show trial finally held in October 1938 was based, in contrast to those in the USSR, on an abundance of documents, evidently because the Spaniards, unlike the Russians, could not be induced to confess. The documents were of such dubious validity, however, that all the defendants were acquitted of relations with Fascists or Nazis, though several were sentenced for rebellion.[42]

That the aims of the Soviet agents far transcended the Spanish situation is further demonstrated by the simultaneous efforts to prove that Trotsky followers in other countries were active as Gestapo agents. The most serious effort was in Czechoslovakia, like Spain a key country for the application of Popular Front tactics. Through some obscure arrangement with the Czechoslovak police, a German refugee, Anton Grylewicz, was arrested in June 1937; in spite of all the NKVD efforts—including "planting" of forged documents—Grylewicz was exonerated a few months later.[43] Evidently this affair was part of a larger scheme for "proving" the ramifications of Trotsky-Nazi espionage in Central Europe.[44] As will be shown in the next chapter, the affair was closely related to the purge of the Red Army.

The destruction of the POUM turned some leftist segments of world opinion against the USSR, but on the balance it probably served the interests both of Soviet foreign policy and of the Republican cause. The subsequent destruction of a large proportion of the higher Soviet officers who had served in Spain was an unmitigated loss to Soviet power. David Cattell has argued in his exhaustive study that the USSR did not use Spain as a major testing ground for new military weapons or techniques.[45] Nevertheless, the brilliant subsequent careers of several officers who served in Spain strongly suggest that their first-hand experience in coping with German and Italian forces—the only opportunity of this kind open to considerable numbers of Soviet military men before 1941—was very useful. But these officers were only the fortunate remnant of the group which had gone to Spain. According to Khrushchev, in 1937-41 "the cadre of leaders who had gained military experience in Spain and in the Far East was almost completely liquidated." [46] Among the outstanding examples are Berzin, the intelligence chief, and "Kleber," the "savior" of Madrid, both recalled in 1937 and shot.

The liquidation of the political and NKVD advisors did not have such long-range importance, but it weakened the power of the Soviet regime to control the course of events in Spain. The ambassador, Marcel Rosenberg;

Staevsky, the consul in Barcelona; and V. A. Antonov-Ovseenko, an old Russian revolutionary used as political advisor, disappeared in 1937. Perhaps their ruin arose in part from their apparent effort to curb the extreme terrorism of Orlov and A. A. Slutskii, the chief of the foreign section of the NKVD, who as "Marcos" spent some time in Spain. The latters' turn came a few months later, however; Orlov succeeded in fleeing abroad, but Slutskii suddenly and mysteriously died after his return to the USSR.

The fate of all these men is properly a part of the story of the Great Purge in the Soviet Union itself, but their destruction also points up, in the present context, an important feature of Soviet politics under Stalin. All was subordinated to the demand of the dictator for absolute power. No consideration of the standing of the Soviet Union in public opinion, no concern for the military capacity of the country, and no regard for the position of a foreign Communist party, even as a pliable tool of Soviet policy, could stand in the way of what Stalin considered his interest. But, as we shall see, in these years Stalin still knew his limitations, and however ruthless, remained prudent.

The destruction of the Soviet Spanish veterans was paralleled by a purge of foreign Communists which was even more injurious to the prospects of international Communism than was the destruction of the Soviet Spanish veterans to the interests of the defense and foreign policy of the USSR. By and large, leaders of legal Communist parties were beyond the reach of Stalin's power, and were left untouched. Communist refugees from their own countries were in a much more vulnerable position. Those residing in Western countries could not be dealt with summarily, but some were effectively deprived of power.

Perhaps the outstanding case of this type is that of Willi Münzenberg, a German Communist who had done more than anyone else to build up the network of "front" organizations and communications media designed to support Soviet policies without revealing their real Communist nature. As early as 1934, Münzenberg was criticized by the Comintern press for inflating his role in the foundation of the Communist International of Youth, and for failing to attack Social Democrats and Trotskyites sufficiently in his newspapers.[47]

When the period of severe purges began in the USSR, Münzenberg was compromised by his association with the one-time prominent Trotskyite Karl Radek and an earlier allegiance to the dissident German Communist Heinz Neumann. In private Münzenberg was apparently accused of having failed to save the German Communist leader Ernst Thälmann from the

Nazis.[48] Münzenberg was ordered to go to the USSR to stand charges, but prudently confined himself to a written defense to the Comintern.[49] This was, by Communist standards, intolerable insubordination, but for some reason the Comintern did not take strong measures against him for more than a year. As late as August 1937 *Kommunisticheskii Internatsional*, while sharply criticizing his book on Nazi propaganda as lacking Marxist analysis, granted that it contained "much carefully gathered material" and "deserves attention." Even this amount of praise for a renegade is almost unheard of in Communist practice. Perhaps the Comintern hoped still to utilize Münzenberg's extraordinary propaganda talents, or it may have wished to lull him into a sense of security in order to gain control of his front organizations. Perhaps the NKVD forces then in control of the Comintern even hoped to lure him to the USSR.

In fact Münzenberg did turn over his organizations to the Comintern representative Bohumir Šmeral, but then he went into hiding. It was not until April 1939, however, that the Comintern publicly confirmed Münzenberg's expulsion from the German party.[50] By this time the value of the "fronts" was much diminished by the breakdown of collective security and the prospect of a Nazi-Soviet rapprochement. The notice accused Münzenberg not only of the old contact with Heinz Neumann, but of writing in periodicals to which Trotskyites contributed and of refusing to denounce the POUM. But the most remarkable feature of the notice was that it accused Münzenberg of publishing books and brochures without authorization of the German Communist Party. This was in effect an admission not only that Münzenberg himself had always been subject to complete Communist discipline, but that the supposedly "anti-Fascist" press he had organized was under complete Communist control.

When World War II began, Münzenberg was arrested by the French authorities. In the confusion following the French military defeat in 1940, he escaped from the concentration camp—but was found hanged a short distance away.[51] It is possible that he committed suicide.

Many other German Communist leaders came to the same end as Willi Münzenberg, but by a more direct route; they were either in the USSR when the purge began, or obeyed the order to return for trial.[52] The upper levels of the Comintern apparatus were also terribly depleted by the purge. Ossip Piatnitskii and Béla Kún, two of the most powerful directors of the organization, disappeared, as did most of the apparatus section directors.[53] Aside from Germans, these men were predominantly from East European countries where Communism was outlawed, or from Japan. The heaviest blows were reserved, however, for the Polish and Korean Communist parties, which in 1938 were abolished altogether. The Korean affair involved the removal to Central Asia of thousands of Koreans living in the Soviet Far East, but it is not clear how many were executed.

The abolition of the Polish Communist Party was initiated by assembling the leaders in Moscow on the pretext of a meeting.[54] Just what proportion came from the Polish underground, and what proportion were among Polish Communists who had fled to the USSR (said to number 4,500) is not known.[55] When the Polish leaders reached Moscow they were apparently confronted by a commission composed of Manuil'skii, Dimitrov, Togliatti, and Otto V. Kuusinen, who charged them with treason and espionage.[56] All, or nearly all, were executed or died in concentration camps. The Polish party—together with its autonomous national sections, the Communist parties of West Belorussia and the West Ukraine—was officially dissolved.[57]

Strangely enough, the Polish ("Dombrowski") International Brigade continued to receive high praise from the Comintern press and from Manuil'skii himself.[58] This praise, and the fact that a number of members of the Polish party were employed, though only in obscure positions, in the Soviet occupation of eastern Poland a year later, suggest that there was some plan for reactivating Polish Communism. It is said also that underground Communist cells were formed in Warsaw as early as 1939.[59] These developments certainly cast doubt on the theory that Stalin liquidated the Polish party in order to remove an obstacle to his agreement with the Nazis.[60] The official charge that the Polish party was ridden with spies very likely contained a grain of truth, in spite of the fact that the accusation was later declared the work of provocateurs. Probably the principal reason for the unprecedented treatment of the Poles, however, lay in their special relation to the origins of Soviet Bolshevism. Stalin doubtless never forgot the rebuff to Communism given by the mass of the Polish population during the Soviet invasion of 1920. Moreover, since the main body of the Polish party had been an integral part of the Bolshevik Party, he reacted as sharply to its deviations—and there had undoubtedly been several—as to deviations within the Soviet Party itself.

While the events just described were shattering the framework of international Communism, the Popular Front was coming to an end in France. The year 1937 passed with the Communist Party providing uneasy support for Popular Front governments while engaging in bitter recriminations with

Blum and other left-wing political figures over Spain and other issues. As late as January 1938 the party supported Blum's proposal for a "national government" embracing all parties from center to extreme left, including Communists. The scheme was defeated, however, and in April Blum was forced to resign. The Communists showed less sympathy for subsequent governments, Edouard Daladier's especially.[61] His willingness to join in the Munich agreement was, of course, a severe blow to the Communists, and by the end of 1938 Thorez was bitterly attacking the government.

The results of the Popular Front period were very mixed. The intricate control apparatus of the Comintern and its "fronts" abroad were destroyed. Most old-line European Communists were dead, alienated, or at least disheartened. These developments were largely hidden even to those who took some interest in Soviet affairs and the international workers' movement. To some, especially the more conservative, among those who did catch a glimpse of the destruction of the old cadres, the process appeared to be a healthy removal of dangerous fanatics, preliminary to the return to traditional policies in the USSR and to patriotic attitudes among Communist parties abroad. On the other hand, the vociferous Soviet support of the League of Nations and collective security, the feverish Communist efforts to mobilize organizations and opinion in the democratic countries against Fascist tendencies, and the real sacrifices of the Communists in Spain, combined to create a new group of Soviet sympathizers, especially among the intellectuals. The process was most pronounced in France, where intellectual and strong working-class support combined to build rapidly an amazingly large and influential Communist Party. After numerous vicissitudes this party would provide the keystone for Communist strength in West Europe during and after World War II. Results in the United States were less striking, but the Popular Front period started a wave of sympathy for Soviet aims which could later be put to use. Even in Great Britain and Scandinavia there was a tendency in the same direction, though the continued firm opposition of the Socialist parties in those countries to Communist overtures provided a counterweight.

The Communist position in international affairs does much to explain why, with certain striking exceptions such as John Dewey, Western liberal and left-wing observers failed to realize the import of the devastating purges described in the next chapter. Probably Stalin realized that under the screen of support for democracy he had an unparalleled opportunity for establishing absolute control over world Communism. One Communist

Party, however, was an exception to this development, and an exception of incalculable importance. At the very time that all other major parties were being ruthlessly purged, the Chinese Communists were evidently pursuing a course markedly more independent than that they had followed in the twenties.

Until 1935 at least Moscow had generally insisted that Chinese Communism follow essentially the pattern of development laid down for European countries. The principal practical features of this pattern were hegemony of the urban proletariat and the maintenance of party headquarters in the cities. A rising Chinese leader, Mao Tse-tung, on the other hand, relied in practice on a Communist-controlled coalition of forces based on a rebellious peasantry. Using this organization, Communists under his direction established extensive "soviet" areas defended by strong guerrilla-type armies. In the meantime, the futility of the reliance on urban centers was demonstrated by the fact that in 1932 or 1933 the underground Central Committee of the Chinese party was forced by government police pressure to flee from Shanghai to the "soviet" area. Then, or somewhat later, Mao assumed factual leadership over the entire Chinese Communist movement. Probably the confusion attendant upon removal of the principal "soviet" base from south-central to northwest China (Shensi) contributed to Mao's ability to pursue his plans during 1935. In any case, as Benjamin Schwartz has pointed out, Mao's "deviation" did not consist of theoretical opposition to the Moscow line, but of practical divergence from it.[62]

Just at the time that Mao, in the "Long March," was transferring his base, an extraordinarily interesting discussion of the broader implications of the Chinese experience was carried on in *Kommunisticheskii Internatsional.* One V. Miro argued that, as in China, Communist parties in "semicolonial countries" such as those of Latin America could set up "soviet" areas based on pre-existing peasant uprisings and partisan movements, even where revolutionary conditions did not prevail in the country as a whole.[63] He admitted that "if the workers' movement is definitely backward, the creation of a strong proletarian nucleus of a revolutionary insurgent army would be extremely difficult or even entirely excluded," but stressed throughout the importance of the peasant insurgents.[64]

In the next issue a writer named Li attacked Miro.[65] "The success of the soviet movement," Li wrote, "was decided by the battles in Canton and Changsha, the concentration of the work of the Communist Party in the manufacturing areas, in Shanghai, in Wuhan, the work of the Party in the proletariat."[66] Areas with a purely peasant partisan tradition but with

weak proletarian influence, like Manchuria, were, contrary to Miro, backward in developing "soviets." In a passage which in retrospect seems
directly aimed at Mao, Li ridiculed the "Northwest theory." [67] This concept,
rejected in 1927, for basing Communist strength in Shansi, Kansu, and
Inner Mongolia, was untenable, Li wrote, because *the center of gravity of
the work of the Communist Party must remain in the proletariat, in the
large manufacturing centers.* [68]

This discussion suggests that at the beginning of 1935 the Comintern was
not yet fully reconciled to "Mao's way." However, Li's essay also pointed in
another direction which was not only fully in accord with the emerging
Comintern line, but which was to prove extremely valuable to Mao. In
opposition to Miro, Li pointed out that in many countries Communists
should not for the present advance the slogan of "soviet power" at all, but
should strive for creation of an "anti-imperialist, popular-revolutionary
power" in areas they controlled. Such were the countries where "the level
of hegemony achieved by the proletariat in the movement, the level of
consciousness of the masses may still be insufficient." [69] In China, he said,
it had been especially important to draw the petite bourgeoisie into the
anti-imperialist movement. This obviously suited the emerging Popular
Front line; but, as we shall see later, it also sounded like a forecast of
Mao's tactics in his time of victory.

Although the Chinese Communists made certain overtures to the Kuomintang at the time of the Comintern Seventh Congress, and had advanced
less ambiguous proposals in 1936, the Chinese implementation of the
Popular Front line itself came three years after its success in France.[70]
Following a series of political maneuvers too complicated to relate here,
the Kuomintang leader, Chiang Kai-shek, proposed terms for Communist
submission in March 1937. After several months' negotiations, during which
the Japanese began all-out war on China, agreement was reached in August
—after Moscow and the Nanking (Kuomintang) government had signed a
nonaggression treaty.[71] Essentially, the "Chinese Soviet Republic" in
Shensi was left undisturbed but it was nominally redesignated the "Frontier
Region" of the Chinese Republic, and its armies (Fourth and Eighth)
were subsidized by the Kuomintang national government. The national
government nominally determined the area of Communist military operations but the forces remained essentially under Communist control. On the
other hand, the Communists did stop or reduce seizure of landlords' property and other measures of "sovietization." [72]

After the Kuomintang-Communist pact both sides remained intensely suspicious, and both maneuvered constantly against each other. Serious military collaboration ceased after 1938.[73] Nevertheless, Soviet support of a Popular Front lasted far longer in China than in Europe. In the absence of an agreement with Japan paralleling the Nazi-Soviet pact, the Moscow leadership evidently was eager to have all available Chinese forces engaged in operations which tied down a substantial portion of Japanese military power.[74] A subsidiary reason was that, although the Communists regarded the United States as a warmonger for its aid to Great Britain, they hoped for American support for both Chinese Communist and Soviet policy in the Far East. In early 1939, for example, Mao wrote of his hope of obtaining help against Japan from the United States and Britain, as well as the USSR.[75] During the Nazi-Soviet pact period the United States Communist Party supported Chiang Kai-shek against the Japanese.[76]

In 1940, however, Communist writings on China began to stress the danger of "capitulator" elements in the Kuomintang who erroneously felt the war against Japan could be continued only if the United States and Great Britain aided.[77] In January 1941 there was a serious armed clash between the Communist armies, evidently trying to extend their area of control, and Kuomintang forces.[78] Even at this point, however, the Comintern press took the conciliatory line that the conflict was Japanese-inspired, and perhaps unknown to Chiang.[79] In line with a tactic which would later become much more important, the Comintern praised certain Americans who were trying to close the Communist-Kuomintang breach.[80]

In April 1941 the USSR concluded a nonaggression pact with Japan; it is possible that this might have brought about a major change in its Chinese policy.[81] Within little more than two months, however, the Soviet Union was itself at war, and a new period in its relations with foreign Communists began.

As Charles McLane has pointed out, it is unlikely that there was continuous contact between the Comintern and the Chinese Communists between at least 1938 and 1941. It is still less likely that Moscow sent detailed directives to Yenan, the Chinese Communist capital in Shensi.[82] In a generally discouraging international picture, however, the relative success of Chinese Communists was undoubtedly of great comfort to the Soviet leaders. The mere existence in China of the only major Communist-ruled area—whether called "soviet" or not—outside the USSR was psychologically important.[83] The continued struggle of China against Japan provided some guarantee that the full Japanese strength could not be applied to the Soviet Union's back door. The Chinese war also enhanced the chance that a war in the Pacific would see the United States ranged against Japan. Beyond these tangible advantages, there was the immense prospect, however remote it may have appeared to the Soviet rulers, that complete Chinese Communist success would open in Asia. Under these circumstances, it is easy to see why Stalin may have tolerated Mao's practical deviation, even though concrete evidence on the point is lacking. As we have seen, Stalin sometimes put his personal power interests above the interests of Communist power. He was, however, a realist, and patient. He might have succeeded in removing Mao in 1934, but he might have failed. If Mao were eventually successful in his tactics, the gain for Communism as a whole would be great; if he failed, his deviation would disappear. For the time being, in view of Mao's care to avoid elevating his practices to the level of explicit theory, the deviation did not threaten Stalin's unchallenged power over world Communism.

CHAPTER
IV

THE GREAT PURGE: I

The August 1936 condemnation of Zinoviev, Kamenev, and the remaining defendants of the "sixteen" cast a shadow over the upper levels of the Party. Even before the verdict was in, men like Khristian Rakovskii, desperately trying to atone for their association with Trotsky, were forced to debase themselves by calling for merciless punishment of the accused. On August 24, two days before the trial ended, *Pravda* demanded editorially that the connection between the defendants and the "Rights" (Tomskii, Bukharin, and Rykov) be investigated. It also called for tracing the relations of Karl Radek and G. L. Piatakov to the Zinoviev-Kamenev group.[1] Radek's association with Trotsky was of long standing, although in recent years Stalin had appeared to show some favor to Radek. Piatakov, who occupied a key position in Soviet industry, had apparently severed his connections with Trotsky in the late twenties.

Tomskii did not wait for Stalin's further moves; on the day the editorial appeared, he shot himself.[2] *Pravda* reported, in effect, that Tomskii had taken the easy way out. But on September 10 there appeared the unexpected announcement that because the evidence was insufficient, charges would not be pressed against Bukharin and Rykov. The parallel to the treatment of Zinoviev and Kamenev in December 1934 was too close to permit Bukharin and Rykov, or those who feared implication with them, to be much relieved. Moreover, the charges against others continued; in November a trial in Kemerovo (West Siberia) implicating Piatakov as a member of the "Trotskyite directorate" indicated that he was doomed.[3]

Until January 17, 1937, Bukharin was listed as editor of *Izvestia*; at the same time the Constitution which he had played a large part in composing

51

was the dominant feature of the Soviet press. In effect "Stalin's" Constitution served primarily to divert uninitiated Soviet opinion from the dictator's preparation of his next move. While retaining the nominally federal structure of the country, the Constitution (formally adopted December 5, 1936) provided for direct instead of pyramidal elections to the various levels of Soviets, or legislatures. To some foreign observers, including Americans, who rather naïvely associated pyramidal elections with the ward heeler, the party "boss," and other alleged evils of the convention system of nominations, this change appeared a step toward democracy, as did the introduction of the secret ballot. Actually, of course, no opposition candidates have ever appeared (although Stalin suggested at one point that they might), and with a very few local exceptions the official candidates have won by votes approaching unanimity. The reason is clear enough in the Constitution itself, though not stressed in publicity aimed at non-Communists: Article 126 provides that "the most active and politically conscious citizens . . . unite in the All-Union Communist Party (Bolshevik), which is the vanguard of the toilers in their struggle for strengthening and development of the socialist structure, and is the directing core of all organizations of the toilers, social as well as state." [4]

While this provision formalized the extragovernmental control which had always existed in the Soviet state, Article 135 granting universal suffrage (*except* of course to the considerable number of concentration-camp inmates) was in line with the reduction of the special prestige of Party members noted earlier. Officially, however, this was a recognition of the fact that only two classes—workers and peasants, constituting together "the working people"—existed in the USSR.

The right to vote and the numerous rights formally granted in Articles 118-128—including those traditional to liberal states, such as freedom of speech, and those felt proper to a socialist regime, such as the right to work—impressed many foreigners. The whole content of this and succeeding chapters of the present history may provide a basis for judging the validity of these provisions.

The real decisions in the Soviet Union were made by small groups gathered behind closed doors, as has been the case in many other countries; but rarely have these decisions proceeded to execution so inexorably as in the USSR. Consequently, one is more than ordinarily perplexed when a Soviet political development, apparently completely planned in advance, is suddenly interrupted. Many observers have sought to explain the failure to proceed immediately to the arrest of the "Right" group. The most common explanation assumes that the older members of the Party ruling group, shocked by the suicide of Tomskii, forced moderation upon Stalin. Abdurakhman Avtorkhanov contends that Stalin was compelled by a majority of the Central Committee to drop the charges against Bukharin.[5]

If we accept as valid Khrushchev's remarks in his secret speech to the Twentieth Party Congress, this version is scarcely tenable. According to Khrushchev, Stalin and Andrei Zhdanov sent a telegram to the Politburo on September 25 (fifteen days after the charges against Bukharin and Rykov were dropped), alleging that the political police was "four years behind" in "unmasking the Trotskyite-Zinovievite bloc." Stalin therefore demanded that Ezhov replace Iagoda as Commissar of the Interior.[6] Stalin's complete command of the situation is shown by the fact that he did not even need to interrupt his Caucasian vacation to secure the instantaneous fall of such a key figure as Iagoda.[7] Evidently Iagoda's removal had been decided at least two weeks earlier.[8] Radek was interrogated in mid-September; consequently he must have been arrested earlier.[9] All of these circumstances indicate that if there was opposition at this time to the intensified purge, it was not effective. What appears most likely is that Stalin, in his usual cautious manner, simply wanted to prepare his position thoroughly before taking the next steps against the "Rights."

Ezhov's appointment as Commissar of the Interior considerably enhanced his—and thereby Stalin's—control of the machinery for investigation and purge. Ezhov apparently remained Chairman of the Commission of Party Control and Central Committee Secretary, although direct control over Party personnel was transferred to his lieutenant, Georgii Malenkov. Henceforward, however, the purge was to be carried out primarily through the direct agency of the police. Even the process of taking control of the police was a gradual one, however. Iagoda was nominally made Commissar of Communications; he did not officially "retire" from active duty as Commissar of State Security until January 28, 1937, when Ezhov assumed that post.[10] G. A. Molchanov was replaced very quickly as Vice-Commissar by M. P. Frinovskii, until then commander of frontier troops.[11] For the time being, most other high officials of the NKVD were not touched.

From January 23 through January 30, Radek, Piatakov, and their co-defendants were tried publicly. The group was known officially as the "Anti-Soviet Trotskyite Centre," and informally as the "seventeen." In its broad outlines the trial—which Ezhov had evidently started to prepare long before he became Commissar of the Interior—was remarkably similar

to the proceedings against Zinoviev and Kamenev.[12] The defendants were
even more compliant in their confessions. In an effort to save his life, Radek,
a cunning orator, seemed to be exercising his talents almost enthusiastically
to destroy his reputation. Indeed, he, and three minor defendants, were
spared the death penalty, although Radek apparently died in prison not
long afterward.[13]

Far more important than Radek was G. L. Piatakov, Deputy Commissar
of Heavy Industry. His trial was part of the unleashing of a devastating
attack upon old-line industrial directors. The effect upon the economic
managers as a functional group will be described later; here only certain
salient aspects need be described. The charges of "wrecking"—i.e., sabotage
designed to undermine the Soviet system—were directed against directors
in a broad range of industry; only a few of the accused were tried in public.
The "wreckers" were distributed over the entire country, although they
were "discovered" principally in areas like West Siberia, the Urals, and
the southern Ukraine where heavy industry prevailed.

The hunt had been keenest in Kemerovo (West Siberia), where in 1935
a group of engineers and technicians, directed by Ia. N. Drobnis, had
allegedly begun widespread sabotage resulting in the death of many innocent workers. Piatakov (and through him Trotsky) was linked to this
"plot" when the group went on trial in November 1936, and again in
January 1937, when Drobnis was one of his codefendants.

The Kemerovo affair points up two aspects of the accusations which to
some extent distinguish the later trials from the Zinoviev-Kamenev proceedings: the fantastic allegation that the opposition elements intensified
their activities *after* the country was engulfed in the wave of "vigilance"
following Kirov's assassination; and the charge that they murdered innocent Soviet citizens. The first aspect was evidently designed to demonstrate that the new trials were not the "mop-up" of enemies who had already
been rendered harmless, but opening moves in a continued campaign
against opponents of the regime. The "murder of the workers" was designed
to substantiate the allegation that the opposition members were "enemies
of the people," and not merely of Stalin's regime.

The August 1936 trial had advanced the charge that the oppositions were
linked to the German police in a scheme to aid in the defeat of the USSR;
this accusation was greatly intensified in January 1937. Piatakov maintained
Trotsky plotted with Hitler's lieutenant, Rudolf Hess, to allow Germany
to seize the Ukraine if the Nazis helped the Trotsky opposition obtain

power.[14] Other defendants elaborated this theory of Trotsky's "defeatism." In spite of the vast effort which the accused and their prompters expended to make this theme plausible, the elements of the confessions which could be independently checked proved as baseless as those in the earlier trial. Alleged meetings between defendants and Trotsky in Norway and France, described in detail by the defendants, were subsequently demonstrated to have been nearly, if not quite, impossible.[15]

The trial marked the end of the brief reprieve for Bukharin and Rykov. Radek testified that Bukharin's "guilt was the same" as his own "if not juridically, then in essence." [16] If the "Rights" were now to be saved, the whole course of the purge would have to be reversed. But it was not only they who were endangered; aside from various secondary figures like the economic theorist and radical E. A. Preobrazhenskii, suspicion was now directed at the military. General Vitvot Putna, former military attaché in London, was directly accused, and certain seemingly innocent remarks concerning the leading Red Army marshal, M. N. Tukhachevskii, suggested to the initiated that he too was in danger.

Before the next round of trials Stalin had to dispose of critics who now ventured to oppose him openly. The first, evidently, was his Georgian compatriot, G. K. Ordzhonikidze. As Commissar of Heavy Industry "Sergo," as Ordzhonikidze was usually called, was undermined by the proliferation of charges against the economic directors, although testimony at the trial had carefully exonerated him. Several defectors, notably Victor Kravchenko, have testified to Ordzhonikidze's loyalty to his subordinates. But whether it was concern for his own position that motivated Ordzhonikidze's clash with Stalin, or real friendship for Piatakov, who is said to have carried the main burden of directing heavy industry, is hard to say.

The climax came on February 18. According to Khrushchev, Stalin and Beria forced Ordzhonikidze to shoot himself.[17] Émigré accounts which have a certain circumstantial plausibility maintain that Stalin had Ordzhonikidze murdered while he lay unconscious following a violent argument with Stalin concerning the fate of Piatakov or other economic directors.[18] These stories are not entirely incompatible with the official announcement that Ordzhonikidze died from a "paralytic stroke" during a "rest period" after he "suddenly began to feel ill." [19] Less important than the manner of Ordzhonikidze's death is the fact that Stalin had eliminated his most formidable critic.

The Central Committee plenum which officially opened five days later on February 23 was the most important of Stalin's later life. It lasted eleven days; and there is reason to believe that preparatory meetings—probably including the one at which Ordzhonikidze was stricken—considerably prolonged the period of tense discussion.

The plenum began with an appearance of Bukharin and Rykov, who sought desperately to defend themselves. While no detailed account of their speeches has been provided, Khrushchev and Zhdanov assailed them in public addresses during the following month for having "tried to deceive" the plenum.[20] At the end of "several days'" discussion they were expelled from the Party, and on February 27 were arrested.[21] It was rumored that they received an eight-year prison term, but it seems somewhat doubtful that at that stage a formal sentence was required to dispose of them temporarily.

On February 26-27 Zhdanov delivered a lengthy report on "Organizational Problems of the Communist Party." The report, the subsequent Committee resolution on it, and the notice of Bukharin's and Rykov's expulsion were the only portions of the plenum proceedings published soon after the meeting ended.[22] The burden of Zhdanov's speeches was the need for collective leadership and for democracy within the Party. The paradox of advancing such themes at the plenum where all difference of opinion was being stifled is only apparent. Secret elections for Party officers, rejection of co-optation of members of Party committees, regular Party elections and meetings, could indeed in some circumstances strengthen the position of the members of the apparatus, if not of the rank and file. During a purge, however, these measures could just as easily be used to weaken the position of the old-line Party secretaries at the raikom and obkom levels. The measures made it a little more difficult for a secretary to stifle his subordinates' criticism inspired by outside sources to undermine his position. Zhdanov himself implied that the measures he proposed would strengthen the ambitious "new cadres" who sought promotion over the political (and usually physical) corpses of their superiors. He said:

> Comrades who spoke here referred to the "paucity" of cadres which, it was claimed, necessitates a constant regrouping and transfer of people. They forget that the reserves and possibilities we possess of advancing new cadres are exceptionally great. Just see how fast Party people and non-Party people develop, just see how rapidly the Stakhanovites develop, and not only the Stakhanovites.[23]

While making these points, Zhdanov left the way open for replacing secretaries who were distrusted. He said that, while new secretaries could not take office officially before confirmation by a plenum of the Party committee which they headed, they could in the meantime serve as "acting secretaries." In fact this designation became almost the usual one during the following months, as the old territorial secretaries were replaced by new men selected by the central apparatus.

In spite of these apparent implications of Zhdanov's remarks, it would be unwise to relate his speeches too closely to the upheaval which was going on in the Party's upper echelon. Stalin's lieutenants, and Zhdanov in particular, whatever their personal interests in the destruction of their enemies, were undoubtedly intent upon preserving the Party as an instrument—indeed in the long run the chief instrument—of continued Soviet rule. Doubtless the instrumental role they envisaged for the Party was rather different from Lenin's concept of it as the basic source of authority in the Soviet system. Nevertheless, the attention devoted to regularity and vitality in Party activity was not entirely hypocritical even in 1937.

After acting on Zhdanov's proposals, the plenum considered "The results of wrecking, diversion and espionage by Japanese-German-Trotskyite agents." The published report on this subject, which appeared suspiciously late (on April 21), indicates that Molotov was the author.[24] A report based on the Party archives indicates that Kaganovich also spoke on the subject.[25] Khrushchev in his secret speech, however, ascribed the document to Ezhov; it does bear all the earmarks of a police report.[26] It was a long résumé of alleged "wrecking" activities, some reported in the January trial, some newly "revealed." The emphasis was on the misdeeds of economic directors. While Ordzhonikidze was praised, the helplessness of those whom he had protected was implied by a reference to a Dnepropetrovsk director, Stefan Birman, who was denounced for complaining to Ordzhonikidze about attacks leveled at economic directors.[27]

This report—or most likely several reports by Molotov, Kaganovich, and Ezhov—must have consumed February 28 and March 1, followed by about a day of discussion. On March 3 Stalin delivered another lengthy report (not published until March 29) on "Deficiencies in Party work and measures for the liquidation of Trotskyites and other double-dealers." He stressed again the theme that the more socialism advanced, the fiercer would its enemies attack it. Stalin compared the position of the USSR in the midst of the capitalist encirclement to that of Napoleon surrounded by enemy states

—a simile which must have sounded odd to those who had taken part in Stalin's earlier struggle against Trotsky's "Bonapartism."

Evidently Stalin was at pains to refute objections to his views made in earlier discussions at the plenum, for he spoke of "the wrong theory that persons who were not always wreckers, and were sometimes successful in their work, cannot now be wreckers," and of "some comrades," "in the center and in the localities" who were naïve in combatting Trotskyites, and even aided their advance.[28] Prominent among those at whom these remarks appear to have been directed was Pavel Postyshev, Politburo candidate and second secretary of the Ukrainian Party. Defending one of his subordinates accused of being a Trotskyite, Postyshev said:

> I personally do not believe that in 1934 an honest Party member who had trod the long road of unrelenting fight against enemies of the party and of socialism would now be in the camp of the enemies. I do not believe it. . . . I cannot imagine how it would be possible to travel with the party during the difficult years and then, in 1934, join the Trotskyites. It is an odd thing. . . .[29]

Stalin himself delivered a brief closing speech on March 5 which gave no sign of concession to criticism. Just what happened after this criticism is puzzling. Khrushchev said in his secret speech that "many members" criticized the "mass repressions." [30] But Khrushchev also indicated that the resolution based on Ezhov's report described above, calling for enhanced police activity, was passed by the plenum.[31] Subsequent events once again showed that Stalin's power was not weakened, although he may have somewhat revised his plan for destroying those whom he considered his opponents.

We can follow most closely the elimination of Postyshev. Within two weeks of the end of the plenum he was relieved of his duties in Kiev and dispatched to the relatively insignificant post of acting secretary of the Kuibyshev obkom.[32] At a meeting of the Kiev Party organization held at about the same time, Stanislav Kosior, first secretary of the Ukrainian Party, spoke rather vaguely of the lack of criticism and self-criticism in the Kiev obkom, but for a time no direct attack on Postyshev appeared. Late in May, however, Kosior said that the Kiev obkom had earlier been penetrated by Trotskyites, because of lack of vigilance at the "top." [33] A few days later Kosior explicitly denounced Postyshev for "co-opting numerous enemies" into the Kiev Party apparatus.[34] In August a central Party journal denounced a "former secretary of the central committee" of the Ukraine who had refused to believe his assistant was a Trotskyite and retained him in a post in which he had access to important documents until he was arrested as an enemy of the people.[35] This statement eliminates any doubt that Postyshev was being condemned for his stand against Stalin. Still Postyshev remained at his post in Kuibyshev oblast, which from time to time was criticized for irregularities. Finally, at the January 1938 plenum of the Central Committee, Postyshev was relieved as candidate member of the Politburo. It is said his health was failing, for he was not apparently formally arrested, but died nearly two years later in the Kremlin hospital.[36]

On March 18, 1937, shortly after Postyshev started on his journey to obscure death, Ezhov advanced by another stage the process of removing those Stalin suspected. Ten months later they appeared in the dock with Iagoda (who had been officially arrested at the beginning of April 1937).[37] During 1937 and early 1938 nearly all the oblast NKVD directors, and several in the union republics, were removed.[38] Estimates of the total number of NKVD personnel eliminated by Ezhov vary from 325 to 3,000 —probably the figure, which must obviously be a guess, depends on the level which the informant is considering. Nearly all the section directors of the NKVD were arrested together with several other high officials.[39]

These were the old "Chekists" who under Felix Dzerzhinskii and Iagoda had built the Soviet secret police; most had served in the ruthless struggle against the "Whites" in the Civil War. Few outsiders could find their characters attractive. In addition to the "Whites," some of whom at least had been armed adversaries, the Chekists had destroyed hundreds of thousands of helpless members of the Tsarist upper classes. They had the major role in exiling millions of kulak families. They were often unscrupulous and licentious in their personal behavior. Reluctantly or not, the very group arrested had directed the extortion of confessions from Kamenev, Zinoviev, and other Old Bolsheviks who had been their comrades. Nevertheless, most old Chekists were dedicated Communists who accepted the doctrine that the political police was the essential defense of the Revolution. Though they employed "third-degree" methods, most used physical brutality reluctantly. They had considerable esprit de corps and loyalty to one another. Even NKVD agents in a remote raion resented the fact that Medved, head of the Leningrad NKVD, was made the scapegoat for Kirov's assassination: "Stalin won't get away with this easily."[40] Naturally, such reactions aroused uneasiness in the Party coterie around Stalin.

Ezhov retained a number of top NKVD officials, and even showed special favor to them. Among them were Frinovskii, mentioned earlier; M. D.

Berman, head of the concentration camps; L. N. Bel'skii, director of the uniformed police; S. F. Redens, director of the Moscow political police; and A. A. Slutskii, head of the foreign section.[41] Ezhov's special protégé was the old Chekist Leonid M. Zakovskii, who was assigned the strategic directorship of the Leningrad political police. Zakovskii was also selected to prove Stalin's thesis that spies were everywhere. Not long after the February-March plenum Zakovskii made a speech to a Leningrad Party conference in which he drew upon many sources having nothing to do with either Communism or Russia, as well as on the stock Soviet spy stories, to show that conspiracy was the essential element of history. This peculiarly un-Marxist essay was given extraordinary distribution in the Communist press abroad as well as in the USSR.[42]

Ezhov was undoubtedly forced to retain some high-ranking old Chekists in order to provide a minimum of technical skill in investigation, as well as to avoid complete disruption of the organizational framework of the NKVD. His principal reliance, however, was on two or three hundred Party officials whom he brought from the Directing Party Organs Section.[43] Unfortunately, with the exception of a few very prominent and typical figures like M. F. Shkiriatov, little is known about these men. They were too obscure to be noticed publicly while in the Party apparatus, and in most cases vanished when Ezhov departed from the NKVD. Consequently, one cannot trace their careers as one can those of the old Chekists. From various sources, however, a vague composite picture of the new political policeman can be derived. He was younger than the old Chekist, and possessed little of the espirit de corps of the latter. Most seem to have been opportunists and careerists, though the fear of failure may often have made them appear more egoistic than they really were. Most witnesses—generally those who experienced the NKVD's methods—agree that the new men, unskilled in interrogation methods, were ready to resort to the most vicious brutality. It is significant that an order of March 1937 permitted physical torture to be used, and that Stalin's own advice (at a later date) was "Beat, beat, and, once again, beat."[44]

Given the large-scale change in personnel (to be followed in late 1938 by a second turnover), it is hard to speak of the NKVD as a continuous body. In 1937 Stalin and his supporters found it convenient to use the NKVD as a ready-made institution for applying extreme pressure to the Party; but if it had not existed, Stalin would have invented something similar. Very likely this would have been an organization along the lines of his and Ezhov's earlier experimentation with the Commission of Party Control and the Section of Directing Party Organs. In later years, the police system became somewhat more stabilized, and no doubt its personnel, having worked together over a number of years, again developed a certain group solidarity. Even then, as we shall see, the police machine was an area of conflicting power groups rather than a unified power system in itself. If at the height of the purge the NKVD did not constitute the power behind the throne in any meaningful sense, it certainly did not in later periods.

While Stalin and Ezhov were transforming the police apparatus, they were also preparing a move against the Red Army command. In 1936 the higher officer corps of the Red Army was even less unified than was the NKVD at that time. There were former Tsarist officers like Marshal Tukhachevskii and General (still nominally called "Commander First Class") B. M. Shaposhnikov; there were men like Marshal S. M. Budennyi who had risen from the ranks to command a cavalry army in the Civil War, and had learned little since; and political officers on the model of Ian Gamarnik, chief of the Main Political Administration. Increasingly, however, the middle-level line and political officers were men who had entered one of the central military academies at an early age and thereafter devoted themselves to the military career. There was still some friction between the line and the political officers; on the whole, however, a tradition of professional solidarity, fostered especially by Tukhachevskii, appeared to be developing. On the social side, the increasing emphasis on the *wives* of officers, who were given, to use the sociological term, an "ascribed" status derived from their husbands', not their own, accomplishments, was a departure from Soviet custom. It suggested that military officers had become a recognized privileged group.[45] The introduction of the rank of marshal and various lower officer ranks in September 1935 symbolized the change.

On the military side, more fundamental trends were the emphasis on mechanization and the dropping (in the 1936 Field Regulations edited by Tukhachevskii) of the old doctrines concerning special "proletarian" tactics.[46] Of both military and political importance was the gradual elimination of units formed on a territorial basis. Especially important in this regard were the nationality formations. Although as late as 1935 the role of the Uzbek National Division in instructing Uzbeks in the Russian language and Communist theory was stressed, Gamarnik (who is said to have played the leading role in eliminating nationality formations) apparently felt that both military efficiency and political reliability of the armed forces would be increased by distributing non-Russians throughout the army.[47] The initial moves, made at the same time, for reintroducing Cossack units seemed a completely contradictory trend. The Cossack units, however, seem to have been favored by Stalin personally, who regarded them as symbols of patriotism and loyalty to the ruling circle.[48]

Why Stalin was not satisfied with the development of the officer corps, which appeared to many to fit in with conservative and nationalist tendencies of the regime in other regards, is still unclear. It has been suggested that any element of Soviet society which tended to develop a stable tradition and sense of group solidarity was a threat to his intention of maintaining absolute power.[49] Another reason, no doubt, was simply that many of the high officers like Gamarnik were Old Bolsheviks or men like Tukhachevskii who had associated with them in the Civil War; against some of these (Tukhachevskii in particular) Stalin had reason to bear a personal grudge. It has also been suggested that Stalin feared that the higher officers were plotting to remove him or at least curb his power. There is considerable circumstantial evidence that in 1933 at the height of the collectivization campaign V. K. Bliukher ("Galen"), commander of the Far East army, informed Stalin that he could not be responsible for defense against Japan unless the unrest arising from collectivization was ended by ameliorative measures.[50] In any event, a special dispensation was made for many peasants in the Far East, who were exempted from taxes and given other privileges on the condition that they be available for military service.

There are less well-substantiated rumors that Tukhachevskii and Gamarnik in Red Army headquarters, and Postyshev and the commander of the forces in the Ukraine, I. E. Iakir, also protested the rigors of collectivization. If this is true, it provides a connecting link to a supposed plan by high officers and Party leaders to overthrow Stalin, which several writers, notably Isaac Deutscher, have accepted as fact.[51] The essence of the various reported versions of this plan is that in late 1936 or early 1937 the military figures supposedly involved in the 1933 protests, perhaps joined by Party leaders, felt that a new situation just as disastrous as collectivization was developing from the intensification of the purges. They were especially alarmed by the destruction of the industrial managers, which threatened military production. Consequently, they resolved to remove Stalin by a military coup.[52]

Other witnesses who were in the USSR at the time flatly deny that there was in 1937 any concerted effort by the military to curb Stalin.[53] The existing evidence is too scanty to permit one to choose between these versions. What does seem certain is that Stalin's subsequent charge that high officers had entered into conspiracy with the Germans is completely unfounded. The "rehabilitation" of the accused officers in 1956 is, perhaps, in itself sufficient to dissolve this charge. Stalin's decision to purge the Red Army commanders was probably made by the end of 1936, when Radek's confession, pointing to military implication in the opposition "plot," was drawn up.[54] Not long afterward, the German Gestapo arranged "leaks" of information to the French and Czechoslovak officials concerning a plot in the Soviet High Command; as allies of the USSR, these officials gave the information to the Soviet government, which then had "proof" that its officers were plotting against it. But the very complicated evidence available indicates that Stalin's agents had supplied the information to the Gestapo in the first place! [55]

In May 1937 the overt moves against the Red Army commanders began. On May 11 Shaposhnikov replaced Tukhachevskii as chief of the general staff; Tukhachevskii was sent to command the relatively unimportant Volga Military District. Iakir was sent from the Ukraine to Leningrad.[56] On the same day a government decree reintroduced the Civil War institution of commissars in the larger military units.[57] This war measure for increasing political control was broadened a few months later by explicitly giving the commissar authority equal to that of the commander.[58] The measure was not, however, aimed at increasing Gamarnik's power; on June 1 appeared the announcement that, "embroiled with anti-Soviet elements," he had committed suicide.[59] Ten days later came the notice of the arrests "at different times" of Tukhachevskii, Iakir, Putna, and five other high officers, who were said to have confessed to treason and espionage for foreign powers. All were tried, condemned, and shot.[60]

This sudden and secret trial was just the beginning of the Red Army purge. Within a few months most of the high officers listed as judges at the trial disappeared. The two most prominent were Bliukher and Ia. I. Alksnis, commander of the air force. It seems probable that the removal of Alksnis is related to a purge of the large émigré colony of Latvians in the Soviet service.[61] The Latvian Communists, like the Poles, had formed a constituent part of the Bolshevik Party at its beginning, and were deeply embroiled in the factional conflicts of the twenties. As a result, Latvians figured prominently in some of the local purges.[62] Their most prominent representative, Ia. E. Rudzutak, Politburo candidate and Deputy Chairman of the Council of People's Commissars, is rumored to have opposed Stalin at the February-March plenum. Though not denounced until December, he, too, disappeared in mid-1937.

Stalin probably distrusted Marshal Bliukher even more than the officers around Tukhachevskii. In addition to the fairly well-substantiated reports of Bliukher's clash with Stalin in 1933, there is a rumor that Bliukher took advantage of his popularity following the Soviet campaign in Manchuria in 1929 to join a group opposed to Stalin.[63] Nevertheless, since Bliukher commanded in an area which might conceivably have sustained a rebellion against Moscow, Stalin moved cautiously against him. It is reported that evidence was being prepared against Bliukher as far back as 1936. In May 1937 a large-scale "conspiracy" was "discovered" on the Far East railroads.[64] Some months later G. M. Shtern became Bliukher's chief of staff. Though Bliukher was reported as commanding in the Far East as late as August 1938,[65] his position appears by then to have been completely undermined by a vast purge which practically destroyed the top command of the Far East forces. Bliukher himself was dead, probably summarily shot, before the year was out.

Various well-informed sources have estimated the total arrests among Red Army officers, line and political, at 15,000 to 35,000—one-fifth to one-half of the total.[66] The most careful available analysis of the evidence indicates that the latter proportion is most likely correct for the officer corps as a whole.[67] The proportion of higher officers purged is calculated to have reached 65 per cent.[68] Not all of these were shot; a number of arrested officers reappeared in World War II as major commanders. The immediate impact on the Soviet armed forces, however, was to reduce drastically its military capability and its reputation among prospective enemies and allies abroad. This was the price which Stalin and his supporters paid for destroying all potential independence in the Red Army.

In the longer view, the results of the army purge were not entirely negative from the standpoint of Soviet power. The effects on morale appear to have been mixed. Soon after Stalin's one-time secretary Lev Mekhlis became chief of the Political Administration of the Army, he accused Gamarnik, his predecessor, of having held back promotions. In this way Mekhlis appealed to the ambitions of junior officers, and especially noncommissioned officers, who were able to rise rapidly to fill the places of their purged superiors. In view of the lack of training of many of the Civil War commanders, their replacement may have eventually improved the quality of the officer corps.[69] Here, as in other areas of purge, Stalin's ruthless actions were not simply arbitrary despotism, but a way to the creation of a new equilibrium of forces.

CHAPTER

V

THE GREAT PURGE: II

During the very week that Marshal Tukhachevskii was accused, the aviator V. P. Chkalov and his crew made a spectacular flight over the Arctic to San Francisco. To the outside world, and to many an ordinary Soviet citizen, this flight and simultaneous Soviet explorations in the Arctic were demonstrations of Soviet technical accomplishments and an expression of international good will. To the Communist, they pointed up the contrast between "socialist organized-planned heroism" and the "individual," "bourgeois" heroism of Charles A. Lindbergh, or still worse the barbarism of the Fascist bombers of Guernica.[1] To the worker in the Party apparatus, a high point of the Arctic exploration was a Party meeting near the North Pole which unanimously demanded the "supreme penalty" for Tukhachevskii and his companions.[2]

Such diverse reactions to a single set of events were typical of the Soviet scene as the mass arrests, torture, and executions known as the "Great Purge" reached their peak in mid-1937. This was a purge unlike any that had gone before, for to be caught in it did not mean mere expulsion from the Party, or even banishment to a concentration camp. Khrushchev has admitted that arrests for "counterrevolution" increased tenfold in 1937, as compared even to 1936, scarcely a tranquil year.[3] He has also indicated that the purpose of the arrests was the "physical annihilation" of the victims. We do not know, and perhaps will never know, the numerical extent of the killings. The most revealing indication was provided in 1943 when the German occupation forces discovered a mass grave in the city of Vinnitsa containing thousands of bodies of persons executed in 1937 and 1938. Although the Germans of course used the discovery for propaganda purposes, its authenticity appears indisputable. Vinnitsa was then a frontier city, in an area where one might expect the hunt for "enemies" would be especially fierce; but the whole province in which it is located contained only a million people. Hence one can conclude that in certain areas at least the Great Purge killed a measurable proportion of the population.

Confronted by this slaughter, the Soviet population seemed to take refuge in a kind of schizophrenia. There was little or no violent resistance. Men sought their individual safety in silence. The typical peasant or worker (now that a very large proportion of workers were of recent peasant origin) in 1937-38 had no immediate reason to risk his life, his limited liberty, and his slowly rising standard of living by openly opposing the regime. Most of the victims of the purge were of the "intelligentsia" or the pre-Revolutionary working class. They included at first officials of the Party and the government and industrial directors—all usually Communists of long standing. Since it was precisely these men who carried out the drastic repression of the peasantry during collectivization, there was no obvious reason for the latter to rally to their support.[4] The case was somewhat different with the intelligentsia in a non-Russian region; but they too had long been cut off from the peasant mass of their nation by the necessity of collaborating with the regime.

The brutalizing effects of the collectivization period itself also undoubtedly helped make the excesses of the Great Purge possible. Having seen hundreds of thousands of families packed off to Siberia in the dead of winter, even larger numbers begging for scraps of bread at the railroad stations, and untold numbers of starving children shot for pilfering, the average Soviet citizen was sufficiently calloused to others' suffering to put his own safety first. The careerists who denounced their superiors, and very likely Ezhov's new Party recruits for the NKVD, had dulled their sensibilities to suffering while participating in the brutal repression of the peasants. It is little wonder that many were just as ready to resort to brutal treatment of their erstwhile Party comrades. Rarely has a group so quickly reaped what it sowed as did the Party officials who carried through collectivization.

At the same time, the regime took every precaution to prevent violent reactions to the purge. As was described earlier, it carefully infiltrated the NKVD and had beheaded the Red Army, the principal instruments which the older officials might have used for resistance. At the same time—unlike the Nazis and the Fascists—the regime avoided arousing sudden revulsion against its tactics by refraining from public brutality. "Up to the door of the NKVD, all men are equal," remained a cynical byword even at the height of the purge. Behind the closed doors and in the distant concentration camps there was brutality aplenty, but members of the general public knew only that neighbors had vanished in the night—and seeing no evil, refused to hear of it.

The Ukraine was especially severely affected in 1937-38, as it had been in 1930-33. As noted earlier, Stalin had been aroused years before by the tendency of some Ukrainian Party leaders to identify Ukrainian national expression with the slogan "away from Moscow." One may imagine that Stalin's suspicions were reawakened by the opposition of Postyshev, Ukrainian second secretary. To be sure, Postyshev, a Russian, had been involved four years earlier in the suppression of the Ukrainian "national Communists." Since the criticisms following his expulsion from Kiev do not link him to a "national deviation," it is impossible to say with assurance that he encouraged Ukrainian feeling, though such a theory has been advanced.[5] Other major Ukrainian Communist leaders purged in 1937 have, however, been explicitly accused of this deviation.

Undoubtedly the reasons for the almost complete purge of the higher echelons of the Ukrainian Party were complex. As early as October 1935 the NKVD in the Ukraine reported the discovery of a Trotskyite "wrecking" group in Kharkov.[6] Hryhoryi Kostiuk, a systematic investigator of this period in the Ukraine, maintains that the NKVD began to "discover" a Ukrainian Trotskyite center as early as January 1935.[7] The trials of August 1936 and January 1937 pointed to various Ukrainian opposition elements; arrests were numerous, especially among industrial directors. High Party officials were struck down suddenly and inexplicably. For example, P. F. Markitan, Chernigov obkom secretary, was praised in *Pravda* on May 30 and bitterly denounced in the same paper on July 17, 1937.

The climax of the purge in the Ukraine came at the end of August 1937. The only immediate published evidence was an obscure notice that Panas Liubchenko, chairman of the Ukrainian council of people's commissars, "embroiled in anti-Soviet activities," had committed suicide.[8] Just what happened at this time is difficult to determine. Avtorkhanov gives a dramatic account of the arrival in Kiev of Molotov, Ezhov, and Khrushchev, accompanied by a force of NKVD agents.[9] An interesting Yugoslav account agrees that a trio of Politburo members headed by Molotov carried out the purge of the Ukrainian Party leaders.[10] Unfortunately, both accounts contain so many demonstrable inaccuracies—such as the report that the Ukrainian first secretary Kosior was arrested then—that they must be treated with great reserve.

A comparison of later Soviet official allegations indicates that the condemned Ukrainian leaders were divided into at least two groups. One group was implicated directly in the Trotskyite "conspiracy." It included Iakir, the commander of the Kiev Military District, who had been shot in June; V. A. Balitskii, director of the NKVD in the Ukraine, who was transferred to the Far East about the same time; and M. M. Popov, secretary of the Ukrainian central committee. Probably there were some real connections—though scarcely conspiratorial ones—between the Jewish and the Russian members of this group, and major victims of the purge like Gamarnik, Bukharin, and Iagoda. Consequently, their elimination was part of the general purge. The second group evidently included Liubchenko, V. P. Zatonskii, A. A. Khvylia, and G. I. Petrovskii.[11] Although these men were Communists above all, and had even persecuted Skrypnyk's "national Communists," they were native Ukrainians. Apparently they wished to preserve some independence for Ukrainian culture. During the autumn of 1937 charges of Ukrainian nationalism mounted. For example, the press of the Vinnitsa "frontier oblast" was accused of failing to attack "enemies" and of not combatting nationalist tendencies.[12] In view of the massacre discovered there later, the article has a sinister sound.

The most explicit charges against the Ukrainian Party leaders were not made until June 1938, when Nikita Khrushchev accused several of trying to turn the Ukraine over to foreign enemies.[13] Apparently by that time the accused group (except for G. I. Petrovskii, who was assigned an obscure job in Moscow) had long been condemned and shot. The role of Khrushchev in the Ukrainian purge, though much discussed, is still unclear. The story that he went to the Ukraine for the initial purge is suspect, because he remained officially in Moscow for over four months following the supposed trip, and his activities there were frequently reported. It is not so certain that Stanislav Kosior, the Polish-born Ukrainian first secretary whom Khrushchev officially replaced at the end of January 1938, actually remained in Kiev until that time. But even after his official departure for Moscow Kosior enjoyed at least some weeks of liberty; according to a report by the American diplomat Charles Bohlen he seemed to be "quite obviously enjoying the limelight" in Supreme Soviet meetings.[14] Whether or not Khrushchev played a direct part in eliminating his predecessors, he almost certainly directed the removal of many of their followers. The Ukraine experienced a greater turnover in Party leadership between mid-1937 and mid-1938 (when Party congresses were held) than any other large area of the USSR. Of all the members of the 1937 central committee only one—the purely honorary member Marshal Timoshenko—was re-elected in 1938. As far as can be determined, only one other—G. I. Petrovskii—ever reappeared in the Soviet press. Only two of the thirty-eight candidate members, including the highly publicized Stakhanovite P. F. Krivonos, continued in public life. At lower levels of the apparatus the purge in the Ukraine was by no means so complete, but it was more intense than in most other areas of the USSR.[15]

Both the intrinsic importance of the Ukraine and the intensity of the purge there have made a somewhat extended treatment desirable. The purge in Belorussia was nearly as severe. As two good accounts are already available, a brief summary of its main features is sufficient here.[16] The purge began considerably before 1937, and passed through several stages. Personal rivalries seem to have played a major role, although eventually all local Party factions were eliminated and replaced by men sent from Moscow. Charges of treasonable relations with Poland played a larger role than in the Ukraine. They led to an especially devastating purge in the border regions of former Civil War fighters *against* the Poles.

Apparently the height of the Belorussian purge came slightly before the climax in Kiev. The main campaign against "deviationists" and "nationalists" in most of the other national republics seems to have taken place in September. *Pravda* published attacks on "nationalists" in such diverse areas as Karelia, Buriat-Mongolia, Kazakhstan, and Tadzhikstan.

Only scattered reports are available from most of the Asian Republics. In Kirgizia the purge in September appears to have been directed mainly against Kirgiz Communist leaders who were accused of "tolerating bourgeois nationalism," though there was at least one accusation of "Trotskyism." Charges of this kind had been mounting ever since the Kirov assassination. In addition, the NKVD utilized pre-existing conflicts between northern and southern groups in the country.[17] In Uzbekistan, accusations of F. Khodiaev and A. Ikramov, leaders tried later with Bukharin, indicate that a special effort was made to link the purged Communists to the "Right" opposition as well.[18]

The Great Purge at this time seems to have taken on a sweeping and concerted nature which differentiates it from earlier phases of Stalin's destruction of his opponents. Having prepared the ground and tested the overhauled NKVD machinery, he apparently no longer saw any reason to delay. Perhaps the sheer momentum of Ezhov's apparatus had something to do with the extent of the purge at this time, but the fact that Politburo members accompanied the NKVD "mobile groups" to some of the peripheral areas indicates that the concerted campaign had Stalin's sanction.[19]

On December 16 A. S. Enukidze was finally tried *in camera* and condemned to death. With him was sentenced an oddly composed group of seven, including a "former baron," a Georgian Party official charged with nationalism, and the famous Soviet diplomat Lev Karakhan, accused of betraying state secrets.[20]

Bukharin and Rykov had to wait three more months for a final condemnation. They appeared in the last public trial, that of the "twenty-one," officially called "the Bloc of Rights and Trotskyites" on March 2-13, 1938. Perhaps no more complicated explanation of the delay is required than that Stalin, Ezhov, and their minions were fascinated by the prospect of bringing all threads of the huge "conspiracy" together in the persons of one group of defendants. The list of those denounced at the March trial, though not personally present—often because they had already been executed—was a résumé of the entire Great Purge. The Comintern leader Béla Kún, the Ukrainians Liubchenko and Zatonskii, the Belorussian Goloded, the Georgian Mdivani, the Latvian Rudzutak, Tukhachevskii and the officers condemned with him, Karakhan, Enukidze—these and many others were again excoriated.

Several of the defendants present, for the most part figures of secondary importance, were accused principally of "bourgeois nationalism." This, at least as a matter of major emphasis, was a new theme for the public trials. The nationalists were supposed to have been linked with the Trotskyites, the Rights, and others in a single conspiracy. All were still connected to treason and espionage for Germany, and Khristian Rakovskii, an actual follower of Trotsky, was accused of trying to undermine the Franco-Soviet alliance.[21] However, the prosecutor, Vyshinskii, noted that Bukharin had hoped to bring Great Britain "over to the side of the aggressor" against the USSR.[22]

A bizarre new accusation was introduced in this trial: that the defendants had covertly murdered most of the prominent men who had died in the Soviet Union in the years immediately preceding the trial. Iagoda, as described earlier, was charged with Kirov's death. He, in collaboration with the other principal defendants, his NKVD lieutenants, and several prominent physicians, was accused of bringing about the deaths of Kuibyshev,

Menzhinskii (an earlier director of the political police), Gor'kii, and Gor'kii's son.

The role of the physicians is especially interesting. D. D. Pletnev, long in attendance at the Kremlin, had been accused in June 1937 of a sadistic attack on a woman patient.[23] As sexual crimes are rarely mentioned in the Soviet central press, the accusation seemed to hide some other charge. A possible clue to the real reason for Pletnev's disgrace is the testimony of a defector, who claims to have been his assistant, that Pletnev was accidentally present when Ordzhonikidze was murdered.[24] There appears to be no such special reason for the implication of the two other physicians, I. N. Kazakov and L. G. Levin. But at the close of the latter's testimony his defense counsel (chosen of course from the official panel) asked an odd question: "Perhaps you belonged to some national party, Jewish, for example?" Levin replied, "Not to any party, only to the physicians' party."[25]

One way or another, all the defendants confessed. But N. N. Krestinskii, a former diplomat, flatly denied the charges when he first appeared, although he confessed freely the following day. Bukharin and each of the other principal defendants confessed crimes sufficient to justify many death sentences; but several of them obstinately refused to admit certain charges, such as the murders mentioned above.

Two months before the trial just described, a plenum of the Central Committee met to consider a broad range of questions. These included the forthcoming Supreme Soviet session, economic matters, the elevation of Khrushchev to candidate member of the Politburo, the removal of Postyshev from that category, and the naming of Mekhlis to the Orgburo. Much the most important subject of the meeting, however, concerned "mistakes" in the exclusion of Party members. The gist of the plenum resolution was that many Party organizations had excluded members *en masse*, without considering individual cases; that "careerists" had falsely accused their comrades; and that "masked enemies" had secured the expulsion of good Communists to weaken the Party. S. O. Kudriatsev, Postyshev's successor in Kiev, was the horrible example of the last category. This did not, however, appear to exonerate Postyshev, for similar practices were noted in the Kuibyshev oblast; nor was the NKVD implicated, for it was said to have reviewed the Kuibyshev cases and exonerated the innocent Communists.[26] But the resolution did mean that some part of the purge process was finally reversed.

As the following figures show, Leningrad under Zhdanov (who probably

played an important role in reversing the excesses of the purge), had
begun to exonerate Party members slightly before the January plenum
though the process was much accelerated afterward:

EXPULSION OF PARTY MEMBERS IN LENINGRAD[27]

Month	Number Expelled by Primary Organizations	Expulsions Upheld by Party Authorities	Per Cent Upheld
Sept 1937	61	59	96.7
Oct	40	37	92.5
Nov	85	83	97.6
Dec	150	131	87.3
Jan 1938	148	72	48.7
Feb	102	46	45.1
Mar	70	43	61.4
Apr	42	16	38.1

In the year following the January 1938 plenum, the proportion of reversals
of expulsions mounted to fantastic heights: 57 per cent in Kiev, 60 per cent
in Belorussia; 63 per cent in Arkhangelsk oblast, 70 per cent in Kursk oblast,
72 per cent in Iaroslav oblast, and 85 per cent in Moscow city.[28]

The emphasis was on the renewal of the Party ranks by new admissions
as well as by exoneration of unjustly purged members. Officially admission
of new candidates and members had begun on November 1, 1936. Down to
July 1937, however, admissions had been trivial in number; aside from
special organizations like those in the armed forces, the Party had accepted
only 12,000 new candidates, and raised about 19,000 candidates to full
membership. The situation was not much improved in the remainder of
1937: only 28,000 candidates and 24,000 members were accepted by ordinary
territorial organizations. In the first half of 1938, on the other hand, these
organizations took in over 100,000 candidates and raised nearly 40,000
candidates to membership.[29] Increase in Party membership during the
second half of the year was still higher; an estimate of the total growth for
1938 is 415,000.[30] The striking reversal in the membership trend due to the
dual process of exoneration and accelerated admission is indicated by the
fact that the total number of Communists declined by 60,000 in 1937, but
rose by 400,000 in 1938.

At first the decisions of the January plenum did not appear to have affected the position of Ezhov, whose public recognition had been steadily

rising as the Great Purge increased in intensity. At the third plenum of 1937, in October (in addition to the February-March plenum, there was a June plenum on agriculture), Ezhov became a Politburo candidate—an unprecedented honor for a police chief. His name and his picture appeared with a prominence and frequency second only to Stalin's; adulatory references to the "iron" commissar (a pun on Ezhov's name) whose "iron gauntlets" were cleansing the country became the order of the day. As late as March 1938, at the Bukharin-Rykov trial he had the honorific role of chief intended victim of the "plotters."

The trial was scarcely over, however, before a significant turn in Ezhov's career occurred: he became Commissar of Water Transportation.[31] It is true that he retained the post of Commissar of the Interior, and that the Party press devoted enormous emphasis to the importance of his work in improving water transport. Nevertheless, it was strange that a man who had risen as rapidly as Ezhov should have to concern himself with a single branch of the economy, however important. The parallel to Iagoda's removal must have arisen in many minds.

Even today there is no real evidence explaining the forces leading to Ezhov's decline. Basically, Zbigniew Brzezinski's explanation that the purge, exceeding its designed limits, had become dangerous to Stalin and his associates seems most plausible.[32] Ezhov, then, was primarily a tool which had become too sharp to be used safely any longer.

Personal rivalries probably played a part as well. The role of Anastas Mikoian is suggestive. As member of a four-man Politburo subcommittee in charge of foreign policy, he apparently occupied a major though unpublicized position in the late thirties.[33] For a government economic official, Mikoian took an unusual interest in the NKVD. On July 20, 1936, six weeks before the first hint of Iagoda's fall, Mikoian had addressed the Party organization of the Moscow NKVD. Apparently covertly referring to Iagoda, Mikoian remarked that Felix Dzerzhinskii, who had died ten years earlier, had had "no secrets from the Party," and had known that deviation of Chekists was especially dangerous for the Party.[34]

Aside from this implied unfavorable comparison to Dzerzhinskii, the printed version of this speech, which went to the press on August 19, 1936, just as the Kamenev-Zinoviev trial opened, completely ignored Iagoda. Indeed, aside from Stalin, Kaganovich was the only living Party leader whom Mikoian notably praised. Both Kaganovich and Mikoian seem to have had some role in the rise of Lavrenti Beria to major posts in the Transcaucasus.[35] Consequently, in the light of later developments, it appears just possible that Mikoian was preparing the ground for a new NKVD chief. In fact, as we already know, Ezhov, not Beria, was Stalin's choice in 1936.[36] By 1936 Beria had achieved prominence by publishing a history of the Transcaucasian Party which blithely disregarded the facts in order to give Stalin the major role. As first secretary of Georgia, Beria probably played an important part in purging Stalin's old enemies, particularly the group around Budu Mdivani which was tried *in camera* on July 9, 1937.[37] It is not so clear that he was the guiding force in the wave of intensive purges that hit the Transcaucasian Republics, and especially the North Caucasus, in September-October 1937. These purges appear to have been an integral part of the far-flung but concerted arrests carried out by the NKVD "mobile teams" in August-October 1937. In the North Caucasus, at least, Ezhov's deputy Shkiriatov was in charge.[38] Indeed, if Beria had really been Ezhov's rival, Beria himself may have been in danger at that time.

On December 20, 1937, on the twentieth anniversary of the founding of the Cheka, Mikoian again spoke to the Moscow NKVD.[39] This time he highly praised the incumbent commissar, Ezhov, but it is worth noting that he compared Ezhov's success in reconstructing the NKVD to Kaganovich's in rebuilding rail transportation.[40] As Kaganovich was probably weakened by the precarious position of his brother Iu. M. Kaganovich who is said to have been under arrest during the purge, the comparison was rather odd. Stranger still was the reference to Mikoian himself in the Bukharin-Rykov trial three months later. M. A. Chernov, one of the defendants, testified that he made use of an assignment given him by Mikoian as Commissar of Trade in 1928 to conspire with Rykov. There was no direct implication of Mikoian, just as there was none of Tukhachevskii in the Radek trial; but the introduction of his name in such a connection was hardly intended as a compliment.[41]

In view of these peculiar references, it is interesting to note that Mikoian also addressed workers of the Commissariat of Water Transportation at just about the time that Ezhov took charge of them.[42] Could Mikoian, fearing for his own safety, have played a part in an intricate plan to ease Ezhov out of the Commissariat of the Interior? By late 1937 the Great Purge seems to have been especially directed against non-Russians. L. M. Kaganovich and Mikoian—both non-Russians—were among the few in the top leadership who had survived Ezhov's purge. According to an NKVD defector, L. M. Kaganovich, frightened by his brother's arrest, urged

Stalin to investigate Ezhov. After following this advice, Stalin—who, as a non-Russian himself may have become disturbed at the direction the purge was taking—decided to replace Ezhov by Lavrenti Beria and to place other Georgians in key NKVD posts.[43]

Sometime in the summer of 1938 Beria was transferred from Tbilisi to become Ezhov's deputy; soon he actually directed the police apparatus.[44] Beria brought a relatively small number of key assistants with him from Georgia, and replaced several of the major NKVD officers who had served Ezhov. The old Chekists Zakovskii, Frinkovskii, and V. S. Korzhenko, police representative in the foreign office, disappeared, although not at once.[45] Many of the new men to whom Ezhov had given high police offices in the provinces, like A. I. Uspenskii in the Ukraine, also vanished.

Ezhov nominally remained at his post, though gradually becoming less prominent in the press. On December 8, 1938, however, a notice in *Izvestia* stated that Ezhov was released "according to his request" as Commissar of the Interior while remaining as Commissar of Water Transportation. Beria officially became Commissar of the Interior.[46] Six weeks later Ezhov appeared on the presidium for the celebration of the anniversary of Lenin's death.[47] After that, no word concerning Ezhov appeared in the Soviet press during Stalin's lifetime—the omission of his name from such publications as the second edition (1939) of the *Short Course* is itself an indication of his fall from favor. It is possible he was not arrested, but died, as rumors have variously had it, in a tuberculosis sanitorium or in a madhouse. According to the NKVD defector mentioned above, Ezhov was accused of having been a British agent.[48]

Whatever attention the general public in the USSR might have given the brief announcement of Ezhov's departure from the NKVD was probably completely diverted a week later when the aviator Chkalov died in a crash, thereby doing one last service in diverting public attention from Stalin's deadly political maneuvers.

For those Stalin considered his opponents the change in NKVD command meant nothing. As we have seen, Stanislav Kosior disappeared in the spring of 1938, but he did not die until 1939 after Ezhov himself had disappeared. We know from Khrushchev's speech that the Politburo candidate Eikhe, arrested in April 1938, was not tried and shot until February 1940.[49] A. V. Kosarev, secretary of the Komsomol, was not even deprived of his office until November 1938, when Ezhov's power was clearly minimal.[50] Some foreign Communist leaders, like Béla Kún and the Pole Julian Lenski, lived until 1939 without being released as did, probably, the Politburo member Vlas Chubar'. Marshal A. I. Egorov lived on, doubtless in a concentration camp, until 1941.[51] Arrests of Old Bolsheviks in the Transcaucasus, and of industrial managers in various areas, continued in 1939.[52] Ezhov's decline did indeed mark the end of mass terror, but it by no means dulled the sword of Damocles hanging above the Party leadership.

CHAPTER
VI

THE IDEOLOGY OF TOTALITARIANISM

The forced march of the Party toward rigid internal centralization was paralleled by extension of totalitarian control over all phases of Soviet life. Communist ideology had always claimed a dominant position for the Party in ideological and cultural activities. Until the mid-thirties, however, some play had been allowed to differing schools of interpretation in certain spheres of intellectual endeavor, and some leeway permitted to localist or national tendencies.

Many observers of the Soviet Union during Stalin's lifetime were inclined to regard the cultural changes which became apparent in the mid-thirties as a conservative development. Some even spoke of a "restoration," in the sense of a return to traditional patterns of Russian society. It seems indisputable that a major effect of the changes was to stabilize social and cultural conditions in the USSR. The measures taken in 1934 to reduce tensions and permit establishment of some degree of stable living conditions among the masses of the rural population were part of this pattern. Beyond the negative aim of reducing tensions and burdens, the regime felt a compelling need to take longer-range measures to repair the drain on human resources which occurred during collectivization. Stalin's remarks of May 4, 1935, that "we have not yet learned to value people" sounded hypocritical in the light of the approaching purge; but it did point to a new emphasis in population policy.[1]

While neither Marx nor Lenin had favored highly unconventional behavior in sexual and familial relations, many Bolsheviks had regarded complete freedom "to dispose of one's own body" as a major gain of the Revolution. Consequently, the proposal to restrict divorce and limit abortion to cases of medical necessity, advanced in May 1936, aroused much opposition, especially among the articulate women in the Party. Practical objections centered around the incontestable fact that housing limitations and women's necessity of performing arduous work usually made stable family life and bearing of children a severe burden. Nevertheless, the proposed law was passed on June 27, 1936.[2]

An interesting aspect of the discussion preceding this measure is the Communist admission that the prohibition of abortion was designed solely for Soviet conditions. Under capitalism, a Comintern journal declared, the workers are right to fight the prohibition of abortion, as that system makes no provision for children.[3] In this way, in line with Lenin's dictum that "morality is that which serves to destroy the old exploiting society and to unite all toilers around the proletariat,"[4] a dual standard of social behavior was recognized. There is abundant evidence that, in accord with the assumptions behind this dual standard, laxity in other aspects of sexual behavior was tacitly sanctioned for non-Soviet Communists, and very probably for special groups such as the higher Party and NKVD officials within the USSR itself.[5] This distinction makes it easier to understand how the concern with improvement of the demographic position of the USSR could be combined with the drastic "blood" purges of 1937-38. The demographic health of the country would be assured if the masses followed the new population policy; the politically undesirable minority was expendable.

The ideological keynote of this period, and indeed of Stalin's whole life, was the necessity of strengthening the Soviet state as long as it existed in a capitalist environment. He returned again and again to this theme, harshly rejecting, as in his "Letter to Comrade Ivanov," any tendency to minimize the role of the state.[6] Closely related to this principle were two others: that socialism had already been built "in the main," and that a society "of working people" had been substantially achieved. The former principle was constantly reiterated by Soviet leaders, and the latter was enshrined in the 1936 Constitution.[7] Together the three principles implied a static society; consequently, it is not surprising that for long periods Stalin made slight reference to the eschatological aspect of Marxism-Leninism, the advent of complete Communism.[8]

Again, however, the "conservative" developments are only part of the picture. The ultimate inevitability of world revolution continued to be stressed in Party indoctrination. In spite of Stalin's declaration to an American journalist that "we never had such plans and intentions" of fostering world revolution, the role of the USSR as the "fortress" of the working class was still proclaimed.[9] On the domestic side Stalin in 1935 referred to the Stakhanovite work system—itself an unsettling process—as the "first feeble" preparation for the transition to true Communism.[10] Stalin's principal ideological pronouncement of the thirties, *The History of the Communist Party of the Soviet Union (Bolshevik): Short Course,* is full of such superficially contradictory elements.

The importance of the *Short Course* is so great that its various aspects must be touched upon again and again in this treatment. Issued in November 1938, at the very end of the Great Purge, it represented Stalin's effort to provide an ideological and pedagogical foundation for his control of the Party. The use of a history to serve this purpose was based on the Marxist principle that practical experience and theory are inextricably intertwined. Consequently, study of Party history (as revised to fit Stalin's wishes) was to be the principal means of indoctrination for Communists.

In spite of this basic approach, which greatly reduced the role of abstract ideas in Party training, Stalin found it necessary to deal with purely theoretical matters separately in the section entitled "Dialectical and Historical Materialism." The principles Stalin advances (for he apparently wrote much of this section, at least, himself) seem only indirectly related to the development of the Party; but certain of them had a fundamental significance for the development of Communist ideology during the following decade.

Stalin was no systematizer of ideas, and his presentation of dialectical materialism contained little that Lenin had not introduced. Any innovation, therefore, is all the more important. The one which has received the most attention is Stalin's omission of one of the three basic laws of the Marxist dialectic, "the negation of the negation."[11] It would require an extended treatment of the dialectic theory to explain the full significance of the complicated and ambiguous concept of "the negation of the negation." Briefly, it means that all development takes place in a spiral form, with each succeeding phase repeating an earlier one, but at a higher level. Hence, change is progress. Some writers have pointed out that the "negation of the negation" is implicitly contained in the first two laws of the dialectic, which Stalin repeated.[12] However, as Herbert Marcuse writes, Stalin's omission of the third law was a step in the formation of the new "conception of dialectic . . . most suitable to serve the ideological stabilization of the established state."[13] By reducing the role of change, the new formulation laid the theoretical basis for the assertion that under socialism transitions were gradual rather than sudden. Stalin's characteristic caution is evident, however; he continued to expound the accepted Marxist theory of the "dialectic leap," in which developments "occur not gradually, but rapidly, suddenly."[14]

The juggling of Marxist theoretical concepts just described may appear to be very remote from the fierce suppression of the opposition. In fact, though, a major theme for the purge was the allegation that opposition elements had infiltrated the ideological sphere:

> . . . Trotskyites, Zinovievites, nationalists, and other class enemies, driven from a number of the most important branches of socialist construction, at the present time are trying to steal into the institutions of higher education, the schools, the publishing houses, the editorial boards of newspapers, and similar branches of work which have a direct relation to the ideological "reworking" of students and readers.[15]

The search for "Trotskyites," and later for "Rights," was closely related to the condemnation of theorists who had advanced radical theories of social innovation. As in the case of marital regulation, such theories were often related to legal development. The dominant figure of early Soviet jurisprudence was P. I. Stuchka, a Latvian. He advanced the theory that law under Soviet rule must be "a changing social phenomenon rather than an eternal category" aimed at upholding "the system of social relationships which conforms to the interests of the toiling masses." [16] After Stuchka died his work was carried on by E. B. Pashukanis. His theories were, in a sense, still more destructive of legal stability than Stuchka's. Pashukanis maintained that law emerged as an aspect of "commodity-exchange" in the capitalist and precapitalist marketplace; consequently law would begin to wither away as soon as socialism was established.[17]

Pashukanis' ideas were closely related to Bukharin's concept of gradual withering away of the state; consequently, they were in direct opposition to Stalin's theory. As early as 1931 Pashukanis had to retract some of his concepts. However, he continued to occupy a dominant position in Soviet jurisprudence during the early stages of the purge, although occasionally sharply criticized by jurists closer to Stalin's ideas.[18] As late as November 1936—during Bukharin's reprieve—Pashukanis was given the important post of Deputy Commissar of Justice.[19] Suddenly—on January 20, 1937, just after Bukharin's ouster from *Izvestia*—*Pravda* attacked Pashukanis as an "enemy of the people." During the following months, his basic concepts were scathingly attacked, especially by Andrei Vyshinskii, who succeeded

him as director of the Institute of Law of the Academy of Sciences. Vyshinskii advanced the basic concept that law under socialism would be just
as lasting as the state, which prescribed the legal norms in the interest of
the dominant class of toilers.[20] This concept was said to have been embodied in the 1936 Constitution, which Pashukanis had allegedly undermined in his activity in the Commissariat of Justice.

Evidently there were two elements in Pashukanis' fall from grace: his
association with the opposition, and his theoretical antipathy to the new
process of stabilization. The first element probably explains the severe
punishment undoubtedly inflicted on him—he was accused of treason, and
disappeared completely. The second element made it necessary to destroy
his legal doctrines, and to remove many of his disciples from the legal field.

The stabilizing trend in Soviet ideology during the thirties was, therefore,
closely related to the elimination of earlier opposition groups. Vyshinskii's
new formula for socialist law clearly implied, however, that stability was
not to mean traditionalism but the acceptance of indisputable norms established by an omnipotent state. These norms were envisaged as relatively
stable; but they were entirely dependent on the will of the state acting in
the interests of the "toilers." In practice, Soviet law in Stalin's time was
frequently and unpredictably altered. Moreover, its sphere of operation
was narrowly limited. For example, a Ukrainian Komsomol organization
was criticized during this period for not making its own decision on expulsion of a member accused of loafing, but awaiting a formal court decision.[21] The strictest adherence to previously defined legal norms, therefore,
did not provide complete security for the Soviet citizen even in nonpolitical
matters. The powers of the NKVD in political cases were, of course, entirely arbitrary.

Similarly—as we have seen in the case of the Red Army officers corps—
stability did not mean tolerance of permanent institutions which might
develop solidarity tending to limit manipulation by the regime. The stability introduced by Stalin in the thirties, therefore, consisted of a degree of
regularity in personal relationships sufficient to enable the mass of the
population to maintain and to reproduce itself. At a more abstract level,
theories which emphasized change and innovation were de-emphasized,
though not always abandoned, in favor of those which stressed a degree
of permanence in existing social and political relations.

The dominant role of Stuchka and Pashukanis in early Soviet legal
theory was exceeded by M. N. Pokrovskii's pre-eminence in historiography.
Like the jurists, Pokrovskii completely rejected the customary approach of

his subject in favor of what he considered a thorough Marxist treatment. Actually Pokrovskii drew almost exclusively upon one element of Marxism, economic determinism. Applying this unicausal principle, he developed a highly schematic interpretation of history based on relationships of productive forces and on class conflict. Pokrovskii applied his theory especially to the history of Russia. He devoted slight attention to events and personages; when he treated them at all it was almost exclusively as examples of unprogressive, socially harmful forces.[22]

Pokrovskii died in 1932, but his followers continued to dominate the field of history. On May 16, 1934, however, the Council of People's Commissars and the Central Committee issued a decision "On the teaching of civic history in the schools of the USSR." This decree rejected Pokrovskii's approach as un-Marxist because of its omission of the dialectic in favor of simple economic materialism, and as unsuitable for pedagogical purposes because of its abstract character. The decree, and subsequent discussions, also criticized Pokrovskii's neglect of historic personages, especially those who had defended Russia against foreign invaders.[23]

The elimination of Pokrovskii's economic interpretation was necessary if history was to become the central element in the revival of Russian patriotism, for if his contention that the Tsarist regime was essentially oppressive were accepted, only the post-Revolutionary system could be used as an object of patriotic veneration. Love for the Soviet "native land" was, of course, inculcated; considerable efforts were devoted to evolving a "Soviet patriotism" and even the "Soviet people" became a common term at the end of the thirties.[24] But Stalin and his adherents evidently felt the need for a longer historical perspective for loyalty to their regime. Soviet patriotism was essentially loyalty to Communist ideas and accomplishments alone. As such, it might have been sufficient for the Party members; but "non-Party masses" cultivated after 1934 required a more traditional attachment. A large proportion of the latter—especially those drawn from the peasantry —could be most effectively reached by appeals to Russian nationalism.

The stress on Russian national feeling was developed gradually and was frequently linked to Soviet patriotism. There were, however, striking exceptions, such as the revival of Mikhail Glinka's opera A Life for the Tsar. The composition was, to be sure, renamed Ivan Susanin, with Izvestia carefully "explaining" that Tsarist courtiers had forced the earlier title on Glinka. Although some changes were also made in the libretto, the theme of the heroic struggle of Tsarist Russia against Poles and Germans was fully retained.[25]

The major difficulty encountered by the program of basing loyalty to the regime on appeals to the national spirit of the Russians arose from the fact that the numerous other nationalities were not only unattracted to Russian nationalism in its traditional form but were usually alienated by it. Consequently, special methods were required to "adapt" the new line to the non-Russian nationalities, and them to it. The negative aspect of Stalin's policy, discussed earlier, included suppression of the concept of separate cultural development symbolized by the slogan "away from Moscow," and liquidation of Party leaders and intellectuals suspected of favoring non-Russian nationalist tendencies. The positive side—from the standpoint of the Soviet regime—consisted of drawing non-Russians (often referred to as "minorities," although they now constitute about one-half of the USSR's population) closer to the Russian national culture.

Throughout the thirties, the principal historical interpretation for positively relating non-Russians to the Russian past was the stress on the Russians as the leading force in the 1917 Revolution. The Russian proletariat was given an honored place in socialist development. Only a beginning was made, however, in presenting the pre-Revolutionary Russians as "first" among the "equal nations." The "lesser-evil" theory was advanced in 1937. This theory held that incorporation of peripheral nations in the Russian Empire, though in the abstract undesirable for them, was much preferable to the real alternative of subjugation by some other aggressive nation such as the Poles.[26] Throughout the thirties, however, a more important line remained the negative one of attacking non-Russian historians who expressed too sharp criticism of the Russian past.

The principal effort to bring the other nationalities closer to the Russians was in the field of language. Until the late thirties the Latin alphabet was considered most appropriate for introduction among preliterate peoples, or for the Moslem nations whose Arabic alphabet was criticized as too cumbersome and too closely related to religious influences. Until the end of 1937 there was even a Committee for Latinization of the Russian Alphabet, though it carried on no practical activity. In 1938-39, however, all major national groups which had used Latin alphabets changed to modified forms of the (Cyrillic) Russian alphabet.[27]

Much was written about the superior adaptability of the Russian alphabet, with its many characters, to the phonetic qualities of the various languages involved. The real reasons for the change, however, appear to have been political. At one stroke the "national Communist" writings of the twenties, published in Latin scripts, were made unavailable to future generations trained to read their native languages only in the quasi-Cyrillic scripts. Probably even more important was the regime's desire to facilitate learning of the Russian language. The effort to make Russian an effective and accepted medium of communication for all Soviet citizens was a basic feature of policy long before the thirties. Knowledge of Russian was necessary for effective use of personnel in both military and civilian service. At the same time, a major value of the Red Army to the regime was its role as a huge school for training non-Russians in the Russian language, as well as for indoctrinating "political illiterates" of all nations in Communist ideology. Indeed, as Communist sources often pointed out, the two processes inevitably went hand in hand.[28]

Aside from the utilitarian value to the regime, increased instruction in Russian language and literature was favored as a device for transmitting Russian patriotism to the rising generation of non-Russians. The campaign for more intensive instruction in Russian in the national Union Republics was greatly intensified during the 1937-38 purge in those areas. For example, the Ukrainian commissariat of education—headed by Zatonskii until his purge—was sharply attacked for the poor quality of instruction in Russian and the shortness of time devoted to the language.[29] Subsequently the number of hours allotted to Russian in Ukrainian elementary schools was increased from 240 to about 400 per year.[30] The stress on language instruction may have had a purely utilitarian purpose. But a simultaneous attack on Ukrainian "nationalists" for substituting "native" Ukrainian words for words of Russian origin common in the Ukrainian speech could scarcely have been necessary from the purely utilitarian standpoint; the relatively small number of words involved could not have significantly decreased ease of communication between Ukrainians and Russians.[31] The attack appeared, therefore, to emphasize the similarity between the two languages in order to avoid the development of the feeling that Ukrainians and Russians were distinct nations.

While an explicit and vigorous campaign was necessary to bring a nation such as the Ukrainian into accord with the Russian "linguistic imperialism," mere suggestion was evidently felt adequate for such groups as the Finnic Mordvins from the Upper Volga. *Pravda* recounts with obvious approval the story of a Mordvin living in Moscow who insisted on being registered as a Russian during the census, because he "had more in common with the Russians than with the Mordvins." [32]

While Russian patriotism—or even Russian nationalism—was unquestionably emphasized, there are numerous indications that the regime took this step in order to utilize Russian feeling as an instrument for increasing the cohesion of the Soviet peoples. Here again there is little evidence of fundamental change in the Communist ideology. Indeed, as in *Pravda's* speculation that Russian might become "the international language of socialist culture," nationalism might become the handmaid of world revolution as well as of "socialism in one country." [33] Aside from these considerations, it is difficult to see why Stalin, who always spoke Russian with a slight Georgian accent, should have become a fervent convert to Russian nationalism. Conversely, it is easy to see why he found it a convenient instrument for strengthening his control. From the purely defensive standpoint, Stalin may also have felt it desirable to appear to embrace Russian patriotism. Most of those he purged were Jews or other non-Russians, but Bukharin, an outstanding opponent, as a "real" Russian might have secured some sympathy from the largest national group. It is interesting to note that a determined effort was made to picture Bukharin as anti-Russian on the basis of his isolated reference to the Russians as a "nation of Oblomovs" i.e., of sluggards.[34] On the other hand, Stalin may well have felt that an excessive return to Russian nationalism might endanger his own position. One of the few occasions on which his name was omitted from a group accorded high praise was in the list of "true" Russians (contrasted to Bukharin) which included Ezhov, Molotov, and even Kaganovich.[35] Also interesting in this connection is that fact that Georgia and Armenia were always permitted to retain their native alphabets; when the small Caucasian nation of Abkhazians dropped its Latin alphabet, it adopted the Georgian, not the Russian characters.[36] Stalin evidently regarded Georgian national aspirations in quite a different light from those of the other non-Russian groups condemned for "bourgeois nationalism."

Another indication that Russian patriotism was designed as a cohesive influence rather than a reversion to traditional ideology was the increasing emphasis placed upon Moscow as the heart of the country. For example, Leonid Leonov's novel, *Road to the Ocean*, published in 1936, imagined a future Soviet capital "in the east"; the 1940 revision deleted this passage.[37] The principal emphasis on Moscow came, however, during World War II, when the identification Moscow-Stalin-center-of-war-effort appeared in innumerable contexts. Moscow is, of course, highly important in Russian history; but the attention devoted to it, in comparison to other Russian cities like Leningrad, strongly suggests that symbols of centralized control rather than those related to Russian patriotism alone constituted the real core of the new indoctrination.[38]

The most striking extension of control in the thirties was in fields seemingly remote from politics: music and the theater. The key moves in this direction were the publication of two *Pravda* articles in early 1936. "Dissonance instead of Music" (January 28) attacked Dmitrii Shostakovich's opera *Lady Macbeth of Mtsensk County*. The opera was said to be "formalist," to neglect "simplicity" and "realism," to distort the natural sound of words, and to substitute cacophony for melody. A week later Shostakovich's *Bright Brook* was similarly attacked, with the added charge that it gave an unrealistic picture of kolkhoz life.

To trace these criticisms to any ideological issue of real significance to the regime would seem a most difficult undertaking, though *Pravda* claimed Shostakovich concealed an "inimical world outlook" behind his artistic "defects." Fortunately, there is relatively complete and reliable information concerning the real inspiration of the criticism. Two weeks earlier Stalin and Molotov had visited an operatic adaptation of Mikhail Sholokhov's *Quiet Flows the Don*. Stalin personally congratulated the composer, Ivan Dzerzhinskii, and his theatrical associates. The theme, Cossack life, appealed to Stalin, for he was restoring the Cossacks to favor. Moreover, he thoroughly enjoyed the folk songs, his favorite kind of music, and he appreciated the straightforward and unsophisticated story.

Stalin's personal views completely outweighed the fact that, in the judgment of outside critics and Soviet musicians who have been able to comment freely, the opera was superficial and immature. Dzerzhinskii's composition was acclaimed by the entire Soviet press. It was almost inevitable that Stalin should be repelled by Shostakovich's highly contrasting opera which appeared so soon afterward. Soviet music critics were at once compelled to reverse their initial approval of *Lady Macbeth*, but Shostakovich himself was not arrested.[39] Some years later it was publicly stated that the criticisms of Shostakovich were written under Stalin's personal direction, although it has also been said that Zhdanov actually wrote them.[40]

Whoever the instigator of these criticisms was, they were expanded to include other aspects of cultural activity. In February 1936 certain writers were accused of formalism. A little later the campaign was linked to the drive against "art for art's sake": "Simplicity and popularity, heroism and stateliness, joy and beauty—such are the fundamental qualities of our

Soviet art." [41] In this way the campaign came to have a definite political implication: "formalism" was bad because it encouraged individualism and made art inaccessible to the mass of the people. It was also clearly related to "proletarian experimentalism," already condemned in literature.

A year after the first articles appeared, P. Kerzhentsev, Chairman of the Committee on the Arts, wrote that the articles applied to all branches of artistic activity, from the theater to architecture. All were bound to renounce "formalism," experimentalist techniques in which the form of artistic expression was more important than the content, in favor of "socialist realism," which was really the idealization of Soviet life.

The principal immediate target of Kerzhentsev was the stage director Vsevolod Meierhold. Meierhold was an extreme example of "formalism"; he had also made the mistake of once dedicating a play to Trotsky. At a congress of theater directors in June 1939 Meierhold openly accused "socialist realism" of having ruined the Soviet theater. The next day—in spite of the fact that the Great Purge was over—he was arrested and disappeared.[42] As this instance shows, the extension of the antiformalist campaign, and the more drastic cases of suppression which arose under it, were based on more complicated motives than Stalin's personal tastes alone. Quite clearly, however, his whims—such as the preference for "wedding-cake" architecture—were thenceforward a major force in control of the arts.

Undoubtedly one of Stalin's major reasons for imposing controls in several fields of intellectual activity was his desire to open the way for elevation of the role of historic personalities. This motive probably played some part in the attacks directed at literature, music, and the theater, since "formalism" did not easily lend itself to adulatory treatment of individuals. It played a major role in the denigration of Pokrovskii. His schematic economic determinism was still less suited to the personal idealizations of historic figures, such as Peter the Great and Ivan the Terrible, than it was to glorification of their role as Russian patriots.

The theoretical justification for emphasizing the role of individual leaders was handled somewhat cautiously since the regime felt it necessary to contrast the Soviet Marxist view to the Fascist and Nazi cult of the leader. Revived public attention to G. V. Plekhanov, Lenin's greatest predecessor in Russian Marxism, was one way in which a solution to the dilemma could be sought. Plekhanov's work on the role of the individual in history received a great deal of attention, but at the same time his emphasis on the dependence of the individual leader on social forces was fully recognized.[43] The same cautious approach to theoretical justification of individual leadership was found in the *Short Course*. Communist policy must be based, it pointed out, "not on the good wishes of 'great men,' but on the real needs of development of the material life of society." [44]

The implicit glorification of Stalin throughout the *Short Course* in fact negated the theoretical limitations on individual leadership. As Bertram Wolfe has shown, this book is an amazing distortion of the entire course of Party history.[45] Stalin's position among the Old Bolsheviks who made the Revolution was actually secondary, if not insignificant; but in the *Short Course* his role is so magnified as to leave no room for anyone else except Lenin. Having destroyed his rivals physically, Stalin obliterated their place in history. In fact, it is difficult to tell in many cases—such as Enukidze's—whether Stalin eliminated prominent Old Bolsheviks because he suspected them of disloyalty or because he wished to be free to rewrite history without their being present to give his version the lie.

Stalin not only had history rewritten to glorify himself; he took credit for the rewriting. The original edition of the *Short Course* was officially "edited by a commission of the Central Committee." In 1940, however, Emelian Iaroslavskii—who probably actually composed most of the book himself—wrote:

> In the course of four months Comrade Stalin worked on the "Short Course." He went through all Marxist-Leninist literature, trying to illuminate each stage in the life of our Party fully and deeply from the point of view of the theory of Marx-Engels-Lenin. . . . Almost all chapters were written by him anew, and the second section of the fourth chapter "On dialectical and historical materialism" was completely written by Comrade Stalin.[46]

Stalin's self-glorification was so extreme that it is hard to accept Isaac Deutscher's view that it was primarily an effort to stabilize the Soviet regime.[47] Moreover, as Bertram Wolfe has shown, there is some evidence that long before he became dictator Stalin began rewriting Transcaucasian history to magnify his own role.[48]

An analysis of the development of Soviet totalitarianism in the thirties can point out the complex of factors involved, but it can scarcely assess their relative weight. Stabilization of social relationships, ideological emphasis on stability rather than change, the appeal to Russian national patriotism, the elevation of the role of the central power, cultivation of artistic productions which appealed to the mass of the population, and even some aspects of the glorification of Stalin served a utilitarian purpose in strengthening the Soviet regime. Undoubtedly the cohesive effect of these measures helped to prepare the USSR to withstand the difficulties of World War II. If survival of a system is regarded as the highest goal, the measures had a pragmatic justification, however abhorrent they were to Western liberal concepts.

Constantly recurring throughout the process of totalitarianization were elements which had little or no utility in strengthening the system. In several cases the direct impact of Stalin's personal tastes, or of his boundless need to satisfy his ego are clearly discernible. Yet, when one examines such cases as the interference in operatic music, he finds that the process initiated by Stalin's whim was gradually broadened into a campaign for increased control over many branches of Soviet culture. Moreover, as the campaign proceeded, a theoretical justification was developed for it which has some plausibility in terms of the needs of the Soviet system. Confronted with this process one is tempted to think that the whole program of control of the arts, at least, was merely a rationalization for Stalin's wish to impose his personal tastes. Undoubtedly, however, the situation here, too, was more complex. Totalitarian statesmanship and self-gratification for the ruler are inextricably bound together.

When one turns from examining the reasons for the extension of totalitarianism to a consideration of its impact upon the people of the USSR, the results appear no less complex. An appraisal of the effect on the esthetic value of Soviet cultural life is beyond the scope of this treatment; the impact upon artists and scholars can only be touched upon. As noted in an earlier chapter, not all members of these groups suffered from the change in policies accompanying increased totalitarian control. Some of the intellectuals earlier banished as "bourgeois" were permitted to resume activity in line with the greater tolerance of traditional cultural themes.

However, the general effect on the intellectual, whether he was a Party ideologist, an artist, or a scholar, was to make him still more helpless in relation to the regime. As Cyril Black has pointed out, historians continued to find some leeway for self-expression through evasion of assigned tasks and concentration on remote periods.[49] Other intellectuals also found some narrow loopholes in the system of controls. But the intellectual, like all Soviet citizens, had been deprived of the principal bulwarks which might have provided a degree of security, even under a dictatorship. Group solidarity was not tolerated by the regime. Faithful obedience to superior

orders was as likely to be a trap as a safeguard when the alleged involvement of high officials in opposition activities led to the arrest of their subordinates. Strict adherence to the law provided some stability for personal
relations, but none in matters the regime chose to consider political. In
view of the fluctuations in the ideological line, the most careful attempt
to conform to official interpretations of Marxist theory was almost bound
to fail eventually.

In these circumstances, the advancement, the security, and even the life
of the articulate individual depended not only on conformity, but "conformity in advance" to the demands of the regime. As these demands were
determined to a considerable extent by the dictator's personal desires, the
personality most likely to succeed in the USSR was vastly different from
that envisaged by earlier theories of the "liberating" role of socialism.

CHAPTER
VII

THE ECONOMY IN THE PURGE ERA

While the ruling elite was in the grip of the Great Purge, Soviet mass media were predominantly concerned with economic developments. Though this emphasis was deliberately directed by the regime, it was also in accord with the basic concerns of the average Soviet citizen. As we have seen, the mass of the Soviet population was not as deeply affected by the Great Purge as it had been by collectivization. At the same time, the average man was very deeply concerned with his job and his standard of living, which were directly related to the economy but only indirectly related to the purge. Even the Party apparatus—although its members were certainly much more deeply concerned with the purge—of necessity devoted a very large part of its attention to economic supervision.

The aspect of economic activity which was most prominent during the second half of the thirties was the Stakhanovite movement. Ostensibly the movement was initiated by a Donbas miner, Aleksei Stakhanov. On August 31, 1935, Stakhanov achieved the remarkable output of 102 tons of coal in a six-hour day, instead of the established "norm" of six to seven tons. The feat was performed in the presence of the local editor and representatives of the Party organization. A competition for increased output was announced, and by October 1935 another miner, Andrei Gorbatiuk, had produced 405 tons of coal in a single day.[1]

"Stakhanovite" methods rapidly spread to other aspects of economic life. To the foreign observer, the new technique was impressive:

> The bricklayer smoothed the mortar and splashed it against the next brick with his left hand, while placing the brick with his right; when all was going smoothly at a rate approaching one brick a second. . . .

I have never seen three people move so fast and accurately. It was heavy
work and must have been very tiring. . . . An English bricklayer, a member
of a trade union delegation, had been there a fortnight earlier. His comment
was "That is not brick laying—it's brick murder!"[2]

Obviously there was more manipulation than spontaneity in these per-
formances. Apparently the real initial move was Stalin's speech to the
graduates of the Red Army academies on May 4, 1935, in which he emphasized cadres as contrasted to technique. Ten days later Ordzhonikidze
(Commissar of Heavy Industry) demanded revision of technical standards
and extension of piecework.[3] Aside from being extraordinarily strong and
skilled, Stakhanov and his imitators were given special advantages, such
as tools and machinery not ordinarily available. In addition, all preliminary
steps in production were carried out in advance of the record-setting in
order that the Stakhanovites could concentrate on measurable output alone.
Under these circumstances it is evident that most of the gains in production
were spurious. Nevertheless, there was a certain real increase in work
efficiency, which, as the ratios of production to man-hours indicate, was
very low in most branches of Soviet industry. Improvement was achieved
both by encouraging the workers to put forth greater effort, and by devoting attention to rationalization of work processes.

The social effect of the movement was a still greater emphasis on individual self-interest. The Stakhanovite was, of course, paid for his "above-
norm" output. Within a short time, however, the norms themselves were
raised from 15 to 50 per cent in various industries.[4] Workers were in effect
paid on a piece-rate basis, with those failing to achieve the norm suffering
a decline in wages. Although by 1939 one-third of all workers were classed
as Stakhanovites, and 18.7 per cent more as "shock workers" (a lower
category), half of the industrial force did not secure a place in the preferred
categories.[5] In its subsequent stages, modifications in the Stakhanovite
movement somewhat loosened the direct money-output nexus. For example,
various marks of distinction, such as the order "Hero of Soviet Toil," were
introduced. The Stakhanovite was flattered by being selected to head
mass organizations, while his presence in this role simultaneously enhanced
the appeal of Party and trade-union agitational campaigns. Some observers
have even concluded that the Party organizations were more interested
in the participation in Party work and the enthusiasm aroused by the
Stakhanovite campaign than by its practical effect on production.[6]

In its later stages (especially after the Eighteenth Party Congress in
March 1939), the Stakhanovite movement directed more attention to in-

creasing the quality of production as compared to the quantity. Economic directors also endeavored to increase the skills of the best workers by training each to operate several different types of machines. This was hailed as a step toward freeing the individual from lifetime dependence on one type of work; apparently, however, the elevation of skills among the minority meant that the unskilled were left aside.[7]

The December 21-25, 1935, plenum of the Central Committee officially approved the Stakhanovite movement, and directed that the Party organizations extend it to all spheres of industry and transport. Heavy industry (including mining) and rail transportation continued to receive special emphasis.[8] P. F. Krivonos, the leading Stakhanovite in railroad work, received even greater Party recognition than Stakhanov himself, for Krivonos was elected to the Ukrainian central committee and to the Central Auditing Commission of the All-Union Party. Even kolkhoz farmers and tractor drivers were brought into the movement through the example of two women, Maria Demchenko and Praskov'ia Angelina.

For all its advantages to Party propaganda, and its somewhat less obvious aid in increasing production, the Stakhanovite movement led to serious complications in Soviet economic management. Although Stakhanovism was officially entirely different from "storming," which had been condemned in the early thirties, the two types of campaign were often similar. Both tended to increase the output of a minority of workers or shops for a brief period, at the expense of the smooth flow of production. Frequently, delicate machinery was overstrained. These disadvantages, and the fact that initial high production in a factory led the government to set a higher, and often unattainable, quota of production for it in the next plan, turned many managers against the Stakhanovite movement. The managers were supposed to control and lead the Stakhanovites, and sometimes were able to use them satisfactorily to fulfill assigned plans. Often, however, young enthusiasts forced the manager's hand.[9] In this way, in some factories a wedge was driven between manager and worker.[10]

The position of the Soviet industrial managers was weak enough in 1936 without this additional handicap. According to David Granick's systematic study, 97 per cent of the managers were Party members; of these nearly three-quarters had joined the Party before 1921. Their superiors, the directors of Chief Administrations (Glavki), had even longer Party tenure; they included many Old Bolsheviks. The Glavki directors were better educated than the factory managers. A majority of the latter had been

young laborers of proletarian parentage when they joined the Party. After
entering the Party, the future manager had been transferred from one post
to another in all aspects of Party, government, and army work, before
becoming an economic director. What education the manager had—and
his education level was increasing—he had usually obtained in special
industrial training academies. Three-quarters had held their managerial
posts less than three years, and one-quarter less than a year.[11]

Nearly all their background characteristics placed the factory managers
in the category most likely to be purged. In fact, the Great Purge took
an especially heavy toll of these men. In this respect, the 1937-38 purge
differed sharply from earlier "wrecking" trials, which had concentrated
upon well-educated engineers of middle-class origin; these were relatively
unmolested by the Great Purge.[12] This factor undoubtedly assured a continuity of operation and technical proficiency which helps to explain how
it was possible to decimate the managerial class without bringing production to a halt. One report indicates a decline of 20 per cent in pig-iron
production in a Urals factory as a result of the purge,[13] but the effect
was only temporary. As was noted in Chapter IV, arrests of the industrial
managers began in 1936, considerably before the climax of the purge in
1937-38.[14] The most drastic period of elimination of the old economic
directors came in 1937, after Piatakov's condemnation and the death of
Ordzhonikidze. The Old Bolshevik Glavki heads were almost eliminated,
and the composition of the factory managerial force drastically altered.

The new managers and Glavki directors had much better formal training
than those who had been purged, and were more homogeneous in background. They spent as little time in a given managerial position as did their
predecessors, but their transfers were usually to other industrial management posts.[15] As Joseph Berliner, who has studied the group intensively,
puts it:

> Officials in ministry [as the commissariat was redesignated in 1946] and
> enterprise are, moreover, the same kind of people. Gone are the days of
> ideological conflict between the Red Directors and their bourgeois engineers.
> Since the great purges of the thirties the leaders of industry have become more
> homogeneous socially, and one hears remarks oddly reminiscent of "the old
> school tie." . . . Such ties remain after one friend is promoted to a ministry.
> And there are many proud references to professional colleagueship.[16]

Accompanying the growth in professionalism was a decline in ideological
fervor. The new manager's prime objective was success in his career; and

to some extent he desired material reward for its own sake. Because of the conflicting demands and extreme pressure for increasing production to which he was exposed, the manager's position remained precarious. Failure often led to imprisonment, though not so frequently to execution as in 1937-38. The manager tended to feel that he was entitled, if successful, to all the privileges he could obtain. While there had of course been an egotistic element among the older "Red" managers, the change in spirit was distinct. It was remarkably similar to emphasis on self-interest inculcated among the factory workers by Stakhanovism. Both developments followed logically from Stalin's 1931 condemnation of "equality-mongering."[17]

During the purge of the managerial group, the regime did not find it necessary to introduce major changes in the organization of industrial direction. A new Commissariat of Defense Industry, supervising enterprises until then directed by Ordzhonikidze's Commissariat of Heavy Industry, was created in December 1936. As late as 1938, however, there were only 14 commissariats. By 1940, on the other hand, there were 34, and of these 24 were engaged in economic direction.[18] As Molotov noted at the Eighteenth Party Congress, the multiplication of commissariats was designed to shorten the chain of command from the commissar to the enterprise. At the same time, however, the reorganization raised serious problems of co-ordination at the top level of industrial control.[19]

The problem of co-ordination was all the more important because the principal co-ordinating agency, the Party, was itself undergoing considerable change. Superficially, the lowest level of Party-industrial contact was not greatly changed by the purge. The proportion of Communists in large industrial plants remained about 5 to 15 per cent, with a total of 1,200,000 Communists (more than one-third of the entire Party) in industry and transportation.[20]

The number of Communists in an enterprise was less important, however, than the position of the primary Party organization secretary (a full-time member of the apparatus in the larger factories). In his address to the Eighteenth Congress, Andrei Zhdanov stressed the importance of "control" of the Party organization in the enterprise, while sharply warning the Party against trying to *direct* management.[21] It is doubtful, however, that the secretaries were able in practice to supervise the managers. By 1939 the latter were nearly all Communists; their political background made them the equals of the Party secretaries. Moreover, the managers apparently had far better educations than the secretaries. Seventy-seven per cent of managers of large and medium enterprises in Leningrad had higher educations, and 13 per cent secondary educations; of the Party secretaries in these enterprises only 37.3 per cent had higher education, and 22.2 per cent secondary.[22]

Under these circumstances, the manager was evidently able to get his way with the Party secretary. Official directives provided that Party meetings were to be scheduled so as not to interfere with production. Economic directors were not to be assigned burdensome Party tasks.[23] In some cases the manager evidently used something very close to outright bribery. For example, the Party press found it necessary to attack the practice of economic organizations which made awards or presented medals to Party workers who were not employed by them. As the article delicately put it, this "may make possible weakening of criticism of the deficiencies in the work of the enterprise."[24]

The seriousness of these weaknesses of the primary organizations was enhanced by the fact that much of the higher Party industrial control apparatus had been abolished by the Eighteenth Congress. All of the "production-branch" sections which had been created in 1934, except Agriculture, were eliminated. Zhdanov explained this move on the ground that the production-branch sections did "not know what their functions are," and encroached on managerial organizations.[25]

Within a very short time after their abolition, however, it became apparent that Party sections were needed in some spheres of industrial activity. By late 1940 the Ukrainian Party secretariat had several industrial sections.[26] Probably the first area in which such sections were quietly introduced was in Donbas coal mining. Voroshilovgrad obkom had a section for coal production by mid-1940.[27] Georgii Malenkov—by then a Secretary of the Central Committee—appears to have had especially close contact with the Donbas. At the Eighteenth Party Conference (February 1941), Malenkov maintained that the commissariats and the Glavki alone were incapable of fully controlling industry. In accordance with his proposal industrial sections were formed once again at the obkom level.[28]

At the same conference, Zhdanov devoted considerable attention to another Party device for industrial control, the "Party organizers of the Central Committee." In 1941 an organizer, selected by the regional Party organization from among its officials, was assigned to each major industrial firm in the Ukraine, and probably in other parts of the USSR.[29] The organizer reported directly to the Central Committee, however.

In spite of the drastic change in its managerial personnel attendant upon the Great Purge and the lesser organizational difficulties encountered in 1938-41, Soviet industry continued its phenomenally rapid expansion. Official Soviet figures indicate an overall industrial production increase of about 190 per cent between 1934 and 1940. The Soviet annual indexes do not suggest that the Great Purge had any marked effect upon production, since the increase shown for 1937-40 is about the same as for 1934-37. An independent calculation indicates, however, that three-quarters of the total 1934-40 increase occurred before the purge of the industrial managers in 1937. But even after 1937 there was a marked, though slower, increase.[30]

After 1937 the USSR released fewer details concerning its industrial production; hence non-Soviet calculations are difficult. Evidently the emphasis on heavy industry—the production of new plants and arms—continued at an even higher level than during the earlier years of the five year plans. In the third Five Year Plan (begun in 1938) 93,900,000,000 rubles were allocated for heavy industry, as compared to 18,000,000,000 for consumer goods, a ratio of more than five to one. The corresponding ratio for the second Five Year Plan had been only a little more than two to one.[31] As a result, according to an independent calculation, production of consumer goods by large-scale industry increased only 80 per cent from 1934 to 1940.[32] All of this gain was made during the 1934-37 period, while the subsequent period showed a slight absolute loss in consumer goods output, and a considerable per capita decline considering the population increase arising from annexations in 1939-40.

The continued shortage of consumer goods was one factor creating labor difficulties for Soviet management. The rapid inflation of the currency and the shortage of items which the workers desired led them to shift jobs frequently in the hope of finding better living conditions. Lack of habituation to the rigidity of factory schedules, the need for spending much time in queues for scarce goods, and the confidence that one could always find another job, led to absenteeism and tardiness as well.

A decree of December 28, 1938, sought to curb these practices by making three cases of absenteeism or tardiness grounds for dismissal with loss of social-security rights.[33] Because of the great demand for labor, the measure was ineffective. On June 26, 1940, however, these offenses against work discipline were made punishable by two- to four-months' imprisonment and workers were forbidden to leave their jobs without permission of management.[34] For Party members there was an additional means of enforcing the prohibition of job change. The primary Party organization

Central Committee Plenums, 1934-41

DATE	TOPICS DISCUSSED		
	Industry	*Agriculture*	*Other*
Feb 10, 1934			Election of Politburo, Orgburo, Secretariat (After XVII Cong.)
June 29- July 1, 1934		Increase in production of animal products	
Nov 25- 28, 1934		Ending of bread rationing; abolition of MTS political sections	(Decision to transfer Kirov to Moscow?)*
Feb 28, 1935			Election to Secretariat (Andreev); to Chairmanship of Commission of Party Control (Ezhov); removal of Kaganovich from latter post and as 1st secretary of Moscow obkom
Feb 1, 1935			Election to Politburo (Chubar' and Mikoian as members, Zhdanov and Eikhe as candidates); to Secretariat (Ezhov); proposals for Constitution
June 5-7, 1935		Harvest and state procurement of products	Apparatus of Central Executive Committee (Enukidze affair)
Dec 21- 25, 1935	Stakhanovite movement		Results of verification of Party documents
June 1-4, 1936		Harvest and state procurement of products	Party admissions and appeals of exclusion; Constitution draft
Feb 23- Mar. 5, 1937	"Economic questions"	"Economic questions"	Exclusion of Bukharin and Rykov from Party; discussion of "enemies"; Party democracy and role of Party in Supreme Soviet elections

* As indicated in Chapter II, the rumors concerning this decision are not substantiated by the official record.

CENTRAL COMMITTEE PLENUMS, 1934-41

DATE	TOPICS DISCUSSED		
	Industry	*Agriculture*	*Other*
June 23-29, 1937		Improvement of grain culture; crop rotation; improvement of MTS work	*102548*
Oct 11-12, 1937			Party propaganda in Supreme Soviet elections; election to Politburo (Ezhov as candidate)
Jan, 1938	"Economic questions"	"Economic questions"	Matters for Supreme Soviet sessions; mistakes in expulsion from Party; Election to Politburo candid. (Khrushchev; Postyshev removed); to Orgburo (Mekhlis)
Jan, 1939			Convocation of XVIII Congress
Mar 22, 1939			Election of Politburo, Orgburo, Secretariat (after XVIII Congress)
May 21-24, 27, 1939		Protection of kolkhoz land from encroachment; harvest and state procurement of products	Election of Commission of Party Control; Party role in local Soviet elections
Mar 26-28, 1940	Change in work of Economic Council of Council of Commissars	Change in system of purchase and procurement of products	Foreign policy; Soviet-Finnish war; convocation of XVIII Conference
July 29-31, 1940	Control over; Restrictions on leaving jobs	Harvest and state procurement of products	Approval of formation of Commissariat of State Control
Feb 21, 1941	Approval of XVIII Conference measures on work of Party in industry and transportation	Approval of XVIII Conference measures on 1941 state plan	Approval of XVIII Conference; exclusion of Central Committee members and candidates

was forbidden to transfer a member's records to another organization until he had obtained permission for his job transfer from the enterprise management.[35]

In addition to these measures, which drastically reduced one of the few remaining areas in which the average Soviet citizen had enjoyed a measure of freedom, a labor draft was provided for farm boys. Eight hundred thousand to one million boys between the ages of fourteen and seventeen were to be selected for compulsory training in trade schools; after completion of their training they were given mandatory job assignments.[36] As in the case of the Party reorganizations mentioned above, the full impact of these measures was obscured by the outbreak of war.

Even though the Great Purge had led to an unusual preoccupation with Party organization and personnel between 1934 and 1941, as the accompanying table shows most Central Committee plenums during the period dealt with agricultural matters. With the exception of 1938—when the Central Committee was too depleted to permit formal gatherings—a plenum on harvesting or some other farm question was always held in the late spring or early summer; frequently other plenums dealt with agricultural matters. This picture is in sharp contrast to the lack of consideration of industrial matters by Central Committee plenums. To be sure, the Party press redressed the balance by devoting a great deal of space to industrial activity. Especially after the Great Purge, however, the Council of People's Commissars carried on the bulk of the direction of industry. While the Council worked closely with the central Party Secretariat, the territorial Party organization was not deeply involved. On the other hand, the secretary was the key figure in agricultural supervision. Since a major purpose of Central Committee meetings was to bring together the obkom secretaries, who comprised much of its membership, the plenum emphasized agriculture.

In the late thirties the Party secretary in an agricultural area was still essentially the commander of a small occupation force in a hostile or indifferent sea of peasants. In 1937, 57.9 per cent of the Soviet population consisted of kolkhoz peasants and co-operative workers.[37] If one adds the few remaining individual farmers and the larger group of rural "intelligentsia" —teachers, agricultural specialists, minor officials, and the like—the rural population at that time was well over two-thirds of the total. Only one-fifth of the Party membership was in the rural areas, however—some 600,000 Communists. The backbone of this rather slender force consisted of non-peasant elements. Only 350,000 Communists were in primary Party organizations in the collective farms themselves; the remainder were in 27,600 primary organizations or candidate groups formed in the territorial sub-divisions of the raion. The reason for this arrangement—a departure from the rule of organizing Party units at places of work—was that the territorial organization brought together the village intelligensia and officials, together with whatever peasants were sufficiently active politically to enter the Party.[38] Until the number of peasant Communists could be greatly increased, or the number of collective farms reduced, this was the only feasible solution.

The two most important agricultural problems facing the thin Party organizations in the rural areas were general increase of production and effective use of labor. The second problem was, of course, closely related to the increasing industrial labor shortage noted above. One non-Soviet analyst estimates that 4.7 per cent of the men in the kolkhozes and 14.7 per cent of the women were not effectively employed.[39] The draft of hundreds of thousands of youths for industrial training reduced this surplus, but the regime still found it difficult to compel the remaining peasants to work on the "collective sector" of the farms. Most peasants preferred to devote as much of their time as possible to their individual garden plots, and to increase the area of their own plots by encroaching on lands assigned to collective use.[40]

While restricting private-farm enterprise the regime tried to make collective farming more attractive. The April 1940 plenum of the Central Committee made delivery of animal products to the state dependent upon the area of the kolkhoz for raising animals instead of the number of animals which the farm possessed. The aim, of course, was to induce the kolkhoz to raise as many animals as it could; similar measures were introduced for vegetable and fruit culture.[41]

The most important trend in agricultural policy in the immediate prewar period related to the organization of kolkhoz work. In accordance with the general emphasis on inequality of monetary reward, kolkhoz peasants were nominally paid according to their contribution to the farm labor. It was difficult to apply the piecework system in agriculture, however, because there was no clear-cut way of distinguishing an individual peasant's output. This was especially the case when the work force was organized in brigades of several dozen peasants each. As a result A. A. Andreev, the Politburo member in charge of agricultural supervision, sharply condemned the brigade system; he demanded that the link, or small work team of a half-dozen members (often members of the same family, or at least related to one another) be the principal form of kolkhoz work organization for grain as well as for industrial crops.[42] As the link was assigned a plot of land for an entire crop year, its production could be measured; consequently, its members' reward could be fairly closely adjusted to the results of their work.[43] The activities of the link were directed by the kolkhoz management; nevertheless, the new organization of farm labor seemed to be a step back toward reliance on the initiative of the individual peasant household.

In the economy as in other aspects of Soviet life, the period of the Great Purge presented a confusing picture of "conservative" and "radical" tendencies. From the Marxist point of view, the extreme concessions to the spirit of individual gain, if not unorthodox, were at least regrettable necessities in the march toward true Communism. On the other hand, the thoroughness with which the regime manipulated the labor force, the drastic restrictions imposed upon individual job movement, and the curb on individual peasant gardens indicated that private economic interests were to be allowed no real freedom.

Taken as a whole, Soviet economic development between 1934 and 1941 was a success. Agriculture made little progress, but the worst losses of the collectivization were repaired. The food supply, though barely adequate, was sufficient in normal times to prevent starvation. The stationary level of consumer-goods reproduction caused much dissatisfaction. However, in the essential field, the output of machinery and arms, the Soviet economy triumphed.

CHAPTER
VIII

EIGHTEENTH CONGRESS AND
THE NEW CADRES

The Eighteenth Congress of the Soviet Communist Party, held between March 10 and 21, 1939, proclaimed no momentous changes in policy. Ezhov's removal had come three months earlier, and the purge tempo had sharply declined even earlier in 1938. The reversal of foreign policy embodied in the Nazi-Soviet pact was still five months in the future. Nevertheless, the Eighteenth Congress was in many respects a more significant landmark in Party history than the Seventeenth Congress of "Victors" held five years earlier. For the Eighteenth Congress was in a very real sense a "congress of victors" itself—and this time the assembled Party leaders were to live to enjoy their victory.

In his opening speech, Stalin indicated the role of the Congress as a symbol of relaxation and consolidation. He assured the delegates that "we shall have no further need to resort to the method of mass purges."[1] Andrei Zhdanov expanded this theme by pointing (as he had done at the January 1938 plenum) to the unjust expulsions which had occurred during the purge. He maintained that "the largest group" of expellees had been condemned merely for the trivial dereliction designated as "passivity." Both Zhdanov and Stalin, however, staunchly defended the most drastic feature of the purge period, the mass arrests of "enemy elements." Zhdanov asserted that "the most important work of purifying the ranks of the Party of enemies of the people, traitors, spreaders of treason, and Fascist agents, was performed after the mass purges"—i.e., in 1937-38.[2] As we have seen, some imprisoned Party leaders were condemned to death in 1939-40; arrests continued at a reduced rate. It was clear that Stalin's reassurance to the new Party leadership represented at the Eighteenth Congress was a highly

qualified one; it meant in effect that their security depended on their complete loyalty to him.

The establishment of Stalin's unquestioned supremacy did not mean that
the "monolithic unity" which the Party had boasted for so many years
—even when it was in fact torn by factional rivalries—was really attained.
Throughout the vast apparatus which the dictator had developed, fierce
bureaucratic infighting continued. Overt indications of these struggles were
concealed by the universal panegyrics to Stalin, and indeed he was the final
arbiter of all disputes. In some ways, however, his supremacy enhanced the
ferocity of the power struggle below him. No doubt the intrigues in any
despot's entourage are merciless, but a special effect of the Great Purge
was to make strikingly clear to all the Soviet leadership that the struggle
for power was a matter of life and death. As far as we are aware, for more
than ten years after the close of the Great Purge no major official was
executed as a result of defeat in this struggle; but the threat was always
present.

Under these circumstances we can hypothesize—although direct evidence
is lacking except in a few instances—that the apparatus officials sought
some means of guaranteeing their personal security. As noted in Chapter
VI, such security could not be attained by strict adherence to laws, regulations, or even ideological principles. Neither could security be attained by
mere conformity to superior orders. One possibility was open, however
—a kind of personal allegiance to a higher-ranking member of the apparatus. Such a patron could serve both as a protector and as a provider of
subtle hints concerning the changes in the Party "line," the expectations of
the regime for "conformity in advance." To be sure, attachment to a patron
of this kind presented dangers of its own, for if he fell from grace he might
drag his protégés to destruction. At the lower level such alignments (often
designated "family circles") are frequently disclosed by the Soviet press,
always in a negative context related to corruption or avoidance of mutual
responsibility for errors. Overt reference to such relationships at higher
levels is very uncommon. But the evidence—while far from conclusive
—suggests that most middle- and upper-level Soviet officials found it more
profitable and less risky to enter into such a patron-protégé relationship.[3]

Such evidence as there is indicates that officials rarely change their allegiances except under extraordinary pressure, at least after they have

reached the higher bureaucratic posts.[4] Moreover, it appears that such allegiances have usually been formed in the course of the official's career since, under Stalin, at least, the regime deliberately limited other opportunities for intimate contact between Soviet officials.[5] If these assumptions are accurate, one can approach the study of personal followings (and at higher levels the equivalent power groupings) by tracing the career patterns of individual officials, though the process is necessarily complicated and tentative.

The starting point for examining career connections is ordinarily the institutional framework of the Soviet bureaucracies. Very frequently, however, relatively unnoticed subdivisions of major bureaucratic structures are more important as centers of personal groupings than are the larger, better-known institutions such as the police and the army. For example (as noted below), for many years higher officers of the frontier troops of the police agencies have evidently constituted a group somewhat distinct from the secret police. Often in such cases the subdivision (e.g., of the police) will have closer ties with a subdivision of another apparatus with which it works closely (frequently because of geographical proximity) than it has with the institution to which it is formally attached. For example (as discussed in Chapter XVIII), the frontier troop officers seem to have been more sympathetic to Party officials in frontier areas than to the top police officials.[6] In general, however, especially for geographically separated officials, institutional ties seem to be necessary prerequisites for personal followings. While this is probably due in large part to common interests and earlier background associations, it is also true that communication between distant officials, unless in line-of-duty, would expose them to the suspicion of participating in "fractional" groupings, prohibited in principle by the Party since Lenin's time. Under the guise of official communication within the framework of institutional activity, however, officials evidently can employ "esoteric" communication (occasionally even in print) to indicate their attitudes to associates.[7]

In the following chapters we shall frequently resort to evidence of power alignments derived from examination of career patterns and of esoteric communication. We are fully aware of the pitfalls of such evidence, which when incautiously used deserves the derogatory appellation of "Kremlinology." The deliberate concealment by the Soviet regime of the basic circumstances of its political development, especially in the years following the Great Purge, forces the scholar to resort to whatever procedures for attaining evidence are available, however indirect and inconclusive they may be.

Of all levels of Party leadership, the Politburo appeared least altered by the purge. Stalin, of course, remained its chairman. Despite the upheaval in the armed forces, Voroshilov, Commissar of Defense, remained in the post which he had held five years earlier, without any apparent gain or loss in influence. Kalinin was still nominal chief of state.

Andreev, now Deputy Chairman of the Council of People's Commissars in charge of agriculture, appeared to have increased slightly in influence. Molotov, still Chairman of the Council of Commissars, and soon to become Commissar for Foreign Affairs as well, had also increased his power. His role in the Nazi-Soviet pact apparently strengthened his position. In 1941, however, when the German alliance was almost at an end, Molotov's Jewish wife was removed from the Central Committee.[8]

The only Jew remaining in the Politburo in 1939 no longer seemed the commanding figure he had been in 1934. Kaganovich's position is somewhat puzzling. As Deputy Chairman of the Council of Commissars he had very considerably increased his role in economic direction; he controlled both heavy industry and rail transportation. But he no longer exercised a major influence on Party organizational matters. He had gradually relinquished control over the Moscow Party organization, and had apparently ceased to deal with agriculture soon after the abolition of the MTS political sections in 1934. About the same time he had surrendered the chairmanship of the Party Control Commission to Ezhov. Quite possibly Kaganovich was affected by the underground current of anti-Semitism which accompanied the Great Purge. At any rate, in contrast to 1934, the organizational measures passed by the Eighteenth Congress seemed to have been designed not only without Lazar Kaganovich's participation, but in sharp departure from his earlier concepts.

Of the 1934 candidate members of the Politburo, only one, Anastas Mikoian, survived in a high post; he had become a full member in 1935 and Deputy Chairman of the Council of Commissars in 1937. His principal field of operation was commerce, but, as we have seen, he exerted influence in foreign policy and police affairs as well. Of the new members of the Politburo, Andrei Zhdanov, still a Central Committee Secretary, had enormously increased in influence. As we shall see, he was involved in most of the major aspects of Party activity. The other new member, Nikita Khrushchev, first secretary in the Ukraine, appeared to be somewhat less important.

The 1939 Politburo contained only two candidate members. Nikolai M. Shvernik, trade-union secretary, was always a third-rate figure. Lavrenti Beria, on the other hand, was already one of Stalin's principal lieutenants. By the time the Eighteenth Congress opened, Beria had rid the police of Ezhov's men, and some of the remaining old Chekists as well. As Commissar of the Interior, however, Beria seemed to avoid the public attention which Ezhov had received in his final year of power. Some of the higher officials, like the Georgian Lavrenti Tsanava, who headed the NKVD in Belorussia, were evidently Beria's own protégés. Others, however, like Ivan Serov in charge of the Ukrainian NKVD, seemed to have a different background. The prominence accorded the frontier guard detachments in the 1939-41 period suggests that the police branch which was least directly associated with Beria was being favored.[9]

Similarly, while Beria retained a large measure of influence over the Transcaucasian Party organizations, he does not seem to have exercised supreme power there. As later events demonstrated, his successor as Georgian first secretary, K. N. Charkviani, was not wholly devoted to Beria's interests. These circumstances suggest that a delicate balance of power had been created—very likely at Stalin's instigation—to prevent Beria from securing absolute control of the crucial police machine or the important Transcaucasian Party complex. On the other hand, Beria was permitted to extend his influence in other fields. Especially significant was the appointment of his Georgian collaborator, V. G. Dekanozov, as Deputy Commissar of Foreign Affairs, and later as ambassador to Germany.[10] The division of the NKVD by the formation of a new Commissariat of State Security (NKGB) in February 1941 implied no lessening of Beria's power, for the new commissariat was headed by his lieutenant, also a Georgian, V. N. Merkulov.[11]

If the 1939 Politburo resembled that of 1934, the Central Committee had changed almost completely. According to Nikita Khrushchev's secret speech 70 per cent of the Central Committee elected at the Seventeenth Congress was liquidated during the purge.[12] A comparison of the Congress election lists indicates that only 16 of 71 full members, and 7 of 68 candidates were re-elected in 1939.[13] A few of the missing may be accounted for by natural deaths or other nonpolitical reasons, but the vast majority was shot. At the Eighteenth Congress itself, the lack of security of Central Committee members was formally indicated by a change in the Party rules permitting a member's replacement by a Party conference as well as by a Congress. In

1941 this new rule was utilized to oust four members and fifteen candidates, and to elect six members and eighteen candidates.[14]

The largest single group of officials represented in the Central Committee comprised secretaries of the obkoms and other major territorial divisions of the Party. As was described in earlier chapters, the industrial directors and the army officers suffered heavily from the Great Purge but the most severe turnover in personnel appears to have taken place in the territorial Party organization. The almost complete liquidation of the 1937 Ukrainian central committee, and similar drastic treatment of major officials in other Union Republics has already been noted. In general the impact of the purge seemed to vary in direct proportion to the importance of the Party posts involved. Nevertheless, the lower levels were heavily depleted.[15] At the Eighteenth Congress Zhdanov summarized the extremely high rate of turnover by pointing out that 60 per cent of the Party committees at the oblast level, 46 per cent of the city committees, 41 per cent of the raion committees, and 35 per cent of the primary Party organization committees consisted of persons elected for the first time.[16]

The Great Purge almost eliminated from the apparatus the Old Bolsheviks, who had entered the Party before the Revolution, and drastically reduced the proportion of Civil War entrants. At the Seventeenth Congress, Ezhov had boasted that 80 per cent of the voting delegates fell in these categories, although the proportion in the Party as a whole was only 10 per cent.[17] By 1939 the proportion of Old Bolsheviks and Civil War veterans among Party members had declined to 8.3 per cent. The relative drop in the proportion of Old Bolsheviks and Civil War Communists in the Congress membership was far greater, however; only 19.4 per cent of the delegates fell in these categories.[18]

Although 70 per cent of the 1939 Party membership consisted of persons who had joined in 1929 or later, only 43 per cent of the delegates had entered the Party that recently; other information indicates that most such recent entrants held relatively low positions. On the other hand, while slightly more than 20 per cent of the Party members had entered between 1920 and 1929, almost 40 per cent of the delegates, including a very high proportion of those in major posts, fell in this category. Nearly half of the delegates were under thirty-six years old, and a third between thirty-six and forty.[19] Other evidence supplementing these statistics indicates that most of the "middle-level" Party officials at this time, and for many years to come, were men who had entered the Party in the twenties, when Stalin was consolidating his power over the apparatus. They constituted a remarkably young ruling group; the vast majority, born between 1900 and 1910, were between thirty and forty years old in 1939.[20] In non-Russian areas where the Party had experienced difficulty in finding satisfactory recruits for its apparatus, the age level was still lower.[21] Many, if not most, of the officials in Kirgizia, for example, were very recent entrants in their twenties. Doubtless, circumstances such as these led the Eighteenth Congress to reduce greatly the length of Party membership required for those elected to secretaryships. Henceforward, the primary Party organization secretary could have been in the Party as little as one year, the obkom secretary as little as five.[22]

Along with the drop in length of Party membership of higher- and middle-level officials went a moderate increase in educational level. Whereas only 10 per cent of the 1934 Congress delegates had higher educations, 26.5 per cent of those at the 1939 Congress had attained this level. Of the latter group, 27.5 per cent had secondary or incomplete higher educations, compared to 31 per cent in 1934. Consequently, less than half of the 1939 delegates had only elementary educations, as compared to nearly three-fifths in 1934.[23]

In spite of these definite gains, the Party leadership as a whole was by no means a highly educated group. In general education and cultural background higher- and middle-level Party officials appear to have fallen into three groups. One consisted of men whose parents were middle- or upper-class in the period before the Revolution. Andrei Zhdanov was a fairly typical example. Born in 1896, he was slightly older than the average Communist apparatus official of 1939. A Soviet student describes Zhdanov's father, a school inspector, as a "cultured, advanced man" of unusually progressive views. Zhdanov is said to have learned Marxism from him, but evidently the father was not a Bolshevik.[24] Like a large majority of the leaders after the elimination of most of the Old Bolshevik Jews, Latvians, and Poles, Zhdanov was a pure Russian. Though he was born in Mariupol' (now Zhdanov), few then considered that Donbas city to be part of the Ukraine. In any case, the family moved to the north Russian city of Tver' (later Kalinin) in 1912; Zhdanov received a good secondary education, and some higher education, before leaving school to devote himself to the Bolshevik Party, which he had entered in 1915. He carried on his Party activity in the army, where he obtained an officer's commission. After the Revolution Zhdanov's principal post, until he succeeded Kirov, was as first secretary in Nizhnii Novgorod (later renamed Gor'kii). There he evidently began to exhibit his penchant for enforcing ruthless ideological conformity which, as we have seen, was displayed on a broader field at the First Soviet Writers' Congress, and was later to make his name a byword in the Soviet Union.[25]

In contrast to men like Zhdanov, who could have had an established place in Russian society had there been no Revolution, the majority of Party leaders owed everything to the Soviet order of society. Some—for the most part those who were children or adolescents when the Revolution took place—had obtained a systematic education under the Soviet regime. Most men in this group were technically schooled; training as an engineer was regarded as the ideal for a promising young Communist in the late twenties and after. Many of the engineering students, of course, went on to become practicing engineers or even economic directors; as described in Chapter VII, most of the new managers fell in this category. Here, however, we are concerned primarily with the fact that a significant portion used their engineering training as a bridge to careers in the Party apparatus. In 1939 this group was still, with few exceptions, in the middle and lower levels of apparatus officialdom. As time went on, however, they profited from the Party's urgent need for technically knowledgeable officials to supervise a society of increasing technological complexity.[26]

The third, and probably the largest, group of Party leaders emerging in 1939 also owed its position entirely to the Soviet regime. Unlike those described in the preceding paragraph, however, officials in this group had little formal education. Of peasant or worker parentage, they had themselves begun heavy physical labor at an early age. After entering the Party (usually in their late teens) they frequently continued as workers for a few years, sometimes obtaining some formal education in the Rabfaks (special schools for workers). Often what education these men received was in agricultural technique or in mechanical training—for example, tractor maintenance. Usually it was at some point in this training, or on the jobs to which they went afterward, that they attracted the attention of higher Party officials. Once singled out for work in the apparatus, such men tended to rise rapidly, as the more experienced officials whom Stalin distrusted were eliminated. Their decisive advancement occurred, of course, during the Great Purge.

A good example of this type of official, except for the fact that he was several years older and began his Party career somewhat earlier, was Nikita Khrushchev. Born in 1894 into a miner's family, Khrushchev (unlike most of the younger men whose careers otherwise resembled his) served obscurely in the Civil War. For several years after the Bolsheviks triumphed, however, he continued as a worker, with some Rabfak training. Only in 1925 did he enter the apparatus; his first major assignment, as second secretary of Moscow obkom, did not come until seven years later. Although agriculture was secondary in the Moscow oblast, Khrushchev's assignment to the Ukraine in 1938 placed him in a position where the farm problem was of major significance. He soon became a leading Party spokesman on agricultural questions. In this respect Khrushchev was also typical of the less-educated Party leader, who tended to be a territorial secretary in an agricultural region. With a familiar, if rough-and-ready approach to the peasant and a keen sense for political manipulation, this group formed the backbone of the territorial apparatus.[27]

The differences among the groups of Party officials just described were latent in 1939, for the cohesive forces uniting them were very strong. Even those who had obtained educations before the Revolution owed their rapid advancement to Stalin's machine. Most, if not all, had developed a callous and egoistic spirit in the course of their repression of the peasantry during collectivization, and their sudden promotions over the corpses of their superiors in the apparatus. Like the new industrial managers, the new officials seemed to be sharply imbued with a faith in their own ability and right to direct Soviet affairs, while devoting little thought to the more abstract aspects of Marxism.

The pre-purge Party official, unless he was an Old Bolshevik (frequently an intellectual who had joined the Party out of deep conviction) was usually of proletarian origin. While many of the new Communist leaders also came from working-class families, a large proportion were apparently of peasant origin. Reports to the Seventeenth Congress in 1934, and to a Ukrainian Party congress as late as 1938, had stressed the proportion of delegates of proletarian background; but the record of the Eighteenth Congress contains no information on the social background of its delegates. Moreover, in accord with Party practice from 1936 on the Eighteenth Congress changed the rules to eliminate the preferential treatment which had formally been accorded workers wishing to enter the Party. All persons applying for admission were now required to submit recommendations from only three Party members of three years' standing who had worked with the applicant for one year.[28]

Partly as a result of this relaxation in requirements for admission, the acceleration of Party growth which had begun in 1938 continued until the Soviet entry into World War II. At the beginning of 1939 there were

1,500,000 members and 800,000 candidates; a year later there were 2,000,000 members and 1,500,000 candidates; by January 1941, though the number of candidates had dropped slightly because of promotions to membership, the full members totaled 2,500,000.[29] Since the beginning of 1938, when the purge had brought overall membership to its lowest point since the twenties, the Party had doubled in size.

The Russian areas of the Soviet Union were disproportionately represented at the Eighteenth Congress. Three hundred fifty-one of the 1,574 voting delegates came from Moscow and Leningrad oblasts alone; fourteen of the next largest RSFSR oblasts had over 400 delegates.[30] The delegation from the Ukraine comprised 272 persons, and the Belorussian, 37, less than one-fifth of the voting strength of the Congress, although these two Republics had almost one-fourth of the USSR's population. The nationality of the delegates themselves was not indicated in the Party records. Since Russians comprised over 37 per cent of the delegates at the Ukrainian Party congress the following year, and only 60 per cent of delegates at the Belorussian congress (held at the same time) were Belorussians, one may assume that the Eighteenth Congress delegations from the smaller Slavic Union Republics were also heavily weighted with persons of Russian nationality.[31] The same was very likely the case with the Central Asian Republics. Probably the Transcaucasian Republics sent a heavier proportion of native delegates; although Georgia had only 2 per cent of the Union's population, it had 2.5 per cent of the Communists.[32] As we have seen before, the Great Purge increased the Russian ascendancy, but the Russians were not the sole dominant nationality.

The altered composition of the Party, and especially that of its directing apparatus, was accompanied by a number of major changes in Party organization. The revised indoctrination organization was directly keyed to the new type of official. After the Eighteenth Congress, all indoctrination activities were directed by propaganda and agitation (agitprop) sections headed by the Propaganda and Agitation Administration of the Central Committee Secretariat. Shortly before the Congress opened, Zhdanov assumed control of propaganda; he continued to direct this activity until September 1940, when he was succeeded by a rising young Marxist theorist, G. F. Aleksandrov.[33]

Under Zhdanov's direction—with, as usual, his Leningrad Party organization setting the pace—the *Short Course* was made the core of indoctrination. We have already seen what this book was like, and its close relation to

Stalin's growing megalomania. From the organizational point of view, its use meant an increasing emphasis on individual study, rather than on group indoctrination in study circles. Individual students of the *Short Course* were guided by propaganda officials, especially in the raikom "cabinets" equipped with Communist literature and other study aids. The principal guidance, however, was through the press, which was given renewed emphasis.[34] A principal theme in the new process of indoctrination was the need to differentiate training according to the recipients' level of education, and especially according to their level of responsibility in the Party, state, or economic bureaucracies. For example, the leading Party organizational journal strongly condemned the Party organization in the Commissariat of Justice for presenting the same lectures to responsible officials as to janitors, and in general keying indoctrination work primarily to the lower level of technicians and laborers.[35] Since, according to a very ingenious, though necessarily speculative estimate, 60 to 80 per cent of all Communists were officials in the various bureaucracies of the Soviet system, these indoctrinational distinctions were crucially important.[36]

Extensive as was the revision of the indoctrinational system, it was far less sweeping than the change in control of personnel. The Eighteenth Congress abolished all "production-branch sections," except the agricultural section, thereby eliminating the supervision (see Chapter I) which these sections had exercised over the assignment of personnel in all fields of activity except the Party itself. Instead, a unified Cadres Administration supervised assignment of all personnel throughout the Soviet system, assuming the personnel functions of the Section of Directing Party Organs (now abolished), as well as those of the industrial branch sections.

As several penetrating non-Soviet analysts, Merle Fainsod, Leonard Schapiro, and Boris Meissner, have pointed out, the change in personnel organization which Zhdanov proposed to the Eighteenth Congress was in diametrical opposition to the organizational scheme set forth by Kaganovich at the Seventeenth Congress.[37] As discussed in Chapter II, the Party leadership soon felt the complete elimination of special personnel sections in 1934 was excessive. The gorkom cadres sections reintroduced in 1935, ostensibly for apparatus personnel alone, were especially well publicized in Leningrad. Consequently, Zhdanov appears to have been the prime advocate of the special cadres organization.

Later events suggest that Georgii Malenkov may have disliked the new cadres organization. He furthered the reintroduction of some production branch sections in 1940-41, and in 1948, during his ascendancy following

Zhdanov's death, the Cadres Administration was abolished. Malenkov had been well entrenched in the Section of Directing Party Organs, which he headed after Ezhov became Commissar of the Interior. Malenkov may, therefore, have preferred the retention of the old system. On the other hand, the key to his rapid rise in the late thirties appears to have been his control of Party personnel records and assignments in the Section of Directing Party Organs. Malenkov became a Secretary of the Central Committee at the Eighteenth Congress, and in this capacity retained control of expanded personnel functions under the Cadres Administration.[38] Moreover, a number of Malenkov's former subordinates, like Mikhail Burmistenko, second secretary in the Ukraine, continued to direct personnel operations.[39] Schapiro and Meissner believe that Malenkov and Zhdanov were united in favoring the concentrated personnel organization, which strengthened the position of the Party secretaries.[40]

Be that as it may, in 1939 there were strong reasons for the Party as a whole, and Stalin in particular, to accept the principle of unified personnel direction. The depletion of the ranks of trained directors in all spheres of activity by the Great Purge made prompt, careful distribution of the remaining skilled directing cadres essential. Moreover, it was very important to keep careful watch over the performance of the newly promoted younger personnel, as yet unproven in major assignments.

The scope of the apparatus devoted to cadres supervision was imposing. The Central Committee Cadres Administration included a cadres section for each of the thirty-four commissariats, in addition to sections for Party organizations, press and publishing, scientific institutions, Komsomol organizations, and trade unions. At the oblast level the cadres sections were somewhat less extensive, but included sectors for personnel in Party organizations, Soviet organizations, manufacturing, transportation and communication, agriculture, procurement of agricultural products, trade and co-operatives, NKVD and defense organizations, procurator and judicial offices, educational and cultural institutions, health departments, and Komsomol organizations. The obkom cadres section also included a special section for supervising the important paper work involving accounting for cadres.[41] A raikom cadres section in the city of Leningrad had four sectors (manufacturing, schools, Soviet and trade institutions, health department), with a director, eight assistant directors, and two instructors for personnel accounting.[42] Later, sectors seem to have been eliminated in the raikom and gorkom cadres sections.[43] Probably the number of Party personnel specialists at this level was not reduced, however, for the task confronting them was enormous. A single Moscow city raikom cadres section had eight hundred officials in its *nomenklatura* (sphere of personnel assignment), of whom slightly more than half were Party apparatus officials.[44]

Not all of the functions of the Directing Party Organs Section were transferred to the Cadres Administration. The duty of supervising the day-to-day work of the lower levels of the Party apparatus was assigned to the Organization-Instruction Section of the Central Committee. The organization-instruction sections at various levels saw that the lower Party organizations promptly provided their superiors with information concerning their activities, and were in turn given such information as the higher bodies felt it desirable to impart. These sections provided instructors (a long-established designation for supervisory officials) to train Party units in the proper procedures for carrying on meetings and elections, and in organizing the work of their full-time officials. The instructors also watched to see that lower Party conferences and bureaus took decisions in accord with the general Party line or specific instructions from above and promptly carried out the decisions taken.

To perform these tasks, the organization-instruction apparatus was made almost as extensive as the personnel administration. According to a Central Committee decree of September 21, 1943, the central Organization-Instruction Section was to have an instructor to supervise the work of the Party organization in each oblast, Union Republic, and *krai* (territory). In addition, the Section was to contain sectors for information, for membership accounting and Party statistics, and for accounting for Party cards.[45] Similar though less extensive subdivisions were contained in organization-instruction sections at lower levels. For example, a Leningrad city raikom organization-instruction section had a director, four instructors assigned to groups of primary Party organizations, two instructors for membership accounting, and one for channeling the flow of Party information.[46]

In the parlance of Western public administration, the cadres and the organization-instruction sections constituted "staff" agencies. Their function was not to direct the substantive operations of the Party and subordinate spheres of Soviet life, but to see that these operations proceeded efficiently in accord with the will of the central authorities. Together with the Central Committee organizers for major factories, these agencies constituted a powerful mechanism for centralized control. One might well think that in the totalitarian system ruled by Stalin such agencies would be the linchpin of dictatorship. For a time, between 1939 and 1941, Party administrative development did, indeed, seem to move in the direction of making the staff agencies supreme. The entry of the Soviet Union into the war apparently destroyed the primacy of the staff agencies, although most of the 1939 organization was retained until 1948.

It is difficult to determine why the staff agencies were allowed to decline in power. One set of reasons appears related to the personalities involved. With the outbreak of war Malenkov, who had been turning more and more to economic direction, devoted himself to supervising war production. The other major proponent of the staff agencies, Zhdanov, had always retained his place as the first among territorial secretaries, supervising, as a "line" director, all spheres of Soviet life in Leningrad. During the war he was preoccupied with affairs in the besieged city. Burmistenko, the most powerful and vigorous of the regional secretaries concerned primarily with staff agencies, vanished early in the war.

The shortage of trained and competent personnel, endemic to the Soviet system but particularly acute after the Great Purge, had helped call the staff agencies into existence. Paradoxically, this very shortage limited their role, for the Party could not afford to hamper the work of the territorial Party first secretary. With relatively few first-rate men available, the central authorities probably considered it more effective in the long run to let a single vigorous Party leader be "on a small scale God and Tsar in the oblast," judging him solely on overall results.[47] If the first secretary was inefficient, or disregarded instructions which the regime felt were really important, he was dealt with ruthlessly. In any case, he was usually transferred within two or three years, before he had entrenched himself in a single province.

Aside from these practical considerations, Stalin himself may well have feared that efficient, all-powerful staff agencies under the direction of such a vigorous leader as Malenkov or Zhdanov might become a greater threat to his personal rule than the dispersed territorial secretaries. Most important, no doubt, the disruption of normal Party functions by the German invasion and the new mechanisms created to cope with the emergency channeled Party organizational development in different directions.

CHAPTER

NAZI PACT AND EXPANSION

The culmination of the reversal of international alignments which the Nazi-Soviet nonaggression pact of August 1939 signalized did not result in major changes in the Soviet Communist Party. The most significant international implications of the pact are outside the scope of this work. Nevertheless, the event is sufficiently important to warrant a brief examination of its relation to internal Soviet politics, and a more extended discussion of its effects on international Communism and Soviet expansion.

Unquestionably the Great Purge facilitated the formation of the Nazi alliance. As has already been discussed (in Chapters III and IV), the theory that Stalin preferred an alliance with Hitler, and destroyed opposition Party and military leaders to secure it, is of doubtful validity. All the same, the drastic policy change which the unheralded signature of the pact involved would hardly have been as easy to make had the Soviet Party contained even moderately independent leaders. As it was, there was not the slightest sign of overt opposition within the USSR.

If there was no opposition to the alliance, there do seem to have been certain figures in the Soviet Communist Party, aside from Stalin himself, who furthered it. Andrei Zhdanov's speeches contained bitter denunciations of the British and the French; he seemed to reject all possibilities of an anti-Nazi front.[1] Molotov's appointment as Commissar of Foreign Affairs was the signal that negotiations for the Nazi alliance were to proceed in earnest. There is no evidence, however, to warrant the belief that either of these men favored the Nazis; rather, they were bitterly opposed to all non-Communists. Part of their antipathy toward the West doubtless arose from a feeling that Great Britain and France had betrayed the USSR at

Munich. Russian ethnocentrism may have played a role; both men were Russians by origin, and had spent little if any time abroad. Probably, however, a generalized contempt for all Western "bourgeois" society, as distinguished from the ambivalent love-hate attitude of the typical Old Bolshevik toward the West was their major motivation.

If the direct effect of the pact on the Soviet Party was slight, the foreign Communist parties were inevitably deeply involved. The very manner in which the pact was made indicates how little regard Stalin had for these parties. The French Communist Party was by far the most important instrument of the Comintern in West Europe, but it was given no advance information. All but one of its politburo members were on vacation.[2] As late as September 2 the French Communist legislators voted for war credits.[3] The Party congratulated Maurice Thorez and other leaders who accepted the call to mobilization in the French army.[4] There was even an effort to petition the Soviet embassy for aid against Germany, but Thorez, though he said privately that he had had no advance warning of the pact, was too well trained to permit interference in Soviet affairs.[5] The British Communist Party, equally affected by the shift of alliances, but perhaps less thoroughly indoctrinated, planned to issue an anti-Fascist manifesto.[6] Before the manifesto could be released, however, the Comintern ordered it scrapped, and after some demurral the British Communist leaders complied.[7]

About the same time—in mid-September—the French Communist Party was compelled to support fully the Nazi-Soviet pact.[8] Soviet motives for not informing the Communist Parties in advance of the agreement are still unclear. The negotiations leading up to the pact were secret, but foreign governments were generally aware that a German-Soviet alignment was at least a strong possibility. It seems unlikely, therefore, that Soviet desire to avoid premature revelation of the agreement was the major factor. Angelo Rossi, one of the most penetrating students of this episode, argues that Stalin did not immediately instruct the French and British Communists to press for peace between their countries and Germany because he wanted the war to begin in order that the USSR would obtain the opportunity to profit from it.[9] This is possible, and even likely. At the same time, the timing of the instructions to the foreign Communist parties, which almost coincided with the Soviet invasion of Poland, suggests that at first Stalin may have been suspicious of German fidelity to the pact. Other evidence fits into this pattern. A page 2 article in *Pravda* on September 16, 1939, reported that a German bomber which had violated the Soviet frontier had been shot down the previous day. On September 17, however, at German urging, the Red Army began to occupy the half of Poland assigned the Soviet Union by the pact. This did not mean that the Soviet Party had determined to maintain real friendship with the Nazis. A secret directive of September 22, 1939, to a major portion of Soviet troops read:

> The German command, knowing that it must evacuate its troops from the cities and settlements where the units of the Red Army are to advance, strove to rob the population "culturally," not to embitter it. All commanders and Red Army political workers must take this into account. The population will compare two armies and two orders represented by them. In all our activities and external appearance we must show the incomparable superiority of the Worker-Peasant Red Army to the German Army.[10]

Nevertheless, Soviet co-operation in the destruction of Poland did mean that the USSR was prepared for a considerable period of close collaboration with the Nazis.

The arguments presented to non-Soviet Communists for the formation of the alliance with Nazi Germany centered on the benefits which would accrue to the USSR. The Western capitalist states, it was said, had been trying to induce Germany to attack the Soviet Union, which had forestalled this machination by making the pact; in this way the regime preserved the Soviet people from war. The war was an imperialist struggle between the older capitalist states which were trying to preserve their empires, and capitalist states which were trying to expand; consequently, it was no concern of the proletariat. The USSR had brought a population of thirteen million under socialism by acquiring former Polish territory.[11] Privately the foreign Communists were told that it was desirable to have the capitalist states fight among themselves.[12]

From the theoretical Marxist standpoint, these arguments indicated that there was really nothing to choose between the two sides in the European war. This had the desirable long-run effect, from the Soviet standpoint, of reindoctrinating Communists, lulled by the emotions engendered by the Popular Front, with the belief that everything which was not Communist was indistinguishably wrong. In the short run Communist propaganda outside the USSR was directed against the Western allies alone. They were condemned for continuing the war after Germany, having obtained its aims, was prepared to make peace. Moreover, especially after the outbreak of the Finnish war, France and Britain were accused of preparing intervention against the USSR. In addition to verbal assaults on the allies, the Communist Party in France, at least, sabotaged the war effort. Thorez set the example by deserting from the army, while Communist workers covertly sabotaged airplanes and other military material.[13] These activities were, of course, in line with the Soviet policy of furnishing Germany with strategic materials and providing facilities for the German naval operations.[14] The abrupt change from an all-out anti-Fascist line to one which at least tacitly favored the Nazis led at first to numerous defections and a severe decline in Communist influence in all Western countries. Nevertheless, the changed conditions in West Europe, especially after the collapse of resistance by France and her Continental allies, seemed to open new opportunities for Communism.

With tacit permission of the Wehrmacht, the Belgian Communists were able for a time to seize power in the Liège and Charleroi areas.[15] French Communists approached the German Kommandantur in Paris to propose a similar arrangement, and were accorded some privileges.[16] After a short time, however, the Germans became wary of giving the Communists political advantages in the occupied areas. Possibly in reaction to this lack of co-operation, and also as an expression of Soviet uneasiness over the rapid German conquest of most of West Europe, various covert criticisms of Germany began to appear in the Communist press. *Kommunisticheskii Internatsional* of June 1940 criticized harsh labor legislation in Germany as well as in other countries.[17] A Comintern spokesman pointed out that the French Communist Party continued to influence the masses by "legal and illegal means," although he did not specifically refer to its activities in the German occupation zone.[18] The prototype Quisling government in Norway, and other regimes under German occupation, were criticized for suppressing the Communist parties in their countries.[19]

Even the early immunity to criticism which the Communists accorded the Nazi regime was never extended to other "Fascist" regimes, particularly to Franco's, which the Comintern press attacked almost as frequently as during the Popular Front period. Indeed, Dimitrov himself hastened to point out soon after the Nazi-Soviet pact was signed that the Popular Front policy was still valid in colonial areas and in China, although elsewhere the policy was a mask for imperialist war.[20] Not long afterward, Spain was implicitly included among the areas where the struggle was "national-revolutionary," and therefore justified.[21]

The position on Italian Fascism was more ambiguous, probably because Italy was fighting the arch-imperialists, the British. The Greek Communists were ordered to sabotage their country's defense against Italian aggression during the winter of 1940-41.[22] The German conflict with Yugoslavia ushered in a distinct change in Communist and Soviet attitudes, however. At first the Comintern press cautiously described the Yugoslav uprising against the pro-Axis policy of the Regent, Prince Paul, by quoting the *Journal de Genève* which called the uprising "the political expression of the unanimous feelings of the nation." [23] A little later the USSR signed a nonaggression pact with the new Yugoslav government. When Germany and its allies attacked Yugoslavia in April 1941 Communists were privately informed that the Yugoslavs were waging a justified war, and underground Communist publications in France, at least, accused the Germans of "incendiarism." [24] The Soviet press did not go that far, but it did criticize Bulgaria and Rumania for aligning with the Axis against Yugoslavia.[25] A few weeks later, when the German conquest of the Balkans was complete, the Soviet leaders appear to have had second thoughts. The envoys of the conquered states in Moscow were deprived of accreditation; the USSR even recognized a pro-Axis regime set up in Iraq. In the final weeks before the German invasion of the Soviet Union on June 22, 1941, Soviet statesmen seemed intent on a last-minute effort to appease the Nazis.

While the maneuvers of the Comintern are the most spectacular aspect of Communist policy in the pact period, territorial expansion had a considerably more intimate relation to the development of the Soviet Communist Party. The first and much the most important territorial acquisitions were in Poland. Nearly one hundred thousand square miles, with a population of thirteen million, were added to the USSR, and the frontier was advanced on the average one hundred fifty miles westward. Even more important was the effect on the ethnic composition of the Soviet Union. The large Jewish population of the USSR was considerably increased, and numerous Poles were added. The bulk of the newly acquired population consisted, however, of Belorussians and Ukrainians. The alleged desire of the Soviet majorities of these nations "to come to the aid" of their brothers in Poland formed a major part of the Soviet justification for the invasion of Poland.

In view of this circumstance, it is understandable that the Soviet occupation regime sought at first to appeal to the national sentiments of the Belorussians and the Ukrainians. Since nationalism was little developed among the Belorussians, and no major cultural centers were included in the Soviet-annexed Polish territory which they inhabited, this theme had relatively little importance in what Soviet sources called "West Belorussia." In the West Ukraine, on the other hand, it was of crucial significance. The Soviet occupation regime "Ukrainized" the University of L'vov, and established Ukrainian in place of Polish as the dominant language in other schools and cultural institutions. Evidently the Communists anticipated that these measures would win them the support of the West Ukrainian population, which had suffered severely from the nationalist oppression of the Polish authorities.

The Communists, however, miscalculated the nature and cohesive force of the Ukrainian nationalist organizations. At the very beginning of the occupation, the Soviet authorities seized the newspapers and cultural establishments which had been maintained by the West Ukrainian nationalist organizations, and arrested such leaders as did not flee to the German-occupied part of Poland. Consequently, Soviet "Ukrainization" of Polish cultural institutions was recognized by most of the West Ukrainian population as a maneuver to provide the appearance of a concession to national feeling, while actually establishing totalitarian control over all institutions of education and communication. Ukrainian nationalist organizations were able to offer only very limited active opposition to the Soviet forces, but the general population revealed its passive hostility to the new rulers. As a result, Soviet policy in the West Ukraine appears to have changed in mid-1940. Ukrainian occupation troops were replaced by Central Asians and harsher measures were taken to control the local population.[26]

This change in occupation policy coincided roughly with the incorporation of additional Ukrainian-inhabited territories into the USSR. In July 1940, following the collapse of France, the Soviet Union presented an ultimatum to Rumania demanding the surrender of Bessarabia and the northern half of Bukovina. The latter territory, and parts of the former, were incorporated in the Ukrainian SSR. On the other hand, a small portion of the Moldavian ASSR, which had been a subdivision of the Ukrainian SSR, was joined to most of Bessarabia to constitute a new Moldavian SSR. The new unit, while nominally co-ordinate in rank with the Ukrainian SSR, evidently continued to be factually subordinated to the Ukrainian Party apparatus.

The arrangements for extending Soviet rule to the newly acquired areas constitute an interesting chapter in the history of the Party. In the areas forcibly seized from Poland (Belorussian and Ukrainian) and in those acquired from Rumania, the initial stage of occupation was military. Political direction, however, was in the hands of the political administrations of the "fronts," the principal Red Army commands involved. The political administrations in turn co-operated closely with the territorial Party organizations of the Ukraine and Belorussia. For example, Nikita Khrushchev, Ukrainian first secretary, accompanied the forces occupying the West Ukraine. The army political officers set up provisional administrations in the occupied areas, but the directors of these administrations in a number of major cities at least were territorial Party officials from the older parts of the USSR.[27]

A major task of the provisional administrations was to prepare for "national congresses" in the West Ukrainian and West Belorussian territories to give a semblance of popular support for their formal annexation to the USSR. Nominal elections to the congresses were quickly held, and they met before the end of October 1939. As a result, by early November the Soviet officials were able to obtain formal petitions requesting annexation of the western areas; a few days later the Supreme Soviets of the two Union Republics and the USSR "complied" with these requests.

By early 1940, the army-controlled provisional administrations had been dissolved and the Communist Party organization, as well as the Soviet governmental administration, had been formally extended to the new territories.[28] Since East Ukrainian and East Belorussian Party officials had already occupied the most prominent positions in the occupation administrations, the change was not of major importance. Down to Soviet entry into World War II, and indeed for many years after Soviet recovery of the territories following the war, outside officials continued to predominate in the western areas acquired from Poland and from Rumania (where formal Party and Soviet organizations had been introduced somewhat more quickly than in the former Polish areas). A Soviet source admits that soon after Soviet reconquest of West Belorussia, in 1944-46, the Belorussian central committee sent 1,026 officials, including 734 for the Party apparatus, to the newer part of the Republic.[29] Probably some of these officials were Russians, for, as one student of the problem points out, even in 1939 the Belorussian Party apparatus was too small to fill all posts in the new territories, which nearly doubled the size of the Republic. As a result, officials had to be secured from the central provinces of the RSFSR.[30]

Prior to World War II, at least, the Ukrainian Party apparatus appears to have been able to fill the new posts in the West Ukraine, although some RSFSR apparatus officials were sent in after the end of hostilities. At first few West Ukrainians were found suitable for promotion to responsible posts in the Party. Remaining members of the Communist Party of the West Ukraine, which like the Communist Party of West Belorussia had been an autonomous part of the Polish Communist Party until all were dissolved in 1938, were used to some extent, but were apparently distrusted.[31] The relatively few local intellectuals who embraced Communism after the occupation were generally given figurehead posts until they had undergone years of indoctrination.[32] Consequently, the vast majority of the key posts were assigned to officials from the East Ukrainian apparatus. Most of these "imported" officials were indeed Ukrainians, but a significant minority were Russians who had resided in the East Ukraine. The influx of "foreign" officials undoubtedly exacerbated Ukrainian nationalist feeling, and contributed to the continued vitality of nationalist organizations.

The Baltic territories annexed to the USSR in 1940 were considerably smaller than the areas acquired from Poland and Rumania, but they presented in many respects a more difficult problem for the Soviet authorities. Unlike the annexed areas to the south, the Baltic lands were swallowed in two "bites." In the autumn of 1939, under the implicit threat of invasion, the strongly anti-Communist governments of Estonia, Latvia, and Lithuania agreed to the establishment of Soviet bases on their territories.[33] Lithuania was nominally rewarded by the acquisition of the former Polish city of Vilna. The influx of Soviet military personnel soon gave the USSR a commanding position in all three countries. Apparently the Soviet rulers decided that the rapid growth of German power in the summer of 1940 made it necessary to extend complete Communist control to the Baltic lands. The Soviet authorities declared that the existing governments were anti-Soviet, and demanded their replacement. Under Soviet pressure, transmitted by Vyshinskii in Latvia, Zhdanov in Estonia, and Dekanozov in Lithuania, left-wing governments, including small Communist groups, were formed. Soon the Communists, assisted by the Red Army, which overcame the resistance of the local police and home guards, forcibly ousted the other parties in the governments.[34] Soon thereafter new parliaments chosen in manipulated elections asked the USSR Supreme Soviet to admit each Baltic country as a Union Republic.

A little later Soviet administrations and Communist Party apparatuses were established in each country.[35] Some concessions were made to existing national institutions, especially the armies. For example, a considerable number of generals with Baltic names were appointed in December 1940.[36] However, military units which showed signs of independence were deported to distant parts of the Soviet Union and the members imprisoned there.[37] The Soviet regime evidently experienced considerable difficulty in finding suitable officials, for the Communist parties in Estonia and Lithuania had been very small. Moreover, the difference between the Baltic languages and Russian made officials sent from older parts of the USSR extremely conspicuous. Consequently, the search for reliable "natives" for the apparatus went to extreme lengths. For example, Aleksei Müürisepp, who became a leading Party official in Estonia, had lived in Russia from childhood, and was a railroad substation master in Piatagorsk when he was called upon to enter the Estonian apparatus.[38] As late as 1953, less than half of the raikom secretaries in Latvia were Latvians, while 44.7 per cent were Russians.[39]

In all the annexed territories the first concern of the Soviet authorities was to secure control of newspapers and other media of communication. All political organizations—Polish, Zionist, and Jewish Socialist (Bund), as well as those of the majority nationality in each area—were completely suppressed, and many of the leaders arrested. As the national organizations had operated many of the cultural institutions, they were seized at the same time. Schools and cultural facilities controlled by religious organizations were confiscated soon afterward. The purely religious activities of the churches were not banned in the prewar period, but the churches were hampered in many ways, and atheist propaganda was initiated. After the war all churches were subjected to severe restrictions similar to those placed upon religion in the older parts of the USSR. The bishops of one of the largest religious bodies, the Ukrainian Greek Catholic Church, were deported to Siberia, and their congregations forcibly incorporated in the Orthodox Church.[40]

A somewhat similar pattern was followed in economic affairs. All large-scale enterprises were "socialized" soon after the Soviet occupation forces arrived. However, while land was nominally nationalized, the support of the poorer peasants was sought by a redistribution of agrarian holdings. Relatively few kolkhozes were established before World War II. Some progress in this direction was made in the West Ukraine, which by June 1941 had 2,589 collective farms, including 13 per cent of the peasant households.[41] There were only thirty kolkhozes in Latvia, however, and by the end of the war even these had disappeared. There were only four collective farms there as late as May 1947.[42]

In the two following years the number of kolkhozes increased rapidly, but the real drive for collectivization did not take place in Latvia until the spring of 1949; in March and April of that year alone 60 per cent of the peasant households were incorporated in kolkhozes.[43] Similarly, there were only 926 kolkhozes in Lithuania in February 1949, but 5,778 by the end of the year.[44] These kolkhozes included 60 per cent of the Lithuanian peasant households, a figure almost identical with that attained in the West Ukraine at the same date, though the increase had been much more gradual there.[45]

As in the older parts of the USSR, the extension of the kolkhoz system was accompanied by an extension of rural Party apparatus. In the West Ukraine before the war only 2 per cent of the members of rural governing bodies had been Communist; by 1948, however, there were 9,000 Party members in the villages, and over 20,000 in 1952.[46] Similarly, nearly 200 new primary party organizations were created in rural Latvia in 1946 alone.[47] A main support for Party work in rural areas in the western regions after the war, however, were the MTS political sections, which were retained there long after they had been eliminated in the older parts of the USSR.[48]

The discussion of collectivization in the annexed regions, which constitutes a distinct aspect of Soviet political development, has taken us far beyond the general chronological confines of this chapter. One additional feature of the Soviet expansionist policy of 1939-40 requires a brief description, however. Apparently the Soviet rulers had planned to subject Finland to the same pattern of "two-bite" incorporation used in the Baltic states. When in November 1939, Finland balked at the first "bite," the granting of bases and certain frontier districts to the USSR, the Soviet regime put in operation an alternative plan. The Red Army invaded Finland, and a "Finnish Democratic Republic" under Otto Kuusinen, an old Finnish Communist émigré living in the USSR, was formed in the captured border city of Terijoki. It was provided with an "army" said to have been composed mainly of "Finns for the day" drafted from the Belorussian Military District.[49] Neither this token force, nor the large Red Army contingents, apparently drawn primarily from the Leningrad Military District, were able to make much headway against the Finns during the first months of the war. Eventually Finland was forced to concede the bases originally demanded, and to make minor territorial concessions; but it never suffered the fate of the Baltic states. The "Finnish Democratic Republic" was quietly disbanded, although the areas annexed from Finland were used to round out the Karelian ASSR which, as the Karelo-Finnish Republic, was promoted to Union Republic status.[50]

The Finnish episode had important repercussions in Soviet domestic politics. It has been rumored that Andrei Zhdanov suffered a decline in prestige because he had advocated the formation of the puppet "government" on the ground that it could secure popular support in Finland. This is not clearly demonstrable. It is evident, on the other hand, that the political administration of the Red Army did lose ground because of the Finnish fiasco.

After the 1937 purge of the Red Army command, the political administration under Lev Mekhlis appeared to have attained a height of power which it had not known since the 1920's. While the political workers in the army had numbered only 15,000 at the beginning of 1934, they totaled 34,000 in early 1939.[51] A new oath, introduced in February 1939, had the Red Army soldier stress his obligations as a Soviet citizen and his loyalty to the nation and government.[52] After the Eighteenth Party Congress the link between army and territorial Party organizations was stressed by the interchange of lecturers and other means.[53] In December 1939, the twentieth anniversary of the foundation of the Lenin Academy for the preparation of commissars was the occasion for increased public recognition of their role.[54] The prominent role of the political administrations in the Polish annexations has already been noted, and the commissars were equally praised for their activity in the frontier conflicts with Japanese forces in Manchukuo.

The Finnish war did not lead to an abrupt, obvious change in the position of the political administration. Very soon after the close of the war, however, the prestige of the military commanders, as contrasted to the commissars, seemed to increase. The institution of the rank of general, conferred on a large number of officers, was given extraordinary publicity in June 1940.[55] Two months later the position of military commissar was formally abolished. This did not mean that political specialists were no longer to work in the armed forces, for the post of deputy commander for political affairs was instituted, and the political "members of the Military Council" were retained at the army level and higher. The deputy commander was, however, strictly subordinated to the military commander of the unit, whereas the commissar had possessed a veto on the commander's orders. The unit Party bureau was told it must act as an adjunct of the plenipotentiary commander, assisting him in both political and military work.[56] Moreover, the political workers of all ranks were to concentrate on increasing their ability as military officers.[57] In a very unusual statement, army political personnel were informed that "Political propaganda and agitation are not goals in themselves, but means for raising the battle preparedness of the Red Army, strengthening Soviet military discipline and the high political-moral content of the personnel component." [58]

In addition to strengthening the command function of the line officer, the new policies of 1940 increased his personal status. Renewed attention was directed to increasing the educational level of the wives of officers, and drawing them into cultural, political, and auxiliary military work in the armed forces.[59] These measures tended to place the officers and their families in a social group sharply distinguished from the rank and file. In spite of the fact that 47.3 per cent of the army recruits were members of the Party or the Komsomol, less than two-fifths had gone beyond the sixth grade.[60] In training and indoctrinating this uneducated mass, great emphasis was laid on strengthening discipline. Commanders and political workers were criticized for considering themselves "great democrats" and permitting enlisted men to address them by the familiar pronoun "ty." [61] These measures were obviously aimed at enhancing the military efficiency of the Red Army, badly shaken by its dubious victory in Finland, coming so soon after the demoralization of the Great Purge. For despite their denials of friction with Germany, it was obvious to the Soviet leaders by the end of 1940 that the USSR was in mortal danger of attack by the seemingly invincible Wehrmacht.

CHAPTER

IMPACT OF WAR

Although there were numerous indications in June 1941 of an impending
German invasion, the Soviet defense did not profit from them. The initial
German attack not only broke through the frontier installations, but destroyed much of the available first-line air and tank strength of the Soviet
forces. The most crushing defeat came in the vital central area where the
Germans, advancing three hundred miles in eighteen days, claimed over
three hundred thousand prisoners. As many more were captured in the
further German advance to Smolensk during the remainder of July. The
German victories in the Ukraine were not quite as imposing. By July 4
(twelve days after the war began) the recent Soviet acquisitions in the
West Ukraine had been conquered, however, and by August most of the
area west of the Dnepr River, except Kiev and Odessa, was in German
hands. Meanwhile, a still more rapid advance—though one which netted
few prisoners—cost the Soviet forces the Baltic countries, and brought the
Germans to the suburbs of Leningrad.[1]

The official explanation for the vast Soviet defeat presented during the
war stressed the surprise achieved by the Germans; the battle experience
of their troops; German accomplishment of full mobilization before the
attack, at a time when the Soviet forces were only partly mobilized; and
German ability to draw on the resources of conquered and satellite states
in Europe.[2] To analyze these arguments fully would require a lengthy
study, but a few general observations may throw some light on their validity.
Even with the addition of Hungarian, Rumanian, and Finnish allies, the
German ground forces were probably numerically slightly inferior to the
Soviet at the outbreak of the war. In planes, tanks, and artillery the Soviet

129

forces also apparently possessed a numerical advantage at the very beginning, but it was quickly lost. Soviet arguments have never stressed the
qualitative inferiority of their planes and tanks, but it is likely that a large
number were obsolescent compared to the Germans'. The battle experience
of the German army was an imponderable, but important factor, which no
amount of Soviet preparation could have overcome—once the USSR had
stood aside while the Germans acquired the experience by destroying their
other Continental opponents.

The principal Soviet controversy concerning responsibility for the initial
defeats has centered around the surprise element. As suggested earlier,
there were numerous indications of an impending German attack. In 1956,
Soviet spokesmen, including Nikita Khrushchev, denounced Stalin for
failing to take account of these indications, to say nothing of direct warnings from Western statesmen.[3] It is likely that Stalin feared to precipitate a
German attack by taking obvious defense measures; but this scarcely explains the failure to alert the troops, or to dispose the more vulnerable
elements at a greater distance from the frontier. Probably Stalin was most
influenced by a reluctance to admit that his Nazi pact policy was a failure.
It is still more difficult to assess the responsibility of the army command.
After the fall from grace of Marshal Zhukov in October 1957, he, as deputy
chief of staff in June 1941, was blamed for the lack of preparedness; but
this charge may have been entirely political.[4]

Whatever Stalin's personal responsibility for the Soviet losses, his behavior at the beginning of the war evidently cost him considerable prestige.
For eleven days he did not appear in public, or even meet the British
military mission; varied rumors circulated concerning his whereabouts.[5]
When Stalin finally addressed the Soviet nation on July 3, he adopted an
unusually humble tone, referring to his auditors as "brothers and sisters."
He also went to considerable lengths to offer an excuse for having made the
pact with Germany.[6] Nevertheless, Stalin left no doubt that he intended to
continue to direct affairs, and before July was over he had underlined his
position by becoming Commissar of Defense.[7]

The initial measures of the Soviet regime seemed to indicate its intention
of mastering the crisis of invasion by utilizing the same instruments of
centralized power which had helped it to weather the Great Purge. On
July 16 the commissar system was restored in the Red Army.[8] The role of
the police was enlarged. In the first days of the war, NKVD officials in
several cities near the frontier massacred political prisoners who could not
be evacuated before the Germans arrived. According to a secret German

report, four thousand recently slain prisoners were found in the NKVD cellars in L'vov alone. A circumstantial émigré report says that police officials in Minsk, on radio orders from Moscow, slaughtered the prisoners there and set fire to the jail.[9]

More apposite to the defense of the regime was the work of the NKVD in forming "block-the-road" detachments to shoot or turn back soldiers trying to flee from the front lines. Martial law was declared for the part of the USSR west of the Tula-Krasnodar' line (extended later to the Caucasus and Lower Volga areas), and severe penalties were dealt by summary courts, apparently directed by NKVD officers, to civilians who shirked defense work or spread rumors.[10] As will be described later, a major task of the NKVD in the first weeks of the war was the establishment of a partisan and underground network.

During July the German advance toward Moscow seemed irresistible; but the Wehrmacht was held up in the south by the stubborn defense of Kiev. Fascinated by the industrial and agricultural wealth of the Ukraine, Hitler ordered the diversion of major forces from the crucial central front. His action temporarily eliminated the danger to Moscow, and probably saved the principal Soviet armies from annihilation; in the Ukraine, however, the German drive led to severe losses for the Party as well as the Red Army. In the German encirclement of Kiev a considerable number of Party officials disappeared, including M. A. Burmistenko, the highest-ranking member of the apparatus lost as a result of enemy action. Throughout the Soviet Union, in these first months of war, the losses in rank-and-file Party members were enormous. In June 1941 there were 3,900,000 Communists, and these were augmented by 343,000 new entrants (170,000 of them in army Party organizations) after the outbreak of war.[11] Nevertheless, the total membership by the end of the year stood at about 3,100,000 —a gross loss of over one million.[12]

Under these circumstances it is understandable that panic gripped all levels of the Soviet Communist Party. In October the situation became most critical in Moscow. Reinforced by troops returned from the south, the German command rapidly approached the capital. Between October 5 and 15 the Soviet authorities began a hasty evacuation of skilled personnel and industrial machinery. The principal government departments were also evacuated. At the same time, thousands of civilians fled east independently.[13] Central Committee members assembled in Moscow for a plenum, but Stalin refused to meet with them.[14] As the diplomatic corps left for Kuibyshev on

October 15, Molotov said that he and Stalin would leave Moscow to join them.[15]

On October 16 *Pravda* carried a full-page headline on the threat to Moscow, evoking the memory of its successful defense during the Civil War. Feverish efforts were made to build fortifications through the use of conscripted civilian labor, and half-prepared militia and training units were sent to the front. At the same time, however, NKVD units and even the ordinary police disappeared from the streets. One Communist source refers to an order of October 16 for the evacuation of the civilian population.[16] There was panic and some looting, but no effort to form a non-Soviet administration. By October 20 it was apparent that the German advance could be halted. Moscow was declared to be in a state of siege; the police returned, taking stern measures to restore order.[17] On November 7 most members of the Politburo, including Stalin, appeared at the customary celebrations of the Bolshevik Revolution.[18]

Leningrad's trial was less sudden, but far grimmer. According to rumors Alexander Werth, an unusually percipient war correspondent, reported, the Soviet forces under Voroshilov prepared to evacuate the city when confronted by the initial German advance. Stalin, however, countermanded the evacuation order, and sent Zhukov to defend the city.[19] In September 1941 Malenkov and Molotov also arrived in Leningrad to help organize its defenses.[20] Voroshilov issued an order appealing to the revolutionary traditions of the Leningrad workers.[21] From August on, however, the city was isolated from land contact with the rest of the Soviet Union. In this desperate situation, according to a Soviet report, dissident elements constituted an anti-Soviet "government" which intended to seek German confirmation when the Wehrmacht entered the city.[22] Throughout the winter similar elements are said to have sent up rockets to guide the German bombers.[23]

As the siege continued, the circumstances of the Leningrad population became horrible. In December 1941 the bread ration for workers sank to 250 grams (9 ounces) per day.[24] Children and other nonworkers, who received only half that amount, died by the thousands. Altogether, over 600,000 died of famine and accompanying diseases. As over 1,500,000 were evacuated, the population of Leningrad, which before the war had been 3,200,000, reached a low point of less than 1,000,000 in 1942.[25]

In spite of these conditions, the Party grimly held on to Leningrad. Zhdanov himself apparently spent most of his time in the city, and is credited with the concept of a road laid out across the ice of Lake Ladoga which enabled supplies to evade the German siege lines.[26] Steps were taken to prepare a house-by-house defense, and Party work, usually conducted in the enterprises, was in large part organized around the apartment houses.[27] Eighty per cent of the Komsomols and 60 per cent of the Party membership were sent to the front. Nearly all the survivors remaining in Leningrad were engaged in producing munitions, which were provided not only to the city's defenders, but were sent by air to Soviet forces on other fronts.[28] In 1942, however, munitions output was not sufficient even for the Leningrad defense, though production recovered rapidly after the siege was raised in early 1943.[29]

In the early stages of the war, sweeping changes were made in the Soviet system of political supervision. The most important innovation was the creation, on June 30, 1941, by joint decree of the Supreme Soviet Presidium, Council of People's Commissars, and the Central Committee, of the State Defense Committee (*Gosudarstvennyi Komitet Oborony*—GOKO). The decree provided for the "concentration of the complete powers of the state" in the committee, and ordered "all citizens and all Party, Soviet, Komsomol, and military organs unconditionally to carry out the decisions and instructions of the State Defense Committee." [30] During the first two years of the war, at least, the GOKO does in fact seem to have functioned as the supreme governing body. With the nominal concurrence of the Central Committee (which in fact did not convene during the war), the GOKO formed a number of new commissariats and committees of crucial importance in the direction of the war.[31] It issued such important decrees as that declaring the state of siege in Moscow in October 1941. Its plenipotentiaries assumed supreme direction of the defense of crucial sectors of the front.

In the light of the extensive power of the GOKO it is instructive to compare its membership to that of the Politburo, which it seems in a sense to have superseded. Stalin was, of course, chairman at all times; Molotov was his deputy. Initially the other members were Malenkov, Voroshilov, and Beria.[32] In February 1942 Mikoian and N. A. Voznesenskii were added, but Kaganovich did not become a member until 1944, when N. A. Bulganin was also added.[33] Older and relatively inactive Politburo members (Kalinin, Andreev, and Shvernik) were omitted; but so also were the very active members Zhdanov and Khrushchev, who had based their power almost entirely on Party activities, especially in the territorial apparatus. On the other hand, Politburo members who had been active in extra-Party affairs

(Molotov, Voroshilov, and Beria), augmented by the younger men who
were not in the Politburo, but who had concentrated on economic and
military matters, gained the center of the stage. Beria obviously increased
both his power and his public prestige. In addition to supervision of the
expanded police activities, which included much economic activity, he
took charge of the entire defense of the Caucasus area when it was
threatened in 1942.[34] The major gain from the new arrangements, however,
fell to Malenkov, not yet a Politburo member. Probably he retained control
of the Cadres Administration, which continued to be centralized, throughout
the war. As we have seen, he was dispatched to Leningrad at a crucial
time; the following year he acted as plenipotentiary of the GOKO throughout the defense of Stalingrad.[35] His chief claim to fame, however, was in
munitions production, where he succeeded Voznesenskii as chairman of the
vital Economic Committee for Armament Production.[36]

Among the major instrumentalities for supervising the war effort were
the plenipotentiaries of the GOKO, whose authority superseded that of all
local officials. As noted above, members of the GOKO themselves went as
plenipotentiaries to the most crucial areas. Others, according to a recent
Soviet source, were appointed by the Council of People's Commissars and
the Central Committee, and received their initial assignments from these
bodies rather than the GOKO itself, but this does not seem to have much
reduced the latter's influence.[37]

In addition to the plenipotentiaries, day-to-day supervision in major
cities threatened by the enemy was exercised by City Defense Committees
(*Gorodskie Komitety Oborony*—GorKO). In Kiev a "defense staff," composed of an obkom secretary, a gorkom secretary, the oblast executive
committee chairman, and the military commander, was formed as early as
July 6.[38] Similarly, a military Defense Council was established in Leningrad on August 20.[39] In their composition these bodies seem to have been
prototypes of the GorKO, but the latter, properly so called, were evidently
formed slightly later in 1941. Such committees were organized in Stalingrad, Tula, Murmansk, Astrakhan, Ivanovo, Kazan', Sevastopol, and Rostov.[40] Only the last two cities eventually fell to the Germans.

The chairman of the GorKO was always the Party first secretary of the
raion or oblast in which the city was located. The other members were the
chairman of the state (oblast or raion) executive committee, the military
commandant of the city, and the NKVD chief.[41] If one compares this group
to the obkom bureau, the dominant local governing body just before the
outbreak of the war, the evidence of decline of Party predominance is

striking. A bureau typically included four or five Party obkom secretaries, the Party secretary of the chief city of the oblast, the newspaper editor and the Komsomol secretary (both in effect Party officials), in addition to the oblast executive committee chairman, the NKVD chief, and less frequently a military commander.[42] Consequently, the prewar Party apparatus had enjoyed a majority of seven or eight to two or three non-Party officials; after the formation of the GorKO, one Party representative, though still chairman, faced three members of other bureaucracies in the local governing body.

It is important, however, to note that the GorKO pattern was confined to a few places, though very important ones. Aside from Leningrad and Moscow, which never had City Defense Committees (although the GOKO seems to have exercised close supervision over Moscow), the GorKO's were not introduced in the major economic centers far behind the front lines, nor were they established in the Caucasus even when it was threatened by the Germans in 1942. The absence of the GorKO did not necessarily mean that the Party apparatus retained its prewar ascendancy, however. While Beria assumed overall supervision in the Caucasus, the GOKO formed a "Central Quintet" composed of M. D. Bagirov, the Azerbaidzhani first secretary; V. N. Merkulov, an old henchman of Beria; Nazarov, Commissar for the USSR Petroleum Industry; Mir Iakubov, head of the Azerbaidzhan NKVD; and the latter's deputy, Emelianov. The "Quintet" was to arrange evacuation, and especially to destroy the Baku oil installations rather than allow them to fall to the Germans.[43] Although this arrangement differed in form from the GorKO, the relative position of the Party in it seems to have been no higher.

The biggest task confronting the Soviet regime in the first two years of the war, other than the actual conduct of military operations, was the evacuation of personnel and industrial facilities from regions threatened by the Germans, and the resumption, with the help of these facilities, of munitions production in areas far behind the front lines. Since the civilian leaders played only a secondary part in directing combat, it seems safe to say that their principal contribution to the war effort was the maintenance of production. Too few details are known of the process of evacuation and reconstruction of industry to permit the non-Soviet observer to make a complete appraisal of this gigantic effort. Even the available facts have not been fully analyzed by the economists, industrial engineers, and others outside the USSR most competent to evaluate them. Enough is known, however, to enable the nonspecialist to hazard the guess that the economic accomplishments of the Soviet system in World War II constitute its greatest single achievement.

Very little seems to have been done to evacuate personnel and material from the large territories overrun during the first months of the war. Orders were given to pursue a "scorched-earth" policy, leaving nothing behind which the Germans might utilize; but the civilian population, unconvinced of the ultimate viability of the Soviet regime, often hampered the destruction of facilities which would be useful in permitting the restoration of economic life under German occupation.[44] Soviet sources admit that there was confusion over military and economic priorities in the use of transport facilities, and that some local officials panicked. For example, most farm tractors in the Ukraine west of the Dnepr could not be transported across the river.[45] Fortunately for the Soviet war effort Belorussia, the Baltic lands, and the Ukrainian areas close to the frontier contained relatively little industry. By the time the German forces approached Leningrad, the Moscow region, and the Donbas, the westernmost of the great industrial regions, the GOKO had set up a Council for Evacuation headed by Shvernik, and including Mikoian and A. N. Kosygin, to supervise orderly evacuation.[46]

An important, but secondary, aspect of the evacuation process was the removal of cultural and governmental institutions. In October 1941 the provisional capital of the country was established in Kuibyshev on the great bend of the Volga. The principal noneconomic agencies, including Foreign Affairs, Defense, Internal Affairs, Transportation, and the State Planning Commission (Gosplan) were transferred there. Volga cities within a radius of a few hundred miles from Kuibyshev sheltered other noneconomic commissariats and administrations, and some commissariats in charge of light industries.[47] Most of the cultural institutions from Leningrad were evacuated to Saratov, also on the Volga.[48] Describing the parade in Kuibyshev on the twenty-fourth anniversary of the Bolshevik Revolution, *Pravda* wrote that "the people of the Volga region—the Russian heartland—go by."[49] With the defense of Moscow highly uncertain, the Soviet regime evidently contemplated directing its continued resistance from the middle Volga region.

Other cultural and governmental offices were scattered far and wide in the extreme eastern European portions of the USSR, and in its Asian territories. This was particularly true of the Ukrainian institutions which, aside from those from Moscow and Leningrad, constituted most of the offices successfully evacuated. Nominally the Ukrainian capital-in-exile was in Ufa, in the southern Urals; the Ukrainian Academy of Sciences and other principal cultural institutions were relocated there. Many Ukrainian governmental and Party offices were placed in such scattered points as Saratov and Moscow, however. A few cultural institutions, like the University of Odessa, were first transferred to the Caucasus; but as this region was itself too exposed, they were later sent to Central Asia.[50]

Organizations and persons not essential to the war effort were generally sent wherever a minimum of living facilities was available; often evacuation points lacked even this minimum. Despite the relatively backward oasis economy of Turkestan, over two million evacuees were sent to the Uzbek SSR; according to eyewitness accounts the struggle for survival in this region became desperate.[51]

Much greater care was taken in the evacuation of industrial facilities essential to the war effort. Again, the relocation of the commissariats provides a clue to the plan. The central Urals cities received most of the major industrial commissariats. In Molotov (later renamed Perm') were the Commissariats for the Armaments, Coal, Chemical, and Paper Industries; Sverdlovsk, only two hundred miles away, received the Commissariats of Ferrous Metallurgy, Non-Ferrous Metallurgy, Heavy Industry, Construction Material, the Chief Army Construction Office, and the Chief Administration of Labor Reserves; in Cheliabinsk, a hundred miles south of Sverdlovsk, were the Commissariats for Construction, Electric Stations, Military Supplies, the Tank Industry, and Medium Machine Construction. Cities in the southern and western Urals and West Siberia became the temporary headquarters of commissariats dealing only with light industry and agriculture, with a few exceptions such as the Commissariat for the Petroleum Industry in Ufa, heart of the "Second Baku" oil field. A few important industrial commissariats remained in cities relatively far to the west like Gor'kii.[52]

The available information suggests that factories were generally relocated in the same areas as the commissariats which supervised them. According to N. A. Voznesenskii, of 1,360 large enterprises evacuated in three months of 1941, 455 went to the Urals, 210 to West Siberia, and 250 to Central Asia and Kazakhstan. Moreover, 400 of those sent to the Urals were back in production by the end of 1942.[53] Probably the Urals received the majority of the 220 large enterprises evacuated from Moscow; the region also obtained most of the refugee Donbas industry. The most detailed Soviet account of the Donbas evacuation suggests that the plan in the early autumn of 1941 was to dispatch machinery from the Donbas through Stalingrad to the Urals. When the rail lines in that direction became clogged, components of some factory installations had to be diverted over a tortuous rail and ferry route through the Caucasus and the Caspian to Central Asia, and from there rerouted to the Urals.[54]

The Urals became, to quote Voznesenskii, "the basic" Soviet economic region.[55] While before the war the region had been of major importance, providing a third of the coal and steel output of the USSR, it produced half of these products in the postwar period.[56] Its relative gain in petroleum production was even greater. Moreover, while the Urals' share in overall manufacturing output before the war had still been small, general industrial production there grew faster during the war than did that of other areas to which industrial facilities were evacuated.[57] Between 1940 and 1943 the Urals ratio of increase was 3.5, as compared to 3 for West Siberia, and 1.5 for Central Asia and Kazakhstan.[58] In military supplies in the narrower sense, the proportionate increase of the Urals was smaller than that of West Siberia or the Volga region; but it seems likely that the absolute gain in Urals production of munitions was the largest.[59] Probably the reason why the Urals rather than other areas—where greater distance from the front conferred even more security from potential land or air attack—was made the center of the Soviet war effort was its relatively ready access to the other major portions of the USSR. From the Volga administrative center, with its rail connections to Moscow, Leningrad, and the front, and its river-sea route to the Caucasus, several major railroads led to the Urals. Beyond the Urals, however, only two rail lines went on to West Siberia and Central Asia.

Even the amazingly rapid recovery of industrial plants moved to the Urals could not, however, immediately make up for the terrible losses suffered by the Soviet economy in 1941. It is estimated that the value of overall industrial production declined from 138.5 billion rubles in 1940 to 103.3 billion in 1942.[60] The low point in production of munitions was reached between December 1941 and March 1942.[61] The areas occupied by the Germans in 1941 had contained 40 per cent of the Soviet population; and had provided 63 per cent of the USSR's coal, 58 per cent of its steel, 38 per cent of its grain, and 84 per cent of its sugar.[62] Millions of the people were saved for the war effort by evacuation, but they were partly offset by vast military losses, and deaths from starvation. As a result of losses and mobilization, the 31,500,000 workers and white-collar employees in the economy in 1940 had shrunk by the end of 1941 to 18,500,000.[63]

As the industrial labor force filled out in the succeeding months, women and youths became its dominant elements. In the Moscow area and some Urals factories over half the workers were women; in one plant 50 per cent of the force consisted of youths, as compared to 6.3 per cent over forty years old.[64] These circumstances posed special problems for the Party organizations. The young men and women had to be trained for efficient work, and both the youths and women of all ages posed special disciplinary problems. The housing situation, which in the new industrial centers was even more primitive than before the war, was especially urgent, for it affected morale as well as output. A gorkom secretary in the Urals was expelled from the Party for failure to work effectively to provide for the needs of the increased population in his city.[65]

While the position of the urban Party organizations was difficult, the rural organizations were in an almost desperate situation. Food supply was one of the weakest aspects of the wartime Soviet economy; here, as in some branches of military activity, particularly motor transport, Anglo-American aid may have made the difference between defeat and victory. While in 1939 women had constituted only 52 per cent of the labor force in agriculture, by the beginning of 1943 they were 71 per cent.[66] Women performed nearly all the agricultural work in some areas; the number of labor-days performed by women and youths increased by 50 per cent.[67] In work such as tractor operation, women replaced four hundred thousand men. Most other workers in this kind of agricultural activity were new at their jobs and unable to cope with machinery breakdowns.[68] This kind of farm laborer required firm discipline, but in many cases it was also necessary to select women as chairmen, who had difficulty in maintaining their authority.[69]

The Party, too, was compelled to turn to women to fill out its apparatus, especially in agricultural areas. By mid-1943, 40 per cent of the apparatus in Kalinin oblast (a large part of which had been occupied by the Germans earlier) consisted of women, including several raikom secretaries.[70] Special training courses were instituted to prepare the new apparatus recruits for their jobs, but the necessity of reintroducing MTS political sections indicates that there were difficulties in maintaining the proper functioning of the Party machinery.

In the first years of the war, at least, there seems to have been a tendency for the Party organizations to confine themselves to secondary tasks such as propaganda and care for the social and physical living conditions of the population. Even in these fields many members, absorbed in the overriding tasks of war production, tended to lose interest in indoctrinational activity.

In front-line areas, such as Tula in 1941, the Party organization tended to become an adjunct of the military command, aiding it by giving defense training to the population, providing auxiliary services in the military hospitals, and raising war loans.[71]

Doubtless to prevent deterioration of the fabric of Party morale and organization, A. S. Shcherbakov and other Party spokesmen stressed the importance of the regular convocation of plenums of Party committees.[72] In view of the fact that Stalin refused to hold a Central Committee plenum in October 1941, and apparently did not convene the Central Committee at any time during the war, this emphasis sounds ironic.[73] Nevertheless, a plenum of the Tula obkom convened on January 16, 1942, a few weeks after the Germans retreated from the province.[74] Throughout the war the Party press continued to stress the requirement for regular plenums and frequently reported their convocation in various areas. Very few Party conferences were held at the oblast level, however.[75]

An order of January 1942 provided for regular election of officers in civilian primary Party organizations.[76] In front-line military units, however, elections were suspended in Party organizations, and Party organizers were appointed from above.[77] At the same time, steps were taken to simplify some aspects of Party operation; for example, the flood of new appointments made it necessary to relax the requirement that candidates for apparatus posts be interviewed personally by the Party bureaus.[78]

All levels of personnel of the Party organization were heavily depleted by the demands of the military forces. Altogether 1,500,000 Communists left for the front, including over 1,000,000 during the first year of war.[79] Sixteen thousand of 37,000 in the Kiev city organization went to the Red Army, half of the Moscow members, and 22,000 of 24,000 from Odessa.[80] 400,000 Communists had died in the army by mid-1942; since the overall loss to the Party in 1941 alone was above 1,000,000, it is evident that numerous Communists surrendered or were cut off in occupied areas.[81]

At first, admissions to the Party did not keep up with losses. On August 19, 1941, however, Party rules were relaxed to permit the entry of distinguished soldiers on the recommendation of three Party members who had known them *less* than a year. On December 9 the period of candidacy for such soldiers was reduced to three months.[82] The Party had embarked on a drive to bring all outstanding military men into its ranks, with little regard for their level of political preparation. In 1942, the influx was enormous: of a total of 1,349,000 new entrants, 425,000 were accepted in the first half of the year, and 640,000 in the second half in the armed forces alone, which contained two million Communists by the end of 1942.[83] By that time the total Party membership (approximately 3,700,000) was still somewhat below that attained by the outbreak of war (almost 3,900,000).[84] By the end of 1943, the Party comprised about 5,000,000, however, of whom some 3,000,000 were in the military forces.[85] By the end of the war overall membership was 5,800,000, of whom the same proportion (60 per cent) were in the armed forces.[86] As about two-thirds of all members at that time had entered during the war years,[87] about 2,000,000 of the roughly 3,900,000 Party members of June 1941 must have died, disappeared, or been expelled for improper conduct during the war. The same fate had also overtaken at least 1,400,000 of the 5,300,000 wartime Party entrants.[88] The overall loss was of the same order as that which the Party had experienced during the purges of the thirties. Considering the 10,000,000 deaths in the armed forces and the partisans, where so many Communists were active, and the 15,000,000 civilian dead in the war and its aftermath, it is likely, however, that by far the larger share of the wartime decrease was due to what the Party would consider "honorable causes."

The contribution of the Party to the military effort cannot be measured in terms of manpower alone. A very considerable proportion of the apparatus officials also departed for military service. For the most part, this level of Party personnel seems to have been used for army political work. By August 1941, 962 of 3,556 primary Party organization secretaries in Moscow oblast had entered the armed forces.[89] Up to December 1941, 47,000 officials of the Party, Komsomols, and trade unions had gone to the Red Army, and during approximately the same period 93,000 Communists and Komsomols under forty years old with military preparation were dispatched to the front as political workers.[90] According to an émigré source, however, the new army political workers tended to constitute a group apart from the regular army commissars.[91] Higher Party officials, at least, were apparently assigned military duties approximately corresponding in nature and rank to their civilian posts. An oblast newspaper editor, for example, became the editor of a divisional paper; a propagandist entered the corresponding section of army political work; the chairman of an oblast court became a member of a military tribunal; and a Union Republic central committee secretary became the political member of the military council of a "front."[92]

At first the influx of Party officials into the Red Army did not mean a heightening of political control. As we have seen, the initial reaction of Stalin's regime, when confronted by the catastrophe of the invasion, was to fall back on the commissars and the police system. As defeat followed defeat, however, the inadequacy of this expedient must have become clear even to Stalin. By early autumn the initial successes of the army commanders in defensive actions in the south and at Leningrad began to increase their self-assurance. Since the war, Party officials have occasionally openly expressed their resentment at high-handed military attitudes during this period.[93] The tremendous defeat of the Germans before Moscow in December 1941, which for a time appeared to be turning into a rout like Napoleon's Russian retreat, raised the prestige of the Red Army to a point which it had never before attained. During the winter of 1941-42 the military commands seemed to be picking up a thousand broken threads of the Soviet system, for example, in the partisan movement. The names of the famous field commanders like Georgii Zhukov far outshone those of all Party leaders, except Stalin, in the popular imagination.[94]

The spring and early summer of 1942 was a period of relative stability at the front and consolidation in the rear areas. It was also, apparently, a period when the Party and police machinery caught its second wind, and regained control over the Soviet system. The subject is very obscure, and much might be learned from painstaking investigation of all available sources. Drawing upon the readily accessible evidence, one can only hypothesize that the recovery of political dominance by the Party and the police was signaled by such actions as the formation of the Central Staff of the Partisan Movement in June 1942. Ostensibly, however, the prestige of the military commanders continued to rise throughout the year. Marshal (then Lieutenant General) Rodion Malinovskii spoke to Alexander Werth of "revolutionary" changes in the Red Army in the summer of 1942.[95] Commissars were cautioned to avoid oversevere disciplinary measures, which the line officers resented.[96] Finally, on October 9 the commissars themselves were once again replaced by deputy commanders for political affairs fully subordinate to the line commanders.

The territorial Party apparatus reassumed a larger and larger role in the front areas as the war went on. In the spring of 1942 the secretary of the Party bureau of a military unit held a political meeting for the inhabitants of a reoccupied village.[97] A little earlier, Party representatives in the reconquered city of Kerch carried on their activity in providing food and hospital facilities with the permission of the commissar of the Red Fleet unit.[98] Immediately after the recapture of Kharkov in February 1943, however, the prewar first secretary arrived to assume control of the city's affairs. From then on the Party seems to have been intent on reinstalling its apparatus in regained areas as soon as the Germans were driven out.[99] Army political officers continued to assist in the reconstitution of administrative institutions in the reoccupied areas, but they did this, it was emphasized, in close contact with the local Party and Soviet organizations.[100]

Although the circumstances just described appear to point to a certain rivalry between army and territorial apparatus, it is interesting to note that it was precisely the major Party leaders from the territorial apparatus who worked most closely with the military. As noted earlier, all of these leaders remained outside the GOKO. Shcherbakov, who during the war rose faster than any other Party leader except those in the GOKO, was simultaneously head of the Main Political Administration of the army, with the rank of colonel general, and first secretary of Moscow oblast. Late in the war he was succeeded as head of the Main Political Administration by Lieutenant General I. V. Shikin, apparently a protégé of Zhdanov.[101] Zhdanov himself attained the rank of colonel general, and co-operated closely with the commands in the Leningrad area. Khrushchev, who became a lieutenant general, was the political member of the military councils of several of the "fronts" in the south. These leaders, like entire categories of lower officials in the Soviet bureaucracy who obtained epaulets for their uniforms at about the same time that these signs of rank were given to the military officers, "borrowed" some of the prestige of the army for themselves and for the political control system in general. In this and in other ways the Party "contained" the unwonted prestige of the military commanders and prepared for a resumption of its absolute control.

CHAPTER

DEFENSE OF THE RUSSIAN FATHERLAND

The far-reaching though transient changes in the relationships among Soviet institutions which occurred during World War II were paralleled by important shifts in ideological emphasis. During the first three years of Soviet involvement in the war, the usual themes of Communist indoctrination, while still present, were muted. In their place in the foreground of the propaganda distributed through mass media appeared appeals to patriotism. Moreover, the sentiment which the propaganda sought to arouse was Russian patriotism.

This development was not, of course, an abrupt departure from earlier ideological tendencies. As was described in Chapter VI, the somewhat vague and rootless concept of the "Soviet native land" was gradually being given a Russian content throughout the decade preceding the war. Wartime propaganda intensified this tendency without fundamentally altering its themes. The heroes of Russian tradition were glorified in popular history. Patriotic operas like Glinka's *Ivan Susanin* were more in vogue than ever. Speeches and orders of the day were studded with references to great military leaders of Tsarist times.

The major new element in the concession to traditional Russian feeling was the stress on the Russian Orthodox Church, which, in contrast to the semipersecution which it had suffered before the war, received a quasi-official status. At the highest level, the Patriarchate of Moscow was restored in 1943; to co-ordinate government relations to it, a Council for Affairs of the Orthodox Church was established. While the lower levels of the Soviet regime did not abandon the propagation of atheism, the extreme antireligious campaign of the immediate prewar period was relaxed.[1]

Much more than during peacetime, of course, patriotic appeals were addressed to the Red Army. While it is very difficult to secure direct evidence on the real feelings of high army officers, this group was probably more imbued with Russian nationalism than any other segment of the Soviet elite. The highest level of the officer corps consisted of Russians, or Russified Ukrainians and Belorussians. There were exceptions like the Armenian I. K. Bagramian, one of the dozen great Soviet commanders produced by the war, but there was no non-Slavic minority in the high command comparable to the cohesive Georgian group in the police and in the Party apparatus.[2] Moreover, most professional military officers who survived the Great Purge had been trained as a closed stratum of Soviet society in military academies which uniformly stressed Russian language and the Russian military tradition.[3]

After the initial months of the war, the rank and file of the Red Army was scarcely less Russian in basic composition than the high officers. Occasionally Soviet sources indicate that as early as the autumn of 1941 the best remaining troops were Russian. For example, the role of Siberian units in the defeat of the Germans at Moscow is well known; one Soviet writer also maintains that its cadres from the Volga region made the "Central Front" outstanding.[4] The need to conserve some skilled workers for war industry, and the greater adaptability of peasant youths to the extreme rigors of wartime military service, made the rural districts the principal source of recruits. Most areas still under Soviet control at the end of 1941 were more solidly Russian than the urban melting pots, and the peasants were relatively more susceptible to traditional and national appeals than were the city dwellers who had received a longer and more intense Communist indoctrination.[5]

The stress on Russian patriotism was combined with extreme expressions of hatred for the Germans. Observers report that literary figures like Il'ia Ehrenburg, Mikhail Sholokhov, and Konstantin Simonov who stressed the anti-German themes were the most popular in the Red Army.[6] As the war went on, initial propaganda efforts to distinguish between "good" Germans and "bad" Nazis faded away. As early as August 1941 an article stressed the immense difficulty of the task of rehabilitating German youth, once "heavy blows" at the front had compelled them to recognize defeat:

German industry provides tanks and airplanes, the Hitler youth—human material. In those tanks and airplanes eighteen and twenty year old German boys feel themselves to be gods of death and destruction. They are harnessed to the Hitlerite war machine, are themselves part of this machine. For them to kill as many people as possible is not only sport, but dark intoxication, the triumph of cruelty.[7]

It is true that as late as November 1941 Stalin denied that the Red Army was imbued with racial hatred, or that it aimed at exterminating the German people.[8] In his November 6, 1943, speech, however, Stalin made no distinction among Germans:

> Like the medieval barbarians or Attila's hordes, the German villains trample the fields, burn down villages and cities, and demolish manufacturing enterprises and cultural institutions. . . . Our people will not forgive these crimes of the German monsters. We shall make the German criminals answer for all their misdeeds.[9]

The anti-German ideological campaign went so far as to lead to a revision of some of the "classics" of Marxism. Curiously enough, the first step in this direction was taken just *before* the German invasion. In the ninth (1941) number of *Bol'shevik* (sent to the printer on May 18) appeared an essay by Stalin entitled "On Engels' Article 'The Foreign Policy of Russian Tsarism.'" In this essay, ostensibly written in 1934, Stalin vigorously criticized Marx's closest associate for having asserted that in certain circumstances a German attack on the reactionary Russian Empire would be justified, instead of insisting (anachronistically, of course) on the "Leninist" principle of transforming an imperialist war which might arise between the two countries into a civil war.[10] During the war itself, even a minor Soviet writer was permitted to attack the German Engels for his derogatory comments concerning Marshal M. I. Kutuzov. The latter had become a particular favorite of Soviet propaganda because his Fabian strategy in the Napoleonic invasion was supposed to have been a forerunner of Stalin's "wisdom" in retreating to draw the German forces to defeat.[11]

With the Ukraine, Belorussia, the Baltic lands, and Moldavia in German hands until mid-1943 or later, the appeal to Russian national feeling was an obviously useful tactic, if only because nearly three-quarters of the population remaining under Soviet rule was Russian. Aleksandr Shcherbakov, who was an especially vigorous exponent of the Russian patriotic line, expressed this fact in a speech of January 7, 1942. "The Russian people—the first among equals in the family of people of the USSR," he said, "takes upon itself the basic burden of the struggle with the German occupiers."[12] The emphasis upon Russian nationalism did not diminish, however, when the western territories were recovered. Indeed, the culmination of this trend is often considered to be Stalin's brief address at the victory reception of Red Army commanders on May 23, 1945. Offering a toast to "our Soviet people, and first of all, the Russian people," Stalin called the Russians "the most distinguished nation of all nations constituting the USSR," "the directing force" in the war, and the "deciding force" which through its steadfast loyalty to the regime made victory possible.[13]

One possible reason why Soviet propaganda continued to stress Russian nationalism in the latter stage of the war was the desire to maintain the loyalty of the troops, still overwhelmingly Russian, who were exposed to increasing anti-Soviet Russian nationalist propaganda. In the late winter of 1942-43 the former Soviet general Andrei Vlasov launched his first public appeal to the Russian people. Vlasov, who had been induced to take his anti-Soviet stand after his capture by the Germans, secured the support of a number of other high Soviet line officers among the prisoners of war, and of a few captive political officers. In general, however, Communist officials were scarce among the elements collaborating with the Germans, primarily because the latter, during the early stage of the war, shot all who were known to be "commissars."[14] The program which Vlasov and his advisors elaborated during 1943-44 called for the overthrow of Communism in the Soviet Union, but for the preservation of major aspects of the socialist system.[15]

While Vlasov's Committee for the Liberation of the Peoples of Russia, formed in 1944, tried to secure the participation of non-Russian anti-Soviet organizations it was only partly successful. Basically the Vlasov movement remained Russian in leadership as well as in name. Hitler never permitted Vlasov more than the vaguest shadow of authority over the hundreds of thousands of ex-Soviet citizens enrolled in auxiliary military formations under German command, to say nothing of the millions under German occupation. Powerful voices in Nazi political circles continued to further the aims of the non-Russian nationalists who opposed the whole Vlasov program.[16] Nevertheless, the mere recognition of Vlasov as the spokesman for Russian national aspirations was a considerable departure from earlier Nazi policy, which, while occasionally making verbal concessions to non-Russian national feeling in the USSR, had condemned Russians to complete subjugation.

By the time the Vlasov movement began, the fortunes of battle had already turned heavily against the Germans. It is doubtful that even a strongly supported Russian "liberation" movement could have had a decisive effect on the course of the war. Moreover, the fact that Stalin stressed the Russian nationalist theme long after the Vlasov threat was ended, just as he continued it long after the need to placate the military command had lessened, suggests that he had deeper grounds for this ideological policy. During the war, Stalin's earlier mistrust of the Ukrainians and other non-Russians increased. At the same time, his authority seemed to depend more and more upon centralizing elements in the USSR. For example, as soon as it became clear that Moscow would hold out, enormous emphasis was placed on the city as a shrine and inspiration of all Soviet people.[17] The furthering of Russian nationalism was a natural part of this pattern.

The emphasis on patriotic themes was much the most impressive ideological development during the war. Certain other developments seemed to continue the stabilizing, if not conservative, tendencies apparent in the thirties. Such, for example, were various 1944 decrees strengthening the position of legal marriage, and encouraging childbearing.[18] A more theoretical development was the trend toward substitution of immutable, or at least stable, social and normative laws for the flux of the dialectic. Some tentative steps in the direction of recognizing unchangeable economic laws were taken.[19] Father Henri Chambre, a profound student of Soviet ideology, has also interpreted Stalin's statement of July 3, 1941, that "our cause is just" as the forerunner of recognition of an "absolute morality."[20] It is perhaps unnecessary to believe that the basic Soviet creed was departing so sharply from Lenin's teaching.[21] It does seem clear, however, that Stalin was willing at this time to pry apart the foundations of "Marxism-Leninism" to further his own ends. This was most evident in the enormous impetus given to the "cult" of Stalin. Six weeks before the USSR entered the war, Stalin became Chairman of the Council of People's Commissars; in this way he became official chief of the government as well as of the Party. Becoming Chairman of the State Defense Committee and Commissar of Defense during the first weeks of the war, and Commander in Chief in the autumn, Stalin seemed to be assuming new titles to compensate for his lowered prestige resulting from the Soviet reverses and his own odd behavior in the first days of the invasion. Public glorification of Stalin grew rather than diminished as the war proceeded to a victorious end, however. On March 6, 1943, he became Marshal of the Soviet Union, and on June 26, 1945, acquired the unprecedented title of Generalissimo.[22]

At the same time, theoretical discussions of the role of the individual leader were departing more and more from traditional Marxist concepts. The decisive role of social forces, and even of the organized Party, was put in question by the statement that in the absence of the individual leader the course of events might be so impeded that historical development would be different.[23] In his 1946 pamphlet, F. V. Konstantinov, a leading theoretician, seemed to place the influence of the leaders on a par with that of the Party and the "masses":

> The mighty force of the influence of Lenin and Stalin on the course of world history is inseparably connected to the activity of our entire Party, whose creators and leaders they have been. . . . The prophetic foresight of Lenin has been verified: the victory was won, and it was won because at the head of the armed people which achieved the Great October Socialist Revolution stood its experienced leaders—Lenin and Stalin. . . . [Stalin] sees more profoundly, more clearly than anyone else on earth, not only how events are unfolding today, but the direction in which they will unfold in the future.[24]

Hand in hand with the restoration of Russian nationalism went a revival of the Panslav ideology of Tsarist times. In 1940 *Bol'shevik* had bitterly rebuked Anglo-French newspaper assertions that the USSR was pursuing a Panslav policy in the Balkans; this, the Soviet journal said, was an attempt to make Balkan Slavs distrust the Soviet Union by recalling the aggressive Tsarist policy of World War I.[25] Very soon after the USSR itself became involved in the war, however, a conference of Slavs met in Moscow. It was, to be sure, called an "All-Slav (*Vseslavanskii*) Meeting," but the difference between this affair and the "Panslav Congresses" of Tsarist days was etymological rather than semantic. The Second All-Slav Meeting took place in Moscow at the beginning of 1942; a third in the same city in May 1943.[26] The purpose was to enlist Slav solidarity to aid the Russians, "the largest Slavic people," against Hitler. An All-Slav Committee, composed mainly of Soviet and pro-Communist figures, formed at the first meeting, served as a permanent organ for propaganda to the West and South Slav nations.

Several of the leaders of the All-Slav Committee were Belorussian or Ukrainian, and Soviet writers stressed the USSR as the home of three of the Slavic nations. One may wonder why still greater efforts were not made at this time to foster a general East Slavic nationalism within the USSR. Three major reasons appear to have lain behind the stress on specifically Russian nationalism. Russified Ukrainians and Belorussians in the elite, especially in the army high command, tended to regard themselves as thoroughly Russian. In addition, as already noted, it was necessary to concentrate propaganda appeals on the Russians, who formed the vast bulk of the population under Soviet control in 1941-43. The third, and perhaps the most important reason, was that Stalin, and probably other major leaders, felt that the second-largest East Slavic nation, the Ukrainians, had failed to meet the test of loyalty to the regime. As Khrushchev later related, Stalin would have banished the Ukrainians after the war if there had been any place to send them.[27]

Stalin probably regarded the rapid conquest of the Ukraine by the Germans as confirmation of his earlier suspicions of Ukrainian loyalty. However, special Ukrainian disaffection cannot be definitely separated from other factors leading to the German conquest, such as the general initial demoralization of the Soviet forces, the adaptability of Ukrainian terrain to mechanized military advances, and Hitler's determination to seize the Ukrainian resources. On the other hand, there is abundant evidence that much of the Ukrainian civilian population welcomed German occupation. It cannot be conclusively demonstrated that this willingness was greater than that of the Russian population under German control, since by the time the Germans had acquired an extensive Russian-inhabited area their atrocities and their treatment of Slavs as serfs had alienated the former Soviet population everywhere. On the whole, however, it seems probable that more intense Ukrainian opposition to the kolkhoz, and a certain amount of anti-Russian national feeling, led Ukrainians to object more strongly to a return of the Soviet system than did most Russians. The considerable success of nationalist groups in recruiting support even when the German authorities tried to suppress them also indicates that there was a reservoir of support for anti-Soviet Ukrainian nationalism.[28]

As in the case of the Russians, however, the leaders and organizers of Ukrainian nationalist activity (aside from émigrés and West Ukrainians) were predominantly intellectuals. Few Communist officials joined the nationalists or collaborated in the German occupation administration in the Ukraine. Indeed, the loyalty of the Ukrainian Party apparatus to the Soviet system is attested by the relatively few changes in its higher levels after the war.[29]

Although the Russian patriotic theme predominated in the first years of the war, the Soviet regime tried hard to win Ukrainian loyalty. The reopening of evacuated Ukrainian cultural institutions was well publicized. According to a postwar Soviet source Ukrainian-language schools were established for evacuated children in such centers as Saratov, Kuibyshev, Chkalov, Molotov, Sverdlovsk, Novosibirsk, Omsk, and the Tatar ASSR.[30] Ukrainian-language publications were issued for the refugee population, and for distribution by clandestine means behind the German line. The twenty-fifth anniversary of the founding of the Ukrainian Soviet Republic was publicly celebrated.[31] The Ukrainian Party headquarters, and especially its propaganda branch, was maintained as near to Ukrainian territory as was militarily feasible.[32] As described in Chapter XII, the principal means of maintaining the Communist "presence" in the Ukraine during the first two years of war was through partisan and underground activity.

Frederick Barghoorn, the most comprehensive analyst of Soviet nationality policy, writes that by late 1943 the Kremlin was convinced that it could withdraw its concessions to national sentiments, especially among the non-Russians.[33] Many formal gestures were made after that, but the general trend appears to have been against expression of Ukrainian national feeling. The amendment of the Soviet Constitution in January 1944 to permit the establishment of separate commissariats of defense and foreign affairs in the Union Republics appears to have been designed to further the Soviet objective of securing increased United Nations representation. The defense commissariat established in Kiev quietly disappeared some time later, while the foreign affairs commissariat, under the shrewd direction of the veteran Comintern leader Dmitrii Manuil'skii, was no more than a valuable propaganda adjunct of Soviet foreign policy. Similarly, a press campaign in early 1944 urged that Chelm and other Ukrainian-inhabited territories in Poland be ceded to the Ukrainian SSR; but when a reliably pro-Communist regime was safely installed in Warsaw these claims were dropped.[34]

If the Soviet regime's wartime attitude toward the Ukrainians was complicated, it maintained an ambiguous position toward the smaller Moslem nationalities of the European USSR only for tactical reasons. The first Moslems in territory overrun by the Germans were the Crimean Tatars. These descendants of the Tatar suzerains of Muscovy, a group of about two hundred thousand, had historical, religious, cultural, and economic reasons to dislike Russians as well as Communists. Consequently, when Communist partisans became active, the Tatars co-operated with the Germans.

> But it was not only the natural conditions which made the partisans' activity difficult. Many Tatar villages were around the woods, and from the beginning of the war many Tatars became traitors. Consequently, the Crimean partisans were deprived of the support of the local population.[35]

As a result, Communist propaganda in the Crimea was more outspoken in its appeal to Russian sentiments than in other mixed areas: "Remember that you are Russian people, and Russian people never betray their native land."[36] Higher-level Russian leaders deeply resented the Crimean Tatar behavior.[37] Not long after the Crimea was reconquered, it was reduced to an oblast of the RSFSR, and the Tatar population deported to Central Asia; unlike other autonomous areas dissolved at the end of the war, this Republic has never been reconstituted.

In some respects the hatred of the North Caucasian Moslems for Communism was greater than that of the Crimean Tatars, for the customs of the tribal mountaineers were deeply violated by the Soviet system. Nevertheless —according to an émigré report—Party and Soviet authorities in the Chechen-Ingush ASSR requested in November 1941 that they be permitted to form a volunteer national division. As soon as they were armed, 90 per cent of the men fled to the mountains to carry on guerrilla warfare against the Soviet authorities.[38] In spite of this experience, Communist leaders in the Caucasus proceeded with a plan for creating nationality units to bolster Soviet armed strength in the area. A cavalry division was formed in the Kabardo-Balkarian Autonomous Republic, with a large Communist and Komsomol component, and a divisional paper in the Kabardian language. It was sent to the front in May 1942, and apparently performed satisfactorily, as did cavalry units from Dagestan.[39] More numerous national formations of divisional strength were formed in the Transcaucasian Union Republics and other areas of the USSR.[40]

The directing force behind this limited return to the territorial principle of military organization was apparently Lev Mekhlis. In 1940 Mekhlis had been replaced as chief of the Main Political Administration, but in 1941 he went as special Politburo plenipotentiary to the southern fronts. When the renewed German advance began in the summer of 1942, however, Mekhlis is said to have come in conflict with Beria, who (probably backed by Malenkov and Shcherbakov) took charge of the defense of the Transcaucasus.[41] Mekhlis was transferred to other fronts.

When the Germans reached the Karachai, Balkarian, Chechen, and Ingush districts, the local populations apparently greeted them warmly. The Communist authorities tried to convince the Moslems that the Germans considered them barbarians.[42] In the Chechen-Ingush Republic, which was bisected by the front line, the Communist authorities endeavored to utilize the tribal structure to reach the native population. Village elders, including Civil War veterans (in loose alliance with the Bolsheviks, the mountaineers had enthusiastically fought Denikin's strongly Russian nationalist "White" regime) spread propaganda in the occupied areas and among Chechen and Ingush troops at the front.[43]

These efforts fell far short of satisfying the Soviet regime. No indication of mass reprisal against the Moslem mountaineers appeared until the German forces had been driven far back, however. As late as February 25, 1944, for example, *Izvestia* reported a plenum of the Kabardo-Balkarian obkom in the reconquered Republic. Even as the item was printed, however, the Chechens and the Ingushes were being rounded up for deportation. The Karachais and the Buddhist Kalmyks had already been sent to Central Asia, and the Balkars were removed in April. The Kabardians were left as the sole titular occupants of their Republic. Some Kabardians, however, including kolkhoz chairmen, had helped dissolve the kolkhoz system under German occupation, and the Party found it necessary to carry out a purge of its members.[44] The other autonomous districts disappeared, although the official decrees on the abolition of some of the areas were not issued until 1946.[45] Significantly, not all of their territory was incorporated in subdivisions of the Russian Republic; perhaps as a token of its loyalty to Stalin, the Georgian SSR received a strip of Chechen-Ingush land.

Evidently there was considerable unrest among the larger Moslem populations of Central Asia and the middle Volga. A Polish observer reports a violent NKVD repression of unrest which arose in the Turkmen Republic as the Germans neared the Caspian Sea in 1942.[46] In this period the Soviet authorities used traditional national themes to appeal to the Central Asians.[47] In 1944, however, Volga Tatar and Central Asian literary figures were sharply criticized for "nationalist deviations" consisting of emphasizing anti-Russian historical themes. A Central Committee decree especially attacked the Volga Tatar obkom for insufficient attention to indoctrinational matters, permitting historians to glorify the Golden Horde (the Tatar suzerains of Russia) and to minimize the co-operation of Russians and non-Russians against Tsarism and foreign enemies.[48] Clearly the Party was determined to root out ideological elements which had contributed to the Moslem defections in other areas.

Soviet Jews were in an especially dangerous position during the war, for they were singled out for extermination by the Nazi invaders. The Soviet authorities did little to save the Jewish population by timely evacuation. This was no doubt partly due to the fact that the most concentrated Jewish settlements lay in Belorussia and the "Right-Bank" Ukraine, where all evacuation measures broke down. Postwar Soviet accounts have expressed sympathy for the plight of the Jews under German occupation, and have indicated that partisan units sometimes helped Jews who escaped to the forests.[49] Other sources, however, maintain that there was more friction than co-operation between Red partisans and Jewish refugees.[50]

Soviet propaganda, especially after 1941, failed to emphasize the extent of the Nazi extermination drive against the Jews. Probably one reason for this omission was the unwillingness of the regime to risk alienating support by espousing an unpopular cause, for the evidence is strong that popular anti-Semitism increased very rapidly in the USSR during the early phase of the war. Some defectors attribute this rise to the grasping behavior of Jewish evacuees, and Jewish unwillingness to fight; the proportion of Jews among soldiers awarded medals indicates, however, that as a group they did their share for the war effort.[51] A more important factor, probably, was officially-sponsored anti-Semitism. According to a story told the present writer by a Soviet literary figure, Aleksandr Shcherbakov came into a propaganda section one day, exclaiming, "You are supposed to be writing of Russian patriotism here, but most of the workers are Jews!" Not long afterward, official but secret quotas prescribed the numbers of Jews who might work in propaganda offices; gradually these were extended to most other aspects of Soviet life. This story cannot be fully substantiated, but there is other information to support the allegation that secret quotas were established during the war.[52]

It is significant that the anti-Semitic action was linked to the rising emphasis on Russian nationalism. Quite likely the steps taken against Jews in general were linked to rivalries in the upper stratum of the regime, especially Shcherbakov's, and probably Malenkov's and Beria's antipathy toward Mekhlis, the most prominent Jew (other than Kaganovich) remaining in high office. In the closing days of the war anti-Semitism may have been linked with a desire to conciliate the Germans; G. F. Aleksandrov sharply attacked Ehrenburg for his extreme anti-German writings.[53] Other Jewish writers were condemned for setting Jews apart from other Soviet citizens as the special victims of the Nazi.[54] Hostility toward Jews returning to their homes in the former occupied areas was widespread, and real pogroms apparently took place in the Ukraine.[55]

The early tendency toward nationalism in domestic ideology was a major factor in reassuring the other partners of the "Grand Alliance." In the first months of the war Stalin endeavored to reassure his allies more directly by seeming to recognize, contrary to earlier Communist theory, an essential difference between Fascist and other capitalist regimes:

> To conceal their reactionary, black-hundred essence, the Hitlerites assail the Anglo-American internal regime as a plutocratic regime. But in England and the United States there are elementary democratic liberties. . . .[56]

Early in the war Soviet publications had a real interest in stressing the contribution of the United States and Great Britain to the war effort. At a time when Soviet forces themselves seemed near collapse, awareness that powerful allies would ultimately defeat the Germans might serve to strengthen the morale of the population of the USSR. Hence it was pointed out that the British did not panic even when they alone faced the superior German forces; the immensity of American production was adduced as a guarantee of victory in a struggle which was basically a "war of motors."[57]

In those first desperate months of the invasion, Soviet policy seemed to clutch at every straw which might afford some help. As noted above, Slav solidarity was stressed; Czechoslovak and Polish units were allowed to form in the USSR. At the same time, occasional appeals to working-class solidarity were voiced, including vain efforts to arouse disaffection in Finland, Hungary, and even Germany.[58] As the war went on, the Soviet regime was both disappointed in the expectations of foreign assistance, and more sure of its own ability to defend itself. The Soviet press no longer frequently praised Western military efforts and gave less attention to the substantial Anglo-American aid which was actually arriving in the USSR than it had earlier given to the potential strength of Britain and the United States. Instead, Soviet spokesmen berated the Western powers for failure to establish a second military front.[59] In March 1943 the USSR broke off relations with the émigré Polish government, and thereafter moved steadily toward a policy of unilateral domination in East Europe.

In one area, however, the Soviet regime seemed intent on conciliating the Western powers well into the latter stages of the war. Shortly after the war the principal Comintern office was evacuated to Ufa. The Foreign Language Publishing House staff was sent to Engel's, and other personnel were scattered in Kuibyshev, Tomsk, and Central Asia.[60] In these remote districts the remaining Comintern leaders apparently had little to do, and no influence.

Doubtless the Soviet rulers, who had long regarded the international Communist movement as an expendable tool, and not a very useful one at that, were more disillusioned than ever by the failure of the Communists in most European countries to render substantial services against the Germans. Various Comintern auxiliary organizations had been disbanded between 1936 and 1942.[61] Elimination of the formal Comintern organization itself would enable the USSR to disavow Communist parties abroad if their activities became embarrassing. Foreign opinion would see the dissolution of the Comintern as a sign of the intention of the USSR to pursue a peaceful policy, or at least to abandon unlimited world revolution for the pursuit of limited national interest. Elimination of the Comintern would also relieve the Soviet Party of the formal responsibility of intervening in disputes which might arise among foreign Communist parties in the aftermath of war, and would permit the development of more covert and flexible means of control.[62]

The public announcement of the dissolution of the Comintern on May 15, 1943, hinted at some of these reasons in its stress on "new political conditions"; but it undoubtedly concealed the real situation when it declared that the development of the Communist parties had made a controlling agency superfluous.[63] High Comintern officials went to great lengths to convince their subordinates that the dissolution had nothing to do with a desire to please Great Britain and the United States.[64]

In fact, provision was made for maintaining the Comintern staff. Georgi Dimitrov received an office in Soviet Party headquarters in Moscow.[65] The Foreign Section of the Soviet Central Committee evidently became a major channel for control of foreign Communists. For example, a special "study bureau" was established in mid-1943 to consider the expulsion of Germans and Magyars from Czechoslovakia and Rumania; it included the Czech Rudolf Slánský, the Magyar János Kádár, and the Rumanian (of Ukrainian-German origin) Emile Bodnăraş.[66] For the routine propaganda activities such as supplying foreign language broadcasts and newspaper material, and for dealing with the "national committees" then being established, an organization known as "Institute No. 205" was set up in the old Comintern headquarters in Moscow. The Czechoslovak Communist Bedřich Geminder played a leading role there, under the Central Committee Foreign Section.[67] Very important were the special schools for training young foreign Communists for activities in their native countries; one near Ufa had sections for each of the major countries of occupied Europe, but none apparently for other areas except Korea.[68]

Unfortunately not much evidence is available on the relation of the Soviet Communist leaders to this complicated and covert structure. The most circumstantial reports indicate that Zhdanov was not important in its direction until 1945, although one ex-Communist maintains that Zhdanov, as chief of the Central Committee Foreign Section, gave orders to Dimitrov. Other reports indicate, however, that Shcherbakov directed the successors to the Comintern through Manuil'skii and the Hungarian Communist Ernö Gerö. There are other indications that Beria, too, was involved in directing the foreign Communists at this time.[69]

The careful preservation of the apparatus for directing Communist activity abroad shows that the Soviet rulers had by no means abandoned the aim of expansion through revolution and subversion. Consequently, any tendencies toward nationalism stopped far short of a return to historical Russian policies in the international field. Likewise, the strong national patriotic element in domestic propaganda was by no means the only current in the wartime scene. Communist theory and Communist tactics were always below the surface, when, indeed, they were not openly proclaimed in the press directed to Party members, youth, and others susceptible to the customary Marxist-Leninist line.

CHAPTER

XII

THE PARTISANS AND THE
ADVANCE INTO EAST EUROPE

From the purely military standpoint, Communist guerrilla and underground activities in East Europe during World War II were of minor significance. The real importance of the partisan episode lies in a different direction. While the institutional setting and the ideological emphasis of the Soviet system seemed to tend to stability resting on Russian national interest, partisan and underground operations revealed the continued power of Party and police. More than this, these aspects of the Soviet war effort showed that even on its home ground Communism throve on unrest. This it could do because it was willing and able when necessary to pay in traditional human values for its own success. Nor was this all; the pattern which served, at a cost, in the USSR was applied with even greater success abroad, indicating that frontiers were still to be respected or disregarded as suited Communist interests.

Many aspects of the partisan movement are still extremely obscure, largely because detailed, systematic analyses have not been published. This is especially true of the evolution of the Soviet concept of partisan warfare in the prewar period. Guerrilla or partisan tactics have a long tradition in Russia, as in most countries where the terrain is suitable for such activity. In the Civil War period, with its heterogeneous forces, shifting fronts, and uncertain political alignments, partisan warfare was at a premium; the Communist guerrilla tradition draws heavily on the feats of Red bands at that time.

The conditions of the Civil War were not likely, however, to be duplicated in a conflict between well-equipped professional armies. Apparently the Communists devoted some thought to the matter of effectively employing small, half-armed forces in such a struggle. During the Spanish Civil War, where the hastily assembled armies somewhat resembled the Civil War forces in Russia, the Communist press praised the activity of Republican guerrillas.[1] A subsequent, more analytic Soviet study has, however, made what appears to be a sounder estimate of the partisans in Spain. It points out that the Republican guerrillas never constituted a mass movement holding a considerable territory. Most units, formed in Republican-held territory, went on special missions behind the enemy lines, then returned to their own forces.[2] One reason for the ineffectiveness of these partisans was, probably, that the Communists feared the undisciplined activity of Spanish guerrillas. Nevertheless, East European Communist agents in Spain learned something from these operations.

Apparently the Chinese experience made a deeper impression on Soviet observers. Articles on Chinese partisans—frequently not distinguishing between Communist and Kuomintang groups—appeared in the Soviet and in the Comintern press.[3] The most interesting was published in June 1940.[4] It stressed the aspect of the Chinese partisan movement which contrasted most sharply with the Spanish experience: the ability of the guerrillas to control continuously the population of large areas behind the enemy lines. According to these articles five hundred of the nine hundred districts nominally occupied by the Japanese were actually bases for the partisans where Chinese authorities named the officials, mobilized men for the army, and levied taxes. In four hundred more districts, the report said, the partisans were able to carry on a "war of maneuver" against the occupation forces.

While the Spanish and the Chinese experiences impressed Soviet writers, their precise relation to the Soviet partisan movement in World War II is still uncertain. On July 3, 1941, Stalin publicly called for the formation of partisan units in the occupied areas.[5] Considering the speed with which the complex directives for implementing this order appeared—one Soviet source claims the complete scheme was worked out by July 5—it seems probable that some preliminary planning at a very high level had been done before war started.[6] German intelligence officers reached the same conclusion:

> It is not surprising, therefore, that the Soviet government (using the NKVD) prepared for band-warfare before the start of the war, by making an organizational plan, securing former members of bands, conducting secret training courses, [issuing] directions to responsible workers, etc.[7]

Moreover the fact that within a few weeks partisan detachments in widely removed areas had been similarly outfitted suggests that some material preparations had been made earlier.[8]

The elaborate plan called for a complete network of underground Party organizations parallel to those of the existing Party. The underground obkoms and raikoms were to direct all activities in their territories, except those of "diversionist" groups sent for specific missions from the Soviet army fronts. Clandestine operations included "underground" work (propaganda, sabotage, espionage) and partisan operations. Each raikom was to have its partisan detachment, while the obkom was to have a stronger unit at its disposal.[9]

While the underground network mirrored the normal Party organization, much evidence indicates that the NKVD played a major role in its formation. German reports indicate that NKVD officers and troops were numerous in the partisan detachments; even Soviet sources indicate that Party officials who had been closely associated with the NKVD, like M. A. Burmistenko in the Ukraine, were the guiding figures in partisan and underground organization.[10]

The well-nigh complete failure of the initial partisan network in the summer and autumn of 1941 must have told heavily against the prestige of the NKVD and the Party officials involved in its organization. Soviet sources admit that no underground or partisan elements could be established in the West Ukraine before the German conquest.[11] The same appears to be true of almost the entire Ukraine west of the Dnepr River, except for Kiev, Odessa, and the environs of those cities, where Soviet troops held out long enough to permit the underground to complete its preparations. No serious effort seems to have been made to organize partisans in West Belorussia or the Baltic states.

Even where elaborate partisan and underground networks had been set up before the Germans arrived, they almost universally proved ineffective as a harassment to the Germans. This was particularly true in the steppe regions of the Ukraine. Some partisan groups withdrew to isolated swamps or forests where they were surrounded and destroyed by the Germans.[12] In the Donbas the extensive underground apparatus collapsed through the flight or defection of its members and had to be rebuilt from the start.[13] A large partisan force was developed in the Crimean mountains. Hampered by a huge mass of civilian refugees, and harassed by the Tatars, it seems, however, to have been a greater drain on Soviet resources than on the Germans'.[14] Even in East Belorussia, where the greatest effort was made and the most favorable terrain existed, partisans were scattered and ineffective throughout the autumn.[15] Only in the Leningrad area, where Zhdanov's Party organization directed an extensive partisan movement in close proximity to the army fronts, did the original network survive more or less intact.

Lack of complete evidence and the peripheral nature of the subject to this study preclude a full explanation of the initial failure of the partisan movement. One factor of considerable importance, however, was the schematic and overambitious nature of the network. The numerous small detachments were distributed without much regard to terrain. In the southern Ukraine the terrain was extremely unfavorable for sustained partisan activity; consequently, partisans there were "sitting ducks" for German countermeasures. Possibly the overextended effort was influenced by the Soviet conception of Chinese Communist experience, which had stressed the number of districts controlled by the partisans.

During the winter of 1941-42, the partisan movement revived. No doubt the most important cause was the series of Soviet victories, which convinced the general population of the occupied areas, potential recruits, and the surviving partisans themselves that resistance to the Germans meant being on the winning side. German atrocities, especially starvation of prisoners of war, induced thousands of Red Army stragglers to form partisan bands or join existing ones.[16] Most important from the organizational point of view was the role of the Red Army in contacting and reorganizing the scattered and demoralized partisans. According to some reports, the Red Army front commands took over direction of the partisans from the NKVD as early as mid-July 1941.[17] The military commanders were not markedly successful in reviving the partisan movement, however, until the German defeat at Moscow in December 1941. During the following winter the Germans were unable to reconstitute a continuous defense line. Consequently, the partisans were able to maintain direct contact with the Red Army through large gaps in the front near Vitebsk and north of Briansk.[18]

From this time on, the Red Army maintained a measure of control over the activities of partisans operating near the front lines. The partisans were of some value to the military in securing information on German activities. Their greatest contribution to Red Army operations, however, was the disruption of German communications. From the beginning of the war the partisans tried to disrupt rail and highway transport serving the German army, but at first were not very successful. During 1942-43, however, the Red Army made an intensive effort to strengthen partisan units near the front by sending in militarily competent officers and specialists.[19] As a result, the partisan detachments in the Briansk area and Belorussia were able by a "war on the railroads" to hamper seriously German efforts to halt the Soviet offensives in 1943.[20] In proportion to the number of men engaged in partisan activities, however, the military accomplishments were meager.[21]

By the spring of 1942, the Soviet regime had begun to regain its equilibrium; it could afford to consider long-range political objectives as well as sheer military survival. It was time, therefore, to return to the first, and in the long run the most important purpose of the partisan movement: to maintain the Communist "presence" in the occupied territories. As one early partisan leader puts it,

> The very fact of the distribution of leaflets demonstrated most clearly to the people tortured and suffering under the occupiers' yoke that regardless of the temporary departure of the Red Army from the West Ukraine the Soviet power had not gone. It existed, it lived, it was expressed by the activities of the underground organization of Soviet patriots.[22]

To achieve the dominant political objective, a new organization was needed to supervise the partisans. On May 30, 1942, the Central Staff seemed to reinforce Red Army control over the partisans, for the nominal director was Marshal Voroshilov.[23] Real power, however, was evidently in the hands of the Chief of Staff, P. K. Ponomarenko, a high Party official, who signed operational orders.[24] Nikita Khrushchev was the director of the Ukrainian staff, with T. A. Strokach, deputy commissar of the interior of the Ukraine, as his chief of staff.[25] Moreover, both the Central Staff and the Ukrainian staff remained in Moscow, where they were in close contact with the central Party direction.[26]

At lower levels, the Red Army continued to exercise somewhat more influence. Regional staffs in charge of partisan activities within approximately one hundred miles of the military fronts remained attached to army commands.[27] Even in these staffs, however, Party and police officials predominated. For example, the chief of the Orel oblast staff, which directed most of the partisans in the Briansk forest, was the obkom first secretary, a former "Chekist," and his principal lieutenant was a state security officer.[28] In the NKVD itself the Fourth Administration dealt with partisan affairs; significantly, the second in command of this administration was one Major

General Eitingon, who had advised the Spanish Republicans on partisan operations.[29]

Most partisan officers in the field were also closely connected to the police or the Party apparatus. Some were the survivors of the initial phase of partisan organization, or had been sent later to the occupied areas to organize partisan groups. Other Party and NKVD officials had fled to the woods to avoid capture and probable execution by the Germans. Once there, they joined with Red Army men who had been cut off by the rapid German advance to form resistance groups which gradually became organized partisan units.[30] After the autumn of 1942 the partisan units received a heavy influx of peasants seeking to avoid conscription for labor in Germany. As a result, if one considers the war period as a whole, the share of Communists in the rank and file of the partisan movement was not much higher than the proportion of Communists in the general male population of military age. A recent Soviet source—which makes the very probably exaggerated claim that the total number of persons in the partisan movement by 1943 was over one million—maintains that Communists constituted 16.2 per cent of all partisans.[31] More specific data from Soviet sources indicate a much lower Party contribution. In the Ukraine there were only 14,875 Communists and 26,000 Komsomols in a total of 220,000 enrolled in partisan and underground activities.[32] In the much larger Belorussian partisan and underground movement there were ultimately 25,000 Communists and 73,000 Komsomols.[33] If there were only 40,000 Communists in all aspects of partisan and underground work in these major areas of activity, it seems extremely doubtful that the general proportion exceeded 7 or 8 per cent.

The politically diluted composition of the partisans made discipline hard to maintain. In spite of the efforts of their veteran Party, police, or regular army commanders, rank-and-file partisans (and some officers) tended, after a protracted period of quasi-independence, to resent the imposition of firm discipline which followed re-establishment of regular air and radio contact with the Soviet hinterland. Even when the members of a unit were not locally recruited, they often formed romantic attachments in nearby villages. The relative security of these familiar villages softened the partisans, who dreaded bringing down German reprisals by too active operations.[34]

This "quiet" state of affairs did not please the Soviet regime. The population of the occupied regions had to be convinced that a settled life was impossible under German occupation. The key to the partisan attainment of this political objective was willingness to incur an enormous amount of human suffering and loss of life. Ordinarily this sacrifice was justified by an appeal to military necessity:

> I knew, of course, that the Hitlerites might send a punitive expedition to the village, accuse its citizens of contacts with the partisans and cruelly avenge themselves on the peaceful population. But I also knew that the population, which was driven to repair the enemy's roads, whether voluntarily or involuntarily, delayed the hour of victory by some time. But who can determine what a minute of military activity costs?[35]

Later on, however, the same writer admits that political considerations prevailed even where the military importance of embroiling the population in partisan activities was slight:

> From the purely military standpoint this was insignificant, simple diversion, but its political significance was enormous. Henceforth the enemy could no longer count on helpers in these villages. They had become those of the partisans.[36]

The willingness of the regime to sacrifice its citizens for political objectives is once again evident.

The solution to the attachment of the partisans to the local population was the formation of "raiding detachments." During the autumn of 1942, overcoming the resistance of partisans who objected to leaving "their" villages, the most forceful partisan officers organized a half-dozen mobile groups of one to two thousand men each. Once formed, these detachments were placed under the direct command of the Central Staff and the Ukrainian staff, for they were destined to serve a special political objective. Down to the end of 1942, Soviet partisans were confined almost exclusively (aside from the ill-fated Crimean units) to the forest and swamp regions of Belorussia, Leningrad, and Briansk. While, as noted above, the partisans had some secondary military value in those areas, they could do little to disrupt German economic exploitation of the occupied territories. The regions in which the partisans operated had a food deficit in peacetime; hence the Germans even if undisturbed could not have obtained many agricultural products there. These regions also had comparatively little industry; almost the only important resource which the partisans could deny the Germans was timber. The far richer and more heavily populated areas of the western and southern Ukraine, on the other hand, were practically undisturbed by partisan activity.

The principal mission assigned the raiding bands, therefore, was to push southward and westward, disrupting economic and social life as they advanced. While some raiding detachments operated in Belorussia, the most important went to the Ukraine. Five major groups entered the Ukraine from the Briansk forest in the winter of 1942-43, and others followed from Briansk and Belorussia in subsequent months. A mounted band under Mikhail Naumov, an NKVD officer, moved across the wooded steppe region, crossed the Dnepr River on the ice, and then moved north to the forest above Kiev and Zhitomir.[37] The four other groups, under Aleksei Fedorov, Ia. I. Mel'nik, Sidor Kovpak, and Aleksandr Saburov (also an NKVD officer), moved directly across the northern wooded area of the Ukraine to the Volhynian area annexed from Poland in 1939.[38] There they came into contact with Ukrainian nationalist forces. The latter reacted by forming their own partisan movement; but to some extent this development also suited the Communist purpose of disrupting normal life in the West Ukraine. In the summer of 1943 Kovpak's detachment increased the area of disruption by a daring raid across Volhynia and Galicia to the Carpathians. There, however, the hostility of the peasantry, combined with German countermeasures, proved too much for the Red partisans, who were almost annihilated.[39]

As they moved into the former Polish territories of West Belorussia and the West Ukraine, the Red partisans were already beginning to serve Communist expansionist aims. Polish nationalist underground forces were important only in the northwest corner of the West Ukraine, for they were limited by the fierce opposition of the Ukrainian nationalists.[40] The Poles maintained, however, a strong underground throughout West Belorussia. As the Communist partisans increased in strength, they sought to destroy the influence of the Poles.[41] One method was ruthless military armed assault. In addition, the Communists sought to win the support of the local population by the formation of "anti-Fascist committees" in place of the usual restoration of Soviet administrative authority.[42]

The partisan issue was no small factor behind the eventual all-out attack of Soviet forces on the Polish "Home Army." In the early days of the war the Soviet and the Comintern press was full of appeals to the conquered nations of Europe to rise in armed rebellion against the occupying forces. At this stage it is quite likely that the overriding, if not the only, aim of the Soviet regime was to obtain a measure of relief from the terrifying

German attack. At a time when the USSR was suffering millions of military and civilian deaths to hold off the Germans, Soviet spokesmen resented any sign of "humanity" on the part of allied nations. For example, General Douglas MacArthur was sharply criticized for declaring Manila an open city to avoid subjecting its population to Japanese attack.[43] A little later when Winston Churchill told Stalin that he feared a premature landing in France would bring down Hitler's vengeance on the French people, Stalin's reply was "an oppressive silence." [44]

Given this Soviet reaction to "mild" tactics by major allies in distant theaters, one can readily guess the Soviet attitude toward the unwillingness of the large, well-organized Polish underground to make an immediate all-out attack on the Germans. With most of the lines of communication from Germany to the Soviet fronts passing through Poland, an early uprising of the Polish underground might have had a significant, though hardly decisive, effect on the German forces in the USSR. Undoubtedly, however, such an attack would have led to horrible German reprisals in Poland, where the dense population and lack of extensive wooded areas made sustained partisan operations difficult.

At first the Soviet press appeared to think there was a chance of inciting widespread fighting in Poland.[45] When these overtures failed, the premier-in-exile, General Władysław Sikorski, was denounced for referring to the danger of "drowning the nation in a sea of blood," for the Germans were already doing this in spite of Polish passivity.[46] Later the Polish underground was attacked by the Soviet press for not leading an uprising to rescue the Jews of the Warsaw ghetto.[47] Meanwhile, Soviet and Comintern leaders took secret steps to revive Polish Communist activity. As early as September 1941 a group of Polish Communists in the USSR prepared to go to Polish territory, and some were actually parachuted into Poland by the end of the year.[48] Within Poland a small group of Communists organized a partisan movement, known as the "National Guard," distinct from the much larger nationalist underground. A "Kósciuszko" radio station supposedly representing this body, but actually in Soviet territory, sent greetings to Stalin as early as the autumn of 1942.[49] The "National Guard" partisans strictly limited their activities to territory the USSR recognized as Polish, although they did send a contact group to Soviet partisans operating in the Polish-claimed West Ukraine.[50] By 1944, on the other hand, Soviet partisan groups, including Naumov's raiding detachment, were operating within what even the Soviet Union recognized as the Polish frontier.[51] The aim of the Soviet bands was to assist the Red Army advance, and to disrupt the underground organization of the Home Army. Apparently their success among the hostile Polish peasantry was limited, for the Soviet partisan groups were disbanded soon after the main body of the Red Army entered ethnic Polish territory.[52]

The relation of the Soviet partisans to Communism in Czechoslovakia was more complex. The Soviet press also complained about Czech passivity toward the German occupation. Probably because the Czech underground constituted a much slighter obstacle than the Polish Home Army to Communist plans for expansion, and was in a less strategic position to aid the Soviet forces by disrupting German communications, the complaints were not as strident as those directed at the Poles.[53]

Real Soviet interest in partisans in Czechoslovakia first centered on the Carpatho-Ruthenian province in the extreme east which had been under Hungarian control since 1939. This area was ethnically Ukrainian; the Soviet regime apparently decided at an early stage of the war to try to acquire it. The Carpatho-Ruthenian (or Transcarpathian) Ukrainian Communist Party was moderately strong, and was able to carry out minor partisan operations. The backbone of the Communist organizational force in this area was composed, however, of nominally loyal Czechoslovak officers in units accompanying the Red Army in 1944.[54]

The next, and most important, Czechoslovak area where the Soviet regime sought to arouse partisan activity was Slovakia, since 1939 nominally independent but actually a German puppet. In 1943, it is said, the Central Staff of the partisan movement began collecting Slovaks who had defected from Slovak occupation forces in the USSR to form a nucleus for a partisan uprising in Slovakia.[55] In 1944 the Ukrainian staff of the partisan movement (which had moved to Kiev after the recapture of the city) began active preparations for sending parachutist teams to Slovakia. The most prominent Czechoslovak Communist leaders who participated were Ján Šverma, who was killed in the subsequent uprising, and Rudolf Slánský.[56] In April 1944 a training school was set up near Rovno for Czech, Slovak, and Polish partisans. Experienced Soviet partisan commanders were detailed to guide them, and accompanied the parachute teams returning to their native countries.[57]

In August 1944 the Communist-led partisans, without informing the principal anti-Nazi body, the Slovak National Council, suddenly greatly increased their activities. As a result, the Germans began to occupy Slovakia, while the rank-and-file anti-Nazi Slovaks rallied to the Communist partisans as the only force actively opposing the Germans. At this point the Slovak

National Council ordered the Slovak army, led by Colonel Ján Golian, to begin a general uprising against the Germans. Golian hoped for a quick Red Army advance. When this did not occur—either for strategic reasons or because the Communists were glad to see the non-Communist military element in the uprising eliminated—Golian's regular military forces were destroyed.[58] The Communist-led partisans, fighting against heavy German attacks, but reinforced from the USSR by air, and later by Soviet partisan groups penetrating the eastern portion of Slovakia, contributed to the continuing turmoil in the country. The resultant disruption of the social fabric and the destruction of the administrative framework were significant factors favoring the rise of Slovak Communism after the German defeat.[59] For example, the Communists as a result of the uprising secured 50 per cent of all official posts after the Germans were driven from Slovakia, and obtained a dominant position in the unified Marxist parties.[60]

The partisan movement played a very much smaller part in the development of Communist control of the remaining countries bordering on the USSR. In spite of the large Soviet partisan concentrations near their borders, neither Rumania nor Finland seems to have been troubled by guerrilla incursions or by native partisan activities.[61] Probably the strong and united opposition of the peasantry in these countries to Communism convinced the Soviet planners that a partisan effort there would be too costly.

The situation in Hungary was slightly more favorable from the Soviet standpoint. Some old Hungarian Communists from the period of Béla Kún's government still lived in the USSR, and other pro-Communists deserted from Hungarian occupation units.[62] With such recruits, several small partisan detachments were formed, including one commanded by a Hungarian officer who had gained experience in Fedorov's band. In 1944 these detachments arrived with, or just ahead of, the Red Army advance in eastern Slovakia and Transcarpathia. There they recruited members from among the Magyar minority, then advanced into north Hungary. Their activities had an almost negligible influence politically as well as militarily, however, since the Red Army itself had entered Hungary by that time.[63]

Paradoxically, the success of Communist partisans in East Europe was enormously greater in Balkan countries which did not adjoin the USSR than it was in those countries where the Soviet partisans could offer direct aid to the native units. No doubt a major reason was the long-standing antipathy of neighboring countries to the USSR, combined with their growing fear of Communist expansion. The major source of Balkan partisan success, however, was the early and successful start of the Yugoslav Communists.

Yugoslavia was an extremely favorable area for guerrilla activity, both because of its long tradition of guerrilla resistance to invaders, and because of its mountainous terrain. The first guerrilla groups to take advantage of these factors in World War II, however, were not Communists, but Chetniks under the royal Yugoslav officer Draža Mihajlović, who began activities against the Germans while the USSR was still bound by the Nazi-Soviet pact. Apparently there was considerable argument in the Communist Party over the wisdom of placing principal reliance on partisans, as contrasted to relying on underground organizational work in the cities.[64] Josip Broz-Tito, the general secretary of the Yugoslav Party, decided on the partisan effort, however, and some weeks after the German invasion of the USSR transferred Party headquarters to the partisan groups. In the autumn of 1941, Tito and Mihajlović, after a brief period of co-operation, came into open conflict. The Chetniks operated in relatively small areas where they had been recruited. Consequently, they were reluctant to undertake operations which would bring down harsh German reprisals on their families. The nucleus of the partisans, on the other hand, consisted of hardened Communists who had no such scruples. The Communists had come to the mountains from distant parts of the country; moreover, as dedicated members of the prewar Communist underground they had long been isolated from normal society.[65] At the same time, the Communists secretly viewed the partisan uprising as an opportunity to destroy the framework of "bourgeois" administration.[66] They doubtless also realized that the extensive social disruption which would accompany drastic partisan activities and the consequent German reprisals would prepare the ground for Communism.

After their break with Mihajlović, the partisans, under strong German attack, quickly abandoned their original territorial scheme of organization and placed their headquarters in a large group which moved considerable distances over the central part of Yugoslavia.[67] Gradually they came to be much stronger than Mihajlović's forces. The reasons are so complex that they can only be suggested here. They included the affinity of partisan intransigence to the reckless martial tradition of a large portion of the Yugoslav people; the supranational character of the partisans, as compared to the narrowly Serbian attitude of the Chetniks; and the decision of the British to confine dispatch of munitions to the partisans, as the group which was most actively combatting the Germans.

Until more research—especially on Yugoslav sources—can be undertaken, one cannot say with assurance whether the remarkable parallels between Yugoslav and Soviet partisan tactics and programs were due to systematic exchange of information, or to spontaneous reactions, following from mutually shared Communist objectives, to similar situations. According to an early Comintern report, 500 International Brigade veterans were in the Yugoslav partisans by mid-1942, including 42 junior officers, 39 sergeants, and 15 political commissars of the Republican army.[68] Some of these men may have been familiar with Communist direction of Spanish partisan activities, and with whatever "principles" Soviet intelligence may have deduced from this experience. At the same time the internal Soviet press stressed the importance of political indoctrination in the Yugoslav partisans, and noted that they studied (apparently on the basis of radio broadcasts) the experience of the Red Army and the Soviet partisans.[69]

In 1942 the Soviet Union was reluctant to identify itself with the Communist partisans of Yugoslavia. Consequently, the stress on the political background and indoctrination of the partisans of Yugoslavia, and their use of Soviet experience was all the more remarkable. It probably indicates the extreme desire of the Soviet regime to impress upon the Yugoslavs and other Communists the importance of utilizing Soviet experience. As early as 1942 a secret Soviet handbook stated that "the Red partisans of the Ukraine must be a model for other countries in the organization of the Red partisan movement." [70]

This was a vital matter because, as *Bol'shevik* put it as early as 1943, "the Yugoslav partisans by their example are stimulating the partisan struggle in Albania and Greece." [71] William H. McNeill, an American correspondent in Greece, has contended that there was probably no direct contact between Soviet and Greek Communists between the outbreak of war and 1944.[72] McNeill and C. E. M. Woodhouse, chief of the British mission to the Greek partisans, and the other principal Western source on wartime Greek Communist activities, place contacts between the Yugoslav and the Greek Communists much later than a recent Soviet source, which states that a representative of the Yugoslav partisan general staff came to Macedonia to establish contact with Greek and Bulgarian partisans in the autumn of 1942.[73] It seems likely, therefore, that the Yugoslavs were in close contact with the Greeks at least a year before regular Soviet-Greek Communist communications were established. At a later period Yugoslav spokesmen talked as though the Greek partisans were their special protégés.[74] In contrast, however, to the really determined attack of the Yugoslavs on German communications, ELAS, as the Communist-led Greek partisan organization was called, tended to avoid important military attacks on the Germans, and even made agreements with their Greek puppets. This difference does not necessarily mean, as Woodhouse contends, however, that the Greek Communists were departing from general Communist policy.[75] By the time they became effective in late 1942 the pressure on the USSR had diminished, and Greek partisan activities would have directly benefited only the British forces in Egypt. At the same time, by avoiding major clashes with the occupation troops, ELAS was able to turn its forces to the destruction of non-Communist partisans.

Balkan Communist partisan co-operation extended to the Albanians, who were under close Yugoslav supervision, but followed the same general tactics toward the occupation forces and rival Communist groups as did the Greeks. The Bulgarian partisans, who started with Yugoslav co-operation in 1941, were slow in developing, since Bulgaria was on the temporarily victorious side. In 1944 increased Bulgarian partisan strength played a part in the exceptionally harsh and rapid destruction of non-Communist elements in the government which brought about Bulgaria's change of sides in the war.[76]

Despite their utility to the Soviet regime while it was confronted by German occupation forces, the Soviet partisans tended to become a liability when the war was drawing to a close. As noted earlier, some large units were used for raids beyond the Soviet frontier. They were not very effective, but whatever losses they incurred conveniently disposed of men who were no longer useful. Partisans were sometimes used as cadres for re-establishment of the Communist apparatus and Soviet administration. Soviet sources comment, however, that former partisans used in these capacities tended to "live in the past" or to employ methods "appropriate to the partisan struggle" rather than persuasion, but "one way or another" these faults were corrected.[77] Other partisans were incorporated wholesale into the Red Army.[78] Finally, according to émigré reports, many intractable partisans were liquidated.

These "solutions" applied to the rank and file and the lower officers of the partisans, whose experience of relative independence and addiction to violence made them unsettling elements in the postwar Soviet society. Higher officers, on the other hand, formed a valuable element of the Party and police apparatus. Since the war a remarkable number of major posts have gone to men whose leadership abilities and loyalty were tested under the extremely difficult conditions of partisan and underground warfare.[79]

In the postwar years the partisan movement in general received enormous attention in the Soviet Union. Nikita Khrushchev and other regional Party leaders devoted a large part of their speeches in the first postwar Party congresses to the partisans. General accounts of the war period devote much space to partisan and underground activities. Stories of specific partisan operations, published in large editions designed especially for Soviet youths, appeared frequently. A recent Soviet bibliography of memoir material on World War II devotes eight of twenty-seven pages to partisan accounts.[80] For a long time no special organization of partisan veterans was permitted, but by 1957 a "Section of Former Partisans" had appeared in the Soviet Committee of Veterans of the War.[81]

It is not hard to see why the Communist Party of the Soviet Union has stressed the wartime partisan movement. In contrast to other spheres of active fighting, it could be treated (with the NKVD role conveniently minimized) as the creation of the Party alone. While the essential inhumanity of partisan tactics has been glossed over, sacrificial, disciplined obedience to Party orders, and even ruthless dedication to attainment of political goals, are qualities which the Party wishes to inculcate in the rising generation of Soviet youth. Presentation of these qualities through the readily dramatized history of the partisan movement has evidently proved an effective weapon of political indoctrination.

CHAPTER
XIII

THE "ZHDANOVSHCHINA"

The Soviet Union completely triumphed over its enemies in World War II, although the cost in human lives and material destruction was greater absolutely, and probably relatively, than that incurred by any of the vanquished nations. For the totalitarian Soviet system, however, such losses were endurable if the framework of control over the surviving population could be maintained. The physical instruments of control were intact, but the underlying ideological framework was badly shaken. About one-fourth of the postwar population had lived in German-occupied areas where, as Communist observers uneasily noted, it had been cut off from Soviet information and exposed to "Fascist" ideology.[1] As noted in Chapter XIV, the regime found it especially hard to restore full regimentation of the peasants in the collective farms after reoccupation of these areas. Soviet co-operation with Great Britain and the United States during World War II enabled some Soviet citizens to catch a glimpse of Western life. Official Soviet expressions of friendship for the Western allies, though very restricted in the domestic press during most periods of the war, gave many elements in the USSR the impression that the policy of hostility to all "bourgeois" ideas was somewhat relaxed. To many, vistas of continued postwar collaboration with the West held out the hope of real diminution of totalitarianism at home.

A recent Soviet study implicitly recognizes the danger which these foreign contacts presented to the Soviet control system by charging that the Western allies used their magazines distributed in the USSR to "propagandize the superiority of the American way of life among the Soviet people," revivifying "survivals of capitalism" in the consciousness of "backward elements" of the population. Even the increased contacts with the outside world resulting from United Nations membership were regarded as dangerous.[2]

Most of the Soviet population, however, had obtained only second-hand acquaintance with life and thought outside the Soviet Union. The position of the returning Soviet prisoners of war and *Ostarbeiter* was considerably more delicate. It is true that they had suffered at least as much as the occupied population from Nazi misdeeds; at the same time, however, they had seen at first hand the enormously higher living standards and the considerably greater personal freedom even in much of Nazi-dominated Central and Western Europe compared to the USSR.[3]

According to Soviet statistics, 5,115,709 Soviet citizens were freed from the Germans beyond the 1941 boundary of the USSR. Somewhat more than half were recovered in territory occupied by the Red Army; the rest were returned to Soviet control (in part, forcibly) by the British and American forces.[4] The latter did, however, permit refugees from the territory annexed by the USSR in 1939 and later to remain in the West.

A special Central Committee decree appeared in 1945 on measures for reindoctrinating repatriated Soviet citizens. Reindoctrination started at the frontier. For example, on the Moldavian border there was a "TASS window" which provided photographic displays from the Soviet news agency concerning the Yalta conference, the defeat of Japan, and similar themes, as well as hundreds of copies of Soviet newspapers and magazines, and an extensive lecture program.[5] These measures, however, were only the "soft sell" of the Soviet campaign for reintegrating the returnees, all of whom were regarded as having at least passively collaborated with the enemy. Accounts which maintain that all were sent to concentration camps exaggerate, but it is evident that many were, and the remainder were at least suspect.[6] To underline the complete determination of the regime to tolerate no subversive element, important collaborators with the Germans, including Andrei Vlasov, were publicly announced to have been *hanged,* in contrast to the almost furtive executions of the prewar period.[7]

Even the ordinary demobilized Red Army men constituted a certain threat to the stability of the Soviet system, for most had had at least a glimpse of the outside world. The extent of the problem is indicated by the fact that over 144,000 demobilized men were in Kharkov oblast alone by the end of 1946, including nearly 17,000 ex-officers. Well over half of the former officers, and about 17 per cent of the ex-enlisted men were

Party members.[8] These demobilized Communists must have constituted a majority of the Kharkov Party membership, and they formed nearly two-thirds of that of the Ukraine as a whole.[9]

As noted in Chapter X, requirements for entrance into the Party, especially in the Red Army, were very low during the war. As soon as victory was gained, the ready access to Party membership ended. On June 26, 1946, a Central Committee decree officially provided that improvement of quality rather than further growth be the chief objective of the Party.[10] During the following years, admissions very slightly exceeded the many expulsions of members who had proved unreliable or recalcitrant to political schooling. Consequently, the six million membership at the beginning of 1946, when Party rolls were fairly stabilized, was not much changed before 1953. Of these six million, a somewhat higher proportion than before the war (32.1 as compared to 24.4 per cent) were workers, but the general educational level was higher in 1946. About half had at least secondary educations; the Party was already tending to become representative of the better-schooled portion of the population. This increased educational level was partly due to the influx of younger age groups who had profited from rising educational standards in the thirties. In 1946, 18.3 per cent (as compared to 8.9 per cent before the war) were youths under twenty-five, and 63.6 per cent were under thirty-five.[11]

Even in 1946 the age level of the general membership was beginning to diverge from that of the postpurge apparatus officials, who had entered the Party ten or more years earlier and were approaching middle age. As late as 1948, 85 per cent of a large group of newly elected raikom secretaries had entered the Party between 1920 and 1940, while nearly one-third had entered between 1920 and 1930.[12] As yet, however, no signs of friction had appeared between the two age groups. There was, indeed, no lack of opportunity for young Communists to enter the apparatus, for the turnover in its lower ranks (though not at the middle and higher levels) during and immediately following the war was extensive. In one Siberian oblast an absolute majority of primary Party organization secretaries had entered the Party during the war.[13] Forty to 50 per cent of raikom Party officials in the Ukraine and Belorussia were changed in 1945-46.[14] In Kazakhstan, far from the war zone, the turnover was even greater. In one oblast, 31.5 per cent of the obkom officials, half of the gorkom officials, and nearly half of the raikom officials were changed in 1946; and the proportion changed in 1947 was even higher.[15]

Initial moves in the process of tightening ideological control considerably preceded the end of the war. Some of the measures directed against "national deviations," such as the Central Committee decree on the Volga Tatar Party organizations, have already been noted. Other Central Committee decrees in 1944-45 provided for increased ideological work, especially by newspapers, in Belorussia and other areas.[16] The Ninth Plenum of the Soviet Writers' Union (February 1944) called for greater attention to ideological work.[17] In mid-1944 a *Bol'shevik* article complained that, due to a failure of literary critics, writers were not following Party directives.[18] A few months later, the journals *Sovetskaia Muzika* (Soviet Music) and *Sovetskoe Iskusstvo* (Soviet Art) specifically warned Soviet operatic composers against exhibiting pro-Western tendencies.[19]

A more important move in the direction of discrediting foreign influences in Soviet culture was the sharp denunciation of the third volume of the *History of Philosophy* for overestimating the value of Hegel's philosophical work.[20] The attack was the more significant because the principal editor of the work was G. F. Aleksandrov, Deputy Director of the Propaganda and Agitation Administration. Aleksandrov, a young and highly trained indoctrination specialist, had been rising very rapidly and was rumored to have intimate connections with Stalin.[21] The attack on the *History of Philosophy* was apparently not directed against him personally, however, for several other major Soviet philosophers were on its editorial board. At any rate, Aleksandrov was able the following year to take the lead in reversing the "hate-the-German" line.[22]

Undoubtedly the further development of the reindoctrination campaign was related to personal alignments and rivalries at the top of the Soviet power structure. Unfortunately, these complex intrigues remain very obscure. Three careful attempts by outside observers (Boris Meissner, Boris Nicolaevsky, and N. Gradoboev) to explain them are helpful, but to a considerable extent contradictory.[23] Nevertheless, the developments were so important that a brief sketch of the ascertainable facts is essential.

At the close of the war Stalin was sixty-six; for the first time published photographs showed that he was graying.[24] He apparently spent the late summer and autumn of each year in secluded rest in the Caucasus. Under these circumstances, the question of succession was an obvious one. Stalin was vigorous enough, however, to destroy anyone who seemed to compete with him for public attention. The most popular hero of the war, Marshal Georgii Zhukov, was suddenly dispatched to command the obscure Urals Military District in the autumn of 1946, and dismissed from the Central

Committee.[25] It is said that other officers who showed signs of independence were imprisoned.[26] A. N. Poskrebyshev, Stalin's faithful chief secretary, was made a major general, perhaps in ironic recognition of his role in curbing the military.[27]

The most rapidly rising among Stalin's lieutenants, however, was Georgii Malenkov. The State Defense Committee (GOKO) was abolished at the end of the war, but Malenkov remained important as a Deputy Chairman of the Council of Commissars as well as a Central Committee Secretary. A well-informed defector has maintained that Malenkov lost prestige in mid-1945 because of failures in the industries he supervised, but down to the second half of 1946 he was mentioned very prominently in the Soviet press, and appeared close to Stalin on public occasions.[28] In mid-March 1946 the first Central Committee plenum in five years made Malenkov a full member of the Politburo.[29]

The March plenum also raised Beria to full Politburo membership, indicating that his resignation two months earlier as Commissar of the Interior had not reduced his importance.[30] A little later, however, he evidently suffered a severe loss of power when the Party Secretary A. A. Kuznetsov was delegated to supervise the police.[31]

The new Orgburo and the Secretariat confirmed by the March 1946 plenum indicated the advance of a number of little-known officials; as far as their affiliations can be determined, however, the new promotees were fairly evenly distributed among rival groups in the leadership. It is also hard to guess the political leanings in that period of N. A. Bulganin, who was made a Politburo candidate. A. N. Kosygin, the other new Politburo candidate, had had an important role in the supervision of war industry, where he was associated with Mikoian.

Nearly all observers agree, however, that Malenkov's principal rival was Andrei Zhdanov. During the early stage of the war Zhdanov was occupied with the defense of Leningrad; he may also have been under a cloud because of the Finnish fiasco of 1939-40, but this is impossible to prove. In the later stages of the war, on the other hand, the raising of the Leningrad siege appeared to free Zhdanov for broader tasks. Nevertheless, he was not named to the GOKO, and Malenkov and Molotov rather than Zhdanov received the principal credit for the defense of Leningrad at the January 1945 ceremonies celebrating the event.[32] It is rumored that shortly before this Zhdanov had suffered an additional loss of prestige through a rebellion of Leningrad partisans, with whom he had been closely associated.[33] In 1944 Zhdanov had been designated to supervise the fulfillment of the

Finnish armistice. This assignment probably kept him in Helsinki during considerable periods, but he appeared fairly often in Moscow during 1944-45.[34]

Perhaps as important as Zhdanov's availability was the illness and death of Aleksandr Shcherbakov in the spring of 1945. There has been much speculation about the relation between the two men. Shcherbakov's career history fairly clearly indicates his early dependence on Zhdanov; it is even said that Shcherbakov married Zhdanov's daughter. It is also rumored, however, that Shcherbakov deserted Zhdanov when the latter's prestige declined, joining Malenkov's rising group.[35] In any case, during the war Shcherbakov, as Central Committee Secretary, apparently supervised the important propaganda apparatus which had been Zhdanov's special province, although Aleksandrov was the immediate director. Within slightly more than a year after Shcherbakov's death, Zhdanov resumed control of propaganda affairs, becoming the spokesman for the most intensive campaign for ideological "purity" ever conducted in the USSR. This campaign, which became known as the "Zhdanovshchina," or "Zhdanov affair," was a continuation of the trend to reindoctrination which had set in in 1944.

Zhdanov was, however, by no means all-powerful. Several major appointments, for example, went to men who were not closely associated with him. Perhaps the most important was that of V. M. Andrianov who, in the autumn of 1946, became director of the Administration for Verification of Party Organs, which had been formed to replace the Organization-Instruction Section, but had more extensive powers.[36] About the same time Andrianov became a vice-chairman of the Council on Kolkhoz Affairs, established to deal with the critical agricultural problem.[37] As the very important deputy directors for political affairs of the MTS reported to the Administration for Verification, Andrianov was in a key position in farm matters.[38]

Some observers have maintained that Andrianov was a close adherent of Malenkov; others contend he was one of Beria's henchmen. In any case, Malenkov and Andrianov must have worked together during 1946-47. Malenkov, as Deputy Chairman of the Council of Ministers (as the Council of Commissars was renamed in March 1946) was placed in charge of agricultural matters; he was given credit for supervising the increased harvest of 1947.[39] Nevertheless, Malenkov was at that time no longer mentioned as a Central Committee Secretary, the listed Secretaries at the end of 1947 being Stalin, Zhdanov, G. M. Popov, Zhdanov's close associate A. A. Kuznetsov, and a new Secretary, M. A. Suslov, who presumably replaced Malenkov.[40]

While the changes just described were taking place, a second postwar plenum of the Central Committee, probably the last until 1952, convened. The February 1947 plenum was devoted primarily to agricultural matters, with Andreev, not Malenkov, reporting. In addition, the plenum elected N. A. Voznesenskii to full membership in the Politburo.[41]

The shift in Party balance in 1946-48 seemed reflected at lower Party levels as well as in the Politburo. Even before the war had ended, the Union Republic Parties began to hold plenums regularly. Agriculture continued to be the principal single topic discussed at the plenums, especially during the drought crisis of early 1947. Between June 1946 and the end of 1948, however, a large group of Union Republic plenums dealt with economic matters only seventy times, as compared to one hundred considerations of political questions.[42] In the latter category, about one-third were questions of mass indoctrination or cultural control. An even larger proportion of plenums held in the areas formerly occupied by the Germans considered questions of propaganda and ideology. In Belorussia, seven of the nine plenums for which information is available considered these subjects; four of eight in Moldavia; eleven of sixteen in Estonia; five of nine in Lithuania; nine of eleven in Latvia. Plenum consideration of indoctrinational questions was less evident in Azerbaidzhan (three of seven) and Armenia (five of thirteen), and scarcely greater than during the prewar period in Georgia and the Central Asian Republics. At the same time, indoctrination specialists such as the propaganda secretaries, who ordinarily occupied rather obscure positions in the apparatus compared to the "line" secretaries, achieved an unparalleled prominence in plenum discussions.[43]

Of the various aspects of the emphasis on ideological matters in 1946-48, the new system of Party training is perhaps the least spectacular, but among the most important in its long-range effects. During the Great Purge the structure of high-level Party schooling had been disrupted by the abolition of institutions like the Institute of the Red Professors, "infested" by Old Bolsheviks. The new program of study centering around the *Short Course* was intended to secure complete ideological conformity among Party officials as well as rank-and-file Communists. The Society for the Propagation of Political and Scientific Knowledge, formed in May 1947, was designed to reach an even larger audience with lectures and popular treatises. One of its principal purposes was to propagate atheism, in opposition to the revival of religion which had been permitted during the war.[44] None of these indoctrination systems, however, could provide the concentrated, high-level training necessary for the apparatus officials. The "Evening Universities of Marxism-Leninism" provided somewhat more comprehensive training, but their part-time programs were designed primarily for intellectuals and technicians not in the Party apparatus itself. In early 1942 two-month courses for propagandists were started in a few major cities, and in 1944 the Central Committee ordered the establishment of year-long courses for a broader range of apparatus workers in some fifty cities.[45]

Probably the circumstances of the war delayed the full implementation of this decree. The real foundation for Party training seems to have been laid by a Central Committee decree of August 2, 1946, "On Preparation and Re-preparation of Directing Party and Soviet Workers." [46] The new decree systematized the middle level of Party schools by providing that they be established in the Union Republic capitals and in thirty-five other Ukrainian and Russian regional centers. The schools were to provide two-year, full-time training courses, though the shorter programs were also continued. The schools provided instruction for the lowest levels of the apparatus: raikom secretaries and instructors, directors of sections of the raikom or of the state raion executive committee; and full-time secretaries of primary Party organizations. The course in the Ukrainian Republic school was gradually extended during the next decade to four years, placing it on a par with the Higher Party School of the Central Committee.[47] The latter formed the apex of the regular training system, providing nine-month short courses and correspondence courses in addition to the full program, initially set at three years.

In the Higher Party School the full-time faculty was of university-level competence, although, of course, the members were selected for political reliability. The students, who numbered several hundred in each class, included important middle-level officials such as obkom first secretaries. The curricula were varied, including special programs for state officials, Party "line" officials (generalists), and propaganda and newspaper directors, for the schools were designed as professional in-service training institutions.[48] At the same time, practical training for increased efficiency was very closely linked to enhancement of political reliability:

> A most important task of the Party schools and courses is to arm students with a deep knowledge of Marxist-Leninist theory, to inculcate habits of independent study of the works of classics of Marxism-Leninism, to teach the students of the Party schools to use the knowledge which they have obtained for the decision of real questions of Party and Soviet work in contemporary conditions.[49]

In addition to the ordinary training schools, the Central Committee decree of August 2, 1946, established an Academy of Social Sciences. This institution, with a very limited and highly qualified student body, was designed for intensive theoretical training and investigation through advanced independent research, conducted, however, under careful supervision.[50] The Academy was equipped, therefore, to play an important part in maintaining ideological control at the highest level. Its importance, and that of the new training system as a whole, is demonstrated by the very large investment of high-level Party officials in the student bodies as well as in the faculties of the schools.[51]

The ideological campaign which so deeply affected the Party apparatus reached fever pitch with the issuance on August 14, 1946, of the Central Committee decree "On the journals *Zvezda* and *Leningrad*." Both periodicals were, significantly, published in Leningrad; the fairly brief Central Committee statement was considerably amplified by a speech by Zhdanov to Leningrad writers on September 21. In the meantime, the Central Committee had issued other decisions reprimanding the theaters and the motion picture *The Great Life*.[52] The central objection was that the cultural activities involved lacked *"partiinost'."* As the first decree put it, Mikhail Zoshchenko, a popular humorist, had "preached rotten lack of ideas, banality, and apoliticalness."[53] In 1948 Zhdanov clearly set forth the basic concept behind the terms *"partiinost'"* and "socialist realism":

> Soviet literature must be able to show our heroes, must be able to look ahead to our tomorrow. This will not be Utopia, for our tomorrow is already being prepared by planned, deliberate work today.[54]

In other words, the only realistic literature serving Party interests was that which pictured things not as they were, but as they ought to be according to Party concepts. For example, the film *The Great Life* was criticized not for being against the existing state of affairs in Soviet society, but for *failing* to portray the Donbas workers as highly cultured persons living in comfortable quarters and using "the most up-to-date machinery" in the immediate postwar reconstruction when these amenities were obviously lacking.[55]

The second, closely related, line of attack accused cultural figures of "artistic incompetence." The major reason for this incompetence, however, was the fact that the writers "stand aloof from the vital contemporary issues," and do not "actively propagandize the policy of the Soviet state."[56]

At a slightly later date, glorification of Soviet policy was extended to include explicit emphasis on the role of the Party. Numerous works, including Aleksandr Fadeev's *The Young Guard*, which had been widely acclaimed when it appeared in 1945, had to be revised to express this emphasis.[57]

The third major theme, stressed throughout the "Zhdanovshchina" and for many years afterward, was rejection of "the spirit of servility in relation to everything foreign."[58] This, too, was closely linked to the theme of *partiinost'*. Well before the major campaign had begun, Soviet citizens were warned that foreigners would try to undermine their ideological loyalty not by direct assaults, but by treating ideology as a matter of indifference:

> As is known, a very widespread method to which the bourgeois always resorts for strengthening its ideological influence is to try to subject the social relations of people to the relations of things. Here is a quite typical expression of one of the representatives of the American business world who, being in Moscow, said, "We like your manganese. Your manganese has one incredibly remarkable feature. It doesn't know that it is socialist. It is just as ready to go into the furnace in Pittsburgh as in Stalingrad. You like our machine tools in just the same way. They don't know that they are capitalist. They are just as ready to cut metal in Kharkov as in Detroit."[59]

In the early period of the campaign, and to some extent as long as Zhdanov lived, the rejection of foreign cultural influences tended to stress their bourgeois or aristocratic nature, and to contrast them to Communist principles. Zhdanov himself emphasized that the development of national elements was a basis for heightened international outlook: "As in everything else, it is impossible to be an internationalist in music if one is not a thorough patriot of his native land."[60] Nevertheless, the ethnocentric campaign readily fitted in with the Russian nationalism which had emerged during the war. For example, the Soviet theater was criticized for producing plays which "idealize kings, khans, and courtiers"—but all of the rulers and nobles mentioned were West European or Moslem, not the Russian Tsars whose idealized stories so frequently appeared on the Soviet stage.[61]

In line with this discrimination, the literary figures in the Union Republics were especially harshly attacked. Intensive criticism began in the Ukraine at about the time of the first Central Committee decree. The important author Ostap Vishnia was criticized for his "mocking tone" concerning the evacuees of 1941, but was most sharply attacked for defending the right of the author to make mistakes and to create unreal situations.[62] A major meeting of Kiev writers was held to "correct" the Ukrainian literary line.[63] Most attention was devoted to the insidious ideas of Ukrainian nationalism. Mykhailo Hrushevs'kyi, the greatest Ukrainian historian, had received an honorable, if obscure, obituary when he died in the thirties. When the war period revealed the potent appeal of his nationalist concepts, however, he posthumously became the chief target for Communist attacks.[64] The most extreme attacks on Ukrainian writers who used national themes did not, however, occur until after Zhdanov's death. Similarly, although the writers and historians of the Turkic peoples, and even the Armenians, were criticized for nationalist tendencies, the full weight of compulsion to glorify Russia at the expense of the smaller Soviet nations did not come until several years later.

In 1947 and 1948 the campaign for ideological "purity" extended to all branches of Soviet culture. For the most part, the themes of criticism were similar to those used in literature and drama. Three aspects of the campaign, however, suggest that certain other factors were involved.

The attack on the Hungarian-Jewish economist Eugene Varga was directed not by Zhdanov, but by Voznesenskii, who as a member of the Politburo and a professional economist was the Party spokesman in economic matters. The object of Voznesenskii's criticism was Varga's *Changes in the Economy of Capitalism as a Result of the Second World War.* This book, while denouncing capitalism, had advanced the theory that monopoly capitalism enlisting state supervision could overcome crises without resorting to war. As will appear in Chapter XIV, this contradicted Zhdanov's theory of the sharpening opposition of the "two camps." After a long discussion in May 1947 Varga lost his economics institute and his journal on international economics. He was not otherwise punished, nor was his discomfiture entirely Zhdanov's and Voznesenskii's work, for Varga did not make full confession of his errors until both these critics had disappeared from the Soviet scene.[65]

The "Zhdanovshchina" in philosophy involved more complicated themes than the economics debate. A considerable effort seemed underway to relate basic Leninist concepts to the demands of the ideological campaign. For example, M. D. Kammari, a prominent philosopher, endeavored to reconcile Zhdanov's *partiinost'* with the philosophical realism which Leninism had stressed. Kammari maintained that Marxism, pursuing the interests of the proletariat, moves in the same direction as objective history itself; consequently the interests of the proletariat and history are identical.[66]

Zhdanov's occasion for intervening directly in philosophy, however, was the discussion of Aleksandrov's newest book, *The History of Western*

European Philosophy. When the work appeared in 1946, it was highly praised; but in early 1947, evidently on direction from above, a critical discussion of the book began in the Institute of Philosophy.[67] In June Zhdanov intervened with a sweeping denunciation of the work. The most important aspects of his attack resembled those used in the criticism of literature. Aleksandrov, Zhdanov said, regarded Russian philosophy as a branch of West European philosophy. According to Zhdanov, the author failed to show that Marxist and bourgeois philosophy were fundamentally opposed:

> Such a conception [as Aleksandrov's], among us would inevitably lead to objectivism, to cringing before bourgeois philosophers and magnification of their accomplishments, to deprivation of our philosophy of a militant, aggressive spirit. But that would be a departure from the basic principle of materialism—its directedness, its *partiinost'*.[68]

At the same time, however, Zhdanov undertook to discuss certain abstract questions which had little direct relation to the general themes of the ideological campaign. Criticizing Aleksandrov's view that philosophy was an "independent sphere of knowledge," Zhdanov contended that under socialism, philosophy became a *method* for scientific research on nature and society.[69] On another point, the meaning of contradictions under socialism, however, he scarcely bothered to relate his exposition to Aleksandrov's work. "That special form of discovery and overcoming of the contradictions of socialist society (and there are these contradictions, and philosophers because of cowardice do not want to write about them)," Zhdanov said, is "criticism and self-criticism."[70] Evidently, Zhdanov's main purpose was not to demolish Aleksandrov (who lost his journal and his post as Deputy Director of the Propaganda and Agitation Section, but remained active in other directions), but to force the philosophers to become more pliant tools for the ideological campaign. He criticized the "scholastic" tendencies of the Institute of Philosophy in general, and demanded that philosophy be made accessible to nonspecialists. Philosophical works, moreover, must become more contemporary in treatment; they must enter the fight against bourgeois philosophies.[71]

As a result of Zhdanov's admonitions, a new philosophical journal, *Voprosy Filosofii,* was created in addition to the new ideological journal, *Kultura i Zhizn',* which often intervened in philosophical matters. The editor of *Voprosy Filosofii,* B. M. Kedrov, apparently took seriously the injunction to develop Marxist-Leninist philosophical concepts; for example, he permitted a lively discussion of the relation of Leninism to physics. He was also relatively moderate on matters of Russian nationalism. After Zhdanov's death, however, Kedrov was attacked for permitting the physics discussion, and removed as editor.[72]

The intrusion of the ideological campaign into musical composition came considerably later than the attacks on the other arts. Musicians assembled for a special meeting in early January 1948, where Zhdanov spoke scathingly on the deficiencies of Soviet music. Early in February the Central Committee issued a decree, primarily directed against V. Muradeli's opera *The Great Friendship,* but extending to the entire "present unsatisfactory state of Soviet music."

Many of the themes of the critiques by Zhdanov and by the Central Committee were the same as those employed earlier. Composers were accused of departing from the traditions of the "Russian school of music" and inclining toward formalism reminiscent of the "contemporary modernist bourgeois music of Europe and America which is a reflection of the morass of bourgeois culture."[73] "Anti-popular" tendencies in Soviet music were related to the earlier Central Committee decrees on literature, the theater, and motion pictures.[74]

The emphasis, however, and certain new features of the criticism, clearly distinguish the Muradeli decree from those of 1946. Zhdanov's role in the attack on musical tendencies is, of course, indisputable. Nevertheless, there is considerable evidence that by early 1948 his personal health as well as his political power was declining; and another hand seems to hover behind the music decree. It will be recalled that Zhdanov also took the public lead in the attack on operatic compositions in 1936, although the impetus was clearly Stalin's. One émigré conversant with Soviet cultural developments even maintains that the Muradeli decree was not prepared by Party officials at all, but by a group of musicians in Stalin's favor.[75]

Some aspects of the decree, while related to the general themes of the ideological campaign, clearly reflect Stalin's personal tastes. The "modernist," "formalist," and "innovationist" aspects of *The Great Friendship* were unfavorably contrasted to the traditional musical treatments Stalin preferred. Its "disharmonious" sounds were disparaged by comparison to the "wealth of folk melodies, songs, tunes, and dance motifs" which Stalin admired.[76] Moreover, the only clearly political aspect of the opera, its treatment of relations between Caucasians and Russians during the Civil War, was singled out for special criticism. Muradeli (a Georgian, as was the librettist, Mdivani) had, it was said, given the impression that Georgians and Ossetians, rather than the Ingushes and Chechens, had been anti-Russian, while (the decree proclaimed) just the reverse was true.[77] After Stalin's death, the Party officially declared that all these national distinctions were false products of Stalin's prejudice.[78]

As the preceding paragraphs suggest, the term "Zhdanovshchina" so often applied to the intense ideological campaign of 1946-48 is misleading, if it is taken to mean that Andrei Zhdanov personally conceived and carried out the campaign. Deep political undercurrents seem to have been more important than any personal factors. Toward the end of World War II the Soviet regime had two major alternatives for its future development. The emphasis on Russian nationalism and on the virtues of the ordinary citizens could have been extended. In that case, sweeping concessions to material needs and the desire for personal freedom would probably have been necessary, for the large masses of returning soldiers and deportees familiar with foreign conditions would probably have constituted a focal point for unrest. The framework of Stalin's dictatorship might have been preserved, but it would have tended to become a traditional autocracy gradually relaxing its control over the private sphere of life. In its foreign policy the Soviet state would have closely adhered to the demands of Russian national interest. The limitations these demands would have imposed on the freedom of action of the regime would have been reinforced by the fact that a crippled postwar Soviet economy which had to satisfy the needs of the population would not have been adequate to support an aggressive foreign policy.

There were, however, powerful forces in Soviet society which would not accept such a solution. The élan of the early Bolsheviks had been broken, but the interests and habits of the Party apparatus were a potent substitute. As the partisan episode showed, Party and police officials who were at first intent on devising an expedient to limit Soviet losses, quickly moved when the opportunity arose to use their instrument for aggrandizing their own power and extending the sphere of Communism. We can guess that the two factors—continued political dominance for the individual official and the apparatus, and the extension of Communism abroad—were inextricably mingled in the minds of the postpurge Party leaders, who accepted the virtues of "Marxism-Leninism" unquestioningly without much thought as to the niceties of its application.

To such men, the "Zhdanovshchina" must have seemed an indispensable program for reasserting Party primacy. If he had lived, Shcherbakov, the

dynamic territorial secretary, with a record of continued interest in ideological matters, might very well have brought the program of reindoctrination
to fruition, for there is little doubt but that the regime had decided on that
course by 1944. Whatever the complete story behind Zhdanov's assuming
the role of chief "purifier," he too seems to have been an excellent representative of the political undercurrents just described. Also a territorial secretary who had long dealt with ideology, little associated with the primary
economic emphasis of the war period, but intimately involved in the
partisan movement, Zhdanov typified the most dynamic and the most
ruthless forces in the Party.

This analysis seems at first glance to leave Stalin out, although his decisive
role is apparent. After the war Stalin seems to have been more intent on
maintaining absolute personal control even than during the Great Purge.
To be absolute, his control had to be totalitarian; to that extent the impulse
to tighten Party controls over all aspects of Soviet life thoroughly suited
his purpose. At the same time, the more radical expressions of *partiinost'*,
especially in philosophy, may have seemed to Stalin to be somewhat contrary to his long-range tendency to stability in ideological questions. Moreover, Stalin feared the rise of individual leaders or groups in any sphere of
Soviet life who might threaten his position. In 1946 Zhdanov probably
seemed a useful counterweight to Malenkov and Beria, who had risen so
fast. By 1948 Zhdanov's prominence—after Ezhov's fall no one but Stalin
himself had received so much attention in the Soviet press—was probably
somewhat disturbing. Then the real personal power behind Soviet politics
became visible in the criticisms of music, and soon in much more important
respects.

CHAPTER
XIV

THE FORWARD LINE IN
INTERNATIONAL COMMUNISM

Initial Soviet recognition of the significance of the Anglo-American war effort against the Axis did not outlast the extreme crisis of Soviet defense. With the Teheran Conference in late 1943, however, began a new period of relatively cordial relations.[1] Six months later the Soviet press highly praised implementation of the promise for a landing in France. Nevertheless, the period between Teheran and the Normandy invasion, and especially the remaining months of 1944 were filled with subdued but irritating clashes of opinion between the USSR and the Western allies.

In West Europe and in Greece, which the USSR had by then definitely recognized as part of a British sphere of influence, Communist operations did not lead to open friction between the USSR and its allies. It seems clear, nevertheless, at least in retrospect, that the Communist parties were engaged in "probing" operations throughout the European area being freed of Nazi occupation.

Much the most spectacular of these Communist probes was in Greece. As noted in Chapter XII, the ELAS Communist-dominated partisans had, wherever possible, ruthlessly destroyed anti-Communist resistance groups. Consequently, when British forces and those of the royal government-in-exile landed in Greece in October 1944, almost the entire country was controlled by the Communists. During the following two months EAM (the civilian counterpart of ELAS) ostensibly collaborated with the royal government, while really trying to maintain control of the country. In December, however, ELAS and royal forces clashed openly. With strong British support the royal government triumphed, and was able for the time being to disband the partisan armed units.[2]

The role of international Communism in this affair is still very obscure. The Soviet press had acclaimed the "Political Committee of National Liberation" established by EAM before the British landing. EAM collaboration with the royal government followed soon after the visit of a Soviet military mission in July 1944.[3] The Yugoslav press displayed relatively little sympathy for the Greek Communists in this clash with the royalists and the British; Markos Vafiades, the ELAS leader in Macedonia who was evidently especially close to the Yugoslav Communists, avoided fighting the British.[4] Since some of the other Greek partisan leaders were almost pathologically inclined to violence, it is possible that Moscow and Belgrade could not restrain them.

On the other hand, the Greek Communist bid for power, while perhaps more violent than intended, appears to fit into a pattern of European Communist activities. In Belgium, too, British troops had to forestall a Communist armed coup. In April 1945 Stalin declared his disinterest in both countries; in his reply, Churchill recognized Soviet noninterference in Greece but did not comment on the Belgian situation.[5]

The biggest stakes, however, were in France and Italy. The Italian Communist Party was evidently determined to avoid large-scale violence and Soviet policy toward the Allied occupation regime in Italy was devious and probably insignificant in its effects. The French Communist Party, on the other hand, made a definite though cautious attempt to obtain a decisive role in the country at the time of liberation. French Communist partisans had resorted to assassination of German troops and similar extreme measures soon after the USSR entered the war.[6] Though the measures were hailed by the Comintern press, the violence of German reprisals, including the execution of Communist hostages, plus General Charles de Gaulle's denunciation of acts which would provoke the Germans unnecessarily, led the underground Communist party to disavow terrorism.[7] Nevertheless, during the following three years the Communists secured a dominant position in the French underground. Evidently they hoped to seize de facto control of much of the country by a general uprising following the Allied invasion. De Gaulle, however, ordered the underground to limit itself to carefully selected operations which would serve definite military purposes. Obliquely at the time, and later openly, the Communist press accused de Gaulle of deliberate sabotage of the partisans' efforts to fight the Germans.[8] Where they could, Communist partisans seized control of local administrations and slaughtered their opponents. The Communist leadership recognized, however, that de Gaulle was too popular to be opposed openly, and in the autumn of 1944, after a bitter dispute, obeyed his order to disband the partisans.[9]

That the French Communist leaders were closely attuned to Soviet policy at this time is indicated by the fact that in April 1945 Jacques Duclos was chosen to signal the shift to open Communist hostility toward the Western democracies. In an article primarily directed at the American Communist leader Earl Browder, Duclos denounced the formal dissolution of the U.S. Communist Party.[10] For the benefit of all Western Communist parties, Duclos stressed that capitalism was basically reactionary and that socialism could be attained only by a "preliminary conquest of power." [11] While his article still distinguished between "democratic" and "fascist" sympathizers in the Western governments, he significantly warned against Browder's concept that "the greatest part of Europe, west of the Soviet Union, will probably be reconstituted on a bourgeois-democratic basis and not on a fascist-capitalist or Soviet basis." [12] As Stalin later told Tito, the USSR was too weak following the war to intervene actively to aid the West European Communists; but henceforth there was apparently to be no limit to what Communists might be permitted to achieve locally if the conditions were favorable.[13]

Perhaps the most significant overt Soviet reaffirmation of the cleavage between the Communist and non-Communist worlds came ten months after Duclos' article in Stalin's electoral speech of February 9, 1946.[14] While still admitting differences between the Western states and the "Fascists," Stalin clearly implied that the former would become involved in a new war, and sharply emphasized the superiority of the Soviet system. A few weeks later Winston Churchill's sharp attack (in his Fulton, Missouri, speech) on Soviet oppression in East Europe seemed to be a riposte (albeit unplanned) to Stalin's declaration of "cold war."

If there was an "irrepressible conflict" between the USSR and its wartime allies, the basic immediate source was not the peripheral friction in West Europe and the Middle East, but Communist expansion in East Europe. In this area, the scope of Soviet and Communist activities was so vast that in this general study one can only sketch the principal features, emphasizing those which help to explain the nature of Soviet policy and the elements in the Soviet Communist Party which were involved in East Europe. Even in this limited approach, the paucity of monographs on the establishment of Soviet control in specific countries is a severe handicap.

A crucial point is the time at which the Soviet regime decided that it

would be feasible to maintain permanent control over the territories occupied by the Red Army. Some light is cast on this matter by the behavior
of the Soviet occupation administration in East Germany. According to a
defector from this administration, the Soviet Council of Commissars, convinced at the end of 1944 that a prolonged occupation of Germany would
be impossible, organized a special committee headed by Malenkov to carry
out wholesale dismantling of German plants to be sent as reparations to the
USSR. In the early stages of occupation, officials representing Malenkov,
Beria, and Kaganovich competed for machinery for the industries supervised by their superiors. Later in 1945, however, Mikoian, responsible for a
longer-range flow of reparations, secured the temporary support of various
high-level officials for a reduction of dismantling to permit revival of German
production.[15] If this account is essentially correct—and there is a certain
amount of corroborating evidence—the Soviet regime decided to stay in
Germany some time during the summer of 1945. It is possible, however,
that pressing needs of the Soviet economy and the personal prestige of
powerful Party leaders may have been sufficient to secure the initial dismantling regardless of long-range policy considerations.

In contrast to its vacillations in East Germany, and perhaps in other
Central European countries, the Soviet regime appears to have planned
permanent Communist domination of most of the countries bordering the
USSR at least as early as 1944. A Communist "National Home Council"
was secretly formed in Warsaw, according to a contemporary Polish source
published in the Soviet press, early in 1944.[16] In July 1944 a Communist-
dominated Polish Committee of National Liberation was established under
Red Army protection in Chelm, later moving to Lublin.[17] Shortly afterward,
Stalin refused to permit aid to the Warsaw uprising of the Home Army on
the ground that the nationalist organization was conducting a reckless and
"inhumane" operation. The Germans destroyed a large part of the nationalist underground in suppressing this rebellion, and the rest was later hunted
down by Soviet partisans, Polish Communist military and police units, and
the Red Army. In these ways the Soviet regime had by the end of 1944
eliminated all elements which could have offered forcible resistance to
permanent Communist control of Poland. In Rumania, Andrei Vyshinskii,
backed by the Red Army, openly installed a Communist government in
early March 1945. In September 1944, two days after the Red Army had
entered Bulgaria, the Communist-dominated "Fatherland Front" seized
control of the government, and proceeded rapidly to destroy all non-Communist forces.[18]

Vyshinskii's position in Bucharest recalls his role in the Communist take-over in Latvia four years earlier. Similarly, Voroshilov, as head of the Allied Control Commission in Budapest, seems to have been the principal channel for Soviet instructions to the local Communists.[19] In most areas, however, the Red Army commanders and their political officers seem to have been in charge in the initial phases of Soviet occupation.[20] Aside from specific intervention against anti-Communist underground groups and political parties, the Red Army contributed enormously to the feeling of terror and insecurity which weakened resistance to Communism. Mass rape by Soviet soldiers horrified and demoralized the civilian population. Official Red Army requisitions and unauthorized plunder depleted the food reserves and disrupted the war-shaken economies of the East European countries. On one occasion at least, Voroshilov used the food requirements of the Red Army as a political weapon, threatening to starve Hungary by quartering vast numbers of troops in the country if the non-Communist political leaders did not acquiesce in his demands.[21]

While the Red Army broke down resistance to Communism in East Europe, the Soviet secret police played an important role in channeling its activities. It is impossible to determine just how influential Beria was in the formation of Soviet East European policy, but it is certain that he was deeply involved in several major aspects. Early in the war, he was in charge of arranging a Jewish Anti-Fascist Committee. In this capacity he dealt with Henryk Ehrlich and Wiktor Alter, leaders of the Polish Jewish Bund, and eventually had them shot.[22] At a later stage of the war Beria also dealt with personnel for the Polish Communist regime, but it is not clear whether he did this as supervisor of Communist activities, or as keeper of the con-centration camps and execution chambers where the earlier Polish Com-munist leaders had disappeared.[23] In the period immediately following the war, native Communists in charge of the Polish and Hungarian police forces took orders from Beria or other NKVD officials.[24] V. N. Merkulov, one of Beria's henchmen, worked closely with Mikoian in reparations policy.[25] With almost incredible cynicism, other Soviet agencies privately admitted the activity of the NKVD agents in Eastern Europe, yet dis-claimed responsibility for them.[26]

Nevertheless, it seems doubtful that the NKVD was the principal channel for instructions to East European Communist regimes. As noted in Chapter XI, several detailed accounts agree in making Shcherbakov, as supervisor of the Foreign Section of the Central Committee Secretariat, the principal Soviet source of instructions for foreign Communists in 1943-44. At some point after Shcherbakov's death, Zhdanov seems to have inherited this function, along with Shcherbakov's ideological role.

Zhdanov's guidance of the East European Communists becomes evident when one examines the development of the Cominform (Communist Information Bureau). The constitutive session was held between September 22 and September 27, 1947 in Szklarska Poręba, a spa in Poland. Representatives from the French, the Italian, and all the East European parties except the German and the Albanian appeared.[27] Both Zhdanov and Malenkov represented the Soviet Party, but Zhdanov was clearly dominant; this appears not only from the accounts of participants, but from the treatment accorded the two figures in the Soviet press, which published Zhdanov's speech weeks before Malenkov's.[28] Just as clearly, however, Zhdanov was entirely subordinate to Stalin, who intervened by telephone to prescribe even such details as the absurdly cumbersome name of the Cominform journal, *For a Lasting Peace, for a People's Democracy*.[29] Zhdanov told the participating Communist representatives that the reason for the meeting was the heightening international tension. Pursuing this theme in his opening speech, Zhdanov pointed to the development of "two camps." The "camp of capitalism" was demonstrating its enmity toward "democracy" and its aversion to peace by such measures as the Truman Doctrine and the Marshall Plan. The "camp of socialism" was nevertheless strengthened through the "leading role" of the USSR in the war, which had discredited capitalism, and by the formation of the "people's republics" in East Europe. Under these circumstances, Zhdanov said, "those comrades" who hesitated to meet with other Communists for fear of being accused of subservience to "the hand of Moscow" were wrong; a permanent organization, the Cominform, was needed for mutual consultation and co-ordination of Communist activities.[30]

In the opinion of Eugenio Reale, an Italian participant, the real purpose of the meeting was somewhat different. It was designed, he thinks, to outline to lagging Communist parties the tactics by which their fellows had obtained complete power, and in this way to develop a concerted plan for ousting non-Communist groups remaining in East European governments.[31] The principal "lesson" was provided by the Bulgarian leader Vŭlko Chervenkov, for the process of establishing a purely Communist government was practically completed in Bulgaria. József Révai dealt with the Hungarian tactics. As the Hungarian Communists had not yet attained absolute power, however, a later account by Révai, of undoubted authenticity, more clearly reveals the nature of Communist tactics:

> We were in a minority in Parliament and in the government, but at the same time we represented the leading force. Our force, the force of our Party and the working class, was multiplied by the fact that the Soviet Union, and the Soviet Army, were always there to support us with their assistance. In the first phase of our transformation, when we struggled directly and apparently only for a steadfast achievement of bourgeois-democratic tasks, we fought as well for the establishment and assurance of the conditions which made possible the Socialistic transformation. The change in the development of our People's Democracy into the dictatorship of the proletariat began with the destruction of the right wing of the Smallholder's Party, with the liquidation of the conspiracy and the fall of Ferenc Nagy [the Smallholder premier]. Then the kulak became an enemy, then the leading role of our Party and the working class was strengthened. . . . Rendering innocuous the agents of the imperialists, and the oppression of the class enemy within are not at all secondary tasks; on the contrary, they are conditions of the work of building Socialism. Furthermore, we must also clearly realize that periods may come in our evolution when the chief function of the dictatorship of the proletariat will consist of exercising force against enemies from within and from without. Whoever forgets that commits the crime of pacifism, demobilizes the Party and the working class, and overlooks the building up of our state security organization as well as our army.[32]

The examples of Bulgaria and Hungary seemed to have particular relevance for Czechoslovakia. The Communists and their allies had a commanding position in the government, where their leader Klement Gottwald was premier. In July 1947, however, Soviet orders to reject participation in the Marshall Plan had aroused resentment, and the non-Communist parties were trying to resist Communist domination. Rudolf Slánský, in his report to the Cominform, endorsed Gottwald's leadership, although there had been rumors in Communist circles that Gottwald was regarded as too weak.[33] Slánsky expressed misgivings, however, over the attitude of Edvard Beneš, the non-Communist president.[34]

Five months after the Cominform meeting, the Czechoslovak Communists carried out their part of the general program of reducing non-Communists in East Europe to impotence. Helped by covert Soviet threats of intervention, the Czechoslovak Communists intimidated all opposition elements by manipulated mass demonstrations and mob violence. When Beneš failed to support the non-Communist ministers they were forced from the government, which then became the instrument for rapid achievement of complete Communist control.[35]

A special feature of the first Cominform conference was the severe criticism, especially by the Yugoslav delegates, of the "parliamentarianism" and "legalism" of the French and the Italian parties. Years later the Yugoslavs maintained that Zhdanov and Malenkov had treacherously incited them to attack the French and the Italian Communists in order to deprive Yugoslavia of potential support in the European Communist movement.[36]

It is probable that a hidden Soviet motive for the foundation of the Cominform was the desire to prepare an instrument to deal with the Yugoslav situation. In comparison to the other East European Communist parties, the Yugoslavs were altogether too independent for Soviet tastes. As we have seen, the Yugoslav partisans drew on Soviet experience to some extent, and "Grandpa" (Molotov) passed on major orders to them; but no special political emissaries, and above all no NKVD representatives, guided them. During the war the NKVD followed its "normal" procedure of forming a net of secret agents, pledged to spy on their fellow-Communist Yugoslavs, in the First Yugoslav Brigade organized in the USSR; but Tito refused to permit the development of an NKVD informers' net in Yugoslavia itself. He politely—but quite out of line with Communist practice —offered to supply himself any information the Soviet authorities needed.[37] Tito was initially successful in maintaining complete control because after the war, which had cost the lives of many of the small group of prewar Communists, key posts in both party and government were assigned to partisan officers who were loyal to him personally. Later, Soviet sources were to accuse Tito, with considerable justification, of employing military methods of control (which to Soviet polemicists was equivalent to "Bonapartism"); but this technique, combined with the intense Yugoslav nationalist resentment of foreign interference, preserved his independence.[38]

There seems little doubt but that the real source of Soviet dissatisfaction with Tito was his ability to evade the control which Stalin has fastened on all European Communists for two decades. At the same time, the extreme nationalism of the Yugoslav Communists, combined with their intransigent partisan tradition, gave rise to specific disputes. At the start of their partisan movement, the Yugoslav leaders complained of the lack of Soviet aid, and resented Soviet hesitancy to disavow Mihajlović and the royal government.[39] In October 1943 Tito aroused Stalin's anger by refusing to follow his advice to recognize the Yugoslav king, and by threatening to resist a

British landing by force.[40] To the Soviet regime, Tito was placing local Communist interests above the demands of Soviet policy, for Stalin wished to temporize with Churchill on the Yugoslav question. In 1945 Tito almost brought on an armed clash with the British and the Americans in his effort to seize Trieste; and when the USSR failed to offer more than verbal support, he grumbled that "we do not want to pay for others." Though Tito denied that his complaint was directed at the Soviet Union, Stalin apparently never forgave the thrust.[41]

In their general attitude toward the Western powers, as in their specific disputes, the Yugoslav Communists were openly belligerent while the Soviet spokesmen were trying to conceal their expansionist aims. This was true of purely theoretical debates in international organizations, where the Yugoslavs attacked every formulation which did not accord with Marxism-Leninism.[42] It was true in regard to Greece, where the Yugoslavs—in contrast to their attitude in 1944—favored greatly increased support for the civil war which had resumed in the summer of 1946.[43]

An additional factor which exacerbated Soviet-Yugoslav relations was a Yugoslav scheme to form a Balkan federation. The details are far too involved to describe here, but the essence of this dispute was, apparently, Stalin's fear that Tito was using his personal prestige to create an East European Communist bloc which would have been strong enough to maintain a degree of independence from the USSR. Tito traveled extensively in East Europe, and was greeted enthusiastically by crowds which apparently admired him more as a national hero than as a Communist leader.[44]

The first postwar All-Slav Congress convened in Belgrade in late 1946, and as late as May 1948 the chairman of the All-Slav Committee, the Yugoslav Božidar Maslarić, pointed out that the organization was linked to non-Slavs as well as Slavs in the East European "new democracies."[45] The first public sign of Soviet displeasure with the Balkan Communists was a sudden denunciation in the January 28, 1948, *Pravda* of a speech in which Georgi Dimitrov (who after the war returned to Bulgaria) advocated an eventual federation of East European states.[46] In February Edvard Kardelj and other Yugoslav representatives were called to a session in the Kremlin with Stalin, Molotov, Zhdanov, Malenkov, the Deputy Foreign Minister V. A. Zorin, and significantly, the new Central Committee Secretary M. A. Suslov.[47] According to the Yugoslav version, Stalin had already decided to demand complete self-abasement of the Yugoslavs. Indeed, the published correspondence between the Yugoslav and the Soviet Central Committees which followed strongly indicates that by February 1948 Stalin was making out a case against Tito which would inevitably result in his downfall if he capitulated.[48] The Soviet letters referred briefly to the basic issue of NKVD infiltration, but they accurately stressed Tito's attempts to embroil the Soviet Union in dangerous foreign policies, and falsely accused him of a whole series of departures from Marxist-Leninist principles.

The correspondence lasted through the spring of 1948. When Tito and his party refused to submit the controversy to the Soviet-dominated parties represented in the Cominform, a second general session nevertheless assembled in Bucharest. The Cominform delegates, led by Zhdanov, Malenkov, and Suslov (who seems to have been in charge of the arrangements), publicly repeated the charges contained in the earlier Soviet correspondence, and expressed their belief that if the Yugoslav leaders failed to reform they would be replaced by "new internationalist leaders" supported by the "sound elements" in the Yugoslav party.[49] After the Bucharest meeting, the Cominform countries provided bases for an extensive network of Stalinist émigrés from Yugoslavia, who continued to appeal vainly for the overthrow of Tito.[50]

While Tito was able to maintain control in Yugoslavia, however, he did not become the leader of an anti-Stalinist Communist bloc. According to Vittorio Vidali, the "loyal" Communist leader in Trieste (then a free city under Anglo-American protection), Tito unsuccessfully endeavored to subvert the Communist Party there.[51] Even in Albania, which had practically been a Yugoslav satellite, the Stalinist faction triumphed.

In Greece the situation was more complicated. A "provisional government" under General Markos Vafiades, who was apparently especially close to the Yugoslavs, had been set up by the Greek Communists in December 1947.[52] While neither the USSR nor its satellites recognized the Markos regime, even after the Soviet-Yugoslav dispute began the Cominform journal published accounts of the efforts in the East European Communist states, especially Yugoslavia, to provide aid and mobilize opinion in favor of the insurgents.[53] In December 1948, however, Nicholas Zachariades, the general secretary of the Greek Communist Party, who had few ties to Yugoslavia, denounced various blunders of the immediate postwar leadership of his party.[54] In February 1949 Markos resigned and retired to Rumania. Five months later Yugoslavia officially closed its border to the Greek rebels.[55] This move probably assured the Greek Communists' defeat.

The evidence is too scanty to relate with any assurance these complicated East European developments to power rivalries within the USSR.

Several careful analysts of the Tito dispute, including notably Hamilton Fish Armstrong and the late Franz Borkenau, have speculated that Tito was an ally of Zhdanov, whose intransigent foreign and domestic pronouncements resembled those of the Yugoslavs.[56] On the other hand, the published Yugoslav statements, and the memoir of Eugenio Reale, maintain that as far back as 1947 Zhdanov was endeavoring to isolate and undermine the Yugoslav Communists.

Probably observers have tended to overrate the independence of Zhdanov's foreign policy as much as they have his personal role in the domestic ideological campaign. Abroad as well as at home he may well have represented strong currents of Party opinion, but Stalin, as Reale's account demonstrates, always maintained ultimate control. Quite possibly, however, Stalin's bitter experience with Tito was an additional factor inducing him to restrict Zhdanov. Zhdanov's intimate involvement in the unsuccessful dealings with the Yugoslavs—whether or not he was responsible for the ultimate failure to bridle them—probably aroused Stalin's displeasure if not his suspicion. The sudden emergence in 1948 of Suslov as a major Soviet representative in dealing with East European Communists suggests that Stalin was seeking a replacement for Zhdanov. Until more evidence is available, however, one can only speculate on the impact of foreign developments on Zhdanov's passage from the Soviet scene.

CHAPTER

XV

DISSENSION IN THE PARTY

It is characteristic of the undispelled murkiness of Soviet politics that the world still does not know whether Andrei Zhdanov, perhaps the most striking personality on the Soviet political scene under Stalin, died a natural death. We have the announcement in the "doctors'-plot" accusation of 1952 that medical mistreatment hastened Zhdanov's death; but a few months later an official communique maintained that Zhdanov had been correctly treated.[1] Since then, among the many fascinating revelations of Khrushchev and his cohorts, no single hint has been dropped concerning Zhdanov's personal position in the Soviet power struggle or his ultimate fate.

While it is impossible to prove conclusively that Zhdanov's power was diminishing before his death on August 31, 1948, there are many indications that this was the case. Stalin's personal intervention in the ideological campaign and Suslov's emergence as a principal factor in the control of East European Communists are two of the most important. If it is true that Shcherbakov had been married to Zhdanov's daughter, the unusual prominence given the death of an older woman described as Shcherbakov's "true consort" was a direct slap at Zhdanov.[2] Unhappily, this kind of hint which members of the Soviet elite might understand immediately is more tantilizing than useful to us. On the other hand, the gradual diminution of Zhdanov's newspaper prominence during 1948, and the published description of Malenkov as "Central Committee Secretary" in July 1948, seem to be definite signs of a shift in the power balance.[3]

None of these indications, of course, really substantiates the charge that Zhdanov met foul play. Unimpeachable sources testify that he was actually ill long before his political decline, which may indeed have been the result of failing energy as much as the work of his rivals.[4] Some speculation centered around the fact that his body was brought to Moscow by railroad from the west. One writer guesses that he may have died during a conference with the Polish Communist Party, but in view of the fact that many Politburo members lived northwest of Moscow the movement of the corpse by rail may have been simply a matter of convenience.[5]

The consideration of such dubious evidence is necessary because of the extreme importance of the events which followed Zhdanov's disappearance from Soviet political life. In early 1949, N. A. Voznesenskii, one of the newest Politburo members; A. A. Kuznetsov, Central Committee Secretary; M. I. Rodionov, Chairman of the RSFSR Council of Ministers; and P. S. Popkov, secretary of Leningrad obkom, disappeared; all were killed or died in prison some months later.[6] These were the highest officials whom Stalin executed after the Great Purge, and they were all close associates of Zhdanov. Several other associates of Zhdanov, like the Central Committee Secretary, G. M. Popov, and the head of the political administration of the army, I. V. Shikin, disappeared or were given obscure posts, but were not executed.

Only in Voznesenskii's case did an official accusation appear. On July 13, 1949, the editors of *Bol'shevik* (including G. F. Aleksandrov) were sharply criticized and removed for ideological shortcomings, including emphasis on Voznesenskii's book, *The War Economy of the USSR in the Period of the Patriotic War*. The decree was not published, however, until December 1952, when M. A. Suslov denounced the book—which had received the Stalin prize in May 1948—for advocating "voluntarism" through the contention that planning was the fundamental economic law of socialist society.[7]

It is far from certain that this theoretical deviation really doomed Voznesenskii. As noted in Chapter XVII, Stalin himself continued to advance "voluntaristic" doctrines long after Voznesenskii had been condemned. When Stalin reversed his position in 1952, it is not surprising that Voznesenskii posthumously became a scapegoat for having advanced the discarded doctrines. In 1948 there were probably more practical reasons for condemning Voznesenskii. He had pursued a relatively independent line within the Soviet leadership, especially during the war years and immediately afterward in connection with German occupation policy. Later, however, Voznesenskii seems to have worked closely with Zhdanov.[8] Moreover, like the other condemned officials, he had once been associated with the Leningrad apparatus.[9] Apparently the Leningrad Party organization as a whole was under attack after Zhdanov's death. According to a later Soviet statement it was "subjected to intolerable discrimination, its militant tradition scorned, and its cadres suffered great losses." [10] An Italian Communist source relates that the official charge against the Leningrad group was conspiracy to form a separatist Russian government in Leningrad.[11]

The Italian correspondent points out that this charge was absurd, and he is almost certainly correct. Nevertheless, it does seem that a certain measure of independent thinking (by Stalinist standards) had appeared in the Leningrad Party organization. Ever since the Revolution the Leningrad Party organization had symbolized the international attachments of Soviet Communism, as opposed to the withdrawn ethnocentrism symbolized by Moscow. During Zhdanov's final years Leningrad had been increasing in prestige. Yugoslav Communist visitors in early 1948 exhibited a suspicious interest in affairs in Leningrad.[12] Voznesenskii, it is said, opposed severance of economic relations with Yugoslavia.[13]

There are some signs that the Leningrad Party apparatus was used as the source for key Party replacements in the RSFSR.[14] In November 1947 Rodionov quoted Kirov's description of Leningrad as "a great foundry of cadres for our new socialist constructions and the scientific research institutes of the whole Soviet Union," adding that "this striking characterization of the role of the Leningradites may in truth be applied to the whole Russian people." [15] This was an unusual note, for during more than a decade Moscow, not Leningrad, had been praised as the great Russian center. According to a foreign diplomatic report, the Leningrad Party group was accused in 1949 of "Great Russian chauvinism" for slighting non-Russian Soviet nationalities in connection with arrangements for an international trade fair planned for Leningrad.[16] It is possible that Stalin's suspicions of the Leningrad organization, which had been the stronghold of his enemies in the twenties, were aroused by these incidents. He may even have had second thoughts concerning the stress on Russian nationalism if Leningrad, not the centralized power structure in Moscow, was to be regarded as the focal point of Russian sentiment. It is scarcely surprising that Beria, his henchman, the Minister of State Security V. S. Abakumov, and other central police officials have since Stalin's death been blamed for inciting Stalin to order the executions in the "Leningrad affair." [17] The charge that A. N. Rapava, also Beria's henchman but not otherwise identified as active outside of Georgia, co-operated with Beria and Abakumov in this plot also suggests that the nationality factor may have played a part, with Stalin relying on his fellow countrymen to eliminate the Russian leaders whom he had come to suspect.[18]

At the same time, Khrushchev's subsequent charge that Malenkov, too, was responsible for the destruction of the Leningrad leaders probably has some factual basis, for Malenkov, not Beria, profited most from the elimination of Zhdanov and his associates.[19] The depleted ranks of the Secretariat were filled by P. K. Ponomarenko and Khrushchev.[20] Apparently neither of these men was then an especially strong supporter of Malenkov; this suggests that Stalin was still careful to maintain a balance in the most important bodies. Malenkov presided over the Secretariat, however, and was undoubtedly its strongest member, apart from Stalin himself.[21] Between 1947 and 1951 the Politburo remained nominally unchanged, except for the promotion of Bulganin and Kosygin to full membership. In fact, however, Stalin refused to permit some members, like Andreev, to attend, and evidently held few if any Politburo meetings during the final years of his life.[22] In 1946 a "Sextet" or committee of the Politburo had been assigned the most important supervisory tasks, but, as this body was dominated by Zhdanov and his adherents, it is questionable whether it survived after 1948.[23] Probably the Orgburo—where Malenkov also presided—became more important than the Politburo, although the Secretariat remained, of course, the key directing body of the Party.[24]

While major changes in the upper stratum of the Party were taking place, the structure of the Party apparatus was being drastically revised. During World War II the cadres sections, in some areas at least, had tended to retain only supervisory powers in selection of personnel for economic posts, leaving the principal role to industrial sections.[25] After the war, various minor revisions in the control of personnel were made. The bureaus of Party committees again required all prospective appointees to appear in person for interviews before their appointments were confirmed, instead of relying on information derived from questionnaires prepared by the cadres sections. This change probably increased the power of the line secretaries who dominated the bureaus, as compared to the cadres officials.[26] Deputy ministers for cadres supervised personnel throughout each ministry and its local branches. Presumably this system somewhat reduced the role of the Party cadres organization in industry, although the Central Committee Cadres Administration retained general supervisory powers over economic personnel.[27]

At the end of 1948 a Central Committee decree abolished both the Cadres Administration and the Administration for Verification of Party Organs, as well as the corresponding sections at lower levels of the Party structure.[28] In their place the decree established sections of Party, trade-union, and Komsomol organizations which supervised all aspects of Party affairs, including personnel. "Industrial-branch" sections were established to supervise all phases, including personnel, of each major aspect of the economy. The indoctrination organization was less drastically affected, but probably declined somewhat in influence. The Propaganda and Agitation "Administration" of the Central Committee was changed to a "Section." Somewhat later the post of secretary for propaganda was abolished at lower levels. Separate sections of propaganda and agitation, science and higher education, and literature and arts were established in at least one Union Republic.[29]

While the formal changes in the other aspects of the apparatus were abrupt, a considerable measure of continuity was maintained at lower levels by retaining the former propaganda secretaries to supervise indoctrination, and the cadres secretaries to supervise internal Party activities.[30] Taken as a whole, however, the new system was a reversion to that which had prevailed between 1934 and 1939. As we have seen (Chapter I), the principal advocate of the 1934-39 system had been Kaganovich. Malenkov, whose influence increased rapidly under that system, may also have preferred it to the one introduced by the Eighteenth Congress.[31] If that is the case, the reorganization following so soon after Zhdanov's death is an additional indication of Malenkov's command of the apparatus.

After Zhdanov's death there appears to have been a distinct though moderate shift in the emphasis of Party activities from political to economic matters. Since there were no Central Committee plenums between his death and the middle of 1952, one cannot form a very accurate estimate of central Party activities; but plenums continued to be held regularly at lower levels. Whereas during the period June 1946-December 1948, when Zhdanov's influence was strong, the ratio of political to economic questions considered by Union Republic plenums had been nearly four to three, in the next three and one-half years the ratio was one to one.[32] Matters of indoctrination and cultural control continued, of course, to occupy the Party meetings, and more attention was given to internal Party training than in Zhdanov's day.

Moreover, the proportion of Party officials taking part in discussion on economic matters rose considerably. This was true especially in agriculture, where raikom and obkom secretaries seem to have regained influence which had to a limited extent gone to state officials in the years immediately after the war. In view of the lack of sharp career cleavage between the Party and the state bureaucracies at the lower level, this shift is probably of no great significance.[33] The role of the Party officials in local agricultural discussions does tend, however, to cast doubt on the generalization that the Party declined in relative importance during the last years of Stalin's life, for no question was more important than agriculture. But, as noted below, central non-Party agencies, especially the Ministry of Agriculture, played the major role in directing agricultural matters in that period.

The general economic situation of the USSR in the immediate postwar period was extremely difficult. Industrial production in 1946 fell to 70 per cent of that of 1940, the last prewar year.[34] The worst difficulties were in the food supply, however, which was gravely endangered by the severe drought of 1946. An official announcement maintained that the effects of the drought were not as great as in 1921, but in view of the famine conditions of that year, this was scarcely reassuring.[35] The agricultural situation in 1946 was, moreover, much worsened by the fact that the former German-occupied territories had by no means recovered their productive capacity. The losses in farm machinery and livestock were especially important for they could not be replaced in a single year. As a result, only 80 per cent of the prewar cultivated land in the Ukraine was sown in 1946 even though dairy cows were used as draft animals.[36]

The considerable quantity of supplies—mainly American in origin—delivered to Belorussia and the Ukraine by the United Nations Relief and Rehabilitation Administration (UNRRA) helped avert widespread famine. Some 287,519 metric tons of food, worth nearly one hundred million dollars, were shipped to the Ukraine alone up to the end of January 1947. Since the state rationing system obtained very little locally produced food for the urban population, this supply played a major role in averting widespread famine.[37] In 1947 the Soviet regime felt able to end rationing, while reducing the extreme inflationary pressures produced by the deficit of food and other consumer goods by a 90 per cent devaluation of the currency, which was especially effective in almost eliminating the peasants' hoarded wartime profits.[38]

Prior to the period of extreme economic crisis in early 1947, state and Party leadership had been combined in the Ukraine, Belorussia, Leningrad, and other crucial areas. For example, from the end of the war until 1947, Khrushchev was both first secretary and chairman of the council of commissars in the Ukraine. On March 8, 1947, however, he was relieved as secretary by Kaganovich.[39] Much speculation has been devoted to the reasons for this change, and its effects on Khrushchev's relative position in the Party command. Since 1957 Party spokesmen have denounced Kaganovich's activities in the Ukraine. At the time, however, there was little evidence that Khrushchev suffered from Kaganovich's mission. Khrushchev had been Kaganovich's protégé in Moscow in the thirties; Kaganovich's assistance in the Ukraine during the critical drought period may have helped Khrushchev to avoid a catastrophic loss of prestige.

Khrushchev retained his Politburo membership, and regained the Ukrainian first secretaryship on December 26, 1947, after the agricultural crisis had been surmounted. Khrushchev did not, however, retain the chairmanship of the council of ministers, which passed on to his associate D. S. Korotchenko.[40] This step appears to have been part of a general reinstitution of separation of Party and state functions in 1947. For example, the first secretary of the important Dnepropetrovsk obkom was relieved of his post for "subjugating" Soviet administrative offices and economic organizations instead of directing activities through them, and for permitting these organizations to present demands and threats to lower Party organizations.[41]

The agricultural crisis of 1946-47 which we have noted in the Ukraine was only the most critical aspect of the general farm problem immediately following World War II. On October 8, 1946, the Council of Ministers formed a new Council on Kolkhoz Affairs, headed by Andreev, with Andrianov and N. S. Patolichev as vice-chairmen.[42] The steps taken by the new council closely resembled those advocated by Andreev in the immediate prewar period. It took strong measures to preserve the collective farm as the basic productive unit in agriculture. These measures included recovery of fourteen million acres of collective fields which peasant "squatters" had appropriated for their private gardens, and stern insistence on the peasants' fullfilling their quota of labor in the kolkhoz. At the same time, the peasants were encouraged to devote themselves to kolkhoz production by adjusting rewards to achievements. The "link" of five to seven workers cultivated specified lands for at least a year in order that the members could be paid in proportion to the harvest.[43]

The scarcity of draft animals and tractors was an important factor in inducing the Soviet regime to encourage such small-scale organization of cultivation. As soon as possible, however, the drive to mechanize the countryside resumed. The February 1947 Central Committee plenum ordered the formation of a special *glavk* (chief administration) in the Ministry of Agriculture to supervise the MTS, which until then had been directed for the most part by the obkoms. The plenum also placed special emphasis on appointing technically qualified persons as MTS directors.[44] For the post of deputy director for political affairs in the MTS, reintroduced at the same time, the qualifications were Party reliability and experience. Of 165 deputy directors appointed in Orel oblast, half were manual workers, half white-collar workers, and none peasants.[45]

The deputy directors for political affairs had, like the earlier political section directors, a key role in Party supervision of rural areas. In the immediate postwar period the Party seemed temporarily resigned to the impracticability of establishing primary organizations in each kolkhoz. This was especially true in Belorussia and the northwestern parts of the RSFSR, where the kolkhozes were very small. In Kalinin oblast, for example, less than 10 per cent of the kolkhozes had Party organizations. There were twice as many village (territorial) primary organizations, which included a high proportion of the peasants who had joined the Party while in military service.[46]

At the same time, however, the Party press stressed the limited rights of the territorial primary organization, which was not permitted to control the work of the kolkhozes in its area.[47] The kolkhoz party organization, on the other hand, could directly influence production. Raikoms which tended to prefer the less numerous, more easily supervised territorial organizations were rebuked for assigning demobilized peasants to them instead of forming new kolkhoz organizations. As a result of Party pressure, kolkhoz party organization and membership increased fivefold in 1945 in Orel oblast, a black-earth province with large farms; but Party membership in the territorial and MTS primary organizations still outnumbered those in the kolkhoz organizations by nearly six to one.[48]

By 1950 the Party apparently felt that agriculture had recovered sufficiently to make it safe to proceed to a thorough reorganization which would adapt farm controls to the political and economic aims of the regime. There is some evidence that Stalin himself may have set the keynote for the new policy.[49] Publicly, however, the key figure in the reorganization was Nikita Khrushchev, who in December 1949 left the Ukraine to become Secretary of the Central Committee and first secretary of Moscow obkom. In the following winter and spring Khrushchev led a twofold attack on the prevailing agricultural system. He and other Party spokesmen denounced the tendency to weaken the large, permanent "brigade," a work unit comprising dozens of peasants, in favor of the "link," which, the Party spokesmen said, should be only an impermanent subdivision of the brigade. The key role of the brigade was related to the MTS, for both were declared indispensable for large-scale, mechanized agriculture. In addition, Party officials envisaged the brigade as a unit for future Party work, when each would have its Party group to organize socialist competition to stimulate production.[50]

In the second element of the agricultural revision—consolidation of the existing kolkhozes in larger units—Khrushchev and his former subordinates in the Ukrainian apparatus were especially active. In April 1950 Khrushchev declared that the small kolkhozes required too large overhead expenditures, and restricted the use of machinery.[51] Within ten months, the number of kolkhozes in the USSR had been reduced from 252,000 to 123,000 and by the end of 1952, when the process was substantially complete, the number had fallen to 97,000.[52] Amalgamation was stressed as particularly urgently needed in the nonblack-soil regions, including Khrushchev's Moscow oblast, where the farms had been much smaller than average.[53] Nevertheless, the program was carried to a still greater length in the Ukraine, where the number of kolkhozes fell to one-fourth of the 1949 total.[54]

The pressure to consolidate farms which were already fairly large strongly suggests that political motives played a far greater part in the program than did technical reasons. In the Ukraine, for example, in spite of the fact that half of the Party membership lived in rural areas in 1949, only 60 per cent of the large kolkhozes had primary organizations. After consolidation, practically every farm had its Party organization.[55] A single Belorussian raion doubled its kolkhoz Party organizations and tripled their membership by recruiting peasants and sending out town workers (a common practice) to serve as organizers.[56]

The establishment of primary organizations in the vast majority of kolkhozes would permit the Party to exercise direct supervision of the basic units of agricultural organization. The physical possibilities of supervision would remain limited, however, as long as the kolkhoz members did not live in a single settlement. Since the original kolkhoz had been formed on the basis of a pre-existing village, the new enlarged kolkhoz included two or three villages located inconvenient distances (in view of the poor roads and the scarcity of automobiles and telephones) from one another. Doubtless at least partly to overcome this hindrance to Party supervision—though he stressed the advantages of providing "city" amenities for the peasants— Khrushchev advanced the most extreme feature of the revision program, the "agrogorod" or "agricultural city."

In late 1949, when he still headed the Ukrainian apparatus, Khrushchev cunningly had a prototype of the agrogorod constructed near Kherson as a "gift" to Stalin on his seventieth birthday. During 1950 and early 1951 Khrushchev and other high officials elaborated the scheme.[57] One village on the enlarged collective farm was selected as the nucleus of the amalgamated settlement, and the rest were demolished. Their inhabitants moved to two-family houses (some four-family apartment buildings were proposed) in the new settlement. Ostensibly to reduce the expense of electricity and water by compact arrangement of the houses, the size of the garden allotment adjoining the peasant's living quarters was reduced from more than an acre to about a quarter acre, restricted to vegetable and fruit cultivation. The peasants' personal livestock was to be kept on additional "garden" allotments outside the city. Since many of the collective fields would have been located a considerable distance from the settlements, peasants working in them would have had to live for considerable periods in outlying labor camps. Obviously these measures would have drastically reduced the peasant's chance to work covertly on his own garden when he was supposed to be working for the kolkhoz. Just as surely they would have disrupted family life, thereby making the individual more subject to official indoctrination and pressure.

By the summer of 1950, plans were being drawn for fifty thousand new settlements of this type.[58] Khrushchev presented his most vigorous and detailed proposal at a conference in Moscow oblast in mid-January 1951. His speech did not appear in the press, however, until March 4, the eve of a Supreme Soviet session.[59] By that time there were strong indications that powerful elements in the Soviet agricultural administration, including I. A. Benediktov, the Minister of Agriculture, had doubts about the amalgamated settlement. Various publications under his control, while devoting much space to the administrative consolidation of the farms and the emphasis on brigades, said little or nothing about physical amalgamation of villages.[60] On March 5, the day after it printed Khrushchev's speech, *Pravda* took the highly unusual step of announcing that it had inadvertently omitted a note explaining that his proposals were for discussion only.[61]

Within a few days, sweeping denunciations of Khrushchev's plan appeared. It is significant that the denunciations stressed the disruptive effect upon agricultural production which the vast village reconstruction would require (especially since the peasants were to provide the building materials as well as construct the buildings themselves), rather than the disruption of the social pattern of the village. There were, however, some references to the importance of the peasant's private garden, to which he was entitled if he worked conscientiously in the collective sector.

Very interesting also is the fact that the most sweeping attacks on Khrushchev began in the Transcaucasus. On March 21 G. A. Ariutinov, the Armenian first secretary said, "I am of the opinion that these proposals [for the agrogorods, "those hybrids"] are closer to fantasy than to the real requirements of the collective farm countryside." [62] Two months later M. D. Bagirov, the Azerbaidzhani first secretary, warned that "we must decisively block attempts to reduce the size of the private gardens belonging to the households of collective farm members or to move part of these garden plots beyond the bounds of the village." [63] Since Beria apparently still dominated the Transcaucasian Party organizations, it is probable that he was a major force behind the rejection of Khrushchev's scheme. Considerably later, at the Nineteenth Congress in October 1952, Malenkov explicitly joined the attack on Khrushchev's ideas, stressing the theme that "certain of our leading officials have indulged in a wrong approach, a consumer's approach" by "forcing" village amalgamation, while the principal task had to be production.[64]

The rebuff on agricultural policy did not, apparently, greatly weaken Khrushchev's standing in the regime. Indeed, it is quite possible that the effort to convince Stalin to abandon the plan—which he very likely at first supported, if he did not instigate—weakened Beria's and possibly even Malenkov's positions more than it did Khrushchev's. As yet, however, it is impossible to separate the repercussions of this controversy from the tangle of maneuvers within the inner circle of the regime during the last two years of Stalin's life.

CHAPTER
XVI

RIGIDITY AT HOME AND ABROAD

Though the system and the personnel of Party control were drastically changed after Zhdanov died, the "Zhdanovshchina" survived. Or, to put it another way, the campaign for ideological conformity, whether Zhdanov was really the author or not, not only continued but became more strident. In the purely artistic field, there were some minor ameliorations, beginning as early as the latter part of 1949.[1] In April 1952 a *Pravda* article attacked the theory that literature should not portray conflicts in contemporary Soviet society.[2] At the Nineteenth Congress (October 1952), Malenkov urged that writers and artists "boldly show the contradictions and conflicts of life."[3] After the 1946 decrees on literature and art writers had become afraid to portray *any* aspect of Soviet life in an unfavorable light, or even to present any "bad" characters (except foreigners). As a result their works became stiflingly dull. If Malenkov's admonition offered some slight relief on this score, however, he insisted in the same passage that "our artists, writers and workers in the arts must constantly remember that the typical is not only what is encountered most frequently, but that which most fully and vividly expresses the essence of the given social force . . . the problem of the typical is always a political problem."[4] This, of course, meant that "socialist realism" remained in full force.

The non-Russian writers of the USSR were especially severely attacked after 1945. In 1951 *Pravda* condemned Volodymyr Sosiura, a major Ukrainian poet, for his poem "Love the Ukraine," published in 1944.[5] It failed, the article said, to distinguish love for the old Ukraine from love for the new, Soviet Ukraine, and therefore played into the hands of bourgeois nationalists. Even the Party favorites Aleksandr Korneichuk and his Polish wife

Wanda Wasilewska were criticized sharply for the "nationalist tendency" of their Ukrainian opera *Bohdan Khmel'nyts'kyi.*[6] The Ukrainian central committee, which was blamed for these deviations, was compelled to issue a decree condemning the writers.[7]

In 1951, too, the theory of the "lesser evil"—that the incorporation of the border nationalities into the former Russian Empire was really a "blessing" for them, because it preserved them from conquest by more oppressive countries, and stimulated their economic and cultural life—first attained official force.[8] During 1950 and 1951 critics attacked as nationalist, pan-Turkic, and pan-Islamic a wide range of historical and belletristic writing in the Moslem Caucasus, such as the Azerbaidzhani epic *Dede Korkut* and treatments of the story of the nineteenth-century rebel against Russia, the Imam Shamil.[9] By 1952, however, even the "lesser-evil" formula was obsolete; M. D. Bagirov, the Azerbaidzhani first secretary, attacked the principal Soviet historical journal, *Voprosy Istorii*, for even conducting a "pointless, abstract discussion about the so-called 'lesser-evil' formula." [10] Thenceforth, annexation to Russia was to be presented as an unmitigated good for the peripheral nations.

The principal change in emphasis after 1948, however, was the sweeping denunciation of "cosmopolitanism," "an indifferent and scornful attitude toward one's fatherland." For years the cosmopolitanism of the big capitalist had been contrasted to the true patriotism of the proletarian.[11] In Zhdanov's time some references to "cosmopolitans" as persons without deep national roots, "passportless wanderers in humanity," also appeared.[12]

The Soviet ideologists were especially concerned with the ideas of world government and allegiance to the UN which had gained considerable support among Western intellectuals. At the end of 1948 *Voprosy Filosofii* printed an editorial denouncing cosmopolitanism as preaching "a nihilistic attitude for the individual toward his nationality," and maintained that it was a tool of United States policy. The editorial contrasted cosmopolitanism to "proletarian internationalism, organically combined among us with Soviet patriotism," and stressed the primacy of Russia in culture and in revolutionary activity. The theme was linked, however, to Zhdanov's "two-camps" theory, with a strong coloring of militant Communism as well as Russian nationalism.[13] On the other hand, an article by the ideologist D. Zaslavskii, which appeared shortly afterward, emphasized naked Russian supremacy:

> Looking ahead into the New Year, into the future, we see the Russian tongue as the world language of socialism. . . . All previous world languages were

cosmopolitan tongues. . . . Even now it is impossible to be a genuinely educated person without Russian. . . ."[14]

The attack on cosmopolitans quickly extended to musicians, philosophers (including Kedrov, although the *Voprosy Filosofii* article cited above had been published when he was editor), and drama critics. Assailing the latter group, the Soviet press openly stated for the first time since the war that intellectuals had been expelled from the Party for ideological deviation—which doubtless meant that they were in concentration camps.[15] The special fury of the anticosmopolitan campaign was directed at the Jews. As was noted in Chapter XI, there is strong evidence that official anti-Semitism began during World War II. The Soviet regime was even more careful to conceal this policy from the outside world than it was its other repressive actions, for it wished to gain the good will of the great body of world opinion which abhorred the savage Nazi persecution of the Jews.

In September 1941 the Soviet authorities—apparently Beria was in charge—began the formation of an international Jewish committee to mobilize opinion to support the Allied war effort, especially that of the USSR. The leaders, in addition to the Soviet Jewish actor and writer, Solomon Mikhoels, were to include Henryk Ehrlich and Wiktor Alter, leaders of the Jewish Socialist Bund in Poland who had been held in a Soviet concentration camp since 1939. In December 1941, however, the Soviet police arrested and shot the two Polish Jews.[16] The published reason, that they were Nazi spies, was fantastic; other Jewish leaders in the USSR were told that Ehrlich and Alter had "meddled in internal Soviet affairs."[17] The real reason was probably the strong influence Ehrlich and Alter exercised in the labor movement; had they survived they might have been serious obstacles to Communist domination in Poland. Possibly another reason was the fact that Ehrlich, as a leader of the Second International, had protested the wave of arrests following Kirov's death—an act that Stalin was unlikely to forgive or forget.[18] Despite this sinister beginning, the Anti-Fascist Committee, under Solomon Mikhoels and Itsik Fefer, was able to arouse considerable enthusiasm for the Soviet war effort. This was especially true in the United States, in spite of the fact that the Anti-Fascist Committee refused to cooperate with the principal American Jewish relief agency, the Joint Distribution Committee.[19]

In the immediate postwar period the Soviet regime apparently felt that it could continue to exploit the good will it had gained for its major role in the destruction of Nazism, and in addition utilize for its own purposes the unhappy situation of the surviving European Jews. Most East European

Jews strongly desired to leave the area where they had suffered so greatly, and where popular anti-Semitism was still strong. The Communist authorities encouraged, and even organized, the flight of Jews to West Europe, where their presence increased the pressure for lifting curbs on emigration to Palestine.[20] At the same time, in order to inflame Jewish opinion, the Soviet press seized upon British efforts to restrict the influx into Palestine.[21] Great Britain, the Soviet press said, was plotting to form an anti-Soviet bloc in the Middle East, and at the same time to retain control of the area for her oil monopolies. In order to do so, Britain was urging the Arab ruling circles and landlords to launch an aggressive war against the Jews in Palestine.[22]

In early 1948 the USSR supported the creation of a Jewish state by partition of Palestine, and when Israel was proclaimed, the Soviet Union and its satellites hastened to recognize it. Satellite delegates even refused to take part in a UNESCO conference held in an Arab country at that time.[23] More than that, soon after the Communists seized power in Prague the Czechoslovak Communist general secretary, Rudolf Slánský, organized a clandestine airlift of arms for the Jewish forces.[24]

Very soon after the foundation of Israel, however, the Soviet attitude changed. Even earlier, Communist publications, continuing the decades-old line of the Palestinian Communist Party, had attacked the predominance of the "bourgeois" groups among the Palestine Jews.[25] Very likely the Soviet rulers were disappointed, though not entirely surprised, when democratic socialist forces predominated in the new state. They may also have been disappointed by the failure of the Progressive Party in the United States, which combined fervent pro-Soviet and pro-Israeli positions, to attract the bulk of American Jewish voters.[26] Another important factor was the strong Zionist feeling aroused among Soviet Jews by the arrival of the Israeli ambassadress in Moscow. It is also possible—though not demonstrable—that Zhdanov and his adherents, whose disappearance from the Soviet scene closely coincided with the changed attitude toward Israel, were more inclined to tolerate Jews than were their successors in Party control.

The heightened anti-Semitic campaign in the latter part of 1948 included direct attacks on Israel and Zionism, such as an especially severe denunciation by Il'ia Ehrenburg (himself a Jew) in September 1948. Such attacks, while restrained since 1941, were in full accord with basic Communist policy. The beginning of open attacks on Jewish cultural institutions indicated a new tendency. As late as January 1948, the death of Solomon Mikhoels had been commemorated by an obituary in *Pravda,* followed by a long list of signatures, most apparently of Jews, including members of the Anti-Fascist Committee.[27] In autumn, however, this committee was quietly dissolved. So were practically all of the Yiddish-language cultural institutions in the USSR.[28] In December a number of major Jewish cultural leaders were secretly arrested. All Soviet Jews, however, whether Zionist, Yiddish-speaking, or completely Communist and Russified, were threatened by the campaign against "homeless cosmopolitans."

The increasing harshness and rigidity of the anticosmopolitan campaign were in part the result of the bitter propaganda war of the USSR against the Western powers which accompanied the Berlin "blockade" in 1948-49. Another factor which doubtless greatly heightened Stalin's suspicions of all foreign influences was Tito's successful defection. Since both factors affected the Soviet-dominated sphere in East Europe, it is not surprising that this area felt the full force of the anticosmopolitan campaign.

In Russia, opposition to cosmopolitanism was at least combined with deeply rooted nationalism. In the East European satellites, on the other hand, it meant naked subordination to Soviet power:

> The genuine internationalist, the genuine Communist, is he who combines love for his people, for the working class, with his love for the Soviet Union—the homeland of Socialism, the country which is now building Communism—he who is irreconcilable towards any deviation from the position of internationalism, who is imbued with boundless love for, and fidelity to, the leader and teacher of working mankind, Comrade Stalin.[29]

Because Tito's successful defiance was based on the independent triumph of the Communist forces in Yugoslavia, all other satellite leaders were forced to admit—despite the inevitable damage to their standing in their own countries and to the Communist propaganda position in the world at large —that they had been installed in power by the Soviet forces. As early as April 1949, the Soviet Cominform leader, P. F. Iudin, said:

> With the arrival of the Soviet Army the national liberation war in the countries enslaved by Hitlerite Germany, and the struggle of the working people in the states allied with Germany, began to turn into a revolutionary struggle for liberation not only from foreign oppressors, but also for the overthrow of the landowners and the bourgeoisie, who were allies of Hitler. Herein was expressed the magnificent liberating force of the army of the socialist state.[30]

At the same time, even Western Communist leaders were obliged to express openly their willingness to help the USSR subdue their countries. Maurice

Thorez, for example, declared on February 23, 1949, that the French Communist Party would collaborate with the Soviet army if it occupied France.[31]

For the satellite Communist leaders, the corollary of admitting that the Red Army had given them their jobs was complete submission to Soviet directives:

> We must emphasize the fact that we received the decisive stimulation and assistance for the clarification of our future development from the Communist (Bolshevik) Party of the Soviet Union, from the teachings of Comrade Stalin. The two sessions of the Cominform, the first in the fall of 1947, the second in the summer of 1948, were of fundamental help for us . . . as regards the fundamental questions of transformation into Socialism, the Soviet Union is our model and . . . the way of the People's Democracies differs only in certain external forms, and not in essence, from the way of the Soviet Union.[32]

The statement just quoted very probably exaggerated the extent of Soviet direction prior to 1949, but the mere fact that a prominent satellite ideologist felt compelled to exaggerate his party's earlier dependence on the Soviet Communist Party is a convincing demonstration of the latter's absolute supremacy after that date.

Only one satellite Communist leader dared differ even slightly with the Soviet blueprint for his country. Władysław Gomułka, the Polish secretary general, fanatically suppressed anti-Communist elements, yet he apparently regarded himself as the representative of a "Polish way to socialism" differing from the Soviet pattern. Down to 1948 the peasants and the Catholic Church were more leniently treated in Poland than in other East European Communist countries, including Yugoslavia. At the June plenum of the Polish party Gomułka struck a discordant note by speaking of the independent national origins of Polish socialism. Although he had represented Poland at the founding of the Cominform, he was not sent to its second meeting, which denounced Tito. In August 1948 a second plenum elected Bolesław Bierut general secretary in Gomułka's place; the plenum also wrung a confession of error from Gomułka—but he continued to defend "some elements of a Polish road to socialism." [33]

On the surface, then, this opening act of the East European purges—for Gomułka was the first major satellite leader to suffer disgrace—arose from his recalcitrance toward Soviet demands of the moment. According to an extremely well-informed defector, however, Gomułka would have been replaced sooner or later even had he exhibited no independence. His essential fault, according to this version, was that he had remained in

Poland (in prison and then in the underground) instead of living in the USSR as an exile, subject to the full discipline of the Soviet Party and secret police, like his successor Bolesław Bierut. Working in the underground, Gomułka had developed habits of independence which on a small scale resembled Tito's: he had signed a memorandum urging anti-Nazi activity while the USSR and Germany were still allied, and had not waited for Soviet approval to begin his underground work.[34]

Apparently the only real reason Moscow permitted the purge in the spring of 1948 of a group of veteran Bulgarian Communist leaders headed by Traicho Kostov was the fact that they had remained in the Bulgarian underground throughout the war, instead of becoming "Muscovites" in Soviet exile. At the same time, the term "permitted" probably accurately reflects the role of the Soviet regime in the affair, for the real instigator of Kostov's downfall and eventual execution seems to have been the "Muscovite" Vŭlko Chervenkov.[35] Probably similar personal rivalry had much to do with the execution in the summer of 1949 of László Rajk, the Hungarian Foreign Minister.[36] Because he was of German descent and had spent most of the war in Hungary, Rajk had a much stronger following in the Communist Party (which included many former members of pro-Nazi groups) than the general secretary, the Jew Mátyás Rákosi, who had spent many years in Soviet exile.[37] Rajk had also apparently criticized the Nazi-Soviet pact.[38]

Just how the "Muscovite" Rákosi managed to discredit Rajk with Moscow (which certainly directed the political police which arranged the trial) is still unknown. Like Kostov, Rajk was accused of secret collaboration with Tito in the service of Anglo-American espionage; but leaving aside the second half of the accusation, it appears that before 1948 Rákosi himself had been much more sympathetic to Tito than Rajk had been.[39] Undoubtedly Rajk's lack of a background of Soviet indoctrination weakened the Soviet leaders' confidence in him. A second factor which tended to compromise Rajk was his involvement in the Spanish Civil War. As we have seen, Tito drew heavily on the "Spaniards," as the international volunteers were called, to officer his partisans. Later, real Spanish refugees under Communist influence were recruited in France and sent through Yugoslavia to enter an "international brigade" helping the Greek rebels.[40] After his break with Stalin, Tito continued to use veterans of the Spanish Civil War —Sreten Žujović, a leading Yugoslav Communist who at first sided with Stalin, but later recanted, was one—and there were even rumors that he intended to use Jésus Hernández, a major Spanish Communist leader who had broken with Stalin, to set up an "anti-Cominform." [41]

Some of the developments just mentioned occurred after Rajk's execution, but even in late 1949 the Hungarian Communist regime had considerable reason to make sure that the Spanish veterans were kept thoroughly in line. Veterans of the Spanish International Brigades formed an important part of the Hungarian army officer corps.[42] There was evidently some plan to concentrate in Hungary Spanish and non-Spanish veterans of the Civil War for use against Tito.[43] Consequently, the "Spaniards" were not denounced *en masse*. A certain Hungarian group headed by Ernö Gerö, who had gone from Spain to Comintern headquarters in Moscow, was even favored.[44] The Rajk accusation was broadened, however, to embrace a large number of the Spanish Civil War veterans who had spent World War II in France: Tito was alleged to have arranged a deal with the Gestapo to secure their release.[45]

In this way the circle of incriminated Communists widened. Even at this early stage of the purge in East Europe it was apparent that the Soviet regime was more concerned with eradicating tendencies which could be taken to indicate an anti-Stalinist "international conspiracy" than it was with national deviations alone.

It was inevitable that the purge in East Europe, like the Great Purge in the USSR in 1937-38, meant a great increase in police power. According to one important defector, a systematic plan for increasing the role of MVD controls in East Europe was worked out in 1947 when the first signs of Tito's deviation became evident, and was put into force after the Soviet-Yugoslav break.[46] As the essential features of the system he described are the same as those revealed by later defectors, a considerable augmentation of MVD control seems very probable, although the precise time at which it occurred is not certain.[47] Within each satellite representatives of its police ministry were placed in every government department to control personnel and current operations. Police agencies in the different satellites maintained close contact with one another. An MVD advisory staff directed each satellite police ministry.[48]

Stalin was careful, however, to keep the ultimate power in his own hands. Top-ranking satellite party chiefs obtained their basic directives in Moscow directly from Stalin, or through Malenkov or some other member of the ruling Party circle.[49] Current orders were transmitted through the secret Soviet Party representative in each satellite capital, or through the satellite party representative in Moscow.[50] Above all, satellite Communists tried desperately to prove their reliability by anticipating Stalin's interpretations of Marxist orthodoxy.[51]

Nevertheless, the whole system of satellite Communism, like the Comintern in the later thirties, came more and more to resemble a police operation instead of a political organization. A distinctly secondary feature of East European Communism was its role as an adjunct of the Soviet propaganda machine. This role was underlined by the appointment in 1947 of the ideologist Iudin as director of the Cominform bureau, and heightened in 1948 by the appearance of Suslov, the Secretary in charge of Soviet propaganda, as a major Cominform representative.

The third, and final, Cominform general meeting, which convened in Hungary in late November 1949, seemed almost entirely designed for international propaganda effect. The only Soviet delegates were Suslov, who spoke on "Defense of Peace and Struggle against the Warmongers," and Iudin. Though several "native" leaders appeared among the satellite delegates "Muscovites" predominated. While savage attacks were directed against the Yugoslav "murderers and spies," the burden of speeches was the duty of Communists and workers everywhere to struggle against the North Atlantic Treaty Organization, and particularly its social democratic supporters.[52]

After 1949 the Cominform fell into desuetude, although its formal existence was prolonged for nearly seven years. Its weekly, *For a Lasting Peace, for a People's Democracy* continued to play a part, although a minor one, in Communist propaganda. The major share of propaganda activities outside the Communist sphere itself, however, went to the vast network of "front" organizations formed after the dissolution of the Comintern. As was described in Chapter III, the prototype "fronts" of the Popular Front period were deeply shaken by the defection of Willi Münzenberg. Some agents of the Münzenberg organization, like the Czechoslovak André Simone, continued to play an important part in covert manipulation of public opinion in Western countries, however.[53] The war period, with its emphasis on anti-Axis unity, provided fertile ground for these tactics. By 1945 the Communists were ready to make a serious effort to dominate and use as "fronts" major international associations.

The first and most important to fall into their hands was the World Federation of Trade Unions. Communist organizers captured this body largely through the disproportionate representation accorded the Soviet trade unions, which were of course mere instruments of the regime, and through Communist domination of the large French and Italian labor federations.[54] Evidently the Communists had hoped to use the WFTU in turn to influence the United Nations, for the Soviet press berated the United States and the British foreign ministers for refusing to provide a consultative vote for the labor organization in the UN Charter.[55] Largely through British Labour insistence, the WFTU was also rendered innocuous for the most part as far as taking *action* in labor matters was concerned. Nevertheless at the end of 1949 the democratic trade unions found it desirable to withdraw and form their own organization, leaving the Communists a restricted, but still powerful, propaganda weapon.

Other organizations, like the World Student Union, which originally united many liberal democratic as well as Communist groups, had a similar history of Communist infiltration and domination, with eventual withdrawal of non-Communist participants. Still other organizations, like the International Union of Democratic Jurists, were founded under Communist inspiration to provide vehicles for special propaganda appeals.[56] During the "forward" period of international Communism, these organizations (which usually had their headquarters in West Europe at that time), were used to support Communist policy by such steps as undertaking propaganda campaigns for the "democratic" Greek insurgents.[57]

Not long after the Tito break, the Stalinist Communists organized a general international movement specifically designed to support their propaganda. The first meeting of the "World Peace Congress" was held in Paris in April 1949, but under official French pressure soon transferred its activities to Prague. It was specifically designed to combat NATO, and perhaps also to provide moral support for the proclamation of the "German Democratic Republic" in East Germany.[58] The following year a second meeting was held in Warsaw. A permanent World Peace Council, with an "executive council" studded with high functionaries (mainly French and Italian) of earlier "fronts" like the WFTU was created to serve as a permanent overall directing body for anti-Western propaganda. During the height of Soviet opposition to the United Nations defense of South Korea, there were even rumors that the Communists intended to use the World Peace Council as the nucleus for an "anti-UN." [59] Probably because the USSR continued to secure some support for its aims in the United Nations, no formal opposition organization was formed, however.

Like the satellite organizations, a key function of the "fronts" in the international Communist system remained their utility as auxiliaries of the Soviet "agitprop." More subdued, but very significant, was the role of the "fronts" as auxiliaries of the secret police; they served as a recruiting ground for Communist sympathizers, some of whom, after passing into the Party itself, became Soviet espionage agents.[60]

While the European and the North American Communist movements, in all their ramifications, were even more restricted to the role of tools of Soviet policy than they had been in the thirties, Communism in the Far East continued to present a startling contrast. The complicated history of the rise of the Communist Party of China to dominate its country, and the vast implications of this cannot be treated in this study. Nevertheless, some indication of its relation to Soviet policy toward international Communism is essential.

Among the many factors leading to the Communist victory in China— such as the unfavorable geographical position of the Kuomintang government in Chungking during the war, and its increasing corruption and inefficiency—the skill and determination of the Communists in organizational and propaganda techniques stand out. These techniques were especially valuable in the development of the Communist partisan movement in Japanese-occupied areas, which eventually enabled the Communists to take over as the Japanese evacuated at the end of the war.[61] In spite of the parallel to Soviet and Yugoslav tactics, there is no direct evidence that the Chinese Communists drew on European Communist experience in partisan operations; if anything, as suggested in Chapter X, the flow of information was in the other direction. If there were Soviet agents or advisors in Yenan during the war, their activity was extremely circumspect.[62]

More conventional assistance from the USSR to the Chinese Communists undoubtedly existed, but it is hard to estimate its extent. There have been repeated rumors of secret training of numbers of Chinese Communist leaders in Moscow, but they cannot be substantiated.[63] Some Soviet munitions reached the Yenan Communist base across Mongolia, but the amount was apparently not great. More substantial was the indirect aid which the Red Army gave the Communists in Manchuria in 1945; in many places Soviet withdrawals were timed to permit Communist partisans to take over the areas (which sometimes contained militarily useful Japanese munitions stockpiles) in advance of the Nationalist troops.[64] On the other hand, Soviet looting of Manchurian industries paralleled the situation in East Germany; hence one may conclude either that domestic Soviet pressures for machinery outweighed long-range foreign policy considerations, or that the Soviet regime did not anticipate permanent Communist dominance in Manchuria. Quite likely, as in Germany, two or more Soviet agencies were pursuing independent, if not contradictory policies.[65]

There is a good bit of additional evidence—too complicated to describe here—to indicate that as late as 1947, at least, the Soviet regime did not expect a Communist triumph in China.[66] During the war there were some indications, though minor ones, that the USSR considered that even the Kuomintang regime might be indirectly useful in overthrowing the Western "imperialists." For example—in strange though undoubtedly unknowing anticipation of the situation of 1960—the Comintern press wrote that a Sino-Iraqi treaty of early 1942 "opened a new page in the histories of the Arab and the Chinese peoples, a page which will have enormous significance in strengthening co-operation of all eastern countries in their struggle for freedom and independence." [67] Of more practical value to Communism was the fact that Kuomintang military commanders in north Indo-China at the close of the war at least tolerated Communist-infiltrated Vietminh's maintenance of control of local administrations.[68]

During the war, the Japanese and the Korean Communist parties, at Soviet direction, transferred their headquarters to Yenan.[69] As late as February 1948, however, a major "front" organization, the World Federation of Democratic Youth, (WFDY) held a "conference of youth of Asia" in Calcutta. This conference apparently served as a major transmission point for Soviet instructions to the South Asian Communists, although the nature of these instructions is still unclear. Late in 1949, however, a major WFTU trade union conference for Asia and Oceania was held in Peking, where the victorious Chinese Communists had established their capital. Subsequently many more conferences of "front" organizations were held in Peking, and co-ordinating bodies for East Asia established there.[70] The policy was apparently accelerated by the Korean war. It seems clear that the North Korean Communist party was under Moscow control in 1950, and that the Soviet authorities at least had prior knowledge of the invasion of South Korea, if they did not order it.[71] When the Chinese Communist military forces entered the conflict, however, Chinese influence in Korean affairs, and perhaps in Japanese as well, seems to have increased relative to Soviet, but the Soviet influence probably continued dominant.

At least as important as the delegation of organizational control over Asian Communism to the Chinese was the explicit Soviet endorsement of the use of Chinese Communist tactics in other Asian countries. One tactic acclaimed by the Soviet press in early 1950 was the union of all anti-imperialist forces, without regard to class affiliation, in the Communist-led struggle; this tactic was to apply to all East Asia. The second Communist tactic, the use of a Communist-led army as the main instrument for securing power in semicolonial countries was endorsed for the smaller Southeast Asian countries, but not for India.[72] Up to 1953, then, the Soviet regime had made unusual concessions, at least verbally, to Chinese Communist autonomy, and even to the extension of its influence to a broader sphere, although as yet this sphere was, in the main, restricted to China's neighbors in East and Southeast Asia.

In the ideological field the period 1950-52 was marked by unusual drastic personal interventions by Stalin. The first pronouncement, published in the summer of 1950, was "Marxism and Questions of Linguistics," a series of replies to questions concerning the theories of N. Ia. Marr. Marr, of Irish-Georgian ancestry, and a special protégé of Stalin, had died in 1934. His idea that all existing languages arose through the prehistoric fusion of earlier, completely dissimilar tongues, although rejected by practically all non-Soviet specialists, had become the mandatory creed of Soviet linguistics. From the Communist point of view, Marr's theories seemed favorable because they maintained that one language proceeded from many under the influence of economic changes; hence, the proletarian revolution would eventually lead to a single world language.[73]

One explanation of Stalin's rejection of Marr's system points out that his world language would differ from any existing language; therefore, it would not be Russian. Throughout the late thirties and the forties Russian was more and more stressed as an essential centralizing linguistic element in the Soviet realm. By 1949, as noted earlier in this chapter, Russian was proclaimed as the future international language. Marr's theory obstructed the study of Russian, and made difficult the tracing of its relation to the other Slavic languages.[74] Against this explanation, however, is the fact that a 1951 publication by Poskrebyshev—who presumably mirrored Stalin's views—pointed out that "Linguistics" confirmed Stalin's earlier view that the future international language would differ from Russian.[75] Quite possibly it is significant that initial moves against Marr came from a fellow Georgian linguist who also occupied an important Party post.

In "Linguistics" Stalin pointed accurately to the close relation of Marr's ideas to the vulgar Marxist theories of the twenties and early thirties on literature.[76] The lengthy interval between the condemnation of these early "radical Communists" and Stalin's belated decision to intervene against

Marr is very puzzling. Herbert Marcuse speculates that "the Marrist doctrines had to give way to more universalist, 'normal,' and internationalist conceptions," when Stalin, having overcome the Soviet Union's technical backwardness, prepared to orient "Soviet society toward a long period of economic as well as political 'coexistence.'" [77] It is evident, however, that acceptance of this explanation rules out the supposition that the "Linguistics" pronouncement was designed to foster Russian nationalism—a dilemma that is typical of outside efforts to probe the obscurity of Stalin's thought.

Marcuse's concept of Stalin's general tendency to provide a theoretical basis for a more flexible foreign policy is directly relevant to Stalin's second pronouncement, "The Economic Problems of Socialism in the USSR." The "Economic Problems" was also a series of replies to questions, published in October 1952, but written in large part as early as February 1952. A principal theme of "Economic Problems" is the avoidability of war between the "Socialist camp" and the "imperialist [i.e., Western] camp." [78] Though Stalin denied that the "world peace movement" led by the USSR was designed to overthrow capitalism, this was hardly reassuring in view of his reiterated disavowals of spreading Communism, combined, as we have seen, with covert but highly successful efforts to do exactly that. [79] On the other hand, his stress on the "inevitability" of war between capitalist powers, while pointing to the desirability of destroying "imperialism" to eliminate war, did suggest that the USSR should avoid hostilities while awaiting the self-destruction of the capitalist world. [80] Some observers have seen in his emphasis on the "exploitation" of the defeated powers, Germany and Japan, a special effort to secure a realignment of international forces by attracting these powers to the side of the USSR. [81]

While the full implications of the nationalist and internationalist aspects of Stalin's pronouncement are not clear, one can at least readily discern their practical relevance to Soviet politics. The significance of certain other aspects of his statements lies at a deeper level. One strain appears to be related to Stalin's hesitant search for stability in ideology and institutions. There is almost a touch of pathos in his question, "How can an existing language be destroyed and a new one erected in its stead in a few years' time without introducing chaos into the life of society and introducing a threat of social disintegration?" [82] "Linguistics" squarely faced the question —which earlier Marxists had inclined to evade—of whether there are immutable elements of culture not a part of the "base" (productive relationships) or the "superstructure" (derivative social and political features). Stalin replied that language did not change with the changes in productive relations, nor did a revolution alter it—specifically, the Russian language remained the same before as after the Bolshevik Revolution.[83] Following Stalin's lead, Soviet ideologists extended the category of "immutable" elements to include logic, mathematics, and, with some qualifications, the natural sciences.[84] It is significant that Trofim Lysenko, the arbiter of Soviet biology after 1948, was criticized in the USSR during 1951-52, and that Albert Einstein's relativity theory again became respectable. Although there were countertendencies, after 1950 the abstract sciences appeared to enjoy somewhat greater freedom to use traditionally accepted theories without regard to their supposed conflict with dialectic materialism.[85]

The mere postulation of an unchanging language implied social stability, for language provided a factor which bound together all classes of a nation throughout history.[86] In further limiting the scope of the dialectic the development fitted a trend which most analysts agree was an important aspect of Stalin's ideological statements.[87] Stalin's rejection of "explosions" (vzryvy) as a necessary form of transition for such elements as language heightened the impression that he was seeking a less revolutionary theory of historical development. In the socialist phase of history, moreover, Stalin ruled out "explosive" development altogether.[88] As B. M. Kedrov—by then restored to favor—explained it, the "dialectic leap" (skachka) was universally valid, but the decisive transition from quantity to quality, need occur as an "explosion" only in overcoming the antagonistic contradictions of capitalist society, not in surmounting the nonantagonistic contradictions of socialism.[89]

In "Economic Problems" Stalin dwelt at considerably greater length on this crucial problem of resolution of socialist contradictions. He concluded "that under socialism matters do not usually reach [the point of] conflict between production relations and productive forces, that society is able to bring the lagging production relations into conformity with the character of the productive forces in good time." [90] In other words, such a contradiction (which Stalin admitted existed) as that between an essentially socialist economy and the continuing private-garden cultivation of the peasantry, could be peacefully solved when the time was ripe.[91] As Father Henri Chambre puts it, "the dialectic of development of the USSR under the direction of the state is reduced to a simple continuous, inevitable progress, the type of progress which the French encyclopedists made fashionable at the end of the Eighteenth century and which the 'utopian socialists' lauded to the skies in the first half of the nineteenth." [92] At the same time, attainment of the goal of complete Communism required the fulfillment of so many difficult conditions that it became an eschatological image rather than a practical objective.[93]

While continuing to emphasize the role of the state in guiding Soviet development, "Economic Problems" contradicts "Linguistics" on one important aspect of state activity. The latter continued to stress the "revolution from above" concept which Stalin had already set forth in the *Short Course*.[94] Official commentaries immediately following the pronouncement explicitly alluded to planning as the way in which Soviet society developed.[95] In "Economic Problems," on the other hand, Stalin denounced those who contended that "the law of planned development of the national economy in proper proportions" is the fundamental economic law under socialism. One explanation for Stalin's attitude is his desire to curb the tendency of economists and managers—typified by the late N. A. Voznesenskii, who shortly afterward was attacked for his "voluntaristic" views on the supremacy of planning—to replace the political basis of Soviet ideology by a functional or "technocratic" attitude toward production.[96] The "law" which Stalin postulated for socialist production—"to assure maximum satisfaction of the constantly growing material and cultural requirements of all society through the constant growth and improvement of socialist production"—was purely normative, however. Consequently, it heightened rather than restricted the role of the state.[97]

In his final ideological pronouncements, Stalin touched upon, but failed to consider systematically, so many questions that careful non-Soviet analysts have reached sharply differing opinions concerning his real meaning. In this brief survey one can scarcely expect to resolve these matters, but at least the complexity of Stalin's views and some of their possible implications have been indicated. Perhaps, however, one hypothesis is worth offering. As Stalin increased his despotic control in the thirties, the totalitarian control of all phases of life implicit in Communism seemed a necessary corollary to his personal absolutism, although he restrained the "radical" aspects of Communism in order to achieve a measure of stability. In his declining years, on the other hand, stability, and even the search for the immutable, may well have seemed to Stalin to offer security against the unsettling dynamics of Communism.[98] In ideology as in personnel policies Stalin was engaged in a perpetual balancing act—and it is most likely that he could not fully understand, much less foresee, the complete implications of the steps he took.

CHAPTER

XVII

THE ENIGMA OF THE
NINETEENTH CONGRESS

During the years following World War II, the power of the Soviet police machine greatly increased in comparison with the years after the Great Purge had ended. The police never had absolute power in the Soviet system, but the extent of its dominion was enormous. As noted earlier, the principal day-to-day mechanism for controlling the satellites was the police network. Within the USSR, the police controlled large segments of the economy, including those operated with concentration-camp labor, and especially the growing nuclear weapons production.[1]

Until the end of 1951 Beria appeared to be the master, subject only to Stalin, of this police empire; his personal influence was even expanding. For example, when Lev Mekhlis was replaced as Minister of State Control in October 1950, his successor was V. N. Merkulov, one of Beria's closest associates.[2] In November 1951 Beria himself delivered the important speech celebrating the thirty-fourth anniversary of the Bolshevik Revolution. It is true that since 1946 Beria had not formally headed the police system. As noted several times before, Stalin apparently took care to prevent Beria from assuming absolute control over the entire personnel of the police. The Minister of the Interior, S. N. Kruglov, was apparently no close supporter of Beria. Branches of the MVD like the frontier troops were full of officers whose careers showed no special dependence on Beria. The key instrument, however, was the Ministry of State Security which controlled the secret police; since 1946 its minister had been V. S. Abakumov, one of Beria's longtime henchmen from the Caucasus. Consequently, Abakumov's unpublicized replacement, sometime in late 1951 or early 1952, by a territorial Party secretary, S. D. Ignat'ev, was an almost certain sign that Beria's position was shaken.[3]

Simultaneously, Beria was involved in difficulties in his early base, Georgia. The political alignments there were exceedingly complicated, and many of their ramifications are still unclear.[4] It is apparent, however, that Stalin did not trust Beria sufficiently to allow him to retain full control over the Georgian apparatus after he became head of the NKVD in 1938. Soon after Beria's departure for Moscow, the new Georgian first secretary, K. N. Charkviani, had reversed the policy of broad cultural autonomy for the non-Georgian minorities of the Republic in favor of a campaign of "Georgification."[5] Although Georgians constituted only three-fifths of the Republic's population, they apparently had a near-monopoly of Party posts. As late as 1954, according to the newspaper *Zaria Vostoka* (February 19, 1954), 82 per cent of the delegates to a Party congress were Georgians. In the autumn of 1951 Charkviani and the Minister of the Interior, N. M. Rukhadze, accused the second secretary N. I. Baramiia, and A. N. Rapava, the Minister of Justice (a former NKVD official), both close supporters of Beria, of corruption in office and supporting nationalist movements among non-Georgians.

Although Beria personally intervened at the April 1952 plenum of the Georgian central committee to secure the dismissal of Charkviani, the purge continued. A. I. Mgeladze, the new first secretary, had until then been in charge of the Party organization in the Abkhazian ASSR. Mgeladze had apparently completely suppressed instruction in the native Abkhazian language in this area, where Beria—apparently himself a pure Georgian—had been born, and had instead promoted the use of Georgian.[6] Mgeladze carried out an extreme attack on the non-Georgians during the second half of 1952. He accused the Party organization in the Adzharian ASSR, an area inhabited by ethnic Georgians (who were, however, traditionally Moslem rather than Christian), of corrupting the Georgian language and of friendship for Turkey.[7] While Mgeladze emphasized the Georgian language, he insisted that more stress also be placed on Russian, which he claimed had been neglected in favor of the non-Georgian minority languages.[8] His most severe attack, however, was directed at officials who tried to "break up Georgia into separate 'duchies'" by extending their "patronage" over individual districts.[9]

All these accusations seemed to be directed against Beria's adherents in the lower levels of the apparatus as well as at Baramiia and Rapava. In early 1953 Mgeladze noted significantly that many new officials had been chosen,

> for the most part specialists—engineers, agronomists, economists, jurists, scientific personnel. In the past year alone 427 new workers were elected and assigned as secretaries of obkoms, gorkoms, raikoms of the Party, and as directors of sections.[10]

The old Party and police apparatus of Georgia, which had furnished so many lieutenants to Beria for his operations on the All-Union scale, seemed on the way to replacement by a new type of technician.

While it is possible to trace with a reasonable certainty the impact of the Georgian changes upon Beria's position, it is impossible to discern Stalin's motives. That he personally intervened is clear not only from the extent of the changes and the violence of the charges—which a lower official could scarcely have made—but also from Khrushchev's subsequent reference to Stalin's concoction of "the Mingrelian affair" relating to alleged nationalism in Georgia.[11] Whether Stalin's initial motive was derived from his congenital involvement in obscure Georgian local and family politics or arose from distrust of Beria as a power factor in general Soviet politics cannot be determined. The situation is rendered still more complicated by the fact that personnel changes of considerable importance took place in other parts of the USSR during the summer of 1952, especially in the Ukraine where V. V. Matskevich, deputy chairman of the council of ministers in charge of argiculture, was ousted from the politburo.[12]

The events just described were soon overshadowed by the announcement on August 20, 1952, that a Central Committee plenum had resolved to hold the Nineteenth Congress of the Party in October. As the Central Committee had not convened for more than five years, the announcement of the plenum itself was noteworthy. The approach of a Congress, after an interval of thirteen and one-half years, was still greater cause for wonder. At first, the delay in convoking the Congress—due, according to the Party rules, in 1942—was easily explained by the war. The convocation of Union Republic congresses in late 1948 and early 1949, about three years after the close of hostilities, seemed to herald an approaching All-Union Congress, but none was held. Consequently, the inevitable question in 1952 was: Why a Congress at this particular time?

The content of the speeches at the Nineteenth Congress did little to answer this question.[13] The most dramatic event was negative—Stalin's failure, after more than a quarter of a century of precedents, to deliver the major speech, the lengthy report of the Central Committee. While this circumstance—and photographs taken at the Congress—indicated that the seventy-three-year-old dictator was no longer physically fit, it did not diminish his commanding role; the "Economic Problems of Socialism," published at the opening of the Congress, set the tone for all the speeches.

Malenkov, who delivered the Central Committee report, adhered especially closely to the theme of "Economic Problems." In dealing with foreign policy he emphasized contradictions in the capitalist world and expanded Stalin's suggestion that the former Axis powers would free themselves from the "American yoke." [14] In domestic economic affairs, the principal subject of his speech, Malenkov, in addition to attacking the "agrogorod" concept, stressed the continued priority to be given heavy industry.[15]

Easily second in importance among the Congress speeches was Khrushchev's report on changes in the Party statutes.[16] Although the subject was narrower than Malenkov's, the innovations proposed were actually much more important. The change of the official name of the Party from "All-Union Communist Party (Bolshevik)" was indeed of secondary significance, although it produced a startling effect. Actually the "Bolsheviks" of the Revolution had been almost entirely eliminated fifteen years earlier, and in practice the new name, "Communist Party of the Soviet Union" (CPSU), had been more and more frequently employed to distinguish the Soviet from the satellite parties. Similarly, the extension of the official interval between Congresses to four years, that between plenums to six months, and the elimination of the Party Conference, were scarcely of practical significance in view of the utter disregard of the earlier stipulations on convocation of Party meetings. The change of the "Commission of Party Control" to the "Committee of Party Control" was apparently purely formal. The reduction in the period of candidacy for Party membership to one year was a significant, though minor, step to reduce the endless probation periods which had become common.

Much the most important change, however, was the replacement of the Politburo and the Orgburo by a new permanent body, the Presidium. Neither the new name nor the emergence of a single body (since the Orgburo appears to have been the only one functioning regularly for several years prior to 1952) was in itself especially important. The vast increase in the size of the Presidium as compared to either of the other bodies or (since their membership had overlapped) of both together, was, on the other hand, crucially significant.[17] With twenty-four full members and eleven candidate members, the Presidium was obviously too unwieldy to serve as a committee for formulating policy. Consequently, Stalin, or whoever else could master the directing apparatus of the Soviet regime, needed to feel little concern over interference by the Presidium. The old Politburo members, moreover, were completely submerged in the new body. While all but Andreev were elected to the Presidium, they constituted less than a third of its membership.

The Party Secretariat was doubled in size by the addition of five new members. This enlargement suggests that Stalin did not feel complete confidence in the old Secretaries. Apparently he intended to rely more closely on his personal secretariat, headed by Poskrebyshev, who made a relatively important speech at the Congress, rather than on the official Secretariat. The organizational changes just described, which simultaneously surrounded the old Party leaders with new men and reduced the efficiency of the nominal directing bodies of the Party, go a long way to substantiate Khrushchev's later statement that Stalin was at this time planning the destruction of the older members of the Politburo.[18]

That Beria was the prime target of Stalin's intended purge is suggested not only by the threats to his position preceding the Congress, but by the relatively insignificant place of his speech in the Congress proceedings. On the other hand, speculation that Stalin's ultimate targets were the "technocrats," or industrial directors, is scarcely substantiated by examination of the Congress record itself.[19] Malenkov, one of the Party leaders closest to economic direction, appeared to have attained a new height of prestige. Other officials associated with industrial direction, like M. Z. Saburov, who gave the third most important speech (on the Five Year Plan), were more prominent than at any preceding Congress.[20] Several of them entered the new Presidium. However many members of the Party apparatus (especially territorial first secretaries) appeared there also; no one group seems to have been allowed to predominate.[21] An analysis of the composition of the Central Committee elected by the Nineteenth Congress also indicates a high proportion of economic directors.[22] Eighty representatives of the territorial Party and state apparatus, including a very high proportion of full members, constituted by far the largest Central Committee group. Nevertheless, approximately thirty ministers—nearly all engaged in economic direction—and half a dozen other officials engaged in economic supervision secured places in the Central Committee. The remaining fourth of the Central Committee membership was composed of nineteen high officers of the armed forces (mainly, however, candidate members only) and a scattering of cultural figures, Komsomol officials, and foreign service officers. Only four Central Committee places went, as far as can be determined, to police officials—and neither Abakumov nor another of Beria's close supporters, V. G. Dekanozov (who had been made a Central Committee candidate member in 1939), was among them.

The very incomplete data presented at the Congress on the background of voting delegates does not indicate any very significant change in the backgrounds of the upper- and middle-level apparatus officials.[23] The Old Bolsheviks and Civil War veterans were only 7.4 per cent. At the same time, the entire group of entrants since the start of World War II constituted only a little more than 20 per cent. The vast majority of the delegates, then, were those who had entered the Party approximately between the time of Stalin's emergence as General Secretary, and the close of the Great Purge. The men (women constituted nearly one-eighth of the delegates, but were probably mostly from the lower levels of officialdom) were about evenly divided between entrants of the 1921-30 period, and those of the 1931-40 period.

In 1939 officials at the upper and middle levels of the apparatus had constituted one of the youngest elites ever to govern a modern industrial power; by 1952, however, these men were predominantly middle-aged.[24] Over three-fifths of the delegates fell in the forty-one to fifty age group alone, while 17.7 per cent were just a little younger (thirty-six to forty) and 15.3 per cent, including men like Khrushchev, were already past fifty. Less than 6 per cent of the delegates were under thirty-five. Whatever storm the convocation of the Nineteenth Congress foreshadowed had to be faced primarily by the generation that had weathered the Great Purge fifteen years before.

In mid-August 1952, just prior to the convocation of the Nineteenth Congress, the official but clandestine anti-Semitic campaign approached a climax. A considerable number of prominent Jews, including several cultural leaders arrested after the dissolution of the Anti-Fascist Committee in 1948, but also the Party propagandist S. A. Lozovskii, were secretly put to death. The most fantastic accusation brought against them was that they had plotted to make the Crimea an area of Jewish settlement with the prospect of its becoming an Anglo-American base.[25] The paranoiac nature of the accusation vividly indicates its relation to subsequent events. It is characteristic of the changed position of Communism in the world, however, that the first public indication that a new "Great Purge" might be approaching appeared not in the USSR itself, but in a satellite. It will be recalled that Stalin had tried in 1937 to make his Great Purge more credible by arranging foreign trials of Trotsky's followers on charges of conspiracy with the Nazis. Since, however, Stalin's absolute power did not then extend even to Spain, his efforts were abortive. The situation in 1952 was quite changed. It is still not clear to what extent Stalin really feared an Anglo-American–Zionist conspiracy against his regime, and to what extent he merely used this charge as a pretext for the destruction of those whom he suspected in his own ruling group. Perhaps this is another instance in which Communists attributed to their opponents a mirror-image of their own conspiratorial intentions. In any case, Stalin was able to use his control of the East European satellites to introduce the overt "fever" stage of the purge campaign within the USSR.

The public charge of "Zionist conspiracy" had been slow in developing. At the Rajk trial in Budapest in 1949 considerable attention was devoted to the alleged espionage activities of Noel Field, an American who had directed relief activities of the Unitarian Committee in France during the war itself. According to the witnesses at the Rajk trial, Field (who had disappeared in East Europe several months earlier) had recruited Spanish Civil War veterans and other Communists in France as espionage agents for the Gestapo and for the Anglo-American intelligence services.[26] In 1949 no mention was made of Field's Zionist connections, although he was apparently of Jewish background. However, a minor witness at the Budapest trial confessed that he had learned (while in Switzerland) of the "close co-operation" between the Zionist movement in general and the United States intelligence service. Some of his subordinates in the "American spy group," he said, were Zionists.[27] While these remarks were scarcely noticeable, Field's involvement caused a wave of nervousness among high-ranking Jewish Communists in East Europe, several of whom were connected to him indirectly through their subordinates who had known him in West Europe.[28] Since Jews constituted a large share of the top party officials in Poland, Czechoslovakia, Rumania, East Germany, and Hungary, the circle of uncertainty was broad.

In mid-1951 the general Soviet charges that Israel was a tool of Anglo-American imperialism began to include specific allegations that Israel was co-operating with the American intelligence agencies. The Soviet press also accused Israel of enticing Jews to emigrate there from East Europe.[29] This complete reversal of Soviet policy obviously put the East European Communists who had implemented the 1945-48 policies of support to the Palestine Jews and encouragement of East European Jewish emigration in a delicate position—especially if the Communists were themselves of Jewish origin. The most important Jewish Communist directly affected was Rudolf Slánský, the Czechoslovak general secretary, who had supervised the arms airlift to Israel.[30] When Slánský engaged in this activity in 1948 he was at the height of his prestige, for he had directed the Communist seizure of power in Prague. The other outstanding figure of the Czechoslovak party, Klement Gottwald was, it was rumored, in disfavor because of his hesitation in taking strong measures against the non-Communist parties. Shortly after Zhdanov's death, however, Gottwald reported to Stalin personally, and appears to have won his favor.[31] In May 1949 Malenkov and Suslov visited Prague; their appearance apparently bolstered the positions of Gottwald (who had become President of Czechoslovakia) and Antonín Zápotocký, his successor as Premier.[32]

Nevertheless, the first major party leader to be accused in Czechoslovakia was Vlado Clementis, a close associate of Gottwald's, who was forced to resign as Foreign Minister in March 1950. Clementis, a Slovak, had spent the war in London with the émigré Czechoslovak government, and during the 1939-41 period he had criticized the Nazi-Soviet pact. He was therefore an easy target for the drive against "bourgeois nationalist" deviationists who lacked Moscow indoctrination, and who had shown signs of independence. During 1949-50 many other officials were arrested on charges of deviation and Titoism, including "Spaniards" and members of the Slovak partisan movement.[33]

Until late 1951 the Czechoslovak purge seemed to be following the same course as those in Poland, Hungary, and Bulgaria, with the "Muscovites" profiting from the disgrace of the "natives." In early September, however, a plenum of the Czechoslovak Communist central committee abolished Slánský's post of general secretary and turned over his functions to Gottwald as party chairman.[34] According to one report, the secret protocol of this meeting shows that Gottwald accused Slánský of substituting the party apparatus for the central committee, a charge which tends to substantiate the view that Gottwald favored the Communists in charge of economic and other state posts over the secretariat and the police machinery.[35]

Before September was out, Slánský was arrested; in December Gottwald charged that Slánský was the real leader of the Clementis group, and had infiltrated his clique into government as well as the party.[36] The secret police was purged of such figures as General Josef Pavel, a former International Brigade member.[37] Slánský, Clementis, and others in disfavor were attacked as "cosmopolitan" traitors who failed to praise the Russian leaders, Slav poets, and the fifteenth-century Czech reformer Jan Hus.[38] Finally, in November 1952, Slánský was publicly tried. Clementis, who evidently had no real connection with Slánský and his group, was put on trial at the same time.[39]

A large majority of the defendants, however, were Jews. The most important, next to Slánský, was Bedřich Geminder. After spending the war in Moscow in the inner circle of Comintern and post-Comintern operations, Geminder directed from his Prague headquarters an extensive Communist underground in West Europe. Another was André Simone, the "front" manipulator of many years' standing.

The group was accused of Trotskyite leanings, of Titoism, and of espionage for the Western powers—by now standard themes of the satellite purges. Much the greatest stress, however, was laid on their originally Jewish names (which most, like Slánský—*alias* Salzmann—had changed). Some, like Geminder, were ridiculed for mistakes in speaking Czech. Simon Ohrenstein, a former assistant to the commercial attaché of the Israeli legation in Prague, was the key witness of the trial. According to his testimony Ben Gurion, subsequently the Israeli premier, and the Zionist leader Moshe Sharett met with President Harry Truman, Dean Acheson, and the prominent American-Jewish statesman Henry Morgenthau in Washington in 1947. There they agreed to a "Morgenthau-Acheson plan" whereby in return for American support for the foundation of the Israeli state all Zionist organizations in East Europe were to become auxiliaries of American espionage.[40] Apparently no greater care was taken in concocting this story than in arranging the confessions of the 1936-38 trials, for it is certain that Ben Gurion did not visit the United States in 1947. Moreover, George Marshall, who was then Secretary of State, would logically have been present at the alleged "high-level" meeting the witnesses referred to, instead of Acheson, who succeeded Marshall the following year. In spite of these dubious points, Slánský, Geminder, and other defendants swore that they had been Zionists (as well as Trotskyites) from boyhood, and that they had eagerly entered into the conspiracy with the aid of Tito's principal Jewish supporter, Moša Pijade and the Jewish relief organization, the Joint Distribution Committee.

In order to dispel any doubt as to which group was implicated by the Slánský trial, Gottwald carefully stated in the Cominform press that the Zionists had abused the sympathy aroused by Hitler's persecution of the Jews for their own ends. All Zionist groups had become American agents. Nevertheless, Gottwald continued, Jewish descent and Zionism were not identical; the decisive factors were loyalty to one's homeland and class origin. From this statement it was evident that all Jews who, like Slánský and Geminder, were of "bourgeois" origin were suspect. The group included the large majority of the East European Jewish Communist leaders, such as Jakub Berman in Poland and Ernö Gerö in Hungary.[41] Even before the Slánský trial took place, the criterion of "Jewish bourgeois" seemed to have been applied in Rumania, where a rabbi's daughter, Ana Pauker, though a "Muscovite" and one of the most powerful figures in the regime, had been denounced for tolerating kulaks and forming a factional party group.[42]

There are many indirect indications and some direct evidence that the Slánský trial was ordered and prepared by Moscow.[43] The principal Soviet newspapers devoted extraordinary attention to the trial, stressing heavily the "American-Zionist" plot.[44] This press campaign was the immediate prelude to a direct public attack, which had evidently been months in preparation, upon the Soviet Jews themselves. On January 13, 1953, *Pravda* made the startling allegation that a group of physicians (most of whom had recognizably Jewish names) had tried to "wipe out the leading cadres of the USSR" by incorrect medical treatment. The accusation said they had actually shortened Zhdanov's and Shcherbakov's lives, and were planning to destroy the health of a number of top military leaders.[45] The principals of the "doctors' plot," as the affair became known, had acted on orders from the United States transmitted through "Joint" (the Jewish Joint Distribution Committee) and the deceased head of the Anti-Fascist Committee, Solomon Mikhoels.

During the following seven weeks, the Soviet press was full of similar charges against various groups throughout the USSR. Physicians were especially singled out, but officials were also attacked for nepotism, speculation, and embezzlement.[46] While not all the accused were Jews, the Soviet press emphasized that many were, by printing their original names or by physical descriptions calculated to arouse anti-Semitic sentiment:

And now this "underground millionaire," "Senka-Nose," stands before the court, unmasked, in his true light. His long, fleshy nose points mournfully downward, his puffy lips tremble with fear, his small, ratlike eyes roam uneasily.[47]

The campaign was especially intense in the Ukraine, with its large Jewish population. An article in the principal Kiev newspaper at the very end of the campaign stressed the themes which propagandists must use in dealing with the "conspiracy":

The physician-murders as the dregs of society recruited by American intelligence and professional spies of "Joint"; Slánský's trial in Czechoslovakia; the terrorist assault against the Soviet legation in Israel; the need for a decisive struggle against Ukrainian bourgeois nationalists, the worst enemies of the Ukrainian people, hirelings of American imperialism.[48]

As the last item indicates, the campaign, while centering on the Jews, had much wider implications. These were brought out at the very beginning by Frol R. Kozlov, a secretary of the Leningrad obkom, in a major article in the Party journal *Kommunist,* sent to press just *before* the "doctors' plot" was announced.[49] Kozlov, who had become secretary in Leningrad shortly after the "Leningrad affair," denounced the Party there for having facilitated imperialist and Titoist efforts to infiltrate agents by allowing "alien" elements, including ex-kulaks falsely claiming to have been partisan and former Jewish Bund members, to obtain membership. Ominously, Kozlov referred to the Central Committee letter following Kirov's assassination, and praised the 1935-36 verification of Party documents.

The resemblance of the pattern of accusations to those made during the Great Purge was unmistakable, though the emphases were altered. At the beginning of the campaign a *Pravda* editorial (January 13, 1953) specifically pointed to the connection:

> The organs of state security did not discover the wrecking, terrorist organizations among the physicians in time. In this regard these organs should have been especially vigilant, as history has examples of foul murderers and traitors to their native land acting under the mask of "physicians," such as the "physicians" Levin, and Pletnev who, on the assignment of enemies of the Soviet Union, murdered the great Russian writer A. M. Gor'kii and the outstanding Soviet statesmen V. V. Kuibyshev and V. R. Menzhinskii by using deliberately incorrect treatment.

It was obvious, too, that the chief victims were not to be the obscure physicians and trade officials publicly accused. Mekhlis, one of the few prominent Jews, died in mid-February, and although he was given a ceremonial funeral, rumors of foul play spread.[50] Kaganovich had long played a minor role. Molotov's Jewish wife was said to be in a concentration camp, and Molotov himself had played a notably obscure part in the Nineteenth Congress.[51] It is significant that Andreev, not elected to the Presidium, and Voroshilov, whom Stalin suspected of being a British spy, both had Jewish wives.[52] Apparently, however, the chief figure in immediate danger was Beria, for he could be blamed for failing to uncover the "doctors' plot," discovered after his henchmen had been removed from control of state security. Because of the Soviet police involvement in satellite control, the "Zionist" conspiracy there, too, seemed to point to Beria. This was especially the case in Czechoslovakia, where Slánský-Geminder control of the police apparatus and the West European espionage network must have entailed close co-operation with Soviet police agencies. But few if any among Stalin's lieutenants could feel secure with a new Great Purge beginning.

CHAPTER

XVIII

THE DEPARTURE OF STALIN
AND BERIA

On the morning of March 4, 1953, the ominous sequence of developments described in the preceding chapter was dramatically interrupted by an official announcement that Joseph Stalin had suffered a cerebral hemorrhage.[1] Two days later the Soviet press announced that he had died during the evening of March 5.[2]

It is inevitable that the coincidence of Stalin's death and the purge campaign should have been viewed with suspicion. Various changes of personnel in the period immediately preceding Stalin's death, it has been suggested, undermined the forces protecting him.[3] General S. M. Shtemenko, chief of the Soviet army general staff, who had risen unusually rapidly, was transferred to Germany shortly before February 23. The commander of the Moscow Military District, General P. A. Artemev was transferred some time during this period, and several of his most important subordinates, including Stalin's son Vasilii, who had commanded the air force in this district, disappeared. On February 17 the death of a Major General Kosynkin of the Kremlin staff, thought to be commander of its guards, was announced. Exactly a year after Stalin's death, the minister of health who had supervised the treatment of his last illness was dismissed.[4] The Soviet press never again mentioned Poskrebyshev, the head of Stalin's secretariat, except for a brief criticism of his interference in legislation.[5]

These very slight and indirect bits of evidence are hardly enough to justify a charge that Stalin was assassinated. On the other hand, there is more reason to believe that the official Soviet accounts have not been entirely frank concerning the time and the precise manner of Stalin's death. The first official bulletin stated that Stalin's hemorrhage occurred on the night of March 1-2 while he was in his Moscow apartment.[6] Six years later, however, Khrushchev told an eminent American visitor, W. Averell Harriman, that Stalin was staying at his *dacha* (country house) when Khrushchev last saw him on February 28, and that Stalin failed to make an expected telephone call to Khrushchev and the other leaders on March 1.[7] They were not informed of Stalin's illness by his bodyguard until the evening of March 2, when they (Khrushchev, Malenkov, Beria, and Bulganin) hurried out to the *dacha* and remained with Stalin until his death on March 5. This account helps to explain the delay in issuing the first announcement of Stalin's illness, but it raises the interesting question of where Stalin really died and how his bodyguard dared delay at least twelve hours in informing this group of major leaders. There is also the story, apparently circulated by P. K. Ponomarenko, a Presidium member at the time, that Stalin suffered his stroke when angered by Voroshilov's refusal to go along with the anti-Semitic campaign.[8] Given the fact that no foreigner saw Stalin after February 17, and the admitted delays in making the public announcement, one is bound to wonder if the ruling group did not put off notifying the world of Stalin's fatal illness still longer, while they temporarily resolved their own differences.

The front which the Soviet officials presented was at first a firmly united one. Obviously the Soviet leaders were deeply concerned with reactions within the USSR and abroad to the news that the man who had ruled the USSR for nearly thirty years was gone. While the Soviet state, unlike most totalitarian regimes, had already surmounted one crisis arising from the death of its leader, the transition from Stalin's dictatorship was bound to be more perilous than had been the change after Lenin's death in 1924. The latter had not exercised the absolute power Stalin insisted upon, especially in his final years. Moreover, by the time of Lenin's death, Stalin had already established control over the key position in the Party.

For a short time it appeared as though Malenkov could assure a smooth transition of rule by repeating Stalin's feat. According to one circumstantial report, he and Beria immediately reached an agreement on a redistribution of top posts in the regime; they confronted the Presidium and the Central Committee with a *fait accompli*.[9] If this is true, the deal must have been arranged quickly for, on March 7, the day after the announcement of Stalin's death, the decisions of a joint meeting of the Central Committee plenum, the Council of Ministers, and the Supreme Soviet Presidium appeared.[10] After calling for "the greatest unity of leadership and prevention of any kind of disorder and panic," the announcement stated that Malenkov had taken over Stalin's post as Chairman of the Council of Ministers. Henceforward, he and four first vice-chairmen—Beria, Molotov, Bulganin, and Kaganovich—were to comprise the Presidium of the Council of Ministers. The swollen Central Committee Presidium established by the Nineteenth Congress was replaced by a Presidium of ten members and four candidates. In composition it very closely resembled the Politburo as it had existed between 1948 and 1952. Malenkov, Beria, Molotov, Voroshilov, Khrushchev, Bulganin, Kaganovich, and Mikoian (listed in that order) were all members, and Shvernik was a candidate. Andreev was still excluded, however, and Kosygin was not even a candidate. Of the large group of new men elected in 1952, only M. Z. Saburov and M. G. Pervukhin remained as full members; Ponomarenko and L. G. Mel'nikov remained too, but were demoted to candidates.

One new candidate, M. D. Bagirov, who had never before appeared in the highest Party bodies, was added. As Bagirov had for decades been Beria's associate in the Caucasus, this appointment suggested a rise in Beria's strength. So did the fact that Beria, along with Malenkov and Molotov, delivered an oration at Stalin's funeral.[11] Still more important was the reunion of the MGB and the MVD under Beria's personal direction.[12] To an on-the-spot observer, these indications of Beria's power were underscored by the dramatic speed and efficiency with which police units established complete physical control of Moscow immediately following Stalin's death.[13]

In the first week without Stalin, however, Malenkov appeared to be the dominant figure. As Chairman of the Council of Ministers he was formal head of the government while remaining the senior Party Secretary. The relatively minor changes in the Secretariat seemed to leave his strength there unimpaired. Ponomarenko and N. G. Ignatov, who were transferred to state functions, were not known as close supporters of Malenkov, while the third Secretary transferred, L. I. Brezhnev, had come from Khrushchev's Ukrainian apparatus. Their replacements were the former Minister of State Security, S. D. Ignat'ev, whose leanings were then an enigma; P. N. Pospelov, an ideologist with no apparent affiliations in the top leadership; and N. N. Shatalin, a cadres specialist close to Malenkov.[14] Malenkov's gain in the Party Presidium was clearer. Saburov and Pervukhin both belonged to the group of industrial managers close to him, while (as noted in Chapter XIII) Kosygin, who was left out, had been associated with Mikoian.

Malenkov's personal advancement following Stalin's death, and especially that of the economic directors, had been one factor causing speculation that the ultimate aim of Stalin's purge had been the "technocrats." Aside from the rather slight animus against this group evident in "Economic Problems of Socialism," the charges of corruption against economic directors—not all Jews—following the "doctors' plot" are cited to substantiate this theory.[15] Most of the accused directors, however, were in consumer-goods industries, rather than in the heavy industries where Malenkov apparently had most support. Whatever the validity of this theory, it was to be expected (given the ruthlessness of Soviet politics) that Malenkov should try to use his position as the most prominent figure below Stalin to replace the dictator once he had died. During the week of March 7-14, there were clear signs that this was Malenkov's intention, the most striking being the publication of a photomontage from which most of the original figures had been clipped to leave Malenkov alone with Stalin and Mao Tse-tung.[16]

On March 21, however, appeared the week-late announcement that a Central Committee plenum on March 14 had relieved Malenkov, at his request, as Secretary.[17] At the same time, the Secretariat was reduced to Khrushchev, Suslov, Pospelov, Shatalin, and Ignat'ev. Since the order departed from the alphabetical listing provided earlier, it was clear that Khrushchev was the first among the Secretaries.

Until late March charges relating to the "doctors' plot" continued to appear, although less blatantly than before Stalin's death. The issue of *Bloknot Agitatora* (The Agitator's Notebook) which went to the press on March 10 had denounced the physicians and other criminals, including some with Jewish names, and had cited Malenkov's speech to the Nineteenth Congress on the need for enlisting the "masses" in control work.[18] A secretary of the Latvian Party referred in the March 15 *Pravda* to Stalin's demand for vigilance in warning against the danger of Zionists and Trotskyites in Latvia.[19] On March 22 a Belorussian report listed a number of embezzlers, including several with obviously Jewish names.[20] On March 25 *Izvestia* carried a similar article by the Leningrad oblast procurator.

Whoever was responsible for permitting the continuance of this aspect of the purge campaign, it is clear that Beria (whether or not in concert with other leaders) undertook to stop it. On March 28 a Supreme Soviet decree appeared amnestying minor offenders, including those accused of economic crimes and crimes committed in official capacities.[21] On April 3, the MVD itself published a communique announcing that the "doctors' plot" was a complete fabrication.[22] Two days later a *Pravda* editorial denounced M. D. Riumin, the deputy security minister who had obtained the physicians' confessions by "investigation methods which are inadmissible and strictly forbidden by Soviet law." Riumin was arrested, and his former superior, Ignat'ev, was accused of "political blindness and heedlessness." [23] On April 7, it was announced that a Central Committee plenum—the third since Stalin's death—had relieved Ignat'ev as Secretary.[24] On the heels of these charges came a widespread reshuffling of MVD officers. Jewish police officials who had been in disgrace were restored to active duty.[25] T. A. Strokach, who had supervised the crucially important Ukrainian police system, was apparently secretly accused of persecuting Ukrainians or Jews.[26] He was replaced by Pavel Iakovlevich Meshik, very probably a Jew.[27]

What could have induced Beria to take the risky step of striking at such an important figure as Strokach, a long-term associate of Khrushchev? The complete answer is, of course, unattainable, but it is easy to speculate that Beria felt that the only way he could preserve his power, and perhaps his life, was by siding with hitherto submerged forces in Soviet society. As director of the dreaded police agencies for nearly fifteen years, he was identified with the most hated aspect of Stalin's regime. Consequently, unless he enlisted new support, Beria would be the logical choice to go down when the new directorate decided to jettison some of the liabilities of the Stalin era.

For years rumors had circulated in Moscow that Beria was himself Jewish, or partly Jewish.[28] There is, however, no substantiating evidence for this rumor. Nevertheless, Beria and the Jews had been in the same boat as Stalin's intended victims. Jews constituted less than 2 per cent of the total Soviet population, and were very poorly represented in the high military officer corps and in the Party apparatus (even in Belorussia, where they were relatively most numerous, Jews constituted only 6.1 per cent of the officials).[29] But Jews made up about 10 per cent of the nonmanual workers, 10 per cent of students in higher education, 11 per cent of scientific workers, and one-sixth of the physicians.[30] They were also significantly numerous, apparently, in the police. While Beria could scarcely have expected that these Jewish elements alone would provide strong support, their influence might be of some value. In addition, many more Soviet citizens, shamed by the affront to revolutionary tradition as well as to customary concepts of human rights involved in the anti-Semitic campaign, might rally to his support.

Reversal of anti-Semitism was, of course, only one aspect of the "liberalization" program, though one which defectors have testified was advanced by Beria himself. Various observers have speculated that the general trend toward "liberalization," far from being Beria's doing, was forced upon him by the other Party leaders. The initial amnesty and continued emphasis on strict observance of Soviet laws did hold out some promise of curbing the characteristic arbitrariness of the Communist regime. Tied to this theme was an unwonted concern for the "well-being of the Soviet man and the prosperity of the Soviet people [which] are the supreme law for our Party." [31] But this theme was in turn directly connected to a theme which seemed especially favorable to Beria personally, the defense of non-Russians. The *Pravda* article just cited stated that "any direct or indirect limitation whatever of the rights or, on the contrary, the establishment of direct or indirect preferences for citizens on the basis of their race or nationality" were punishable by law.[32] Most articles in this vein merely implied that Russian nationalism was at fault, but occasionally direct reference was made to this essential point. In spite of the fact that since 1934, at least, Stalin had regarded non-Russian nationalism as the chief, if not the only nationalist deviation, he was cited as putting Russian and non-Russian nationalism on a par:

> J. V. Stalin said that national deviation—and it is all the same, whether a deviation toward great-Russian nationalism or a deviation toward local national-ism—is an adaptation of the internationalist policy of the working class to the nationalist policy of the bourgeoisie, an attempt on the part of the national-ist bourgeoisie to undermine the Soviet regime and restore capitalism.[33]

In recovering control of his erstwhile Georgian bailiwick, however, Beria's emphasis on the question of nationalism was slightly different. On April 14 Mgeladze, the Georgian first secretary, was replaced by I. A. Mirtskhulava.[34] The former minister of the interior, Rukhadze (who had been removed by Mgeladze in the summer of 1952), was arrested.[35] Beria's close associate, Dekanozov, became head of the Georgian MVD, but strangely enough the minister of state security under Mgeladze was made his deputy.[36] The Georgian press explicitly compared Rukhadze to Riumin, as an "enemy of the Party and the people" who had fabricated a nonexistent case—in this instance, non-Georgian nationalism. Rapava, Baramiia, and other supporters of Beria were exonerated, while Mgeladze was accused of taking an active part in their arrest. Both he and his predecessor, Charkviani, were accused of bureaucratic methods of administration and of filling the apparatus with their personal adherents.[37] The latter, of course, lost their posts, especially in Abkhazia; among their replacements was one A. Beria, elected first secretary of the gorkom in Tkvarcheli, a city a few miles from Lavrenti Beria's birthplace.[38] The secretary of the Georgian supreme soviet, a cousin of Stalin, was removed, as was the Komsomol secretary, a member of the Kandelaki family which had been close to Stalin.[39] Nevertheless, the Georgian press quoted Stalin himself on the need for inner Party democracy. In addition—implicitly recognizing Beria as the author of the purge reversal—the Georgian press referred to Beria as the "director of the Georgian Party organization for many years," the "talented pupil of Lenin" —and the "advisor of Stalin." [40]

There were, of course, compelling reasons for Beria to avoid an explicit rejection of Stalin, however glad he may have been to have the opportunity to get rid of Stalin's Georgian protégés. In spite of their alienation after 1951, Beria more than most Soviet leaders owed his prominence to Stalin's patronage. Moreover, despite the Georgian Stalin's encouragement of Russian nationalism, an open attack on him would further discredit non-Russians in the eyes of the dominant Russian population. Consequently, it is by no means certain that Beria played during the spring of 1953 a major role in the incipient effort to downgrade Stalin. It is fairly certain that a whole complex of forces in the Soviet leadership was pushing for some measure of change at this time.

In fact, the effort to downgrade Stalin was a cautious one. The Party as a whole and the Central Committee were praised instead of Stalin personally.[41] The principle of "collectivity" of leadership was stressed, for example, by L. Slepov, director of the "Party Life" section of *Pravda* and certainly not intimately connected with Beria's group. Slepov condemned the failure (prevalent during Stalin's lifetime) to hold Party bureau and plenum meetings regularly, and to conduct full discussion in them.[42] The philosopher, F. V. Konstantinov, hinted slightly more directly at Stalin's shortcomings. "Acceptance of the will and acts of outstanding personalities as the chief motive force of history is an expression of subjectivism and voluntarism in social science." [43]

That Beria's position was a key one in the developments of spring 1953 is indicated by numerous bits of evidence, small or uncertain individually, but convincing when viewed as a whole. On May 7, N. A. Mukhitdinov, later a protégé of Khrushchev, was demoted from chairman to first deputy chairman of the Uzbek SSR.[44] A few weeks later, A. Niiazov, the Uzbek Party first secretary—later dismissed for "arbitrary actions"—published an article, "In the Fraternal Family of Peoples of the Soviet Union," in which he used Beria's speech to the Nineteenth Congress as a source, while not referring to any other living Soviet leader.[45] As Central Asia was an area in which the MVD had long had special influence this sequence of events appeared significant. A reference in an Abkhazian Party conference to the fact that kolkhozniks had been forced illegally to make work contributions to unplanned construction seemed to be directed against Khrushchev's abortive "agrogorod" program.[46] Still more startling was the fact that at the May Day celebrations in Kiev as well as in Tbilisi Beria's picture was more prominently displayed than any other living leader's.[47]

There is also evidence that Beria had much broader plans for increasing his power in the Ukraine. Sometime earlier in the spring he had made a special trip to the West Ukraine. According to an accusation made against him after his downfall, Beria did this to establish contacts with Ukrainian nationalists as part of a scheme for creating an independent, capitalist Ukraine. This charge is doubtlessly greatly exaggerated, but the companion accusation that he placed the West Ukrainian police apparatus under the complete control of his adherents, headed by one Menshtein (an obviously Jewish name) in L'vov is probably accurate.[48]

Having prepared the ground in the West Ukraine, it seems probable that Beria was ready in June to act in a wider field. About this time, the Central Committee Presidium sent a letter to the Ukrainian central committee denouncing its nationality policy in the West Ukraine.[49] While it was later charged that Beria forged this letter, it seems more likely that Beria confronted the Presidium with highly embarrassing evidence gathered by his minions in the West Ukraine and by Meshik in Kiev concerning Soviet policy in the western areas. In any case, it is certain that the other Presidium members for a while at least tacitly acquiesced in the charges against the Ukrainian apparatus, for they were endorsed by the central newspaper *Izvestia*.[50]

The substance of the charges was that the Ukrainian Party apparatus had assigned East Ukrainians rather than native West Ukrainians to Party and state posts in the West Ukraine, had made Russian the language of instruction in the institutions of higher education in that area, and had made mistakes in developing the kolkhozes there.[51] While the Ukrainian central committee plenum was considering these serious accusations, obkom plenums began to meet in the West Ukraine; the timing suggests that Beria's forces were prepared in advance to press the issue there. Between June 12 and 17 plenums of nearly all the West Ukrainian obkoms considered the three charges described above, except that the question of kolkhoz organization was not taken up in the mountainous provinces.[52] The obkom bureaus were severely criticized.

The major target in the Ukraine, however, was the first secretary, L. G. Mel'nikov. The central committee plenum made him personally responsible for the faulty nationality policy, and elected the second secretary, A. I. Kirichenko, in his place. Aleksandr Korneichuk, the writer accused of Ukrainian nationalism in 1951-52, was elected to the Party bureau.[53]

It is still extremely difficult to understand how Beria was able to carry out such a sweeping attack on the Ukrainian apparatus. Some observers have assumed, therefore, that he carried out no far-reaching attack at all; according to this version, the other leaders simply chose him as a scapegoat on whom to place the irrepressible blame for the evils of Stalin's regime.

On the other hand, it has also frequently been supposed that Beria was in direct conflict with Khrushchev. According to this theory, Khrushchev, as former head of the Ukrainian apparatus, had been responsible for the special harshness of the anti-Semitic campaign in the Ukraine during the preceding winter.[54] There is, indeed, much to recommend this explanation. Khrushchev may well have borne a grudge against Beria because of the leading part played by Transcaucasian apparatus officials in denouncing the "agrogorod" scheme two years earlier. Khrushchev and the Ukrainian minister of the interior of that period, Strokach, had been intimately connected in the past. Moreover, retribution for the "doctors'-plot" campaign had a part in the upheaval in the Ukrainian Party organization in June. In Dnepropetrovsk, high Party officials were assailed for having permitted unjustified attacks on medical workers in the preceding February.[55] On the other hand, the publicized Ukrainian campaign against the Jews at least had become intense only after the Moscow press had rebuked the Kiev press for insufficient zeal in the matter.[56]

Additional doubt is cast on the theory of a direct Khrushchev-Beria clash by a consideration of the personnel changes. While Mel'nikov had served under Khrushchev when the latter headed the Ukrainian apparatus, there are many aspects of Mel'nikov's early career which suggest an affiliation to Malenkov.[57] Moreover, for about a month after Beria's fall, Mel'nikov was not rehabilitated; then he obtained successively the comparatively unimportant jobs of ambassador to Rumania and Minister for Coal Mine Construction. He never reappeared in the Presidium. Later, after Khrushchev had finally triumphed over Malenkov, Mel'nikov was reduced to the position of chairman of the Kazakh state planning commission, and even in this minor post was officially reprimanded—on a ground that seemed to imply his association with Malenkov.[58] Since Mel'nikov's successor, Kirichenko, turned out to be an especially close adherent of Khrushchev, one cannot escape the feeling that Beria plunged into a carefully set trap when he entered upon his Ukrainian adventure, which in the end profited only Khrushchev and his associates.

In spite of the importance of the Ukrainian affair, it is impossible to determine whether it was the immediate cause of Beria's downfall. As will be described in the next chapter, Beria was very probably simultaneously engaged in far-reaching operations designed to increase his influence in East Europe. Charges that the Party organizations in Latvia and Lithuania had failed to employ local cadres seemed to presage the removal of important Party officials in those Union Republics as well as in the Ukraine, Georgia, and Uzbekistan.[59] If Beria could have gained control of all of these areas he would have dominated a vast belt of Communist territory along the Soviet western and southern frontiers. In such case, the other members of the Soviet regime could hardly have dislodged him without undertaking a civil war which would have threatened the Soviet position in the world balance of power. Even in the spring of 1953, fear of weakening the Soviet power position by internecine struggle may have been a considerable factor in influencing the other Soviet leaders to let Beria have his way.

In mid-June, however, the workers' uprisings in East Berlin and other parts of East Germany seemed to indicate that the risks of Beria's course were as severe as those which would be incurred by deposing him. Probably such reasoning was especially prevalent in the Soviet army, which was most deeply involved in holding the East German position.[60]

Once the decision was made to overthrow Beria by force, his power structure collapsed quickly. The portion of the MVD most important to his control of the periphery, the frontier troops, had long been distinct from, and probably unsympathetic to, the secret police which formed the core of Beria's power.[61] Apparently, however, some even of the latter group helped in his arrest, which was effected quietly and smoothly on June 26 or 27.[62] On the evening of June 27 all members of the Presidium except Beria, his protégé Bagirov, and the disgraced Mel'nikov appeared together at the Bol'shoi Theater.[63] This was a rather transparent hint to the sophisticated observer of Soviet politics that Beria was in disfavor, and similar hints followed. The leadership took two weeks, however, to consolidate its control over the police and to deliberate on future moves before publicly announcing Beria's arrest.

Although—according to the official version, at least—Beria was not tried and executed until December 1953, an unusually long Central Committee plenum in early July expelled him from the Party and submitted his case to the USSR Supreme Court.[64] According to the plenum report and later accusations, Beria had been since adolescence an agent of the Caucasian nationalist organizations "Dashnak" and "Mussavat" and of the British intelligence. The fact that Beria's predecessor Ezhov had also been accused (secretly) fifteen years earlier of being a British agent is a singular indication of the fantastic operation of the Soviet police mentality.[65]

In addition, the charges said, Beria had fostered national discord and disrupted the kolkhoz system. In a secret letter, according to one report, the Central Committee accused Beria of endeavoring to make contacts with Tito and of wishing to liquidate the Soviet occupation in East Germany— although he was later publicly blamed for Stalin's antagonism toward Tito.[66] Another report indicates that the official indictment charged Beria with having established contact with British Conservative government circles.[67] After Beria's execution, Soviet spokesmen—especially Khrushchev —tended to implicate him in all the misdeeds that were charged to Stalin and his other lieutenants. All, that is, save one: the "doctors' plot."

The major count against Beria, adumbrated in the public indictment and elaborated in the restricted version, was his effort to seize power by using the police apparatus. To do this, the charges read, he had endeavored to make police officials gather material on Party leaders, and had replaced those recalcitrant to this demand by his own supporters.[68] Consequently, Beria's arrest was followed by the destruction of his lieutenants. Six, including Merkulov, Dekanozov, and Meshik, were executed with him.[69] The purge of the Georgian apparatus took place in several stages. In July Dekanozov and other MVD officials were expelled from the Party, while Mirtskhulava, the first secretary, and V. M. Bakradze, the chairman of the council of ministers (an especially close supporter of Beria), tried to save themselves by attacks on Beria.[70] In September, however, they lost their posts, but Mgeladze, Charkviani, and others purged in earlier years were not rehabilitated.[71] Late in 1955 Rapava and other especially close collaborators of Beria were executed.[72]

Similarly, there was a delay ranging up to two and one-half months in the destruction of other close supporters of Beria. The fate of the group around Abakumov was evidently tied closely to power rivalries among Beria's successors. The same may have been true of the Azerbaidzhani Party chief, Bagirov. Though his disgrace was not revealed at once, he was denounced at the July 1953 plenum for collaborating with Beria.[73] A little later, under the supervision of the CPSU Secretary Pospelov, the Azerbaidzhani central committee plenum removed Bagirov from the Party bureau and recommended his dismissal as chairman of the council of ministers. Although the plenum participants "drew political lessons from the Beria affair," explicit charges against Bagirov were almost trivial—arbitrary and incorrect style of leadership, rejection of criticism, and the like.[74] Hints concerning lack of control of MVD organs by the Azerbaidzhani Party appeared, however; later in the year the first secretary, an old MVD associate of Beria's and Bagirov's, was replaced.[75] Not until the time of the Twentieth Congress in February 1956, however, was Bagirov accused of the capital crimes of the "cult of the individual" and persecution of Old Bolsheviks.[76] Later that spring he was tried along with several MVD officials from Azerbaidzhan, and was executed.[77]

The strange delay in the case of Bagirov seemed to point to the operation of hidden forces in his favor. One suggestion is that the Soviet regime feared offending Middle Eastern opinion by publicly condemning the most prominent Communist of Moslem origin.[78] It is also possible that his fate was a pawn in the continuing internal Soviet power rivalry. While it is very likely that Bagirov aided Beria in 1953, his speeches did not indicate complete commitment to the Beria line. He and his subordinates seemed to be making a special effort during the spring of 1953 to express continued Azerbaidzhani devotion to the Russians. At the same time, Bagirov appeared to go out of his way to describe Malenkov as Stalin's "closest comrade in arms." [79]

These indications suggest that the contest for Stalin's heritage merged in the summer of 1953 into a struggle for the special sphere of influence left masterless by Beria's downfall. Because the events of the spring and summer of 1953 set the stage for the further development of the struggle for supremacy in the USSR, it has been necessary to consider them in great detail. Moreover, as the ramifications of this struggle transcended the USSR itself, it is necessary to consider the satellite situation before continuing the examination of Soviet domestic events.

CHAPTER

XIX

STRUGGLE FOR SUCCESSION

The reverberations of the Soviet power struggle spread widely in the satellite zone of East Europe. The exposed position of East Germany and the concentration of Soviet military and police forces there made this area especially sensitive. According to Boris Meissner, a careful student of East German developments, Beria and Malenkov collaborated in the founding, under Soviet aegis, of the "German Democratic Republic" in 1949.[1] In 1951, however, Malenkov, who made a special visit to Berlin, reversed the policy of the previous two years by stressing the danger of "German imperialism" instead of pressing for a "national front" designed to attract support in West Germany.[2] From this period until well after Stalin's death Soviet policies in Germany paralleled those in the other satellites. Little regard was paid to the discontent of the population; the raising of labor norms in the spring of 1953 caused special dissatisfaction. At the same time, a purge of the Socialist Unity Party (SED—entirely Communist-dominated) struck the prominent Spanish veteran Franz Dahlem, who was accused of allowing "imperialist agents" (including some with obviously Jewish names) to penetrate the party.[3]

East German officials who later defected report that rumors that Beria favored a more lenient line were current as early as May.[4] On June 9— shortly after the Soviet high commissioner had returned from a conference in Moscow—the SED politburo reversed the policies of the Stalin period.[5] It criticized mistakes in rationing and rigidity of tax collection, and promised measures to ameliorate the living standard. The new measures, the politburo said, were designed to help individual peasant farmers, artisans, retail traders—in other words, "bourgeois" elements. In addition, the intelligentsia was encouraged; dismissed teachers and students were to be reinstated. The SED appealed to persons who had fled to West Germany to return, and even promised a relaxed passport system.[6]

The concessions were too slight to win support for the distrusted Communist regime. On June 16 spontaneous workers' demonstrations began in East Berlin and other East German cities. By June 17 the demonstrations had reached the proportion of an uprising, and Soviet army units began to suppress them. Both the East German and the Soviet press blamed "Fascist agents" for inciting the uprising, but admitted that the harsh measures taken earlier by the government had been partly to blame.[7] The labor quotas were reduced and on June 21 a plenum of the SED central committee promised to continue the reforms instituted by the politburo.[8]

A second plenum in late July (after Beria's arrest) continued this theme. At the same time, however, it implied that Beria was linked to the uprisings by thanking the CPSU Central Committee for exposing him and for "showing the international ramifications of the Berlin provocation." According to one report, a secret Central Committee letter to satellite Communist leaders accused Beria of having proposed after the riots to liquidate the East German regime in order to unify Germany in agreement with the Western powers.[9] Simultaneously the SED resumed the denunciation of Dahlem and broadened the investigation of the "anti-party" faction to include a number of other high officials.[10]

In the remaining East European satellites there is no clear indication that Beria's brief ascendancy changed the policies started before Stalin's death. The death of Gottwald two weeks after Stalin died (according to the official statement his death resulted from pneumonia contracted at Stalin's funeral) did not lead to a reversal of the Slánský charges. At the end of April, in the midst of the reversal of the anti-Semitic campaign in the USSR, the Czech Communist Party secretary Antonín Novotný praised Gottwald for exposing and smashing the "conspiracy" headed by Rudolf Slánský.[11] In June Slánský's brother Richard and several other Jews received long prison terms.[12]

After Beria's arrest, according to a highly placed defector, the Polish Workers Party (i.e., Communist) central committee, acting in co-ordination with the CPSU, formed a special sector to control the police machine.[13] Probably the other satellite parties took similar measures; very quickly the lowered status of their police apparatus became noticeable. While in the earlier period the charges of abuse of police power had been made in closed sessions, or at least not emphasized in the public purge trials, in 1954 they became a dominant theme. For example, Clementis' son-in-law, Daniel Okalyi, the minister of the interior in Slovakia, was accused of preventing members of the partisans and the working class from entering the police. At the same time the prosecution attacked Okalyi, a Jew, for supporting Zionist groups such as the Joint Committee, and even for permitting "Jewish capitalists" to flee the country with their property.[14] In June 1954, on a visit to the Czechoslovak Communists, Khrushchev openly placed his seal of approval on the Slánský purge by praising the Czechoslovak party's exposure "in recent years" of "a gang of contemptible agents of the imperialist bourgeoisie." [15]

In Hungary the chief of the security police, Gábor Péter, who had apparently been especially closely linked to Beria, disappeared from public view at the beginning of 1953, while Stalin still lived. In March 1954 Péter was sentenced to life imprisonment for crimes against the people and the state. The Jewish aspect, though not publicized, was also present in this trial. Péter and another Jew, Gyula Décsi, the Minister of Justice, convicted at the same time, had, it is said, organized the transport of Jews to Palestine in 1945-46.[16] In Rumania arrests of Jews continued in late 1953, while in Poland the purge of Jews from the party apparatus which had begun in 1951 was extended in 1954 to the army and state officials.[17]

The continued anti-Semitic aspects of the satellite policies were scarcely "liberalizing"; insofar as the purges were directed against the oppressive police apparatus, they tended, however, to win a measure of popular support. In Hungary the effort to make the Communist regime acceptable to the native population took a much more drastic form. In June 1953 Mátyás Rákosi visited Moscow; on his return (while he remained general secretary) his power was visibly reduced. On July 4, Imre Nagy, who like Rákosi had spent several years of exile in Moscow, but who retained a considerably greater popularity, became Prime Minister. According to Nagy, the Soviet leadership compelled Rákosi to surrender the premiership.[18] One journalist's report, presumably based on high Hungarian officials' accounts, pictures Beria as especially severe in his attitude toward Rákosi.[19] Nagy was evidently accused later of having had Beria's support, for Nagy's apologia is careful to deny this connection.[20] But it seems likely that Nagy's contention that in May-June 1953 all the other major Soviet leaders—Malenkov, Molotov, Khrushchev, and Mikoian—supported the change in Hungary is accurate.[21]

While there is no demonstrable link between Nagy's rise and the session of the CPSU plenum which announced Beria's fall, the coincidence is striking. Nagy immediately began to put into effect an economic program which anticipated, but considerably surpassed in its innovating tendencies, that introduced in the USSR later in the summer. Nagy explicitly declared that industrialization had been exaggerated, that in the future "the development of heavy industry must be slowed," and that "the emphasis must be on the production of consumer goods and food." Nagy curbed the police and made conciliatory gestures to workers, private merchants, intellectuals, and even the church. He promised peasants who had sold their land to the state (to avoid classification as kulaks) that they could have the land back.[22]

Nagy's "new course" on paper went at least as far as the June reforms in East Germany. Rákosi, however, immediately expressed strong reservations; apparently the party apparatus did all it could to prevent the realization of Nagy's program. In fact, little appears to have been accomplished and popular discontent increased rather than diminished.[23] Groups associated with Nagy and Rákosi engaged in a bitter struggle; the Hungarian party congress scheduled for April had to be postponed. Before it was finally held in May Rákosi and Nagy both journeyed to Moscow, where the Soviet leaders considered the dispute. According to Nagy's account—revealed several years later—all of the top Soviet leaders sharply criticized Rákosi a little later.[24] One report has Kaganovich backing Rákosi. Nagy's account, however, conveys the impression that Malenkov and Kaganovich were much less sympathetic to Rákosi than was Khrushchev.[25] Moreover, a secret CPSU statement later declared that it was Malenkov who had supported Nagy.[26] During the autumn of 1954 Rákosi and Nagy engaged in public recriminations. Shortly before the end of the year, Rákosi, after returning from a visit in the Soviet Union, announced that emphasis on heavy industry must be resumed. On February 20, 1955, Nagy went on sick leave. Ten days later the Hungarian central committee denounced him for "right-wing" views in speaking "demagogically" of raising living standards before productivity had increased, of minimizing the successes of the party, and of failing to fight the kulaks.[27]

Rapproachment with Tito, the sole independent East European Communist, seems to have been a major objective for most dominant CPSU leaders in 1953-54. Immediately after Stalin's death there were small but significant signs that the extreme tension between Yugoslavia and the USSR had abated. Probably several of Stalin's successors simultaneously realized the advantages which might be derived from renewed friendship with Yugoslavia. According to defector reports, one Party accusation against Beria was that he had made an abortive effort to establish personal contacts with Tito.[28]

In June 1953 Molotov suggested that the two states again exchange full ambassadors; Tito replied publicly that "we need normal diplomatic relations." [29] Shortly afterward, the USSR sent an ambassador to Yugoslavia. In October 1954 the Soviet ambassador joined with the Jewish Yugoslav leader, Moša Pijade, and Alexandar Ranković, the Yugoslav Minister of the Interior (who had been, next to Tito, the chief target of Cominform attacks), in laying a wreath on the graves of Soviet and Yugoslav soldiers who had fallen in the capture of Belgrade from the Germans.[30] This symbolic reconciliation implied that the USSR no longer regarded as valid two principal elements in the satellite purges—the "Zionist-Tito" link and the "Yugoslav spy network." In November the logical conclusion was drawn in Budapest by freeing Noel Field.[31] The return of Rákosi to favor in Moscow the following month, however, tended to undo much of this advance toward re-establishment of Soviet-Yugoslav links, for he was Tito's bitterest enemy in the satellites.

In other parts of the world, too, Soviet policy exhibited numerous contradictions. In the Far East, the new Soviet leadership indicated its respect for the Chinese Communist regime immediately following Stalin's death. On March 10, 1953, a high-ranking Soviet official, V. V. Kuznetsov, was dispatched as ambassador to Peking.[32] The same newspapers which carried this announcement displayed a lengthy tribute to Stalin and to the CPSU from Mao Tse-tung.[33] In September of 1953 the USSR made an agreement promising major economic and technical aid to the Peking government.

Apparently the new Soviet regime also exerted considerable influence on Communist Chinese foreign policy. In July 1953 the Chinese Communist and North Korean delegates finally agreed to substantially the same armistice terms which the United Nations representatives had offered the preceding year. Communist assistance to the Vietminh rebels in Indo-China continued, however, reaching a climax in the spring of 1954, when the French government felt compelled to come to terms with the Communist insurrectionists. While the Communist bloc in the Far East demonstrated

its continued aggressiveness, it did not press matters to the point of provok-
ing the Western powers to a major war.

There is no demonstrable connection between these developments and
the simultaneous Soviet domestic power rivalries. On the broader issue of
war and peace, however, there was a visible cleavage between Malenkov
and Khrushchev. In January 1954 Malenkov significantly departed from
the customary Soviet line that war would mean the end of capitalism alone
by saying that a new war (involving nuclear weapons) would mean the
"destruction of civilization." [34] In early 1954 Malenkov and his adherents
also seemed to be de-emphasizing military aspects of the Soviet budget.[35]
In mid-June Khrushchev made an extremely belligerent speech in Prague,
in which he boasted that "we have even gone ahead of the capitalist class
in creating the hydrogen bomb before it did" and defied the "capitalists"
by saying that "nothing can scare us for we know as well as they what a
bomb is." When the speech appeared in *Pravda* the next day, however, its
tone was notably softened to emphasize that Soviet disarmament proposals
were made "not because we are weak, but in line with our policy of peace
in the interest of the toiling masses really mean it seriously." [36]

The entire period of Malenkov's premiership (March 1953-February 1955)
was influenced by the struggle for succession. Even such a broad issue as
the nature of Soviet relations with the major foreign powers was complicated by the clash of rival Soviet leaders. It would be wrong, however,
to regard Soviet policy developments in 1953 and 1954 as solely or even
primarily the results of power rivalries. Until his death Stalin had been able
to dominate the main trends of Soviet life; his intricate control system and
forceful personality had of course been major factors in his success. After
the enormous blood-lettings of collectivization, Great Purge, and war, the
sheer exhaustion of the Soviet social body rendered it more easily dominated. Obtaining the bare essentials of livelihood absorbed the attention
of the mass of the population. The intellectual and administrative strata,
though more privileged in a material sense, were so thoroughly cowed by
repeated repression that they, too, were preoccupied with sheer survival.
By 1953, however, the situation was changing rapidly. Whatever the
defects of the Soviet system, it continued to exhibit its tremendous capacity for expansion in heavy industry. According to Soviet figures, the
industrial output for 1951 was two and one-half times as large as in 1946

(the postwar low) and double the 1940 production. A more credible independent analysis indicates that the 1951 production was 75 per cent greater
than that of 1940.[37] Some amelioration in living conditions had taken place;
the dugouts which had been the only shelter of millions during several
harsh winters in reoccupied areas such as Belorussia had been virtually all
replaced by at least primitive houses. The famine of 1946-47 was not
repeated. According to the independent analysis just cited the total output
of manufactured consumer goods was only 10 per cent greater in 1951 than
in 1940.[38] As the total population at that time was still five or six million
below the prewar figure, however, this output meant that there were
slightly more consumer goods per capita. The average man could begin to
imagine, at least, a real increase in living standards, and to hope for a
measure of individual freedom.[39]

The attitudes of the upper strata of the Soviet population were somewhat
more complex. They, too, welcomed improvements in living conditions, and
they were glad to be freed from Stalin's arbitrary and terroristic methods.
They had, however, a much larger stake in maintaining the system than had
the lower strata. The Party, state, and industrial bureaucracies owed their
material privileges to their places in the system, and, as noted in Chapters
VII and VIII, were firmly convinced of their right to these privileges. The
war enhanced the pride of the privileged elements—including military
officers—in the strength of the Soviet system (as contrasted to the simpler
patriotism of the lower strata).

Consequently, any efforts to change the direction of Soviet development
had to take into account two distinct and partially conflicting currents:
the unambiguous desire of the mass of the population, and of many
intellectuals, for better living conditions and greater freedom; and the
determination of the bureaucratic upper strata to maintain the strength of
the Soviet system and their own position in it. Rival leaders endeavored
to use these currents to reach their own goals. The leaders also sought, no
doubt, to channel the currents in directions which they themselves felt
were best for the future of the Soviet system. Unlike Stalin, they could not
afford to disregard or swim against the currents of Soviet life.

In the field of internal controls there seems to have been a general con-
sensus among the Soviet leaders that the harsh terroristic aspects of
Stalinism must be ameliorated. The elimination of Beria, whose efforts to
pose as the champion of legality and mildness were constantly hampered
by his association with the police machine, made it much easier for the

remaining leaders to make sweeping changes. At the same time, the urgency of such measures was made clear in July 1953 by a startling revolt in Vorkuta, one of the principal concentration camps.[40]

The most drastic measure taken in 1953 after Beria's arrest was the abolition (in September) of the "special tribunals" of the MVD, which had been the principal instruments by which persons suspected of disloyalty were confined without judicial proceeding.[41] Many (estimates of the numbers have varied enormously) were released from concentration camps as a result of an amnesty in September 1955, as well as that proclaimed in March 1953 during the Beria period.[42] In early 1955 regulations to prevent interference by local officials in the work of the courts and the prosecutors appeared. A decree of September 1953 revoked the injunction against marriage between Soviet citizens and foreigners. In 1954 or earlier the Military Collegium of the Supreme Court began to "rehabilitate" (for the most part, no doubt, posthumously) the victims of the Great Purge.[43]

It has been rumored that the police apparatus itself was diminished by the transfer in late 1953 of its frontier and internal troops to the Soviet army; this cannot be confirmed, however, and it is certain that the frontier guards at least were back under control of the police agencies by early 1956.[44] In March 1954 the MVD (from Beria's arrest until February 1955 again under Kruglov) was reduced in scope by the establishment of the Committee of State Security (KGB), headed by I. A. Serov.[45] While the exact functions of the KGB and its counterparts in the Union Republics were not publicized, it is clear that they were given the politically most important assignments.

Just as important as the diminution of repression was the promise of an increased supply of consumer goods. This and other economic policies of the 1953-54 period seem to have been more intimately related to the power struggle than were the legal reforms. The first important step in this direction was taken by Malenkov in August 1953. Acting as Chairman of the Council of Ministers, he stated in his speech to a Supreme Soviet session that, having built up heavy industry, "the foundation of foundations of our socialist industry," the USSR was in a position to develop heavy and consumer-goods' industry at the *same* rate in the future.

Hitherto we have not had the opportunity to develop light and food industry at the same rate as heavy industry. Now we can and consequently we must accelerate the development of light industry in every way in the interest of securing a faster rise in the living standards and cultural level of the people.[46]

A decree on increased food and consumer goods production appeared in September; during the autumn the Soviet press was filled with articles on specific deficiencies in consumer goods which needed correction, and on the justification of the workers' demands for a better living standard.[47]

In view of the importance of the campaign for increasing output of manufactured consumer goods it is amazing that the matter was never discussed at a Central Committee plenum. Moreover, only one Union Republic plenum (in Turkmenistan, where Khrushchev later expelled the first secretary from the Party) discussed the topic during the entire period from July 1953 to January 1955. On the other hand, the topic occupied an important position on the agenda of the Ukrainian central committee plenum which met June 29-30, 1953—i.e., just after Beria was arrested, but before the CPSU Central Committee had officially condemned him, and just four days before Imre Nagy became Hungarian Premier.[48] After Malenkov was ousted as Soviet Council of Ministers Chairman in February 1955, on the other hand, several Party plenums considered the question of increasing consumer-goods output.

The chronological sequences just described appear to be convincing proof that the territorial Party organizations were ignoring Malenkov's consumer-goods campaign, which was heavily stressed by state organs and by some central Party organs, like the newspaper *Pravda*. At the same time, the Party plenums devoted enormous attention to Khrushchev's program for increasing agricultural production. Every Central Committee plenum between September 1953 and January 1955 considered the topic, while it came up for discussion over fifty times in various Union Republic plenums during that period. It is interesting to note that local state officials were heavily represented in the Union Republic discussions. This seems additional evidence that the state officials at the territorial level, who are closely linked in their career patterns to their Party counterparts, share the same interests even when the higher state officials in Moscow are alienated from the Party apparatus. It is also interesting that the Republic Party apparatuses endeavored during this period (and later) to enhance the appearance of popular participation in the work of the plenums by bringing a large number of lower officials such as kolkhoz chairmen, MTS directors, scientists, educators, and writers into the discussions.

On August 10, 1953, *Pravda* announced a major step to reduce the tax of kolkhoz peasants.[49] The principal agricultural measures, however, were taken at the September 3-7 plenum of the Central Committee.[50] Khrushchev, who officially became First Secretary at this plenum, took the lead in the discussion of these measures. The most striking feature of Khrushchev's speech was the blunt admission that past agricultural policies had failed, that the country was in a serious position as far as its food supply was concerned. Some months later Khrushchev told a foreign interrogator that he did not mean to contradict Malenkov's and Stalin's earlier assurances that there was enough grain to feed the Soviet people, but added that "man does not live by bread alone." [51] On the other aspects of consumer goods Khrushchev's emphasis was definitely, though not obviously, different from Malenkov's. Khrushchev carefully avoided a commitment to *equal* development of heavy and light industry, saying that past inadequacies were due to the fact that

> We did not have the means for high speed simultaneous development of heavy industry, agriculture, and light industry. For this it was necessary to provide needed prerequisites. Now these prerequisites exist. [52]

In addition to measures to increase grain production, the Central Committee September plenum resolved on improvements in many other branches of agriculture, especially in animal husbandry, which Khrushchev admitted had never recovered from the losses of collectivization. From the point of view of the Party apparatus, the most important innovation was the complete reorganization of political supervision of the countryside. The post of MTS deputy director for political affairs was abolished. In one oblast at least the majority of these officials became secretaries of the MTS primary Party organizations. [53] In this capacity they were restricted to supervising political work among the MTS personnel (which was, to be sure, more than doubled by the transfer of tractor drivers from the kolkhoz to the MTS payroll). Since, as noted in Chapters XIII and XV, the MTS deputy directors for political affairs had been partly dependent on the central Party apparatus, and perhaps the MVD, this step reduced the influence of these agencies.

Still more important was the appointment of a raikom secretary with a staff of instructors for each MTS zone. Henceforth the secretary was to supervise the work of both the MTS primary organization and of the kolkhoz primary Party organization, including the latter's economic activities. [54] As four-fifths of the MTS zone secretaries (in one oblast, at least) had been ordinary raikom secretaries or section directors before their appointment, while less than one-tenth had been MTS primary Party organization secretaries, the gain in influence for the territorial Party organization was clear. [55] The September plenum also directed the central

Ministries of Agriculture and Procurements to turn over a large part of their technical personnel to the MTS and the kolkhozes. Consequently, considerably larger staffs were supervised directly or indirectly by the territorial Party organizations.[56] As the RSFSR ministries were given primary responsibility for supervision of Russian agriculture the central ministries were still further curbed.[57] During January-February 1954 a number of highly publicized meetings of agricultural workers, including MTS zone raikom secretaries and MTS primary Party-organization secretaries, took place under Khrushchev's aegis in Moscow.[58]

At the next Central Committee plenum (February 23-March 2, 1954) Khrushchev criticized the central ministers directly.[59] The plenum further strengthened the territorial apparatus by placing the post of kolkhoz chairman in the direct *nomenklatura* (assignment sphere) of the obkom. The principal business, however, was Khrushchev's proposal for an enormous extension of land devoted to grain culture.[60] Most of the "virgin lands" were in semi-arid regions in Kazakhstan, the Volga–southern Urals area, Siberia, and the North Caucasus. In order to provide labor for the new fields Khrushchev directed an intense campaign to induce Komsomols and other young people to leave the European USSR for these areas.

In spite of the Party approval of the new program, only thirteen million acres of new land were devoted to grain in 1954; the total grain harvest of eighty-six million metric tons, while slightly larger than that of 1953, fell somewhat below the harvest of 1952, even when that was calculated in the more accurate system of "barn" yields.[61] Much later Khrushchev and his supporters blamed the poor results in 1954 on the bitter opposition of Malenkov, Molotov, and Kaganovich. According to these allegations, the group assailed the new program as unrealistic and excessively expensive; Malenkov, as head of the government, was said to have forbidden increases in sowing.[62] If this is true, it partially explains the initial failure of Khrushchev's program, although unfavorable weather and poor management were important factors.

Once Malenkov had been displaced in early 1955, however, the program was resumed with increased vigor. In 1955 alone thirty-four million new acres were plowed for grain; according to the official statistics the harvest, aided by favorable weather, reached 107,000,000 metric tons. In 1956 (with the same acreage) the official figures showed the phenomenal yield of 127,000,000 tons, though the following year less favorable weather led to a reversion to the 1955 yield. Similarly, the 1958 crop was extraordinarily large (141,000,000 tons) but the 1959 harvest fell back to 125,000,000 tons.

By then it was fairly clear that the "virgin-lands" program had been successful in raising the long-run average of grain yields. But the net gain would probably not be enormous (especially in view of the rapid growth of the Soviet population after 1952) and the wide harvest fluctuations from year to year might cause grave complications in an emergency situation. Consequently, while Khrushchev's program had alleviated the food production difficulty, it remained one of the most serious weaknesses of the Soviet system.

While the muted controversy over agricultural measures was proceeding, the factions represented by Khrushchev and Malenkov were engaged in an intricate struggle for ascendancy over the Party and the state apparatus. While it is unnecessary to detail all the moves in this game, a few of the most important deserve mention. In September 1953 Khrushchev's side apparently profited from a purge of Beria's adherents in Georgia, for the new first secretary, V. P. Mzhvanadze, a professional army political officer, had served in areas where Khrushchev was active during the war, and more recently had been associated with Khrushchev's friends in the Ukraine.[63] A much more important move was Khrushchev's direct participation in the replacement of V. M. Andrianov as first secretary of the Leningrad obkom by Frol R. Kozlov, the third secretary.[64] There is some doubt as to whether Andrianov was a supporter of Beria or of Malenkov, but by removing Andrianov (who had replaced P. S. Popkov when the latter was arrested in the "Leningrad affair") Khrushchev seemed to invite the support of Zhdanov's one-time adherents.

The almost simultaneous appointment of Saburov, Pervukhin, and V.A. Malyshev (with Mikoian's associates Kosygin and I. F. Tevosian) as vice-chairmen of the Council of Ministers seemed, however, to indicate that Malenkov was strengthening his control over industrial management agencies of the government.[65] As yet the tempo of personnel changes was low, though increasing. The series of Union Republic Party congresses held during January-February 1954 did not result in striking changes in the corps of secretaries.[66] On the other hand, the rate of change of the RSFSR obkom secretaries was significantly higher than in earlier years.[67]

During the spring of 1954 there were some small indications that Khrushchev was preparing to invade Malenkov's sphere of industrial control. In a speech to the Supreme Soviet in late April, Khrushchev referred to the need for dividing the existing ministries into smaller units while avoiding an increase in total staff, scornfully remarking that, "I think that

such a proposal will not encounter much sympathy on the part of individual ministers." [68] The June plenum of the Central Committee (following closely upon the *Pravda* censorship of Khrushchev's belligerent
speech in Prague) does not appear to have been a very successful occasion
for the Khrushchev group, however. While the RSFSR ministers whom
Khrushchev favored spoke on the agricultural matters, and the "virgin-
lands" plan was backed, the principal reporter apparently was Benediktov,
the USSR Minister of Agriculture. [69] Many observers have speculated that
the trial of Riumin in July was also aimed at Khrushchev, who was apparently protecting Riumin's superior, Ignat'ev.

In October 1954 Khrushchev became the first major Soviet leader to visit
Communist China. After he returned from Peking, Khrushchev appeared
to feel strong enough to take the offensive. In November, the Party newspaper *Pravda* gave much more prominence to Khrushchev, while the
state organ, *Izvestia*, emphasized Malenkov. [70] About this time Ignat'ev was
restored to Party good graces by being assigned as first secretary of the
Bashkir ASSR. At the end of December, the trial of Abakumov and his
MGB associates before a large, though restricted audience, dramatically
resurrected the "Leningrad affair." [71] As the prosecutor was Khrushchev's
old supporter, R. A. Rudenko (appointed Procurator General in September
1953), Khrushchev seemed to be preparing for the implication of Malenkov.
Four days later *Pravda* published a lengthy speech delivered by Khrushchev in early December, in which he openly contradicted Malenkov's
economic emphasis by saying that "only on the basis of a further development of heavy industry will we be able successfully to promote all branches
of the national economy, steadily raise the well-being of the people, and
ensure the inviolability of the frontiers of the Soviet Union." [72] However,
the public award of the Order of Lenin to Malenkov's chief supporter in
the Secretariat, N. N. Shatalin, seemed to indicate that Malenkov retained
some strength. [73]

A number of non-Soviet observers have pointed out that Malenkov's
program for increasing consumer goods was so slight as to have a negligible
effect on heavy industrial emphasis. Output of cotton fabrics, for example,
was to increase only 2 per cent and woolens only 5 per cent, although somewhat more substantial advances were to be achieved in luxury items (by
Soviet standards) such as electrical appliances. In the proposed 1955
budget only 8.8 per cent of the capital investments would have gone for
consumer-goods production facilities, as compared to 69.1 per cent for
heavy industry and transportation; this was scarcely more than the 83.4 to

7.3 ratio during Stalin's lifetime.[74] Consequently, it is still uncertain why Khrushchev chose, successfully, to make Malenkov's pronouncements on the equal rate of development of the two branches of industry his chief public point of assault.

Among other still unexplained elements of the Malenkov-Khrushchev conflict, the most mysterious is the position of Anastas Mikoian who, as Minister of Trade, was deeply involved in the question of consumer goods. There was much speculation abroad that Mikoian had been weakened by Beria's fall. The two men had at one time been intimately associated, and G. A. Ariutinov, the Armenian first secretary removed in September 1953, had been accounted an adherent of Mikoian.

Consequently, when Mikoian resigned as Minister of Trade "at his own request" on January 22, 1955, the move seemed to be an integral part of the power struggle. On the other hand, Mikoian's resignation may just as easily have been a belated effort to dissociate himself from Malenkov's lagging "consumer-goods" program.

Two days later D. T. Shepilov, then known as a close supporter of Khrushchev, delivered a sharp attack on the proponents of consumer-goods emphasis. Describing them as "some economists and teachers in our higher educational institutions," he said they resembled the "right restorationists" who would fatally weaken the USSR in the capitalist encirclement.[75] The next day Khrushchev practically repeated these views to the Central Committee plenum, but even more ominously linked the consumer-goods proponents to "regurgitation of the right deviation, regurgitation of views hostile to Leninism, views which Rykov, Bukharin and their ilk once preached." [76] The Central Committee resolution (which ostensibly dealt with agricultural matters) supported Khrushchev by declaring that the "main task is the further development of heavy industry, which is the firm basis of the entire national economy and the inviolable defensive capacity of our homeland and the source of undeviating improvement of the Soviet people's well-being." [77]

Such was the public record of the January 1955 plenum. Apparently, however, much more serious measures were taken to discredit Malenkov. He was accused of association with Beria both in the events immediately following Stalin's death, and in the "Leningrad affair." More generally, Malenkov's record, as principal Secretary (under Stalin) was used against him; he was accused of suppressing information and distorting agricultural statistics.[78]

Immediately following the plenum Malenkov's position remained publicly unaltered. On February 8, however, Malenkov ostensibly sent a message to the Supreme Soviet session submitting his resignation.[79] According to this message, Malenkov admitted that heavy industrial development must be emphasized. He also took upon himself the responsibility for lack of progress in agriculture and recognized the dominant role of the Central Committee (i.e., of the Party as compared to the government) in directing agricultural affairs. In addition Malenkov hinted at the superiority of the territorial organizations by pointing to his own deficient experience in "local work." Malenkov (who retained a subordinate post in the Council of Ministers) was succeeded by Bulganin, but it was evident to all that Khrushchev and his supporters were the real victors. And on February 28 Anastas Mikoian became First Deputy Chairman of the Council of Ministers.

THE PERIOD OF THE TWENTIETH
CONGRESS: ORGANIZATIONAL CHANGES

Malenkov's confession of failure in February 1955 ended one phase of the struggle for Stalin's heritage, but it began another phase even more protracted and bitter, though not so evenly balanced. From the purely formal point of view, the partnership between Party and state continued. Now, however, the representatives of the two elements were not Khrushchev and Malenkov, but Khrushchev and Bulganin; and Khrushchev left little room for doubt that his shift of partners meant his complete ascendancy in the duumvirate. Whether Khrushchev was acting as Stalin's successor or as the representative of the triumphant Party remained an open question, however.

In foreign affairs Khrushchev was bound to associate himself with Bulganin, for the latter as head of government was the formal spokesman for Soviet foreign policy. At the Geneva conference in July 1955, the first meeting between top-ranking Soviet and Western statesmen since World War II, Bulganin was publicly most prominent. While this was the most highly publicized international event of the year, the Soviet leaders' tour of South Asia in November-December, and their visit to Yugoslavia in May, were more important for the development of Soviet policies. On both these trips Khrushchev not only accompanied Bulganin, but—especially in Yugoslavia, where interparty relations were at issue—was obviously the real spokesman of the Soviet regime.

Issues of foreign policy were also intimately related to Khrushchev's continued veiled attack on his rivals in the leadership. He undoubtedly was gratified by the strong statements issued by Marshals I. S. Konev and G. K. Zhukov on the tenth anniversary of the World War II victory in May

1955. Zhukov, for example, emphasized the devastation which the hydrogen bomb could inflict on Europe and America, without indicating that it represented a fatal danger to the USSR.[1] More significant, however, was the attack on Molotov. On February 8 Khrushchev had remained silent while Molotov accused Yugoslavia of "departing from the positions" which she had maintained immediately after World War II.[2] Perhaps Khrushchev's desire to see the defeat of Malenkov sealed that same day led him to refrain from challenging Molotov, though the incident threatened to impede efforts to form a rapprochement with Tito. There is little doubt but that disagreements over this and other aspects of foreign policy (discussed below) were the real grounds for the conflict between Molotov and Khrushchev.

In the February 8 speech, however, Molotov made a curious statement that later furnished an ostensible ground for his decline in prestige:

> Together with the Soviet Union, where the bases of socialist society are already constructed, there are also the people's democratic countries, which have accomplished only the first, but extremely important, steps in the direction of socialism.[3]

Since for nearly two decades (for example, at the Eighteenth Congress) Molotov had stressed the concept that socialism was built "in the main" in the USSR, it is hard to see how he could have accidentally employed the phrase "the bases [or foundations] of socialism" to describe Soviet conditions in 1955. Quite possibly Molotov wished to stress the vast amount remaining to be accomplished, as an argument for a cautious continuance of the Stalinist policy he seemed to favor.

For nearly eight months no comment appeared on Molotov's remarks. Then the Party journal *Kommunist* published a scathing attack on "the theoretical worthlessness and the political harm of attempts to apply to the present day formulas and descriptions that relate only to a stage that was passed through long ago—to claim that so far only the foundations of socialism . . . have been built in our country." [4] In a letter to the editor in the same issue, Molotov humbly confessed not only to a slip of the tongue, but to the exaggerated implications stressed in the magazine's editorial.[5]

This incident provides a convincing demonstration of the importance in Soviet politics of seemingly minor shifts in phraseology. In a careful examination of Soviet publications between 1954 and 1957, Myron Rush has endeavored to trace the fluctuations in Khrushchev's position as revealed by such "Aesopian" or esoteric language.[6] While it is impossible even to summarize all of the subtle indications he lists, some of the main features of the analysis are crucial for the understanding of one of the major interpretations of recent Soviet political developments. One basic feature of the 1955 period, according to Rush, was Khrushchev's effort to preserve Stalin's prestige, in order that he, Khrushchev, might succeed to it.[7] The treatment of the Stalin "myth" as such will be dealt with in Chapter XXI, but here we may note that the closely related effort of Khrushchev to enhance his title of "First Secretary" appears to be well demonstrated. Unquestionably —in view of later developments—Khrushchev saw his post as something apart from and, at least in a practical sense, above the Presidium. To the many observers who have identified "collective leadership" with the half-dozen major leaders who occupied high posts at Stalin's death, this attitude of Khrushchev has seemed to indicate a definite effort to revert to one-man rule.

Aside from manipulating the symbols associated with high Party posts, Khrushchev appeared to be engaged in a subtle contest to magnify his own position in recent Soviet history. For obvious reasons neither Khrushchev nor his rivals were inclined to boast of their activities during the thirties; and the history of the period after World War II had few aspects which could be adapted to the glorification of individual leaders. On the other hand, World War II itself was rapidly assuming a place alongside the Revolution and Civil War as a Soviet heroic age. Obviously, references to the war period had a far greater emotional appeal to the generation active in Soviet politics in 1955, and especially to the professional military officers. Consequently, reference to the role of the Party leaders in achieving victory was fraught with political meaning.[8]

Malenkov's claim to a major part in the victory rested primarily, as we have seen, on his part in the tremendous achievement of industrial evacuation and production. The symbol of his claim was the GOKO (State Defense Committee), to which Khrushchev had never belonged; consequently emphasis on this body in historical allusions seemed to indicate Malenkov's ascendancy. The situation is somewhat complicated, however, by the fact that most of the other Soviet leaders (including notably Mikoian) had also been members of the GOKO. Bulganin and Khrushchev, on the other hand, were unique among the highest living Soviet leaders in having spent most of the war as political representatives at the military fronts. By alluding to this aspect of his background, Khrushchev could enhance his prestige in several directions. Since the dead leaders Shcherbakov and Zhdanov had also served at the front, Khrushchev may have strengthened his appeal to the remnants of their following. He identified his past with that of at least some major military commanders. Moreover, since the front political representatives had acted as Party leaders, in contrast to the subordination of Party identification to governmental status in the GOKO, Khrushchev was indirectly but forcefully appealing to the tradition of Party supremacy.

The evidence just summarized provides considerable support for the thesis that Khrushchev was endeavoring to become a personal dictator. As we shall see in Chapter XXI, however, even the treatment of World War II which magnified his role seemed also to serve the interests of a considerable group of Party leaders. Aside from this, many circumstances have led the present writer to doubt that the overwhelmingly dominant factor in Khrushchev's rise in power during 1955-56 was his personal effort to succeed Stalin as absolute dictator.

The most important arguments for the view that Khrushchev was the *chosen* leader, and in a sense the representative of the higher levels of the territorial Party apparatus can be summarized briefly.[9] Khrushchev was representative of the territorial Party elite in a biographical sense.[10] His entire career in high place (before he became a Central Committee Secretary) was spent directing territorial branches of the apparatus in Moscow and the Ukraine. Most rival leaders, on the other hand, had spent much of their careers in state posts, or in relatively remote and anonymous manipulation of the central Party machinery. This applied, of course, especially to Malenkov, who had been in the cadres section under Ezhov, had directed it as Ezhov's successor, and subsequently had been engaged in state economic direction. It applied to a lesser degree to Kaganovich, Molotov, Mikoian, and Suslov.

In his direction of the territorial apparatus, Khrushchev had been heavy-handed enough, but he had been accessible. In the Ukraine Party meetings had convened regularly; subordinate officials at least took part in discussion, however circumspect they may have been. Khrushchev's jovial and familiar manner, though it undoubtedly concealed much shrewdness and ruthlessness, was a welcome change from Stalin's aloof inscrutability. Khrushchev, in other words, resembled a "boss" in the American political sense of the term, rather than a Byzantine despot.

Khrushchev was a "self-made man" with little formal education, a relatively late start in major Party work, and a considerable practical familiarity with rural matters. This background very likely endeared him to the Party officials, still very numerous in the territorial apparatus, who had similar backgrounds. They presented a marked contrast to the official (typified by Malenkov, Saburov, and Pervukhin) with a relatively high level of technical education acquired early in life. Finally, a simple but important consideration must have occurred to the elite: Khrushchev in 1955 was sixty-one years old. Molotov was indeed sixty-five; but he was too rigidly linked to Stalin's record. Kaganovich was sixty-one, Mikoian sixty, but they were members of disliked national minorities. Malenkov, however, was only fifty-three, and Khrushchev's other possible competitors were about as young as Malenkov. They (like Stalin, who was fifty-four at the "Congress of Victors") had the time to make themselves absolute masters of the Soviet system by destroying a generation of the Party elite; Khrushchev, in all likelihood, did not. If an individual had to be recognized as the Soviet leader—and absolute parity among a group of high officials is difficult if not impossible to maintain even in a democratic system—Khrushchev was the safest choice.

These arguments are unconvincing, however, if, as those who believe that Khrushchev was striving to become absolute dictator contend, he achieved power by "packing" the Party governing bodies with men who were devoted to him personally. With a few exceptions, Khrushchev's personal following must have come from the Ukrainian apparatus. As suggested above, Khrushchev's appeal to the Ukrainian apparatus may have arisen as much from his "regular" conduct of Party affairs as from efforts to build personal loyalties. With this reservation, however, one may regard movement of Ukrainian apparatus officials to key posts as signs of Khrushchev's personal ascendancy. The easily available evidence on personnel transfers is far from complete; conclusions drawn from it are, therefore, necessarily somewhat ambiguous. As was noted in Chapter XIX, various crucial transfers in late 1953 and 1954 apparently strengthened Khrushchev's position, insofar as they represented the replacement of officials who had been closely associated with Beria and Malenkov by men who had no such ties. In several cases (such as the appointment of Mzhvanadze in Georgia and of A. I. Struev in the important Molotov industrial province in the Urals) officials associated in the past with Khrushchev were the beneficiaries of the changes. As noted earlier, however, these appointments were partially offset by promotion of men who had been associated with Malenkov. But if Khrushchev personally had assumed a dominating position after Malenkov's resignation, one might anticipate still more changes designed to place his adherents in key positions before the convocation of the Twentieth Party Congress in February 1956. In fact, however, changes in the key level of the territorial apparatus were very limited for nearly two years prior to the Twentieth Congress.

In July 1955 the first plenum following Malenkov's removal met.[11] The plenum decided to convene the Twentieth Congress. Khrushchev reported on the Soviet-Yugoslav negotiations.

Molotov stubbornly opposed both the rapprochement with Yugoslavia and the peace treaty with Austria, but was isolated in the plenum. Khrushchev and Mikoian both openly criticized the Ministry of Foreign Affairs (which Molotov had directed).[12] Bulganin reported on industrial development; according to a later Communist report he sharply criticized the direction of industry. In pointing out the effect of the anti-"cosmopolitan" campaign on Soviet utilization of foreign technical advances, Bulganin indirectly criticized Stalin.[13] Various high agricultural officials (including the Deputy Minister of Agriculture, V. V. Matskevich, who had been transferred from the Ukraine in late 1953 and who was soon to become Minister of Agriculture) reported on the 1955 farm year. Kirichenko and Suslov were made full Presidium members; A. B. Aristov, N. I. Beliaev, and Shepilov were appointed Secretaries. Kirichenko's appointment undoubtedly strengthened Khrushchev's position in the Presidium. Shepilov, an economist and a propagandist by career, was known as Khrushchev's supporter, although their ties were not of long standing. Beliaev had been a territorial secretary in the RSFSR. Aristov assumed supervision of the vital Party Organs Section. He replaced Shatalin (a close associate of Malenkov) who had been sent to a minor post in the distant Maritime oblast several months earlier. Since Aristov (although he had been a Secretary for a short time in 1953) had an extensive background as a territorial secretary, the gain for the *group* which Khrushchev *led* was evident. That it represented a *personal* triumph for Khrushchev is not so clear.

Three Ukrainian officials assumed direction of RSFSR oblasts in the autumn of 1955.[14] Much the most important of these transfers was A. P. Kirilenko's appointment as first secretary of the major Urals industrial province of Sverdlovsk, especially since it followed close upon severe criticism (at the July plenum) of the Sverdlovsk obkom for failing to see that the Party directed manufacturing adequately.[15] Apart from these instances it is very difficult to substantiate the contention that Khrushchev was "packing" the territorial apparatus *in 1955*. While precise information on the overall turnover of officials is unobtainable, it is possible, thanks to painstaking compilations by several non-Soviet sources, to make a fairly accurate estimate.[16] Of fifteen Union Republic first secretaries, only three were replaced between early 1954 and the Twentieth Congress. The replacement in the tiny Karelo-Finnish Republic was unimportant. P. K. Ponomarenko's appointment as ambassador to Warsaw may indeed have been intended to remove him from control of the "virgin lands" of Kazakhstan. The most interesting replacement, however, was that of A. I. Niiasov, the Uzbek first secretary who had seemed to be currying favor with Beria in 1953. On his way back from South Asia Khrushchev stopped over in Tashkent; shortly after his visit, Niiasov was dismissed on charges similar to those initially brought against Bagirov ("arbitrary methods," failure to work collectively with the Uzbek central committee), and the post given to N. A. Mukhitdinov, a young man who appeared to be Khrushchev's protégé.[17]

In spite of this one striking instance of Khrushchev's intervention, the 20 per cent general turnover in Union Republic first secretaries between April 1954 and the opening of the Twentieth Congress was no more than usual for a two-year period. Similarly, only one of the Autonomous Republic secretaries was replaced in this period. Much the most important group was the body of RSFSR first secretaries. Of fifty-nine oblast and *krai* (territory) first secretaries, thirty-nine retained their posts, or were transferred to direct provinces of approximately equal importance. Aside from the two or three replacements of key importance noted earlier, the one-third turnover in RSFSR provincial secretaries seems to have been no more than normal for the interval involved. Between 1950 and 1953, for example, almost half of the secretaries were replaced, while in the single year from April 1953 to April 1954 there had been a 30 per cent turnover. In order to assume that Khrushchev *personally* "packed" the Central Committee one would have to contend that his power over high territorial Party appointments was so great during the period *before* Malenkov and Molotov were defeated that Khrushchev was able then to make the vast majority of changes which he desired. If that had been the case, of course, Khrushchev would indeed have needed to make few changes among the territorial secretaries *after* April 1954. But it seems far more probable that the numerous changes in 1953 and early 1954 represented the removal of a group of secretaries obnoxious to the majority of the territorial apparatus because they had been protégés of Beria, or in some instances, perhaps, of Poskrebyshev. If that is the case, it is easy to understand why after the removal of such men the majority of the territorial secretaries would have sought stability in their group, regardless of Khrushchev's personal wishes.

The role of the territorial secretaries is crucially important because of the dominant role they assumed in the Central Committee elected at the Twentieth Congress.[18] Of its 133 full members, 55 were territorial first secretaries, as were 27 of its 122 candidates. If one adds the 13 second secretaries and members of territorial state organizations (intimately linked in their careers to their Party counterparts) who were full members of the Central Committee, the territorial organizations had a slight majority of the votes in the body. With 14 additional candidates they comprised one-third of the nonvoting members. In contrast, the central Party apparatus was only represented by 8 members and 4 candidates; the central industrial ministries and departments by 15 and 20 respectively. It is also interesting to note that the 1956 Central Committee was still basically the same in membership as that elected before Stalin's death; 81 of its members had served (as full members or candidates) at least since 1952, as had 54 of the candidates.

Throughout the Twentieth Congress proceedings, the delegates hailed the Central Committee (elected in 1952) as the true repository of collective leadership. To Khrushchev, "the plenums of the Central Committee of the Communist Party, which took place regularly during the period under review, played an exceptionally important part in the life of the Party and of the entire country." [19] Suslov—senior to Khrushchev in length of service as a Secretary, and scarcely his protégé—said,

> One may say without the slightest doubt that the principle of collective leadership has been fully established in the Central Committee. The decision of all the most important questions has passed into the hands of the regularly assembling plenum of the Central Committee—this broad, collegially functioning Party center, which is most intimately connected to the decisive sections of the structure of Communist society.[20]

Certainly one may doubt that the actual process of decision-making could be carried out by a body of more than two hundred assembling three or four times a year for a week at a time. But what Suslov may have really meant was that the views of the Central Committee members, as representatives of the upper levels of the Soviet bureaucracies, must be considered in every action taken by the regime.

The Presidium remained, of course, the arena of day-to-day decision-making, and there the group led by Khrushchev was not yet ready to establish full control.[21] No further changes were made in its full members; apart from the removal of Beria and the addition of Kirichenko and Suslov they remained those elected in March 1953. Of the candidates, Bagirov and Mel'nikov had been dropped in July 1953. Ponomarenko was later dropped, leaving only Shvernik of those elected in March 1953.[22] Five replacements were chosen in February 1956. Marshal Zhukov's appearance was an evident concession to his popularity in some military circles and among the general public. Mukhitdinov, Shepilov, L. I. Brezhnev, and Mme. E. A. Furtseva (like Brezhnev, also elected to the Secretariat) were all accounted Khrushchev's followers.

Since many of the substantive matters considered at the Twentieth Congress will be treated in detail in subsequent chapters, it is sufficient here to indicate their importance. Khrushchev, of course, made the principal public report. He also provided on February 25 the real sensation of the Congress by revealing to a closed session some of the worst of Stalin's despotic excesses.[23] Whatever the factors (discussed in Chapter XXI) influencing Khrushchev to undertake to demolish Stalin's reputation, Khrushchev cleverly turned the occasion to account by linking his chief rivals, Molotov, Kaganovich, and Malenkov, to the most objectionable features of Stalin's regime.[24] Malenkov was portrayed obliquely but unmistakably as Stalin's confidant operating behind the scenes to maintain a screen between him and the "honest" Party and army officers in the field.[25] Simultaneously Khrushchev pictured the territorial Party organizations as the instigators of the curbs put on the NKVD in 1939, and as principal architects of the war victory.[26]

Contrary to what one might have expected, in view of the great emphasis on economic questions which characterized this, like other Congresses, very little was said about the primacy of heavy industrial development over consumer goods. The issue was, of course, settled, for Malenkov plainly conceded that the "line of the predominant development of heavy industry was, is, and will remain the general line of our Party." [27] No recriminations appeared on this matter, possibly because Malenkov's position was somewhat stronger than it had been the previous February. At the same time, this lack of emphasis on the primacy of heavy industrial development suggests that the whole controversy had been contrived to bring about Malenkov's dismissal. By 1956 Khrushchev was proceeding to the second and much more crucial aspect of his economic program: the reduction of the great complex of centralized industrial ministries. At the Twentieth

Congress, however, only the earliest and still obscure phases of this program were evident.

Since the Twentieth Congress met at the height of Khrushchev's emphasis on "peaceful coexistence," Malenkov was not berated for his mild foreign policy line. Molotov, as the representative of intransigence toward the West, and still more toward Yugoslavia, however, received a sharp reminder of his theoretical lapse of the preceding year.[28]

Much more important, in the long run at least, than the verbal fencing of the Party leaders were the Party organizational measures introduced during the period of the Twentieth Congress. Enormous emphasis was placed on the regularity of meetings of Party bodies. To make such meetings more convenient the Congress slightly increased the intervals between them. Speakers at the Congress also stressed the importance of reducing personnel overhead; since 1952, it was reported, the Central Committee apparatus had been reduced 24.7 per cent, while the obkom-level staffs had been cut back to less than one-eighth of those of the lower Party organizations.[29] Somewhat later the position of the lower Party organization was enhanced by the elimination of the special Party organizations in such areas as transportation and police, which had been outside the jurisdiction of the territorial apparatus. The elimination of the special roving plenipotentiaries of the Committee of Party Control (see Chapter II) must also have been gratifying to the lower organizations.[30] In addition, the Central Committee assured the lower bodies that it would continue the practice instituted after Stalin's death of fully informing them of its decisions.[31]

Much the most important organizational measure, however, was the creation of the Central Committee Bureau for the RSFSR at the plenum immediately following the Congress. In 1955 a special Agricultural Section for the RSFSR had been formed to take over all Party supervision of agriculture in Russia.[32] The existing Agricultural Section of the Central Committee was then restricted to the smaller Union Republics. After the RSFSR Bureau was formed, it was given similar parallel sections for most other aspects of Party activity: Party Organs; Propaganda and Agitation; Science, Culture, and Schools; Transport and Industry; and Administrative, Commercial, and Financial Institutions. Certain sections, however, remained the exclusive sphere of the original Secretarial apparatus: Transport and Communications; Heavy Industry; Machine Construction; Light Industry; Construction; Foreign; Administration (Party funds, etc.); and Military.[33]

The broad outlines of this organization did not differ from that introduced in late 1948 (see Chapter XV). Closer examination of the Party Organs Section, the key control body, indicates a certain shift in administrative emphasis, however. The residual general Party Organs Section (for the non-Russian Republics) was now organized on a combination of the functional and the territorial principles. It had four territorial "sectors": Ukraine and Moldavia; Transcaucasus; Kazakhstan and Central Asia; Baltic (presumably including Belorussia). In addition, it had four functional "sectors." One supervised the minor organizations under the Party Organs Section— Komsomols, trade unions, and Soviet bodies. A second sector maintained Party records, although the basic file for all CPSU members was kept in a special office apart from either the regular or the RSFSR Party Organs Sections. The organization sector carried on most of the work handled by the Organization-Instruction Section before 1947: supervision of the fulfillment of Party decisions, collection of statistics, and consideration of expulsions. This sector had at its disposal several former obkom secretaries detailed to serve as high-level inspectors. Probably the most important sector, however, was the cadres sector.[34] While the general sphere of its operations was reduced by delegation to the regional organizations of final appointive powers for lower categories of officials, it retained the power of confirmation not only of medium-level Party officials, but of chairmen and vice-chairmen of state bodies down to the oblast level.[35]

The whole of the work of the Party Organs Section (for the smaller Republics) was carried on by sixty-four political officials and sixty-four technical officials. According to Soviet accounts they were directed to avoid giving orders to lower Party organizations, but were to consult with them concerning their problems. In order to do this the officials of the central apparatus spent, it is said, three-quarters of their time on visits to the field organizations.[36] Obviously Party spokesmen were taking care to stress that the staff agency was to remain, in contrast to the late thirties, a servant rather than a master of the line officials.

The central Secretariat, as reorganized after 1956, continued to be a powerful instrument for centralized control. Party sources were careful to point out that a RSFSR central committee was still unthinkable, as it would constitute a competing power center opposed to the CPSU Central Committee.[37] Similarly, the composition of the RSFSR Bureau was arranged so as to overlap that of the Party Secretariat, with Khrushchev as the head of both organizations.[38] Why, then, the step—odd from the standpoint of normal administrative procedure—of splitting the apparatus into two parallel organizations? Probably Khrushchev and his supporters felt that the old central apparatus, as it had developed under Stalin, Zhdanov, and Malenkov, needed a thorough overhauling to make it susceptible to new tasks as well as more amenable to control. When more than half of the USSR's territory was placed under a new organization undoubtedly many opportunities arose for introducing officials with a fresh point of view in Party and government key posts. The appointment of V. M. Churaev, who had been deputy director of Khrushchev's cadres section when he was first secretary in Kiev, as Director of the RSFSR Party Organs Section was one such move. This, and the reorganization in general, made it easier for Khrushchev to deal with the Russian apparatus, and *may* even have been a step toward his domination of it.

The data released at the Twentieth Congress and in the four years following it enabled one to form, for the first time in nearly two decades, a fairly comprehensive picture of the composition of the Party membership and of the apparatus. As we shall consider in Chapter XXIV the relationship of the changing social and educational structure of the CPSU to Party objectives and operations, it seems preferable to postpone presentation of Twentieth Congress data on these points. Since, however, the very interesting material on geographical and national distribution is especially relevant to questions of Party reorganization just treated, it must be analyzed here.[39]

Unfortunately, Party membership in the RSFSR has not been given. Since (at the beginning of 1956) CPSU members and candidates totaled about 7,200,000, while the other Union Republic membership totaled 2,200,000, one might conclude that the RSFSR total was 5,000,000, or 70 per cent of the CPSU membership. Possibly, however, this residual amount includes the entire military membership, and not merely that of military units stationed in Russia. From the point of view of nationality representation, however, the proportion of 70 per cent of total Party membership for the Russians is probably not exaggerated (in comparison to their proportion of 54 per cent among the population at large), for they were numerous among Party members in Republics other than the RSFSR. For example, over three hundred thousand (28.2 per cent) of the Ukrainian Party members in 1958 were actually Russians,[40] although Russians comprise less than 18 per cent of the Ukraine's population.

Similarly, Russians were very heavily represented in the Party apparatus. In the Ukraine (1956) they constituted 29.6 per cent of the delegates to the Republic congress; in Uzbekistan (1956) 25.7 per cent of the delegates, though Russians constituted only 13.6 per cent of the Uzbek SSR's population; while in Kirgizia (1952) they were 30.5 per cent of the delegates—in this case, to be sure, a proportion almost exactly equal to that of the Russians in the population of the Kirgiz SSR.[41] In Belorussia, at a more remote period (1946) Russians constituted 26.9 per cent of the entire Party apparatus, and 11 per cent of kolkhoz chairmen, though only 9 per cent of the Republic's population is Russian (1959).[42] In Latvia (26.6 per cent Russian in population) 37.6 per cent of the raikom secretaries were Russian (1956).[43]

Russian dominance in the Party was merely one part of the disproportionate representation of Russians in all the more influential spheres of Soviet life. For example, 65 per cent (1954) of scientific workers were Russians, as were 64.5 per cent of Komsomol Congress delegates (1949).[44] In general, Russian predominance had increased over prewar days, when only half of Komsomol Congress delegates were Russians and only two-thirds of the Party membership was in the RSFSR.[45]

In this connection, language distribution of publications (either directly published or strictly supervised by the Party) is revealing.[46] In 1957 Russian-language newspapers accounted for over two-thirds of the total circulation. The huge circulations of the central newspapers like *Pravda* and *Izvestia* helped greatly in establishing the Russian language predominance, but the Russian papers in the Union Republics had circulations disproportionate to the number of Russians in those areas. For example, Russian-language papers in the Ukraine had circulations one-half as large as those of the Ukrainian, although Ukrainians in the Republic outnumbered Russians three to one. In the Central Asian Uzbek Republic the proportions were about the same, while in Belorussia Russian-language papers had three-fourths of the circulation of those in the local language, although Belorussians outnumbered Russians nine to one. Russian predominance in magazine circulation was even more marked: 85 per cent of the total circulation was printed in Russian. Books were only slightly less predominantly Russian (80 per cent). Obviously convenience in administration and education was one factor favoring the use of Russian-language publications. But it is equally true that the enormous emphasis on Russian-language materials strongly tended both to increase the proportion of Russified elements among non-Russian peoples, and to give a decided cultural advantage to persons who were native speakers of Russian.

After Stalin's death (aside from the Beria interval) Russian dominance was in practice as fully recognized as before; but its overt claims were somewhat muted to make them more acceptable to the other nationalities. Khrushchev evidently attributed special importance to reconciling the Ukrainians, whom Stalin had distrusted. Probably Khrushchev's own association with the Ukraine was of minor importance in this regard, for the Ukrainian apparatus officials who supported him were Russians or Russified. Less highly placed Ukrainians, who tended to maintain some sense of national identity when they left their native land, were extremely important to the maintenance of Soviet control in Central Asia, however. In Kirgizia in 1949, 8.9 per cent of the Party congress delegates were Ukrainian (compared to 6.6 per cent Ukrainians in this Republic's population in 1959). The proportion of rank-and-file members in parts of Asia like Kazakhstan, to which Ukrainians emigrated in large numbers (by 1959 they were 8.3 per cent of its population), was probably higher; as early as 1949 Ukrainians constituted 6.3 per cent of the congress of the Kazakh Party organization.[47]

The overtures to the Ukrainians included the rehabilitation of most of the literary figures condemned by Stalin, although the Party continued to wage a vigorous war against "bourgeois nationalist" tendencies. Also symbolically important was the transfer of the Crimea to the Ukrainian SSR, during the highly publicized tricentennial of the "union" of the Ukraine and Russia in 1654. From the practical standpoint the most important change was the very rapid growth of the Ukrainian Party organization. In 1952 it still had slightly under 800,000 members and candidates (16 per cent of CPSU membership at that time, as compared to the 20 per cent which the Ukrainian SSR contributed to the total Soviet population), but by 1960 membership had grown to 1,400,000.[48] The much smaller Belorussian Party registered a similar proportionate gain, increasing from about 140,-000 in 1952 to 184,000 in 1958.[49] Henceforth, the two Slavic nations were to be assiduously cultivated as the Russians' very important younger brothers. Their junior relationship was emphasized, however, by Khrushchev's careful avoidance of too close identification with the Ukraine; he even denied that he felt thoroughly at home in speaking the Ukrainian language.[50] Moreover, some signs, such as the abrupt demotion in late 1959 of Central Committee Secretary A. I. Kirichenko, who had risen higher in the Party than any other native Ukrainian in its history, suggested a reaction against the "younger brothers" in the Party apparatus.

Party composition in the other European Republics can be summarized briefly. In Belorussia, Lithuania, and Moldavia, with their overwhelmingly peasant populations, there was still only one Party member for fifty to sixty persons—less than half the ratio in Russia. In Latvia and Estonia the ratio was higher; but, considering the high proportion of Russian officials in the apparatus, it is likely that many of the Party members, too, were Russians.

In the Transcaucasus, the ratio of Party members and candidates remained about as high as in Russia: one per 24 persons in Armenia, one per 21 in Georgia, and one per 28 in Azerbaidzhan. These high ratios reflected the high level of education in the area (with 4.5 per cent of the Soviet population, the Transcaucasus furnished over 5 per cent of the scientific workers), and in Georgia, at least, the heritage of a privileged Party status under Stalin and Beria.

In Central Asia, the growth of the Party had been enormous since the middle thirties. Whereas there was then only one Party member per 175 persons (Kazakhstan) to one per 500 (Tadzhikstan), in 1957 the ratios throughout the area compared well with that of the Ukraine (one to 40) and considerably surpassed those in most other European Republics. No doubt many of the members were Europeans (in 1945 only 43 per cent of the Kazakh SSR higher officials were Kazakhs) but the Party seems to have had some success in raising the number of its Asian members.[51]

Rumblings of discontent still were heard in Central Asia, however, especially in Kazakhstan. The old Party complaint that Kazakh writers overstressed national traditional themes continued to appear. Apparently Kazakh intellectuals also resented the enormous influx of Slavic technical personnel into the republic. Local resistance to the introduction of Russian terms into the Kazakh language, and efforts to prevent the enrollment of Kazakh children in Russian-language schools were also officially criticized.[52] In summary, in Kazakhstan, at least, the elements of national discontent which the regime had condemned in many areas during the later years of Stalin's rule were still evident.

As yet it is impossible to draw up a satisfactory balance sheet of the changes introduced in the Party during the Twentieth Congress. It seems clear, however, that five powerful, and in large measure disharmonious, forces were at work. One force was Khrushchev's effort to establish himself as the undisputed leader, if not the absolute master, of the USSR. Unless the analysis presented in this chapter is completely wrong, the determination of the powerful officials of the territorial apparatus to obtain greater weight in Party decisions was a second. While the territorial officials' interests were not identical with those of other segments of that large body of bureaucratic officials discussed in Chapter XIX, all of the officials were determined to maintain the strength of the Soviet system and their own privileged positions in it. Then there was the strong, but scarcely articulate, demand of the mass of the Soviet population for better living conditions. Finally, there was the increasing restiveness of the intellectuals, who were, as we shall see, deeply involved in the ideological upheaval associated with the Twentieth Congress.

THE PERIOD OF THE TWENTIETH
CONGRESS: IDEOLOGICAL FINESSE

The first manifestations of the pressure for greater intellectual freedom appeared very soon after Stalin's death. Considering the rigor of the controls imposed during his lifetime, such a reaction was inevitable. In addition, intellectual ferment was stimulated at this time by the growing size and importance of the Soviet system of higher education, which in 1952 and 1953 (after delays arising from slow demobilization and the economic hardships of 1946-47) was turning out its first large graduating classes. While the ideological indoctrination which the students had received during their schooling in many cases increased their confidence in the Soviet system, for others even diluted exposure to non-Communist ideas stimulated a desire for more freedom.

To the extent to which the iron controls of the previous twenty years had been the result of Stalin's personal tastes and morbid suspicion, the new Soviet leadership was willing to make concessions. Consequently, the question of relaxation of intellectual restraints is intimately linked to the process of destruction of the myth of Stalin's infallibility. As we saw in Chapter XIII, however, the motive forces behind the imposition of ideological controls were complex. The campaign for conformity led by Zhdanov was by no means merely an expression of Stalin's craving for absolutism; it represented also the determination of broad strata of Soviet leaders to maintain the dynamic of Communist totalitarianism. These strata, as noted earlier, still held decisive power in the USSR. Consequently, as soon as the campaign for intellectual relaxation touched the fundamental principles of Party control, a sharp reaction could be expected.

In the complex development of cultural affairs in the post-Stalin period, certain incidents stand out because of their close relation to political tendencies in the field of ideological control. Such, it seems, were the controversies centering on Il'ia Ehrenburg's *The Thaw* and on the magazine *Novyi Mir* (New World). Ehrenburg's novella, which appeared early in 1954, was intrinsically much the less important in spite of its expressive title, which symbolized the new period. It did, however, suggest that virtue (in painting) found it difficult to triumph in Soviet conditions.[1] More important was Ehrenburg's explicit denunciation in late 1953 of the efforts of the regime to prescribe themes for writers and artists, thus robbing them of all true creative impulse.[2]

When the attacks on Ehrenburg began in the spring of 1954, they closely resembled those directed against the group of writers, such as Vera Panova (*The Seasons*) associated with *Novyi Mir*. Critics charged that the writers suggested that the upper strata of Soviet society did not adhere to accepted Soviet ideals of behavior, and that individuals who did adhere to them found a very cool reception in influential circles. Generally, however, their accusers admitted that Ehrenburg and Mme. Panova upheld the accepted Soviet standards themselves.[3] Much sharper attacks were directed against critics like V. Pomerantsev (also in *Novyi Mir*) who explicitly defended the writer's right to "sincerity" and "immediacy of expression." The presidium of the Soviet Writers' Union denounced this "subjectivist" attitude, which would have freed the writer from the requirement of producing according to prescription, as a return to the deviations of the twenties.[4]

The coincidence of the attack upon the writers with Malenkov's apparent ascendancy over Khrushchev may be entirely accidental. But the incident does serve to cast doubt upon speculation that Malenkov favored a "new course" in ideological development as well as in other areas of Soviet life.[5] Probably both rivals were guided by expediency in this as in other "policy" matters. In August, after three months' debate, the favored Soviet novelist Konstantin Simonov was appointed editor of *Novyi Mir*. In December 1954 the Second Soviet Writers' Congress (the first, it will be recalled, took place in 1934) convened. An interesting feature was the low relative proportion of Russian delegates (about 35 per cent) and of all Slavs taken together (50 per cent, though the Slavs comprised over three-fourths of the Soviet population), compared to the numerous Transcaucasians (16 per cent for groups which totaled only 4 per cent of the peoples of the USSR).[6] At the very beginning of the Congress, the Party Central Committee laid down the basic principle that writers had a duty to "educate" the Soviet people in Communism and Communist morality, and condemned deviations from socialist realism.[7] But there was apparently a deliberate effort to mute controversy.[8] In his own report Simonov tried to reconcile the attack on writers like Ehrenburg and the *Novyi Mir* group with the rejection of the "no-conflict" theory. According to Simonov, *The Thaw* and other works which had been criticized had made evil the rule instead of the exception in descriptions of Soviet life. Henceforth writers were indeed to portray the "sharp corners" but were to avoid emphasizing the "bad side of life." [9] Simonov's resort to cubistic metaphor was apparently insufficient, for shortly afterward *Novyi Mir* was again criticized for exhibiting tendencies harking back to the radical deviations, and also for harboring "esthetic cosmopolitans." [10]

It would be risky to take indications such as that just mentioned to be proof that the Soviet regime in late 1954 was moving in the direction of reinvigoration of Zhdanov's principles. In the field of antireligious propaganda, which had been reinvigorated during the "Zhdanovshchina," precisely the contrary tendency appeared. On November 11 a Central Committee decree "On Errors in Conducting Scientific-Atheist Propaganda Among the Public" warned that attacks on the loyalty of clergy or believers were harmful. Instead, "positive" educational measures stressing the growth of scientific knowledge were prescribed.[11] Early in December Malenkov himself received the Moscow Patriarch Alexei.[12] The meaning of these maneuvers—which only temporarily reduced the assaults on religion —is unclear; possibly they were designed to create good will abroad for the USSR. Certainly, however, they represent a slight diminution rather than an increase of the Party antireligious campaign which had been one aspect of the "Zhdanovshchina."

In philosophy the tendency was to restore the Leninist elements by removing the Stalinist encrustations on ideology. Since at least the end of World War II, formal logic (which most Western philosophers would regard as *the* logic) had been reintroduced in Soviet schools, with the so-called "dialectic logic," like other aspects of the dialectic, falling into desuetude. Stalin's "Linguistics" and the numerous commentaries which followed it placed formal logic, like language, outside base and superstructure, although recognizing a "higher form" of "dialectic logic." Soviet philosophers, especially in Georgia, tended to ignore the latter completely, however.[13]

Immediately after Stalin's death, Soviet ideologists tended to proceed in several different directions, but gradually certain officially favored lines of development seemed to emerge. In general, the propositions advanced by Stalin concerning the nonantagonistic nature of contradictions in Soviet circumstances were defended. "Any basis for political revolution disappears," it was said. But the same article put somewhat more emphasis on the "contradictions" which arose between the "boundlessly growing need" of the people, and the actual state of production and consumption. Moreover, dialectical materialism as doctrine received considerably greater stress.[14]

It was at least ostensibly on this issue that G. F. Aleksandrov, who had been Stalin's "court philosopher" after the appearance of "Linguistics," lost his place in the new leadership. Aleksandrov had become Minister of Culture shortly after Stalin's death, but by the time of the Second Writers' Congress his influence was obviously waning.[15] Early in March 1955 he was dismissed as Minister. Shortly afterward a *Kommunist* editorial said that his commentary on "Linguistics" "not only does not solve new questions; at times it even obscures questions already answered!" [16] Other attacks followed. The volume on *Dialectic Materialism* which Aleksandrov had edited, wrote B. M. Kedrov (who, it may be recalled, had been demoted shortly after Zhdanov's death), failed to take account of Zhdanov's requirements for a philosophy textbook. Instead of presenting a systematic theory, it reduced the dialectic to a series of examples presented chaotically. It made only vague reference to the law of the negation of the negation. At the same time, Kedrov said, Aleksandrov, who had once devoted too much attention to Western philosophy, went to the opposite extreme of failing to show that Marxism had any roots in older philosophical thought.[17] By implication, Aleksandrov was also linked to the Georgian philosopher K. S. Bakradze in neglecting "dialectic logic." [18] After the Twentieth Congress, the philosopher M. Kammari cast doubt on Stalin's removal of elements like logic from the dialectic process by stating that such phenomena as language might be regarded as parts of the superstructure which were preserved and gradually transformed after their social base had vanished.[19]

Up to 1956 no such frontal attacks on Stalin's teachings were made. It is evident from the discussion above, however, that Stalin's ideological position was being undermined both by indirect attack on specific features and by denigration of his protégés such as Aleksandrov and the members of the Georgian philosophical school. This process of "whittling away" of the

Stalin myth characterized the entire period from his death until the Twentieth Congress.[20]

At first Soviet writers made a valiant effort to condemn the glorification of Stalin by citing his own words. Some of these attempts involved the writers in as far-fetched departures from historical truth as Stalin himself had made. For example, in the autumn of 1953 the Central Committee Secretary P. N. Pospelov denounced the "incorrect, non-Marxist treatment of the question of the role of personality in history." [21] To support his argument he cited a hitherto unknown letter which Stalin allegedly wrote in 1938 to a publishing house which proposed to publish a book entitled *Accounts of the Childhood of Stalin.* Stalin—according to Pospelov—wrote:

> the booklet has a tendency to root in the unconscious of Soviet children (and of people in general) the cult of personality, of leaders, of infallible heroes. This is dangerous, injurious. The theory of "heroes" and "crowds" is not Bolshevik, but a Social Revolutionary theory. . . . I advise you to burn the booklet.[22]

Pospelov neglected to mention, however, that a few years later a book called *Stalin: Childhood and Adolescence. An Epic,* "a poetic story about Stalin, who incarnates in his person the entire greatness of the human spirit, who has become the teacher and the leader of the broad popular masses, [which] ennobles the moral world of the reader" did in fact appear.[23]

On the first anniversary of Stalin's death (March 5, 1954) the Soviet press carried numerous commemorative articles, but even such Stalinist stalwarts as Aleksandrov emphasized the Party rather than the deceased leader as an individual.[24] Somewhat more attention was paid to Stalin personally on the occasion of the seventy-fifth anniversary of his birth (December 27, 1954)—perhaps because writers close to Malenkov wished to emphasize the State Defense Committee by pointing to Stalin's role in it.[25] Similarly, the ideologist F. Konstantinov used the second anniversary of Stalin's death to stress—in accord with Khrushchev's policy—Stalin's constant insistence on the predominance of heavy industry.[26] In May even Zhukov, who had been humiliated by Stalin, praised his role in World War II.[27] A little later the chief historical journal, *Voprosy Istorii,* like Pospelov two years earlier, tried to correct the fantastic concept that the catastrophic retreat of the Soviet forces in 1941 was part of a planned strategy, referring to Stalin's single admission (in his speech of May 24,

1945) that the regime had made mistakes. Like Pospelov, however, the journal distorted Stalin's real position by failing to note that Stalin himself later acclaimed the retreat as a masterpiece of strategy.[28]

Up to this point, though Stalin was being "downgraded," the process was so cautious and oblique that the average Soviet citizen (although not the politically sophisticated) must have regarded his prestige as unimpaired. On his seventy-sixth birthday in December 1955, and even in Khrushchev's opening speech at the Twentieth Congress, this cautious approach prevailed; some observers have even felt that there was a revival of praise for Stalin during this period.[29]

Just before the Congress convened, however, a "conference of the readers of *Voprosy Istorii*" took place in Moscow. At this meeting a deputy editor openly criticized the keystone of Stalin's system of Party education, the *Short Course*.[30] Prior to this speech the members of the conference must at least have received intimations that the Party Presidium was considering Stalin's misdeeds. But it is probably no accident that this first general attack on Stalin's ideas came from a historian. While their particularly sensitive field made them subject to the full pressure for ideological conformity, historians had shown a remarkable ability to resist passively full compliance with Party demands for distortion of the historical record.[31] They—like most Soviet citizens—regarded the USSR's accomplishments in World War II as a source of real patriotic pride, in contrast to the numerous questionable aspects of Soviet history. In this feeling they were undoubtedly at one with the military leaders, with whom they necessarily collaborated in writing war history. Both groups resented the degrading misrepresentation of the real nature of Soviet accomplishments in the war which maintenance of the myth of Stalin's infallibility necessarily entailed.

As we have seen, the effort to destroy the myth through Stalin's own words involved such transparent contradictions as to be untenable. The only other solution was a direct criticism of Stalin. As *Pravda* admitted a little later in 1956, the efforts to cite Stalin against the "cult of personality" could never succeed:

> It cannot be said that there are no passages in J. V. Stalin's works condemning unjustified glorifying of individuals and disparagement of the role of the masses. As a rule these passages did not transcend the boundaries of general, vague declarations, while in fact no resistance was put up to the constantly swelling practice of personal glorification. . . .[32]

The published account of the historians' conference went to press on February 13. By February 16, when Anastas Mikoian addressed the Twentieth Congress, the account may have been in the hands of subscribers. Consequently, Mikoian's remark that Soviet historians could "better explain from the standpoint of Leninism" events described in the *Short Course*, combined with his criticism of the "Economic Problems of Socialism," was official confirmation that Stalin and his ideological pronouncements were now fair target for explicit criticism.[33]

A week later (February 25) Khrushchev delivered his secret speech. Much speculation has been devoted to the relation between this event and Mikoian's remarks. Was Mikoian forcing Khrushchev's hand, or was he (perhaps because as an Armenian his criticism of Stalin would be more palatable in the Transcaucasus) selected to make the first open suggestion that Stalin was fallible?[34] Like so many other aspects of Mikoian's enigmatic career, this one cannot be explained. Khrushchev later explicitly denied that any one had "dragged" him into making the speech.[35] Unless Khrushchev misled his audience, moreover, Party investigations of Stalin's despotism had been underway for a long time; just before the Congress met, the Presidium itself had considered some of the most repulsive cases of his arbitrary repression.[36] Consequently, we may assume that the emotional pressure to break with the policy of adulation of Stalin was gaining considerable force within the upper levels of the Party itself.

Once Khrushchev had determined to denounce Stalin, he did it with a fervor that even a man of his considerable histrionic talents would find hard to feign. There is no need here to describe the substance of the speech, which has already been cited innumerable times in this work in connection with earlier phases of CPSU history. Two themes do need comment at this point, however. Khrushchev not only destroyed Stalin's aura of infallibility, but pictured him as a man of almost inhuman vanity and bloodthirstiness. An inescapable implication of this description of Stalin was that it was dangerous to permit any one leader to dominate the Soviet system. At the same time, however, Khrushchev devoted much of his speech to pointing out the ways in which Stalin had deviated from Lenin's teachings, and had even treated Lenin, personally or in his posthumous reputation, with contempt.[37] In the weeks immediately following the Twentieth Congress, this opposition of Stalin to Lenin was stressed by publication of Lenin's "last testament" recommending Stalin's removal as General Secretary, and by denunciation of Stalin for minimizing Lenin's ability as a military strategist.[38] In this way, the image of a more remote, but equally infallible leader, was put in the place of the soiled portrait of Stalin.

A second, and probably even more important, theme of the secret speech was Khrushchev's insistence that Stalin had been right in destroying "opposition" elements up to and including the "Right Deviation" (Bukharin and his associates). To be sure, Khrushchev said that Party deviationists should be corrected by re-education instead of liquidated; but he emphasized that "class enemies" such as the kulaks must be dealt with ruthlessly.[39] In effect, Khrushchev was taking the Party back to the period of the "Congress of Victors": up to that point, when Stalin began to turn on his supporters in the territorial apparatus, he was justified. Implicitly, Khrushchev seemed to be saying that a leader was indeed necessary, but that he must remain loyal to his own supporters. Like the officials assembled in 1934, however, Khrushchev presented no solution for the psychological contradiction posed by the endorsement of violent repression for those outside the Party along with the advocacy of restraint in internal Party disputes.

While Khrushchev's speech was never published in its entirety in the USSR, the usual Communist practice of gradually revealing the contents of secret Party documents of such importance was followed. Only in Georgia was an effort made to soften the impact of the destruction of the Stalin myth; on the third anniversary of his death he was still moderately praised.[40] Nevertheless, Tbilisi students carried out violent demonstrations or riots when the news of the denunciation of Stalin reached Georgia. The Party immediately began a campaign for heightened political education in the university, and denounced "some professors" for "liberalism" in regard to student behavior.[41] Later the official, public version of Stalin's misdeeds, stressing the harm Stalin's methods had done to Georgians themselves, gradually appeared in Tbilisi.[42] From this time on, however, it appeared that Georgia's favored position in the USSR was ended; two years later, for example, Khrushchev seemed to be taking special care to stress that he had not visited Georgia for a long time.[43]

As might have been anticipated, the reaction in army and historical circles to Stalin's "downgrading" was the opposite from that evidenced in Georgia. The March issue of *Voprosy Istorii*, criticized the *Short Course* and praised a number of persons whom Stalin had purged; it also laid great emphasis on the initial defeats of 1941.[44] Two months later the same journal said that there had been "failures of entire army formations" at that time.[45] Almost simultaneously the theoretical military journal *Voennyi Vestnik* (Military Messenger) emphasized the lack of preparedness for war due to Stalin's refusal to heed warnings of impending Nazi attack.[46] In May, however, *Krasnaia Svezda* (Red Star), which represented the political administration of the army, attacked *Voennyi Vestnik* for minimizing the role of the Party and the Central Committee in preparing for the war and in directing firm rearguard actions.[47]

The rebuke to those elements which appeared to be using the destruction of Stalin's infallibility as an occasion for general criticism of the response of the Soviet system to the war was also implied in the official decree on Stalin's faults issued by the Central Committee on June 30, 1956.[48] The decision endorsed most of Khrushchev's secret speech (which had already been read to Party gatherings and meetings of intellectual workers), but used far more restrained language. The stress was upon the essential soundness of the Soviet system:

> It is known that precisely during the war period members of the Central Committee, and also outstanding Soviet military leaders, took over certain sectors of activity on the home front and at the fighting front, made independent decisions, and through their organizational, political, economic, and military work with local Party and Soviet organizations ensured the Soviet people's victory in the war.[49]

Shortly afterward, *Kommunist* explicitly stressed the theme (to which the above quotation alludes in passing) that the local or territorial Party organizations were relatively unaffected by Stalin's arbitrary behavior:

> At the same time it must be stressed that in local Party organizations the violation of the Leninist norms of Party life was not the same as in those units of the Party which Stalin influenced directly. It is known that meetings in the primary Party organizations were convened systematically. Before and after the war conferences of oblast and *krai* Party organizations, Congresses of Communist Parties of the Union Republics, and plenums of Party committees were held more or less regularly. The congresses, conferences, and plenums collectively discussed and solved the most important problems of economic and cultural work, and sharp criticism was directed at leading Party workers.[50]

This picture—generally true insofar as the actual holding of meetings and participation of officials in discussion was concerned—was an obvious gesture to the territorial organization. At the same time, it exonerated those, like Khrushchev, connected with the territorial Party from participation in

Stalin's arbitrary practices, while casting still deeper suspicion on officials like Malenkov and Molotov who had been intimately involved in the central apparatus. To explain why the "Leninist core" of the Central Committee, which presumably included the representatives of the territorial organization, did not take an "open stand against Stalin and remove him from leadership," however, the June Central Committee decree was forced to fall back on the lame excuse that "if anyone . . . had acted against Stalin, he would not have been supported by the people" and it "would have been regarded . . . as an undermining of the unity of the Party and the entire state, which would have been extremely dangerous in view of the capitalist encirclement." [51]

So far, Khrushchev seemed to have been performing with considerable skill the delicate task of destroying Stalin's prestige without undermining Communism. Khrushchev had even been able to enhance his personal position, in spite of the fact that his official biography had once described him as "an outstanding example of the post-October generation of Party workers trained by Stalin." [52] For a brief time it seemed as though the Party might even sanction considerably greater freedom in literature. The official journal Kommunist in September 1956 published the startling remark that "A. A. Zhdanov's report [of 1946] on the magazines Zvezda and Leningrad . . . which explained the well-known resolution of the Party Central Committee and embodied profound and correct ideas, also contained particular factual errors and some incorrect generalizations." Among the works which Zhdanov had "incorrectly evaluated" were some which had been explicitly denounced as late as 1955.[53]

Within two months of this extreme departure from earlier Party policy, however, the Polish Communist leadership had been overthrown, and Hungary was in open rebellion against Communism itself. Minor but visible tremors were felt even in the USSR, especially among the educated elements. Apparently the Party decided that the time had come to reimpose controls in cultural affairs. The most interesting aspect of the reimposition process related to Vladimir Dudintsev's Not by Bread Alone. The coincidence between the title of this novel and the phrase (both of course derived from the same unacknowledged Source) used by Khrushchev in 1954 to criticize obliquely Stalin and Malenkov is curious. Moreover, Dudintsev's story seemed to support one of Khrushchev's favorite theses by indicating the inefficiency and favoritism prevalent in the higher echelons of industrial direction. As Mikoian later remarked to Khrushchev "he [Dudintsev] has some points which sound as though he had overheard them from you." [54]

When the novel first appeared (in serial form) in *Novyi Mir*, it was highly praised.[55] Late in 1956, however, a writer in *Izvestia* criticized its hero as an "individualist" who was "not drawn toward a collective," and compared this to the philosophy of the "strong personality"—i.e., to the cult of the individual.[56]

The principal charge against Dudintsev, repeated over and over during the winter and the spring of 1957, was that he depicted Soviet society in too dark colors. Significantly, he tried to defend himself by appealing to the memory of the terrible early days of the war, just as had the historians and soldiers who had sought in the previous year to broaden criticism of the Communist system:

> "I remember the early days of the Great Patriotic War," he said. "I lay in a trench. A dogfight was going on overhead. Messerschmitts were shooting down our planes, although our planes were superior in numbers. Something snapped in me, because I had always heard that our planes were the fastest and the best.
>
> "It is said that I express 'blackening' tendencies. That is not so. I simply do not want to see a repetition of what I saw then. I have a right to such a wish."[57]

Dudintsev's opponents' answer was a variation of the appeal to success as justification for their system which Soviet spokesmen have come to employ more and more frequently in dealing with internal and external critics: "How was it that we won the war if everything was as Dudintsev saw it?" [58] (Or, to use the classic American phrase, "If you're so smart, why ain't you rich?")

In May the board of the Soviet Writers' Union officially condemned *Novyi Mir* for publishing *Not by Bread Alone*.[59] About the same time, the majority of the editorial board of *Voprosy Istorii* was replaced because of the views advanced by the periodical on early aspects of Soviet history.[60] During the same period conferences in a number of the most important segments of Soviet cultural life took place. The Central Committee Secretary D. T. Shepilov, who took an active part in the meetings of music composers, denounced bourgeois music as degraded and insisted that art must be for the masses, not the individual.[61]

When, in June 1957, Shepilov lost his post for involvement in the "anti-

Party group," he was nevertheless accused of "liberal" tendencies in regard to cultural conformity. Specifically, he was attacked for neglecting the Central Committee decrees which Zhdanov had fostered in 1946.[62] The following year the Central Committee again affirmed the applicability of these decrees. Even the 1948 decree on Muradeli's opera *The Great Friendship*, the Central Committee resolution said, was valid insofar as it condemned "formalism" and insisted on socialist realism. The resolution admitted that "certain of the decree's incorrect evaluations reflected J. V. Stalin's subjective approach," but even in this respect placed the principal blame on the "bad influence" exerted by Beria, Molotov, and Malenkov on him.[63]

By this time, Khrushchev had partially restored Stalin's general position by declaring him to be a "dedicated and stalwart revolutionary." [64] For the time being, at least, a measure of compromise had been effected in ideological questions. Stalin was still subject to criticism on individual points. Consequently, it was possible to write history without the utter distortion previously required. Writers were allowed a certain freedom to criticize Soviet life. In an important speech at the Third Writers' Congress (May 1959) Khrushchev conceded the need for criticism, and urged its importance; he even recognized some merit in Dudintsev's biting remarks on Soviet society.[65]

In spite of these minor concessions, writers had to remember that they were primarily servants of the Party, portraying not things as they really were, but as the regime promised that they would be in the future. Or, as one Soviet writer ventured to complain, much Soviet literature (and certainly the portion most acceptable officially) sounded "as if our entire life was to pass under azure skies, to the accompaniment of strong and optimistic laughter of 'active' men and women."[66] Artists of all kinds were allowed a certain amount of experimentation with different forms, but they were bound to produce works immediately comprehensible to the mass of the population, rather than those which appealed only to an esthetic elite. Natural scientists, unless they openly attacked one of Khrushchev's favorites like Trofim Lysenko, seemed almost immune from Party criticism.[67]

By and large Soviet intellectuals seemed to be accepting their status (including its material privileges), albeit with a certain amount of unpublished grumbling which occasionally reached foreign ears. Among the younger ones, little discussion groups avowedly devoted to political criticism occasionally arose, but were suppressed—although more gently than in earlier years—by the MVD.[68] More rarely, a writer like Boris Pasternak risked his freedom to attack the fundamental presuppositions of the Soviet system, such as the justification of the Revolution itself. Such isolated rebels could not, however, continue to present their case. How long the Soviet intellectuals as a group would refrain from rebellion remained to be seen.

CHAPTER

XXII

THE FRUITS OF REVISIONISM

While the denigration of Stalin was the most spectacular feature of the Twentieth Party Congress, pronouncements on the development of world Communism attracted almost as much attention. Perhaps the most startling remark was Mikoian's reference to Karl Marx's 1872 statement that the "workers" in England and America could achieve their ends by peaceful means; even Lenin had rejected this possibility.[1] Basically, however, Mikoian's remarks were part of a carefully developed shift in emphasis, in which Khrushchev took the lead. The essence of this new "line" was the insistence that Lenin had not felt that violent means were universally necessary for attaining "socialism" (in the Soviet sense of the term), but had been compelled to use force by the violent resistance of the bourgeoisie.[2] This is not the place to present an extended analysis of the validity of this interpretation of Lenin's thought. However, it is important to note that the exception to the general rule of violent revolution which Lenin envisaged was "some small country," where the capitalists, confronted by the overwhelming force of the "proletarians" victorious in the neighboring countries, surrendered power peacefully to "save their [capitalist] heads."[3]

In this context, Khrushchev's and Mikoian's explicit references to the "European people's democracies," and especially to Czechoslovakia, as countries where "revolution" was achieved without civil war assume a special significance.

As a result of the favorable postwar situation in Czechoslovakia, the socialist revolution was carried out by peaceful means. The Communists came to power after having concluded an alliance not only with the working people's parties

294

that were close to them but also the bourgeois parties which supported the common national front.[4]

Evidently what Mikoian really meant in this passage is that, given the "favorable conditions" of initial Soviet occupation of Czechoslovakia, and the veiled threats which the USSR directed at the bourgeois parties which sought to curb the Communists, the latter were able to triumph by menace of force rather than its actual exercise.

Aside from the question of the necessity of civil war, Khrushchev and other speakers insisted that the transfer of power to "the working class, headed by its advanced detachment," however achieved, must be complete.[5] It must include transfer of the means of production from private to public ownership. Hence, any compromises with the capitalist order, any seeking of concessions rather than fundamental change, continued to be called "reformism" or "revisionism."[6] Nevertheless, Khrushchev and Mikoian declared that conditions had changed sufficiently that it might be possible for the Communists and their allies to win control of parliaments of bourgeois countries, and to use them to bring about fundamental social changes.[7]

All speakers, however, emphasized their belief that in most countries violent revolution would be necessary because the bourgeoisie, controlling the police, army, and state machinery, would resist.[8] Later in the year, however, a *Kommunist* article, while not disputing this judgment, placed greater stress on the use of parliamentary means in Western countries, and even advanced the unusual view that if the Communists attained power in the United States they could permit opposition parties, since by that time the American Communist regime would not be confronted by encircling capitalist states.[9]

Probably the motives of the Soviet leaders who made these carefully hedged, but novel pronouncements were mixed. They evidently felt that there was a real chance as in the Popular Front period of obtaining support abroad for Communism. In West Europe the democratic Socialists were the prime targets for the Communist maneuver. The Italian situation, where the larger portion of the Socialist Party, under Pietro Nenni, had become the "captive" ally of the Communist Party, was held up as the model.[10] Direct overtures were made to major social democratic leaders. Since the Communist insistence on violent revolution had been a stumbling block in earlier efforts at securing socialist support, the "parliamentary method" sanctioned at the Twentieth Congress was a necessary prerequisite to these overtures.

Still more important, probably, was the appeal to the "zone of peace." Instead of the "two camps" into which Zhdanov's 1947 speech had split the world, the Twentieth Congress pronouncements in effect divided all the world into three parts. The "camp of socialism"—i.e., the Communist bloc —remained, but the non-Communist world (lumped together in Zhdanov's formula) was subdivided into a group of "imperialist," "aggressive," capitalist countries like the United States and Great Britain, and countries like India which "actively implemented" "peaceful coexistence," renounced interference in other countries' internal affairs, and refused to enter "military blocs." [11] Obviously, highly publicized disavowal of the necessity of violent revolution aided the Communist claim to constitute a "zone of peace" with these countries. Essentially the move was a reversion to the Popular Front tactic.

While the theme of "peaceful transition to socialism" appears to have been a maneuver to gain support for the "coexistence" aspect of Soviet foreign policy, the theme of "differing roads to socialism" had a deeper significance. In part it was a long overdue recognition of the need to bring Soviet and Chinese ideological positions into accord. After 1948 Soviet ideologists regarded the "people's democracies" of East Europe as dictatorships of the proletariat; Soviet ideology declared that such dictatorships were a necessary prerequisite to the transition to socialism. Chinese Communist ideologists, on the other hand, maintained that their system was proceeding to socialism by educating part of the "exploiting classes" (the peasantry and some sections of the middle class) under the "hegemony" of the proletariat. While the Chinese terminological difference from the Soviet model was not emphasized, it was occasionally explicitly recognized. As late as the end of 1955, on the other hand, Soviet spokesmen seemed to be saying that the Chinese, because they did not recognize the need for a dictatorship of the proletariat, were at a less advanced stage of the road to socialism than were even the East European satellites.[12]

Some observers have felt that the Chinese failure to recognize the necessity for a dictatorship of the proletariat was adopted only for tactical advantage in dealing with foreign countries. It is pointed out, for example, that the USSR sanctioned East German avoidance of the formula of dictatorship of the proletariat, to avoid complications in relations with the Western powers.[13] Nevertheless, the gap in Sino-Soviet ideological positions remained an anomalous element in international Communist practice until 1956.

Khrushchev's statements on "peaceful transition" implicitly recognized the Chinese methods of revolution. Khrushchev went beyond this to praise the "gradual transformation" of the Chinese economy "into a component part of the socialist economy" as an example of the different forms of socialist construction.[14] Later Soviet statements explicitly recognized the Chinese Communist alliance with "the greater part of the bourgeoisie" as historically justified, in contrast to Russia, where the proletariat had had to liquidate the strong bourgeoisie. In return, the Chinese Communists began to call their system a "dictatorship of the proletariat," but only in the sense of a dictatorship representing all elements siding with the Communist-led revolution.[15]

This *détente* did not apparently extend to all aspects of Sino-Soviet differences. In later years subdued controversy revived over such practical matters as Peking's effort to reorganize agriculture in drastically regimented "communes."[16] The Chinese Communists at first maintained that the commune system was a preparation for an immediate transition to complete communism, thereby implying that they had surpassed the Soviet Party.[17] Khrushchev, on the other hand, publicly though unofficially denounced the commune system as unwise and premature. Eventually Peking modified both the practical and the theoretical implications of the commune system, but it remained clear evidence that the Chinese Communists were prepared to take more "radical" measures than was the CPSU. By mid-1960 *Pravda* was pointedly denouncing the "Leftists in international Communism" who hold "that, having power in one's hands, one may forthwith institute communism by passing certain historical stages of its development."[18]

Unquestionably, the Twentieth Congress and its immediate aftermath for a time made it easier for the CPSU to pose as the leader of a group of Communist states rather than as a demanding taskmaster. This relaxed position was especially important in relation to Yugoslavia. The Khrushchev-Bulganin visit of May 1955 and the subsequent rebuffs to Molotov's intransigent attitude had done much to improve relations between the Soviet leadership and Tito. Nevertheless, the latter insisted that, while state relationships should be cultivated vigorously, the time was not ripe for renewed links between the two Communist parties. Khrushchev, on the other hand, made the re-establishment of such relations a major aim of his policy. Tito, with his cordial connections in Southeast Asia and the Arab world, could be a major reinforcement for the Soviet policy of detaching the "peace zone" from Western influence; his influence in West European "neutralist" circles was also considerable. Since the defection of Yugoslavia from the "socialist camp" had been the greatest territorial loss suffered by the Communist system since World War II, Tito's return would enormously enhance Soviet prestige. This prestige would inevitably strengthen the domestic position of the Soviet leader who secured it.

The significance of the matter for internal Soviet politics is demonstrated by the fact that the Central Committee plenum of June 1955 and at least four Union Republic plenums (in the Ukraine, Latvia, Tadzhikstan, and Turkmenistan) discussed the improvement of Soviet-Yugoslav relations following the Khrushchev-Bulganin visit. As far as can be determined, this was the first foreign policy matter dealt with by the Party plenums in more than fifteen years.

As in 1954-55, the satellite situation was a major obstacle to rapprochement between the CPSU and the Yugoslav Communists. As long as the satellite leaders whom Stalin had installed remained in power, insisting on rigid application of Soviet methods in their countries and ruthlessly purging members of their parties who had shown signs of independent attitudes, Tito would scarcely feel secure enough to re-enter a bloc of Communist parties. As late as December 1955, for example, the Rumanian leader Gheorghiu Gheorghiu-Dej, in the presence of A. I. Kirichenko, Khrushchev's Ukrainian henchman, insisted that there was no way to build socialism except the way "tested by the Communist Party of the Soviet Union and the people's democracies."[19]

Other currents in the satellites were gradually undermining this position, however. In November the Polish Communist leader Aleksander Zawadzki openly stated that the 1938 condemnation of the Polish Communist Party had been the result of unjustified suspicions. Posthumous rehabilitation of purged Polish leaders preceded the similar Soviet development by several months.[20]

At the Twentieth Congress Khrushchev explicitly recognized the validity of the Yugoslav approach to Communism:

> In the Federated People's Republic of Yugoslavia, where the toilers hold power, and society is based on public ownership of the means of production, unique concrete forms of economic administration and organization of the state apparatus are arising in the process of socialist construction.[21]

As in the Chinese case, there was no question, of course, of admitting a "peaceful transition" in the recognition of the "Yugoslav path to socialism"; on the contrary, Mikoian heartily praised the "Yugoslav partisan war against fascism [which] merged with the civil war against the bourgeoisie and landlords who had betrayed Yugoslavia."[22] This praise in effect completed the reversal of Stalin's unfavorable attitude toward the East European partisan movements; as noted in Chapter XIX, oppressors of local partisans were being pictured as Party "deviationists" as early as 1954.[23]

The process of restoring the "native" Communist leaders who had fallen into disfavor proceeded at a very slow rate immediately after the Twentieth Congress, however. Early in April Edward Ochab, the first secretary of the Polish party, recognized that the arrest of Władysław Gomułka in 1951 had been unjustified, blaming it on Beria's machinations. Ochab also admitted that Gomułka and Marian Spychalski, another purged leader, had not been guilty of subversion; but the secretary insisted that they had violated party discipline.[24] At the same time the Czechoslovak party, which was among the most reluctant to abandon Stalinism, admitted that a "cult of personality" had developed around the late Klement Gottwald.[25]

In mid-April 1956 the Cominform was dissolved in order to facilitate Communist collaboration with non-Communist groups in the "peace zone" and with the Socialists; but the dissolution was also an overt expression of the loosening of Moscow's control in East Europe.[26] The ferment in the Communist parties outside the Soviet Union increased rapidly as the shocking revelations of Khrushchev's speech spread to wider and wider circles. The lead was taken by the Italian Communist Party, which had always hesitated to follow the violent and intransigent prescriptions issued by Moscow.[27] Italian comments suggested that the evils of Stalin's regime were not the result of personal or accidental factors, but reflected serious deficiencies in the Soviet political and social system. The CPSU Central Committee resolution of June 30, 1956, was a reply to these criticisms. Rather inconsistently, the resolution maintained that no personal faults could alter the progressive force of the Soviet system, yet attributed all the misdeeds of the preceding twenty years to Stalin and Beria.[28]

From the practical standpoint, two other developments of June 1956 outweighed this polemic, however. One was Tito's protracted visit to the USSR, culminating in a joint communique of the CPSU and the Yugoslav Communist party setting forth bases of mutual co-operation.[29] At last Khrushchev seemed on the verge of attaining the goal of returning the Yugoslav Communists to the "camp of socialism."

Within a week after the Soviet-Yugoslav communique had appeared, however, the "socialist camp" was disturbed by the most violent upheaval it had experienced since Tito's defection. The riots which broke out in the western Polish city of Poznań on June 28 were essentially the same as the

East German and Czechoslovak riots of 1953: spontaneous workers' demonstrations against harsh living and working conditions. Like the earlier riots, the Poznań disturbance was indirectly stimulated by the signs of weakening Communist controls. It was, however, far more violent; the insurrectionists were able to control the principal government buildings for a short time, and hundreds were killed and wounded.[30]

Poznań, however, was completely overshadowed by the Polish crisis of October 1956. The "hard" faction of Polish Communists, survivors of the Stalinist era, wished to inflict drastic punishment on the Poznań rioters, and in general to maintain power by imposing severe restrictions on the Polish population.[31] The "liberal" group, supported by demonstrations of students and workers in Warsaw, elected Władysław Gomułka first secretary of the party, despite threatening Soviet troop movements. On October 19, while the Polish central committee plenum was occupied with these matters, Khrushchev, accompanied by Mikoian, Molotov, Kaganovich, Marshal Konev, and the chief of staff General A. I. Antonov, flew to Warsaw. In the ensuing conversations, and in subsequent meetings with the CPSU representatives, the new Polish Communist leadership successfully demanded recognition of its freedom to pursue a "Polish way to socialism." At the same time, the Polish Communists assured the USSR of their complete fidelity to the Communist-bloc (Warsaw Pact) alliance, although the Soviet regime agreed to restrictions on troop dispositions in Poland.[32]

On the Polish side, the success of the struggle for a minimal national independence owed much to the availability of Gomułka as a leader, for, in spite of his dubious early record, he had acquired the aura of a martyr for national aspirations after 1948. It was also due to the firm yet cautious attitude of the Polish population (encouraged by the Catholic Church). The people furnished support to the new party leadership, while avoiding violent disturbances or extreme demands which might provoke forceful Soviet intervention.

It is not so clear what the Soviet forces leading to concessions were. At the time many observers believed that Khrushchev wanted to pursue a mild policy, but that a CPSU faction headed by Molotov and strongly backed by the Soviet army command desired to suppress the Polish "deviation" by force.[33] In the light of subsequent events, Khrushchev's "mildness" is somewhat doubtful; but perhaps he did feel a cautious policy was necessary in Poland. Unquestionably, the Soviet regime was willing ultimately to pay a considerable price to avoid a bloody struggle with the Poles, who had considerable armed forces at their disposal. The price which the Poles demanded was high, but fell just short of being too high: internal autonomy, but under undoubted Communist leadership within the "socialist camp," preserving the essential features of the "socialist" system under the flexible definition of the Twentieth Congress.

Events in Hungary took a different course. There, as in Poland, purged leaders had been rehabilitated in the spring of 1956. The general feeling that the old Communist order was finished was stimulated by the removal of Mátyás Rákosi on July 18, 1956, probably at the demand of Mikoian, who had arrived in Budapest a day earlier. Rákosi, whose departure was very likely part of the price Tito exacted for renewed relations with the CPSU, was succeeded by Ernö Gerö, equally compromised as a "Muscovite." Consequently, dissatisfaction grew within the Communist Party, with many members demanding drastic changes. The ground was prepared for more violent action as soon as events in Poland seemed to indicate that sweeping change was feasible. Shortly after Gomułka's return to power, strong popular demonstrations began in Budapest. When Hungarian Communist security troops and Soviet army units endeavored to suppress the disturbances they became a full-scale rebellion. The Communist party then installed Imre Nagy, Rákosi's old rival, as Premier. On the advice of Mikoian and Suslov, who arrived from Moscow that same day (October 24), Gerö was replaced as party secretary by János Kádár. Moscow announced that Soviet forces were withdrawing from the country, but warned that "socialism" had to be maintained in Hungary.[34]

It is still uncertain whether this announcement was simply a ruse, or whether the Soviet leadership was really undecided upon the course which it should pursue in Hungary. One observer feels that the decision to suppress the revolution was made on October 31, before Mikoian's return from Budapest.[35] At first the new Nagy government did not seem to be substantially different from Gomułka's, although Nagy himself, because of his earlier relation to Malenkov, may have been obnoxious to Khrushchev. It was difficult, however, for the Soviet regime to face the loss of prestige involved in a second publicized rebellion against its policies. Although preparations for the Soviet move must have been made before the French and British intervention at Suez, the distraction afforded by the Anglo-French-Israeli invasion of Egypt made the prospect of violent suppression in Hungary a little less repugnant to the Soviet leaders than it had been in the case of Poland. Unlike the Poles, the Hungarians had no effective military force.

Most important, in all likelihood, were the developments within Hungary itself. The revolutionaries—for the insurrection was developing into a real effort to overthrow Communism, although it was by no means an attempt to restore the old regime—attacked Communist offices and killed security policemen. A multiparty system was developing in which Communists of any brand would probably have been in a weak position. The great emphasis which the Soviet press devoted to these aspects of the struggle indicates that the Soviet regime considered the destruction of the framework of Communist control in a satellite intolerable, and also that it wished to warn its own apparatus members of the fate awaiting them if the control system were ever broken.

It is possible that Nagy's effort, backed by an appeal to the United Nations to withdraw from the Soviet alliance and adopt a neutral status, was an equally important factor in the Soviet decision to crush the Hungarian independence movement, though Mikoian is supposed to have given verbal approval to dissolution of the alliance. Since the Soviet army had begun several days earlier to mass troops in areas convenient for preparing an intervention, Nagy's appeal to the UN may have had no influence on the Soviet decision. On the other hand, it may be argued that Nagy's appeal precipitated a Soviet intervention which had been prepared but not finally decided. On November 4 Soviet troops, including a number of divisions newly arrived in Hungary and several which had never actually withdrawn, moved against the Nagy government. Protests from foreign countries and the United Nations were completely disregarded. Within a few days the independent government was destroyed, although it took many months before the new Soviet-installed premier, János Kádár, could restore order.

The violent suppression of the Hungarian independence movement ended the chances for Communist rapprochement with European socialists. Soviet and Communist popularity in West Europe was probably at a lower point in late 1956 than at any time since 1941. In the Asian-African "peace zone" the repercussions were slighter, because public opinion in those areas was more intimately concerned with the Suez crisis. Gradually, however, the "lesson of Hungary" led many of the more reflective elements in those countries to distrust Communist appeals. For many Asians this distrust was reinforced by similar Chinese Communist violence in Tibet and on the Indian frontier in 1959. In general, however, the USSR escaped the opprobrium of the latter incidents.

The most critical effect of the Hungarian revolution was upon Soviet-Yugoslav relations. Tito, possibly fearing for his own safety if outright anti-

Communism should spread in East Europe, defended Soviet suppression of the "counterrevolution." But Tito also denounced not only the Rákosi-Gerö regime, but the Soviet policies in Hungary, up to and including the initial Soviet armed intervention. Tito—who had visited the Soviet leaders on the Black Sea coast in September—apparently sincerely believed that these "errors" were a result of the machinations of "Stalinists" in the Soviet regime who were seeking to undermine Khrushchev's flexible policy.[36]

The Soviet leadership sharply rejected Tito's criticism.[37] In the following months, however, Tito and Khrushchev made considerable efforts to re-establish cordial relations. Ranković and Kardelj, two of Tito's most important lieutenants, visited Moscow in July, shortly after Khrushchev had defeated his enemies; during the following month he and Tito met in Rumania. At the end of October 1957, however, Tito pleaded illness to avoid going to Moscow for the fortieth anniversary of the Bolshevik Revolution.[38]

It is not clear just what were the immediate reasons for this cooling of Soviet-Yugoslav relations. A few days earlier Marshal Georgii Zhukov had been severely criticized and removed from the Soviet leadership. Zhukov had just returned from a cordial visit in Yugoslavia. On the other hand, Zhukov is said to have favored a drastic policy of suppression in Poland and Hungary, an attitude which could scarcely have endeared him to Tito.[39] Very likely Tito was also disturbed by the tendency of the satellite states (except Poland) to remain hard in the mold of the Stalin period. Kádár, for example, seemed to be taking a step back from the Twentieth Congress pronouncements, to say nothing of the more extreme Polish and Hungarian efforts to achieve independence, when he declared in Moscow (March 1957) that the reason that the "bourgeoisie" could return in November 1956 was that the Communists had not been drastic enough in their destruction of the old state machinery.[40]

Probably a more immediate reason for Tito's reluctance to appear in Moscow was his unwillingness to be involved in the formation of a new "Communist International." On November 14-16, 1957, a "Conference of Representatives of Communist and Workers Parties" gathered in Moscow. A lengthy policy statement, evidently designed to prescribe the limits within which Communist parties could operate, was issued. Noninterference in internal affairs of other "socialist" countries was reaffirmed, but so was "proletarian internationalism," the solidarity of the working class of different countries. The "peace-loving states of Asia and Africa" and "neutralists" were acclaimed as part of the "forces of peace," but the "socialist camp" was identified as a distinct entity. "Peaceful transition to socialism" was still affirmed as the ideal, but "revisionism," "right-wing opportunism," "bourgeois ideology" demanding "capitalist restoration" were considered the principal dangers.[41] Thenceforward, "revisionism" was to be denounced as the principal ideological deviation confronting the world Communist movement. No precise Soviet definition of the elements of revisionism has appeared, but a good non-Soviet analysis describes its principal characteristics as the rejection of the leading role of the USSR in "proletarian internationalism," rejection of a narrow definition of the "dictatorship of the proletariat" in favor of greater scope for parliamentary controls, and rejection of forced collectivization of agriculture and undue emphasis upon heavy industry.[42] After 1957, Soviet sources bitterly condemned all these elements of "revisionism."

In March 1958 "several" Communist parties—probably including most of those in power, at least in Europe—met in Prague to found a joint "theoretical and informational" journal.[43] While no other permanent organizational features were mentioned, this step seemed suspiciously close to a de facto revival of the Cominform, which throughout most of its existence had centered around its journal, *For a Lasting Peace, for a People's Democracy*. The Yugoslavs were not only absent at Prague, but at that very time they were preparing a program for their own party which sharply clashed with Soviet concepts.

The ensuing Soviet critique of the Yugoslav program clearly indicated how far the CPSU had gone in its retreat from the concepts of 1956. The critique (in *Kommunist*) defended Stalin's concept of the state as necessary "right up to the development of the triumphant socialism into full communism."[44] Moreover, the article stated bluntly that Marxism "does not make a fetish either of the state or of democracy as a form of it."[45] Consequently, it strongly rejected Yugoslav allegations that there was an inherent contradiction in the existence of an "administrative-centralist" leadership during the transition to Communism.

The article denounced the concept of "national Communism," and maintained that there was no lasting "uneven development" of socialist countries.[46] Most important, however, it strongly defended the position of the Soviet Union among Communist states:

> The demand for recognition of equality of nations also characterizes petty-bourgeois nationalism . . . proletarian internationalism requires in definite circumstances the subordination of the interests of the proletarian struggle in

one country to the interests of this struggle on a world scale. . . . Which party, which country heads the international workers' movement depends not on someone's subjective wishes, but on objective conditions. This is determined concretely by where the center of the world revolutionary movement is located, by where in practice the urgent tasks of the revolutionary transformation of society are primarily being carried out. . . . The participants in the conference of representatives of the Communist and Workers' Parties of the socialist countries which took place in November 1957 noted in their declaration that the invincible camp of socialist states is headed by the Soviet Union. . . . Fulfilling the role of the leading force of the socialist camp, of the vanguard of the entire world revolutionary movement has nothing in common with "hegemonism."[47]

While, as in the Cominform days, the Soviet press insisted that Yugoslavia must bow to the "majority" of Communist parties, the statement just quoted obviously meant that what was actually required was submission, as in Stalin's time, to Moscow's orders.[48]

As is usually the case in disputes among Communists, doctrinal quarrels presaged conflict over more practical matters. In June 1958 Kádár's government executed Imre Nagy, who had left the sanctuary of the Yugoslav embassy in Budapest in November 1956 when Kádár (obviously with Soviet sanction) gave him a pledge of safe conduct. A bitter Yugoslav protest was met with charges that the Yugoslav government had been the accomplice of Nagy's crimes. As Yugoslav-Soviet relations worsened, the USSR took various economic measures of reprisal.[49]

Just before these events, in a visit to Bulgaria, Khrushchev had declared that the Cominform resolution of 1948 denouncing Yugoslavia had been basically correct. While he recognized "certain errors" on the part of the Soviet regime during the 1949-53 period, he maintained that the Yugoslav Communists had wrongly refused to abandon "erroneous positions."[50] The wheel had made a full turn: Khrushchev's position was almost identical with Molotov's statement of February 1955.

The willingness of Khrushchev to return so bluntly to the "Stalinist" position after he had disposed of his rivals in the CPSU suggests that the entire "Tito gambit," with all its overtones of renunciation of revolutionary violence and relaxation of satellite controls, was nothing but a tactical maneuver designed to bolster Khrushchev's position at home. In a profound sense this may well have been the case. Khrushchev, like other Soviet leaders engaged in the grim contest for supreme power, probably was willing to subordinate all other considerations to the attainment of victory.

At the same time, he was undoubtedly a good enough Leninist to believe that all tactics were justified to hasten the triumph of world Communism.

It seems probable, however, that there was some element of sincerity in the pronouncement of 1956. While there is little reason (as a careful reading of the statements themselves indicates) to believe that the Soviet spokesmen really thought that "peaceful transition" to socialism was feasible on a significant scale, Khrushchev and Mikoian apparently were willing to experiment with looser forms of control of the satellites. The events of 1956 proved that Communism in East Europe was so unpopular that it could not stand without Soviet support. "National communism," unless sharply restricted, would be a halfway house to withdrawal from the Soviet bloc and formation of a democratic society on the Western model. At the same time, the Soviet rulers probably became convinced in 1956 that there was no danger of forceful intervention by the United States and its allies. Indeed, it may have seemed after Suez that the West was amenable to Soviet threats. The striking advances of the Soviet military and scientific power may well have led Khrushchev and his supporters to feel that economic pressure, the threat of force, and possibly force itself would be far safer and more profitable tactics than concessions designed to make Soviet policies appear more attractive to either the non-Communist or the Communist world. At the same time, however, Khrushchev was careful to denounce the "Leftist" deviation (apparently represented principally by Chinese Communists) which would have hampered his tactical flexibility by insisting on unvarying intransigence toward "imperialist" countries.

> . . . we must not now repeat mechanically what Vladimir Ilyich Lenin said about imperialism many decades back, and again and again reiterate that imperialist wars are inevitable until socialism has won all over the world. . . . If Lenin could rise from the grave he would take such people [who repeat this doctrine] by the ear, as they say, and teach them how the essence of the matter should be understood.[51]

In the latter part of 1960 signs of friction between Peking and Moscow over the "inevitability" of war increased, though observers differed sharply on the importance of this apparent controversy on tactics. In December, however, a second "Conference of Representatives of Communist and Workers' Parties" in Moscow issued a statement which appeared for the time to have smoothed over whatever ideological differences may have arisen between the CPSU and the Chinese Communist party, while reiterating the 1957 Condemnation of Yugoslav "revisionism."

CHAPTER

XXIII

INDUSTRIAL REORGANIZATION AND "ANTI-PARTY" AFFAIR

Nikita Khrushchev and his supporters had scarcely won their victory over Malenkov on the issue of emphasis on heavy industry before they turned to the reorganization of the economic administrative system. At the Twentieth Congress a number of speakers—including Khrushchev's henchmen from the Ukraine now installed as secretaries in the crucial Urals obkoms —sharply criticized the prevailing industrial organization.[1] Apparently there was a genuine need for greater flexibility in industrial control. Since the early thirties, the system of industrial ministries (until 1946 called commissariats) had remained essentially the same, although the number of ministries had increased significantly, and at times strong efforts had been made to curb their tendency toward compartmentalized specialization.[2] As a general rule, one ministry controlled an entire branch of Soviet industry (e.g., iron and steel), although there had been some experimentation with division of industrial branches into huge regional complexes (e.g., separate coal ministries for the eastern and the western parts of the USSR).[3] Since World War II Soviet industry had grown enormously in size and, even more important, its products had greatly increased in complexity and technical refinement. The rigidity and overcentralization of the old system tended to impede the adaptation to the new conditions of management.

Aside from these considerations of economic rationalization, there were strong political factors behind reorganization. Under Stalin, the Party had played a relatively minor role in industrial management. To be sure, the overall directors of the industrial machine, including Stalin himself, were also important figures in the Party high command. For day-to-day control of industry, however, these directors relied on a large staff of officials in the industrial ministries in Moscow. While there was some interchange of personnel between these ministries and the central Party apparatus, there was much less interchange with the territorial Party apparatus. Except on peripheral matters such as political indoctrination of workers and provisions for housing them, territorial Party organizations did not deal extensively with heavy industrial questions. Secretaries of primary party organizations in the plants themselves had somewhat more direct contact with production problems but as a general rule could not interfere directly in management.[4]

As noted in Chapters XVI and XVII, there were some indications in the last year of Stalin's life that he was seeking to curb the "technocratic" tendencies of the industrial directors. Some observers—notably Boris Nicolaevsky—have advanced the view that the industrial managerial class as a whole, including the directors in Moscow and the plant managers throughout the USSR, were a major target of the "second Great Purge" which Stalin evidently planned in 1952.[5] Nicolaevsky also views the managers as Malenkov's principal backers in the contest for power with Khrushchev.

There seems little doubt that the economic directors in the central ministries were regarded with suspicion by Khrushchev and his group. The position of the plant managers is rather more doubtful. To the extent to which Malenkov really did foster emphasis on consumer goods at the expense of heavy industry, he would seem to have been going contrary to the vested interests of the managers. As one penetrating analyst of the Soviet industrial economy has pointed out, transfer of emphasis to consumer-goods production would not lessen the strains which the Soviet system imposes on the manager.[6] At the same time, such a transfer would seem likely to diminish the role of the large plants headed by the most important managers.

During 1955-56 Khrushchev and his adherents seemed to be trying to play off the plant managers against the central directors. At the July 1955 plenum, for example, Bulganin was applauded when he said that the rights of the enterprise director were too limited. While he emphasized the role of the Party in industrial supervision, Bulganin also criticized the ineffectiveness of the territorial Party organizations in this respect.[7] About the same time *Kommunist* wrote that the basic principle of one-man management in industry must be respected. It recognized the need for "centralized guidance of all branches of production," but said that such guidance "does not at all mean that the apparatus of ministries and departments should replace the local economic apparatus." [8]

The initial moves to reduce the power of the central ministries involved delegation of greater authority to the Union Republics. We have already seen that in agricultural direction, as well as in Party operation, RSFSR agencies were given far greater power in 1955-56 than they had possessed earlier. At the same time, some of the most important industrial ministries, which had hitherto been organized on the strictly centralized "All-Union" model, were transformed into Union-Republic ministries; i.e., in addition to the central ministry in Moscow, corresponding ministries, jointly responsible to the central ministry and to the Republic Council of Ministers, were formed in one or more Union Republics. The most important new Union-Republic ministries were for coal and ferrous metallurgy in the Ukraine; petroleum in Azerbaidzhan; and nonferrous metallurgy in Kazakhstan.[9] According to official reports, by 1957 about one-half of Soviet industrial production was under the direction of Union-Republic ministries and Republic Ministries (those without central offices in Moscow) as compared to less than one-third at the time of Stalin's death.[10]

These innovations were only the opening moves in the plan for industrial reorganization. The matter came to a head at the December 1956 plenum of the Central Committee. After hearing reports from Bulganin, N. K. Baibakov, Chairman of the State Planning Commission (Gosplan), and M. Z. Saburov, First Deputy Chairman of the Council of Ministers, the plenum severely criticized the state of industrial direction. Contact of the central agencies with local administrative divisions and individual enterprises was weak, the plenum resolution maintained. Consequently, it continued, improvement of industrial direction required expansion of the rights of the Union Republics in the industrial field. Activities of the central ministries were to be transferred in part to "regions where the enterprise of the corresponding branches of the national economy are located." [11] At the same time, however, the Central Committee resolution directed a "further extension of the rights of the ministries" themselves.[12]

In the light of the latter statement, which seemed to run contrary to the earlier trend toward reducing the sphere of activity of the central ministries, some observers have felt that the December plenum represented a setback for Khrushchev's policy.[13] That Saburov, who was one of Malenkov's closest associates in economic direction, gave the report seems to substantiate this interpretation. Saburov was indeed relieved of his post as Chairman of the Commission for Current Economic Planning a few days after his speech, but his successor, M. G. Pervukhin, was also close to Malenkov.[14]

If Khrushchev did feel obliged to give way temporarily to opposing views, he must have been influenced by the tendency of his old rivals in the Presidium to draw together. At the time, foreign observers felt that Khrushchev had been weakened to some extent by the Hungarian revolution, which seemed to show that his policy of reconciliation with Tito endangered continued Soviet control in East Europe.[15]

In retrospect it seems rather doubtful that Khrushchev and his supporters were really so weakened as to have to submit to a reversal of their economic reorganization plan. Quite possibly, however, they felt that it was wise to retreat a step before presenting the complete scheme with all its implications of a fundamental shift in the relative power of the Soviet bureaucracies. At the February 1957 plenum of the Central Committee this scheme began to appear more clearly. The plenum resolution said nothing more about broadening the powers of the ministries. Instead, the ministries were condemned for "weakening and injuring the normal territorial connections between enterprises of different branches of production located in one economic region." [16] The ministries prevented on-the-spot operative decisions, and retained in the central offices highly qualified technical experts needed in the enterprises. The remedy was to be direction of industry "on the territorial principle on the basis of definite regions." [17] The Central Committee Presidium and the Council of Ministers were directed to work out concrete proposals for the reorganization.

The principle of territorial control of industry was a drastic departure from the system which had prevailed for a quarter of a century. Still, the devolution of power to large economic areas was in general accord with the transfers to the Union Republics which had taken place during the preceding two years. Apparently most Soviet as well as foreign observers anticipated that the "regions" to which the Central Committee resolution referred would approximately correspond to the customary major economic subdivisions of the USSR.[18] These included four regions for the non-Russian Republics (corresponding exactly to the territorial sectors of the Party Organs Section of the CPSU), and nine for the RSFSR. As recently as September 1955 an article in *Kommunist* had pointed out that the territorial administrative subdivisions were "as a rule" *parts* of the economic regions, although the administrative units were also supposed to be formed on the basis of economic criteria.[19] The same article had discussed the need for a modest increase in the number of economic regions, but would have left unchanged their essential framework. On February 12, 1957, however, a Supreme Soviet deputy had stated (in another context) that

> The Soviet administrative-territorial structure takes into account the natural and historical conditions and the economic profile of the region and is closely linked with the tasks of developing the economy, planned guidance of the national economy, and the most effective distribution of productive forces in our country.[20]

On March 30 Khrushchev's "theses" on the reorganization of industry made this principle the basis of the new plan of industrial reorganization. The theses maintained that

> it is apparently necessary to change over from the former organizational forms of management through branch ministries and administrations to new forms of management on the territorial principle. One form of such management may be, for instance, the economic councils. . . . The economic councils should be organized, as a rule, in accordance with existing administrative division, taking into consideration the level of industrial development in the province, territory, or republic.[21]

Despite the seemingly hesitant, half-apologetic tone of his remarks, Khrushchev's proposal had dramatic implications. If the oblast (for this was the predominant form of administrative subdivision at the level to which he referred) became the center for economic direction, the obkom first secretary would have a strong, if not a dominant voice in economic decisions. Obviously the Party as a whole would attain full ascendancy over the apparatus of industrial direction. Equally important would be the greatly extended powers of Khrushchev's principal body of supporters in the territorial Party organizations.[22]

Khrushchev backed up his proposal by a sweeping attack on the prevailing system of industrial direction. He pointed to the top-heavy staffs and inordinately extensive paper work of the ministries, but was careful to point out that their engineers and technicians were generally highly qualified, and should be transferred to equally important jobs when the ministries were abolished. Khrushchev criticized the ministries for incurring unnecessary transshipment costs in moving the products of their industries about the huge territory of the USSR. He maintained that three-

quarters of the industrial and construction research institutes were concentrated in Leningrad and Moscow instead of near the industries they
served. Apartment houses on the same street, he said, were built by many
different construction organizations; this resulted in waste and duplication
of effort.[23]

Much of the discussion which followed reflected the importance of the
proposal to establish economic councils in each oblast. Although Khrushchev had specifically rejected the establishment of a single council for
the Urals, the director of the Urals Machinery Trust argued that separate
councils for each province in the area would endanger the close ties of
its industry. In addition, he trenchantly pointed out that the total number
of new councils should be smaller than that of the ministries they were
to replace.[24] Another Urals trust director criticized the proposal for a
single Urals council, however. It would be "unwieldy," he said; separate
councils would make industrial ties in the region even more direct.[25] At
the Supreme Soviet session which convened in May to consider Khrushchev's theses, Kirilenko—whom Khrushchev had installed as first secretary
of Sverdlovsk obkom in the Urals a year and a half earlier—said, ". . . we
recognize the need for preserving some co-operation with factories situated
outside the province," but insisted that Sverdlovsk must have its own
council.[26]

At the Supreme Soviet meeting Khrushchev repeated the arguments he
had made earlier, but made some show of compromise. For example, he
agreed to the retention of the Union-Republic heavy industrial ministries
which had been formed in the preceding two years, although he remarked
that "our Ukrainian comrades" consider them unnecessary.[27] Only eleven
sovnarkhozes (councils of national economy, as they were eventually
called) were to be provided for the twenty-six oblasts of the Ukraine
(which Khrushchev's supporters completely controlled). The Leningrad
oblast Party organization already effectively supervised the small adjoining
oblasts; only one sovnarkhoz was to be formed for the entire group. For
the time being, however, Khrushchev agreed to the retention, without direct
managerial authority, of ministries for six of the industries most vital to
national defense.

Despite these trivial concessions the plan as adopted by the Supreme
Soviet on May 10, 1957, was a complete victory for Khrushchev and his
territorial apparatus supporters.[28] Of twenty Central Committee members
and candidates heading ministries or similar departments abolished in
1956, six became chairmen of major sovnarkhozes, nine received new

assignments in central economic direction (mostly as deputy chairmen of the Gosplan), two obtained important territorial administrative posts, one became an ambassador, and two were not mentioned subsequent to the dissolution of their ministries.[29] Apparently slightly lower officials of the central ministries received most of the sovnarkhoz chairmanships in the RSFSR. In the small Union Republics, the chairmen of the Republic council of ministers usually became sovnarkhoz chairmen.[30] Central economic officials assigned to the sovnarkhozes or to similar territorial administrative posts were kept under close supervision, however, and sharply reprimanded for departing from the scheme of economic development which Khrushchev outlined.[31] Discussions in subsequent Party meetings suggested strongly, moreover, that the territorial first secretaries really had the decisive voice in direction of industrial activities in their provinces. One of the most striking statements on the subordination of the sovnarkhoz officials to the Party was made in early 1960 by V. V. Skriabin, first secretary of the Zaporozh'e obkom:

At the bottom of the matter was the poor provision of building materials, equipment, etc. The administration and the sections of the sovnarkhoz to which the [Berdiansk] gorkom of the CP of the Ukraine had turned did not act in response to its request. The workers of the sovnarkhoz explained that the main thing for them was the primary objective of ferrous metallurgy, not Berdiansk's manufacturing.

The city committee of the Party had to turn to the oblast committee of the Party with the request that responsible workers of the sovnarkhoz go to Berdiansk and review the complex of questions on the spot.

The obkom of the Party decided to send secretaries of the obkom, the chairman of the sovnarkhoz Comrade Ivanovskii and his deputy, the directors for questions of construction and machinery manufacture, and the responsible workers of the oblast organizations. Having arrived on the spot, they spent several days carefully analyzing all questions of manufacturing and construction, planned concrete measures, set schedules, and appointed responsible persons to carry them out. The obkom of the Party took over supervision [*kontrol'*] of the implementation of the measures which had been planned for the construction and rebuilding of the Berdiansk enterprises.[32]

Later Skriabin makes it clear that the actual directing agency was the obkom bureau.[33] It is especially interesting to note that Skriabin had attained a moderately important position in the Ukrainian Party apparatus while Khrushchev was still its director; while G. I. Ivanovskii, the target of Skriabin's criticism, was one of the Moscow industrial officials who had been sent to work in the provinces when the ministerial apparatus was disbanded. There could scarcely be a clearer indication of the victory of Khrushchev's adherents in the territorial apparatus.

The results were more doubtful from the standpoint of administrative efficiency. One critic outside the USSR has estimated that the sovnarkhozes would require an administrative staff totaling at least 210,000. Consequently the new organization would require a greater personnel overhead than the old ministries.[34] This estimate may be slightly exaggerated. In December 1957, however, a Soviet source complained that the heavy industrial sections of each sovnarkhoz contained 350 to 1,600 staff members. As there were over one hundred sovnarkhozes (the number varied slightly in 1957-59), each of which also had light industrial sections and doubtless some other administrative overhead, the total personnel must have been in the neighborhood of two hundred thousand.[35]

Even more important was the question of co-ordination of the work of such a large number of directing bodies. From the inception of the reorganization plan, the Party press had warned against "localism" and "autarky." The terms meant, the press explained, the subordination of general to local economic interests, as contrasted to the praiseworthy effort to make one's own region successful.[36] At the May Supreme Soviet session Khrushchev remarked sardonically, but pointedly, that he agreed with "the American radio" that the plan meant "not less but greater centralization." [37]

Khrushchev's object was, indeed, to use the highly centralized Party organization to ensure complete control of all phases of the economy. While "one-man management" was retained in the factories, primary Party organizations later formed special commissions empowered to report managerial shortcomings to higher Party authorities or to the sovnarkhozes.[38] Party organizations were enjoined to see that autarkical tendencies did not result in violations of the state plans.[39] At the center, the Gosplan, at first under a relatively obscure official, I. I. Kuzmin, then (after March 1959) under A. N. Kosygin, Mikoian's old associate in directing wartime evacuation, co-ordinated industrial activities in close collaboration with the Party Secretariat. Nevertheless, there were many complaints of the encroachment of local interests.[40] Khrushchev continued to acclaim the overall result of the industrial reorganization.[41] By the end of 1958, however, some indications seemed to point to a reconsideration of the wisdom of delegating industrial direction to the myriad of provincial councils. The traditional system of large economic regions was again mentioned favorably:

> The change to the new order of planning, increasing the role of the Union Republic and local organs in direction of the national economy has sometimes

been understood as a departure from planning by large complex economic regions. Planning by Union Republics and economic administrative regions, however, cannot take the place of planning by large complex regions, as the function of the one and the other are different. Economic administrative regions were formed primarily for operative direction of the economy in the localities. But large complex regions also were used for decision of major national economic problems transcending the frame of individual oblasts and republics. . . .

Given the gigantic dimensions of our country and the existence of over one hundred sovnarkhozes, many important problems of territorial planning can be correctly decided only at the level of the large economic regions.[42]

In subsequent months, more concrete proposals for reorganization of economic planning around large economic regions or "zones" appeared.[43] One proposal even suggested the alteration of the boundaries of territorial administrative divisions, such as the oblasts and the Union Republics, to make them conform more closely to the requirements of economic planning.[44]

One may speculate that Khrushchev, having pushed through the industrial reorganization with the support of the territorial Party apparatus, hedged somewhat in later years on giving it the reward of full control of industry. In 1957, however, he was in no position to dispense with the assistance of the territorial secretaries. According to later Soviet accounts (which, of course, are all derived from Khrushchev's supporters), Kaganovich, Malenkov, and Molotov had opposed Khrushchev's agricultural plans as far back as 1953.[45] In addition, there was the long-standing dispute with Molotov over foreign policy; although Malenkov had scarcely shared Molotov's position in 1954-55, by the end of 1956 the two seemed to have found common ground in attacking Khrushchev's handling of foreign affairs. Malenkov, Molotov, and Kaganovich alike had been intimately associated with the central governing apparatus (state and Party) for many years. Consequently it is probably true, as one of Khrushchev's adherents charged, that Malenkov, Molotov, and Kaganovich regarded the program of transferring authority to the territorial organizations as anti-Leninist and apt to result in anarchy. Aside from the sincerity of this view, all three stood to lose their last possible cohesive body of supporters if the staffs of high economic directors were dispersed.

It would appear, therefore, that the "increased activity" of the group in late 1956 or early 1957 was as much a "last-ditch" fight to preserve their influence as an effort to use Khrushchev's embarrassment over the Hungarian crisis.[46] That the urgency of curbing Khrushchev and his group was clear to a fairly wide group of Soviet officials seems probable in view of the important recruits whom the dissident trio was able to secure. D. T. Shepilov, who, after acting as Foreign Minister for a time, resumed his duties as Secretary in charge of ideological matters in February 1957, had been accounted a firm adherent of Khrushchev. His defection to the Malenkov group illustrates the constant possibility that one can be seriously misled in estimating Soviet political alignments on the basis of the past affiliations of officials. On the other hand, the frequent indignant references to Shepilov's behavior after his defection was discovered indicate that such shifts are rare and unexpected; very likely his behavior is the exception which proves the rule.

Bulganin, the second recruit of the "anti-Party" group (as the Malenkov-Molotov-Kaganovich alignment later became known officially) was much more important than Shepilov, for Bulganin was nominally head of the Soviet government. Bulganin evidently had some doubts concerning the wisdom of open opposition to Khrushchev, but permitted the "conspirators" to meet in his office.[47] Evidently he would have provided the official sanction for the formation of a new government and Party directorate had the plan to oust Khrushchev succeeded. The "anti-Party" group could count on at least the neutrality of several other Presidium members. Pervukhin sided openly with the group on opposing the industrial reorganization scheme, although he later said he objected to the other aspects of the opposition program.[48] Since Khrushchev's group punished Pervukhin less severely than Saburov, the latter probably was still more closely linked to the opposition. Consequently, the group had at least as many voting members as Khrushchev and his supporters, who included Mikoian, Kirichenko, and apparently Suslov.[49] On the occasion they chose to challenge Khrushchev—a Presidium meeting beginning on June 18, 1957, which had been called to discuss the relatively insignificant question of the dispatch of a ceremonial delegation to Leningrad—the "anti-Party" group certainly had a majority, for at first Kirichenko and possibly others were absent.[50] Just what the "anti-Party" group did at the meeting is not entirely clear; apparently they made sweeping attacks on the various phases of Khrushchev's policy which they had opposed in the past, and demanded his resignation as First Secretary.

Instead of complying, Khrushchev, probably using the Secretariat apparatus, hurriedly called for a Central Committee plenum.[51] Although such an appeal from the Presidium was unprecedented, Khrushchev may well have acted within the formal Party rules in taking this action, for they permitted one-fourth of the Central Committee members to demand a plenum.[52] Discussions at the plenum lasted an entire week (June 22-29, 1957). Under severe pressure, Pervukhin and Saburov reversed their positions at the Presidium session, "recognizing their mistakes."[53] The result was a complete victory for Khrushchev. The Central Committee voted unanimously (with Molotov abstaining) to expel Malenkov, Molotov, Kaganovich, and Shepilov from the Presidium and from the Central Committee itself, as an "anti-Party" group which had used "factional methods" in opposing Khrushchev's policies. Shepilov was also dismissed as Secretary, Saburov was removed from the Presidium, and Pervukhin was demoted to a candidate member.[54] A few days later all six lost their major government posts.

The defeat of the "anti-Party" group was undoubtedly due in large measure to the solid phalanx of territorial secretaries who dominated the Central Committee. From one point of view, the new Presidium reflected their predominance. To the remaining full members (Khrushchev, Bulganin, Voroshilov, Kirichenko, Mikoian, Suslov) were added Marshal Zhukov, N. M. Shvernik, A. B. Aristov, N. I. Beliaev, L. I. Brezhnev, E. A. Furtseva, O. V. Kuusinen, F. R. Kozlov, and N. G. Ignatov. Nearly all of these had been associated throughout much of their careers with the territorial Party organization; and the new candidate members seemed to be chosen almost entirely as representatives of the territorial Party.

At the same time, however, the changes gave the Secretariat an unprecedented representation in the Presidium. Seven of the voting members (Khrushchev, Aristov, Beliaev, Brezhnev, Suslov, Furtseva, and Kuusinen) were Secretaries. At the December 1957 plenum Kirichenko and Ignatov were also elected Central Committee Secretaries, as was Mukhitdinov, who simultaneously became a full member of the Presidium.[55] The Secretariat acquired an overwhelming majority in the highest continuously operating Party body. This development obviously strengthened the central Party organization as compared to the local organizations. It might also make it possible for Khrushchev, if he could dominate the other Secretaries, most of whom were newcomers to positions of first rank, to assume gradually the powers of an absolute dictator by employing the central machinery to enforce his will on all levels of the Party.

While these are possible implications of the events following the defeat of the "anti-Party" group, they do not appear to be necessary consequences. After 1957 the large group of territorial officials who had provided Khrushchev's chief support were probably no longer in a position to determine his fate. As discussed in Chapter XX, however, the territorial secretaries may have backed Khrushchev because they realized that they had to choose a leader and preferred one most likely to permit them to share in power. If Khrushchev did continue to respect their position, a kind of "collective leadership" could still exist. Up to the present (mid-1960) the majority of the territorial Party secretaries have retained their positions. Eleven of the fourteen Union Republic first secretaries, and at least thirty-four of the fifty-eight major obkom and *kraikom* secretaries in the RSFSR have remained in the posts they held at the Twentieth Congress, or have received equally important assignments.[56] Nevertheless, there are some indications—though by no means sure evidence—that the central Party machinery under Khrushchev has been regaining the position of complete dominance over the territorial apparatus which it had attained under Stalin after 1936.

During the months following the overthrow of the "anti-Party" group, bitter accusations were made against its members.[57] The most dangerous charges were directed at Malenkov. Khrushchev said that Malenkov had been responsible for the "Leningrad affair," that he had been Beria's tool, and that he had played upon the bad side of Stalin's personality.[58] Still, the group was not expelled from the Party, although Khrushchev said that "the tongue will simply not call such men comrades." [59] Bulganin's case was handled differently. For months he was retained as Chairman of the Council of Ministers, doubtless to avoid the public shock of revealing the full extent of Presidium opposition to Khrushchev and of removing the head of the government until the initial impact of the overthrow of the "anti-Party" group had diminished. Bulganin's influence was obviously minimal, however, and rumors of his participation in the "conspiracy" spread. In March 1958 Khrushchev assumed the post of Chairman of the Council of Ministers (while remaining First Secretary).[60] At the September 1958 Central Committee plenum Bulganin was harshly, though privately denounced, and removed from the Presidium; at the December plenum he was publicly castigated.[61] Like other members of the "anti-Party" group, however, he retained a minor administrative position. Speakers at the Twenty-first Party Congress (January 1959) assailed the entire opposition group, including Pervukhin and Saburov, who had not been denounced publicly before that time. Nevertheless, Pervukhin retained his position as Presidium candidate; Saburov continued to be in the Central Committee.

Long before these events, another minor but dramatic upheaval in the

Soviet ruling group had occurred. Marshal Georgii Zhukov, the Minister of Defense, had profited from the defeat of the "anti-Party" group by becoming the first Soviet professional military officer ever elected to full membership in the Party Presidium. Many foreign observers even credited Zhukov with a decisive role in the overthrow of the "anti-Party" group; his warning that the army would not permit Khrushchev's ouster was supposed to have thwarted the opposition's plan. In fact, this estimate of Zhukov's power seems to have been highly exaggerated. Most likely Khrushchev, supported by the Party apparatus, triumphed without any need for military intervention. Possibly the rumors of Zhukov's decisive role alarmed the Party leadership, however. In other directions too, there had been small but significant indications that the Party was dissatisfied with Zhukov's dominant position in the armed forces. We have already noted the subdued, but distinct, differences on the interpretation of World War II.[62] In 1956 Party organs began to complain of the failure of the army political administration to urge soldiers due for demobilization to migrate to the "virgin-soil" lands.[63] Complaints of insufficient contacts between the military units and territorial Party organizations in the areas where the troops were stationed also appeared.[64]

The denouement came at the end of October 1957. The plenum held at that time removed Zhukov as a Presidium and a Central Committee member on the ground that he had undermined the leadership of the Party, the Central Committee, and the Soviet government over the military forces. In addition, the resolution said that Zhukov indulged in self-glorification and was "disposed to adventurism" in foreign policy.[65] Speeches at the October plenum showed that some of Zhukov's fellow military officers, as well as the Party leaders, had resented his influence and popularity. Marshal I. S. Konev, for example, said that Zhukov had failed to "rely on local Party organizations" in army indoctrinational work, had reduced the military Party organizations to the status of "purely educational agencies," and had made many mistakes as a commander in World War II.[66]

Immediately after the plenum Marshal Rodion Malinovskii replaced Zhukov as Minister of Defense. The Party quickly regained its dominant position in the armed forces. "After the plenum the army and the fleet Party organizations began to live anew." [67] During the first half of 1958 one-fifth more candidates entered military Party organizations than in the last half of 1957. Military line officers soon adjusted to the new circumstances by exhibiting a greater interest in political affairs. The position of the line-officer corps was made uncomfortable by large-scale demobiliza-

tions which sent many of the officers to relatively humble positions in
civilian life. The Party organs were quick to defend the remaining officers'
prerogatives in command matters, however, and to stress the continuing
importance of the armed forces. While the important position and high
educational qualifications of the secretaries of military Party organizations
were stressed, it was also emphasized that they were men of considerable
combat experience.[68]

By the end of 1957 the Communist Party of the Soviet Union had attained
a place of undisputed supremacy in all aspects of Soviet life. Many an
official with a long memory must have reflected on Nikita Khrushchev's
words, pronounced in the Ukraine many years earlier when after the Great
Purge the Party seemed to have become just one among several competing
bureaucracies in Stalin's dictatorship:

> The Party is responsible for everything. Whether it is Army work, Chekist
> work, economic work, Soviet work—all is subordinate to the Party leadership,
> and if anyone thinks otherwise, that means he is no Bolshevik.[69]

CHAPTER
XXIV

THE RESTLESS SOCIETY

For more than two years after the ejection of Marshal Zhukov and the "anti-Party" group, there were no drastic changes in the composition of the top Soviet leadership. A few administrative changes attracted some attention, such as the appointment of A. I. Kirichenko and N. G. Ignatov to the Secretariat, and the removal (December 1958) of I. A. Serov from the post of Chairman of the State Security Committee (some months later the USSR Ministry of the Interior—but not the State Security Committee— was abolished ostensibly to devolve police supervision to the Republics). In January 1960, however, two major changes occurred: N. I. Beliaev was removed as first secretary of the Kazakh Party, obviously because of the meager harvest in his area, and presumably ceased to act as a Presidium member. The demotion of A. I. Kirichenko from his commanding position in the Secretariat (where he had evidently supervised cadres) to the relatively obscure post of secretary of Rostov obkom (in June 1960 he lost even this position) was more puzzling. Much later Kirichenko was also accused of failure in agricultural supervision; but this seems a questionable ground for his removal, considering that he had long been one of Khrushchev's principal lieutenants, and indeed appeared to be his special favorite.

On May 4, 1960, a Central Committee plenum officially removed Kirichenko and Beliaev from their high posts in the central apparatus. Three candidate members were elevated to Presidium membership: the Ukrainian Party first secretary N. V. Podgornyi; D. S. Polianskii, chairman of the Russian Republic council of ministers; and A. N. Kosygin (appointed deputy chairman of the USSR Council of Ministers the same day). At the same time the plenum drastically altered the composition of the Secretariat. Only five of the eight Secretaries were retained, but Frol R. Kozlov was added to the group.[1] Since most of the Secretaries who were removed had appeared to be protégés of Khrushchev, there was some speculation that his position had been weakened. This view was related to the fact that the plenum action occurred shortly after Soviet forces had succeeded in bringing down an American high-altitude airplane ("U-2") engaged in a reconnaissance flight across the USSR, and just before Khrushchev's sharp reversal in the Soviet policy of *détente* toward the United States. In the months immediately following these events, however, Khrushchev ostensibly retained his dominant position—he was able to denounce "Leftist critics" of his foreign policy more vigorously than ever—and there is no direct evidence to show that he had suffered a real setback.[2]

During these same two years a growing body of evidence has accumulated concerning less dramatic, but more profound tensions in the social structure of the Soviet Union, and especially within the membership of the CPSU itself. Much of the evidence has appeared in connection with sudden and surprising innovations undertaken by Khrushchev and his lieutenants. There seems little doubt but that the ruling group is aware that the present equilibrium in Soviet politics is an unstable one. To hold their own positions, and still more to maintain the civic solidarity and national strength of the USSR, the Party leaders, unlike Stalin, are resorting to constant experimentation to adjust the totalitarian system to underlying social changes. In this respect, their practice differs sharply from Stalin's emphasis in his later years on stability bolstered by rigid controls. At times the experimentation of the present rulers—reflecting, no doubt, Khrushchev's own restless personality—verges on the erratic.[3] But observing the shifts and turns of policy in the past two years, against the background of the basic data of Soviet social structure, one can learn much concerning the true nature of latter-day Communism.

A typically unexpected and seemingly paradoxical development was the abolition of the machine tractor stations. For four and one-half years subsequent to the September 1953 plenum, the MTS seemed to constitute a basic organizational feature in Khrushchev's program for Soviet agriculture. As noted in Chapter XIX, the abolition of the post of deputy director for political affairs, and the institution of the position of raikom secretary for the MTS zone seemed to establish territorial Party supremacy in agricultural direction. Quite possibly the territorial secretaries continued to feel uneasy concerning the MTS as an institution. Nevertheless, it is difficult to see that Khrushchev or his principal body of supporters could derive any marked political advantage from its abolition.

Consequently, one is inclined for once to accept at their face value Khrushchev's reasons for the abolition of the MTS. When he broached the matter in Belorussia on January 22, 1958, he emphasized on the one hand the increasing strength of the kolkhoz technical personnel and the kolkhoz Party organizations, which enabled the collective farms to conduct mechanized agricultural operations without close supervision. At the same time, Khrushchev said, the existence of the MTS led to excessive overhead, uneconomical utilization of machinery, and bureaucratic inefficiency.[4] At the February 1958 Central Committee plenum he repeated these arguments. The plenum resolved to abolish gradually both the MTS and the raikom instructor groups which had operated in conjunction with them. Tacitly refuting Stalin's argument in "Economic Problems" that dissolution of the MTS would be a step backward from socialism, Khrushchev's proposal to the plenum contended that strengthening the collective farms at the expense of the state-owned MTS would not weaken the public sector of society because the "indivisible funds" of the kolkhoz (including the machinery which it would acquire from the MTS) "essentially approach" the status of "public property," for, he said, the kolkhoz "wealth essentially belongs to the whole people." [5]

Evidently Khrushchev envisaged the transfer of agricultural machinery to the collective farms as a step toward the transformation of the peasant into a kind of rural industrial laborer. This was, of course, in some measure a return to his abortive "agrogorod" scheme of 1950. It was also in line with the emphasis devoted since 1953 to the sovkhoz (state farm), where all workers were hired employees of the state. Using his native village of Kalinovka (Kursk oblast) as a model, Khrushchev proposed that the kolkhoz peasants' privately owned cows be turned over to the collective, and that communal kitchens be established—all in the name of relieving the women (the great majority of farm workers) from domestic drudgery and freeing them for work in the collectivized sector of agriculture.[6]

But Khrushchev as leader of the USSR was much more cautious in taking these steps than, apparently, he had been in a subordinate capacity eight years earlier. Perhaps he was influenced by the alarm which Soviet leaders seemed to feel concerning the drastic Chinese Communist measures for establishing tightly regimented, egalitarian communes. Khrushchev's plans, far from envisaging a leveling of kolkhoz labor, evidently were designed to strengthen the appeal of the system of material incentives. Many local Party officials, including an especially large contingent of Khrushchev's close adherents in the Ukraine, took the "voluntary" prescription for the sale of privately owned cows to the kolkhoz with a large grain of salt, for various kinds of pressure were exerted to force the reluctant peasants to surrender their cattle. In the spring of 1959, however, the Party intervened firmly to stop these excesses.[7]

Industrial labor was equally subjected to seemingly contradictory policies. On April 25, 1956, a decree of the Supreme Soviet abolished the criminal penalties established in 1940 for workers who changed jobs without permission or were guilty of absenteeism.[8] For the common man in the USSR this measure was probably the most important step taken after Stalin's death to restore a measure of personal liberty. While the hesitant steps toward freedom of private expression and abolition of arbitrary arrest might have a deeper significance for the development of the Soviet system, the right to change jobs without restriction, if fully granted, could greatly reduce the impact of totalitarianism on everyday life.

Very soon, however, it became apparent that the Soviet system would balk at relying upon material incentives alone to control the flow of labor. The regime retained full power over Party and Komsomol members, who could be expelled in disgrace from their organizations for refusal to accept job assignments. It could exert strong pressure on other Soviet workers. The April 25, 1956, decree provided for the temporary loss of social security benefits for those leaving jobs without permission.[9] The police were authorized to expel unemployed persons from major cities.[10] All of these measures, however, were inadequate, for the Soviet press increasingly emphasized the number of persons who managed to evade doing "socially useful" work.

In 1957 a nation-wide campaign was instituted to pass legislation authorizing mass meetings of the residents of a given area or apartment house to sentence a neighbor to banishment at compulsory labor if he was found to be socially unproductive. Several smaller Union Republics (including all those with predominantly Moslem-Turkic populations) actually made provision for such "courts." A number of Soviet jurists expressed alarm at the development, pointing out that it violated the basic Soviet legal and constitutional principles. Khrushchev's regime (which had, of course, instituted the campaign in the first place) then drew back, and the new system was not extended to the larger European Republics.[11]

The problem of securing maximum use of labor, which was closely linked to the growing volume of hoodlum activity in the USSR, remained. Fundamentally, the regime was more concerned with a direct attack on the problem than with nice questions of legality. In March 1959 a decree established "voluntary detachments" of "leading workers" to act "primarily through persuasion and warning" to curb delinquents and rowdies, but it was evident that the measure in effect placed a special police power in the hands of the Party and its auxiliary agencies.[12]

At the end of 1959 a more drastic interference with the private lives of individuals was officially introduced in the Supreme Soviet. "Comradely courts" composed of persons elected at biennial meetings in places of work and apartment houses were to be established. The courts were to "try" cases of violation of labor discipline—tardiness, absence, drunkenness, poor quality of work, unsafe or negligent practices, illegal use of materials— and derelictions in private life such as "parasitical living," slander, failure to care for children or parents, petty speculation, and violation of apart- ment-house regulations. In other words, the jurisdiction of the "comradely courts" was to resemble that of the mass meetings which had been dropped two years earlier. The penalties—reprimands and small fines—were much lighter, however, and provision for review of fines by the courts appeared in the draft law. Essentially the new measure appeared to be a compromise between the regime's desire to exert strong pressures for social and labor discipline, and its reluctance to disregard legal procedures blatantly.[13]

Party membership policies did not undergo drastic change at the end of the fifties. According to a very careful estimate by T. H. Rigby, 30 to 40 per cent of the Communists in 1954 were officials of the Party itself, the state, or one of the "mass organizations."[14] This figure contrasts very sharply with the Soviet official assertion five years later that fewer than 15 per cent of the Communists were officials in the administrative apparatus in industry, agriculture, state, Party, trade unions, Komsomols, or "social organizations."[15] While the apparatus has undoubtedly shrunk in recent years, the Soviet claim very probably exaggerates the shrinkage.

The high proportion of officials in the Party was closely related to the dominance of white-collar workers, although, as we shall see, the two categories were not identical. Higher officials concerned with the growth of the Party membership were disturbed by the tendency, unaltered by the changes following Stalin's death, to neglect recruitment of workers and peasants. During 1955 only 34.2 per cent of those admitted to the Party in the RSFSR were workers; only 17.5 were kolkhoz peasants, as compared to 46 per cent white-collar workers.[16] While the proportion of kolkhozniks admitted in the smaller Republics was also about one-sixth, the worker Party recruits formed an even smaller contingent there than in the RSFSR.[17] By 1957, however, the new RSFSR Party Bureau claimed to have increased the proportion of worker admissions to 40.8 per cent, and kolkhozniks to 20 per cent, as compared to 37.8 per cent white-collar employees. In some of the larger industrial oblasts the workers formed a majority of those admitted.[18] Official data for the entire USSR indicate that 65.4 per cent of all persons admitted to the Party in 1959 were workers or kolkhozniks.[19] Rank-and-file Communists were represented in much smaller numbers in even the nominally authoritative bodies of the Party, however. Even if 399 workers and kolkhozniks reported as delegates to the Twenty-first Congress included nothing but full-time industrial and farm laborers, they constituted only half of the Congress membership, while Party officials alone constituted 31 per cent.[20]

Precise data on the Party's social composition are available for the Ukraine, although it would be unwise to consider this area, with its large peasant population and extraordinarily rapid Party growth after 1953, as typical of the Soviet Union as a whole. Of the total membership in 1958, slightly over one-fifth (225,000) were workers.[21] As the total number of workers in the Ukraine was probably between 4,000,000 and 4,500,000, the Party members constituted about 5 per cent of this group.[22] There were over 10,000,000 kolkhozniks, but this figure included many women and children who worked only part time.[23] The 155,000 kolkhoz Party members, therefore, constituted about 1.5 per cent of the kolkhoz work force; but there were more than 100,000 more Party members working in agriculture in the MTS and similar agencies. In 1959 in the USSR as a whole, according to an official source, 3,500,000 Communists were employed in agriculture.[24]

The Party's efforts to recruit highly trained personnel were indicated by the official statement that 62 per cent of those admitted to the CPSU in 1958 were specialists such as engineers, technicians, agricultural specialists, teachers, and physicians,[25] though such specialists comprised only about 6 per cent of the general adult population. About 12 per cent of the total Ukrainian Party membership consisted of specialists with higher educations; of the 534,000 specialists with higher education, 30 per cent were Communists.[26] About half of the 97,000 engineers—a highly favored group—and nearly half of the agricultural specialists were in the party. Only 24 per cent of the physicians, and less than one-fifth of the teachers—professions in which women heavily predominated—were Party members, however.[27]

Though the Party has stressed recruitment of highly educated specialists, the trend toward higher educational attainments among delegates to Party Congresses has been slightly but significantly reversed since Khrushchev and his adherents became dominant in the apparatus. Whereas 59 per cent of the delegates to the Nineteenth Party Congress (1952) had some higher education, and only 15 per cent had only primary education, at the Twenty-first Congress the ratio was 56 to 27. The decline in the educational level of Ukrainian Party congress delegates was more notable: from 71.7 per cent with some higher education, and 11.6 per cent with primary educations only, in 1954, to 58.4 and 29.9 per cent respectively in 1959.[28] The comparatively small, but definite decrease in the proportion of the highly educated tended to bring Congress representation somewhat more closely in line with the rank-and-file Party membership, which (in 1956) included 14.7 per cent with higher or incomplete higher education and 22.2 per cent with secondary educations. If one adds to the groups just listed Communists with incomplete secondary education (i.e., with more than seven but less than ten years' schooling), one obtains a total of 64.6 per cent with more than elementary schooling, as compared to only 33.7 per cent in 1939.[29] For the dominant Party in a modern technological society the educational level of the membership is not very impressive; but it represents a vast increase over earlier periods.

It is notable, however, that the largest single category of territorial Party officials, the raikom secretaries, were only moderately better educated than the rank-and-file Communists. While by 1954 nearly all (83.8 per cent) of the secretaries had at least secondary educations, less than one-tenth had completed higher educational institutions.[30] It is significant, too, that much of the increased educational level of the Party apparatus was due to training received in the network of Party schools established after World War II. Between 1946 and 1957, 130,000 persons had been graduated from these institutions—the vast majority from the relatively short-term courses in the territorial centers. Practically all of the graduates went to official duties; over 77,000 became Party or propaganda officials alone.[31] While all Soviet education contains a strong element of ideological indoctrination, graduates of the Party schools had, of course, received an inordinately strong dose. Consequently, while the level of the apparatus officials' education was rising in rough correspondence to the general increase of education among the Soviet population, their training was by no means the same as that of the average educated man.

The background of Khrushchev and many other members of the Party apparatus who have "risen from the ranks" makes it easier to understand why they may have entertained a certain suspicion of the rapidly increasing contingent of highly educated persons in the USSR.[32] As Khrushchev has pointed out, only 30 to 40 per cent of the students in Moscow institutions of higher learning were (in 1958) children of workers or kolkhozniks.[33] While this percentage corresponded almost exactly to the proportion of workers and peasants in the Party membership itself, it was evidently far removed from Khrushchev's image of the ideal Soviet ruling strata. As an American sociologist has recently pointed out, Soviet propaganda has placed much more emphasis upon the worker in recent years, and some concrete measures have been taken to reduce the gross inequalities in pay of workers and more highly educated white-collar employees.[34]

Two other factors undoubtedly increased the regime's uneasiness concerning the educated youth. The Nineteenth Congress had made the achievement of secondary education a universal goal for Soviet citizens, and in fact the number of graduates from the secondary schools increased rapidly in the following years. But only one-sixth of them were admitted to institutions of higher education. The remainder tended to form a somewhat dissatisfied group. They were not easily absorbed in manual work, in spite of the fact that, due to the low birth rate of the war period, the Soviet economy was hard pressed to satisfy its needs for ordinary labor.[35] Consequently, in the short run the increased educational level seemed an economic liability.

The second factor disturbing Khrushchev and his associates was the tendency of university students or at least those in studies containing a fairly large humanistic element to question official prescriptions. After the recognition of Stalin's faults at the Twentieth Congress, and especially after the upheavals in East Europe, students began open protests. Some of their activities, like the craze for American jazz and "strikes" against the mediocre food in the student dining halls, may have reflected nothing more than the proverbial rebelliousness of youth; but they were new phenomena in the

Soviet system. Boycotts of stereotyped lectures and protests against the refusal of instructors to discuss controversial questions concerning events in East Europe indicated a real tendency toward political disaffection. In early 1957 *Komsomolskaia Pravda* issued a vigorous denunciation of such "demagogues." [36] At about the same time Khrushchev told the Moscow Komsomols how the Rumanian workers had warned students in their country:

> For the time being you are living on what we are creating, so you should study well. If you do not like our ways, which we have established with blood and toil, go and work, and others will come and study in your place.[37]

The regime's dissatisfaction with the educational system assumed a more concrete form in 1958. Khrushchev said that some lacked "respect for manual labor." Consequently, he continued, the schools must train all for physical work.[38] He proceeded to outline a drastically revised educational system, which was partially implemented early in 1959. Under the revised system the basic compulsory school term was to be eight rather than seven years, but the students were to receive a considerable amount of what the Soviet spokesmen called "polytechnic training"—manual arts in American educational terminology. After completing the eighth grade, most students were to go to work immediately, finishing their secondary education by correspondence, part-time, or night courses, if at all. Similarly, those finishing secondary schools and accepted for higher education were to combine the first two or three years of such training with practical work experience.[39]

A "gifted" minority of 5 to 8 per cent was excepted from the requirement of interrupting its education by working.[40] Apparently the great majority of such students were to study science or engineering. Even the less talented students in such subjects could combine their studies with work which would enhance their abilities. No such solicitude was shown for the ideologically recalcitrant humanities student:

> As for the humanities faculties of universities and pedagogical and other higher educational institutions, the students' work here need not necessarily be related to their future specialty. Their practical work at various enterprises will enable them to acquire definite labor skills, to study production and to take an active part in the constructive labor and socio-political life of the people.[41]

Apparently the regime's curbs on education have not solved the problem of students' disaffection. In late 1959 an unusual report described how a group of students

> went so far as to decide to start a kind of "review" setting forth their "political" opinions. . . . In the last analysis they unquestionably represented an anti-Soviet group, though a very small and insignificant and not even a very serious one. Later they confessed that one of the group had even proposed to write and circulate disgusting leaflets.[42]

Though the report stressed the "penitence" of the youths and their "lenient" treatment by the MVD, it was clear that they presented an annoying problem—and that the regime was just as determined to suppress any circulation of dissenting opinions as it had been in Stalin's time.

Alongside the cleavage in educational background between the Party ruling elite and the Soviet intellectual elite was the increasing gap in age level between the ruling group and the younger Party generation. Young Party members were, to be sure, much better indoctrinated than the average Soviet youth. During the fifties a considerable majority of those admitted to the Party had previously gone through Komsomol training.[43] Between 1950 and 1954 the Komsomols increased in number from eleven million to nearly nineteen million.[44] At that point the total membership of the organization was stabilized, for it included the great bulk of the eligible Soviet youth. The turnover remained very considerable, however, with six million entering the Komsomol in 1956-59 alone.[45] Apparently this increment was approximately balanced by those leaving the organization.

Just because the organization did include such a large proportion of the younger generation, however, Komsomol membership was no guarantee of complete ideological conformity. One may assume that the minority of Komsomol members who went on to become Party members (only 675,000 of about six million leaving the youth organization in 1956-59)[46] were more enthusiastic supporters of Communism—or more intent on appearing as such. But it was precisely the careerist element among young Communists which was apt to be alienated by the near-monopoly of older officials in the upper levels of the apparatus.

Basically, the higher- and the middle-apparatus strata were still the "men of '38" who had received their positions as a result of the Great Purge. A voluminous body of statistics (some of which have been presented earlier) could be adduced to prove this statement; but a simple comparison of the delegations at the Eighteenth and the Twenty-first Party Congresses, held almost exactly twenty years apart, is sufficient to show the essential continuity of the Party elite.[47] Over 80 per cent of the delegates to the Eighteenth Congress (1939) were *under* forty. At the Twenty-first Congress (1959) 78.9 per cent of the delegates were *over* forty. At the Eighteenth Congress 81 per cent of the delegates had entered the Party between 1921 and 1929; twenty years later the proportion in this group had somewhat declined (to about 53 per cent), but still represented a clear majority of the total Congress membership.[48] In contrast, Communists *under forty* (in the Ukraine, at least) comprised well over half the general Party membership in 1958, while about *80* per cent had been admitted since 1940.[49] While the increase of elderly pensioners in the Party membership (evidently mostly retired army officers) was sufficient to lead to the formation of some primary Party organizations in apartment houses (in addition to places of work), the number was too small to alter the predominance of youth in the Party ranks.[50]

The portrait of the typical Soviet political elite member, then, is that of a man fifty years old, with a generation of Party service behind him. While the Soviet elite was in 1939 one of the youngest groups to rule a modern industrial state, it is now one of the oldest.

This circumstance may well be related to the attitude of Khrushchev (even older than the average elite member) and his supporters to the educational system. As noted earlier, Khrushchev is a "self-made" man, with very little formal education; many high officials have similar backgrounds. Certainly it would be natural for middle-aged or elderly men lacking extensive educational qualifications but determined to maintain their grip on political power to be suspicious of a well-educated younger generation which has in some measure indicated that it does not feel entirely satisfied with the present state of the Soviet system. In recent years a few more direct indications of tension between the generations have appeared. At least one recent Soviet student of personnel problems has felt it necessary to recognize the problem:

. . . the strength of our Party lies in the fact that there is no schism between the old and the new generations of cadres. We are victorious because our old and young cadres go together in one front, in one rank.[51]

A few years later, Kirichenko alluded to the problem in less euphoric terms. Stressing the importance of promoting new men, he sharply reminded the middle-aged officials at the Twenty-first Congress that "many of these

leaders forget that they were themselves promoted to positions of responsibility by the Party when they were 30 or 35." [52]

At the present time, therefore, the top level of the Party leadership
recognizes the potential danger of a conflict of generations. The moderate
increase in the number of younger men at the past two Congresses indicates that cautious steps are being taken to give the rising generation a
position in the elite. The turnover of personnel at lower levels of the
apparatus has been much more extensive. In the RSFSR over half of rural
raikom first secretaries have held their positions no more than three years,
while less than one per cent have over ten years' service in this post.[53]
A high Party official, in an article which is a thinly veiled directive on the
manipulation of elections in Party organizations, speaks of the need to
"balance old and young cadres." But, he insists, too frequent change of
personnel is as bad as too lengthy terms for officials, noting that the 30 to
40 per cent annual turnover in primary party organization secretaries may
be excessive.[54]

As long as Khrushchev relies on his supporters in the territorial apparatus,
however, it is hard to see how the process of replacing the middle and
higher levels of the apparatus can be carried very far. While the present
higher Party leaders are over forty, very few are over fifty-five; under
normal circumstances they have ten years or more of active life ahead of
them, and it is difficult to see how they can be persuaded to relinquish their
posts gracefully to younger men. Stalin's solution—the wholesale purge of
the older generation—is, of course, always possible. That Khrushchev at
his advanced age (sixty-six in 1960) would risk his position and alienate his
supporters merely to appease the younger generation is scarcely likely.
If, as some observers think he will, he should seek absolute power by
destroying the men who helped him defeat his rivals, their replacements
are readily available. In the opinion of the present writer, however, the
oligarchic tendencies of the present regime are too strong to make such a
development, with all its unforeseeable implications, likely.

It seems more probable that the solution to the generations problem will
come later, after Khrushchev has passed from the Soviet scene. The present
"oligarchy" is, as noted earlier, divided between men like Khrushchev who
have little formal education of any kind, and those like Kozlov and
Brezhnev who have advanced technical training. For the time being, the
two elements, linked by common experience in the territorial Party organization and similar in age, have held together. As the rising generation of
highly trained officials increases its pressure for a greater voice in the

direction of the Soviet system, however, the second element may decide to make common cause with them. The present restrictions on academic training and the tendency to renewed emphasis on the role of common workers in the Party may, therefore, represent the last effort of the old-line Party "boss" to turn back the tide which has been bringing an elite of training to the commanding posts in the increasingly complex technological society of the Soviet Union.

CENTRAL COMMITTEE PLENUMS, 1946-59

DATE	TOPICS DISCUSSED		
	Industry	*Agriculture*	*Other Action*
March 1946			Considered questions to be reviewed by Supreme Soviet; Elected Orgburo
Feb., 1947		Measures to improve agriculture, especially violations of work day, expropriation of kolkhoz property	Elected Voznesenskii to Politburo
(Feb. 1948)* (based on remark in Bulganin's biography in BSE, 2nd ed., VI, 260. Of dubious validity)			Elected Bulganin to Politburo (?)
Mid-Aug., 1952			Convocation of XIX Congress
Oct. 16, 1952			Election of Presidium and Secretariat after XIX Congress
(c. Mar. 6, 1953)			Joint action with Supreme Soviet Presidium and Council of Ministers to form new government and Presidium
Mar. 14, 1953			Elected new Secretariat (relieving Malenkov); elected Central Committee member (Shatalin)

* Plenums listed in parentheses were not officially listed as such, but the nature of the actions taken indicates that plenums may have been held.

CENTRAL COMMITTEE PLENUMS, 1946-59 (CONTINUED)

DATE	TOPICS DISCUSSED		
	Industry	*Agriculture*	*Other Action*
c. Apr. 6, 1953			Dismissed S. D. Ignat'ev as Secretary
July 2-7, 1953			Expelled Beria from Central Committee and Party
Sept. 3-7, 1953		Improvement of agriculture (including raikom secretaries for MTS zones)	Elected Khrushchev First Secretary
Feb. 23-Mar. 2, 1954		Improvement of grain culture and other agricultural measures, especially "virgin lands"	
c. June 26, 1954		Result of spring sowing, 1954 procurement plan, other agricultural measures	(Decision to try Riumin?)
Jan. 25-31, 1955	Resolution mentioned in passing stress on heavy industry	Livestock	
July 4-12, 1955	Development of industry; improvement of its organization	Results of spring sowing; 1955 procurement plan; other agricultural measures	Convocation of XX Congress; Khrushchev report on Soviet-Yugoslav talks; election of Kirichenko, Suslov to Presidium; of Aristov, Beliaev, Shepilov to Secretariat
Feb. 27, 1956			Election of Presidium and Secretariat after XX Congress; formation of Central Committee RSFSR Bureau
(June 30, 1956?)			(Resolution on cult of individual?)

CENTRAL COMMITTEE PLENUMS, 1946-59 (CONTINUED)

DATE	TOPICS DISCUSSED		
	Industry	*Agriculture*	*Other Action*
Dec. 20-24, 1956	Sixth Five Year Plan; direction of industry		
Feb. 13-14, 1957	Improvement of management in industry and construction (replacement of ministries by sovnarkhozes)		Election of Kozlov to Presidium; Shepilov to Secretariat
June 22-29, 1957			Removal of "anti-Party" group from Presidium and Central Committee; election of new Presidium and Secretariat
Oct. 29, 1957			Party work in armed forces; removal of Zhukov from Presidium and Central Committee
Dec. 16-17, 1957	Trade union work		Discussion of Conference of Communist and Worker Parties; Mukhitdinov elected to Presidium; Ignatov, Kirichenko, Mukhitdinov to Secretariat
Feb. 25-26,1958		Development of kolkhozes; reorganization of MTS	
May 6-7, 1958	Chemical industry		
June 17-18, 1958		Abolition of compulsory deliveries and payments in kind to MTS; new agricultural price system	Podgornyi and Polianskii elected candidates of Presidium

CENTRAL COMMITTEE PLENUMS, 1946-59 (CONTINUED)

DATE	TOPICS DISCUSSED		
	Industry	*Agriculture*	*Other Action*
Sept. 5, 1958			Convocation of XXI Congress; removal of Bulganin from Presidium
Nov. 12, 1958	7 Year Plan		Educational "reforms"; Beliaev removed as Secretary
Dec. 15-19, 1958		Results of 5 years in agriculture; further tasks	Denunciation of "anti-Party" group
June 24-29, 1959	Technical and industrial progress		
Dec. 22-25, 1959		Further development of agriculture	
May 4, 1960			Supreme Soviet session; organizational questions: Kosygin, Podgornyi, Polianskii elected to Presidium; Kirichenko, Beliaev relieved; Kozlov elected to Secretariat; Aristov, Pospelov, Ignatov, Furtseva relieved
July 13-16, 1960			Foreign policy "peaceful coexistence." Removal of Voroshilov from Presidium, Brezhnev from Secretariat

CHAPTER
XXV

THE POLITICS OF TOTALITARIANISM

The preceding chapters trace only a quarter-century of the history of the Soviet Communist Party. The long ferment of Russian Marxism, culminating in the formation of Lenin's Bolshevik party, lies outside the scope of the study as do the Revolution, the triumph of the Bolsheviks over their enemies, and the formative years of the Soviet system itself. The climax of the history of the Communist Party of the Soviet Union, whatever it may be, is still hidden in the future.

Despite these limitations, there is a certain unity in the period we have treated. By 1934 the Soviet regime was no longer a frail, experimental structure. It had weathered the Civil War, the first great effort to overthrow Communism by force. Lenin, the regime's founder, had died, but his power had been transmitted peacefully, however deviously, to Stalin. Half a decade later the "second revolution" of collectivization and forced industrialization began, accompanied by untold suffering, but successful in terms of the objectives of the regime. In 1934 the USSR was still a relatively weak member of international society, while in 1959 its leaders could boast (subject to dispute, but not ridicule) that it was the strongest power on earth. Even in 1934, however, the Soviet Union was definitely a "going concern."

The most obvious discontinuity in the period 1934-60 arises, of course, from Stalin's death. It would be difficult to exaggerate the pervasiveness of Stalin's influence on the Soviet system between 1934 and 1953. Even phenomena which have popularly been associated with his lieutenants, like the "Zhdanovshchina" and the Cominform formation, were in large measure reflections of Stalin's personal views, or at least were decisively shaped by him. In matters like the imposition of controls in music his hand was clearly the guiding one. The relative eclipse of the Communist Party itself, especially during the last five years of Stalin's life, is an indication of the dictator's influence, for he would not tolerate the concentration of power in a single institution, even the nominally ruling party.

At the same time, it is important to note the limits of Stalin's dictatorial powers. Supreme though he was, he required lieutenants. With very few exceptions these men had passed large portions of their careers in the upper strata of the Party apparatus. This was true even of the police machine, for the new men introduced by Ezhov and Beria had for the most part been Party officials. As was emphasized in the last chapter, the "men of 1938" are still in the commanding posts of the CPSU and the other bureaucracies of the Soviet regime.

In a sense 1959, with its Twenty-first Congress "of victors" over the "anti-Party" group, resembles 1934 more than any intervening year. Again the united Party secretaries, for the most part drawn from the territorial apparatus, intolerantly condemn the opposition while holding out bright promises for the future. Again the leader who has triumphed both through his personal cunning and the support of the dominant Party leaders demonstrates his primacy. But—unless the analysis pursued earlier in this work is wrong—Khrushchev is no second Stalin. Even if Khrushchev's personality were such as to induce him to emulate the despotic features of Stalin's rule, it is most doubtful that the present balance of forces in Soviet society, especially within the ruling elite, would permit such a course.

This conclusion is not an argument that limited government, even in the loosest sense of the term, has been achieved in the Soviet Union. If anything, the events since Stalin's death have served to demonstrate how inadequate "democratic centralism" is as a device for attaining the orderly transfer of power and resolution of conflicts within the ruling circle. The mysterious manner in which Beria secured a "falsified" Presidium decision on the "incorrect nationality policy" of the Ukrainian Party organization and his arrest immediately afterward by the same Presidium is an example of the devious workings of democratic centralism in the nominally supreme "continuously operating" body of the Party.[1]

Much more has been made outside the USSR of Khrushchev's refusal to bow to the Presidium majority in June 1957; many foreign observers have interpreted the move as a clear violation of democratic centralism. In fact, as noted in Chapter XXIII, it is possible that Khrushchev adhered to the letter of the Party rules in convening the Central Committee. Before and after this event the latter body has been proclaimed as the real repository of "collective leadership." We have argued that these proclamations have some meaning, for in a sense the Central Committee is representative of the oligarchic groups of officials who exert real power in the Soviet system. The representative character of the Central Committee is purely a sociological phenomenon, however, for its members are in no formal sense delegates of the ruling strata of officials. Aside from this consideration, the irregular and lengthy intervals between Central Committee meetings, and the considerable though reduced turnover in its membership between the formal elections by the Party Congresses, prevent the Central Committee from becoming even a quasi-constitutional device for settling power disputes. Instead, the Central Committee is itself one of the factors (at times a crucial one) in the institutionally uncontrolled power struggle. Consequently, even accepting the presuppositions of Communist ideology, all power in the USSR is ultimately illegitimate.

Under Stalin defeat in the power struggle meant ignominious death. It appears that this bloody sanction was not always due to Stalin's ferocity. In the "Leningrad affair" the jealousy of his lieutenants—quite possibly including some like Suslov who are still in power—may well have motivated the execution of Voznesenskii and his associates. Since Stalin's death, except for those linked to the police apparatus, the penalty for defeat has been reduced to disgrace. In the Soviet system, however, this is a severe enough sanction, for there is no private sphere in which the publicly disgraced official can exercise his talents. And the revival of the capital penalty is always possible.

Because of the grim nature of the struggle for power the individual contestant subordinates all other considerations to his effort to win. Lenin, of course, expressly sanctioned disregard by the Party of scruples in the choice of means.[2] His personal conduct in fighting for power within the Party implied that the limits of such a struggle were, to say the least, flexible. While there is no overt inculcation of the principle that all means are legitimate in intra-Party conflict, the present generation of leaders during their apprenticeship in the Great Purge probably took the principle to be a practical corollary of Leninism. In the extreme case, the welfare and safety of the Soviet system itself might become a pawn in the power struggle.

If our analysis of Beria's maneuvers in the spring of 1953 is correct, he was willing to disrupt the Soviet system to maintain his position, or was trying to blackmail the other leaders with the threat of such disruption. To enhance his own power Stalin also risked injury to the Communist movement, though to a far more limited degree, by his destruction of the

Soviet control system in Spain, and somewhat more significantly by the break with Tito. In these cases, the strength of the Communist system was to some degree diminished or imperiled to serve the personal ends of leaders; but the non-Communist world stood to profit from the maneuvers. The reverse effect is equally possible in the future, however: a contestant for Soviet power may precipitate catastrophic world war to enhance his domestic power position. Khrushchev's threats against Turkey in October 1957 at a time when Marshal Zhukov's fate was being decided may have been an example of such dangerous incitement of international crisis for domestic motives.[3]

In June 1960, Khrushchev boasted of his success in deterring Western "aggressors" by the threats just mentioned, as well as those he made during the Suez crisis of 1956 and the Lebanese crisis of 1958.[4] In linking these boasts to unrestrained verbal assaults on President Dwight D. Eisenhower and other American leaders, Khrushchev may only have been pursuing a "war of nerves" against the Western powers. As noted earlier, he simultaneously rejected "Leftist" attempts to rule out peaceful relations with these countries, and his personal power position seemed secure. But his behavior might well form a precedent for a Soviet leader who felt a foreign policy of unlimited risk was necessary to maintain his position at home.

To date, indeed, the lack of a mechanism for legitimizing power has not fatally impaired the operation of the Soviet system. After an interval of upheaval (limited, however, to the ruling circle), political stability has apparently been attained. Since (from the point of view of governmental stability) essentially the same result was secured by Stalin after Lenin's death, one might hypothesize that there is some inherent element in the Soviet system which prevents power rivalries from disrupting the system itself. If the two historical cases just referred to are too few to permit a firm conclusion, one can at least point to certain features which tend to restrict political upheaval.

Warned by the fate of earlier regimes which lacked recognized mechanisms for legitimizing power, the Soviet leaders have always feared "Bonapartism," i.e., seizure of power through support of the military. From Stalin's early cautions against Trotsky through the "Tukhachevskii plot" to the dismissal of Zhukov in 1957 this has been a frequent theme of Soviet polemics. Foreign observers, too, have often predicted a military coup in the USSR; most recently such observers ascribed the Soviet abandonment of "coexistence" and "summit diplomacy" themes in its relations with the

United States to the determining influence of Soviet military circles. The mere listing of the cases in which "Bonapartism" supposedly threatened suggests, however, that the danger has been chimerical. This view is bolstered by the lack of a tradition of military dictatorship in Russia. The ease with which Zhukov and Tukhachevskii were ousted, and the complete failure of the Red Army to consolidate the power which it secured by default in late 1941, convincingly show the weakness of the military as an autonomous power factor. For better or worse, the Soviet system seems most unlikely to succumb to military dictatorship.

The strong oligarchic tendencies of the higher bureaucratic officials limit the extent to which the power struggle may undermine the system. As discussed in Chapters VIII and XXIII, the comparative uniformity in age and experience of the present elite members tends to give all a similar stake in the preservation of the system. While the marked differences in educational background at present may lead to some divergencies in the ruling group, this would appear to be a transitory phase, after which almost the entire elite will possess the additional cohesive attribute of a common technological higher education. For more than two decades the elite group has been inculcated with the belief in its right to a disproportionate share of the material rewards and of the prestige available in Soviet society; it is not likely to acquiesce willingly in any development which threatens these rewards. Since the emphasis on material rewards in proportion to one's contribution to the Soviet society has been emphasized for far broader groups of the population and has had a real meaning for many (e.g., extraordinarily efficient industrial workers), the spirit of self-interest is a powerful prop for the present system. The very real diminution of terror through the introduction of curbs on the police system and the substantial increase in food and manufactured consumer goods available to the general public have tended to reconcile even the least privileged elements to the system.

Stabilization under Stalin, who at the height of his power undoubtedly possessed the strength to wreck the Soviet system by injudicious policies, resulted from a somewhat different equilibrium. As we have seen, Stalin's caution set limits to the extent to which he would risk the safety of the Soviet system. Hostile as was Soviet policy toward the outside world in his later years, it never courted major war.

At the same time, Stalin encouraged a force which turned out to be a mighty support for the system when his own failure of judgment in dealing with the Nazis had almost fatally endangered it during World War II. The gradual enrichment in the thirties of the concept of Soviet patriotism by the traditional element of Russian nationalism made it easier for the regime to appeal unrestrainedly to the national spirit of the unconquered Russian "core" of the USSR. Stalin's real motive in fostering Russian nationalism was the enhancement of the centralizing forces of the system. Consequently purely Russian centers other than Moscow, such as Leningrad, were slighted. In addition, of course, Stalin's own Georgian affiliation and his reliance on the Georgians and other Caucasians in the police limited his use of Russian nationalism as a support for the regime. Even more important, probably, was his prejudice against the Ukrainians, which (together with the military situation during part of the war) prevented an unambiguous effort to base Soviet strength on an embracing East Slav nationalism.

The present leadership is less hampered by such prejudices. While the Russians remain the "elder brothers," the Belorussians and especially the far more numerous Ukrainians are offered junior partnerships in controlling the Soviet empire. Ukrainians have become much more numerous among the higher Party, state, government, and police officials, and they were always strongly represented in the military command.[5] Especially important is the Russian-Ukrainian partnership in controlling and developing Central Asia. At a lower level, the phenomenal growth of Ukrainian Party membership since 1956 testifies to the regime's effort to enlist Ukrainian support. Whether these gestures will really enlist the undivided support of the Ukrainian population for the Soviet system remains to be seen. The continued disproportionate number of Russians in the Ukrainian Party organization, the strong antipathies of the West Ukrainians to the Soviet system, and the widespread memories of earlier oppression combine to make the Ukrainians' loyalty doubtful. But the regime's effort to deepen this loyalty is wholly logical, for the Ukraine, with its large population, vast resources, and strategic location could be either the Achilles heel or the bastion of the Soviet system.

Stalin's ambiguous attitude toward the appeals of nationalism reflects the general ambiguity of his attitude toward stabilizing factors. In his later years he sternly restricted social radicalism in such fields as family relations, imposed rigidly philistine standards of cultural taste, and minimized the revolutionary aspects of Marxist ideology. At the same time, Stalin could not tolerate the development of a system in which strict lines of authority would permit the individual to shelter himself behind the orders of his hierarchical superior. Consequently, Stalin disrupted the Red Army command (the model of a hierarchical system) in 1937 and constantly avoided formally compartmented spheres of authority in the Party. Similarly, neither regulations nor laws hindered the direct, arbitrary exercise of political power. As the ideology itself was reinterpreted by Stalin, it no longer preserved a real dogmatic character, but became a wholly flexible and arbitrary instrument of political control.

These developments, as noted earlier, were essential aspects of Stalin's drive for absolute power. But it would be incorrect to attribute them entirely to Stalin. Neither strict hierarchical lines of authority nor reliance upon the rule of law has been established under Stalin's successors, and while it is too early to make positive statements concerning ideological developments it is certainly not clear that this sphere has been removed from the area of political manipulation. There is good reason to believe that the dynamism of Communist totalitarianism requires the blurring of lines of authority, regulatory prescriptions, and even ideological principles.[6] Otherwise the individual (and particularly the individual official) lacks the feeling of insecurity which at present induces him to throw his entire effort into satisfying the undefined, and hence insatiable, demands of the regime. If one contrasts the achievements of Soviet industry and technology, which even the most severe critics of Communism must recognize as impressive, to the nonchalant inefficiency of many pre-Revolutionary bureaucrats, one can appreciate the importance of these "institutionalized" psychological spurs.[7]

The reverse side of the disregard for fixed principles is, of course, only too tragically evident. The dual standard of morality in personal relationships has already been suggested in the case of the power struggle; apparently a similar "license for the elite" is implicitly accepted in familial matters. The flagrant contradiction of Marxist concepts as well as of traditional morality embodied in Stalin's violent anti-Semitism, which Khrushchev has cynically perpetuated at home and in the satellites, is another example. Even more important in terms of human values has been the callous acceptance of enormous loss of life in collectivization, the wartime industrial relocation, and the partisan activities. In the latter instances, especially, it is unlikely that Stalin's own ruthless temperament was the decisive instigating factor, for local authorities and commanders far from Moscow were equally callous. As noted in Chapter IV, the moral sensibilities of the generation of officials who came to power in the thirties were blunted by the experience of collectivization and the Great Purge—and these men are still dominant.

Corruption of traditional virtues and dynamism in action are not incompatible, as the tremendous Soviet effort in World War II showed. Dynamism was evident in the expansion into hostile areas in East Europe as well as in defense of the USSR itself. The inference is strong that a wide range of Party officials was convinced of the desirability of expanding as well as preserving the Communist system, and strove mightily to attain these ends.

As noted in Chapter XXI the desire to use the memory of this "heroic age" of World War II was a major factor leading to the denigration of Stalin in 1956. The ideological campaign following Stalin's death has included numerous other re-emphases on the more dynamic aspects of Communism. In the purely ideological field, the revival of stress on the dialectic (see Chapter XXI) is part of this pattern. In the view of the present writer, however, there is little tendency toward real restoration of the primacy of the complex Marxist doctrine of dialectical materialism. As noted earlier, self interest is a strong prop for the system. But it is not selfishness in the narrow sense which provides the dynamic quality of Soviet society. Increasingly, it appears, the typical educated Soviet citizen accepts uncritically a world view composed of vulgar materialism and atheism. To men of this frame of mind, the evident material success and political power of the Soviet regime are not only reasons why they as individuals should adhere to it, but why it should and shall be the model for all humanity. Such an ideology may not attract the fanatics intent on fulfilling a vision of a perfect society, but it may find just as dynamic adherents among those who are convinced that their own type of society is practically superior, and ought to be extended.

The residual elements of Soviet Marxism provide few detailed prescriptions for positive action; but in addition to contributing to the general feeling that the Soviet system is right and inevitable the Leninist ideological heritage provides a number of negative prescriptions. Of major importance are the demands for totalitarian control of culture set forth in the decrees of 1946-48 associated with Zhdanov. As noted in Chapter XXI, these decrees have been re-emphasized in recent years. Equally important are the implications for the field of Communist international behavior. The hollowness of the Soviet campaign for "coexistence" is indicated by the bitter rejection (also dating back to the Zhdanov period) of even technology as a common, neutral meeting ground for Communists and non-Communists.[8] Similarly, the careful definition (for the initiated Communists) of the real meaning of the Popular Front policy, made at a time when the USSR urgently needed foreign support, indicates the limits of Communist co-operation with the outside world even for tactical purposes. The present devious references to Lenin's "peaceful path to socialism" indicate that the new line is no more sincere.

Undoubtedly there has been more real variation in Moscow's attitude toward control of foreign Communist parties. In all likelihood the Soviet Party has never since 1934 exercised firm control over the Chinese Communists. Gradually, as the latter have increased in power, their early de facto independence has been formally recognized by the Soviet regime. Today in ideological and policy matters Peking stands on a plane little below that of Moscow.

What Moscow has necessarily (whether or not reluctantly) accorded in East Asia it has, after some hesitations, firmly withheld in East Europe. In many ways the aggressive, doctrinaire attitudes of the triumphant Yugoslav Communists of 1945 closely resemble those of the Chinese Communists since 1949. In many respects Yugoslav behavior also fitted in with the dynamic trends of Soviet Communist expansion unleashed by World War II. Nevertheless, this similarity was not sufficient to save Tito's regime from Soviet assault stopping just short of forceful invasion when he refused to bow to complete Soviet control. During the long "thaw" after Stalin's death, his insistence on bringing the Yugoslav Communists to heel was proclaimed to be the result of his megalomania. As discussed in Chapter XXII, it seems likely that Khrushchev's associates were in considerable measure sincere in these statements, for they evidently thought that a more flexible approach could attain the basic Soviet objectives in East Europe. When the Polish and Hungarian events of autumn 1956 dispelled this illusion, Khrushchev's regime, by denouncing Tito in terms which echoed Stalin and Molotov, demonstrated the unswerving Soviet Communist insistence on retaining the realities of control in East Europe. At the moment of writing it appears that the reimposition of full Soviet control even in Poland is only a matter of time. There is no place for those who seek "original, separate roads to socialism for each country individually." [9]

In the broader perspective, the development of CPSU policies abroad closely resembles the internal transformation of the Party. The old dedication to world revolution as the answer to burning social problems has almost vanished. In its place is the constantly reiterated theme that the USSR must be emulated because it is—aside from "historical accidents" like the United States—the most successful country on earth. At the same time, the USSR insinuates, its wishes must be followed and its controls accepted because it is the world's strongest country. These themes were already visible in 1934 in the boasts concerning the success of collectivization and the first Five Year Plan, and the reiterated reference to the USSR as "one-sixth of the world's land surface." Given the real weaknesses of the Soviet power position, and the misery of its citizens, such themes could not, however, attain major success in Stalin's lifetime. With the swelling flood of industrial and technological achievements in the fifties, and the resultant shift in the world balance of power, the appeals to success and to strength as the chief recommendations of the Communist way have begun to submerge all others.

Instead of the fomenting of revolution, the basic Soviet methods of expansion (at least in the industrialized West) since the 1930's have been force of arms, blackmail through threats of force, and the terrifying example of Soviet subjugation of other countries. In this light the extreme cynicism of the Twentieth Party Congress statements pointing to Czechoslovakia as an example of the "peaceful path to socialism" are all too apparent.[10] More recently (as in the Suez crisis, the Turkish affair of October 1957, and a whole series of incidents in the summer of 1960) the USSR has begun to employ the threat of force as a blackmailing tactic even in relations with major powers.

These tactics have cost the Communist movement (again, at least in the industrial countries of the West) nearly all of its dedicated supporters. Most Western Communist parties, to the extent to which they are still active at all, have been reduced to adjuncts of the Soviet police and "agitprop" networks. In crucial areas where Soviet threats have real meaning, however, a new group of recruits replaces the dedicated revolutionaries of the interwar period. Those who are attracted by the prospect of power unchecked by moral scruples, and those cunning opportunists who wish merely to ride the "wave of history" align themselves with the Soviet "presence"—the local Communist parties. Consequently, with the whole world today a theater for the exertion of Soviet pressures, it would be foolhardy to dismiss international Communism as a movement without a future. Today as in the past the Communist Party of the Soviet Union occupies a unique historical position as the center and buttress of a world-wide complex with unlimited aims of aggrandizement.

ABBREVIATIONS OF PERIODICAL AND SERIAL PUBLICATIONS

B *Bol'shevik* (Bolshevik)
BO *Biulleten' Oppozitsii* (Bulletin of the Opposition)
BSE *Bol'shaia Sovetskaia Entsiklopediia* (1st and 2nd eds).
Bulletin *Bulletin of the Institute for the Study of the USSR*
CDSP *Current Digest of the Soviet Press*
CSP I Leo Gruliow (ed.), *Current Soviet Policies* (New York: Frederick A. Praeger, 1953)
CSP II Leo Gruliow (ed.), *Current Soviet Policies II* (New York: Frederick A. Praeger, 1956)
CSP III Leo Gruliow (ed.), *Current Soviet Policies III* (New York: Columbia University Press, 1960)
E&O *Est et Ouest* (before 1956 called *Bulletin d'Etudes et d'Information Politique Internationale*)
FLP *For a Lasting Peace, for a People's Democracy*
Iz *Izvestia* (News)
KI *Kommunisticheskii Internatsional*
KPSS *Kommunisticheskaia Partiia Sovetskogo Soiuza v Rezoliutsiiakh i Resheniiakh S"ezdov, Konferentsii i Plenumov TsK* (The Communist Party of the Soviet Union in resolutions and decisions of congresses, conferences, and plenums of the Central Committee)—various editions and volumes as indicated in reference notes
NYT *New York Times*
OE *Osteuropa*
P *Pravda* (Truth)
PS *Partiinoe Stroitel'stvo* (Party Construction)
PZh *Partiinaia Zhizn'* (Party Life)
SV *Sotsialisticheskii Vestnik* (Socialist Messenger)
Vestnik *Vestnik Instituta po Izucheniiu SSSR* (Messenger of the Institute for the Study of the USSR)

REFERENCE NOTES

CHAPTER I   TO THE VICTORS . . .

1. "Chto oznachaet kapituliatsiia Rakovskogo?" (What does Rakovskii's capitulation mean?), BO, No. 40, 1934, p. 12.
2. P, January 27, 1934.
3. *XVII S"ezd Vsesoiuznoi Kommunisticheskoi Partii (b) 26 Ianvaria-10 Fevralia 1934 g.: Stenographicheskii Otchet* (The Seventeenth Congress of the All-Union Communist Party [Bolshevik], January 26-February 10, 1934: Stenographic report) (Moscow: Partizdat, 1934), p. 28. Hereafter cited as `XVII S"ezd.*
4. *Ibid.,* p. 16.
5. Donald R. Hodgman, *Soviet Industrial Product, 1928-1951* (Cambridge, Mass.: Harvard University Press, 1954), p. 73.
6. *Ibid.,* p. 89.
7. *Ibid.,* p. 108.
8. See Max Beloff, *The Foreign Policy of Soviet Russia* (London: Oxford University Press, 1947), I, 40.
9. See especially John Scott, *Behind the Urals* (Boston: Houghton Mifflin Co., 1942).
10. *XVII S"ezd,* p. 188.
11. *Ibid.*
12. *Ibid.,* p. 124.
13. Winston S. Churchill, *The Second World War,* Vol. IV: *The Hinge of Fate* (Boston: Houghton Mifflin Co., 1950), p. 498.
14. Merle Fainsod, *Smolensk under Soviet Rule* (Cambridge, Mass.: Harvard University Press, 1958), p. 241.
15. *Gosudarstvennyi Plan Razvitiia Narodnogo Khoziaistva SSSR na 1941 God (Prilozheniia k Postanovleniiu SNK SSSR i TsK VKP[b] ot 17 Ianvaria 1941 g.)* (State plan of development of the national economy of the USSR for 1941 [Annex to the decree of the Council of People's Commissars of the USSR and the Central Committee of the All-Union Communist Party-Bolshevik of 17 January 1941]. American Council of Learned Societies Reprints: Russian Series No. 30 (Baltimore: Universal Lithographers, n.d.), pp. 612, 618-619. Hereafter cited as *Plan, 1941.*

16. Fainsod, *Smolensk*, p. 56.
17. WKP 177 (unpublished document in Smolensk Archive, National Archives, Washington, D.C.), pp. 134-135.
18. *XVII S"ezd*, pp. 19-20.
19. WKP 351, pp. 125-133.
20. Beloff, *Foreign Policy*, I, 97-99.
21. "Ot rasshatyvaiushcheisia stabilizatsii ko vtoromu turu revoliutsii i voin" (From the shattering of stability to the second round of revolution and war), KI, No. 34, 1934, p. 7.
22. *XVII S"ezd*, p. 303.
23. "Nekotorye itogi chistki partii" (Some results of the purge of the Party), PS, No. 21, 1933, p. 1.
24. Emelian Iaroslavskii, "Pervye itogi chistki partorganizatsii" (The first results of the purge of the Party organizations), B, No. 15, 1934, p. 9. Compare this figure to the growth from 2,212,225 (January 1, 1931) to 3,555,338 (January 1, 1933) reported in PZh, No. 20, 1937, p. 80. "Voprosy chlenstva v VKP(b) (do dokumenstam i tsifram za 30 let)" (Questions of membership in the All-Union Communist Party [Bolshevik] [on documents and figures for 30 years]). The purge was decreed by the January 7-12, 1933, plenum, but evidently did not get well underway until late spring.
25. Fainsod, *Smolensk*, p. 221.
26. Iaroslavskii, in B, No. 15, 1934, p. 9.
27. *XVII S"ezd*, p. 303.
28. For a comprehensive discussion of the evolution of the Party apparatus in Lenin's and Stalin's time, see Merle Fainsod, *How Russia is Ruled* (Cambridge, Mass.: Harvard University Press, 1953), Chapter 6.
29. See especially Alfred E. Meyer, *Leninism* (Cambridge, Mass.: Harvard University Press, 1957), Chapter 5.
30. *XVII S"ezd*, p. 561.
31. Fainsod, *Smolensk*, pp. 288 ff.
32. S. P. Trapeznikov, "Istoricheskaia rol' MTS v sozdanii i ukreplenii kolkhoznogo stroiia" (The historical role of the MTS in the creation and strengthening of the kolkhoz structure), *Voprosy Istorii KPSS*, No. 3, 1958, p. 61.
33. See for example a letter to P, January 1, 1934.
34. *XVII S"ezd*, p. 560.
35. *Ibid.*, p. 672.
36. "Bol'she vnimaniia novym raionam" (More attention to the new raions), PS, No. 7, 1935, p. 1.
37. *XVII S"ezd*, p. 115.
38. *Letter of an Old Bolshevik* (New York: Rand School Press, 1937). This was first published in SV, No. 23-24, 1936, and No. 1-2, 1937. Nearly twenty-three years later Nicolaevsky ("Chetvert' veka nazad" [A quarter of a century ago], *Novoe Russkoe Slovo*, December 6, 1959) acknowledged that he had written the *Letter*, ascribing it to an "Old Bolshevik" both for "conspiratorial" and for literary reasons. Nicolaevsky relates that the material for the *Letter* was obtained in conversations with Bukharin in Paris in March-April

1936, and from other "Old Bolsheviks." Obviously the composite character of the sources and the literary method of presentation complicate the task of determining the authenticity of individual portions of the *Letter*.

39. Boris Nicolaevsky, "Stalin i ubiistvo Kirova" (Stalin and the killing of Kirov), SV, No. 12, 1956, p. 240.

40. Alexander Orlov, *The Secret History of Stalin's Crimes* (New York: Random House, 1953), p. 13; A. Tikhomirov (ed.), "Na sluzhbe u Stalina: Ispoved' Chekista" (In service with Stalin: A Chekist's confession), unpublished manuscript (MS 25) in the Archive of Russian and East European History and Culture, Columbia University. Hereafter cited as Tikhomirov MS. Cf. Isaac Deutscher, *Stalin: A Political Biography* (New York: Oxford University Press, 1949), p. 354.

41. A letter from Moscow, in SV, No. 8, 1934, p. 15.

42. Grigorii A. Tokaev, *Betrayal of an Ideal* (Bloomington, Ind.: Indiana University Press, 1955), p. 241.

43. Stalin was not officially elected General Secretary after the Seventeenth Congress, but Soviet publications continued to ascribe that title to him. Various interpretations have been given to this circumstance; some view the failure to secure official confirmation of the title as a rebuff for Stalin, others regard it as of no significance. For a résumé of the evidence see Myron Rush, *The Rise of Khrushchev* (Washington, D.C.: Public Affairs Press, 1958), p. 95.

44. Boris Nicolaevsky, "Stalin i ubiistvo Kirova," SV, No. 5, 1956, p. 93.

45. P, July 11, 1934.

46. A. Vyshinskii, "Ob ukreplenii revoliutsionnoi zakonosti v period sotsializma" (On strengthening revolutionary legality in the period of socialism), B, No. 18, 1934, p. 37.

47. Simon Wolin and Robert M. Slusser (eds.), *The Soviet Secret Police* (New York: Frederick A. Praeger, 1957), pp. 14-15; Louis Fischer, *Men and Politics* (New York: Duell, Sloan and Pearce, 1941), pp. 225-229.

48. Wolin and Slusser, p. 15.

49. "Chto sdelano dlia ukrepleniia sotsialistecheskoi zakonnosti" (What has been done to strengthen socialist legality), PZh, No. 4, 1957, pp. 66-71.

50. *Inprekorr*, No. 12, 1935, p. 144.

51. E.g., by N. Leontev, "Sotsializm i voprosy ravenstva" (Socialism and questions of equality), B, No. 3-4, 1934, pp. 117-128.

52. Gustav A. Wetter, *Der Dialektische Materialismus* (Rev. ed.) (Freiburg: Verlag Herder, 1958), pp. 154-159.

53. See especially Edward Brown, *The Proletarian Episode in Russian Literature, 1928-1932* (New York: Columbia University Press, 1953), pp. 200-218.

54. Klaus Mehnert, "An Moskaus literarischer Front," OE, IV (1954), 343-344.

55. Jack F. Matlock, Jr., "The 'Governing Organs' of the Union of Soviet Writers," *American Slavic and East European Review*, XV (1956), 382-384.

56. George S. N. Luckyj, *Literary Politics in the Soviet Ukraine, 1917-1934* (New York: Columbia University Press, 1956), pp. 65-67.

57. *XVII S"ezd*, p. 32.

CHAPTER II   KIROV'S ASSASSINS

1. "Rasstrely—ne otvet" (Shootings—no answer), SV, No. 23-24, 1934, pp. 1-2. See also "B. P." (Hryhoryi Kostiuk), "Za shcho bulo vbyto Kirova" (Why was Kirov killed), Vpered, No. 1, 1949, pp. 11-12, for confirmation by a writer who met Nikolaev's cousin in prison.

2. John Dewey, The Case of Leon Trotsky: Report of Hearings on the Charges Made Against Him in the Moscow Trials by the Preliminary Commission of Inquiry (New York: Harper & Bros., 1937), p. 260.

3. Elizabeth Lermolo, Face of a Victim (New York: Harper & Bros., 1955), pp. 20 ff.

4. USSR, People's Commissariat of Justice, Report of Court Proceedings in the case of the Anti-Soviet "Bloc of Rights and Trotskyites." (Moscow: People's Commissariat of Justice of the U.S.S.R., 1938), p. 558. Hereafter cited as Bloc.

5. W. G. Krivitsky, I Was Stalin's Agent (London: Hamish Hamilton, 1939), p. 207, and Orlov, p. 249.

6. Orlov, p. 15; cf. Trotsky, "Vse stanovitsia postepenno na svoe mesto" (Everything gradually falls into place), BO, No. 42, 1935, pp. 10-12.

7. Boris Nicolaevsky, "Stalin i ubiistvo Kirova" (Stalin and the killing of Kirov), SV, No. 12, 1956, pp. 242-243.

8. Orlov, p. 18. Boris Nicolaevsky accepts this date.

9. Krivitsky, p. 205. The prosecutor's accusation (P, December 27, 1934) said that the plan for the killing was made on November 1. Khrushchev's secret speech (N. S. Khrushchev, "The Crimes of the Stalin Era" Special Report to the 20th Congress of the Communist Party of the Soviet Union, annotated by Boris Nicolaevsky [New York: The New Leader, 1956] [hereafter cited as Khrushchev's secret speech]), p. S22, places Nikolaev's arrest "a month and a half" before the assassination.

10. Khrushchev's secret speech, p. S22.

11. J. V. Stalin, Leninism, Selected Writings (New York: International Publishers, 1942), p. 268.

12. Tikhomirov MS.

13. "Vse stanovitsia postepenno na svoe mesto," BO, No. 42, 1935, pp. 10-12.

14. One version—the Tikhomirov MS—discredits Stalin's Leningrad trip, but it is attested by so many other versions that it appears almost certain. Zhdanov was photographed in Leningrad on December 3 (P, December 4, 1934). Cf. Aron L. Kublanov, "Razgrom Fashistsko-Troitskistsko-Bukharinskoi 'Piatoi Kolonny' v SSSR" (The destruction of the Fascist-Trotskyite-Bukharinite "fifth column" in the USSR) (unpublished dissertation, Voroshilov Military-Naval Academy, 1946), p. 215. Kublanov, a Soviet student, asserts that Stalin made the trip; he bases his statement on a reference to the Bloc trial, but the passage cited (p. 558) refers only to "members of the govern-

ment." Probably Kublanov inadvertently relied on unpublished Party archives which he used.

15. P, December 25, 1934, and January 5, 1935.
16. For reference to the secret letter see WKP 316, pp. 98-99.
17. P, December 30, 1934; see also P, December 22, 1934, which presents a somewhat less detailed version, and Andrei Vyshinskii's prosecutor's accusation, P, December 27, 1934; cf. BO, No. 52-53, 1936, p. 13.
18. P, December 23, 1934.
19. P, January 16, 1935.
20. P, January 18, 1935.
21. The most detailed and circumstantial account is by Lermolo.
22. WKP 316, pp. 98-99.
23. WKP 505, p. 47.
24. "O zadachakh partiino-organizatsionnoi i politicheski-vospitatel'noi raboty" (On the tasks of Party-organizational and political-educational work) (Leningrad gorkom decision of March 29, 1935), PS, No. 7, 1935, pp. 7-15.
25. "O reorganizatsii Kultpropa TsK VKP(b)" (On the reorganization of the Culture and Propaganda Section of the Central Committee of the All-Union Communist Party [Bolshevik]), PS, No. 11, 1935, p. 47.
26. P, February 2 and March 1, 1935.
27. See P, November 1, 1937, and subsequent issues, on Poskrebyshev's Supreme Soviet candidacy.
28. For the scanty and in part unverifiable information on Stalin's secretariat, see "Diktator Sovetskogo Soiuza (Pismo iz Moskva)" (Dictator of the Soviet Union [Letter from Moscow]), SV, No. 19, 1933; Boris Nicolaevsky, "Stalin i ubiistvo Kirova," SV, No. 12, 1956, p. 242; and Alexander Barmine, *One Who Survived* (New York: G. P. Putnam's Sons, 1945), pp. 260-262.
29. "Dela i resheniia partkollegii po partiinym prostupkam" (Affairs and decisions of the Party Collegium on Party delinquencies), PS, No. 15, 1935, pp. 47-48, and the article of the same title in PS, No. 6, 1935, pp. 47-48.
30. J. T. Kendrick, Jr., "The Structure of the Central Committee of the CPSU (b)" (unpublished essay, Columbia University, 1951), p. 37.
31. "Tretii plenum Komissii Partkontrolia" (The third plenum of the Commission of Party Control), PS, No. 7, 1936, p. 5.
32. "Podbor, vospitanie i vydvizhenie kadrov—reshaiushchii uchastok partraboty" (Selection, education, and assignment of cadres—a decisive part of Party work), PS, No. 8, 1935, p. 16.
33. Z. Sibiriachka, "Pervye shagi otdela partiinykh kadrov" (The first steps of the section of Party cadres), PS, No. 9, 1935, p. 21.
34. I. Pindiur, "Ozhivlenie partiinoi zhizni kak resul'tat raboty otdelov partkadrov" (Animation of Party life as a result of the work of the sections of Party cadres), PS, No. 10, 1935, pp. 21-26 (based on the organization in Gor'kii).
35. "Struktura otdela rukovodiashchikh partorganov TsK partii" (The structure of the Section of Directing Party Organs of the Central Committee of the Party), PS, No. 17, 1935, pp. 73-78.

36. These calculations (and those on the verification process), admittedly approximate, are based on figures in PZh, No. 20, 1947, p. 81 (article cited above), checked against some contemporary Soviet sources, especially those on the rate of expulsions in local Party organizations. Cf. Zbigniew K. Brzezinski, *The Permanent Purge* (Cambridge, Mass.: Harvard University Press, 1956), pp. 54-58. Hereafter cited as Brzezinski, *Purge*.

37. M. Meksina, "Raionnye kadry v svete itogov chistki" (Raion cadres in the light of the results of the purge), PS, No. 8, 1935, p. 23.

38. WKP 500, p. 308. According to *Istoriia Kommunisticheskoi Partii Sovetskogo Soiuza* (History of the Communist Party of the Soviet Union) (prepared by B. N. Ponomarev *et al.*) (Moscow: Gosudarstvennoe Izdatel'stvo Politicheskoi Literatury, 1959), p. 463 (hereafter cited as *Istoriia KPSS*), the verification began as early as October 1934—weeks before Kirov's death.

39. *Letter of an Old Bolshevik*, pp. 50, 56-58.

40. P, May 26, 1935.

41. *Letter of an Old Bolshevik*, pp. 51-52.

42. P, June 14, 1935.

43. P, June 8, 1935; P, June 13, 1935.

44. Krivitsky, p. 14; *Letter of an Old Bolshevik*, pp. 36-37.

45. P, June 13, 1935 (speech to the Moscow Party activists).

46. P, June 16, 1935.

47. Speeches by Khrushchev (P, June 13, 1935) and Zhdanov (P, June 16, 1935).

48. "Stalinskie amal'gami byli predvideny" (The Stalinist amalgams were foreseen), BO, No. 52-53, 1936, p. 7; USSR, People's Commissariat of Justice, *Report of Court Proceedings in the case of the Trotskyite-Zinovievite Terrorist Centre.* (Moscow: People's Commissariat of Justice of the U.S.S.R., 1936), p. 174. Hereafter cited as *Trotskyite-Zinovievite Centre.*

49. WKP 237, pp. 289-290.

50. See the notes by "P" in SV, No. 16, 1935, p. 16. The writing in question was Enukidze's biographical article in the *Bol'shaia Sovetskaia Entsiklopediia* (1st ed.). Hereafter cited as BSE.

51. Fainsod, *Smolensk*, p. 223.

52. *Ibid.*, p. 375.

53. A. Vinogradov, "Na bor'bu o narusheniiami linii partii v dele vospitanii kadrov" (In the struggle with infractions of the line of the Party in the matter of the education of cadres), PS, No. 14, 1935, p. 19.

54. "Glavnye uroki proverki partiinykh dokumentov" (The principal lessons of the verification of Party documents), PS, No. 2, 1936, p. 12, provides the percentages; the absolute figure is calculated on the basis of the Party's size at the beginning of 1935, allowing for about one hundred thousand expulsions during the final stages of the purge.

55. WKP 54, pp. 202-209.

56. *Trotskyite-Zinovievite Centre* (this abridged version, in various languages, was the only record published).

57. WKP 500, p. 322.

58. The most comprehensive contemporary analyses are in Dewey and Lev Sedov, *Livre Rouge sur le Procès de Moscou* (Paris: Editions Populaires, 1936); Nathan Leites and Elsa Bernaut, *Ritual of Liquidation* (Glencoe, Ill.: The Free Press, 1954), provide the most elaborate effort at explanation.
59. WKP 500, p. 322.
60. Cf. "Po stolbtsam 'Pravdy' " (In the columns of *Pravda*), BO, No. 50, 1936, p. 15 (published before the trial); Trotsky's remarks in Dewey, p. 280; and the listing of Molotov as among Stalin's "closest advisors" in "Trotskistsko-Zinov'evskie bandity—golovnoi otriad kapitalisticheskoi restavratsii" (Trotskyite-Zinovievite bandits—the leading detachment of capitalist restoration), B, No. 18, 1936, p. 19.
61. United States Department of State. *Foreign Relations of the United States: The Soviet Union, 1933-1939* (Washington, D.C.: U.S. Government Printing Office, 1952), p. 302. Hereafter cited as US *Foreign Relations*.
62. *Trotskyite-Zinovievite Centre*, pp. 25, 43.
63. *Ibid.*, p. 100.

CHAPTER III   COMINTERN AND POPULAR FRONT

1. Boris Nicolaevsky, "Stalin i ubiistvo Kirova" (Stalin and the killing of Kirov), SV, No. 10, 1956, p. 186, and No. 12, 1956, pp. 239-240; Franz Borkenau, *European Communism* (New York: Harper & Bros., 1953), pp. 117, 132-135, 234-235.
2. Krivitsky, pp. 18-34, 37-40; Erich Wollenberg, *The Red Army: A Study of the Growth of Soviet Imperialism* (London: Secker & Warburg, 1940), p. 237.
3. Krivitsky, p. 38. The fact of Kandelaki's trade negotiation is recorded in Gerhard L. Weinberg, *Germany and the Soviet Union, 1939-1941* (Leiden: E. J. Brill, 1954), p. 8.
4. Cited by Leonard Schapiro, *The Communist Party of the Soviet Union* (New York: Random House, 1960), p. 485, note 2.
5. Gustav Hilger and Alfred E. Meyer, *The Incompatible Allies: A Memoir-History of German-Soviet Relations, 1918-1941* (New York: The Macmillan Company, 1953), pp. 305-306. See also pp. 269-270. Hilger was for many years an important official in the German Embassy in Moscow.
6. *Partiino-Politicheskaia Rabota v Boevoi Obstanovke: Sbornik Dokumentov, Izdannykh vo Vremia Osvoboditel'nogo Pokhoda v Zapadnuiu Ukrainu i Zapadnuiu Belorussiiu* (Party-political work in battle conditions: A collection of documents published at the time of the liberation campaign in the West Ukraine and West Belorussia) (Moscow: Gosudarstvennoe Voennoe Izdatel'stvo Narkomata Oborony Soiuza SSR, 1940). I was able to use a photostat copy of this book, issued for official use only by the Political Administration of the Red Army, through the kindness of Geroid T. Robinson; cf. Chapter IX, p. 119.

7. O. Piatnitskii, "Piatnadtsat' let kommunisticheskogo internatsionala" (Fifteen years of the Communist International), B, No. 3-4, 1934, p. 27.

8. Borkenau, p. 118.

9. O. Piatnitskii, B, No. 3-4, 1934, p. 27.

10. "O tsentral'nom organe KPCh 'Rude Pravo' " (On the central organ of the Communist Party of Czechoslovakia Rudé Pravo), KI, No. 10, 1934, p. 62.

11. Borkenau, p. 123; US Foreign Relations, p. 164.

12. Beloff, Foreign Policy, I, 188.

13. Ibid.; Borkenau, pp. 124-125.

14. Beloff, Foreign Policy, I, 188; cf. A. Vassar, "Organizatsii bor'by protiv fashizma vo Frantsii" (The organization of the struggle against Fascism in France), KI, No. 23, 1934, pp. 24-25.

15. Ibid.

16. Inprekorr, No. 20, 1936, p. 231.

17. Beloff, Foreign Policy, I, 195.

18. Borkenau, pp. 158-159; Beloff, Foreign Policy, II, 22-24.

19. Abbreviated stenographical report, KI, No. 27, 1935, pp. 12-13.

20. Abbreviated stenographical report, KI, No. 20-21, 1935, pp. 55 ff.

21. Abbreviated stenographical report, KI, No. 23-24, 1935, p. 145.

22. Abbreviated stenographical report, KI, No. 20-21, 1935, p. 44.

23. Proclamation in Inprekorr No. 6, 1936, p. 89.

24. "Obshchee polozhenie v Frantsii" (The general situation in France), KI, No. 11-12, 1936, p. 38; Borkenau, pp. 150-152.

25. M. Thorez, "Frantsiia narodnogo fronta—strana progressa i svobody" (France of the Popular Front—a country of progress and freedom), KI, No. 2, 1938, p. 63.

26. Fulvio Bellini, "The Italian Communist Party; Part I: The Transformation of a Party, 1921-1945," Problems of Communism, V (1956), 36-43.

27. On the background and the course of events in Spain see especially David T. Cattell, Communism and the Spanish Civil War (Berkeley: University of California Press, 1955).

28. Germany, Auswärtiges Amt. Documents on German Foreign Policy, 1918-1945 (Series D, Vol. III) (Washington, D.C.: U.S. Government Printing Office, 1950), pp. 713-715.

29. Cattell, p. 83.

30. José García, Ispaniia Narodnogo Fronta (Spain of the Popular Front) (Moscow: Izdatel'stvo Akademii Nauk SSR, 1957), pp. 56-57.

31. Ibid.

32. XVIII S"ezd Vsesoiuznoi Kommunisticheskoi Partii (b), 10-21 Marta 1939 g.: Stenographicheskii Otchet (The Eighteenth Congress of the All-Union Communist Party [Bolshevik], March 10-21, 1939, stenographic report) (Moscow: Gosudarstvennoe Izdatel'stvo Politicheskoi Literatury, 1939), p. 64. Hereafter cited as XVIII S"ezd (The Land of Socialism Today and Tomorrow [Moscow: Foreign Languages Publishing House, 1939], p. 91).

33. "Internatsional'naia brigada" (The international brigade), KI, No. 18, 1936, pp. 68-69; B. Jan, "Slavnyi put' internatsional'noi brigady im. Dombrovskogo"

(The glorious road of the "Dombrowski" international brigade), KI, No. 11, 1938, pp. 79-82.

34. Sources for the presence of Soviet and East European Communist advisors in Spain are as follows:

García, *Ispaniia,* pp. 46, 48, 59, 63, 65;

José García, "Internatsional'nye brigady v Ispanii (1936-1938 gg.)" (International brigades in Spain [1936-1938]), *Voprosy Istorii,* No. 7, 1956, pp. 33-48;

Cattell, p. 73;

Enrique Castro Delgado, *J'ai Perdu la Foi à Moscou* (Paris: Gallimard, 1950), pp. 14, 124;

L. Fischer, pp. 362, 383, 389, 392, 395, 401, 427, 498;

Valentín González and Julian Gorkin, *El Campesino: Life and Death in Soviet Russia* (translated by Ilsa Barea), (New York: G. P. Putnam's Sons, 1952), pp. 20, 26;

Jesús Hernández, *Yo fuí un Ministro de Stalin* (Mexico: Editorial America, 1953), pp. 40, 43, 44, 57, 59, 66;

Ramón Moreno Hernández, *Rusia al Desnudo: Revelaciónes del Comisario Communista Español Rafael Pelayo de Hungria, Comandante del Ejército Ruso* (Madrid: Ediciones de Actualidad Mondial, 1956), pp. 69-70;

Krivitsky, pp. 114-116, 119-120, 122, 125-126, 130, 132;

Orlov, p. 235;

Richard E. Lauterbach, *These Are the Russians* (New York: Harper & Bros., 1945), p. 124;

Alexander Werth, *The Year of Stalingrad* (New York: Alfred A. Knopf, 1947), p. 474.

35. Cattell, pp. 81-82; Beloff, *Foreign Policy,* II, 26; Krivitsky, p. 132; *Soviet Shipping in the Spanish Civil War* (New York: Research Program on the U.S.S.R., 1954) (mimeographed), p. 18.

36. "Vozhdi II. Internatsionala, SSSR i edinyi front" (The leaders of the Second International, the USSR, and the United Front), KI, No. 4, 1935, pp. 9-10.

37. "Na sud rabochikh organizatsii!" (At the court of the workers' organizations), BO, No. 45, 1935, p. 13.

38. Cattell, pp. 134-137, 141-144, 172-173.

39. D. Jiron, "Bor'ba s trotsistskoi agenturoi fashizma v Ispanii" (The struggle with the Trotskyite agency of Fascism in Spain), KI, No. 5, 1937, p. 75.

40. J. Hernández, p. 125.

41. J. González, "Sud nad POUM" (The court on the POUM), KI, No. 10, 1938, p. 115.

42. Cattell, p. 133.

43. Orlov, pp. 205-208; Victor Serge, *Carnets* (Paris: René Juilliard, 1952), pp. 98-99; Krivitsky, pp. 189-191.

44. See the odd collection of materials published by Karl Kreibich, leader of the German section of the Czechoslovak Communist Party. Karl Kreibich (ed.), *Spione und Verschwörer* (Prague, 1937).

45. Cattell, p. 75.

46. Khrushchev's secret speech, p. S39.

47. "Kak ne nado vesti bor'bu protiv fashizma" (How one should not carry on the struggle against Fascism), KI, No. 11-12, 1934, pp. 77-81; "K piatnadtsa-tiletiiu Kommunisticheskoi Internatsionala Molodezhii (On the fifteenth anniversary of the Communist International of Youth), KI, No. 34, 1934, pp. 46-48.

48. EAP-3a-11/2, Armee Oberkommando 16, Ic, August 18, 1941 (interrogation of NKVD Lieutenant Aleksandr Zhigunov) (English translation), p. 159.

49. Ruth Fischer, Stalin and German Communism: A Study in the Origins of the State Party (Cambridge, Mass.: Harvard University Press, 1948), p. 615, note 5; Krivitsky, pp. 79-80; SV, No. 16, 1937, pp. 12-14; decree in KI, No. 4, 1939, pp. 126-128.

50. Decree in KI, No. 4, 1939, pp. 126-128.

51. Ruth Fischer, p. 615, note 5.

52. Margarete Buber, Under Two Dictators (New York: Dodd, Mead & Co. [n.d.]), pp. 1-23; "Iu. O.," "Sovetskii krisis i Komintern" (The Soviet crisis and the Comintern), SV, No. 16, 1937, pp. 12-14.

53. "Iu. O.," in SV, No. 16, 1937, pp. 12-14; SV, No. 5, 1938, pp. 14-16.

54. Eugenio Reale, Avec Jacques Duclos au Banc des Accusés à la Réunion Constitutive de Kominform à Szlarska Poreba (Paris: Librairie Plon, 1958), pp. 8-9.

55. George W. Strobel, "Taktik, Auflösung und Rehabilitierung der polnischen KP," OE, VI (1956), 280.

56. This is a probable but by no means certain reconstruction from the information which became available during the "rehabilitation" of the Polish Party in 1955-56. The rehabilitation commission included representatives of the Soviet, Bulgarian, Italian, and Finnish parties; hence it is reasonable to suppose that the Comintern representatives of these parties, the men listed in the text of this book, issued the original condemnation. Moreover, it is very probable, that Dimitrov and Manuil'skii would have been involved in such an important decision; we have independent evidence (Reale, p. 8) that Togliatti was involved.

57. B. Dudykevich, "Iz zhizni i deiatel'nosti Kompartii Zapadnoi Ukrainy" (From the life and activity of the Communist Party of the West Ukraine), PZh, No. 12, 1958, pp. 60-64.

58. B. Jan, "Slavnyi put' internatsional'noi brigady im. Dombrovskogo" (The glorious road of the "Dombrowski" international brigade), KI, No. 11, 1938, pp. 79-82; C. Lucani, "International'nye brigady v Ispanii—olitsetvorenie edinstva i solidarnosti mezhdunarodnogo proletariata" (The international brigades in Spain—the embodiment of the unity and solidarity of the international proletariat), KI, No. 1, 1939, p. 79; Dmitrii Manuil'skii in XVIII S"ezd, p. 64 (Land of Socialism, p. 91).

59. Strobel, in OE, VI (1956), 280.

60. Alexander Minc, "The Polish Communist Party: A Political and Organizational History" (an unpublished manuscript, in German, in the Archive of

Russian and East European History and Culture, Columbia University). Hereafter cited as Minc MS.

61. Beloff, *Foreign Policy*, II, 26.
62. Cf. Benjamin I. Schwartz, *Chinese Communism and the Rise of Mao* (Cambridge, Mass.: Harvard University Press, 1958), pp. 185-187; Charles B. McLane, *Soviet Policy and the Chinese Communists, 1931-1946* (New York: Columbia University Press, 1958), pp. 19-40; Robert C. North, *Moscow and Chinese Communists* (Stanford, Calif.: Stanford University Press, 1953), pp. 150-151, for somewhat divergent interpretations.
63. V. Miro, "Bor'ba za sozdanie vnutrennikh sovetskikh raionov v polukolonial'nykh stranakh" (The struggle for the creation of internal soviet areas in semicolonial countries), KI, No. 1, 1935, pp. 38-47.
64. *Ibid.*, p. 42.
65. Li, "K voprosu ob usloviiakh sozdaniia vnutrennikh sovetskikh raionov v polukolonial'nykh stranakh (otvet t. V. Miro)" (On the question of the conditions for the creation of internal soviet areas in semicolonial countries [an answer to Comrade V. Miro]), KI, No. 2, 1935, pp. 40-51. This writer may have been Li Li-San, a major Chinese Communist leader who had been attacked by the Comintern in 1930 for prematurely using the "soviet" forces in a vain attack on Changsa and other cities held by the Kuomintang (cf. McLane, pp. 19-20, 37). But there were, of course, other "Li's" in the Chinese Communist movement.
66. Li, in KI, No. 2, 1935, p. 49.
67. A dissident Chinese Communist leader has maintained that in the autumn of 1934 Moscow authorized Mao's forces to retreat as far as Outer Mongolia if necessary (North, p. 164); McLane, pp. 56-59, casts considerable doubt on this version.
68. Li, in KI, No. 2, 1935, pp. 40-51.
69. *Ibid.*, p. 41.
70. McLane, pp. 66 ff.
71. *Ibid.*, pp. 98-100.
72. Peter S. H. Tang, *Communist China Today* (New York: Frederick A. Praeger, 1957), pp. 59-60; North, pp. 178-180; Beloff, *Foreign Policy*, I, 222-223.
73. McLane, p. 109.
74. On the considerably more complex attitude of the Chinese Communists in this period see *Ibid.*, pp. 132-144.
75. Mao Tse-tung, "Novyi etap razvitiia antiiaponskoi natsional'noi voinyi zadachi kompartii Kitaia" (The new stage in the development of the anti-Japanese national war and the tasks of the Communist Party of China), KI, No. 4, 1939, p. 101.
76. North, p. 186.
77. Lin Biao, "Tri goda natsional'no-osvoboditel'noi voiny kitaiskogo naroda" (Three years of the national-liberation war of the Chinese people), KI, No. 7, 1940, p. 58; cf. McLane, pp. 138-139.

78. See McLane, pp. 140-152, who feels there may have been a divergence of Soviet and Chinese Communist policies at this time.
79. "Vokrug mezhdousobnogo konflikta v Kitae" (Around the internecine conflict in China), KI, No. 2, 1941, pp. 83-86.
80. *Ibid.;* cf. McLane, pp. 186-187.
81. North, p. 188; McLane, p. 136.
82. McLane, pp. 152-155.
83. Apart from the puppet regimes in Tannu Tuva and Outer Mongolia.

CHAPTER IV   THE GREAT PURGE: I

1. P, August 22, 1936. This article seems to me to disprove Leonard Schapiro's contention (p. 409) that Piatakov, because of Ordzhonikidze's favor, was "in favor" at the time of the 1936 trial.
2. P, August 23, 1936.
3. P, November 20, 1936.
4. *Konstitutsiia (Osnovnoi Zakon) SSSR: Konstitutsii (Osnovnye Zakony) Soiuznykh Sovetskikh Sotsialisticheskikh Respublik* (The constitution [basic law] of the USSR: The constitutions [basic laws] of the Union of Soviet Socialist Republics) (Moscow: Izdanie TsIK SSSR, 1937), p. 30.
5. Abdurakhman Avtorkhanov ("Alexander Uralov"), *The Reign of Stalin* (London: The Bodley Head, 1953), pp. 40-47 (hereafter cited as Avtorkhanov, *Reign*); and Abdurakhman Avtorkhanov, *Stalin and the Soviet Communist Party* (New York: Frederick A. Praeger, 1959), p. 223 (hereafter cited as Avtorkhanov, *Stalin*); cf. Boris Nicolaevsky, "Iz istorii Ezhovshchiny: padenie Postysheva" (From the history of the Ezhov affair: the fall of Postyshev), SV, No. 12, 1954, pp. 237-240.
6. Khrushchev's secret speech, p. S23.
7. Ezhov's appointment was announced in P, September 27, 1939.
8. Wolin and Slusser, p. 378.
9. USSR, People's Commissariat of Justice, *Report of Court Proceedings in the case of the Anti-Soviet Trotskyite Centre* (Moscow: People's Commissariat of Justice of the U.S.S.R., 1937), p. 133. Hereafter cited as *Anti-Soviet Centre*.
10. P, January 28, 1937; Iz, January 28, 1937.
11. VI. Posdniakov, "Kak Ezhov prinimal N.K.V.D." (How Ezhov took over the NKVD), *Narodnaia Pravda*, No. 5, 1949, pp. 21-23; cf. P, October 17, 1936.
12. See the remark in *Anti-Soviet Centre*, p. 402.
13. Vladimir and Evdokia Petrov, *Empire of Fear* (London: Andre Deutsch Ltd., 1956), p. 69.
14. *Anti-Soviet Centre*, p. 64.
15. Dewey (full citation, Chapter II above).

16. *Anti-Soviet Centre*, p. 549.

17. Khrushchev's secret speech, p. S53.

18. N. Magus, "La Suppression de S. Ordjonikidze et du professeur D. D. Pletnev," E & O, No. 83, 1953, pp. 8-9.

19. P, February 19, 1937.

20. P, March 6 and March 21, 1937.

21. Kublanov dissertation, p. 385 (based on Leningrad Party archives).

22. P, March 6 and March 11, 1937.

23. A. A. Zhdanov, *Organizational Problems of the Communist Party* (New York: Workers Library Publishers, 1937), p. 31.

24. P, April 21, 1937; published separately as V. M. Molotov, *Uroki Vreditel'stva, Diversii i Spionazha Iapono-Nemetsko-Trotskistskikh Agentov* (The lessons of the wrecking, diversion, and espionage of Japanese-German-Trotskyite agents) (Moscow: Partizdat TsK VKP(b), 1937). Hereafter cited as *Uroki Vreditel'stva*.

25. Kublanov dissertation, p. 384.

26. Khrushchev's secret speech, p. S23.

27. *Uroki Vreditel'stva*, p. 57. Cf. Victor Kravchenko, *I Chose Freedom* (Garden City, N.Y.: Garden City Publishing Co., 1946), pp. 224-225.

28. P, March 29, 1937.

29. Khrushchev's secret speech, p. S26.

30. *Ibid.*

31. *Ibid.*, p. S23.

32. The announcement of Postyshev's transfer appeared in *Pravda*, March 19, 1937.

33. P, May 26, 1937.

34. P, May 29, 1937.

35. R. Rubenov, "Formy maskirovki trotskistskikh i inykh dvurushnikov" (Forms of concealment of Trotskyites and other double-dealers), PS, No. 15, 1937, p. 30.

36. Hryhoryi Kostiuk, *The Fall of Postyshev* (New York: Research Program on the U.S.S.R., 1954) (mimeographed), p. 6. In spite of several inaccuracies, this account is an interesting attempt, published before Khrushchev's secret speech, to reconstruct the events leading to Postyshev's removal from the Ukraine.

37. P, April 4, 1937.

38. List in SV, No. 12, 1938, p. 15; cf. Wolin and Slusser, p. 379.

39. Krivitsky, pp. 166-171; Orlov, pp. 214-216; cf. the account of another defector, Vl. Posdniakov, "Kak Ezhov prinimal N.K.V.D.," *Narodnaia Pravda*, No. 59, 1949, pp. 21-23, who places the ouster of some of these officials in the autumn of 1936.

40. WKP 92, p. 3.

41. Most of the group was praised in P, July 28, 1937; cf. Orlov, p. 214.

42. "O nekotorykh metodakh i priemakh inostrannykh razvedyvatel'nykh organov i ikh trotskistko-bukharinskoi agentury" (On some methods and ways of

foreign intelligence organs and their Trotskyite-Bukharinite agents), *Kommunist RKKA*, No. 11-12, 1937, pp. 25-36; abridged versions in Kreibich and other sources.

43. Roman Gul, *Les Maîtres de la Tcheka* (Paris: Les Editions de France, 1938), p. 224; Orlov, p. 213; cf. Nora Korzhenko Murray, *I Spied for Stalin* (New York: Wilfred Funk, Inc., 1951), p. 112.

44. Khrushchev's secret speech, pp. S34-S49.

45. P, December 21, 1936; cf. Ernest J. Simmons (ed.), *Through the Glass of Soviet Literature* (New York: Columbia University Press, 1953), p. 92.

46. Beloff, *Foreign Policy*, I, 182-184; see also Dmitri D. Fedotoff White, *The Growth of the Red Army* (Princeton: Princeton University Press, 1944), pp. 375-377.

47. Mikhail Soloviev, *My Nine Lives in the Red Army* (New York: David McKay, 1955), p. 57 (on Gamarnik's role in dissolving the Tatar units); Iz, February 23, 1935.

48. Orlov, p. 37; cf. P, April 24, 1936, for a novel reference to "kolkhoz Cossackdom."

49. Tikhomirov MS, pp. 98-101.

50. Erich Wollenberg, in SV, No. 14-15, 1937, pp. 22-23; J. Hernández, p. 308; Krivitsky, p. 245; A. Svetlanin, "Zagovor Tukhachevskogo i OKDVA" (The plot of Tukhachevskii and the Special Red Far East Army), *Posev*, No. 9, 1950, pp. 12-13.

51. Deutscher, *Stalin*, p. 379.

52. *Ibid.*; A. Svetlanin, *Dal'nevostochnyi Zagovor* (The Far East plot) (Frankfurt a. M.: Posev, 1953), and the article cited in note 50 above; Avtorkhanov, *Reign*, pp. 50-52.

53. See especially SV, No. 8-9, 1948, p. 161, "M. N." "Kto vydal Tukhachevskogo?" (Who betrayed Tukhachevskii?); the critique of this article by "M. V." in SV, No. 10, 1948, p. 192; "A. N. R.," "K delu Tukhachevskogo" (On the Tukhachevskii Affair), SV, No. 3, 1949, p. 49; L. Nord, "Eshche o Tukhachevskom" (Still more on Tukhachevskii), *Chasovoi*, No. 3, 1951, pp. 20-21.

54. See above, Chapter IV, pp. 54-55; and Krivitsky, p. 239.

55. A full discussion of this complex plot would require a more detailed presentation than its importance for the present study warrants. See especially Krivitsky, Chapter VII; Robert Coulondre, *Souvenirs de Deux Ambassades, 1936-1939* (Paris: Hachette, 1950); Brzezinski, *Purge*, p. 217; Walter Schellenberg, *The Schellenberg Memoirs* (London: Andre Deutsch, 1956), pp. 46-49; and Wilhelm Hoettl, *The Secret Front: The Story of Nazi Political Espionage* (New York: Frederick A. Praeger, 1954), pp. 78-83.

56. P, May 11, 1937.

57. *Ibid.*

58. Merle Fainsod, *How Russia Is Ruled*, p. 405.

59. P, June 1, 1937.

60. P, June 11, 1937, and June 12, 1937.

61. "Verkhovnyi Sovet pretoriantsev" (The Supreme Soviet of praetorians), BO, No. 62-63, 1938, p. 20.
62. WKP 386, pp. 384 ff.
63. Roman Gul, *Voroshilov, Budennyi, Bliukher, Kotovskii* (N.p.: Izdatel'stvo "Paravolo," n.d.) (received in Library of Congress in 1934), pp. 122-126. Since this book was published long before Bliukher's downfall, the story is not incredible.
64. Kublanov dissertation, p. 468; cf. P, December 20, 1937, for congratulations to Liushkov, head of the Far East NKVD (who later fled to Japan) for security work.
65. Beloff, *Foreign Policy*, II, 193.
66. Barmine, p. 323; Krivitsky, p. 198; Brzezinski, *Purge*, p. 106.
67. Raymond G. Garthoff, *Soviet Military Doctrine* (Glencoe, Ill.: The Free Press, 1953), p. 220.
68. Boris Meissner, "Sowjetmarschälle—Die Macht im Hintergrund," OE, V (1955), 94.
69. Fedotoff White, pp. 377, 390. Many of the newly promoted high officers were also Civil War veterans, though not necessarily commanders in that war (see Chapter 8, note 13), and some, like Budennyi and Timoshenko, who retained Stalin's favor were notorious for "resting" on their Civil War reputations.

CHAPTER V THE GREAT PURGE: II

1. E. Fischer, "Letchiki dvukh mirov" (Aviators of two worlds), KI, No. 7, 1937, p. 33.
2. "Partiinaia rabota v ekspeditsii na severnyi polius" (Party work on the expedition to the North Pole), PS, No. 13, 1937, p. 22.
3. Khrushchev's secret speech, p. S26.
4. See Alex Inkeles and Raymond Bauer (with the assistance of David Gleicher and Irving Rosow), *The Soviet Citizen: Daily Life in a Totalitarian Society* (Cambridge, Mass.: Harvard University Press, 1959), pp. 304 ff., for evidence of some general resentment against intelligentsia among lower strata.
5. Kostiuk, *Postyshev.*
6. P, October 22, 1935.
7. Hryhoryi Kostiuk, *Stalinist Rule in the Ukraine* (New York: Frederick A. Praeger, 1960), p. 105.
8. P, September 2, 1937.
9. Avtorkhanov, *Reign*, pp. 68-69.
10. Vladimir Dedijer, *Tito* (New York: Simon and Schuster, 1953), p. 107.
11. Kublanov dissertation, p. 166; P, June 9, 1938; *Soviet Political Personalities: Seven Profiles* (in Russian) (New York: Research Program on the U.S.S.R.,

1952) (mimeographed), pp. 5-6; Kostiuk, *Stalinist Rule*, pp. 124-126; *Bloc*, p. 67.

12. P, September 2, 1937.

13. P, June 9, 1938.

14. US *Foreign Relations*, p. 511.

15. Cf. Brzezinski, *Purge*, p. 78.

16. *Ibid.*, pp. 180-184; S. Krushinskii, *Belorussian Communism and Nationalism: Personal Recollections* (in Russian) (New York: Research Program on the U.S.S.R., 1953) (mimeographed), pp. 52-66.

17. K. Kudaibergen, "Kirgizstan v Gody Bol'shoi Chistki" (Kirgistan in the years of the Great Purge) (an unpublished manuscript in the Archive of Russian and East European History and Culture, Columbia University), pp. 5, 9, 19, 30-35.

18. *Bloc*, pp. 212 ff., 339 ff.

19. Tikhomirov MS, p. 76.

20. P, December 20, 1937.

21. *Bloc*, p. 763.

22. *Ibid.*, p. 661.

23. P, June 8, 1937.

24. N. Magus, "La Suppression de S. Ordjonikidze et du professeur D. D. Pletnev," E&O, No. 83, 1953, pp. 8-9.

25. *Bloc*, p. 551.

26. *Kommunisticheskaia Partiia Sovetskogo Soiuza v Rezoliutsiiakh i Resheniiakh S"ezdov, Konferentsii i Plenumov TsK* (The Communist Party of the Soviet Union in resolutions and decisions of congresses, conferences, and plenums of the Central Committee) (6th ed.) (Moscow: Gosudarstvennoe Izdatel'-stvo Politicheskoi Literatury, 1953), II, 852, 854. Hereafter cited as *KPSS*.

27. Kublanov dissertation, p. 500 (based on Leningrad Party archives).

28. E. Shvarts, "Otmena massovykh chistok partii" (Abolition of mass purges of the Party), PS, No. 5, 1939, p. 34; A. S. Shcherbakov, "Ob izmeneniakh v ustave VKP(b) (On changes in the statute of the All-Union Communist Party [Bolshevik]) B, No. 4, 1939, pp. 16-34.

29. D. Bakhshiev, *Partiinoe Stroitel'stvo v Usloviiakh Pobedy Sotsializma v SSSR* (Party structure in the conditions of the victory of socialism in the USSR). (Moscow: Gospolitizdat, 1954), p. 65.

30. Brzezinski, *Purge*, p. 121; cf. T. H. Rigby, "The Selection of Leading Personnel in the Soviet State and Communist Party" (unpublished doctoral thesis, University of London, 1954), p. 55.

31. V. Vlasov, "Partiino-politicheskaia rabota na vodnom transporte" (Party-political work in water transport), PS, No. 8, 1938, p. 21; cf. P, March 28 and March 29, 1938.

32. Brzezinski, *Purge*, pp. 118 ff.

33. Fainsod, *How Russia Is Ruled*, p. 282.

34. A. I. Mikoian, "Feliks Dzerzhinskii," B, No. 16, 1936, pp. 26-27; cf. Wolin and Slusser, p. 378.

35. Khrushchev's secret speech, p. S51.

36. Avtorkhanov, *Reign*, p. 80.
37. *Bloc*, p. 6.
38. Brzezinski, *Purge*, pp. 184-188.
39. A. I. Mikoian, "Slavnoe dvadtsatiletie sovetskoi razvedki" (Glorious fifteenth anniversary of the Soviet intelligence), PS, No. 2, 1938, pp. 19-25.
40. *Ibid.*, p. 23.
41. *Bloc*, p. 90. It should be noted, however, that Leites and Bernaut (p. 211) conclude that the testimony weakened Ezhov's position by stressing his impaired health.
42. P, March 28, 1938.
43. EAP-3a-11/2, Armee Oberkommando 16, Ic, August 18, 1941 (interrogation of NKVD Lieutenant Aleksandr Zhigunov) (English translation), p. 119. On Zhigunov's background and reliability see Hilger and Meyer, pp. 281-282.
44. See "X"'s letter from Moscow, in SV, No. 20-21, 1938, p. 24. Beria was reported as "director of the Bolsheviks of Georgia" in P, June 15, 1938.
45. Murray, p. 123.
46. Iz, December 16, 1938.
47. P, January 22, 1939.
48. EAP-3a-11/2 (Zhigunov interrogation), p. 127.
49. Khrushchev's secret speech, p. S29.
50. Ralph Talcott Fisher, Jr., *Pattern for Soviet Youth* (New York: Columbia University Press, 1959), p. 212. According to the NKVD defector Zhigunov (EAP-3a-11/2, p. 127), Kosarev was accused of plotting with Ezhov against the regime.
51. The years in which these men died are recorded in their biographies in *Bol'shaia Sovetskaia Entsiklopediia* (2nd ed., special volume for 1957).
52. Fedor Kubanskii, "Shkola Zhizni," *Rossiia*, July 14, 1953, pp. 3-4; Brzezinski, *Purge*, p. 87.

CHAPTER VI   THE IDEOLOGY OF TOTALITARIANISM

1. Stalin, *Leninism*, p. 364.
2. Henri Chambre, *Le Marxisme en Union Soviétique* (Paris: Editions du Seuil, 1955), pp. 75-78; L. Fischer, pp. 346-348; "Eine Volksdiskussion von beispiellosem Masstab," *Inprekorr*, No. 12, 1936, pp. 205-206.
3. *Inprekorr*, No. 12, 1936, pp. 205-206.
4. Vladimir I. Lenin, *Sochineniia* (Works) (Leningrad: Partizdat, 1935), XXV, 392.
5. For foreign Communists the most striking picture is presented by "Jan Valtin" in *Out of the Night* (New York: Alliance Book Corp., 1941); of the innumerable accounts of family life in high Party and NKVD circles, Nora Korzhenko Murray's *I Spied for Stalin* is especially interesting.

6. "Otvet T-shchu Ivanovu Ivanu Filippovichu" (Answer to Comrade Ivanov, Ivan Filippovich), B, No. 4, 1938, pp. 13-16.
7. On the attainment of socialism see for example Molotov, *XVIII S"ezd*, p. 288 (*Land of Socialism*, p. 113).
8. Thomas S. Rothschild, "The Highest Phase of Communism, According to the Works of Joseph Stalin, 1924-1936" (unpublished essay, Columbia University, 1950), p. 7.
9. For the Howard interview see KI, No. 5-6, 1936, pp. 5-12; cf. Frederick A. Leedy, "National Defense and the Revolutionary Expansion in the Political Education of the Red Army, 1939-1941—A Study of *Krasnaia Zvedzda*" (unpublished essay, Columbia University, 1952), p. 20; R. L. Tuck, "The Relation between the U.S.S.R. and Revolution Abroad, as Treated by Two Popular Soviet Encyclopedias" (unpublished thesis, Columbia University, 1949), pp. 32-35.
10. Herbert Marcuse, *Soviet Marxism* (New York: Columbia University Press, 1958), p. 161.
11. See especially Wetter, pp. 365, 413.
12. Helmut Dahm, "Ontologische Aspekte der sowjetischen Dialektik," OE, VII (1957), 235.
13. Marcuse, p. 153.
14. *Istoriia Vsesoiuznoi Kommunisticheskoi Partii (Bol'shevikov): Kratkii Kurs* (History of the All-Union Communist Party [Bolshevik]: Short Course) (Moscow: Gosudarstvennoe Izdatel'stvo Politicheskoi Literatury, 1938), p. 102. Hereafter cited as *Kratkii Kurs*. The English version is *History of the Communist Party of the Soviet Union (Bolsheviks): Short Course* (New York: International Publishers, 1939), p. 107. Hereafter cited as *Short Course*.
15. D. Ermakov, "Bol'she bditel'nosti pri podbore propagandistov" (More vigilance in the choice of propagandists), PS, No. 6, 1935, p. 8.
16. Hugh W. Babb and John N. Hazard, (ed. and trans.), *Soviet Legal Philosophy* (Cambridge, Mass.: Harvard University Press, 1951), p. xxiv.
17. *Ibid.*, pp. xxv-xxxi; Chambre, *Marxisme*, pp. 223-225.
18. See for example P. Iudin, "O gosudarstve pri sotsialisme" (On the state under socialism), B, No. 8, 1936, p. 54.
19. P, November 17, 1936.
20. Chambre, *Marxisme*, p. 228.
21. A. Koliada, "'Advokaty' iz Kirovogradskogo raikoma" ("Lawyers" from a Kirovograd raikom), *Stalinskoe Plemia* (Kiev), October 26, 1940, p. 2.
22. C. E. Black (ed.), *Rewriting Russian History* (New York: Frederick A. Praeger, 1956), pp. 13-14.
23. *Ibid.*, p. 15; "Istoricheskaia nauka i leninizm" (Historical science and Leninism), B, No. 3, 1936, pp. 7-9.
24. Frederick C. Barghoorn, *Soviet Russian Nationalism* (New York: Oxford University Press, 1956), p. 22.
25. Iz, January 27, 1939.
26. Black, p. 110 (article by Konstantin Shteppa).

27. Hans Niedermeier, "Schriftreform und Nationalitäten in der UdSSR," OE, III (1953), 415.
28. Chapter IV, p. 61 above.
29. P, March 26, 1938.
30. Barghoorn, *Nationalism*, p. 98.
31. P, October 4, 1937.
32. P, January 1, 1937.
33. Barghoorn, *Nationalism*, p. 252.
34. B. Volin, "Velikii russkii narod" (The great Russian people), B, No. 9, 1938, p. 34; P, July 28, 1937.
35. *Ibid.*
36. Hans Niedermeier, "Schriftreform und Nationalitäten in der UdSSR," OE, III (1953), 415.
37. Maurice Friedberg, "Soviet Literature and Retroactive Truth," *Problems of Communism*, III (1954), 31-39.
38. Conversely, Moscow became the symbol of the regime to non-Russian dissidents. Inkeles and Bauer, p. 353.
39. This account is based on the memoirs of a musician intimately acquainted with the circumstances described (Juri Jelagin, *Taming of the Arts* [New York: E. P. Dutton & Co., 1951], pp. 211-213); Genrietta L. Volokhova, "Bor'ba Kommunisticheskoi Partii za Usilenie Ideino-Vospitatel'noi Roli Khudozhestvennoi Literatury v Gody Vtoroi Piatiletki (1933-1937 gg.) (The struggle of the Communist Party for strengthening the idea-educational role of belletristic literature in the years of the second Five Year Plan [1933-1937]) (unpublished dissertation, Moscow University, 1956), pp. 125 ff.; N. Gorchakov, "Repressii protiv sovetskikh teatrov i teatral'nykh deiatelei" (Repression against Soviet theaters and theatrical workers), *Vestnik*, No. 1, 1956, pp. 63-64.
40. Cf. Gorchakov, in *Vestnik*, No. 1, 1956, p. 63, and Jelagin, p. 152.
41. A. Angarov, "Partiinye organizatsii i voprosy iskusstva" (Party organizations and questions of art), PS, No. 12, 1936, p. 52.
42. Jelagin, pp. 153-160, 169-174; and the Gorchakov article cited in note 39 above, pp. 66-70.
43. Leo Yaresh, "The Role of the Individual in History" in Black, pp. 92-93.
44. *Kratkii Kurs*, p. 110 (*Short Course*, pp. 115-116).
45. Bertram Wolfe, *Three Who Made a Revolution* (New York: Dial Press, 1948).
46. Emelian Iaroslavskii, "Ideinaia sokrovishchnitsa partii" (The treasure of ideas of the Party), PS, No. 18, 1940, pp. 11-12.
47. Deutscher, pp. 335-337.
48. Bertram Wolfe, *Six Keys to the Soviet System* (Boston: Beacon Press, 1956), pp. 51-52.
49. Black, p. 30.

CHAPTER VII THE ECONOMY OF THE PURGE ERA

1. Harry Schwartz, *Russia's Soviet Economy* (2nd ed.) (New York: Prentice-Hall, 1954), pp. 546-547; Alexander Baykov, *The Development of the Soviet Economic System* (New York: The Macmillan Company, 1947), p. 336.
2. E. D. Simon *et al.*, *Moscow in the Making* (London: Longmans, Green & Co., 1937), pp. 175-177. (Quoted by permission.)
3. Baykov, p. 336.
4. Baykov, pp. 336 ff.
5. David Granick, *Management of the Industrial Firm in the USSR* (New York: Columbia University Press, 1954), pp. 248-250.
6. Joseph S. Berliner, *Factory and Manager in the USSR* (Cambridge, Mass.: Harvard University Press, 1957), pp. 273-274.
7. Alexander Vucinich, *Soviet Economic Institutions* (Stanford, Calif.: Stanford University Press, 1952), pp. 30-32.
8. *KPSS*, II, 810-822.
9. Berliner, pp. 273-274; Baykov, pp. 341, 337.
10. Kravchenko, *I Chose Freedom*, p. 188.
11. Granick, pp. 51-52.
12. Baykov, p. 281.
13. Scott, p. 195.
14. Kravchenko, p. 197.
15. Granick, p. 51.
16. Berliner, p. 261.
17. *Ibid.*, pp. 49-50.
18. Baykov, pp. 297-298; A. Polozhaev, "Soviet Economic Reorganization: the Background, 1917-56," *Bulletin*, IV, No. 6, p. 7.
19. *XVIII S"ezd*, pp. 494-495 (*Land of Socialism*, p. 160).
20. Granick, p. 211; "Krovnoe delo partiinykh organizatsii" (Vital business of the Party organizations), PS, No. 3, 1941, p. 5.
21. *XVIII S"ezd*, p. 535 (*Land of Socialism*, p. 218).
22. G. Smirnov, "Partiinyi aktiv Leningrada" (The Party activist of Leningrad), PS, No. 5, 1939, p. 27. The level of education of secretaries in the very large factories was considerably higher, however.
23. N. Surovoi, "Kak stroitsia rabota raikoma partii" (How to arrange the work of the Party raikom), PS, No. 17, 1940, p. 25; "Dolzhen li chlen partbiuro imet' postoiannye obiazannosti?" (Should a member of a Party bureau have permanent tasks?), *ibid.*, pp. 70-71.
24. "Mozhet li partiinyi rabotnik premirovat'sia khoziaistvennym organom?" (May a Party worker be given a premium by an economic organ?) PS, No. 7, 1941, pp. 38-39.

25. *XVIII S"ezd,* p. 532 (*Land of Socialism,* p. 212).
26. *Kolhospnyk Ukraïny,* December 3, 1940.
27. P, July 1, 1940; cf. Gregory Bienstock, Solomon M. Schwarz, and Aaron Yugow, *Management in Russian Industry and Agriculture* (London: Oxford University Press, 1944), p. 20.
28. Bienstock, Schwarz, and Yugow, p. 21.
29. Granick, pp. 218-219; John A. Armstrong, *The Soviet Bureaucratic Elite: A Case Study of the Ukrainian Apparatus* (New York: Frederick A. Praeger, 1959), pp. 65, and 71, note 12.
30. Hodgman, p. 89.
31. Baykov, p. 286.
32. Hodgman, p. 89.
33. *Direktivy KPSS i Sovetskogo Pravitel'stva po Khoziaistvennym Voprosam* (Directives of the CPSU and the Soviet government on economic questions) (Moscow: Gosudarstvennoe Izdatel'stvo Politicheskoi Literatury, 1957-58), II, 546-553. Hereafter cited as *Direktivy.*
34. *Ibid.,* pp. 637-638.
35. Central Committee decision of September 17, 1940, in PS, No. 17, 1940, p. 65.
36. *Direktivy,* II, 653-655.
37. *Narodnoe Khoziaistvo,* 1956, p. 19.
38. PS, No. 6, 1941, pp. 78-80.
39. S. Diachenko, *Po Voprosam Organizatsii Kolkhozov v SSSR* (On the question of the organization of kolkhozes in the USSR) (Munich: Institute for the Study of the USSR, 1955) (mimeographed), p. 26; cf. Vucinich, pp. 34-36.
40. *Direktivy,* II, 589; Baykov, p. 314.
41. *KPSS,* II, 947-951.
42. *XVIII S"ezd,* pp. 117-118 (*Land of Socialism,* pp. 259-260); cf. Herbert S. Dinerstein and Leon Gouré, *Communism and the Russian Peasant; Moscow in Crisis* (Glencoe, Ill.: The Free Press, 1955), p. 44.
43. Boris Nicolaevsky, "Neuer Feldzug gegen das Dorf," *Ost-Probleme,* III (1951), 390-400.

CHAPTER VIII   EIGHTEENTH CONGRESS AND NEW CADRES

1. *XVIII S"ezd,* p. 28 (*Land of Socialism,* p. 38).
2. *XVIII S"ezd,* p. 519 (*Land of Socialism,* p. 189).
3. For a detailed case study of such relationships see J. Armstrong, *Elite,* especially pp. 3-5, 142-150.
4. See Chapter XXIII, pp. 315-316.
5. J. Armstrong, *Elite,* pp. 11-13.

6. See also *ibid.*, pp. 56-57.
7. See especially Rush, pp. 88-94; and for a striking indication of institutional divergencies in press coverage see Chapter XV, p. 208.
8. Iz, February 21, 1941. Madame Molotov was listed under her "Party name," P. S. Zhemchuzhina.
9. See the list of awards to NKVD officers in Iz, April 27, 1940.
10. Beloff, *Foreign Policy*, II, 348, note 1.
11. Wolin and Slusser, p. 19; cf. US *Foreign Relations*, pp. 771-772.
12. Khrushchev's secret speech, p. S20.
13. *XVIII S"ezd*, pp. 680-681 (*Land of Socialism*, pp. 485-487); cf. BO, No. 77-78, 1939, p. 19.
14. Iz, February 21, 1941.
15. See especially Brzezinski, *Purge*, Chapter 6.
16. *XVIII S"ezd*, p. 525 (*Land of Socialism*, p. 202).
17. *XVIII S"ezd*, p. 303.
18. *Ibid.*, p. 149. It is interesting to note that the proportion of Civil War entrants among high Red Army officers apparently remained much higher. Twenty-two of fifty generals dying in 1956-58 (for whom information on Party entry is given) had entered 1918-20. Vladimir Hawryluk, "La Mortalité des Généraux en URSS de 1956 à 1958," E&O, No. 214, April 16-30, 1959, p. 14. Obviously those who died tended to be older, and consequently to have entered the Party earlier, than average; but only a small proportion of Party officials' obituaries for the same period indicate such early Party entry.
19. *XVIII S"ezd*, p. 149.
20. J. Armstrong, *Elite*, pp. 19-22.
21. Rigby thesis, p. 101.
22. *XVIII S"ezd*, p. 475 (*Land of Socialism*, p. 462).
23. *XVIII S"ezd*, p. 149.
24. Galina I. Kurbatova, "A. A. Zhdanov—Vydaiushchiisia Teoretik Marksizma" (A. A. Zhdanov—Outstanding Theorist of Marxism) (unpublished dissertation, Moscow University, 1949), p. 1.
25. Most of the details on Zhdanov's life are taken from the standard official biography in B. N. Ponomarev (ed.), *Politicheskii Slovar'* (Political Dictionary) (2nd ed.) (Moscow: Gosudarstvennoe Izdatel'stvo Politicheskoi Literatury, 1958), p. 187. Hereafter cited as *Politicheskii Slovar'*. Interesting additional details are found in the Kurbatova dissertation.
26. See J. Armstrong, *Elite*, pp. 49-50.
27. *Ibid.*, pp. 45-47.
28. *XVIII S"ezd*, pp. 672-673 (*Land of Socialism*, p. 457). On earlier changes in practice on admission see especially Schapiro, p. 438.
29. "Voprosy chlenstva v VKP(b) (po dokumentov i tsifram za 30 let)" (Questions of membership in the All-Union Communist Party [Bolshevik] from documents and figures for 30 years), PZh, No. 20, 1947, p. 81; Report of the Credentials Commission of the Eighteenth Party Conference, PS, No. 4-5, 1941, p. 143.

30. *XVIII S"ezd*, p. 147.
31. J. Armstrong, *Elite*, p. 16; P, May 14, 1940.
32. *XVIII S"ezd*, p. 578.
33. See Zhdanov's obituary in B, No. 16, 1948, p. 15; and P, September 7, 1940.
34. *XVIII S"ezd*, p. 531 (*Land of Socialism*, p. 211).
35. N. Shakhova, "Partiinye organizatsii narkomatakh" (The Party organizations of the People's Commissariats), PS, No. 7, 1941, pp. 17 ff.
36. Rigby thesis, p. 86.
37. Fainsod, *How Russia Is Ruled,* pp. 172-173; Schapiro, pp. 450-451; Boris Meissner, *Russland im Umbruch* (Frankfurt a. M.: Verlag für Geschichte und Politik, 1951), pp. 20-21.
38. Fainsod, *How Russia Is Ruled*, p. 271.
39. J. Armstrong, *Elite*, pp. 72-73.
40. Meissner, *Umbruch*, p. 21; Schapiro, p. 450.
41. "Podniat' delo podbora kadrov na nauchnuiu bol'shevistskuiu vysotu" (Raise the matter of selection of cadres to a scientific, Bolshevik height), PS, No. 13, 1939, p. 6.
42. Andrei S. Favorskii, "Ustav Partii Priniatyi XVIII S"ezdom VKP(b) i Ego Znachenie v Bor'be Kommunisticheskoi Partii za Povyshenie Urovna Partiinnoi Organizatsionnoi Raboty (1939-Iiun' 1941 gg.)" (The Party charter adopted at the Eighteenth Congress of the All-Union Communist Party [Bolshevik] and its significance in the struggle of the Communist Party for heightening the level of Party organizational work [1939-June 1941]), (unpublished dissertation, Leningrad University, 1953), p. 202.
43. "Podniat' delo podbora kadrov na nauchnuiu bol'shevistskuiu vysotu," PS, No. 13, 1939, p. 6.
44. "Otchet otdela kadrov na plenume raikoma" (The report of the cadres section to the plenum of the raikom), PS, No. 21, 1940, pp. 58 ff.
45. Text in PS, No. 17-18, 1943, p. 36.
46. Favorskii dissertation, p. 202.
47. Émigré interviewee quoted in Fainsod, *How Russia Is Ruled,* p. 192.

CHAPTER IX NAZI PACT AND EXPANSION

1. Beloff, *Foreign Policy*, II, 113, 240, 255.
2. Angelo Rossi, *Les Communistes Français pendant la Drôle de Guerre* (Paris: Les Iles d'Or, 1951), p. 16.
3. *Ibid.*, p. 27.
4. *Ibid.*
5. *Ibid.*, p. 35.
6. Douglas Hyde, *I Believed: The Autobiography of a Former British Communist* (London: William Heinemann, Ltd., 1951), p. 70.
7. *Ibid.*
8. Rossi, *Drôle de Guerre*, pp. 37, 47.

9. *Ibid.*, p. 46.
10. *Partiino-Politicheskaia Rabota v Boevoi Obstanovke*, p. 33.
11. "Vozzvanie ispolkoma Kominterna k dvadtsat' vtoroi godovshchine Velikoi Oktiabr'skoi sotsialisticheskoi revoliutsii" (Proclamation of the Executive Committee of the Comintern on the twentieth anniversary of the Great October Socialist Revolution) KI, No. 8-9, 1939, p. 4.
12. J. Hernández, pp. 267-268.
13. Rossi, *Drôle de Guerre*, pp. 67 ff., 208-209.
14. Weinberg, pp. 68-85.
15. Angelo Rossi, *Physiologie du Parti Communiste Français* (Paris: Editions Self, 1948), pp. 398-404.
16. *Ibid.*, pp. 17-20.
17. L. Taylor, "Imperialisticheskaia voina i polozhenie rabochego klassa v kapitalisticheskikh stranakh" (The imperialist war and the position of the working class in the capitalist countries), KI, No. 6, 1940, p. 31.
18. M. Iovchuk, "Materialisticheskaia dialektika—ideinoe oruzhie kommunistov vsekh stran" (The materialist dialectic—the idea-weapon of Communists of all countries), KI, No. 2, 1941, p. 47.
19. R. Magnus, "Kniga o Norvegii" (A book on Norway), KI, No. 2, 1941, p. 122; cf. G. Friedrich, "Pod znakom mezhdunarodnoi proletarskoi solidarnosti (k itogam 1 Maia 1941 g.)" (Under the sign of international proletarian solidarity [on the results of 1 May 1941]), KI, No. 5, 1941, p. 39.
20. G. Dimitrov, "Voina i rabochii klass kapitalisticheskikh stran" (The war and the working class of the capitalist countries), KI, No. 8-9, 1939, p. 31.
21. "Polgoda imperialisticheskoi voiny" (A half year of the imperialist war), KI, No. 2, 1940, p. 30.
22. William Hardy McNeill, *The Greek Dilemma: War and Aftermath* (Philadelphia: J. B. Lippincott Co., 1947), p. 67.
23. A. Clerc, "Khod voiny v otsenke inostrannykh obozrevatelei" (The course of the war in the estimate of foreign observers), KI, No. 4, 1941, p. 109.
24. Hyde, p. 114; Wolfgang Leonhard, *Child of the Revolution* (Chicago: Henry Regnery Co., 1958), pp. 107-108; Rossi, *Physiologie*, pp. 113-114.
25. "SSSR—oplot i nadezhda trudiashchikhsia vsego mira" (The USSR—the stronghold and the hope of the toilers of the whole world), PS, No. 8, 1941, pp. 3-7.
26. John A. Armstrong, *Ukrainian Nationalism, 1939-1945* (New York: Columbia University Press, 1955), pp. 64-70.
27. J. Armstrong, *Elite*, pp. 106-107; P, November 23, 1939; November 27, 1939.
28. J. Armstrong, *Elite*, p. 108.
29. Nadezhda P. Khripko, "Deiatel'nost' KPSS po Podboru, Rasstanovke i Vospitaniiu Partiinykh Kadrov v Chetvertoi Piatiletke—1946-1950 gg. (na Materialakh Belorusskoi SSR)" (The activity of the CPSU in the selection, distribution and training of Party cadres in the fourth Five Year Plan—1946-1950 [from materials of the Belorussian SSR]) (unpublished dissertation, Minsk University, 1956), p. 115.

30. Krushinskii, p. 68.
31. J. Armstrong, *Elite*, pp. 115-117.
32. *Ibid.*, pp. 115, 120-121.
33. Beloff, *Foreign Policy*, II, 286, 330; Irina Saburova, "The Soviet Occupation of the Baltic States," *Russian Review*, XIV (1955), 36-49.
34. Henry W. Mott, III, "The Occupation and Incorporation of Latvia, June 17 to August 5, 1940" (unpublished thesis, Columbia University, 1957), p. 16.
35. The Baltic Communist Parties were incorporated in the All-Union Party in October 1940 (*Istoriia KPSS*, p. 512).
36. P, December 30, 1940.
37. Tadeusz Wittlin, *A Reluctant Traveler in Russia* (New York: Rinehart & Co., 1952), pp. 155-156.
38. Aleksander Kaelas, "Aleksei Müürisepp," OE, VIII (1958), 33.
39. Il'ia A. Fomin, "Podbor, Rasstanovka i Vospitanie Rudovodiashchikh Kadrov Partiinogo i Sovetskogo Apparata v Period Mezhdu XIX i XX S"ezdami KPSS" (Selection, distribution, and training of directing cadres of the Party and the Soviet apparatus in the period between the Nineteenth and the Twentieth congresses of the CPSU) (unpublished dissertation, Academy of Social Sciences, Moscow, 1956), p. 34.
40. J. Armstrong, *Ukrainian Nationalism*, p. 174.
41. A. F. Virnyk, *Ukrainskaia SSR: Kratkii istoriko-ekonomicheskii ocherk* (Ukrainian SSR: A short historic-economic survey) (Moscow: Gosudarstvennoe Izdatel'stvo Politicheskoi Literatury, 1954), p. 97.
42. Mott thesis, p. 32; Petr I. Riabchun, "Kommunisty Latvii v Bor'be za Kollektivizatsiiu Sel'skogo Khoziaistva (1945-1949 gg.) (The Communists of Latvia in the struggle for collectivization of agriculture [1945-1949]) (unpublished dissertation, Moscow University, 1952), p. 38.
43. Riabchun dissertation, p. 328.
44. Liubov' M. Chaiko, "Bor'ba Partiinoi Organizatsii Sovetskoi Litvy za Provedenie Agrarnoi Reformy (1940-1947 gg.)" (The struggle of the Party organization of Soviet Lithuania for the implementation of agrarian reform [1940-1947]) (unpublished dissertation, Leningrad University, 1952), p. 298.
45. *Pravda Ukrainy*, October 30, 1949.
46. J. Armstrong, *Elite*, p. 115; Leo Gruliow (ed.), *Current Soviet Policies* (New York: Frederick A. Praeger, 1953), p. 56. Hereafter cited as CSP I.
47. Riabchun dissertation, p. 104.
48. Bakhshiev, p. 36.
49. I. Dmitriev, *Party and Political Organs in the Soviet Army* (in Russian) (New York: Research Program on the U.S.S.R., 1953) (mimeographed), p. 20.
50. In 1956, however, Karelo-Finland again became an autonomous republic in the RSFSR.
51. *XVIII S"ezd*, p. 200 (*Land of Socialism*, p. 292).
52. Leedy thesis, p. 9.
53. M. Estrakh, "Sviaz' s grazhdanskimi partorganizatsiiami" (Contact with

civil Party organizations), *Partiino-Politicheskaia Rabota v RKKA*, No. 20, 1939, pp. 50-52.

54. P, December 14, 1939.
55. Iz, June 5, 1940, and following issues.
56. P, August 26, 1940.
57. "Po-bol'shevistski perestroit partiino-politicheskuiu rabotu" (Reconstruct Party-political work in the Bolshevik manner), *Partiino-Politicheskaia Rabota v RKKA*, No. 15-16, 1940, pp. 9-16.
58. *Ibid.*, p. 16.
59. *Ibid.*, pp. 9-16; N. Sinitsina, "Zheny komandirov gotoviatsia k oborone" (The wives of commanders prepare themselves for defense), *Partiino-Politicheskaia Rabota v RKKA*, No. 10, 1940, pp. 41-42.
60. A. I. Zaporozhets, Director of Main Administration of Political Propaganda of Red Army, "O perestroike raboty politorganov i partiinykh organizatsii Krasnoi Armii" (On the reconstruction of the work of the political organs and the Party organizations of the Red Army), *Partiino-Politicheskaia Rabota v RKKA*, No. 23-24, 1940, pp. 1-8.
61. Regimental Commissar A. Feshankov, "Protiv lozhnogo demokratisma—za vysokuiu trebovatel'nost'" (Against false democratism—for high exactingness), *Partiino-Politicheskaia Rabota v RKKA*, No. 17, 1940, pp. 6-9.

CHAPTER X IMPACT OF WAR

1. While the sketches of military events in this chapter are based on numerous sources, the most important is Kurt von Tippelskirch, *Geschichte des zweiten Weltkriegs* (2nd ed., revised) (Bonn: Athenäum Verlag, 1956).
2. See for example G. F. Aleksandrov, "O tekushchem momente velikoi otechestvennoi voiny" (On the present moment of the Great Patriotic War), B, No. 1, 1942, pp. 22-42.
3. Khrushchev's secret speech, pp. S37-S38.
4. E.g., in I. M. Shliapin *et al.*, *Kommunisticheskaia Partiia v Period Velikoi Otechestvennoi Voiny* (The Communist Party during the period of the Great Patriotic War) (Moscow: Voennoe Izdatel'stvo Ministerstva Oborony Soiuza SSR, 1958), p. 42.
5. Henry C. Cassidy, *Moscow Dateline, 1941-1943* (Boston: Houghton Mifflin Co., 1943), p. 57.
6. J. V. Stalin, *O Velikoi Otechestvennoi Voine Sovetskogo Soiuza* (The Great Patriotic War of the Soviet Union) (Moscow: Gosudarstvennoe Izdatel'stvo Politicheskoi Literatury, 1952), pp. 9-17. Hereafter cited as *O Velikoi Otechestvennoi Voine*. An English version bearing the translated title given above (New York: International Publishers, 1945) contains the same passage on pp. 9-17; the book is cited hereafter as *Great Patriotic War*.
7. Iz, July 20, 1941.

8. Fainsod, *How Russia Is Ruled,* p. 407.

9. J. Armstrong, *Ukrainian Nationalism,* p. 77; Viacheslav P. Artem'ev, *Rezhim i Okhrana Ispravitel'no-Trudovykh Lagerei MVD* (The living conditions and policing of MVD corrective labor camps) (Munich: Institute for the Study of the USSR, 1956), pp. 108-109.

10. Shliapin *et al.,* p. 56; *Komunist* (Kiev), September 13, 1941.

11. "Rost riadov VKP(b) vo vremia otechestvennoi voiny" (The growth of the ranks of the All-Union Communist Party [Bolshevik] during the time of Patriotic War), PS, No. 7, 1942, pp. 11-21; *Istoriia KPSS,* p. 547.

12. B. S. Tel'pukhovskii, "Kommunisticheskaia partiia—vdokhnovitel' i organizator pobeda sovetskogo naroda v velikoi otechestvennoi voine" (The Communist Party—inspiration and organizer of the victory of the Soviet people in the Great Patriotic War), *Voprosy Istorii KPSS,* No. 2, 1958, p. 56, reports that the 1,300,000 Communists in the military forces at the end of 1941 constituted 42.4 per cent of the total membership.

13. Dinerstein and Gouré, pp. 175 ff.

14. Khrushchev's secret speech, pp. S19-S20.

15. Dinerstein and Gouré, p. 185.

16. Giuseppe Boffa, Moscow correspondent of the Italian Communist newspaper *Unità, La Grande Svolta* (Rome: Editore Riuniti, 1959), p. 82. An English-language version, *Inside the Khrushchev Era* (translated by C. Marzani) (New York: Marzani & Munsell, 1959), has appeared, but the inexact translation and deletion of a few significant passages make the version unreliable.

17. Dinerstein and Gouré, pp. 185-191.

18. P, November 8, 1941.

19. Werth, *Stalingrad,* p. 102. There is no confirmation of this assertion from a Soviet source; but A. V. Karasev, *Leningradtsy v gody blokady, 1941-1943* (Leningraders in the years of the blockade, 1941-1943) (Moscow: Izdatel'-stvo Akademii Nauk SSSR, 1959), pp. 105-106, admits that Stalin expressed his dissatisfaction with Voroshilov and Zhdanov in another connection on August 21.

20. P, January 27, 1945.

21. Alexander Werth, *Moscow War Diary* (New York: Alfred A. Knopf, 1942), p. 59.

22. Vasilii V. Stremilov, "Organizatsionnaia i Massovo-Politicheskaia Rabota Leningradskoi Partiinoi Organizatsii v Period Geroicheskoi Oborony Lenin-grada (Iiun' 1941-Ianviar' 1943)" (Organizational and mass-political work of the Leningrad Party organization in the period of the heroic defense of Leningrad [June 1941-January 1943]) (unpublished dissertation, Academy of Social Sciences, Moscow, 1956), p. 162; cf. Karasev, pp. 120-121, who cites a report that an anti-Soviet group planned to seize power and admit the Germans.

23. Karasev, p. 154; Stremilov dissertation, p. 162.

24. Stremilov dissertation, p. 200.

25. Karasev, pp. 185, 254-257.

26. See the review of *Geroicheskii Leningrad, 1917-1942*, in B, No. 22, 1943, p. 59; much the most complete account of the siege is in Karasev, who notes Zhdanov's presence in the city at frequent intervals.

27. Stremilov dissertation, p. 131; "Politorganizatory v domakh" (Political organizers in houses), PS, No. 2, 1943, p. 47.

28. A. A. Kuznetsov, "Bolsheviki Leningrad na zashchite rodnogo goroda" (The Bolsheviks of Leningrad in the defense of their native city), PS, No. 9-10, 1945, p. 58.

29. P, January 27, 1945; Karasev, pp. 235-236.

30. P, July 1, 1941; cf. A. M. Sinitsyn, "Chrezvychainye organy sovetskogo gosudarstva v gody Velikogo Otechestvennoi Voiny" (Extraordinary organs of the Soviet state during the years of the Great Patriotic War), *Voprosy Istorii*, No. 2, 1955, pp. 32-43.

31. Tel'pukhovskii, in *Voprosy Istorii KPSS*, No. 2, 1958, p. 40.

32. P, July 1, 1941.

33. "H. R.," "Zurück zum Politbüro," *Ost-Probleme*, V (1953), 530-534; A. M. Sinitsyn, "Rol' Sovetskogo Gosudarstva v Ukreplenie Tyla" (The role of the Soviet state in strengthening the rear) (unpublished dissertation, Academy of Social Sciences, Moscow, 1953), p. 45.

34. *Bakinskii Rabochii*, February 25, 1943.

35. Werth, *Stalingrad*, p. 462.

36. Boris Meissner, "Der Nachfolger—Georgij M. Malenkow," OE, III (1953), 86.

37. See Sinitsyn dissertation, p. 49.

38. M. Suprunenko, *Ukraina v Velikoi Otechestvennoi Voine Sovetskogo Soiuza, 1941-1945 gg.* (The Ukraine in the Great Patriotic War of the Soviet Union, 1941-1945) (Kiev: Gosudarstvennoe Izdatel'stvo Politicheskoi Literatury, 1956), p. 46.

39. Karasev, pp. 105-106.

40. Tel'pukhovskii, in *Voprosy Istorii KPSS*, No. 2, 1958, p. 41. On Kazan' see *Istoriia Tatarskoi ASSR* (History of the Tatar ASSR), II (Kazan': Tatarskoe Knizhnoe Izdatel'stvo, 1960), 401.

41. Sinitsyn dissertation, p. 53; cf. P. P. Andreev, *Kommunisticheskaia Partiia v Period Velikoi Otechestvennoi Voiny (Iiun' 1941 g.-1945 g.)* (The Communist Party in the period of the Great Patriotic War [June 1941-1945]) (Moscow: Izdatel'stvo VPSh i AON pri TsK KPSS, 1959), p. 23.

42. See J. Armstrong, *Elite*, pp. 13-14.

43. Moreno Hernández, p. 231 (based on an account of a Spanish émigré in the USSR who was attached to the "Quintet" as demolition expert).

44. Dinerstein and Gouré, p. 155.

45. M. D. Iushchenko, "Komunisty Ukraïny—orhanizatory patriotychnoho pidnesennia trudiashchykh respubliky na vidsich vorohovi v pochatkovyi period velikoï vitchysnianoï viiny" (The Communists of the Ukraine—the organizers of the patriotic rising of the toilers of the Republic to repulse the enemy in the period of the Great Patriotic War), *Ukraïns'kyi Istorychnyi Zhurnal*, No. 3, 1958, pp. 58, 61.

46. Tel'pukhovskii, in *Voprosy Istorii KPSS*, No. 2, 1958, p. 42; cf. P. P. Andreev, pp. 48-51.

47. Based on the translation of captured order No. 022, November 5, 1941, of the Chief of the Rear Areas of the Red Army in Anlage 3 zum Feindnach-richten Blatt 219/42, Armeeoberkommando 11, Ic/Abwehr Offizier (kindly made available to me by the U.S. Army). Hereafter cited as Feindnachrichten Blatt 219/42.

48. Werth, *Stalingrad*, p. 428.

49. P, November 8, 1941.

50. J. Armstrong, *Elite*, p. 133; Suprunenko, pp. 261-264.

51. William H. Standley and Arthur A. Ageton, *Admiral Ambassador to Russia* (Chicago: Henry Regnery Co., 1955), p. 322; González, pp. 88-89; Jan Dubicki, *Elements of Disloyalty in Turkmenistan* (in Russian) (New York: Research Program on the U.S.S.R., 1954) (mimeographed), pp. 43-44.

52. Feindnachrichten Blatt 219/42.

53. Nikolai A. Voznesenskii, *The Economy of the USSR during World War II* (Washington, D.C.: Public Affairs Press, 1948), pp. 24, 29, 34.

54. Boris Galin, *Donbas Sketches* (Moscow: Foreign Languages Publishing House, 1948), pp. 43-44, 48-49.

55. Voznesenskii, p. 29.

56. Joseph J. Baritz, "The Organization and Administration of the Soviet Arma-ment Industry," *Bulletin*, IV (1957), No. 11, p. 17.

57. H. Schwartz, p. 218.

58. Voznesenskii, p. 30.

59. N. Shatagin, *Partiia v Period Velikoi Otechestvennoi Voiny* (The Party in the period of the Great Patriotic War) (Moscow: Gosudarstvennoe Izdatel'-stvo Politicheskoi Literatury, 1959).

60. See H. Schwartz, p. 127.

61. Voznesenskii, p. 25.

62. *Ibid.*, p. 24.

63. Tel'pukhovskii, in *Voprosy Istorii KPSS*, No. 2, 1958, p. 43.

64. Speech of A. S. Shcherbakov to Moscow gorkom, May 5, 1942, in PS, No. 9-10, 1942, pp. 9-18; N. Gusarov, "Rukovodit'—eto znachit predvidet'" (To direct means to foresee), PS, No. 7, 1943, pp. 7 ff.

65. See the notice in PS, No. 1, 1942, p. 41.

66. Shatagin, p. 118.

67. A. Kiselev, "Zametki nachal'nika politotdela MTS" (Remarks of the director of the political section of an MTS), PS, No. 6, 1942, pp. 18-22; "Sovetskaia ekonomika v gody Velikoi Otechestvennoi Voiny" (The Soviet economy in the years of the Great Patriotic War), PS, No. 9-10, 1945, p. 36.

68. Shliapin *et al.*, p. 179; speech of A. S. Shcherbakov to the Moscow Party activists, in PS, No. 23, 1943, pp. 11 ff.

69. Kiselev, in PS, No. 6, 1942, pp. 18-22.

70. P, June 28, 1943.

71. M. I. Pavlova, "Tul'skaia partorganizatsiia v pervyi period velikoi otechestven-

noi voiny" (The Tula Party organization in the first period of the Great Patriotic War), *Voprosy Istorii KPSS*, No. 6, 1958, p. 116.

72. A. S. Shcherbakov to a Leningrad Party meeting, January 21, 1942, in PS, No. 1, 1942, pp. 14-21.

73. See Khrushchev's secret speech, p. S19; in this passage he implicitly recognized that the "plenum" reported for January 27, 1944 (*KPSS*, II, 1018) was fictitious.

74. Pavlova, in *Voprosy Istorii KPSS*, No. 6, 1958, p. 126.

75. L. Slepov, *Mestnye Partiinye Organy* (Local Party organs) (Moscow: Vysshaia Partiinaia Shkola pri TsK KPSS, Kafedra Partiinogo-Stroitel'stva, 1954), p. 19.

76. *Ibid.;* cf. "Ob otchetakh i vyborakh partorganov v pervichnykh partorganizatsiiakh" (On accountings and elections of the Party organs in primary Party organizations), PS, No. 1, 1943, pp. 27-28.

77. Col. V. Kraskevich, "Pervichnaia partorganizatsiia v Krasnoi Armii" (The primary Party organization in the Red Army), PS, No. 12, 1943, pp. 40 ff.

78. N. Senin, "Iz praktiki otdela kadrov obkoma partii" (From the practice of the cadres section of the Party obkom), PS, No. 24, 1943, pp. 26-27.

79. CSP I, p. 223; Tel'pukhovskii, in *Voprosy Istorii KPSS*, No. 2, 1958, p. 40. Shatagin (p. 134) implies that there were about 450,000 Communists in the armed forces at the outbreak of the war, and states that 800,000 entered the army on mobilization.

80. Iushchenko, in *Ukraïns'kyi Istorychnyi Zhurnal*, No. 3, 1958, p. 48; G. Fedotov, "Vovlech' v aktivnuiu rabotu kazhdogo kommunista" (Draw each Communist into active work), PS, No. 21-22, 1943, p. 27.

81. Tel'pukhovskii, in *Voprosy Istorii KPSS*, No. 2, 1958, p. 55, gives the number of deaths; the calculation of the number of Communists lost in 1941 is given in note 12 above. A very large source of error in any calculation of Communists who surrendered is introduced by the fact that a considerable number must have starved in Leningrad and other areas, and very many must have been cut off behind the German lines as civilians. Generally speaking, however, one can consider those who remained in occupied areas without contacting the underground, and prisoners of war, to have been in the same "unreliable" category from the Soviet standpoint.

82. *Ibid.*, p. 40; the text of the decision is in PS, No. 1, 1942, p. 43.

83. Shatagin, pp. 132, 134; cf. (for slightly different figures) Tel'pukhovskii, in *Voprosy Istorii KPSS*, No. 2, 1958, pp. 55-56. *Istoriia KPSS*, p. 547, says 1,368,000 candidates and 573,000 members were added in 1942.

84. See Shatagin, pp. 31, 132.

85. Shatagin, p. 147; a contemporary source, "Zadachi partiino-organizatsionnoi raboty" (Tasks of Party-organizational work), PS, No. 19, 1943, p. 4, suggests a much lower figure ("over" 4,000,000) for Party membership in late 1943.

86. Tel'pukhovskii, in *Voprosy Istorii KPSS*, No. 2, 1958, pp. 55-56.

87. S. S. Kultyshev, "Rost riadov partii v 1945-1950 gg." (The growth of the ranks of the Party in 1945-1950), *Voprosy Istorii KPSS*, No. 2, 1958, p. 60.

88. According to *Istoriia KPSS*, p. 576, 5,319,000 candidates and 3,615,000 members were added to the Party during the war. Since the number of candidates alone exceeds the total wartime entrants still in the Party in 1945 (two-thirds of 5,800,000) by over 1,400,000, this last figure can be taken as the minimum attrition of wartime entrants. As some of the members may have entered without passing through the candidate stage, the actual total (and consequently the attrition of wartime entrants) is probably higher.

89. Shliapin *et al.*, p. 48.

90. *Ibid.;* Tel'pukhovskii, in *Voprosy Istorii KPSS*, No. 2, 1958, p. 40.

91. Dmitriev, p. 4.

92. J. Armstrong, *Elite*, p. 127.

93. Aleksei F. Fedorov, *The Underground Committee Carries On* (Moscow: Foreign Languages Publishing House, 1952), p. 50. "Although I did not like the colonel's manner, I had no choice." This sentence is omitted in later Russian editions of the book.

94. Perhaps the best portrayal of popular attitudes in the Soviet Union at this time is contained in Werth, *Stalingrad.*

95. *Ibid.*, p. 422.

96. *Ibid.*, p. 168.

97. P, March 2, 1942.

98. Ivan Kozlov, *V Krymskom Podpol'e: Vospominaniia* (In the Crimean Underground: A memoir) (Moscow: Sovetskoi Pisatel', 1947), pp. 69-70.

99. J. Armstrong, *Elite*, pp. 133-134; cf. P, February 18, 1943, and March 17, 1943, on similar situations in Smolensk and Orel.

100. Lt. Col. K. Seleznev, "Rabota politorganov deistvuiushchei armii sredi naseleniia" (The work of the political organs of the active army among the population), PS, No. 7-8, 1944, pp. 38-41.

101. Boris Meissner, "Führungswechsel in der Sowjetunion," OE, V (1955), 136.

CHAPTER XI DEFENSE OF THE RUSSIAN FATHERLAND

1. See especially John Shelton Curtiss, *The Russian Church and the Soviet State* (Boston: Little, Brown & Co., 1953), Chapter XV.

2. Cf. Vladimir Hawryluk, "La Mortalité des Généraux en URSS de 1956 à 1958," E&O, No. 214, April 16-30, 1959, p. 14, for the conclusion that eighty-two of eighty-five generals dying during 1956-58 were Russian or Ukrainian by name.

3. On the prevalence of the Russian military tradition see Garthoff, *Soviet Military Doctrine*, pp. 48, 51.

4. V. Andreev, *Narodnaia Voina: Zapiski Partizana* (The people's war: Sketches of a partisan) (Moscow: Gosudarstvennoe Izdatel'stvo Khudozhestvennoi Literatury, 1952), p. 26.

5. Cf. Garthoff, *Soviet Military Doctrine,* pp. 227-228.
6. Werth, *Stalingrad,* pp. 83-84, 135; Alexander Kaempfe, "Konstantin Simonow, Dichter und Propagandist," OE, IV, 354-358.
7. P. Wieden, "Zveryni oblik gitlerovskoi molodezhi" (The bestial aspect of the Hitler Youth), KI, No. 8, 1941, p. 13.
8. *O Velikoi Otechestvennoi Voine,* p. 46 (*Great Patriotic War,* p. 44).
9. *O Velikoi Otechestvennoi Voine,* p. 120 (*Great Patriotic War,* p. 101).
10. "O stat'e Engel'sa 'Vneshniaia politika russkogo tsarizma,'" B, No. 9, 1941, pp. 1-5.
11. Black, pp. 293-294.
12. Text of the speech in B, No. 2, 1942, pp. 7-17; quotation on p. 10.
13. Text of the address in B, No. 10, 1945, pp. 3-4.
14. Cf. J. Armstrong, *Elite,* p. 136; Oleg Anisimov, *The German Occupation in Northern Russia during World War II: Political and Administrative Aspects* (New York: Research Program on the U.S.S.R., 1954) (mimeographed), pp. 13-14.
15. George Fischer, *Soviet Opposition to Hitler: A Case Study in World War II* (Cambridge, Mass.: Harvard University Press, 1952), pp. 59-60.
16. *Ibid.,* pp. 48-49, 81; J. Armstrong, *Ukrainian Nationalism,* pp. 168, 179-184.
17. See Chapter VI, p. 85.
18. Louise E. Luke, "Marxian Women: Soviet Variants," in Simmons, p. 94.
19. Chambre, *Marxisme,* p. 401.
20. *Ibid.,* pp. 282-284; *O Velikoi Otechestvennoi Voine,* p. 12 (*Great Patriotic War,* p. 12).
21. See Chapter VI, p. 78.
22. Julian Towster, *Political Power in the U.S.S.R.* (New York: Oxford University Press, 1948), p. 294.
23. Leo Yaresh, "The Role of the Individual in History," in Black, p. 97.
24. *Rol' lichnosti i narodnykh mass v istorii* (The role of personality and of the popular masses in history) (Moscow: Izdatel'stvo "Pravda," 1946), pp. 38-40.
25. "O panslavizme (istoricheskaia spravka)" (On Panslavism [an historical reference]), B, No. 10, 1940, pp. 85-89.
26. Emelian Iaroslavskii, "Bor'ba slavianskikh narodov protiv germanskogo fashizma" (The struggle of the Slavic peoples against German fascism), B, No. 13, 1941, pp. 10-22; P, August 11, 1941; P, August 12, 1941; Iz, February 4, 1943; P, May 10, 1943; P, October 20, 1943; "Obrashchenie vtorogo Vseslavianskogo mitinga" (Appeal of the Second All-Slav Meeting), *Kommunisticheskii Internatsional,* No. 3-4, 1942, pp. 10-13.
27. Khrushchev's secret speech, pp. S44-S45.
28. See J. Armstrong, *Ukrainain Nationalism.*
29. J. Armstrong, *Elite,* pp. 136-137.
30. Suprunenko, p. 254.
31. P, December 26, 1942.
32. J. Armstrong, *Elite,* p. 133.
33. Barghoorn, *Nationalism,* p. 61.

34. See Khrushchev's speech reported in P, March 16, 1944.
35. Kozlov, p. 76.
36. *Ibid.*, p. 146.
37. See A. Umanskii's strong statement in Werth, *Stalingrad*, p. 155.
38. V. Kirilik, "Iz istorii antibol'shevistskoi bor'by na Kavkaze" (From the history of the anti-Bolshevik struggle in the Caucasus), *Posev*, No. 35, 1950, pp. 2-6.
39. Ivan V. Davydov, "Partiinaia Organizatsiia Kabardinskoi ASSR v Period Velikoi Otechestvennoi Voiny, 1941-45 gg." (The Party organization of the Kabardian ASSR in the period of the Great Patriotic War, 1941-45) (unpublished dissertation, Rostov University, Rostov-on-the-Don, 1954), pp. 38-39; *Bakinskii Rabochii,* February 25, 1943.
40. *Ibid.;* A. Gindin, "Nekotorye voprosy ideinoi zhizni partorganizatsii" (Some questions of the idea-life of the Party organization), PS, No. 17-18, 1943, p. 12; Shatagin, p. 189.
41. See Article "Lew Sacharowitsch Mechlis," *Ost-Probleme,* III (1951), 53-54; Boris Nicolaevsky, "Na komandnykh vysotakh Kremlia" (On the commanding heights of the Kremlin), SV, No. 6, 1946, pp. 142-146.
42. A. Azizian, "Narody Kavkaza nikogda ne budut rabami" (The peoples of the Caucasus will never be slaves), B, No. 15, 1942, p. 28.
43. "Pochetnye stariki Checheno-Ingushetii" (Honorary elders of Checheno-Ingushia), PS, No. 2, 1943, p. 47.
44. Davydov dissertation, pp. 112, 157.
45. On the times at which the nationalities were deported and their autonomous areas abolished see Khrushchev's secret speech, p. S44; Walter Kolarz, "Die Rehabilitierung der liquidierten Sowjetvölker," OE, VII, 414-415.
46. Dubicki, pp. 43-44.
47. V. Gafurov, "O vospitanie kadrov" (On the education of cadres), PS, No. 17-18, 1943, p. 17.
48. *O Partiinoi i Sovetskoi Pechati: Sbornik Dokumentov* (On the Party and the Soviet press: A collection of documents) (Moscow: Izdatel'stvo "Pravda," 1954), pp. 526-529. Hereafter cited as *O . . . Pechati.*
49. Fedorov, *Underground,* pp. 66-67; Kozlov, p. 11; G. Lin'kov, *Voina v Tylu Vraga* (War in the rear of the enemy) (Moscow: Gosudarstvennoe Izdatel'stvo Khudozhestvennoi Literatury, 1951), p. 351.
50. Solomon M. Schwarz, *The Jews in the Soviet Union* (Syracuse, N.Y.: Syracuse University Press, 1951), p. 321 ff.
51. Werth, *Moscow,* p. 177; Vladimir Petrov, *My Retreat from Russia* (New Haven: Yale University Press, 1950), pp. 42-43; Towster, p. 357.
52. Igor Gouzenko, *The Iron Curtain* (New York: E. P. Dutton & Co., 1948), p. 158; S. Schwarz, p. 348.
53. Deutscher, p. 539.
54. Bernard J. Choseed, "Jews in Soviet Literature," in Simmons, pp. 143-145.
55. S. Schwarz, p. 347.
56. *O Velikoi Otechestvennoi Voine,* p. 28 (*Great Patriotic War,* p. 27).
57. "Besposhchadno karat' dezorganizatorov tyla" (Ruthlessly punish disorgani-

zers of the rear area), B, No. 14, 1941, p. 10; A. Shpirt, "Sovremennaia voina—voina motorov" (Contemporary war—a war of motors), B. No. 4, 1942, pp. 54-64.

58. See the series of articles in KI, No. 6-7, 1941, and "Gitlerovskaia Germaniia posle tretei voennoi zimy" (Hitlerite Germany after the third war winter), KI, No. 5, 1942, pp. 24-30, purportedly based on letters from German Communists.

59. See especially Frederick C. Barghoorn, *The Soviet Image of the United States* (New York: Harcourt, Brace & Co., 1950), Chapter III.

60. Alfred Burmeister, *Dissolution and Aftermath of the Comintern: Experiences and Observations, 1937-1947* (New York: Research Program on the U.S.S.R., 1955) (mimeographed), pp. 14-16; Alfred Burmeister, "Rehabilitierte NKVD-Opfer," *Ost-Probleme,* VII (1955), 1225-1230; Castro Delgado, p. 165.

61. Branko Lazitch, "La Dissolution du Comintern et la Dissolution du Kominform" E&O, No. 135, 1955, pp. 1-6.

62. Cf. J. Hernández, p. 348, for speculations by a major foreign Communist leader who discussed dissolution of the Comintern with Dimitrov and Manuil'skii.

63. The decision is printed in KI, No. 5-6, 1943, pp. 8-10.

64. Leonhard, *Child,* p. 226.

65. J. Hernández, p. 348.

66. "B. L.," "Rudolf Slansky," *Ost-Probleme,* III (1951), 1529-1530; L. Lesny, "Der Slansky-Prozess," OE, III (1953), 2.

67. Joseph Wechsberg, "My Schoolmate Germinder—Rise and Fall of A Communist Leader," *Collier's,* February 7, 1953, p. 20.

68. Burmeister, *Dissolution,* pp. 17-25; Leonhard, *Child,* pp. 177-183, 242-249.

69. Cf. Leonhard, *Child,* p. 252; Burmeister, *Dissolution,* p. 25; J. Hernández, p. 342; Castro Delgado, p. 227; also p. 212 for Beria's role in the formation of the Jewish Anti-Fascist Committee.

CHAPTER XII THE PARTISANS AND THE ADVANCE INTO EAST EUROPE

1. "Partizanskaia bor'ba v tylu ispanskikh miatezhnikov" (The partisan struggle in the rear of the Spanish rebels), *Mirovoe Khoziaistvo i Mirovaia Politika,* No. 10, 1938, pp. 124-126.

2. Marklen T. Meshcheriakov, "Kommunisticheskaia Partiia Ispanii v Bor'be za Demokraticheskie Svobody i Natsional'nuiu Nezavisimost' Ispanii (1936-1939 gg.)" (The Communist Party of Spain in the struggle for democratic freedoms and national independence of Spain [1936-1939]) (unpublished dissertation, Lenin Pedagogical Institute, Moscow, 1953), pp. 207-208.

3. See, for example, P, July 6, 1938; "Obzor voennykh deistvii v Kitae" (Review of military activity in China), KI, No. 6, 1939, pp. 87-93.

4. A. Kolan, "Partizanskaia voina v okkupirovannykh raionakh Kitaia" (The partisan war in the occupied regions of China), KI, No. 6, 1940, pp. 60-72. The article asserts that the partisans restored the authority of the Chinese Nationalist government, but in view of the Chinese Communist tactic of maintaining the Popular Front at that time, the assertion is not convincing. The report also makes it clear that *military* operations in the partisan areas were directed by the Communist armies.

5. *O Velikoi Otechestvennoi Voine*, p. 15 (*Great Patriotic War*, p. 15).

6. Fedorov, *Underground*, p. 16.

7. H 14/14. Oberkommando des Heeres, Generalstab des Heeres. Abteilung Fremde Heere Ost, *Nachrichten über Bandenkrieg*, No. 1, May 3, 1943, p. 2. Cf., however, EAP-3a-11/2, Armee Oberkommando 16, Ic, August 18, 1941 (interrogation of NKVD Lieutenant Aleksandr Zhigunov) (English translation), p. 119, for an assertion that the NKVD did not begin partisan work until after the start of the war. Very recent Soviet treatments, such as P. P. Andreev, pp. 43-44, and P. P. Lipilo, *KPB, Organizator i Rukovoditel' Partizanskogo Dvizheniia v Belorussii v Gody Velikoi Otechestvennoi Voiny* (The Communist Party of Belorussia, organizer and director of the partisan movement in Belorussia in the years of the Great Patriotic War) (Minsk: Gosudarstvennoe Izdatel'stvo BSSR, 1959), pp. 32, 36-37, refer only to Party directives for partisan organization issued shortly after the beginning of the war. But the generally bland approach of these works (particularly the complete omission of mention of the unquestionably important role of the NKVD in the partisan movement) does not inspire confidence in their accuracy in discussing the origins of the partisan movement. Moreover, they confirm the rapidity with which the partisan groups were started (especially Lipilo, p. 37), almost incredible unless some advance planning had been done.

8. *Soviet Military Intelligence: Two Sketches* (in Russian) (New York: Research Program on the U.S.S.R., 1952) (mimeographed), p. 6; NOKW 1519 (Report of Feldpolizeidirektor in area of Sicherungsdivision 494, WB 1768A, November 5, 1941).

9. Fedorov, *Underground*, pp. 19, 22-26; EAP-3a-11/2 (Zhigunov interrogation), p. 119.

10. Fedorov, *Underground*, p. 16; J. Armstrong, *Elite*, p. 129.

11. Suprunenko, p. 41.

12. NOKW 1519; J. Armstrong, *Elite*, p. 129.

13. J. Armstrong, *Elite*, p. 130.

14. Kozlov, pp. 77, 90, 324.

15. Lin'kov, p. 74.

16. J. Armstrong, *Ukrainian Nationalism*, pp. 118-119.

17. EAP-3a-11/2 (Zhigunov interrogation), p. 119; cf. Peter Vershigora, *Liudi s chistoi sovest'iu* (People with clean consciences) 1st and 2nd book (Moscow: Moskovskii Rabochii, 1946), p. 390; V. Andreev, pp. 210-211; Fedorov, *Underground*, p. 364.

18. Lavrentii Tsanava, *Vsenarodnaia Partizanskaia Voina v Belorussii Protiv Fashistskikh Zakhvatchikov* (The partisan war of the whole people in

Belorussia against the Fascist aggressors) 2 vols. (Minsk: Gosudarstvennoe Izdatel'stvo BSSR, Redaktsiia Politicheskoi Literatury, 1949, 51), II, 104; Tippelskirch, pp. 210-214.

19. H 14/14, *Nachrichten über Bandenkrieg*, No. 1, May 3, 1943, pp. 4-5.

20. Tsanava, II, 94; V. Andreev, pp. 289, 328.

21. H 14/14, *Nachrichten über Bandenkrieg*, No. 1, May 3, 1943, p. 5.

22. Dmitrii Medvedev, *Sil'nye dukhom* (The strong in spirit) (Moscow: Voennoe Izdatel'stvo Voennogo Ministerstva Soiuza S.S.R., 1951), p. 240.

23. H 14/14, *Nachrichten über Bandenkrieg*, No. 1, May 3, 1943, p. 2.

24. See H 14/14 for various documents (captured by the Germans) showing that Ponomarenko actually signed the orders to the partisan units.

25. B. S. Tel'pukhovskii, "Kommunisticheskaia partiia—vdokhnovitel' i organizator pobeda sovetskogo naroda v velikoi otechestvennoi voine" (The Communist Party—inspiration and organizer of the victory of the Soviet people in the Great Patriotic War), *Voprosy Istorii KPSS*, No. 2, 1958, p. 40.

26. See Aleksei F. Fedorov, *Podpol'nyi obkom deistvuet* (The Underground Committee carries on) (enlarged ed.) (Moscow: Izdatel'stvo VLKSM "Molodaia Gvardiia," 1954), pp. 511-512.

27. H 14/14, *Nachrichten über Bandenkrieg*, No. 1, May 3, 1943, Anlage 2.

28. Vershigora, pp. 42, 49.

29. Cf. Suprunenko, p. 200; N. Khokhlov, "Pravo na sovest'" (The right to conscience), *Posev*, No. 31, 1957, pp. 9-10; Moreno Hernández, p. 70. Eitingon had, apparently, an important role in controlling the NKVD activities outside the USSR prior to 1941.

30. Fedorov, *Podpol'nyi obkom*, pp. 320, 392; Vershigora, p. 187; Lin'kov, pp. 100, 377-378, 406, 417-418; V. Andreev, pp. 85, 98, 182, 230; Tsanava, I, 129; cf. D. Karov, *Partisanskoe Dvizhenie v SSSR v 1941-1945 gg.* (The partisan movement in the USSR in 1941-1945) (Munich: Institute for the Study of the USSR, 1954), who, however, exaggerates the spontaneity and disorganization of the early partisan movement.

31. Shatagin, p. 151.

32. J. Armstrong, *Elite*, p. 131.

33. T. Kiselev, "40 let kommunisticheskoi partii Belorussii" (Forty years of the Communist Party of Belorussia), PZh, No. 23, 1958, pp. 8-14; Shatagin also accepts this figure (p. 164).

34. Fedorov, *Podpol'nyi obkom*, p. 383; Lin'kov, p. 400; Sidor Kovpak, *Ot Putivlia do Karpat* (From Putivl' to the Carpathians) (Moscow: Gosudarstvennoe Izdatel'stvo Detskoi Literatury, 1945), p. 34.

35. Lin'kov, p. 92.

36. *Ibid.*, p. 111.

37. V. Andreev, p. 197; Mikhail I. Naumov, *Khinel'skie Pokhody* (*Vospominaniia Uchastnika Partizanskogo Dvizheniia na Ukraine, 1941-1942 gg.*) (The Khinel' Campaign [Remembrances of a participant of the partisan movement in the Ukraine, 1941-1942]) (Moscow: Voenizdat, 1954), p. 395.

38. J. Armstrong, *Ukrainian Nationalism*, pp. 146-147; Vershigora, pp. 282, 295, 395; I. I. Slyn'ko, "Boiovyi partizans'kyi reid pid Kyïv (1943 r.) (The

military partisan raid toward Kiev [1943]), *Ukraïns'kyi Istorychnyi Zhurnal*, No. 4, 1958, pp. 52-63.

39. J. Armstrong, *Ukrainian Nationalism*, pp. 151-153.
40. *Ibid.*, p. 148, note 45.
41. Vershigora, p. 237; Tsanava, II, 918; Edward J. Rozek, *Allied Wartime Diplomacy: A Pattern in Poland* (New York: John Wiley & Sons, Inc., 1958), p. 166.
42. Lin'kov, p. 392; Tsanava, I, 199.
43. Barghoorn, *Nationalism*, p. 59.
44. Churchill, *The Hinge of Fate*, p. 480.
45. Z. Nejedlj, "Nemetskii fashizm—zakliatyi vrag slavian" (German Fascism —the fiercest foe of the Slavs), KI, No. 8, 1941, p. 54; L. Wolski, "Tri goda gitlerovskogo gospodstva v Pol'she" (Three years of Hitlerite rule in Poland), KI, No. 8-9, 1942, p. 49.
46. A. Iur'ev, "O natsional'no-osvoboditel'noi bor'be protiv okkupantov" (On the national-liberation struggle against the occupiers) *Voina i Rabochii Klass*, No. 5, 1943, pp. 5-12.
47. D. Anishev, "Pol'skii narod na puti k svobode i nezavisimosti" (The Polish people on the road to freedom and independence), B, No. 13-14, 1944, p. 51.
48. Zbigniew K. Brzezinski, *The Soviet Bloc: Unity and Conflict* (Cambridge, Mass.: Harvard University Press, 1960), p. 46.
49. "Privetstvie zashchitnikam Stalingrada ot Narodnoi Gvardii Pol'shi" (Greetings to the defenders of Stalingrad from the National Guard of Poland), KI, No. 10-11, 1942, p. 82.
50. Lin'kov, p. 521.
51. Naumov, p. 399.
52. P. P. Petrov and L. M. Subotskii, *Partizanskie Byli* (Partisan Accounts) (Moscow: Voennoe Izdatel'stvo Ministerstva Oborony Soiuza SSR, 1958), p. 256.
53. Milos Skala, "Novyi etap natsional'no-osvoboditel'noi bor'by cheskskogo naroda" (The new stage of the national-liberation struggle of the Czech people), KI, No. 1-2, 1942, pp. 61-64. Cf. Reale, p. 97; see Paul E. Zinner, "The Strategy and Tactics of the Czechoslovak Communist Party" (Ph.D. thesis, Department of Government, Harvard University, 1953), p. 66, on the weakness of the Communist underground in Bohemia and Moravia.
54. J. Armstrong, *Elite*, pp. 108-110; J. Armstrong, *Ukrainian Nationalism*, p. 176; V. M. Mazilo, "Z istorii komunistychnoï partii Zakarpats'koï Ukraïny (1944-1946 rr.)" (On the history of the Communist Party of Transcarpathian Ukraine [1944-1946]), *Ukraïns'kyi Istorychnyi Zhurnal*, No. 3, 1958, pp. 96-108.
55. D. Karov, "The Future Ambassador to Bonn," *Bulletin*, No. 2, 1955, pp. 14-15; cf. V. Andreev, p. 327.
56. *Rudé Pravo*, November 21, 1952; "B. L.," "Rudolf Slansky," *Ost-Probleme*, III (1951), 1529-1530; L. Lesny, "Der Slansky-Prozess," OE, III (1953), 2; Petrov and Subotskii, p. 541.

57. Petrov and Subotskii, pp. 541-543.
58. Jozef Lettrich, *History of Modern Slovakia* (New York: Frederick A. Praeger, 1955), pp. 202-215.
59. See *ibid.*, pp. 218-219, 230, and Petrov and Subotskii, pp. 549-557. Peter A. Toma, "Soviet Strategy in the Slovak Uprising of 1944," *Journal of Central European Affairs*, XIX (1959), 295, note 19, claims that Šverma said that a partisan war was the most useful form for promoting Communism.
60. Zinner thesis, pp. 256-257.
61. However, two Rumanian divisions, probably composed for the most part of prisoners of war, were formed in the USSR, "F. E. G.," "Emil Bodnaras," OE, V (1955), 447.
62. Petrov and Subotskii, p. 258; Dezsö Nemes, *Osvobozhdenie Vengrii* (The Liberation of Hungary) (Moscow: Izdatel'stvo Inostrannoi Literatury, 1957), p. 129.
63. Nemes, pp. 129-132; cf. Imre Kovaćs, *Im Schatten der Sowjets* (Zurich: Thomas Verlag, 1948), pp. 82-84, 171.
64. Speech of E. Kardelj to the First Cominform Meeting, in FLP, No. 1, 1947.
65. Of the many analyses of the development of the Yugoslav partisans and their relations to the Chetniks see especially Stephen Clissold, *Whirlwind* (New York: Philosophical Library, 1949), one of the earliest and still one of the best. Franz Borkenau (pp. 358 ff.), basing his analysis almost entirely on materials dealing with the Balkan and the West European Communists, came to much the same conclusions concerning the real purpose of the partisans which I have presented in this chapter. Borkenau's accomplishment is the more striking when one considers that he was apparently very little acquainted with Soviet materials on the partisan movement within the USSR, and lacked Reale's revealing account of the arguments of Yugoslav leaders at the first Cominform meeting.
66. Reale, pp. 112-113.
67. Kardelj, in FLP, No. 1, 1947.
68. I. Vlasov, "Molodezh' Iugoslavii v natsional'no-osvoboditel'noi voine" (The Youth of Yugoslavia in the national-liberation war), KI, No. 8-9, 1942, p. 53.
69. "Partizanskaia voina v Iugoslavii" (The partisan war in Yugoslavia), B, No. 14, 1942, pp. 42-43.
70. H 14/14, *Nachrichten über Bandenkrieg*, No. 2, June 6, 1943, Anlage 1.
71. V. Kruzhkov, "Pod znakom novykh pobed Krasnoi Armii" (Under the sign of the new victories of the Red Army), B, No. 15-16, 1943, p. 63.
72. McNeill, p. 145.
73. *Ibid.*; Christopher M. Woodhouse, *Apple of Discord: A Survey of Recent Greek Politics in Their International Setting* (London: Hutchinson & Co. Ltd. [n.d.]), pp. 64, 112; I. V. Ganevich, "Pro uchast' bolgars'kykh trudiashchykh u natsional'no-vyzvol'nyi borot'by Iugoslavs'koho narodu (1941-versen' 1944r.) (On the participation of the Bulgarian toilers in the national-liberation struggle of the Yugoslav people [1941-September 1944]), *Ukraïns'kyi Istorychnyi Zhurnal*, No. 2, 1958, p. 97.

74. Reale, pp. 111, 137.
75. Woodhouse, p. 199.
76. Cf. Ganevich, in *Ukraïns'kyi Istorychnyi Zhurnal,* No. 2, 1958, pp. 94-103; L. B. Valev, *Iz Istorii Otechestvennogo Fronta Bolgarii (Iiul' 1942—Sentiabr' 1944 g.)* (From the history of the Fatherland Front of Bulgaria) (Moscow: Izdatel'stvo Akademii Nauk SSSR, 1950), pp. 62-63.
77. I. Boitsov, "Vydvizhenie i rost kadrov v gody voiny (Assignment and growth of cadres in the years of war)," PS, No. 11, 1945, p. 35; cf. A. Bormotov, "V raione, osvobozhdonnom ot nemetskikh okkupantov" (In a raion freed from the German occupiers), PS, No. 8, 1942, pp. 26-30; Kozlov, pp. 69-70.
78. Tsanava, II, 519.
79. J. Armstrong, *Elite,* pp. 131-132.
80. *Istoriia Sovetskogo Obshchestva v Vospominaniiakh Sovremennikov, 1917-1957* (The history of Soviet society in the remembrances of contemporaries, 1917-1957) (Moscow: Izdatel'stvo Moskovskogo Universiteta, 1958), pp. 261-290.
81. See the introduction in Petrov and Subotskii, pp. 3-4.

CHAPTER XIII THE "ZHDANOVSHCHINA"

1. "Ob ideino-politicheskoi rabote partiinykh organizatsii v sovremennykh usloviiakh" (On the idea-political work of the Party organizations in contemporary conditions), B, No. 17-18, 1945, pp. 1-10.
2. Valentina A. Bondarenko, "Bor'ba Kommunisticheskoi Partii Sovetskogo Soiuza za Povyshenie Politicheskoi Bditel'nosti Sovetskogo Naroda v Poslevoennyi Period" (The struggle of the Communist Party of the Soviet Union for heightening the political vigilance of the Soviet people in the postwar period) (unpublished dissertation, Leningrad University, 1955), pp. 62, 66.
3. Cf. *ibid.,* pp. 60-62, for an interesting recent Soviet analysis of these factors.
4. *Pravda Ukrainy,* September 9, 1945.
5. Bondarenko dissertation, p. 188.
6. See G. Doberauer, "Soviet Political Amnesties in Practice," *Bulletin,* III (1956), No. 6, pp. 27-28; also "Resultaty pravil'noi politiki partii (Tsifry i fakti)" (Results of the correct policy of the Party [figures and facts]), PZh, No. 13, 1957, p. 33, on the amnesty in 1955 for soldiers imprisoned for surrendering to the Germans.
7. P, August 2, 1946; P, January 17, 1947; Vladimir D. Samarin, *Civilian Life under the German Occupation, 1942-1944* (in Russian) (New York: Research Program on the U.S.S.R., 1954) (mimeographed), p. 74.
8. I. T. Pinegin, "Rabota KP Ukrainy po Osushchestvleniiu Reshenii Partii o Podbore, Rasstanovke i Vospitanii Rukovodiashchikh Partiinykh i Sovetskikh Kadrov v Poslevoennyi Period (1946-1955 gg.)" (The work of the Communist Party of the Ukraine in carrying out the decisions of the Party concerning the selection, assignment, and training of directing Party and Soviet

cadres in the postwar period [1946-1955]) (unpublished dissertation, Academy of Social Sciences, Moscow, 1955), p. 58.

9. J. Armstrong, *Elite*, p. 135.
10. S. S. Kultyshev, "Rost riadov partii v 1945-1950 gg." (The growth of the ranks of the Party in 1945-1950), *Voprosy Istorii KPSS*, No. 2, 1958, p. 62.
11. M. Shamberg, "Nekotorye voprosy vnutripartiinoi raboty" (Some questions of internal Party work), PS, No. 4, 1946, p. 28.
12. "Povyshat' rol' raikomov kak organov politicheskogo rukovodstva" (Heighten the role of the raikoms as organs of political direction), PZh, No. 5, 1948, pp. 20-27.
13. Shatagin, p. 174.
14. Brzezinski, *Purge*, pp. 139-140.
15. Vasilii G. Tolkachev, "Rabota Kommunisticheskoi Partii po Podboru, Rasstanovke i Vospitaniiu Rukovodashchikh Partiinykh Kadrov v Poslevoennyi Period (1945-1950 gg.) (na materialakh Kazakhstana)" (The work of the Communist Party in selection, distribution, and training directing Party cadres in the postwar period [1945-1950] [from Kazakhstan materials]) (unpublished dissertation, Kazakh branch of the Institute of Marxism-Leninism, Institute of History of the Party in the Central Committee of the Communist Party of Kazakhstan, Alma Ata, 1956), p. 128.
16. O . . . *Pechati*, pp. 529-540.
17. Ernest H. Swayze, "Soviet Literary Politics, 1946-1956" (unpublished thesis, Harvard University, 1958), pp. 54-55.
18. A. Egolin, "Za vysokuiu ideinost' sovetskoi literatury" (For a high idea-content of Soviet literature), B, No. 10-11, 1944, pp. 39-49.
19. N. Kulikovich, *Sovetskaia Opera na Sluzhbe Partii i Pravitel'stva* (The Soviet opera in the service of the Party and the government) (Munich: Institute for the Study of the USSR, 1955) (mimeographed), p. 34.
20. "O nedostatkakh i oshibkakh v osveshchenii istorii nemetskoi filosofii kontsa XVIII i nachala XIX vv." (On deficiencies and mistakes in the elucidation of the history of German philosophy at the end of the eighteenth and the beginning of the nineteenth centuries), B, No. 7-8, 1944, pp. 15-19; cf. Wetter, p. 219.
21. Boris Nicolaevsky, "Two Soviet Scandals," *The New Leader* (October 13, 1958) XLI, 8-10.
22. Deutscher, p. 539.
23. Meissner, *Umbruch*, p. 23; Boris Nicolaevsky, "Na komandnykh vysotakh Kremlia" (On the commanding heights of the Kremlin), SV, No. 6, 1946, pp. 142-146; N. Gradoboev, "Liudi v Kremle" (People in the Kremlin), *Posev*, No. 10, 1948, pp. 2-5; No. 13, 1948, pp. 2-6; No. 15, 1948, pp. 2-5; No. 18-19, 1948, pp. 3-6; No. 37, 1948, pp. 2-3; see also "L'ordre des préséances au Politbureau soviétique de 1945 à 1952," E&O, No. 19, 1953, pp. 1-5, and "A propos du 'conflit' Jdanov-Malenkov," E&O, No. 92, 1953, pp. 13-14.
24. Boris Nicolaevsky, "Bulganin: Kontury politicheskoi biografii" (Bulganin: contours of a political biography), SV, No. 2-3, 1955, pp. 33-36; Walter

Bedell Smith, *My Three Years in Moscow* (New York: J. B. Lippincott Co., 1950), p. 58.

25. Boris Meissner, "Im Zeichen der Aufrüstung (II)," OE, II (1952), 49.
26. W. Claudius, "In a Soviet Isolator," *St. Anthony's Papers: Soviet Affairs*, No. 1, 1956, p. 141.
27. Boris Meissner, "Poskrebyschew—der Privatsekretär Stalins," OE, I (1951), 45-46.
28. Vladimir Rudolph, "The Execution of Policy, 1945-47," in Robert Slusser (ed.), *Soviet Economic Policy in Postwar Germany: A Collection of Papers by Former Soviet Officials* (New York: Research Program on the U.S.S.R., 1953), p. 41.
29. P, March 20, 1946.
30. P, January 16, 1946.
31. Khrushchev's secret speech, p. S45.
32. P, January 27, 1945; P, January 28, 1945; cf. Hamilton Fish Armstrong, *Tito and Goliath* (New York: The Macmillan Company, 1951), p. 57. The probability of this theory is enhanced by F. R. Kozlov's remarks on the incorrect admission of partisans to the Leningrad Party organization noted in Chapter XVII, p. 236.
33. I am indebted to Boris Nicolaevsky for pointing out this rumor; cf. Gregory Klimov, *The Terror Machine* (New York: Frederick A. Praeger, 1953), pp. 18-19.
34. See P, March 2, 1944; P, April 25, 1945; P, June 6, 1945; P, June 25, 1945.
35. Nicolaevsky, in SV, No. 6, 1946, pp. 142-146.
36. Boris Meissner, "Innenpolitische Entwicklung," OE, IV (1954), 45.
37. *Ibid.;* cf. Vucinich, p. 64.
38. "O rabote zamestitelei direktorov MTS po politicheskoi chasti" (On the work of the deputy directors of the MTS for political affairs), PZh, No. 22, 1947, pp. 61-62.
39. *Vecherniaia Moskva*, November 24, 1947; cf. *Moskovskii Bol'shevik*, November 23, 1947.
40. *Vecherniaia Moskva*, November 24, 1947.
41. P, February 28, 1947.
42. These Union Republic Party plenums are all on which information is available except the Karelo-Finnish (later dissolved) and the Ukrainian (which show similar trends).
43. See J. Armstrong, *Elite*, pp. 99-100, for Ukrainian data, which are most complete; data for other Republics are derived from materials collected by G. J. Svejda.
44. *Pravda Ukrainy*, December 8, 1951; cf. Barghoorn, *Nationalism*, p. 212.
45. Shatagin, p. 175.
46. KPSS, II, 1019-1027.
47. J. Armstrong, *Elite*, p. 34.
48. *Ibid.*, pp. 36-38; Bruno Kalnins, *Der Sowjetische Propagandastaat* (Stockholm: Tidens Förlag, 1956), pp. 45-46; Efim F. Agafonenkov, "Marksistko-

Leninskoe Vospitanie Rukovodiashchikh Partiinykh i Sovetskikh Kadrov v Poslevoennyi Period (1946-1950 gg.)" (Marxist-Leninist training of directing Party and Soviet cadres in the postwar period [1946-1950]) (unpublished dissertation, Academy of Social Sciences, Moscow, 1952), pp. 103-105.

49. Agafonenkov dissertation, p. 114.

50. *Ibid.*, pp. 131-132.

51. J. Armstrong, *Elite*, pp. 38-39. Rigby thesis, p. 168, points out that some important officials secure assignments to Party schools to avoid dismissal for incompetence from their previous posts. I doubt, however, that such officials constitute a significant segment of the student body.

52. The three decrees are contained in *O . . . Pechati*, pp. 564-576. Convenient, though nonliteral, English translations are in *Decisions of the Central Committee, C.P.S.U.(B.) on Literature and Art (1946-1948)* (Moscow: Foreign Languages Publishing House, 1951). Hereafter cited as *Decisions . . . on Literature and Art.*

53. *O . . . Pechati*, p. 565 (*Decisions . . . on Literature and Art*, p. 5).

54. Quoted in "Bor'ba bol'shevistskoi partii za rastsvet sovetskogo iskusstva" (The struggle of the Bolshevik Party for the blossoming of Soviet art), B, No. 6, 1948, p. 7. (In italics in the original.)

55. *O . . . Pechati*, p. 573 (*Decisions . . . on Literature and Art*, pp. 24-25).

56. *O . . . Pechati*, p. 570 (*Decisions . . . on Literature and Art*, p. 15).

57. Klaus Mehnert, "An Moskaus literarischer Front," OE, IV (1954), 345; Swayze thesis, p. 77.

58. *O . . . Pechati*, p. 566 (*Decisions . . . on Literature and Art*, p. 7).

59. B. Leibson, "Sovetskoe gosudarstvo i politicheskoe vospitanie narodov" (The Soviet state and the political education of the peoples), PS, No. 1, 1946, p. 14.

60. Quoted in "Bor'ba bol'shevistskoi partii za rastsvet sovetskogo iskusstva," B, No. 6, 1948, p. 4.

61. *O . . . Pechati*, p. 569 (*Decisions . . . on Literature and Art*, p. 14).

62. P, August 29, 1946.

63. P, September 2, 1946; P, September 26, 1947.

64. See, for example, "Do kintsy vykryty burzhuazno-natsionalistychni konseptsiï Hrushevs'koho i ioho 'shkoly' " (The final unmasking of the bourgeois nationalist conceptions of Hrushevskii and his "school"), *Radians'ka Ukraïna*, September 14, 1946.

65. Cf. Chambre, *Marxisme*, pp. 407-410; Erik Boettcher, "Moskaus Bild der westlichen Wirtschaft—ein Spiegelbild seiner eigenen Probleme und Absichten," OE, VI (1956), 219.

66. I. M. Bochenski, *Der sowjetrussische Dialektische Materialismus* (Bern: A. Francke AG. Verlag, 1950), p. 143.

67. See especially Wetter, pp. 216-218, 296.

68. A. A. Zhdanov, "Vystuplenie na diskussii po knige G. F. Aleksandrova 'Istoriia zapadnoevropeiskoi filosofii' " (Intervention in the discussion on the book of G. F. Aleksandrov, *The History of Western European Philosophy*), PZh, No. 16, 1947, p. 8.

69. *Ibid.*, p. 5. Soviet discussions of the role of philosophy are very complex; generally it is regarded as a combination of *Weltanschauung* and methodology. For a discussion of this matter and its relation to Zhdanov's statement, see Wetter, pp. 293-298.
70. A. A. Zhdanov, in PZh, No. 16, 1947, p. 16.
71. *Ibid.*, p. 13.
72. Wetter, pp. 218-222; Bochenski, p. 58.
73. *O . . . Pechati*, p. 591. (*Decisions . . . on Literature and Art*, p. 33).
74. *O . . . Pechati*, p. 591 (*Decisions . . . on Literature and Art*, p. 33).
75. Jelagin, pp. 328-329.
76. *O . . . Pechati*, p. 590 (*Decisions . . . on Literature and Art*, p. 31).
77. *O . . . Pechati*, p. 590 (*Decisions . . . on Literature and Art*, p. 31).
78. CDSP, X, No. 23, p. 3 (Central Committee decree of May 28, 1958, in P, June 8, 1958).

CHAPTER XIV THE FORWARD LINE IN INTERNATIONAL COMMUNISM

1. Barghoorn, *Image*, pp. 65-66.
2. Major sources for this period of Communist activity in Greece are: Winston Churchill, *The Second World War*, Vol. VI: *Triumph and Tragedy* (Boston: Houghton Mifflin Co., 1953), Chapters 18 and 19; McNeill, pp. 145 ff.; Woodhouse, pp. 112 ff. For excellent summaries see Hugh Seton-Watson, *The East European Revolution* (New York: Frederick A. Praeger, 1956), pp. 318-322, and Borkenau, pp. 429-437.
3. Woodhouse, p. 112.
4. *Ibid.*, pp. 218, 231.
5. Churchill, *Triumph and Tragedy*, p. 495; USSR, Ministerstvo Inostrannykh Del, *Perepiska Predsedatelia Soveta Ministrov SSSR s Presidentami SShA i Prem'er Ministrami Velikobritanii vo Vremia Velikoi Otechestvennoi Voiny, 1941-1945 gg.* (Correspondence of the Chairman of the Council of Ministers of the USSR with the Presidents of the USA and the Prime Ministers of Great Britain during the Great Patriotic War, 1941-1945). 2 vols. (Moscow: Gosudarstvennoe Izdatel'stvo Politicheskoi Literatury, 1957-58), I, 335. Hereafter cited as *Perepiska*. Cf. Borkenau, p. 450.
6. Rossi, *Physiologie*, pp. 195-204.
7. *Ibid.*, p. 441; Angelo Rossi, *La Guerre des Papillons: Quatre Ans de Politique Communiste (1940-1944)* (Paris: Les Iles d'Or, 1954), pp. 228-229; "Narody okkupirovannykh stran usilivaiut bor'bu protiv germanskogo fashizma" (The peoples of the occupied countries strengthen the struggle against German fascism), KI, No. 9, 1941, p. 73.
8. Borkenau, p. 443; P. Vishniakov, "The War and the Resistance Movement in France," *New Times*, No. 23, 1947, pp. 27-28.
9. Borkenau, pp. 448-452; Rossi, *Physiologie*, p. 444.

10. An English translation is contained in U.S. Congress, House Report No. 2244, 84th Congress, 2nd Session, Union Calendar No. 838. *The Communist Conspiracy, Strategy and Tactics of World Communism. Part I; Communism Outside the United States. Section E, The Comintern and the CPUSA* (Washington, D.C.: U.S. Government Printing Office, 1956), pp. 173-189. Hereafter cited as HR 2244. On the importance of the Duclos article see especially David A. Shannon, *The Decline of American Communism* (New York: Harcourt, Brace & Co., 1959), pp. 5 ff.

11. HR 2244, p. 188.

12. *Ibid.*, p. 176.

13. *The Soviet-Yugoslav Dispute: Text of the Published Correspondence* (London: Royal Institute of International Affairs, 1948), p. 51.

14. P, February 10, 1946.

15. Vladimir Rudolph, "The Agencies of Control" and "The Execution of Policy, 1945-47," in Slusser, *Soviet Economic Policy*, pp. 19-34, 37-60; cf. Klimov, p. 148; J. P. Nettl, *The Eastern Zone and Soviet Policy in Germany, 1945-50* (London: Oxford University Press, 1951), pp. 63, 67; Boris Meissner, "Führungswechsel in der Sowjetunion," OE, V (1955), 133.

16. M. Moravski, "Kak byl sozdana Kraeva Rada Narodova" (How the National Home Council was created), *Voina i Rabochii Klass*, No. 12, 1944, pp. 23-26.

17. Rozek, p. 229.

18. For an excellent summary of these developments, see Seton-Watson, pp. 114-118, 171-172, 202-207, 212-214.

19. Ferenc Nagy, *The Struggle Behind the Iron Curtain* (New York: The Macmillan Company, 1948), pp. 148-149; Nicholas Nyárádi, *My Ringside Seat in Moscow* (New York: Thomas Y. Crowell Co., 1952), pp. 10, 266.

20. See Lt. Col. K. Seleznev, "Rabota politorganov deistvuiushchei armii sredi naseleniia" (The work of the political organs of the active army among the population), PS, No. 7-8, 1944, pp. 38-41, for an early admission of the role of the Red Army in spreading propaganda in Rumania. See also Robert W. Ramsey, "Political Indoctrination in the Red Army, 1941-1945: The Concepts of National Defense and Revolutionary Expansion" (unpublished essay, Columbia University, 1953), pp. 39-43.

21. Nyárádi, p. 10.

22. Rozek, pp. 100-101; R. Umiastowski, *Poland, Russia and Great Britain, 1941-1945* (London: Hollis & Carter, 1946), pp. 59-61.

23. Burmeister, *Dissolution*, p. 31.

24. Imre Kovaćs, pp. 131, 271, 283; Nagy, p. 119; Stanisław Mikołajczyk, *The Rape of Poland* (New York: McGraw-Hill Book Co., 1948), p. 233.

25. Nyárádi, p. 56.

26. Zbigniew Stypułkowski, *Invitation to Moscow* (New York: Thames, 1951), p. 325.

27. For the official record of the meeting see FLP, No. 1 and No. 2, 1947; for the much more revealing unofficial record see Reale.

28. P, October 22, 1947, and P, December 9, 1947.

29. Reale, p. 48.
30. FLP, No. 1, 1947.
31. Reale, p. 17.
32. "The Character of a 'Peoples' Democracy,'" *Foreign Affairs*, XVIII (October 1949), 146, 150-151 (translated from *Társadalmi Szemle*, March-April, 1949).
33. Hyde, p. 234. Zinner (thesis, pp. 256-257) doubts that Gottwald was weaker than Slánský.
34. Reale, pp. 103-104.
35. See especially Hubert Ripka, *Czechoslovakia Enslaved* (London: Victor Gollancz Ltd., 1950). A useful summary is contained in Seton-Watson, pp. 187-190.
36. Reale, pp. 34-35; Dedijer, p. 295.
37. *Soviet-Yugoslav Dispute*, pp. 14, 29.
38. P, July 15, 1948.
39. Fitzroy Maclean, *Disputed Barricade: The Life and Times of Josip Broz-Tito, Marshal of Jugoslavia* (London: Jonathan Cape, 1957), p. 206; H. F. Armstrong, pp. 27-28.
40. Adam B. Ulam, *Titoism and the Cominform* (Cambridge, Mass.: Harvard University Press, 1952), p. 76; Dedijer, p. 209.
41. *Soviet-Yugoslav Dispute*, p. 35; H. F. Armstrong, pp. 64-65.
42. J. A. Armstrong, "The Soviet Attitude toward UNESCO," *International Organization*, III (1954), 218-219.
43. Reale, p. 137; Dedijer, pp. 319-320.
44. Dedijer, pp. 304-306; cf. Ulam, pp. 89-95; H. F. Armstrong, p. 67.
45. K. Komarov, "At the Slav Congress in Belgrade," *New Times*, No. 3, 1947, pp. 20-23. "The Slav Movement—a Fighting Unit of the Democratic Camp," FLP, No. 10, 1948, p. 4.
46. P, January 28, 1948.
47. Dedijer, p. 316.
48. *Soviet-Yugoslav Dispute*.
49. FLP, No. 13, 1948, p. 1; cf. Dedijer, p. 356, on Suslov's invitation to Tito to attend a Cominform meeting in the Ukraine. Note also Suslov's major foreign policy speech in P, January 22, 1948.
50. Ernest Bauer, "Die Kominform-Emigration," OE, V (1955), 289-294; cf. P, July 23, 1948; P, September 8, 1948; Ulam, p. 132; H. F. Armstrong, pp. 102-105.
51. FLP, No. 18, 1948, p. 6.
52. H. F. Armstrong, p. 191; Seton-Watson, p. 327; cf. V. Vasil'ev, "Narodno-osvoboditel'naia armiia Gretsii" (The popular liberation army of Greece), PZh, No. 4, 1948, pp. 60-65.
53. FLP, No. 5, 1948, p. 1.
54. "The Struggle for Freedom and Democracy in Greece," FLP, No. 24, 1948, p. 4.
55. H. F. Armstrong, pp. 192-194.

56. H. F. Armstrong, pp. 57-59; Borkenau, pp. 538-540; cf. Paul Barton (pseud.), *Prague à l'heure de Moscou: Analyse d'une démocratie populaire* (Paris: Editions Pierre Horay, 1954), p. 269.

CHAPTER XV DISSENSION IN THE PARTY

1. CSP I, p. 244 (P, January 13, 1953); CSP I, p. 259 (P, April 4, 1953).
2. P, June 10, 1948; cf. N. Gradoboev, "Liudi v Kremle" (People in the Kremlin), *Posev*, No. 18-19, 1948, pp. 3-6, and Boris Nicolaevsky, "Na komandnykh vysotakh Kremlia" (On the commanding heights of the Kremlin), SV, No. 6, 1946, pp. 142-146.
3. See Lazar M. Pistrak, "Georgii Maximilianowitsch Malenkov," *Ost-Probleme*, V (1953), 535-542.
4. Bedell Smith, p. 75.
5. N. Gradoboev, in *Posev*, No. 49, 1948, pp. 4-5; cf. Bedell Smith, p. 57.
6. Khrushchev's secret speech, p. S45; on the dates of Voznesenskii's and Kuznetsov's deaths see BSE (2nd ed.), LI, 60, 168.
7. M. Suslov, "Concerning the Articles by P. Fedoseyev in *Izvestia*, Dec. 12 and 21," CDSP, IV, No. 50, pp. 14-15, (P, December 24, 1952).
8. The most direct evidence on Voznesenskii's relation to Zhdanov is in Vassily Yershov, "Confiscation and Plunder by the Army of Occupation," in Slusser, *Soviet Economic Policy*, pp. 22, 41; but their parallel prominence in 1946-47 provides indirect, though far from conclusive, evidence on this score.
9. BSE (2nd ed.), LI, 60.
10. I. Spiridonov, secretary of Leningrad obkom, "Pod znakom vosstanovleniia leninskikh norm partiinoi zhizni" (Under the sign of revival of Leninist norms of Party life), PZh, No. 2, 1959, p. 21. Spiridonov accuses the "anti-Party group" (See Chapter XXIII) of these misdeeds.
11. Boffa, p. 26.
12. Dedijer, p. 312; *Soviet-Yugoslav Dispute*, p. 40.
13. B. Souvarine, "Confidences d'un Diplomate Communiste," E&O, No. 190, 1958, p. 2.
14. See P, August 15, 1946, which reports that the first secretary of the Crimean obkom, removed for errors, was replaced by N. V. Solov'ev, "recently chairman of the Leningrad oblast soviet." It is extremely unusual for a notice of this kind to give the former post of a new appointee.
15. M. Rodionov, "Tridtsat' let Rossiiskoi Sovetskoi Respubliki" (Thirty years of the Russian Soviet Republic), B, No. 21, 1947, p. 29.
16. NYT, December 26, 1954.
17. Khrushchev's secret speech, p. S46; Report of the Military Collegium of the Supreme Court, CDSP, VI, No. 49, p. 12 (P, December 24, 1954).
18. R. A. Rudenko, "Zadachi dal'neishego ukrepleniia sotsialisticheskoi zakonnosti v svete reshenii XX S"ezda KPSS" (Tasks of the furthermost strengthening

of socialist legality in the light of the decisions of the Twentieth Congress of the CPSU), *Sovetskoe Gosudarstvo i Pravo*, No. 3, 1956, pp. 15-25.

19. N. S. Khrushchev, "Za tesnuiu sviaz' literatury i iskusstva s zhizn'iu naroda" (For a close connection of literature and art with the life of the people), K, No. 12, 1957, p. 20 (CDSP, IX, No. 35, pp. 3-10).

20. See *V Pomoshch' Slushateliam Politshkol* (An aid to the students of political schools) (2nd ed.) (Moscow: Izdatel'stvo "Pravda," 1951), pp. 93-94. Hereafter cited as *V Pomoshch' Slushateliam*.

21. *Plenum Tsentralnogo Komiteta Kommunisticheskoi Partii Sovetskogo Soiuza, 15-19 Dekabria 1958 g.: Stenograficheskii Otchet* (Plenum of the Central Committee of the Communist Party of the Soviet Union, December 15-19, 1958: Stenographic report) (Moscow: Gosudarstvennoe Izdatel'stvo Politicheskoi Literatury, 1958), p. 98. Hereafter cited as *Plenum . . . Dekabria 1958*.

22. Khrushchev's secret speech, pp. S62-S63.

23. *Ibid.*, p. S62.

24. See *Plenum . . . Dekabria 1958*, p. 98, for a remark on the role of the Orgburo in the years immediately preceding Stalin's death.

25. Rigby thesis, p. 152.

26. Zh. Shiakmetov, "Vazhnaia zadacha partiinoi organizatsii Kazakhstana" (An important task of the Party organization of Kazakhstan), PZh, No. 8, 1947, p. 31.

27. E. Andreev, "O rabote s kadrami v ministerstvakh i vedomastvakh" (On work with cadres in ministries and departments), PZh, No. 2, 1946, p. 21.

28. The phrase "end of 1948" is used in Tolkachev dissertation, p. 106, to describe the decree; no Soviet source has ever revealed the exact date or wording of the decree.

29. Report of M. D. Bagirov to the eighteenth Azerbaidzhani Party congress, CDSP, III, No. 24, pp. 3-10 (*Bakinskii Rabochii*, May 26, 1951).

30. J. Armstrong, *Elite*, p. 76.

31. This seems to be Merle Fainsod's judgment (see *How Russia Is Ruled*, p. 174); for a contrary opinion see Meissner, *Umbruch*, p. 21.

32. Based on G. J. Svejda's survey of Union Republic plenums (excluding the Ukrainian and the Karelo-Finnish). Ukrainian data show roughly similar trends, but the role of the Party officials (not strictly comparable because of the great importance of obkom-level officials in the Ukraine) was always dominant.

33. Cf. J. Armstrong, *Elite*, pp. 54-55, 64; Rigby thesis, pp. 181-184.

34. Hodgman, p. 89.

35. *KPSS*, II, 1046.

36. UNRRA European Regional Office, Division of Operational Analysis, *Economic Rehabilitation in the Ukraine: Operational Analysis Papers, No. 39* (London: April, 1947) (mimeographed), pp. 25-30.

37. *Ibid.*, pp. 66-67.

38. H. Schwartz, p. 479.

39. *Radians'ka Ukraïna,* March 9, 1947.
40. *Pravda Ukrainy,* December 27, 1947.
41. N. Alekseev, "Nepravil'nye metody partiinogo rukovodstva (c plenuma Dnepropetrovskogo ogkoma KP [b]U)" (Incorrect methods of Party direction [from the plenum of the Dnepropetrovsk obkom of the KP (b)U]), PZh, No. 23, pp. 50-52.
42. *Direktivy,* III, 105.
43. *Ibid.,* 91-97; Vucinich, pp. 64-65; H. Schwartz, pp. 311-312; Boris Nicolaevsky, "Neuer Feldzug gegen das Dorf," *Ost-Probleme,* III (1951), 390-400.
44. *KPSS,* II, 1045-1054; 1075-1079; 1092-1093; Vucinich, p. 115-116.
45. Vucinich, pp. 124-125.
46. P. Vorotsov, "Sel'skie territorial'nye partiinye organizatsii" (Village Party organizations), PZh, No. 7, 1947, pp. 14 ff.
47. "Kak dolzhna stroit' rabotu sel'skaia territorial'naia partiinaia organizatsiia?" (How must the village territorial Party organization develop its work?), PZh, No. 5, 1947, p. 42.
48. I. Afanas'ev, "Ob ukreplenii pervichnykh partorganizatsii v kolkhozakh" (On the strengthening of the primary Party organizations in the kolkhozes), PS, No. 7-8, 1946, pp. 22-27.
49. Roy D. Laird, *Collective Farming in Russia: A Political Study of the Soviet Kolkhozy* (Lawrence, Kans.: University of Kansas Publications, 1958), p. 124.
50. For a recent scholarly survey of the campaign, see *ibid.,* pp. 123-141; on the contemporary Soviet discussion see especially M. Kraev, "Postoiannaia proizvodstvennaia brigada—osnovnaia forma organizatsii truda v kolkhozakh" (The permanent production brigade—the basic form of organization of labor in the kolkhozes), B, No. 11, 1950, pp. 44-56; letters to the editor of *Pravda* in CDSP, II, No. 10, pp. 14-15 (P, March 2-8, 1950); the article by a brigade leader from Chkalov oblast in CDSP, II, No. 12, pp. 12-14 (Iz, March 19, 1950); and Khrushchev's "On some questions of the further organization and economic strengthening of the collective farms," CDSP, II, No. 17, pp. 3-6 (P, April 25, 1950).
51. Khrushchev, in CDSP, II, No. 17, pp. 3-6 (P, April 25, 1950).
52. H. Schwartz, pp. 312-313.
53. Kraev, in B, No. 11, 1950, pp. 50-56.
54. J. Armstrong, *Elite,* pp. 61-62.
55. *Ibid.*
56. A. Markov, "Work of Party organizations on amalgamated collective farms," CDSP, II, No. 37, p. 26 (P, September 11, 1950).
57. See especially Khrushchev's speech to the Moscow obkom plenum, CDSP, II, No. 52, p. 42 (P, December 25, 1950); L. G. Mel'nikov, Ukrainian first secretary, "Organizational and Economic Consolidation of Amalgamated Collective Farms," CDSP, II, No. 50, pp. 32-35 (P, December 14, 1950); V. Moshchil, deputy director of the administration of village and kolkhoz construction of the Ukrainian council of ministers, "Collective Farm Cities," CDSP, III, No. 3, pp. 33-34 (Iz, January 17, 1951).

58. Dinerstein and Gouré, pp. 134-135.

59. CDSP, III, No. 7, pp. 13-16 (P, March 4, 1951).

60. See, for example, I. A. Benediktov, "Make Use of All Potentialities for New Progress in Soviet Agriculture," CDSP, III, No. 9, pp. 32-33 (*Sotsialisti-cheskoe Zemledelie*, March 3, 1960); cf. Boris Nicolaevsky, "Chruschtchew erlitt eine Niederlage," *Ost-Probleme*, III (1951), pp. 645-649.

61. CDSP, III, No. 7, p. 16.

62. CDSP, III, No. 21, p. 4 (*Kommunist* [Erivan], March 21, 1951).

63. CDSP, III, No. 24, p. 5 (*Bakinskii Rabochii*, May 26, 1951).

64. CSP I, p. 111 (P, October 6, 1952).

CHAPTER XVI   RIGIDITY AT HOME AND ABROAD

1. Swayze thesis, pp. 117-119.

2. *Ibid.*, p. 143.

3. CSP I, p. 115 (P, October 6, 1952).

4. *Ibid.*

5. Swayze thesis, p. 139, considers this to have been the beginning of the campaign to link "bourgeois nationalism" and "cosmopolitanism."

6. "Against Ideological Distortions in Literature," CDSP, III, No. 24, pp. 13-14 (P, July 2, 1951).

7. CDSP, III, No. 25, p. 23 (P, July 13, 1951).

8. Konstantin F. Shteppa, "The 'Lesser Evil' Formula," in Black, p. 110.

9. See for example D. Dzhafarov, "Concerning the Epic 'Dede Korkut,'" CDSP, III, No. 28, p. 15 (P, August 2, 1951). See especially A. Bennigsen, "Les Peuples Musulmans de l'U.R.S.S. et les Soviets," *L'Asie et l'Afrique*, No. 1, 1953, pp. 13-30; No. 2, 1953, pp. 21-32; No. 3, 1953, pp. 15-34.

10. CSP I, p. 144.

11. N. Baltiiskii, "O patriotizme" (On patriotism), *Novoe Vremia*, No. 1, 1945, pp. 3-10.

12. Robert M. Hankin, "Postwar Soviet Ideology and Literary Scholarship," in Simmons, p. 265.

13. "Against the Bourgeois Ideology of Cosmopolitanism," CDSP, I, No. 1, p. 11 (*Voprosy Filosofii*, No. 2, 1948).

14. D. Zaslavskii, "Great Language of Our Epoch," CDSP, I, No. 3, pp. 22-23 (*Literaturnaia Gazeta*, January 1, 1949).

15. Barghoorn, *Nationalism*, pp. 205-206; cf. especially T. Khrennikov, "K novomu pod'emu sovetskoi muzyki" (Toward a new rise of Soviet music), B, No. 3, 1951, pp. 27-35, and "Sovetskaia literatura na novom pod'eme" (Soviet literature in a new rise), B, No. 14, 1951, pp. 1-10.

16. Rozek, pp. 98-101.

17. SV, No. 3-4, 1942, p. 51.

18. "Vozhdi II. Internatsionala, SSSR, i edinyi front" (The leaders of the Second International, the USSR, and the united front), KI, No. 4, 1935, p. 9.

19. S. Mikhoels and I. Fefer, "Poezda v Ameriku" (A trip to America), *Voina i Rabochii Klass*, No. 2, 1944, pp. 27-31; Grigorii Aronson, "Sionizm i Stalinizm" (Zionism and Stalinism), SV, No. 13-14, 1943, p. 161, and "Evreiskaia delegatsiia iz SSSR" (The Jewish delegation from the USSR), SV, No. 15-16, 1943, pp. 187-188; S. Schwarz, p. 204.

20. See "Sturz kommunistischer Parteigrössen in Ungarn," *Neue Zürcher Zeitung*, March 15, 1954 (reprinted in *Ost-Probleme*, VI [1954], 563-565); E. F. Penrose, "Negotiating on Refugees and Displaced Persons, 1946," in Raymond Dennett and Joseph E. Johnson (eds.), *Negotiating with the Russians* (Boston: World Peace Foundation, 1951), pp. 149-150; Arthur Bliss Lane, *I Saw Poland Betrayed* (Indianapolis: Bobbs-Merrill Co., 1948), pp. 252-253; Peter Meyer *et al.*, *The Jews in the Soviet Satellites* (Syracuse, N.Y.: Syracuse University Press, 1953), pp. 458-459, 462.

21. "A Shameful Action," *New Times*, No. 37, 1947, p. 18.

22. See, for example, L. Sedin, "The Arab League," *New Times*, No. 11, 1948, pp. 8-12.

23. J. A. Armstrong, "The Soviet Attitude toward UNESCO," *International Organization*, VIII (1954), 220.

24. L. Lesny, "Der Slansky-Prozess," OE, III (1953), 11-12; cf. Leites and Bernaut, p. 387, who speculate that Moscow intended to make Israel its principal Near Eastern base.

25. S. Mikunis, "The Peoples of Palestine Struggle for National Independence," FLP, No. 18, 1948, p. 5.

26. See "America and Palestine," *New Times*, No. 23, 1948, pp. 18-19, which emphasizes the alleged role of American-Jewish voters in forcing the United States to recognize Israel.

27. P, January 15, 1948.

28. Bernard J. Choseed, "Jews in Soviet Literature," in Simmons, p. 147.

29. I. Răutu, "Mighty Force of Proletarian Internationalism," FLP, No. 5, 1951, pp. 5-6.

30. P. Iudin, "On the 25th Anniversary of J. V. Stalin's Work 'Foundations of Leninism,'" CDSP, I, No. 17, pp. 45-46 (P, April 27, 1949).

31. Rossi, *Drôle de Guerre*, p. 337.

32. "The Character of a 'People's Democracy,'" *Foreign Affairs*, XVIII (October 1949), 147 (translated from József Révai in *Társadalmi Szemle*, March-April, 1949).

33. Ulam, pp. 166-174; H. F. Armstrong, pp. 146-149.

34. "The Swiatlo Story," *News from Behind the Iron Curtain*, IV (1955), No. 3, p. 14; cf. Ulam, pp. 145-159; H. F. Armstrong, 154-156.

35. Ulam, pp. 204-217; H. F. Armstrong, pp. 199-210.

36. For the record of the trial see *László Rajk and His Accomplices Before the People's Court* (Budapest: n.p., 1949).

37. On the general background of the Rajk trial see H. F. Armstrong, pp. 245-255; Ulam, pp. 195-199; "Laszlo Rajk," E&O, No. 181, p. 64.

38. "Rajk rehabilité," E&O, No. 151, 1956, p. 7.

39. H. F. Armstrong, p. 253; cf. Nyárádi, p. 261.

40. Jean Creach, "Repli vers le Glacis," *Le Monde*, December 21, 1950 (partially translated in *Ost-Probleme*, III [1951], 67-71).
41. *Ibid.*
42. Reale, p. 129.
43. Creach, in *Le Monde*, December 21, 1950.
44. "Expose the Provocateurs and Spies," FLP, No. 19, 1949, p. 2; cf. Ignacio Gallego, "Francoites and Titoites—Jackals from the Same Pack," FLP, No. 47, 1950, p. 4.
45. "Expose the Provocateurs and Spies," FLP, No. 19, 1949, p. 2; in fact Tito does seem to have secured release of Spanish veterans from French internment camps, but he did this with the aid of the Comintern during the Nazi-Soviet pact period in order to prepare for a later uprising in Yugoslavia. Clissold, pp. 26-27.
46. Bedřich Brueghel, "Methods of Soviet Domination in Satellite States," *International Affairs*, XXVII (1951), 32-37.
47. "The Swiatlo Story," *News from Behind the Iron Curtain*, IV (1955), No. 3, pp. 4, 22-23; Interview with Lazar Brankov (Yugoslav chargé d'affaires in Budapest tried with Rajk), E&O, No. 203, 1958, pp. 12-14.
48. There may have been, however, a central MVD directory for Southeast Europe. Cf. Interview with Brankov, in E&O, No. 203, 1958, pp. 12-14; Chapter XIV, note 24.
49. "The Swiatlo Story," *News from Behind the Iron Curtain*, IV (1955), No. 3, p. 4.
50. Brueghel, in *International Affairs*, XXVII (1951), 34.
51. See Brzezinski, *Bloc*, p. 96, on Stalin's direct intervention in the Polish Party purge. In Chapter 6 of *Bloc* (which was published after the basic draft of the present volume had been completed) Brzezinski presents a comprehensive interpretation of Soviet control of the satellites during Stalin's lifetime. Brzezinski attributes considerably more importance to ideology as a "source of self-imposed controls" (p. 136) on satellite leaders than I feel is justified, but points out that the ideological factor gradually declined in significance.
52. The notices and part of the speeches are printed in FLP, No. 28, 1949.
53. Ruth Fischer, p. 614, note 5; Barton, p. 54.
54. "Das Netz der Frontorganisationen," *Ost-Probleme*, VI (1954), 1641-1644.
55. *Novoe Vremia*, No. 1, 1945, p. 10.
56. "Das Netz der Frontorganisationen," *Ost-Probleme*, VI (1954), 1650-1652.
57. "Aid to the Greek People" and "Consolidation of the Youth in the Struggle for Peace," FLP, No. 5, 1948, p. 1.
58. See Boris Meissner, *Russland, die Westmächte und Deutschland* (Hamburg: H. H. Nölke Verlag, 1954), pp. 184-185. The term "Partisans of the peace" (Russian *storonniki mira*), sometimes applied to adherents of this movement, is not apparently intended to have any relation to the guerrilla-partisans (Russian *partizany*).
59. "Weltfriedenrat und Kominform," *Ost-Probleme*, III (1951), 289; "Das Netz der Frontorganisationen," *Ost-Probleme*, VI (1954), 1650-1652; "His-

toric Decisions of Great Assembly of Peoples," FLP, No. 9, 1951, p. 1.

60. See especially Canada, Royal Commission to Investigate the Facts Relating to and the Circumstances Surrounding the Communication, by Public Officials and other Persons in Positions of Trust, of Secret and Confidential Information to Agents of a Foreign Power, *The Report of the Royal Commission, June 27, 1946* (Ottawa: Edmond Cloutier, 1946), p. 71.

61. See especially Tang, pp. 63-70; Max Beloff, *Soviet Policy in the Far East, 1944-1951* (London: Oxford University Press, 1953), Chapters II, III; North, Chapter XIII.

62. McLane, p. 175.

63. Eudocio Ravines, *The Yenan Way* (New York: Charles Scribner's Sons, 1951), pp. 148 ff.; González, p. 54; Nyárádi, p. 28.

64. Beloff, *Far East,* pp. 38-41; McLane, pp. 209-217, 230-231.

65. McLane, p. 240.

66. Beloff, *Far East,* p. 36; McLane, pp. 264-265; Howard L. Boorman, "The Sino-Soviet Alliance: The Political Impact," in Howard L. Boorman *et al., Moscow-Peking Axis* (New York: Harper & Bros., 1957), p. 4.

67. "Vozzvanie kompartii Sirii i Livana" (Appeal of the Communist Parties of Syria and Lebanon), KI, No. 7, 1942, p. 66.

68. Beloff, *Far East,* p. 222.

69. *Ibid.,* p. 157; Rodger Swearingen and Paul Langer, *Red Flag in Japan* (Cambridge, Mass.: Harvard University Press, 1952), pp. 73-79.

70. Beloff, *Far East,* pp. 210-211; John Clews, "Führt der Weg nach Paris über Bandung?" *Ost-Probleme,* VII (1955), 637-642.

71. Philip E. Mosely, "The Moscow-Peking Axis in World Politics," in Boorman *et al.,* p. 211; Swearingen and Langer, pp. 240-241.

72. North, pp. 243 ff.; John H. Kautsky, *Moscow and the Communist Party of India* (Cambridge, Mass.: Harvard University Press, 1956), pp. 97-99; cf. Benjamin Schwartz, "Ideology and the Sino-Soviet Alliance," in Boorman *et al.,* pp. 123 ff.

73. See Arnold Klees, "Ethnogenese—eine neue Sowjetwissenschaft," OE, IV (1954), 166-170; and Jindrich Kučera, "Soviet Nationality Policy: the Linguistic Controversy," *Problems of Communism,* III (1954), 24 ff.

74. Kučera, in *Problems of Communism,* III (1954), 24 ff.

75. A. Poskrebyshev and P. Pospelov, *Velikaia Sila Stalinskikh Idei* (The great force of Stalinist ideas) (Moscow: Gospolitizdat, 1951), p. 8.

76. J. V. Stalin, "On Marxism in Linguistics," CDSP, II, No. 21, p. 9 (P, June 20, 1950).

77. Marcuse, pp. 155, 159.

78. J. V. Stalin, "Economic Problems of Socialism in the USSR," CSP I, p. 7 (B, No. 18, 1952, pp. 1-50).

79. CSP I, p. 8.

80. *Ibid.,* p. 7.

81. *Ibid.,* pp. 7-8; Klaus Mehnert, "Über Stalins 'Wirtschaftsprobleme der Sozialismus in der UdSSR,'" OE, II (1952), 406.

82. CDSP, II, No. 21, p. 4.

83. *Ibid.*
84. M. D. Kammari, "J. V. Stalin on Marxism in Linguistics," CDSP, III, No. 3, pp. 11-12 (*Voprosy Filosofii,* No. 2, 1950, pp. 9-30).
85. Arnold Buchholz, "Das Naturwissenschaftlich-ideologische Weltbild der Sowjetunion," OE, VII (1957), 77; Wetter, pp. 480, 486 (but see also p. 388 on the countertendency to extension of the dialectical materialistic concept of matter to the natural sciences).
86. See Wetter, pp. 260-263.
87. See Marcuse, pp. 137 ff., for an interesting interpretation of the role of the dialectic.
88. CDSP, II, No. 21, p. 8.
89. B. Kedrov, "O formakh skachkov v razvitii prirody i obshchestva" (On forms of leaps in the development of nature and society), B, No. 15, 1951, pp. 15-16 (CDSP, III, No. 52, pp. 3-8, 24).
90. CSP I, p. 11.
91. *Ibid.,* p. 14.
92. Chambre, *Marxisme,* p. 469.
93. *Ibid.,* p. 444; but cf. Herman Achminow, "Das gegenwärtige Bild der kommunistichen 'Gesellschaft der Zukunft,'" OE, VII (1957), 783 ff., who regards "Economic Problems" as having simplified and reduced the prerequisites for the transition to Communism. For Stalin's discussion of the prerequisites see CSP I, p. 14.
94. Cf. CDSP, II, No. 21, p. 8, and *Kratkii Kurs,* pp. 291-292 (*Short Course,* p. 305). See also Wetter, p. 255.
95. "Concerning Base and Superstructure," CDSP, II, No. 37, p. 12 (P, October 5, 1950).
96. Chambre, *Marxisme,* p. 437.
97. CSP I, pp. 9, 15; Wetter, p. 265; Chambre, *Marxisme,* p. 472; but cf. Marcuse, p. 106.
98. Cf. Klaus Mehnert, "Neues Licht auf den Fall Vosnessenskij," OE, III (1953), 99-100.

CHAPTER XVII   THE ENIGMA OF THE NINETEENTH CONGRESS

1. Wolin and Slusser, p. 25.
2. Fainsod, *How Russia Is Ruled,* p. 344.
3. For varying versions of the date of this change see NYT, December 25, 1954; and the sources cited in Wolin and Slusser, pp. 56, 382. Abdurakhman Avtorkhanov presents the theory (unique, so far as I can determine) that Abakumov was Stalin's, not Beria's, adherent; consequently, Abakumov's replacement by Ignat'ev (which Avtorkhanov erroneously places at the end of 1950 or the beginning of 1951) was a victory of the Politburo, and particularly Malenkov, over Stalin. Avtorkhanov, *Stalin,* p. 254.

4. See especially NYT, April 17, 1953, April 19, 1953, and September 23, 1953; Boris Meissner, "Georgien," OE, III (1953), 285-289; and "Les crises du parti communiste de la R.S.S. de Géorgie," *Chroniques Etrangères: URSS* (France: Direction de la Documentation), No. 162, 1956, pp. 13-22. Apparently all of these analyses (as well as my own) are based entirely on revelations in the Soviet press, as there is no indication that defectors have provided information on recent events in Georgia. The reconstruction of the events from the Soviet press is greatly complicated by the fact that the Soviet sources tend to attribute all the crimes and shortcomings to every Party official who is discredited at a given time. Since, however, the three analyses listed above (and my own) tend to agree on all the important aspects of the rivalries described in the text, they have at least a measure of probability.

5. *Chroniques Etrangères: URSS*, No. 162, 1956, p. 16.

6. See *Zaria Vostoka*, August 7 and August 23, 1956. Although the suppression in Abkhazia was blamed on Beria, it apparently occurred when Mgeladze was in charge.

7. *Chroniques Etrangères: URSS*, No. 162, 1956, p. 17.

8. CSP I, p. 66 (*Zaria Vostoka*, September 16, 1952).

9. CSP I, p. 62 (*Zaria Vostoka*, September 16, 1952).

10. *Zaria Vostoka*, January 31, 1953.

11. See Khrushchev's secret speech, pp. S46-S47. Khrushchev at that time accused Beria of plotting the "Mingrelian affair" with Stalin, but this accusation is almost certainly false.

12. *Radians'ka Ukraïna*, May 30, 1952.

13. The available record of the Congress, in translation, is in CSP I. The original reports are in the Soviet press for October 1952; contrary to the usual practice, no collected version of the Congress speeches has been published in the USSR.

14. CSP I, pp. 99-106 (P, October 6, 1952).

15. CSP I, pp. 106-114 (P, October 6, 1952).

16. CSP I, pp. 133-139 (P, October 13, 1952).

17. CSP I, p. 242 (P, October 17, 1952). There was also a Bureau of the Presidium (presumably a smaller body), but no information on its membership or activities ever appeared (see CSP I, p. 248—P, March 7, 1953).

18. Khrushchev's secret speech, p. S63.

19. Boris Nicolaevsky, "The Party Men and the Managers," *The New Leader*, July 29, 1957, p. 10. Nicolaevsky (and Schapiro, p. 545) also argues that the article (58, Section 7) of the RSFSR Criminal Code under which Riumin was later tried as perpetrator of the false trial of the physicians is directed against economic sabotage, hence the "technocrats." In fact, however, this section covers a wide range of "counterrevolutionary" acts against government institutions. While all specifically listed are economic, the principle of analogy in Soviet law would make the provision applicable to sabotage of medical institutions.

20. CSP I, pp. 127-132 (P, October 10, 1952).

21. Boris Meissner, "Partei," OE, II (1952), 429.

22. For the list of Central Committee members and candidates, with the posts that they held in 1952, see CSP I, pp. 237-242. Cf. Meissner, in OE, II (1952), 426.

23. CSP I, p. 94 (P, October 9, 1952).

24. As noted in Chapter XIII this generalization refers only to the upper and middle levels, as represented by All-Union and Ukrainian congress delegates (see J. Armstrong, *Elite*, pp. 19-23). At lower levels, including delegates to the smaller Union Republic congresses, younger men predominated (*ibid.*, p. 22, and Rigby thesis, p. 101).

25. See especially "Observer," "Krimskoe delo" (The Crimean Affair), SV, No. 5, 1957, pp. 97-100, based primarily on Khrushchev's revelation to a Canadian Communist and excerpts from the latter's account in *The New Leader*, September 14, 1959, p. 9 (special issue, "Jews in the Soviet Union"). On the earlier background see Bernkhard Terner, "Vstrecha v Lagere s Bergel'sonom i Feferom" (A meeting in a concentration camp with Bergel'son and Fefer), SV, No. 6, 1957, pp. 121-122.

26. Barton, pp. 255 ff.; Ernst Halperin, *The Triumphant Heretic: Tito's Struggle against Stalin* (London: William Heinemann, Ltd., 1958), p. 187.

27. *László Rajk . . . Before the People's Court*, p. 162; cf. Halperin, *Heretic*, p. 189. See also the Soviet propagandist, M. Mitin, "Zionist Agency of U.S. Imperialism," FLP, No. 8, 1953, p. 4, who recalls this obscure testimony.

28. See Jakub Berman's remarks in Alexander Korab, "Die Oktober-Tagung der polnischen KP," OE, VII (1957), 132. According to Meyer *et al.*, p. 154, a quiet purge of prominent Czechoslovak Jews began after the Rajk trial.

29. See, for example, M. Marinin, "Israel—an American Preserve," CDSP, III, No. 16, p. 11 (P, May 13, 1951); L. Vatolina, "Israel, Base of American Imperialism in the Near East," CDSP, III, No. 30, pp. 6-8 (*Voprosy Istorii*, No. 4, 1951, pp. 94-105); P. Khazov, "Trip to Israel: Travel Notes," *New Times*, No. 35, 1951, pp. 22-25; *New Times*, No. 36, 1951, pp. 25-29.

30. A witness at his trial hinted that Slánský was blamed for his part in helping Israel (*Rudé Pravo*, November 2, 1952, testimony of Goldstücker).

31. Barton, p. 144; L. Lesny, "Der Slansky-Prozess," OE, I (1951), 9.

32. Lesny, in OE, I (1951), 10; Barton, p. 193.

33. Barton, pp. 149-156; H. F. Armstrong, pp. 177-184; Lesny, in OE, I (1951), 10-11.

34. "Meeting of Central Committee, Communist Party of Czechoslovakia," FLP, No. 37, 1951, p. 2.

35. Barton, pp. 30-31.

36. Klement Gottwald, "Concerning Certain Matters of Inner-Party Life in the C. P. of Czechoslovakia," FLP, No. 50, 1951, p. 2.

37. Barton, p. 266; cf. *Rudé Pravo*, November 26, 1952.

38. Václav Kopecký, "Against Cosmopolitanism, for Socialist Realism," FLP, No. 14, 1952, p. 3.

39. The published record of the trial appeared in *Rudé Pravo* in late November 1952. For accounts of the trial and various special aspects of its background,

see Barton, pp. 18 ff., 244; Lesny, in OE, I (1951), 1-7, 11-12; Halperin, *Heretic*, p. 204. See also Joseph Wechsberg, "My Schoolmate Geminder —Rise and Fall of a Communist Leader," *Collier's*, February 7, 1953, pp. 20 ff.

40. *Rudé Pravo*, November 26, 1952.
41. Cf. "Le Procès de Prague et la Préparation des Procès de Varsovie," E&O, No. 80, 1953, pp. 15-17.
42. Alexandru Moghioros, "Consolidation of Party of Working Class—Guarantee of Victory of Socialism in Rumania," FLP, No. 23, 1952, p. 3; cf. Halperin, *Heretic*, p. 196.
43. See Meyer *et al.*, p. 203, note 1, for evidence that the indictment was drawn up in Russian; cf. *ibid.*, pp. 189-190.
44. See CDSP, IV, No. 47, pp. 20-22 (P and Iz, November 22 and November 25, 1952), and CDSP, IV, No. 48, pp. 29-30 (P and Iz, November 26 and November 27, 1952).
45. CSP I, p. 244 (P, January 13, 1953).
46. See especially CDSP, V, No. 1, p. 11 (editorials from *Meditsinskii Rabotnik*, January 27, 1953, and January 13, 1953); CDSP, V, No. 1, pp. 12-14 (articles from *Pravda Ukrainy*, January 16 and 23, 1953); CDSP, V, No. 4, pp. 3-4 (*Bloknot Agitatora*, No. 3, 1953, pp. 10-22); CDSP, V, No. 4, pp. 6-8 (P, February 6, 1953); CDSP, V, No. 4, p. 12 (Iz, February 18, 1953); CDSP, V, No. 4, p. 37 (*Sovetskaia Belorussiia*, January 18, 1953).
47. B. Protopopov and I. Shatunovskii, "A Three-Million Trial," CDSP, V, No. 5, p. 6 (*Komsomolskaia Pravda*, February 12, 1953).
48. "Vyshe uroven lektsionnoi propagandy" (A higher level of lecture propaganda), *Pravda Ukrainy*, March 3, 1953.
49. F. R. Kozlov, "Politicheskaia bditel'nost'—obiazannost' chlena partii" (Political vigilance—a responsibility of the member of the Party), K, No. 1, 1953, pp. 46-58.
50. The obituary is in CDSP, V, No. 7, p. 22 (P, February 14, 1953).
51. Harrison E. Salisbury, *American in Russia* (New York: Harper & Bros., 1955), p. 153; on the arrest of Molotov's wife cf. Boffa, p. 27.
52. According to F. R. Kozlov (to American reporters), NYT, July 4, 1959.

CHAPTER XVIII THE DEPARTURE OF STALIN AND BERIA

1. CSP I, p. 246 (P, March 4, 1953).
2. CSP I, pp. 246-247 (P, March 6, 1953).
3. See especially Salisbury, pp. 181-183; Boris Nicolaevsky, "The Rise and Fall of Lavrenti Beria," *The New Leader*, August 5, 1957, pp. 9-10; and Abdurakhman Avtorkhanov, "The Political Outlook after the Twentieth Party Congress," *Bulletin*, III (1956), No. 5, pp. 11-13.
4. Avtorkhanov, in *Bulletin*, III (1956), No. 5, p. 12; cf. NYT, March 3, 1954, on the dismissal of the health minister.

5. "Ukreplenie sotsialisticheskoi zakonnosti i iuridicheskaia nauka," (The strengthening of socialist legality and legal science), K, No. 11, 1956, p. 17. Khrushchev in his secret speech (p. S43) referred sarcastically to Poskrebyshev as Stalin's "loyal shield-bearer."

6. CSP I, p. 246 (P, March 4, 1953).

7. NYT, July 3, 1959.

8. NYT, June 8, 1957. Cf. NYT, March 12, 1958, on legal consideration of this revelation in Poland.

9. Boffa, p. 30, maintains that the Beria-Malenkov deal was discussed at the January 1955 plenum of the Central Committee.

10. CSP I, pp. 247-248 (P, March 7, 1953).

11. CSP I, pp. 251-252 (P, March 10, 1953).

12. CSP I, p. 248 (P, March 7, 1953).

13. Salisbury, pp. 161-171; cf. Boffa, p. 42.

14. CSP I, p. 248 (P, March 7, 1953).

15. Boris Nicolaevsky, "The Party Men and the Managers," *The New Leader,* July 29, 1957, p. 10. See also Chapter XVII, note 19.

16. CSP I, p. 254 (P, February 15, 1953).

17. CSP I, p. 258 (P, March 21, 1953).

18. A. Kruglov, "High Political Vigilance is the Duty of Every Soviet Person," CDSP, V, No. 10, pp. 8-9 (*Bloknot Agitatora*, No. 7, 1953).

19. CDSP, V, No. 11, p. 16 (P, March 15, 1953).

20. "From the Courtroom," CDSP, V, No. 12, p. 21 (*Sovetskaia Belorussiia*, March 22, 1953).

21. CSP I, pp. 258-259 (P, March 28, 1953).

22. CSP I, p. 259 (P, April 4, 1953); cf. Boffa, p. 100.

23. CSP I, pp. 259-260 (P, April 6, 1953).

24. CSP I, p. 260 (P, April 7, 1953).

25. N. Khokhlov, "Pravo na sovest'" (The right to conscience), Posev, No. 36, 1957, pp. 8-9; cf. Unto Parvilahti, *A Slave Laborer's Experiences in the Soviet Utopia* (New York: E. P. Dutton & Co., 1960), p. 233. Peter Meyer has analyzed (mainly on the basis of Khokhlov's report) the position of the Jewish MVD officers in "Has Soviet Anti-Semitism Halted?," *Commentary,* XVIII (July 1954), 8.

26. Ivan A. Fateev, "Bor'ba Kommunisticheskoi Partii Sovetskogo Soiuza za Povyshenie Bditel'nosti Sovetskogo Naroda v Poslevoennyi Period (1945-1953 gg.) (Na Materialakh Kievskoi, Khar'kovskoi i L'vovskoi Oblastei USSR)" (The struggle of the Communist Party of the Soviet Union for heightening the vigilance of the Soviet people in the postwar period [1945-1953] [from materials of Kiev, Kharkov and L'vov oblasts of the Ukrainian SSR]) (unpublished dissertation, Kiev University, 1954), p. 285.

27. CDSP, V, No. 17, p. 3 (*Pravda Ukrainy*, April 11, 1953).

28. Salisbury, pp. 89-91; Bedell Smith, p. 80.

29. Khripko dissertation, p. 121. The group referred to consisted of officials in the Belorussian Central Committee *nomenklatura* in 1946.

30. Bernard J. Choseed, "Jews in Soviet Literature," in Simmons, p. 111;

"L'Edification Culturelle de l'URSS," E&O, No. 195, 1958, p. 21. Since these sources relate respectively to periods six years before and three years after 1953, one cannot be certain that the proportion of Jews at the latter time was precisely that cited in the text. Probably, however, there was no important change in their ratio to the categories of the population discussed. The fact that in all categories except physicians—not a highly favored group in the USSR—the proportion of Jews was at or near 10 per cent suggests that this was a set quota.

31. K. Gorshenin, "Socialist Law on Guard over the People's Interests," CDSP, V, No. 15, pp. 6-7 (P, April 17, 1953).
32. *Ibid.*
33. N. Matiushkin, "Great Principles of Internationalism," CDSP, V, No. 16, p. 18 (*Literaturnaia Gazeta*, April 21, 1953).
34. *Zaria Vostoka*, April 15, 1953.
35. *Ibid.*, April 21, 1953.
36. *Ibid.*, April 22, 1953.
37. *Ibid.*, April 21, 1953.
38. *Ibid.*, May 15, 1953.
39. Boris Meissner, "Georgien," OE, III (1953), 288.
40. *Zaria Vostoka*, April 21, 1953.
41. Boris Meissner, "Nach Stalins Tod," OE, III (1953), 279-281.
42. L. Slepov, "Collectivity is the Highest Principle of Party Leadership," CDSP, V, No. 13, p. 3 (P, April 16, 1953).
43. F. Konstantinov, "The People—Makers of History," CDSP, V, No. 23, p. 6 (P, June 28, 1953).
44. CDSP, V, No. 19, p. 26 (*Pravda Vostoka*, May 7, 1953).
45. A. Niiazov, "V bratskoi sem'e narodov Sovetskogo Soiuza" (In the fraternal family of the peoples of the Soviet Union), K, No. 8, 1953, pp. 25-39.
46. *Zaria Vostoka*, May 23, 1953.
47. *Ibid.*, May 4, 1953; *Pravda Ukrainy*, May 4, 1953.
48. All of these assertions are based on an undocumented passage—probably derived either from the West Ukrainian press or the L'vov Party archives —in Fateev dissertation. Some corroboration is offered by Seweryn Bialer, "I Chose Truth," *News From Behind the Iron Curtain*, V (1955), No. 9, p. 6, who writes that the secret Central Committee letter condemning Beria accused him of having ordered the MVD chief in L'vov to exercise surveillance on a Presidium member visiting there. Apparently this man (who, according to the document Bialer read, informed the Presidium) was replaced by Menshtein.
49. According to Fateev dissertation, which does not explicitly state, however, that this letter caused Mel'nikov's dismissal.
50. Cf. *ibid.;* and N. Nefedov and M. Tiurin, "Friendship of Peoples of the U.S.S.R.—Source of Strength of the Soviet State," CDSP, V, No. 24, pp. 3-4 (Iz, June 19, 1953).
51. *Pravda Ukrainy*, June 13, 1953.
52. See *ibid.*, for June 18, 19, 21, 1953.

53. *Ibid.*, June 13, 1953.
54. See Boris Nicolaevsky, "The Rise and Fall of Lavrentii Beria," *The New Leader*, August 5, 1957, pp. 9-11, for a partial support of this explanation; Nicolaevsky does not, however, argue that Mel'nikov was Khrushchev's protégé.
55. *Pravda Ukrainy*, June 17, 1953.
56. See *ibid.*, February 10, 1953, reprinting a *Pravda* editorial of February 8, 1953, attacking *Pravda Ukrainy* and other newspapers for insufficient zeal in the "vigilance" campaign, and the admission by *Pravda Ukrainy* that it had failed in this respect. While, as noted by Wolfgang Leonhard, *Kreml ohne Stalin* (Cologne: Verlag für Politik und Wirtschaft), p. 73, the Ukrainian press had previously published articles on the "doctors' plot" theme (and even earlier had reported the execution of economic officials for corruption), I fail to find that the campaign was especially vigorously pressed in the Ukraine before the Moscow articles appeared.
57. See J. Armstrong, *Elite*, pp. 51, 67. From 1940 to 1944 Mel'nikov was Deputy Minister of State Control of the USSR.
58. "O grubykh narusheniiakh gosudarstvennoi ditsipliny v ispol'zovanii kapital'nykh vlozhenii i faktakh proiavleniia mestnichestva so storony otdel'nykh rubovoditelei sovnarkhozov" (On the flagrant violations of state discipline in the utilization of capital investments and the facts of the appearance of localism on the part of certain directors of councils of national economy), PZh, No. 15, 1958, pp. 22-24. The fault charged to Mel'nikov was the use of funds alloted to heavy industrial development for construction of amenities for workers; since Khrushchev had earlier based his condemnation of Malenkov on the latter's alleged wish to subordinate industrial development to consumer goods production, the prominent accusation of Mel'nikov appears to tie him to Malenkov's condemned policy. It is worth noting that in the June 1959 plenum Khrushchev himself referred to this episode (though not to Mel'nikov). CDSP, XI, No. 28, p. 6 (P, July 2, 1959).
59. *Pravda Ukrainy*, June 18, 1953; *Kommunist* (Erivan), June 19, 1953; NYT, June 4, 1953.
60. See Chapter XIX, p. 250.
61. See J. Armstrong, *Elite*, pp. 55-57.
62. N. Khokhlov, "Pravo na sovest'" (The right to conscience), *Posev*, No. 31, 1957, pp. 9-10; cf. Salisbury, pp. 188-189. For a summary (marred by some inaccuracies) of the evidence, which seems very weak, that military measures were required to eliminate Beria, see N. Ia. Galai, "Armiia i peremeny v poslestalinskom rukovodstve SSSR" (The army and the changes in the post-Stalin leadership of the USSR), *Vestnik*, No. 1, 1959, pp. 32-34.
63. CDSP, V, No. 24, p. 5 (P and other newspapers, June 28, 1953).
64. CDSP, V, No. 24, p. 9 (P, July 10, 1953); for the dates of the plenum, cf. *Kommunisticheskaia Partiia Sovetskogo Soiuza v Rezoliutsiiakh i Resheniiakh S"ezdov, Konferentsii i Plenumov TsK* (The Communist Party of the Soviet Union in resolutions and decisions of congresses, conferences, and plenums of the Central Committee) (7th ed.) (Moscow: Gosudarstvennoe Izdatel'-

stvo Politicheskoi Literatury, 1954), III, 609. Hereafter cited as *KPSS* (1954).

65. EAP-3a-11/2, Armee Oberkommando 16, Ic, August 18, 1941 (interrogation of NKVD Lieutenant Aleksandr Zhigunov) (English translation), p. 127.

66. N. Khokhlov, in *Posev*, No. 36, 1957, pp. 9-10.

67. Boffa, p. 101.

68. *Ibid.;* N. Khokhlov in *Posev*, No. 36, 1957, pp. 9-10; "Predateli rodiny razoblacheny i unichtozheny" (Traitors to the homeland unmasked and annihilated), K, No. 18, 1953, pp. 13-18.

69. CDSP, V, No. 51, p. 20 (*Zaria Vostoka*, December 24, 1953).

70. *Zaria Vostoka*, July 15, 1953.

71. *Ibid.*, September 22, 1953.

72. "Les crises du parti communiste de la R.S.S. de Géorgie," *Chroniques Etrangères: URSS* (France, Direction de la Documentation), No. 162, 1956, p. 22.

73. Kuznetsov dissertation, p. 135; *Bakinskii Rabochii*, July 21, 1953.

74. *Bakinskii Rabochii*, July 21, 1953. In April 1953 Bagirov was relieved "at his request" as first secretary, but remained chairman of the council of ministers.

75. *Bakinskii Rabochii*, July 22, 1953; see Boris Meissner, "Neuwahl des obersten 'Sowjetparlaments' und Parteisäuberungen," OE, IV (1954), 221.

76. *XX S"ezd Kommunisticheskoi Partii Sovetskogo Soiuza, 14-25 Fevralia 1956 goda: Stenograficheskii Otchet* (The Twentieth Congress of the Communist Party of the Soviet Union, February 14-25, 1956: Stenographic report) (Moscow: Gosudarstvennoe Izdatel'stvo Politicheskoi Literatury, 1956), I, 544. Hereafter cited as *XX S"ezd*.

77. CDSP VIII, No. 21, p. 12 (*Bakinskii Rabochii*, May 27, 1956).

78. "La crise du Parti Communiste d'Azerbaïdjan," *Chroniques Etrangères: URSS* (France, Direction de la Documentation), No. 168, July 31, 1956, pp. 17-18.

79. See Bagirov's speech to the Azerbaidzhan supreme soviet, CDSP, V, No. 17, p. 6 (*Bakinskii Rabochii*, April 19, 1953); D. Dzhafarov, "Great Son of the Azerbaidzhan People," CDSP, V, No. 14, p. 38 (P, April 7, 1953).

CHAPTER XIX   STRUGGLE FOR SUCCESSION

1. Meissner, *Deutschland*, pp. 184-186.

2. *Ibid.*, p. 265.

3. Report in FLP, No. 18, 1953, p. 5.

4. Leonhard, *Kreml*, p. 110.

5. Brzezinski, *Bloc*, p. 157.

6. "Important Decisions of Political Bureau, Central Committee, Social Unity Party of Germany," FLP, No. 25, 1953, p. 2.

7. Wolf G. Contius, "Der 17. Juni in der Sowjetpresse," OE, III (1953), 271-275.

8. "Communiqué of 14th Plenary Meeting, Central Committee, Socialist Unity Party of Germany," FLP, No. 26, 1953; cf. Leonhard, *Kreml,* pp. 110-111.

9. Tibor Meray, *Thirteen Days that Shook the Kremlin* (New York: Frederick A. Praeger, 1959), p. 28. I have seen no other report of secret Central Committee letters of this period which indicate such a specific accusation of Beria.

10. "New Course and Tasks of Party," FLP, No. 32, 1953, p. 2.

11. Antonín Novotný, "Along Great Path of Socialist Construction," FLP, No. 18, 1953, p. 4.

12. Rudolf Urban, "Tschechoslowakei," OE, III (1953), 293.

13. "The Swiatlo Story," *News From Behind the Iron Curtain,* IV (1955), No. 3, p. 22.

14. *Ost-Probleme,* VI (1954), 750-754 (translation from *Pravda,* Bratislava, Czechoslovakia, April 25, 1954).

15. FLP, No. 25, 1954, pp. 3-4.

16. "Sturz Kommunistischer Parteigrossen in Ungarn," *Neue Zürcher Zeitung,* March 15, 1954 (in *Ost-Probleme,* VI [1954], 563-565).

17. Juliusz Burgin, "Contagion," *Problems of Communism,* VI (1957), 39 (from *Przeglad Kulturalny,* Warsaw, No. 6, 1957); cf. *Ost-Probleme,* VI (1954), 756.

18. Imre Nagy, *Imre Nagy on Communism* (New York: Frederick A. Praeger, 1957), pp. 250-251. There seems no doubt but that this work, which was taken out of Hungary following the 1956 revolution, is genuine. It is, therefore, a major source on events in Hungary between 1953 and 1956, although of course a partisan one.

19. *Ibid.,* p. 153. The specific point on which Nagy emphasizes he had Molotov's, not Beria's, support was relaxation of collectivization of agriculture; in view of the charges of disrupting the Soviet kolkhoz system directed against Beria, this is especially significant.

20. *Ibid.,* pp. 106-107, 153, 250-252.

21. Meray, pp. 4, 7. Meray (p. 7) asserts that Beria accused Rákosi of trying to act as a "Jewish king" of Hungary.

22. Karl Piribauer, "Hintergrunde und Vorgeschichte des Ungarischen Aufstandes," OE, VI (1956), 458-459.

23. Piribauer, in OE, VI (1956), 460-461.

24. Meray, p. 25.

25. See Nagy, *On Communism,* pp. 107, 280, 282-283. His account of the attitudes of the Soviet leaders is, however, far from unambiguous.

26. Seweryn Bialer, "The Three Schools of Kremlin Policy," *The New Leader,* July 29, 1957, p. 12.

27. "On the Political Situation and Tasks of the Party," FLP, No. 11, 1955, p. 2.

28. Beria's overtures are recounted in N. Khokhlov, "Pravo na sovest'," (The right to conscience), *Posev,* No. 36, 1957, pp. 8-9; Seweryn Bialer, "I Chose

Truth," *News From Behind the Iron Curtain,* V (1955), No. 9, p. 4. While it cannot be demonstrated that Malenkov *personally* made overtures to Tito, the first public steps toward rapprochement with Yugoslavia were made in 1953-54 when he was premier. Unless we assume that Molotov *personally* favored a Tito rapprochement at that time (in contrast to his bitter opposition to the later development of this policy) it seems evident that Malenkov was at least in favor of the moves.

29. D. Slijepcevic, "New Developments in Relations between Moscow and Belgrade," *Bulletin,* I (1954), No. 8, p. 5; cf. Ernest Bauer, "Tito und die Sowjetunion," OE, IV (1954), 100-101.

30. FLP, No. 43, 1954, p. 4; cf. "National Holiday of the Yugoslav People," FLP, No. 49, 1954, p. 4.

31. Halperin, *Heretic,* p. 250.

32. CSP I, p. 248 (P, March 10, 1953).

33. CSP I, "Supreme Friendship," pp. 253-254 (P, March 10, 1953).

34. Richard P. Stebbins *et al., The United States in World Affairs, 1954* (New York: Harper & Bros., 1955), p. 129.

35. Raymond Garthoff, *Soviet Strategy in the Nuclear Age* (New York: Frederick A. Praeger, 1958), p. 23.

36. Boris Meissner, "Das Duumvirat Malenkow-Chruschtschjow," OE, IV (1954), 445. See P, June 16, 1954.

37. Hodgman, p. 89.

38. *Ibid.*

39. It should be obvious that any appraisal of the attitudes of the Soviet population as a whole, or different strata of it, is conjectural. I base this appraisal on observations during my own trips to the USSR, accounts of other visitors and defectors, and deductions from the course of Soviet political and economic developments.

40. See especially the article by John H. Noble in NYT, April 6, 1955.

41. For a general review of these measures (which may distort the picture to emphasize those taken after Khrushchev's attainment of full control), see "Chto sdelano dlia ukrepleniia sotsialisticheskoi zakonnosti" (What has been done to strengthen socialist legality), PZh, No. 4, 1957, pp. 66-71.

42. O. Yurchenko, "The Latest Soviet Amnesty," *Bulletin,* II (1955), No. 9, pp. 26-28.

43. Khrushchev's secret speech, p. S32.

44. See the account of the meeting in MVD headquarters to celebrate the thirty-fifth anniversary of the founding of the frontier troops, CDSP, VIII, No. 7, pp. 24-25 (P, February 19, 1956). Cf. S. Volin, "Cheka posle Stalina" (The Cheka after Stalin), SV, No. 5, 1958, p. 96.

45. Boris Meissner, "Verwaltungsumbau," OE, IV (1954), 284-287.

46. CDSP, V, No. 30, p. 4 (P, August 9, 1953); cf. Rush, p. 7.

47. See Boffa, p. 30, on the charge that Malenkov used this campaign to increase his personal prestige.

48. "Materialy do istorii KP Ukraïny" (Materials on the History of the Communist Party of the Ukraine), *Ukraïns'kyi Istorychnyi Zhurnal,* No. 3, 1958,

p. 133. Data on other Union Republic plenums are from G. J. Svejda's survey.

49. CDSP, V, No. 35, p. 3 (P, August 10, 1953).

50. *KPSS* (1954), III, 610-653; cf. especially Otto Schiller, "Der neue Kurs der sowjetischen Agrarpolitik," OE, III (1953), 403-412.

51. Interview with J. D. Bernal, FLP, No. 52, 1954, p. 1.

52. CDSP, V, No. 39, p. 12 (P, September 15, 1953).

53. S. Butuzov, "Voprosy partiinoi raboty v mashinnotraktornykh stantsiiakh" (Questions of Party work in machine-tractor stations), K, No. 18, 1953, pp. 67-80.

54. Roy D. Laird, "The Demise of the Machine Tractor Station," *American Slavic and East European Review*, XVII (1958), 420.

55. S. Butuzov, in K, No. 18, 1953, pp. 67-80.

56. *KPSS* (1954), III, 646.

57. *Ibid.*, p. 647.

58. "Umwege zur Agrostadt?", OE, IV (1954), 125.

59. Boris Meissner, "Neuwahl des Obersten 'Sowjetparlaments' und Parteisäuberungen," OE, IV (1954), 220.

60. *KPSS* (1954), III, 654-686.

61. For an analysis of recent data on Soviet food production, see especially "Agrarproduktion und Neulanderträge der UdSSR in Zahlen," OE, X (1960), 415-435. Much of the data is based on figures in USSR, Council of Ministers, Tsentralnoe Statisticheskoe Upravlenie, *Narodnoe Khoziaistvo SSSR: Statisticheskii Sbornik* (The national economy of the USSR: A statistical collection) (Moscow: Gosudarstvennoe Statisticheskoe Izdatel'stvo, 1956), 106 pp.; USSR, Council of Ministers, Tsentralnoe Statisticheskoe Upravlenie, *Narodnoe Khoziaistvo SSSR v 1956 Godu: Statisticheskii Ezhegodnik.* (The national economy of the USSR in 1956: A statistical annual) (Moscow: Gosudarstvennoe Statisticheskoe Izdatel'stvo, 1957), p. 107.

62. *Plenum . . . Dekabria 1958*, pp. 185, 206, 318.

63. J. Armstrong, *Elite*, p. 148.

64. CDSP, V, No. 48, p. 23 (P, November 29, 1953).

65. CDSP, V, No. 50, p. 6 (*Vedomosti Verkhonogo Soveta SSSR*, December 29, 1953, p. 1).

66. Cf. Boris Meissner, "Partei," OE, II (1952), 418-419, and Boris Meissner, "Neuwahl des Obersten 'Sowjetparlaments' und Parteisäuberungen," OE, IV (1954), 221-222.

67. Meissner, in OE, IV (1954), 224-225.

68. CDSP, VI, No. 22, p. 7 (P, April 27, 1954).

69. CDSP, VI, No. 26, p. 4 (P, June 27, 1954).

70. Cf. Especially CDSP, VI, No. 42, p. 9, for the photographs of the Presidium of the Moscow Soviet in *Pravda*, November 7, 1954, and *Izvestia* for the same date.

71. CDSP, VI, No. 49, p. 12 (P, December 24, 1954); Boffa, p. 26.

72. Speech (December 7, 1954) to the All-Union Conference of Builders, Architects, and Workers in Building Materials Industry, in Construction

Machinery and Road Machine Building and in Design and Research Organizations, CDSP, VI, No. 52, p. 7 (P, December 28, 1954).

73. CDSP, VI, No. 52, p. 35 (Iz, December 31, 1954, p. 1).
74. Herman Achminow, "The Change in Soviet Policy," *Bulletin*, II (1955), No. 4, pp. 5-6; cf. the Communist Boffa's similar assertion (p. 29).
75. D. Shepilov, "The Party General Line and the Vulgarizers of Marxism," CDSP, VI, No. 52, p. 4 (P, January 24, 1955).
76. CDSP, VII, No. 6, p. 3 (P, February 3, 1955).
77. "On Increasing Output of Livestock Products," CDSP, VII, No. 4, p. 17 (P, February 2, 1955).
78. Boffa, pp. 29-30, partially corroborated by Bialer in *The New Leader*, July 29, 1957, pp. 11-12.
79. The complete text (in translation) is in NYT, February 9, 1955.

CHAPTER XX   THE PERIOD OF THE TWENTIETH CONGRESS: ORGANIZATIONAL CHANGES

1. G. K. Zhukov, "Tenth Anniversary of the Great Victory," CDSP, VII, No. 17, 1955, p. 5 (P, May 8, 1955). Cf. Rush, p. 94, note 2.
2. P, February 9, 1955.
3. *Ibid.*
4. "Sviaz' teorii s praktikoi i partiinaia propaganda" (The connection of theory with practice and Party propaganda), K, No. 14, 1955, p. 4. (CDSP, VII, No. 38, pp. 3-6).
5. K, No. 14, 1955, pp. 127-128 (CDSP, VII, No. 38, p. 3).
6. See especially Rush, pp. 88-93.
7. *Ibid.*, pp. 21 ff.
8. On the manipulation of war history by Malenkov and Khrushchev—with somewhat different interpretations of the significance of the tactics from that which I present below—see especially Rush, pp. 16-18; and Richard Lowenthal, "Crisis in Moscow," *Problems of Communism*, IV (1955), 1-7.
9. See J. Armstrong, *Elite*, pp. 149-150, 45-47; and J. Armstrong, "Toward Personal Dictatorship or Oligarchy? Soviet Domestic Politics Since the Twentieth Congress," *Midwest Journal of Political Science*, II (1958), 345-356.
10. Cf. Chapter VIII.
11. CDSP, VII, No. 26, p. 6 (P, July 13, 1955).
12. Boffa, p. 31. One cannot, of course, be sure that this Communist correspondent is not merely echoing ex post facto charges by the Khrushchev group (in 1957, after the defeat of the "anti-Party" group, Molotov was publicly accused of opposing the Yugoslav rapprochement at the July 1955 plenum); but Boffa's account closely fits all other available evidence.
13. *Ibid.*, p. 32.
14. I cannot agree with Boris Meissner ("Partei und Personnelles," OE, VI

[1956], 184) that D. S. Polianskii, who had been secretary of the Crimean obkom for many years prior to its transfer to the Ukraine in 1954 was in any political sense a member of the Ukrainian apparatus. Nor can I agree that T. F. Shtykov and N. G. Ignatov, who had been associated with the Leningrad area, were Khrushchev's adherents in any *personal* sense. To me, their transfers to key RSFSR posts are a further indication of the rise of men whose basic careers had been in the territorial apparatus. Obviously, however, a considerable element of speculation is involved in this appraisal.

15. See Bulganin's report "Concerning Tasks in the Further Advance of Industry, Technical Progress and Improvement of Production-Organization," CDSP, VII, No. 28, p. 19 (P, July 17, 1955).

16. Leo Gruliow (ed.), *Current Soviet Policies II* (New York: Frederick A. Praeger, 1957), pp. 196-202. Hereafter cited as CSP II; Boris Meissner, "Neuwahl des Obersten 'Sowjetparlaments' und Parteisäuberungen," OE, IV (1954), 221-225.

17. "S plenuma TsK Kompartii Uzbekistana" (From the plenum of the Central Committee of the Communist Party of Uzbekistan), PZh, No. 1, 1956, p. 38.

18. This analysis is based on the information concerning the backgrounds of the Central Committee members and candidates contained in CSP II, pp. 196-202, and the special supplement of *Bulletin*, III (1956), No. 5; cf. Boris Meissner, "Partei und Personnelles," OE, VI (1956), 182-184.

19. *XX S"ezd*, I, 101 (CSP II, p. 56).

20. *XX S"ezd*, I, 278 (CSP II, p. 78).

21. For the composition of the Presidium see CSP II, 202 (P, February 28, 1956).

22. Kirichenko became a candidate member in 1953 or early 1954; see Meissner, "Das Duumvirat Malenkow-Chruschtschjow," OE, IV (1954), 445. Kirichenko's official biography (BSE, 2nd ed., LI, 152) says he became a candidate in May 1953—i.e., before Mel'nikov's fall.

23. Of the various easily available printed copies, that contained in CSP II, pp. 172-188, and the version (including Boris Nicolaevsky's very valuable annotations) published by *The New Leader* in 1956 are especially noteworthy.

24. Khrushchev's secret speech, p. S23.

25. *Ibid.*, pp. S38, S41.

26. *Ibid.*, pp. S34, S59.

27. *XX S"ezd*, I, 413 (CSP II, p. 92).

28. *XX S"ezd*, I, 115 (CSP II, p. 60).

29. *XX S"ezd*, I, 124 (CSP II, p. 64).

30. Cf. *XX S"ezd*, II, pp. 128-129 and *Problemi e Realtà dell' URSS. Relazione sul viaggio della delegazione del PCI nell' Unione Sovietica* (Rome: Editori Riuniti, 1958), p. 55.

31. *XX S"ezd*, I, 382.

32. The existence of the RSFSR Agricultural Section prior to the Twentieth Congress is demonstrated by the fact that its director reported to that body (*XX S"ezd*, II, 181 ff.). For information on the organization of the RSFSR

Bureau and the regular sections of the CPSU Secretariat, see *Problemi e Realtà*, pp. 44 ff.

33. *Problemi e Realtà*, p. 45; cf. L. Slepov, *Vysshie i Mestnye Organy Partii* (Higher and local organs of the Party) (Moscow: Vysshaia Partiinaia Shkola pri TsK KPSS, Kafedra Partiinogo Stroitel'stva, 1958), p. 107.

34. *Problemi e Realtà*, p. 48.

35. *Ibid.*, pp. 47, 51.

36. *Ibid.*, pp. 49-50.

37. Slepov, *Vysshie . . . Organy*, pp. 9-10.

38. CSP II, p. 202 (P, February 29, 1956).

39. Membership figures for the CPSU and for the Union Republic Parties may be found in BSE (2nd ed.), *Ezhegodnik* 1958, pp. 86, 91, 96-97, 101, 107-108, 112, 116, 121, 126, 160-161, 165-166, 169-170, 175, 185. Population statistics (on which the ratios of membership are based) are from "On Preliminary Results of 1959 All-Union Population Census," CDSP, XI, No. 19, p. 1 (P, May 10, 1959). Actually, fairly accurate estimates (based on the size of Congress delegations and other data) of Union Republic membership were made prior to 1956 (e.g., Rigby thesis, p. 67). Calculations of the ratio of Party members to population were seriously hampered, however, by lack of realistic population estimates for several Republics, such as Belorussia. For a detailed presentation of recent data on Party membership in the Union Republics (computed before the appearance of BSE [2nd ed.], *Ezhegodnik* 1958, and the 1959 census data), see Walter S. Hanchett "Some Observations on Membership Figures of the Communist Party of the Soviet Union," *American Political Science Review*, LII (1958), 1123-1128.

40. "Kommunisticheskaia Partiia Ukrainy v tsifrakh" (The Communist Party of the Ukraine in figures), PZh, No. 12, 1958, pp. 57-59.

41. J. Armstrong, *Elite*, p. 16; *Pravda Vostoka*, January 29, 1956; *Sovetskaia Kirgiziia*, September 22, 1952.

42. Khripko dissertation, p. 121.

43. Fomin dissertation, p. 54.

44. "L'Edification Culturelle de l'URSS," E&O, No. 195, 1958, p. 21; Ralph Fisher, p. 417.

45. Ralph Fisher, p. 417; approximate data on 1934 Party membership can be derived from the list of numbers of members verified, and percentage which they were of the total membership, in the various Union Republics and oblasts of the RSFSR and the Ukraine, contained in Smolensk Archive, T/84, pp. 77-99. The data is incomplete, probably because of omission of army membership.

46. The data in this paragraph is from *Notes: Soviet Affairs*, No. 259, October 12, 1959, pp. 3-9.

47. *Sovetskaia Kirgiziia*, February 13, 1949; *Kazakhstanskaia Pravda*, February 28, 1949.

48. Cf. CSP I, p. 56 (*Pravda Ukrainy*, September 25, 1952) and A. Slepov, A. Chernichenko, and A. Riabokliach, "Congress of the Ukrainian CP," CDSP, XII, No. 8, p. 23 (P, February 21, 1960).

49. The 1952 figure is based on the number of delegates Belorussia sent to the Nineteenth Congress (CSP I, p. 94—from P, October 9, 1952); the 1958 figure is given by T. Kiselev, "40 let Kommunisticheskoi Partii Belorussii" (Forty years of the Communist Party of Belorussia), K, No. 23, 1958, p. 14.
50. Khrushchev interview with the British journalist I. McDonald, CDSP, X, No. 7, p. 16 (P, February 16, 1958).
51. Tolkachev dissertation, p. 62; cf. Rigby thesis, p. 68, for data on the low proportion of Tadzhiks among Party recruits in the Tadzhik SSR.
52. N. D. Dzhandil'din, secretary of the Kazakh Central Committee, "Nekotorye voprosy international'nogo vospitaniia" (Certain questions of international education), K, No. 13, 1959, especially pp. 35-40 (CDSP, XI, No. 39, pp. 3-7, 22).

CHAPTER XXI   THE PERIOD OF THE TWENTIETH CONGRESS: IDEOLOGICAL FINESSE

1. See especially Klaus Mehnert, "An Moskaus literarischer Front," OE, IV (1954), 346-350.
2. *Ibid.*, p. 347.
3. Cf. V. Kochetov, "Which Seasons?" CDSP, VI, No. 20, pp. 3-5 (P, May 27, 1954); and "The Strength of Our Literature Lies in Affirming Life," CDSP, VI, No. 20, pp. 5-6 (*Komsomolskaia Pravda*, June 6, 1954) for attacks on Panova and Ehrenburg; Ehrenburg's reply to the attacks, in "On the Article by K. Simonov," CDSP, VI, No. 32, pp. 13-15 (*Literaturnaia Gazeta*, August 3, 1954); and Jeri Laber, "The Soviet Writer's Search for New Values," *Problems of Communism*, V (1956), 14-19.
4. Resolution in CDSP, VI, No. 36, pp. 3-7 (*Literaturnaia Gazeta*, August 17, 1954).
5. For a more detailed discussion of the period of relaxation (which apparently reached its height in late 1953) and renewed criticism of "deviationists" (which began well before May 1954) see Swayze thesis, pp. 154-179.
6. Report of the credentials commission, CDSP, VII, No. 4, pp. 28-29 (*Literaturnaia Gazeta*, December 18, 1954).
7. CDSP, VI, No. 48, pp. 3-4 (P, December 16, 1954); cf. Gleb Struve, "The Second Congress of Soviet Writers," *Problems of Communism*, IV (1955), pp. 3-11.
8. Swayze thesis, p. 194.
9. CDSP, VII, No. 3, p. 11 (*Literaturnaia Gazeta*, December 18, 1954).
10. "The World View and Work of the Writer," CDSP, VII, No. 21, pp. 31-33 (*Voprosy Filosofii*, No. 6, 1954, pp. 17-33).
11. "On Errors in Conducting Scientific-Atheist Propaganda among the Public," CDSP, VI, No. 43, pp. 13-15 (P, November 11, 1954).
12. CDSP, VI, No. 49, p. 9 (P, December 12, 1954).
13. Cf. Wetter, pp. 598-600; Bochenski, p. 133; Hans Koch, "Sowjetideologie als Weltanschauung und Wissenschaft," OE, VII (1957), 14-16.

14. Ts. Stepanian, "Lecture: Dialectical Materialism Is Scientific Basis for Building Communism," CDSP, V, No. 50, pp. 3-4 (P, December 7, 1953).

15. See the very brief notice of his speech, CDSP, VI, No. 52, p. 23 (P, December 22, 1954). On the rumors concerning Aleksandrov's attachment to Stalin, see Boris Nicolaevsky, "Two Soviet Scandals," *The New Leader*, October 13, 1958, pp. 8-10.

16. Editorial "Nasushchnye voprosy filosofskoi nauki" (Urgent questions of philosophical science), K, No. 5, 1955, p. 15 (CDSP, VII, No. 32, pp. 7-9, 15).

17. V. Kedrov and G. Gurgenidze, "Za glubokuiu razrabotku leninskogo filosofskogo nasledstva" (For profound elaboration of the Leninist philosophical heritage), K, No. 14, 1955, pp. 45-56 (CDSP, VII, No. 46, pp. 3-4); cf. Helmut Dahm, "Ontologische Aspekte der Sowjetischen Dialektik," OE, VII (1957), 236-244.

18. Editorial in K, No. 5, 1955, p. 15, cited above; cf. Wetter, pp. 607-609.

19. M. D. Kammari, "Nekotorye voprosy teorii bazisa i nadstroiki" (Some questions on the theory of the base and the superstructure), K, No. 10, 1956, pp. 42-58.

20. See Rush, especially Chapters II, IV, V, and VI, for a more detailed discussion.

21. P. N. Pospelov, "Piat'desiat let Kommunisticheskoi Partii Sovetskogo Soiuza" (Fifty years of the Communist Party of the Soviet Union), *Voprosy Istorii*, No. 11, 1953, p. 21.

22. *Ibid.*

23. Review by G. Leonidze of *Stalin: Detstvo i Otrochestvo, Epopsiia* (translated from the Georgian, 1944, 141 pp.) in B, No. 23-24, p. 72.

24. G. F. Aleksandrov, "Powerful Force of Creative Marxism," CDSP, VI, No. 9, p. 14 (P, March 5, 1954).

25. See for example D. Kukin, "Stalin—velikii prodolzhatel' dela Lenina" (Stalin —the great continuer of Lenin's work), PZh, No. 17, 1954, p. 16; V. Kruzhkov, "J. V. Stalin—Great Continuer of the Cause of V. I. Lenin," CDSP, VI, No. 51, pp. 3-5 (P, December 21, 1954).

26. F. Konstantinov, "J. V. Stalin and the Problems of Building Communism," CDSP, VII, No. 9, 1955, pp. 17-19 (P, March 3, 1955).

27. G. K. Zhukov, "Tenth Anniversary of the Great Victory," CDSP, VII, No. 17, pp. 3-5 (P, May 8, 1955).

28. "On Historical Treatment of Great Patriotic War of the Soviet Union," CDSP, VII, No. 24, pp. 3-5 (*Voprosy Istorii*, No. 5, 1955, pp. 3-8).

29. Rush, pp. 36-38.

30. *Ibid.*, pp. 45-46.

31. Black, pp. 29-30.

32. "Why Is the Cult of the Individual Alien to the Spirit of Marxism-Leninism," CDSP, VIII, No. 9, p. 3 (P, March 28, 1956).

33. XX S" ezd, I, pp. 323, 325 (CSP II, pp. 87-88).

34. Cf. Rush, pp. 66 ff.; Boris Souvarine, "Le Stalinisme sans démence," E&O, No. 147, 1956, pp. 4-6.

35. Speech to Third Writers' Congress, CDSP, XI, No. 21, p. 4 (P, May 24, 1959).
36. Khrushchev's secret speech, p. S35.
37. *Ibid.*, pp. S9 ff., S66.
38. "New V. I. Lenin Documents," CSP II, pp. 210-211 (P, April 22, 1956) and material on subsequent pages. Col. I. Chashnikov, "An Important Question of Military History," CDSP, VIII, No. 14, pp. 6-8 (*Krasnaia Zvezda*, April 3, 1956).
39. Khrushchev's secret speech, pp. S14-S15, S17.
40. *Zaria Vostoka*, March 9, 1956.
41. *Ibid.*, March 24, 1956.
42. *Ibid.*, August 7, 1956.
43. N. S. Khrushchev, "Za tesnuiu sviaz' literatury i iskusstva s zhizn'iu naroda" (For a close connection of literature and art with the life of the people), K, No. 12, 1957, p. 16 (CDSP, IX, No. 35, pp. 3-10).
44. "XX S"ezda KPSS i zadachi issledovaniia istorii partii" (The Twentieth Congress of the CPSU and tasks of research in the history of the Party), *Voprosy Istorii*, No. 3, 1956, pp. 3-12 (CDSP, VIII, No. 19, pp. 6-9, 18).
45. E. A. Boltin, "Ser'eznye nedostatki 'Ocherkov Istorii Velikoi Otechestvennoi Voiny'" (Grave Mistakes of "Essays on the History of the Great Patriotic War"), *Voprosy Istorii*, No. 5, 1956, p. 148.
46. "A Glorious Anniversary," CDSP, VIII, No. 16, pp. 3-4 (*Voennyi Vestnik*, No. 4, April 1956, pp. 2-9).
47. "Great Exploit of Soviet People," CDSP, VIII, No. 18, pp. 11-13 (*Krasnaia Zvezda*, May 9, 1956).
48. "On Overcoming the Cult of the Individual and Its Consequences," CSP II, pp. 221-227 (P, July 2, 1956).
49. CSP II, p. 224 (P, July 2, 1956).
50. "Za tvorcheskuiu razrabotku istorii KPSS" (For creative elaboration of the history of the CPSU), K, No. 10, 1956, p. 23 (CSP II, p. 219).
51. CSP II, p. 224 (P, July 2, 1956).
52. J. Armstrong, *Elite*, p. 47.
53. A. Metchenko, A. Dementiev, and G. Lomidze, "Za glubokuiu razrabotku istorii sovetskogo literatury" (For profound elaboration of the history of Soviet literature), K, No. 12, 1956, pp. 85-86.
54. Khrushchev's speech to Third Writers' Congress, CDSP, XI, No. 21, p. 5 (P, May 24, 1959).
55. See the report on the discussion of the novel at the Central Writers' Club in Moscow, CDSP, VIII, No. 49, pp. 4 ff. (*Literaturnaia Gazeta*, October 27, 1956).
56. N. Kriuchkova, CDSP, VIII, No. 49, pp. 7-9 (Iz, December 2, 1956).
57. "Summing Up: At the Plenary Session of the Moscow Branch of the USSR Writers' Union," CDSP, IX, No. 13, p. 22 (*Literaturnaia Gazeta*, March 19, 1957).
58. CDSP, IX, No. 13, p. 22 (*Literaturnaia Gazeta*, March 19, 1957).

59. Report of third plenary session of Board of USSR Writers' Union, CDSP, IX, No. 22, pp. 3-10 (*Literaturnaia Gazeta*, May 21, 1957).
60. See "Strogo sobliudat' leninskii printsip partiinosti v istoricheskoi nauke" (Strictly observe the Leninist principle of partyness in historical science), K, No. 4, 1957, pp. 17-29 (CDSP, IX, No. 17, pp. 3-8).
61. CDSP, IX, No. 13, pp. 15-21, 40 (P, April 4, 1957).
62. "Za leninskuiu printsipal'nost' v voprasakh literatury i iskusstva" (For Leninist adherence to principles in questions of literature and art), K, No. 10, 1957, pp. 16-17 (CDSP, IX, No. 33, p. 4).
63. "On Rectifying Errors in Evaluation of Operas 'Great Friendship,' 'Bogdan Khmelnitskii' and 'With All One's Heart,'" CDSP, X, No. 23, p. 3 (P, June 8, 1958).
64. "40 years of the Great October Socialist Revolution," Report to Anniversary Session of Supreme Soviet, CDSP, IX, No. 45, p. 9 (P, November 7, 1957).
65. CDSP, XI, No. 21, p. 5 (P, May 24, 1959).
66. Quoted by Maurice Friedberg, "Socialist Realism: Twenty-five Years Later," *American Slavic and East European Review*, XIX (April 1960), 283. This article is an excellent discussion of the Third Writers' Congress and the contemporary significance of socialist realism.
67. *Plenum . . . Dekabria 1958*, pp. 233 ff.
68. L. Sheinin, "A Writer's Notes: Strength and Faith," CDSP, XI, No. 36, pp. 11-13 (Iz, September 6, 1959).

CHAPTER XXII　　THE FRUITS OF REVISIONISM

1. *XX S"ezd*, I, 314 (CSP II, p. 84).
2. *XX S"ezd*, I, 314 (CSP II, p. 84); Khrushchev, *XX S"ezd*, I, 39 (CSP II, p. 38).
3. Oskar Anweiler, "Lenin und der friedliche Übergang zum Sozialismus," OE, VI (1956), 194.
4. *XX S"ezd*, I, 317 (CSP II, p. 85).
5. *XX S"ezd*, I, 40 (CSP II, p. 38).
6. Mikoian, *XX S"ezd*, I, 318 (CSP II, p. 85).
7. Khrushchev, *XX S"ezd*, I, 40 (CSP II, p. 38); Mikoian, *XX S"ezd*, I, 316 (CSP II, p. 85).
8. Khrushchev, *XX S"ezd*, I, 40 (CSP II, p. 38); note especially the differences in emphasis between Mikoian, *XX S"ezd*, I, 316 (CSP II, p. 85) and Suslov, *XX S"ezd*, I, 274 (CSP II, p. 76).
9. A. Sobelov, "O parlamentskoi forme perekhoda k sotsializmu" (On the parliamentary form of transition to socialism), K, No. 14, 1956, pp. 31-32.
10. B. N. Ponomarev, "Urgent Tasks of International Workers' Movement," CDSP, VIII, No. 13, p. 10 (P, March 31, 1956).
11. Khrushchev, *XX S"ezd*, I, 22 (CSP II, p. 33).
12. Benjamin I. Schwartz, "Ideology and the Sino-Soviet Alliance," in Boorman

et al., pp. 126-131; Klaus Mehnert, "Ideologische Gegensätze zwischen Moskau und Peking," OE, VIII (1958), 99-100.

13. Brzezinski, *Bloc*, p. 131.
14. *XX S"ezd*, I, 38 (CSP II, p. 37).
15. B. Schwartz, in Boorman *et al.*, pp. 133-136; Mehnert, in OE, VIII (1958), 100; F. S. Pavlov, "Soiuz i bor'ba rabochego klassa Kitaia s natsional'noi burzhuaziei v period perekhoda k sotsializmu" (The league and the struggle of the working class of China with the national bourgeoisie in the period of transition to socialism), *Voprosy Istorii KPSS*, No. 2, 1958, pp. 105, 110.
16. See Khrushchev's remarks reported in NYT, July 22, 1959; Mehnert, in OE, VIII (1958), 100-105.
17. See Brzezinski, *Bloc*, pp. 367-368.
18. N. Matkovskii, "Ideological Weapon of Communism—On the 40th Anniversary of the Publication of Lenin's Book 'Left-Wing Communism: An Infantile Disorder,'" CDSP, XII, No. 24, p. 4 (P, June 12, 1960).
19. Report to second congress of Rumanian Communist Party, FLP, No. 52, 1955, pp. 5-6.
20. Aleksander Zawadzki, "The Ideas of the Great October Socialist Revolution Inspire the Polish People to Fresh Achievements in Socialist Construction," FLP, No. 44, 1955, p. 3.
21. Khrushchev, *XX S"ezd*, I, 39 (CSP II, p. 38).
22. *XX S"ezd*, I, 317 (CSP II, p. 85).
23. Chapter XIX, p. 252.
24. Edward Ochab, "Results of the Twentieth Congress of the CPSU and the Tasks of the Polish United Workers' Party," FLP, No. 15, 1956, p. 4.
25. Antonín Novotný, "The Twentieth Congress of the CPSU and the Conclusions to be Drawn by Our Party," FLP, No. 15, 1956, p. 4.
26. FLP, No. 16, 1956, p. 1; CSP II, p. 221 (P, April 18, 1956).
27. See Columbia University, Russian Institute (ed.), *The Anti-Stalin Campaign and International Communism: A Selection of Documents* (New York: Columbia University Press, 1956), pp. 97 ff.
28. "On Overcoming the Cult of the Individual and Its Consequences," CSP II, pp. 221-227 (P, July 2, 1956).
29. CSP II, pp. 228-229 (P, June 21, 1956).
30. See especially Artur Utta, "Die Posener Ereignisse vom 28.Juni 1956," OE, VI (1956), 292-293.
31. NYT, October 18-23, 1956; for a good summary see Zyrill Boldirev, "Frühling im Oktober: der polnische Umbruch und seine Aussichten," OE, VI (1956), 467-484. The literature on the Polish and Hungarian events of 1956 is, of course, enormously voluminous and only a bare summary can be attempted here.
32. *Ibid.*; Joint Soviet-Polish Statement of November 18, 1956, NYT, November 19, 1956.
33. Boldirev, in OE, VI (1956), 467. Apparently the Yugoslavs were one source of this rumor; but foreign diplomats in Moscow saw additional evidence to support the theory.

34. For details see especially Meray; see also NYT, October 25-November 5, 1956, and summary, November 11, 1956; Richard P. Stebbins *et al., The United States in World Affairs, 1956* (New York: Harper & Bros., 1957), pp. 315-322.

35. Meray, p. 203.

36. Speech at Pula, November 11, 1956 (partial text in NYT, November 17, 1956).

37. "For Further Solidarity of Forces of Socialism on Basis of Marxist-Leninist Principles," CSP II, pp. 233-238 (P, November 23, 1956). For a detailed presentation of the complicated evolution of Soviet-Yugoslav positions after the Hungarian rebellion, see Brzezinski, *Bloc*, Chapter 6.

38. Carl G. Ströhm, "Jugoslawien," OE, VIII (1958), 49-55.

39. My information on Zhukov's attitude is derived in part from an oral informant. For Khrushchev's enigmatic "explanation" of his ambiguous reference to Zhukov's "adventurous" foreign policy see the Khrushchev-W. R. Hearst, Jr.-F. Coniff-R. Considine interview, CDSP, IX, No. 46, p. 14 (P, November 29, 1957).

40. CDSP, IX, No. 13, pp. 30-31 (P, March 28, 1957). The Yugoslavs and other Communists were represented at a supplemental meeting.

41. CDSP, IX, No. 47, pp. 3-7 (P, November 22, 1957). See especially p. 5.

42. William E. Griffith, "What Happened to Revisionism?" *Problems of Communism*, IX (1960), No. 2, pp. 2-3.

43. CDSP, X, No. 10, p. 27 (P, March 11, 1958).

44. P. Fedoseev, "O proekte programmy Soiuza Kommunistov Iugoslavii" (On the draft program of the League of Communists of Yugoslavia), K, No. 6, 1958, p. 26. (CDSP, X, No. 18, pp. 3-11).

45. P. Fedoseev, K, No. 6, 1958, p. 26.

46. *Ibid.*, p. 38.

47. *Ibid.*, pp. 33-35.

48. "Unity and Solidarity of Marxist-Leninist Parties—Guarantee of Further Victories of World Socialism," CDSP, X, No. 19, pp. 7-11, 51 (P, May 9, 1958).

49. See especially Ströhm, in OE, VIII (1958), 731-746.

50. CDSP, X, No. 22, p. 8 (P, June 3-4, 1958).

51. Khrushchev to Third Congress of Rumanian Workers' [Communist] Party, CDSP, XII, No. 25, p. 8 (P, June 22, 1960).

CHAPTER XXIII   INDUSTRIAL REORGANIZATION AND "ANTI-PARTY" AFFAIR

1. XX S"ezd, I, 290, 386.

2. See Henri Chambre, *L'Aménagement du Territoire en U.R.S.S.* (The Hague: Mouton & Co., 1959), p. 211.

3. For a survey of industrial organization down to 1956, see John N. Hazard,

The Soviet System of Government (Chicago: University of Chicago Press, 1957), pp. 94-101.

4. See J. Armstrong, *Elite*, pp. 65-69, for a more extended discussion of the relation (which fluctuated considerably during the last years of Stalin's life) between Party and industrial management.

5. Boris Nicolaevsky, "The Party Men and the Managers," *The New Leader*, July 29, 1957, pp. 8-9.

6. Granick, p. 130.

7. "Concerning Tasks in the Further Advance of Industry, Technical Progress and Improvement of Production and Organization," CDSP, VII, No. 28, pp. 13-14, 18-20 (P, July 17, 1955).

8. "Nastoichivo ulushat' khoziaistvennoe rukovodstvo v promyshlennosti" (Persistently improve economic direction in manufacturing), K, No. 10, 1955, p. 10 (CDSP, VII, No. 30, pp. 3-6, 36).

9. A. Polezhaev, "Soviet Economic Reorganization: The Background, 1917-1956," *Bulletin*, IV (1957), No. 6, pp. 6-7.

10. Abdurakhman Avtorkhanov, "Soviet Decentralization," *Bulletin*, IV (1957), No. 3, p. 7; and *Narodnoe Khoziaistvo* 1956, p. 47.

11. *Spravochnik Partiinogo Rabotnika* (Handbook of the Party worker) (Moscow: Gosudarstvennoe Izdatel'stvo Politicheskoi Literatury, 1957), pp. 109-110.

12. *Ibid.*, p. 110.

13. See, for example, the "The News of the Week in Review" section of NYT, July 7, 1957.

14. See especially Philip E. Mosely, "Khrushchev's New Economic Gambit," *Foreign Affairs*, XXXVI (July 1958), 557-568, for an analysis of the political and economic implications of industrial reorganization.

15. See, for example, Meray, pp. 202-203, who attributes the decision to suppress the Hungarian revolution in part to the Molotov-Kaganovich "Stalinist" faction.

16. *Spravochnik*, 1957, p. 114.

17. *Ibid.*, p. 116.

18. George P. Denicke, "Why Khrushchev Revamped Industry," *The New Leader*, February 3, 1958, p. 12; cf. Naum Jasny, "Chruschtschow und die Sowjetwirtschaft," OE, VII (1957), 713-716; Chambre, *Aménagement*, pp. 205-209.

19. V. Kostennikov, "Ob ekonomicheskom raionirovanii i kompleksnom razvitii khoziaistva ekonomicheskikh raionov SSSR" (On economic regionalization and the complex development of the economy of economic regions of the USSR), K, No. 14, 1955, pp. 30-44.

20. Report of Deputy T. M. Zueva, member of Legislative Proposals Committee of Supreme Soviet Council of the Union, CDSP, IX, No. 9, pp. 3-4 (Iz, February 12, 1957).

21. CDSP, IX, No. 13, p. 7 (P, March 30, 1957).

22. See Chapter XX.

23. CDSP, IX, No. 13, pp. 3-15 (P, March 30, 1957).

24. CDSP, IX, No. 14, p. 19 (P, April 4, 1957). It is worth noting that this director (G. Glebovskii) still had his post as of mid-1959.
25. CDSP, IX, No. 14, p. 19 (P, April 10, 1957).
26. CDSP, IX, No. 19, pp. 7-8 (Iz, May 9, 1957).
27. CDSP, IX, No. 18, p. 7 (P, May 8, 1957).
28. CDSP, IX, No. 20, pp. 14-16 (P, May 11, 1957).
29. Based on a comparison of lists in CSP II, pp. 196-202 and Bulletin, VI (1959), No. 6, Supplement.
30. See Bulletin, V (1958), No. 5.
31. "O grubykh narusheniiakh gosudarstvennoi ditsipliny v ispol'zovanii kapital'-nykh vlozhenii i faktakh proiavleniia mestnichestva so storony otdel'nykh rukovoditelei sovnarkhozov" (On the flagrant violations of state discipline in the utilization of capital investments and the facts of the appearance of parochialism on the part of certain directors of councils of national economy), PZh, No. 15, 1958, pp. 22-24.
32. V. Skriabin, Novoe v Rabote Partorganizatsii po Rukovodstvu Promyshlen-nost'iu: Iz Opyta Raboty Zaporozhskoi Oblastnoi Partorganizatsii (What's new in the work of the Party organization in the direction of manufacturing: From the experience of the work of the Zaporozh'e oblast Party organization) (Kiev: Gosudarstvennoe Izdatel'stvo Politicheskoi Literatury USSR, 1960), pp. 32-33.
33. Ibid., p. 96.
34. J. Kholmogorov, "The Dilemma of Economic Planning," Bulletin, VII (1957), No. 7, p. 40.
35. Kh. Kastanaev and F. Savenkov, "For the Organization of Administrative Apparatus on a Scientific Basis," CDSP, IX, No. 51, p. 26 (Iz, December 18, 1957).
36. "Partiinost' khoziaistvennogo rabotnika" (The partyness of the economic worker), PZh, No. 8, 1957, pp. 3-7; "Chto takoe mestnichestvo i avtarkiia" (What are localism and autarky?), PZh, No. 10, 1957, pp. 76-78.
37. CDSP, IX, No. 18, p. 17 (P, May 8, 1957).
38. "New Organizational Forms of Party Control," CDSP, XII, No. 28, pp. 17-18 (P, July 13, 1959).
39. "Partiinost' khoziaistvennogo rabotnika," PZh, No. 10, 1957, pp. 76-78.
40. "Wirtschaft und Sozialverhältnisse," OE, VIII (1958), 729-731.
41. E.g., in his remarks to the Twenty-first Party Congress, Vneocherednoi XXI S"ezd Kommunisticheskoi Partii Sovetskogo Soiuza, 27 Ianvaria-5 Fevralia 1959 Goda: Stenograficheskii Otchet (Extraordinary Twenty-first Congress of the Communist Party of the Soviet Union, 27 January-5 February 1959: Stenographic report) (Moscow: Gosudarstvennoe Izdatel'stvo Politicheskoi Literatury, 1959), II, 14. Hereafter cited as XXI S"ezd; Leo Gruliow (ed.), Current Soviet Policies III (New York: Columbia University Press, 1960), p. 42. Hereafter cited as CSP III.
42. P. Alampiev, V. Kistanov, F. Sukhopara, "Dal'neishee sovershenstvovanie ekonomicheskogo raionirovaniia" (Further perfection of economic regionaliza-tion), K, No. 16, 1958, pp. 57-62.

43. Ia. Feigin, "On Studying Contemporary Problems of the Distribution of Production Forces," CDSP, XII, No. 9, pp. 10-11 (*Voprosy Ekonomiki*, No. 1, 1960, pp. 59-68).

44. A. Vedishchev, "The Question of the Division of the USSR into Economic Regions," CDSP, XII, No. 11, p. 12 (*Voprosy Ekonomiki*, No. 2, 1960, pp. 25-35).

45. See Chapter XIX.

46. On the "increased activity" of the group, see Bulganin's "confession" in *Plenum . . . Dekabria 1958*, p. 338.

47. *Ibid.*

48. Pervukhin's speech to the Twenty-first Congress, *XXI S"ezd*, II, 141, (CSP III, p. 156), and *Istoriia KPSS*, p. 656.

49. This analysis assumes that all publicly identified members of the "anti-Party" group voted against Khrushchev, while Saburov, Pervukhin, and Voroshilov abstained; possibly, however, they too voted against Khrushchev. The Italian Communist Boffa (p. 132) states that the "anti-Party" group could "count on a majority of deliberative votes" in the Presidium. Various rumors have circulated concerning the behavior of Voroshilov (who in view of his age and purely honorary position as Chairman of the Supreme Soviet Presidium was perhaps not worth Khrushchev's vengeance); his failure to support Khrushchev is indicated by his omission from the list of those who spoke against the "anti-Party group," in *Istoriia KPSS*, p. 655. Other sources feel that Suslov may have been against Khrushchev (see NYT, February 2, 1959), but *Istoriia KPSS*, p. 655, lists him among Khrushchev's firm supporters.

50. The most revealing Soviet accounts of the Presidium meeting are Kirichenko's speech to the Twenty-first Congress, *XXI S"ezd*, I, 463 (CSP III, p. 117); and *Istoriia KPSS*, p. 656; cf. NYT, July 9, 1957, and February 2, 1959.

51. For revealing evidence on the way in which the plenum was called see Sydney Gruson's account in NYT, July 6, 1957.

52. KPSS, I, 724 (the rule was adopted in 1923).

53. *Istoriia KPSS*, p. 656.

54. For the official account of the plenum see *Spravochnik*, 1957, pp. 120-126 (also CDSP, IX, No. 27, pp. 5-7).

55. CDSP, IX, No. 50, p. 10 (P, December 19, 1957).

56. Based on a comparison of lists in CSP II, pp. 196-202 and *Bulletin*, VI (1959), No. 6, Supplement. The number of RSFSR secretaries retaining high posts is probably much higher, since only those who were Central Committee members or candidates were checked.

57. See the speeches of various leaders translated in CDSP, IX, No. 24, pp. 5 ff. (P, July 5-7, 1957).

58. N. S. Khrushchev, "Za tesnuiu sviaz' literatury i iskusstva s zhizn'iu naroda" (For a close connection of literature and art with the life of the people), K, No. 12, 1957, p. 20 (CDSP, IX, No. 35, pp. 3-10).

59. *Plenum . . . Dekabria 1958*, p. 10.

60. Resolution of Supreme Soviet, CDSP, X, No. 13, p. 3 (Iz, March 28, 1958).

61. Report of September plenum in CDSP, X, No. 36, p. 3 (P, September 7, 1958); December plenum in *Plenum . . . Dekabria 1958,* especially p. 365.
62. See Chapter XXI.
63. "Zabotlivo vstrechat' demobilizuemykh iz armii" (Meet men being demobilized from the army with solicitude), PZh, No. 12, 1956, pp. 35-37; "Ukrepliat' sviazi grazhdanskikh organizatsii s voinskimi" (Strengthen ties of the civil organizations with the military), PZh, No. 3, 1957, pp. 28-32.
64. PZh, No. 3, 1957, pp. 28-32.
65. "On Improving Party Political Work in the Soviet Army and Navy," CDSP, IX, No. 43, p. 2 (P, November 3, 1957).
66. CDSP, IX, No. 43, pp. 5-8 (P, November 3, 1957).
67. F. Golikov, "Nepreryvno sovershenstvovat' partiino-politicheskuiu rabotu v Sovetskikh Vooruzhenykh Silakh" (Ceaselessly improve Party-political work in the Soviet armed forces), PZh, No. 16 (August 1958), p. 16.
68. *Ibid.*
69. Quoted in J. Armstrong, *Elite,* p. 145.

CHAPTER XXIV   THE RESTLESS SOCIETY

1. CDSP, XII, No. 18, p. 3 (P, May 5, 1960). Up to that point Kirichenko officially remained a Secretary (making the total nine), but very likely ceased to exercise this office in December 1959. Brezhnev left the Secretariat a little later, in 1960.
2. See Chapter XXII, p. 306 above. The most detailed attempt to trace CPSU rivalries after the Twentieth Congress is Boris Meissner's *Russland unter Chruschtschow* (Munich: R. Oldenbourg Verlag, 1960). Unfortunately, this interesting book reached me too late for discussion in the text of the present work. Meissner believes that there is evidence of considerable friction in the Party command during 1958-59. In particular, he feels that Bulganin continued to occupy a position of some influence until early 1958. While Meissner's presentation is interesting, I am still inclined to the view presented in Chapter XXIII that Bulganin was merely tolerated by Khrushchev after June 1957.
3. For Khrushchev's own recognition that he is "a person of restless temperament" see his speech to the Third Writers' Congress, CDSP, XI, No. 21, p. 7 (P, May 24, 1959).
4. CDSP, X, No. 4, pp. 10 ff. (P, January 25, 1958).
5. "Theses: On Further Developing Collective Farm System and Reorganizing M.T.S.," CDSP, X, No. 9, p. 10 (P, March 1, 1958).
6. At the Belorussian agricultural conference, CDSP, X, No. 4, p. 14.
7. "Against Harmful Haste in Accomplishing an Important Task," CDSP, XI, No. 9, pp. 41-42 (P, March 5, 1959).
8. "On Abolishing Legal Liability of Workers and Office Employees for Leaving Employ of Enterprises and Institutions without Permission and for

Absence from Work without Valid Reason," CDSP, VIII, No. 15, p. 3 (*Vedomosti Verkovnogo Soveta*, No. 10, May 8, 1956, pp. 246-248).

9. CDSP, VIII, No. 15, p. 3 (*Vedomosti Verkovnogo Soveta*, No. 10, May 8, 1956, pp. 246-248).

10. V. Gizatullin, "Rehabilitation through Labor," CDSP, IX, No. 42, p. 7 (*Literaturnaia Gazeta*, September 10, 1957, p. 2).

11. Y. Mironenko, "A Soviet Labor Problem," *Bulletin*, IV (1957), No. 12, pp. 20-24; Albert Boiter, "Das neue sowjetische Gesetz gegen Parasiten," OE, VIII (1958), 10-16.

12. "On Participation by the Working People in Safeguarding Public Order," CDSP, XI, No. 10, p. 3 (P, March 10, 1959). Cf. especially Dietrich A. Loeber, "Rechtsverfolgung durch das Kollektiv," *Ost-Probleme*, XI (1959), 658-664.

13. "Draft: Model Statute on Comrades Courts," CDSP, XI, No. 43, pp. 15-17 (Iz, October 24, 1959).

14. Rigby thesis, pp. 85-86.

15. V. Churaev, "Über die Entwicklung der innerparteilichen Demokratie in der KPdSU," *Probleme des Friedens und des Sozialismus* (East Berlin), No. 6, 1959, reprinted in *Ost-Probleme*, XI (1959), 712. Churaev is Director of the Section of Party Organs for the RSFSR. I have not been able to find a Russian-language version of this important article.

16. V. Churaev, Director of the Section of Party Organs for the RSFSR, "Nekotorye voprosy rosta riadov KPSS" (Some questions on the growth of the ranks of the CPSU), PZh, No. 23, 1958, p. 18.

17. "Voprosy priema v partii" (Questions of admission to the Party), PZh, No. 8, 1956, pp. 3-8.

18. Churaev, in PZh, No. 23, 1958, p. 18.

19. V. Gorin and V. Vasiliev, "Admission to the Party and upbringing of Young Communists," CDSP, XII, No. 15, p. 21 (*Partiinaia Zhizn'*, No. 5, 1960, pp. 8-14).

20. Credentials Commission Report, Twenty-first Congress, *XXI S"ezd*, I, 260 (CSP III, p. 40).

21. "Kommunisticheskaia Partiia Ukrainy v tsifrakh" (The Communist Party of the Ukraine in figures), PZh, No. 12, 1958, pp. 57-59, provides the information on Party membership contained in this and the following paragraph.

22. USSR, Council of Ministers, Tsentral'noe Statisticheskoe Upravlenie, Statisticheskoe Upravlenie Ukrainskoi SSR, *Narodne Gospodarstvo Ukraïns'koi RSR: Statystychnyi Zbirnyk* (The national economy of the Ukrainian SSR: A statistical collection) (Kiev: Derzhavne Statystychne Vydavnytstvo, 1957), pp. 24, 385 (hereafter cited as *Narodne Gospodarstvo*), provides the basis for this estimate.

23. *Ibid.*, p. 290.

24. Churaev article translated in *Ost-Probleme*, XI (1959), 712.

25. *Ibid.*

26. *Narodne Gospodarstvo*, p. 388.

27. *Ibid.*

28. Material in this, and subsequent passages concerning Nineteenth Congress delegates, is based on CSP I, p. 94 (P, October 9, 1952); material concerning the Twenty-first Congress is from *XXI S"ezd*, I, 260-261 (CSP III, pp. 39-40). For Ukrainian Party Congress data see J. Armstrong, *Elite*, p. 33, and *Vneocherednoi XX S"ezd Kommunisticheskoi Partii Ukrainy, 16-17 Ianvaria 1959 Goda: Materialy S"ezda* (Extraordinary Twentieth Congress of the Communist Party of the Ukraine, 16-17 January, 1959: Materials of the Congress) (Kiev: Gosudarstvennoe Izdatel'stvo Politicheskoi Literatury USSR, 1959), p. 73.

29. *XX S"ezd*, I, p. 237 (CSP II, p. 67).

30. Ia. Storozhev, "Vospitanie kadrov na prakticheskom rabote" (Training cadres by practical work), PZh, No. 9, 1954, pp. 9-18.

31. M. P. Fil'chenkov, "Iz istorii partiinykh uchebnykh zavedenii" (From the history of Party educational institutions), *Voprosy Istorii KPSS*, No. 1, 1958, p. 121.

32. See Chapter VIII.

33. Khrushchev's memorandum in the Presidium of the Central Committee, CDSP, X, No. 38, p. 6 (P, September 21, 1958).

34. Robert A. Feldmesser, "Equality and Inequality under Khrushchev," *Problems of Communism*, IX (1960), No. 2, pp. 33-34.

35. Nicholas DeWitt, "Upheaval in Education," *Problems of Communism*, VIII (1959), No. 1, pp. 29-33.

36. "Men of Action vs. Phrasemongers," CDSP, VIII, No. 50, p. 15 (*Komsomolskaia Pravda*, December 15, 1956).

37. "Meeting of Moscow Youth Devoted to Awarding of Order of Lenin to Y.C.L.," CDSP, VIII, No. 45, p. 13 (P, November 10, 1956, p. 12).

38. Khrushchev's memorandum in the Presidium of the Central Committee, CDSP, X, No. 38, p. 4 (P, September 21, 1958).

39. "Control Figures for Development of the USSR National Economy in 1959-1965; Theses of Comrade N. S. Khrushchev's Report to 21st Party Congress," CDSP, X, No. 49, pp. 9-10 (P, November 14, 1958).

40. DeWitt, in *Problems of Communism*, VIII (1959), No. 1, p. 33.

41. V. Eliutin, USSR Minister of Higher Education, "Make Higher Schools Equal to Present-Day Demands," CDSP, X, No. 37, pp. 3-4 (P, September 17, 1958).

42. L. Sheinin, "A Writer's Notes: Strength and Faith," CDSP, XI, No. 36, p. 11 (Iz, September 6, 1959).

43. PZh, No. 18, 1958, pp. 57-63.

44. Ralph Fisher, p. 251.

45. Churaev article translated in *Ost-Probleme*, XI (1959), 712.

46. *Ibid.*

47. See Chapters VIII, XVII, XX. For more detailed treatments see Rigby thesis, especially Chapter V, and J. Armstrong, *Elite*, Chapter II.

48. *XVIII S"ezd*, p. 149; Report of Credentials Commission, Twenty-first Congress, *XXI S"ezd*, I, 260-261 (CSP III, pp. 39-40).

49. "Kommunisticheskaia Partiia Ukrainy v tsifrakh," PZh, No. 12, 1958, pp. 57-59.

50. See A. Moiseev, "Politicheskaia rabota po mestu zhitel'stva trudiashchikhsia" (Political work in the dwelling place of the toilers), PZh, No. 8, 1958, pp. 37-41, and "Bol'she vnimaniia partorganizatiiam domoupravlenii" (More attention to the Party organizations of house administrations), PZh, No. 6, 1958, pp. 49-51.
51. Tolkachev dissertation, p. 11.
52. Speech to Twenty-first Congress, *XXI S"ezd*, I, 472 (CSP III, p. 119).
53. Churaev article translated in *Ost-Probleme*, XI (1959), 710.
54. *Ibid.*

CHAPTER XXV   THE POLITICS OF TOTALITARIANISM

1. Chapter XVIII, pp. 245-246.
2. Chapter VI, p. 78.
3. *US in World Affairs*, 1957, pp. 326-330.
4. Khrushchev's speech to the Third Congress of the Rumanian Workers' [Communist] Party, CDSP, XII, No. 25, p. 9 (P, June 22, 1960).
5. See Chapter XI, p. 145.
6. Fainsod, *How Russia Is Ruled*, p. 208.
7. See Berliner, Chapter XVIII.
8. Chapter XIII, p. 182.
9. N. Matkovskii, "Ideological Weapon of Communism—On the 40th Anniversary of the Publication of V. I. Lenin's Book 'Left-Wing Communism: An Infantile Disorder,'" CDSP, XII, No. 24, p. 4 (P, June 12, 1960).
10. Chapter XXII, p. 295.

INDEX

This Index includes authors cited in the Reference Notes.

ABOUT THE AUTHOR

JOHN A. ARMSTRONG was born in St. Augustine, Florida, in 1922, and was educated at the University of Chicago, the University of Frankfurt, and Columbia University. He holds the Ph.D. in Public Law and Government and the Certificate of the Russian Institute at Columbia.

Mr. Armstrong served with the U.S. Army in Europe during World War II, worked as a research analyst for the War Documentation Project in Alexandria, Virginia, and taught international relations and Russian politics at the University of Denver and Columbia University. Since 1954 he has been at the University of Wisconsin, where he is now Professor of Political Science and Executive Secretary in charge of the Russian Area Studies Program.

Mr. Armstrong has traveled extensively in the Soviet Union in recent years, and is the author of *Ukrainian Nationalism, 1939-1945* (1955) and *The Soviet Bureaucratic Elite* (1959).